OF MINDS AND LANGUAGE

OF MINDS AND LANGUAGE

A Dialogue with
Noam Chomsky in the
Basque Country

Edited by

Massimo Piattelli-Palmarini,
Juan Uriagereka, and
Pello Salaburu

OXFORD

UNIVERSITY PRESS

OXFORD
UNIVERSITY PRESS

Great Clarendon Street, Oxford OX2 6DP

Oxford University Press is a department of the University of Oxford.
If furthers the University's objective of excellence in research, scholarship,
and education by publishing worldwide in

Oxford New York

Auckland Cape Town Dar es Salaam Hong Kong Karachi
Kuala Lumpur Madrid Melbourne Mexico City Nairobi
New Delhi Shanghai Taipei Toronto

With offices in

Argentina Austria Brazil Chile Czech Republic France Greece
Guatemala Hungary Italy Japan Poland Portugal Singapore
South Korea Switzerland Thailand Turkey Ukraine Vietnam

Oxford is a registered trade mark of Oxford University Press
in the UK and in certain other countries

Published in the United States
by Oxford University Press Inc., New York

© 2009 editorial matter and organization Massimo Piattelli-Palmarini,
Juan Uriagereka, and Pello Salaburu
© 2009 the chapters their various authors

The moral rights of the authors have been asserted
Database right Oxford University Press (maker)

First published 2009

British Library Cataloguing in Publication Data
Data available

Library of Congress Cataloging in Publication Data
Data available

Typeset by SPI Publisher Services, Pondicherry, India
Printed in Great Britain
on acid-free paper by
CPI Antony Rowe, Chippenham, Wiltshire

ISBN 978-0-19-954466-0

1 3 5 7 9 10 8 6 4 2

Contents

PART 3: ON ACQUISITION

PART 4: OPEN TALKS ON OPEN INQUIRIES

Foreword and Acknowledgments

In mid-2004, the organizers of the Summer Courses at the University of the Basque Country (UBC), San Sebastián Campus, contacted me because they wanted to organize a special event in 2006 to celebrate the twenty-fifth anniversary of our summer program. Their idea was to arrange a conference in which Noam Chomsky would figure as the main speaker.

What immediately came to mind was the Royaumont debate between Jean Piaget and Noam Chomsky, organized in October 1975 by Massimo Piattelli-Palmarini and published in a magnificent book (Piattelli-Palmarini 1980) that greatly influenced scholars at the UBC and helped to put linguistics on a new footing at the University, particularly in the Basque Philology department. A second Royaumont was naturally out of the question, since Jean Piaget was no longer with us and also because Chomsky's own theories had developed spectacularly since 1975, stimulating experts in other disciplines (cognitive science, biology, psychology, etc.) to join in contributing new tools to the study of human language. It seemed therefore like a wonderful opportunity to bring together scientists from various fields and give them the chance to discuss their findings and proposals at length with Noam Chomsky, in an open debate lasting several days. But in order for this to be possible, we would first have to convince Chomsky to come and take part.

Accordingly, I contacted Juan Uriagereka at the University of Maryland and told him my plan. Juan was instantly enthused by the idea and wanted to get started right away, so we talked to Massimo Piattelli-Palmarini about it and immediately set in motion all the machinery that an event of this nature requires. Noam agreed to the project, and all the persons whom we asked to participate gave us an immediate positive response. The result was a vibrant, fascinating week of work, thought, and discussion in San Sebastián, from June 19th–22nd, 2006. The sessions drew large audiences of scholars and students, as well as very ample coverage by the local and national news media. Chomsky himself was particularly engaged in the proceedings, never missed a single talk, and contributed at length to many of the discussions, as readers of this volume will see in the following pages, which contain the main contributions to that week based on the edited transcripts of the talks and discussions of all the participants.

As is natural, a seminar of this kind could not have been organized without the participation of many people, or without extraordinary funding. In this regard, I would like to stress first what a pleasure it has been to work with Massimo and Juan. The harmony between us before, during, and after the Conference has been impressive and very gratifying. Equally impressive was the performance of the Summer Course staff, who worked overtime to make sure that everything went smoothly. Regarding funding, in addition to the usual sponsors of our Summer Courses, we were very fortunate to receive extraordinary contributions from the Basque Government Department of Culture, thanks to the commitment and support of Miren Azkarate, our Minister of Culture and a linguist by profession.

So the Conference week came and went, but the work of the organizers had to continue so that these pages could be published. We were greatly helped during this phase by all the authors, who quickly and generously revised their transcripts, and to M. Dean Johnson, who had done the transcribing and copy-edited the resulting manuscripts. Also in the name of my co-editors, Massimo and Juan, I wish to express our gratitude to Jerid Francom (Department of Linguistics, University of Arizona) for an outstanding job in collating, unifying, checking, and formatting the bibliography and integrating the references with the body of the text, making it ready for publication. The result is the volume you now have in your hands – a book which we trust will be of maximum interest to readers from many fields hopefully for many years to come.

Pello Salaburu

Professor of Basque Linguistics at the University of the Basque Country

Former Rector of the University of the Basque Country

Abbreviations

Adj	Adjective
ASL	AMERICAN SIGN LANGUAGE
Aux	Auxiliary
AxS	Analysis by Synthesis
C	Complementizer
CC	Corpus Callosum
CED	Condition on Extraction Domains
CFC	Canonical Form Constraint
C-I	Conceptual-Intentional
Colag	Computational Language Acquisition Group (CUNY)
CP	Categorical Perception / Complementizer Phrase
CT	Computer Tomography
D	Determiner
Dat	Dative
Dem	Demonstrative
DNA	Deoxyribonucleic Acid
DO	Direct Object
DP	Determiner Phrase
ECM	Exceptional Case Marking
ECP	Empty Category Principle
EEG	Electroencephalography
ELAN	Early Left Anterior Negativity
E-Language	External Language
EM	Evaluation Measure
EPP	Extended Projection Principle
ERP	Event-related Brain Potential
Fo	Pitch
FLB	Language Faculty In The Broad Sense
FLH +	Left-Handed
FLH-	Right-Handed
FLN	Language Faculty In The Narrow Sense
fMRI	Functional Magnetic Resonance Imaging
Foc	Focus
FSG	Finite State Grammar
GEN	Generate
HP	Head Phrase

H-XP	Head–X(Variable) Phrase
IFG	Inferior Frontal Gyrus
I-Language	Internal Language
Intrans	Intransitive
IO	Indirect Object
L1	First Language
L2	Second Language
LCA	Linear Correspondence Axiom
LH	Left Hemisphere
LU	Linguistic Universal
LSLT	*Logical Structure Of Linguistic Theory* (Chomsky 1955)
MEG	Magnetoencephalography
N	Noun
NP	Noun Phrase
Nom	Nominative
Num	Numeral
O	Object
PDA	Push-Down Automaton
PONS	Poverty Of The Negative Stimulus
POPS	Poverty Of The Positive Stimulus
POS	Poverty Of Stimulus
P&P	Principles And Parameters (Model)
PSG	Phrase Structure Grammar
Q	Interrogative
RH	Right Hemisphere
RNA	Ribonucleic Acid
S	Subject
S-M	Sensorimotor
SMT	Strong Minimalist Thesis
SP	Subset Principle
STG	Superior Temporal Gyrus
Top	Topic
TP	Tense Phrase
Trans	Transitive
UG	Universal Grammar
V	Verb
VP	Verb Phrase
XP	X(Variable) Phrase

CHAPTER 1

Introduction

Massimo Piattelli-Palmarini, Pello Salaburu,
and Juan Uriagereka

This whole enterprise grew from a delightful equivocation. Everyone involved assumed we would be learning from Noam Chomsky, while he told us he was looking forward to the encounter in order to learn from the participants. We are convinced that the reader will benefit from this equivocation. It is a tribute to Chomsky and the other protagonists of this rich exchange that the layout of, and spirited exchanges upon, multiple central topics are among the most genuinely interdisciplinary to be found anywhere in the literature. We like to think that readers with quite different disciplinary backgrounds (linguistics, psychology, biology, computer science, or physics) will enjoy at least some sections of this book. The organization into parts and sections has been conceived with a view to facilitating such selective access.

The present ordering does not always reflect the chronology of the conference, though the discussions following each presentation, after minimal editing, are all reported here in "real time." Most of the originality and interest of this volume lies, we think, in these candid discussions, but the reader, depending on concrete interests, may decide to go past some of them and connect to the following sections. In fact, although we tried to organize matters proceeding from the more general to the more specific, it was inevitable that, in the ensuing deliberations, specific, and even sometimes technical, issues be brought to the fore also for quite general presentations.

The book is divided into four parts, almost in contrapuntal fashion. The **Overtures** jointly offer different, but complementary, introductions to the central theme of this volume: biological perspectives on language and related cognitive functions. These presentations are all non-technical and, we think, accessible to readers with different backgrounds. The second part, **On Language**, is a multi-faceted attempt to draw the frontiers of an approach to language seen as a natural object and, therefore, to linguistics conceived as part of the natural sciences. The third part, **On Acquisition**, focuses on how it is possible for every normal child to converge so rapidly and so efficiently onto the specific language of the surrounding community. Like the final entries of a fugue, the explorations in part four (**Open Talks on Open Inquiries**) enter domains of research that are conversant with, but also attempt to go beyond, the present concerns of linguistic theory (ethics, aesthetics, individual differences, neural correlates of emotion and prosody, and more).

Part 1: Overtures

In his **opening remarks**, Chomsky retraces the essential history of the field of biolinguistics and leads us to the present panorama. The chapters that follow explore, from different angles, the present contours of a biology of language. This part could be characterized, paraphrasing a famous paper by W. S. McCulloch,[1] as an attempt to answer the question: What is biology, that language may be part of it?

Starting from very general questions and the premise that the more is packed into the Broad Faculty of Language, the easier it is to understand the overall evolution of this faculty (including its "narrow" aspects), Cedric Boeckx attempts to decompose Merge into more basic operations. He concentrates on endocentric (multiply nested, of the same type) structures specific to language, and seeks to derive this property from elementary "grouping" and "copying" operations, which he speculates may have been recruited from other cognitive systems in animal cognition. This fits into François Jacob's and Steven Jay Gould's dictum that new structures in biology are a recombination of old processes that are put together in new fashion, that being the general origin of evolutionary novelty.

Marc Hauser emphasizes the importance of probing the boundaries of animal cognition through "spontaneous methods." He insists that there is virtually no connection in animals between the sensorimotor output of signaling and the richness of their conceptual systems. In order to bridge this gap, subtle experiments have been carried out to reveal the representation of the singular–plural distinction in monkeys and in prelinguistic children. Hauser then expands the analysis to the mass/count distinction, where he ascertains a contrast between monkeys and infants. He concludes with a proposal for the relations between language and ontological commitments which is sensitive to that mass–count distinction, so that it manifests itself only in some languages.

---

[1] McCulloch (1961).

Charles Randy Gallistel explains why a materialist conception of mind is compatible with the attribution of high-level abstractions even to birds and bees. Experiments on the mastery by jays of thousands of locations of different food caches show that it is based on their memory of what they had hidden where and when. Moreover, on the basis of data on caching while being watched by conspecifics and then re-caching when out of view, Gallistel concludes that nonverbal animals represent the likely intentions, and reason about the probable future actions, of others. The mastery of solar ephemeris in the foraging bees demonstrates the sophistication of the spatial reasoning that goes on in these miniature brains. Such abstractions are both primitive and foundational aspects of mentation that must have emerged early in evolutionary history.

Gabriel Dover introduces a dissenting opinion. In contrast with Chomsky's plea for focusing on optimal computation in language design, Dover is hesitant to embrace the idea of a "rational morphology" that countenances only a limited number of archetypal body-plans. Detailing some factors in the present picture of evolution and development (modularity, redundancy, genetic regulatory networks, turnover, and degeneracy) Dover insists on a distinction in biology between the micro-level of chemical bonds – where the laws of physics are dominant – and a "higher" level where variation and "interactive promiscuity" reign. His position is that development is a "highly personalized" set of operations from the early inception of the networks regulating gene expression through to the ever changing neuronal connections in the brain. Subjectivity is the name of the game at all levels, even though we are only mindful of it in the brain.

Donata Vercelli, in stark contrast with that view, develops her considerations starting with the characteristics of a biological trait L (thinly disguised as being language) and stresses the importance for L of the dimension of plasticity. She then offers a summary of the mechanisms of epigenetics (under intense scrutiny in biology proper in the last half decade), suggesting that they may have a pivotal role in language development and may have had it too in language evolution. Vercelli and Piattelli-Palmarini conclude by suggesting that parametric variation across languages may well represent a genetic mini-max optimal solution, between the extreme of encoding every aspect of language genetically (thereby minimizing learning) and the opposite extreme of leaving all aspects of language to be learned (thereby minimizing the genetic load).

A counterpoint to Dover's view is also presented by Christopher Cherniak, who discusses his idea of a "non-genomic nativism." As a result of computer calculations (previously published in detail by Cherniak et al. 2004), the minimization of connection costs at various levels of nervous systems in vertebrates and invertebrates – from the placement of the brain in the body down to the sub-cellular level of neuron arborizations – emerges as being innate, though not genome-dependent. Models that also cover the optimal design of the best commercial micro-chips show that such optimal design comes "for free," directly from the laws of physics. Cherniak's "non-genomic nativism" stresses the continuity between this finding and Chomsky's strong minimalist hypothesis, according to which narrow syntax is like a snowflake, shaped by natural law.

Part 2: On Language

Still in the same spirit of McCulloch's quote, the second part of this book could be characterized as an attempt to answer the symmetric question to the one posed above: What is language, that it may be part of biology? This general theme is developed in various ways here, even conflicting ones. It is perhaps useful to keep in mind that James Higginbotham will, at the end of the conference, acknowledge that he and Luigi Rizzi identify themselves as being, in some sense at least, abstract biologists – a characterization that probably fairly describes all the language experts presenting their views in this section. That said, it is only natural for "natural philosophers" to explore views like these, rationally disagreeing when the evidence is conflictive.

Wolfram Hinzen defends the radically minimalistic view that structural semantic conditions are satisfied in virtually tautological terms with regard to a corresponding syntax. From his perspective, in effect only syntax is a natural system reflecting Chomsky's familiar "three factor" considerations, and it is (hopefully) rich enough to provide the essential scaffolding for semantic structuring. In a nutshell, syntax creates its own ontologies by virtue of its core mechanisms, and such ontologies are not independently given in any sense; the issue is to then match such ontologies with those needed to conceptualize, at least in their bare essentials. As Hinzen explains, this thesis extends the idea that language – if analytical tools for its structure go minimally beyond mere bracketing – and basic mathematics are virtually isomorphic.

James Higginbotham explores two putative interfaces of the linguistic system: one between syntax and semantics, and one between the latter and the world. The first implies asking how much of compositionality (the meaning of a whole being a function of the meaning of its parts and their mode of composition) belongs to general features of computation, as opposed to anything specific to language. A central issue is to explain where compositionality breaks down and what differences between languages should be explained in terms of parameters at the syntax/semantics interface. The second interface involves the relations of semantics to our systematic beliefs about the world: What causes us to think/speak in the specific modes we do – and is this state of affairs necessary?

Sentences are known to ubiquitously contain parts that are interpreted not where they are pronounced. Yet there are strict, partly language-specific, constraints on what is syntactically allowed to be thus "moved," where and how. Movement to distant sentential locations takes place via successive local steps, called "cyclical." In his contribution, Luigi Rizzi argues that certain conditions on syntactic "impenetrability" can be derived from "intervention" – that is, effects arising when "movement" of a given element takes place over another *of the same type*. Locality is then relativized to skipping over interveners of equal or higher featural richness, so that elements involving fewer features have more leeway: when not involving, say, question sites, merely topicalized constituents result in less specified interveners. Thus, in the end only elements with rich featural arrays are forced into taking cyclic steps to by-pass "minimality" effects.

Juan Uriagereka discusses so-called uninterpretable features (Case being a paradigmatic example), which pose a puzzle for a minimalist program understood as an optimal solution to interface conditions. Why are there, then, uninterpretable features in languages? His suggestion is that their presence relates to a "viral" take on morphology: that is, the view that displacement correlates with the elimination of morphological specifications that bear no interpretive import. This abstractly recalls the workings of the adaptive immune system, and represents a solution to the parsing puzzle posed by compressing complex recursive (thought) structures into simple linear (phonetic) manifestations: the intricate syntax resulting from excising the viral morphology constitutes an effective instantiation of corresponding nuanced semantic types.

Complementing these approaches with a search for brain correlates to language, Angela Friederici's proposal is that the capacity to process hierarchical structures depends on a brain region that is not fully developed in monkeys, and that the phylogenetically younger piece of cortex may be functionally relevant for the acquisition of complex Phrase Structure Grammars. The older cortex may be sufficient to process local dependencies, while the human ability to process hierarchical structures could be based on the fully developed, phylogenetically younger cortex (Broca's area). Similarities and differences with germane studies on humans in other laboratories and with analogous inquiries by Hauser and Fitch into the processing limitations of grammars in tamarin monkeys, as compared to humans, emerge in the important ensuing discussion.

In the **round table on language universals**, Cedric Boeckx invites us to reconsider historically the very idea of language universals, and challenges the notion of parameters as theoretically relevant in a minimalist framework, where universal grammar (or at least narrow syntax) is supposed to be genuinely universal, and all parametric variation (or at least its "macro" version) is discharged onto the morpho-lexicon. Janet Dean Fodor declares herself not so much as a "discoverer" of universals, but a "consumer" thereof. Fodor conveys the idea of how hard it is to explain the child's actual acquisition of grammars, concretely how laborious the process of hypothesis-testing is in the abstract. She candidly declares herself to be "shopping for" hypotheses that can constrain the acquisition of grammars in real life, to avoid hosts of overgeneralizations that are possible on paper, but that no child ever makes. Lila Gleitman emphasizes the puzzle of the acquisition of the meaning of "simple" verbs like *hug* or *give* for ten-month-olds, which combines the "poverty of the stimulus" problem with its virtual opposite: the richness of the stimulus problem. How does a baby know enough to ignore irrelevant accessory objects or events in a scene? She stresses that a mosaic of conspiring cues – each of them inadequate or even obfuscating by itself – are exploited by babies to converge, almost errorlessly, on the lexicon of their native tongue. Finally, Luigi Rizzi retraces the transition from generalizations about particular grammars to the principles of UG and the notion of parameter. He reviews the recent history of Principles and Parameters, from the Extended Standard Theory to consequences ensuing from the current Cartographic Program.

Part 3: On Acquisition

Ever since Chomsky stressed the importance of attaining "explanatory adequacy" for any linguistic theory, all hypotheses on processes, mechanisms, constraints, and computations that are not supposed to be innately available have had to be answerable to the possibility of acquisition by the child on the basis of normal linguistic input. For instance, it is a true descriptive generalization about English that all verbs derived from Latin are regular (form the past tense by adding the suffix -*ed*). But since this is patently a generalization that the monolingual child acquiring English has no access to, a theory based on such a generalization would have no explanatory adequacy whatsoever. This part of the book offers several interesting approaches to theories and data by researchers who are highly sensitive to explanatory adequacy, from various angles.

Rochel Gelman deals with the issues of similarity, causality, and core or "skeletal" (innate) versus non-core (acquired) domains. She insists that appeal to universal innate principles does not exclude learning; rather, it forces us to ask what kind of theory of learning is needed to account for early learnings and the extent to which they help, redirect, or hinder later learnings. Taking up the hard case of counting and natural numbers, and subtraction, Gelman concludes that core domains provide structure to the learning process, because they provide a mental skeletal structure that helps search the environment for relevant data and move readily onto relevant learning paths. The difficulty about non-core domains is that both the structure and the data have to be found. In her words: "It is like having to get to the middle of a lake without a rowboat."

Instead of marveling at how fast children acquire their mother language, Lila Gleitman invites us to wonder why it takes so long. Although prelinguistic infants discriminate kinds of relations, such as containment versus support or force and causation, they tend to understand and talk about objects first. Since objects surface as nouns, these overpopulate the infant vocabulary as compared to verbs and adjectives, which characteristically express events, states, properties, and relations. Why are verbs "hard words" for the infant? Explaining the acquisition of "perspective verbs" (*chase/flee*, *buy/sell*) and "unobservables" (*know*, *think*, *believe*) leads us into a circle: the transition from the word to the world must be made to a world that is observed *in the right way*, that is, under the characterization that fits the word being used. The central datum is that syntax, in itself, is not only a powerful cue, but the *strongest* of all.

Janet Fodor explores plausible linguistic inputs ("triggers") that allow the child to fix syntactic parameters. If ambiguous, such triggers do not solve the acquisition process; in that hypothetical situation, the acquisition mechanism must evaluate (as in Chomsky's original 1965 formulation) competing grammar hypotheses. How this could be done by a learner is not obvious, and the possibility is explored here of building on "partial decoding" of competing grammar hypotheses. The approach is based on organizing grammars (vectors of parametric values) in terms of a lattice that learners must tacitly assume for the orderly setting of parameters. As learning proceeds, the smallest grammars are tried out on input sentences and some fail, then being erased from the learner's mental representation of the language domain. In effect this "keeps track" of disconfirmed grammars, by erasing them from the presumably innate lattice. The paper ends by puzzling over the nature of such a lattice.

Thomas Bever was unable to attend the conference, although his approach to the EPP (Extended Projection Principle) had been discussed at the meeting. In light of exchanges with Chomsky, and after reading relevant sections of the transcripts, Bever offered the present paper. The odd requirement that sentences must "sound" as though they have subjects, even when there is no semantic motivation for this (cf. *It rained,* **There** *are problems,* **It** *seems that he left,* etc.) is still an anomaly within the minimalist program. The condition was initially proposed as a syntactic universal, but while it is roughly correct for English, its presence in other languages is less obvious. Bever takes the EPP out of syntax and explains the vagaries of its generalization by means of a Canonical Form Constraint (CFC). His contribution also explores the implications of this constraint for language comprehension, language acquisition, and Broca's aphasia.

Part 4: Explorations

The final section of the proceedings is based on more open-ended talks, some of which were delivered to a more general audience, after the end of the ordinary sessions. In these, broader speculations are often attempted, although, once again, occasional disparity exists between the normally non-technical character of the presentations and the tone of some of the ensuing discussions, as different participants eagerly engage the speakers in lively discussion.

Marc Hauser anticipated some of the issues that were to appear in his recent book on "Moral Minds." His point of departure, methodologically and conceptually, is Chomsky's insistence on universal innate constraints on humanly possible mental procedures and contents, and the notion of generativity. These are tentatively expanded by Hauser to the domains of ethics (via the work of John Rawls) and aesthetics, with special reference to musical tastes in humans and non-human primates. Universal minimalism is, in his own words, what he is arguing for. Connecting his considerations with other presentations at the conference (especially those by Chomsky, Gallistel, and Cherniak), he offers an interesting panoply of novel experimental data to support his hypotheses. In the discussion, several of Hauser's hypotheses are sympathetically, but also rigorously, challenged by other participants.

Itziar Laka retraces the early steps of the innatist hypothesis for language, probing its limits and suggesting the hardest tests. Thus she takes up a challenge launched by the organizers in the invitation document: thinking about what we know and what we would like to know about minds and language. She examines innate mechanisms disclosed by the study of the perceptual salience of rhythmic/prosodic properties of speech, some specific to humans, some also found in other species. The acquisition of phonemes across different languages suggests that the peculiar thing about human babies is that they are very quickly able to construct something new, using largely an old perceptual mechanism. At the end of her exploration of the conceptual and empirical development of the field of generative linguistics, connecting with several other issues freshly discussed at the conference, Laka cannot help but wonder about the nature of parameters.

Nuria Sebastián-Gallés explores the reasons why some individuals are better than others at acquiring a second language (L2). After discussing the issues the literature has raised with regards to possible causes for this disparity, she presents several data showing differences in brain structure and function in relevant groups tested (of poor versus good L2 learners). Importantly, in general these differences are not in language-related areas. This leads her to conclude that it is probably not the language faculty as such that is involved in proficient L2 learning, but other, perhaps general, cognitive capacities. Inasmuch as such differences are not at all important for the acquisition of a first language, these results suggest that the two processes may be quite distinct.

Angela Friederici examines the different computations carried out by the two hemispheres of the brain and tests the prediction that there are separate, and sequential, phases in processing syntactic and semantic information. She also reports on data suggesting that the right hemisphere is responsible for the processing of prosodic information. The focus of her presentation is intonational phrasing and the hypothesis that it tracks syntactic phrasing. Processing structural hierarchies activates Broca's area, parametrically as a function of the number of syntactic movements involved. A judicious insertion of morphological markers in German allowed her also to conclude that local structure-building processes precede lexical-semantic processes. Curious data on sex differences in the interactions of semantic-emotional and prosodic-emotional processes during language comprehension show women using prosodic-emotional information earlier than men.

In Chomsky's **concluding remarks,** virtually all of the different threads spun during the conference finally come together. Sharing with us his unique impressions, perplexities, excitements, and after-thoughts – and merging some of the issues discussed during the conference, while suggesting disparities between others – Chomsky retraces the main lines of development of the generative enterprise. With his vast knowledge and perspective, after reconstructing historical antecedents, he insists on the strangeness of the amnesia that has struck the cognitive sciences in the last couple of decades. Many of the fundamental problems that still (should) define the agenda for our understanding of mind at work, how it evolved and develops, and how it is embodied in brains, were openly discussed from the eighteenth century on, but appear to have been partially forgotten in our times. Perhaps Chomsky's most lasting message in this book, in our view full of both humility and insight, is that a look into the future must be accompanied by a rediscovery of the intellectually relevant past.

PART I

Overtures

CHAPTER 2

Opening Remarks

Noam Chomsky

I have been thinking about various ways to approach this opportunity, and on balance, it seemed that the most constructive tack would be to review, and rethink, a few leading themes of the biolinguistic program since its inception in the early 1950s, at each stage influenced by developments in the biological sciences. And to try to indicate how the questions now entering the research agenda develop in a natural way from some of the earliest concerns of these inquiries. Needless to say, this is from a personal perspective. The term "biolinguistics" itself was coined by Massimo as the topic for an international conference in 1974[1] that brought together evolutionary biologists, neuroscientists, linguists, and others concerned with language and biology, one of many such initiatives, including the Royaumont conference that Massimo brought up.[2]

As you know, the 1950s was the heyday of the behavioral sciences. B. F. Skinner's William James lectures, which later appeared as *Verbal Behavior* (1957), were widely circulated by 1950, at least in Cambridge, Mass., and soon became close to orthodoxy, particularly as the ideas were taken up by W. V. Quine in his classes and work that appeared a decade later in his *Word and Object* (1960). Much the same was assumed for human capacity and cultural variety generally. Zellig Harris's (1951) *Methods of Structural Linguistics* appeared at the same time, outlining procedures for the analysis of a corpus of materials from sound to sentence, reducing data to organized form, and particularly within American linguistics, was generally assumed to have gone about as far as theoretical linguistics could or should reach. The fact that the study was called *Methods* reflected the prevailing assumption that there could be nothing much in the way of a theory of language, because languages can "differ from each other without limit and in unpredictable ways," so that the

---

[1] May 20–21; Piattelli-Palmarini (1974). (Editors' note)

[2] Piattelli-Palmarini (1980b). (Editors' note)

study of each language must be approached "without any preexistent scheme of what a language must be," the formulation of Martin Joos, summarizing the reigning "Boasian tradition," as he plausibly called it. The dominant picture in general biology was in some ways similar, captured in Gunther Stent's (much later) observation that the variability of organisms is so free as to constitute "a near infinitude of particulars which have to be sorted out case by case."

European structuralism was a little different, but not much: Trubetzkoy's *Anleitung*, a classic introduction of phonological analysis,[3] was similar in conception to the American procedural approaches, and in fact there was very little beyond phonology and morphology, the areas in which languages do appear to differ very widely and in complex ways, a matter of some more general interest, so recent work suggests.

Computers were on the horizon, and it was also commonly assumed that statistical analysis of vast corpora should reveal everything there is to learn about language and its acquisition, a severe misunderstanding of the fundamental issue that has been the primary concern of generative grammar from its origins at about the same time: to determine the structures that underlie semantic and phonetic interpretation of expressions and the principles that enter into growth and development of attainable languages. It was, of course, understood from the early 1950s that as computing power grows, it should ultimately be possible for analysis of vast corpora to produce material that would resemble the data analyzed. Similarly, it would be possible to do the same with videotapes of bees seeking nourishment. The latter might well give better approximations to what bees do than the work of bee scientists, a matter of zero interest to them; they want to discover how bee communication and foraging actually work, what the mechanisms are, resorting to elaborate and ingenious experiments. The former is even more absurd, since it ignores the core problems of the study of language.

A quite separate question is whether various characterizations of the entities and processes of language, and steps in acquisition, might involve statistical analysis and procedural algorithms. That they do was taken for granted in the earliest work in generative grammar, my *Logical Structure of Linguistic Theory* (LSLT) in 1955, for example. I assumed that identification of chunked word-like elements in phonologically analyzed strings was based on analysis of transitional probabilities – which, surprisingly, turns out to be false, as Thomas Gambell and Charles Yang discovered, unless a simple UG prosodic principle is presupposed. LSLT also proposed methods to assign chunked elements to categories, some with an information-theoretic flavor; hand calculations in that

---

[3] Trubetzkoy (1936). For a recent English translation see Trubetzkoy (2001). (Editors' note)

pre-computer age had suggestive results in very simple cases, but to my knowledge, the topic has not been further pursued.

Information theory was taken to be a unifying concept for the behavioral
sciences, along the lines of Warren Weaver's essay in Shannon and Weaver's
famous monograph.[4] Within the engineering professions, highly influential in
these areas, it was a virtual dogma that the properties of language, maybe all
human behavior, could be handled within the framework of Markov sources, in
fact very elementary ones, not even utilizing the capacity of these simple
automata to capture dependencies of arbitrary length. The restriction followed
from the general commitment to associative learning, which excluded such
dependencies. As an aside, my monograph *Syntactic Structures* in 1957 begins
with observations on the inadequacy in principle of finite automata, hence
Markovian sources, but only because it was essentially notes for courses at
MIT, where their adequacy was taken for granted. For similar reasons, the
monograph opens by posing the task of distinguishing grammatical from ungrammatical sentences, on the analogy of well-formedness in formal systems,
then assumed to be an appropriate model for language. In the much longer and
more elaborate unpublished monograph LSLT two years earlier, intended only
for a few friends, there is no mention of finite automata, and a chapter is
devoted to the reasons for rejecting any notion of well-formedness: the task
of the theory of language is to generate sound–meaning relations fully, whatever
the status of an expression, and in fact much important work then and since
has had to do with expressions of intermediate status: the difference, say,
between such deviant expressions as (1) and (2).

(1)   *which book did they wonder why I wrote
(2)   *which author did they wonder why wrote that book

Empty category principle (ECP) vs. subjacency violations, still not fully understood.

There were some prominent critics, like Karl Lashley, but his very important
work on serial order in behavior,[5] undermining prevailing associationist assumptions, was unknown, even at Harvard where he was a distinguished
professor. Another sign of the tenor of the times.

This is a bit of a caricature, but not much. In fact it is understated, because
the prevailing mood was also one of enormous self-confidence that the basic
answers had been found, and what remained was to fill in the details in a
generally accepted picture.

---

[4] Shannon and Weaver (1949 [1998]). (Editors' Note)
[5] Lashley (1951). (Editors' Note)

A few graduate students in the Harvard–MIT complex were skeptics. One was Eric Lenneberg, who went on to found the biology of language; another was Morris Halle. One change over the past fifty years is that we've graduated from sharing a cramped office to being in ample adjacent ones. From the early 1950s, we were reading and discussing work that was then well outside the canon: Lorenz, Tinbergen, Thorpe, and other work in ethology and comparative psychology. Also D'Arcy Thompson,[6] though regrettably we had not come across Turing's work in biology,[7] and his thesis that "we must envisage a living organism as a special kind of system to which the general laws of physics and chemistry apply... and because of the prevalence of homologies, we may well suppose, as D'Arcy Thompson has done, that certain physical processes are of very general occurrence." The most recent evaluation of these aspects of Turing's work that I've seen, by Justin Leiber,[8] concludes that Thompson and Turing "regard teleology, evolutionary phylogeny, natural selection, and history to be largely irrelevant and unfortunately effective distractions from fundamental ahistorical biological explanation," the scientific core of biology. That broad perspective may sound less extreme today after the discovery of master genes, deep homologies, conservation, optimization of neural networks of the kind that Chris Cherniak has demonstrated,[9] and much else, perhaps even restrictions of evolutionary/developmental processes so narrow that "replaying the protein tape of life might be surprisingly repetitive" (quoting a report on feasible mutational paths in *Science* a few weeks ago,[10] reinterpreting a famous image of Steve Gould's). Another major factor in the development of the biolinguistic perspective was work in recursive function theory and the general theory of computation and algorithms, then just becoming readily available, making it possible to undertake more seriously the inquiry into the formal mechanisms of generative grammars that were being explored from the late 1940s.

These various strands could, it seemed, be woven together to develop a very different approach to problems of language and mind, taking behavior and corpora to be not the object of inquiry, as in the behavioral sciences and structural linguistics, but merely data, and not necessarily the best data, for discovery of the properties of the real object of inquiry: the internal mechanisms that generate linguistic expressions and determine their sound and meaning. The whole system would then be regarded as one of the organs of the body,

---

[6] Thompson (1917). (Editors' Note)

[7] Turing (1952). (Editors' Note)

[8] Leiber (2001). (Editors' Note)

[9] See Chapter 8 for details. (Editors' Note)

[10] Weinreich et al. (2006). (Editors' Note)

in this case a cognitive organ, like the systems of planning, interpretation, reflection, and whatever else falls among those aspects of the world loosely "termed mental," which reduce somehow to "the organical structure of the brain." I'm quoting chemist/philosopher Joseph Priestley in the late eighteenth century, articulating a standard conclusion after Newton had demonstrated, to his great dismay and disbelief, that the world is not a machine, contrary to the core assumptions of the seventeenth-century scientific revolution. It follows that we have no choice but to adopt some non-theological version of what historians of philosophy call "Locke's suggestion": that God might have chosen to "superadd to matter a faculty of thinking" just as he "annexed effects to motion which we can in no way conceive motion able to produce" – notably the property of action at a distance, a revival of occult properties, many leading scientists argued (with Newton's partial agreement).

It is of some interest that all of this seems to have been forgotten. The American Academy of Arts and Sciences published a volume summarizing the results of the Decade of the Brain that ended the twentieth century.[11] The guiding theme, formulated by Vernon Mountcastle, is the thesis of the new biology that "Things mental, indeed minds, are emergent properties of brains, [though] these emergences are...produced by principles that...we do not yet understand."[12] The same thesis has been put forth in recent years by prominent scientists and philosophers as an "astonishing hypothesis" of the new biology, a "radical" new idea in the philosophy of mind, "the bold assertion that mental phenomena are entirely natural and caused by the neurophysiological activities of the brain," opening the door to novel and promising inquiries, a rejection of Cartesian mind–body dualism, and so on. All, in fact, reiterate formulations of centuries ago, in virtually the same words, after mind–body dualism became unformulable with the disappearance of the only coherent notion of body (physical, material, etc.) – facts well understood in standard histories of materialism, like Friedrich Lange's nineteenth-century classic.[13]

It is also of some interest that although the traditional mind–body problem dissolved after Newton, the phrase "mind–body problem" has been resurrected for a problem that is only loosely related to the traditional one. The traditional mind–body problem developed in large part within normal science: certain phenomena could not be explained by the principles of the mechanical philosophy, the presupposed scientific theory of nature, so a new principle was proposed, some kind of *res cogitans*, a thinking substance, alongside of material

---

[11] Mountcastle (1998). (Editors' Note)
[12] Mountcastle (1998). (Editors' Note)
[13] Lange (1892). (Editors' Note)

substance. The next task would be to discover its properties and to try to unify the two substances. That task was undertaken, but was effectively terminated when Newton undermined the notion of material substance.

What is now called the mind–body problem is quite different. It is not part of normal science. The new version is based on the distinction between the first person and the third person perspective. The first person perspective yields a view of the world presented by one's own experience – what the world looks like, feels like, sounds like to me, and so on. The third person perspective is the picture developed in its most systematic form in scientific inquiry, which seeks to understand the world from outside any particular personal perspective.

The new version of the mind–body problem resurrects a thought experiment of Bertrand Russell's eighty years ago, though the basic observation traces back to the pre-Socratics. Russell asked us to consider a blind physicist who knows all of physics but doesn't know something we know: what it's like to see the color blue.[14] Russell's conclusion was that the natural sciences seek to discover "the causal skeleton of the world. Other aspects lie beyond their purview."

Recasting Russell's experiment in naturalistic terms, we might say that like all animals, our internal cognitive capacities reflexively provide us with a world of experience – the human Umwelt, in ethological lingo. But being reflective creatures, thanks to the emergence of human intellectual capacities, we go on to seek a deeper understanding of the phenomena of experience. If humans are part of the organic world, we expect that our capacities of understanding and explanation have fixed scope and limits, like any other natural object – a truism that is sometimes thoughtlessly derided as "mysterianism," though it was understood by Descartes and Hume, among others. It could be that these innate capacities do not lead us beyond some theoretical understanding of Russell's causal skeleton of the world. In principle these questions are subject to empirical inquiry into what we might call "the science-forming faculty," another "mental organ," now the topic of some investigation – Susan Carey's work, for example (Carey 1985, 2001; Barner et al. 2005, 2007). But these issues are distinct from traditional dualism, which evaporated after Newton.

This is a rough sketch of the intellectual background of the biolinguistic perspective, in part with the benefit of some hindsight. Adopting this perspective, the term "language" means internal language, a state of the computational system of the mind/brain that generates structured expressions, each of which can be taken to be a set of instructions for the interface systems within which the

---

[14] "It is obvious that a man who can see knows things which a blind man cannot know; but a blind man can know the whole of physics. Thus the knowledge which other men have and he has not is not part of physics." (Reprinted in Russell 2003.) (Editors' note)

faculty of language is embedded. There are at least two such interfaces: the systems of thought that use linguistic expressions for reasoning, interpretation, organizing action, and other mental acts; and the sensorimotor systems that externalize expressions in production and construct them from sensory data in perception. The theory of the genetic endowment for language is commonly called universal grammar (UG), adapting a traditional term to a different framework. Certain configurations are possible human languages, others are not, and a primary concern of the theory of human language is to establish the distinction between the two categories.

Within the biolinguistic framework, several tasks immediately arise. The first is to construct generative grammars for particular languages that yield the facts about sound and meaning. It was quickly learned that the task is formidable. Very little was known about languages, despite millennia of inquiry. The most extensive existing grammars and dictionaries were, basically, lists of examples and exceptions, with some weak generalizations. It was assumed that anything beyond could be determined by unspecified methods of "analogy" or "induction" or "habit." But even the earliest efforts revealed that these notions concealed vast obscurity. Traditional grammars and dictionaries tacitly appeal to the understanding of the reader, either knowledge of the language in question or the shared innate linguistic capacity, or commonly both. But for the study of language as part of biology, it is precisely that presupposed understanding that is the topic of investigation, and as soon as the issue was faced, major problems were quickly unearthed.

The second task is to account for the acquisition of language, later called the problem of explanatory adequacy (when viewed abstractly). In biolinguistic terms, that means discovering the operations that map presented data to the internal language attained. With sufficient progress in approaching explanatory adequacy, a further and deeper task comes to the fore: to transcend explanatory adequacy, asking not just what the mapping principles are, but why language growth is determined by these principles, not innumerable others that can be easily imagined. The question was premature until quite recently, when it has been addressed in what has come to be called the minimalist program, the natural next stage of biolinguistic inquiry, to which I'll briefly return.

Another question is how the faculty of language evolved. There are libraries of books and articles about evolution of language – in rather striking contrast to the literature, say, on the evolution of the communication system of bees. For human language, the problem is vastly more difficult for obvious reasons, and can be undertaken seriously, by definition, only to the extent that some relatively firm conception of UG is available, since that is what evolved.

Still another question is how the properties "termed mental" relate to "the organical structure of the brain," in Priestley's words.[15] And there are hard and important questions about how the internal language is put to use, for example in acts of referring to the world, or in interchange with others, the topic of interesting work in neo-Gricean pragmatics in recent years.

Other cognitive organs can perhaps be studied along similar lines. In the early days of the biolinguistic program, George Miller and others sought to construct a generative theory of planning, modeled on early ideas about generative grammar.[16] Other lines of inquiry trace back to David Hume, who recognized that knowledge and belief are grounded in a "species of natural instincts," part of the "springs and origins" of our inherent mental nature, and that something similar must be true in the domain of moral judgment. The reason is that our moral judgments are unbounded in scope and that we constantly apply them in systematic ways to new circumstances. Hence they too must be founded on general principles that are part of our nature though beyond our "original instincts," those shared with animals. That should lead to efforts to develop something like a grammar of moral judgment. That task was undertaken by John Rawls, who adapted models of generative grammar that were being developed as he was writing his classic *Theory of Justice* (1971) in the 1960s. These ideas have recently been revived and developed and have become a lively field of theoretical and empirical inquiry, which Marc Hauser discusses below.[17]

At the time of the 1974 biolinguistics conference, it seemed that the language faculty must be rich, highly structured, and substantially unique to this cognitive system. In particular, that conclusion followed from considerations of language acquisition. The only plausible idea seemed to be that language acquisition is rather like theory construction. Somehow, the child reflexively categorizes certain sensory data as linguistic experience, and then uses the experience as evidence to construct an internal language – a kind of theory of expressions that enter into the myriad varieties of language use.

To give a few of the early illustrations for concreteness, the internal language that we more or less share determines that sentence (3a) is three-ways ambiguous, though it may take a little reflection to reveal the fact; but the ambiguities are resolved if we ask (3b), understood approximately as (3c):

(3) a. Mary saw the man leaving the store
     b. Which store did Mary see the man leaving?
     c. Which store did Mary see the man leave?

---

[15] See also Chomsky (1998). (Editors' note)
[16] Miller and Johnson-Laird (1976). (Editors' note)
[17] See Chapter 19. (Editors' note)

The phrase *which store* is raised from the position in which its semantic role is determined as object of *leave*, and is then given an additional interpretation as an operator taking scope over a variable in its original position, so the sentence means, roughly:

for which x, x a store, Mary saw the man leav(ing) the store x

– and without going into it here, there is good reason to suppose that the semantic interface really does interpret the variable x as *the store x*, a well-studied phenomenon called "reconstruction." The phrase that serves as the restricted variable is silent in the phonetic output, but must be there for interpretation. Only one of the underlying structures permits the operation, so the ambiguity is resolved in the interrogative, in the manner indicated. The constraints involved – so-called "island conditions" – have been studied intensively for about forty-five years. Recent work indicates that they may reduce in large measure to minimal search conditions of optimal computation, perhaps not coded in UG but more general laws of nature – which, if true, would carry us beyond explanatory adequacy.

Note that even such elementary examples as this illustrate the marginal interest of the notions "well-formed" or "grammatical" or "good approximation to a corpus," however they are characterized.

To take a second example, illustrating the same principles less transparently, consider sentences (4a) and (4b):

(4)   a. John ate an apple
      b. John ate

We can omit *an apple*, yielding (4b), which we understand to mean *John ate something unspecified*. Now consider

(5)   a. John is too angry to eat an apple
      b. John is too angry to eat

We can omit *an apple*, yielding (5b), which, by analogy to (4b) should mean that *John is so angry that he wouldn't eat anything*. That's a natural interpretation, but there is also a different one in this case: namely, *John is so angry that someone or other won't eat him, John* – the natural interpretation for the structurally analogous expression

(6)   John is too angry to invite

In this case, the explanation lies in the fact that the phrase *too angry to eat* does include the object of *eat*, but it is invisible. The invisible object is raised just as *which store* is raised in the previous example (3), again yielding an operator-variable structure. In this case, however, the operator has no content, so the construction is an open sentence with a free variable, hence a predicate. The semantic interpretation follows from general principles. The minimal search conditions that restrict raising of *which store* in example (3) also bar the raising of the empty object of *eat*, yielding standard island properties.

In both cases, the same general computational principles, operating efficiently, provide a specific range of interpretations as an operator-variable construction, with the variable unpronounced in both cases and the operator unpronounced in one. The surface forms in themselves tell us little about the interpretations.

Even the most elementary considerations yield the same conclusions. The simplest lexical items raise hard if not insuperable problems for analytic procedures of segmentation, classification, statistical analysis, and the like. A lexical item is identified by phonological elements that determine its sound along with morphological elements that determine its meaning. But neither the phonological nor morphological elements have the "beads-on-a-string" property required for computational analysis of a corpus. Furthermore, even the simplest words in many languages have phonological and morphological elements that are silent. The elements that constitute lexical items find their place in the generative procedures that yield the expressions, but cannot be detected in the physical signal. For that reason, it seemed then – and still seems – that the language acquired must have the basic properties of an internalized explanatory theory. These are design properties that any account of evolution of language must deal with.

Quite generally, construction of theories must be guided by what Charles Sanders Peirce a century ago called an "abductive principle," which he took to be a genetically determined instinct, like the pecking of a chicken. The abductive principle "puts a limit upon admissible hypotheses" so that the mind is capable of "imagining correct theories of some kind" and discarding infinitely many others consistent with the evidence. Peirce was concerned with what I was calling "the science-forming faculty," but similar problems arise for language acquisition, though it is dramatically unlike scientific discovery. It is rapid, virtually reflexive, convergent among individuals, relying not on controlled experiment or instruction but only on the "blooming, buzzing confusion" that each infant confronts. The format that limits admissible hypotheses about structure, generation, sound, and meaning must therefore be highly restrictive. The conclusions about the specificity and richness of the language faculty follow directly. Plainly such conclusions make it next to impossible to raise questions that go beyond explanatory adequacy – the "why" questions – and also pose serious barriers to inquiry into how the faculty might have evolved, matters discussed inconclusively at the 1974 conference.

A few years later, a new approach suggested ways in which these paradoxes might be overcome. This principles and parameters (P&P) approach was based on the idea that the format consists of invariant principles and a "switch-box" of parameters – to adopt Jim Higginbotham's image. The switches can be set to one or another value on the basis of fairly elementary experience. A choice of parameter settings determines a language. The approach largely emerged from intensive study of a range of languages, but as in the early days of generative grammar, it was also suggested by developments in biology – in this case, François Jacob's ideas about how slight changes in the timing and hierarchy of regulatory mechanisms might yield great superficial differences (a butterfly or an elephant, and so on). The model seemed natural for language as well: slight changes in parameter settings might yield superficial variety, through inter-action of invariant principles with parameter choices. That's discussed a bit in Kant lectures of mine at Stanford in 1978, which appeared a few years later in my book *Rules and Representations* (1980).

The approach crystallized in the early 1980s, and has been pursued with considerable success, with many revisions and improvements along the way. One illustration is Mark Baker's demonstration, in his book *Atoms of Language* (2001), that languages that appear on the surface to be about as different as can be imagined (in his case Mohawk and English) turn out to be remarkably similar when we abstract from the effects of a few choices of values for parameters within a hierarchic organization that he argues to be universal, hence the outcome of evolution of language.

Looking with a broader sweep, the problem of reconciling unity and diversity has constantly arisen in biology and linguistics. The linguistics of the early scientific revolution distinguished universal from particular grammar, though not in the biolinguistic sense. Universal grammar was taken to be the intellec-tual core of the discipline; particular grammars are accidental instantiations. With the flourishing of anthropological linguistics, the pendulum swung in the other direction, towards diversity, well captured in the Boasian formulation to which I referred. In general biology, a similar issue had been raised sharply in the Cuvier–Geoffroy debate in 1830.[18] Cuvier's position, emphasizing diversity, prevailed, particularly after the Darwinian revolution, leading to the conclu-sions about near infinitude of variety that have to be sorted out case by case, which I mentioned earlier. Perhaps the most quoted sentence in biology is Darwin's final observation in *Origin of Species* about how "from so simple a

---

[18] See Appel (1987). (Editors' note)

beginning, endless forms most beautiful and most wonderful have been, and are being, evolved." I don't know if the irony was intended, but these words were taken by Sean Carroll (2005) as the title of his introduction to *The New Science of Evo Devo*, which seeks to show that the forms that have evolved are far from endless, in fact are remarkably uniform, presumably, in important respects, because of factors of the kind that Thompson and Turing thought should constitute the true science of biology. The uniformity had not passed unnoticed in Darwin's day. Thomas Huxley's naturalistic studies led him to observe that there appear to be "predetermined lines of modification" that lead natural selection to "produce varieties of a limited number and kind" for each species.[19]

Over the years, in both general biology and linguistics the pendulum has been swinging towards unity, in the evo-devo revolution in biology and in the somewhat parallel minimalist program.

The principles of traditional universal grammar had something of the status of Joseph Greenberg's universals: they were descriptive generalizations. Within the framework of UG in the contemporary sense, they are observations to be explained by the principles that enter into generative theories, which can be investigated in many other ways. Diversity of language provides an upper bound on what may be attributed to UG: it cannot be so restricted as to exclude attested languages. Poverty of stimulus (POS) considerations provide a lower bound: UG must be at least rich enough to account for the fact that internal languages are attained. POS considerations were first studied seriously by Descartes to my knowledge, in the field of visual perception. Of course they are central to any inquiry into growth and development, though for curious reasons, these truisms are considered controversial only in the case of language and other higher human mental faculties (particular empirical assumptions about POS are of course not truisms, in any domain of growth and development).

For these and many other reasons, the inquiry has more stringent conditions to satisfy than generalization from observed diversity. That is one of many consequences of the shift to the biolinguistic perspective; another is that methodological questions about simplicity, redundancy, and so on, are transmuted into factual questions that can be investigated from comparative and other perspectives, and may reduce to natural law.

---

[19] The passage quoted is, in its entirety: "The importance of natural selection will not be impaired even if further inquiries should prove that variability is definite, and is determined in certain directions rather than in others, by conditions inherent in that which varies. It is quite conceivable that every species tends to produce varieties of a limited number and kind, and that the effect of natural selection is to favour the development of some of these, while it opposes the development of others along their predetermined lines of modification" (Huxley 1893: 223). See also Gates (1916). Huxley's passage is there quoted on page 128. See also Chomsky (2004b). (Editors' note)

Apart from stimulating highly productive investigation of languages of great typological variety, at a depth never before even considered, the P&P approach also reinvigorated neighboring fields, particularly the study of language acquisition, reframed as inquiry into setting of parameters in the early years of life. The shift of perspective led to very fruitful results, enough to suggest that the basic contours of an answer to the problems of explanatory adequacy might be visible. On that tentative assumption, we can turn more seriously to the "why" questions that transcend explanatory adequacy. The minimalist program thus arose in a natural way from the successes of the P&P approach.

The P&P approach also removed the major conceptual barrier to the study of evolution of language. With the divorce of principles of language from acquisition, it no longer follows that the format that "limits admissible hypotheses" must be rich and highly structured to satisfy the empirical conditions of language acquisition, in which case inquiry into evolution would be virtually hopeless. That might turn out to be the case, but it is no longer an apparent conceptual necessity. It therefore became possible to entertain more seriously the recognition, from the earliest days of generative grammar, that acquisition of language involves not just a few years of experience and millions of years of evolution, yielding the genetic endowment, but also "principles of neural organization that may be even more deeply grounded in physical law" (quoting from my *Aspects of the Theory of Syntax* (1965), a question then premature).

Assuming that language has general properties of other biological systems, we should be seeking three factors that enter into its growth in the individual: (1) genetic factors, the topic of UG; (2) experience, which permits variation within a fairly narrow range; (3) principles not specific to language. The third factor includes principles of efficient computation, which would be expected to be of particular significance for systems such as language. UG is the residue when third-factor effects are abstracted. The richer the residue, the harder it will be to account for the evolution of UG, evidently.

Throughout the modern history of generative grammar, the problem of determining the general nature of language has been approached "from top down," so to speak: how much must be attributed to UG to account for language acquisition? The minimalist program seeks to approach the problem "from bottom up": how little can be attributed to UG while still accounting for the variety of internal languages attained, relying on third-factor principles? Let me end with a few words on this approach.

An elementary fact about the language faculty is that it is a system of discrete infinity. In the simplest case, such a system is based on a primitive operation that takes objects already constructed, and constructs from them a new object. Call that operation Merge. There are more complex modes of generation, such as the familiar phrase structure grammars explored in the early years of generative grammar. But a Merge-based system is the most elementary, so we assume it to be true of language unless empirical facts force greater UG complexity. If computation is efficient, then when X and Y are merged, neither will change, so that the outcome can be taken to be simply the set {X,Y}. That is sometimes called the No-Tampering condition, a natural principle of efficient computation, perhaps a special case of laws of nature. With Merge available, we instantly have an unbounded system of hierarchically structured expressions. For language to be usable, these expressions have to link to the interfaces. The generated expressions provide the means to relate sound and meaning in traditional terms, a far more subtle process than had been assumed for millennia. UG must at least include the principle of unbounded Merge.

The conclusion holds whether recursive generation is unique to the language faculty or found elsewhere. If the latter, there still must be a genetic instruction to use unbounded Merge to form linguistic expressions. Nonetheless, it is interesting to ask whether this operation is language-specific. We know that it is not. The classic illustration is the system of natural numbers, raising problems for evolutionary theory noted by Alfred Russel Wallace. A possible solution is that the number system is derivative from language. If the lexicon is reduced to a single element, then unbounded Merge will easily yield arithmetic. Speculations about the origin of the mathematical capacity as an abstraction from language are familiar, as are criticisms, including apparent dissociation with lesions and diversity of localization. The significance of such phenomena, however, is far from clear. As Luigi Rizzi has pointed out,[20] they relate to use of the capacity, not its possession; for similar reasons, dissociations do not show that the capacity to read is not parasitic on the language faculty. The competence–performance distinction should not be obscured. To date, I am not aware of any real examples of unbounded Merge apart from language, or obvious derivatives from language, for example, taking visual arrays as lexical items.

We can regard an account of some linguistic phenomena as principled insofar as it derives them by efficient computation satisfying interface conditions. A very strong proposal, called "the strong minimalist thesis," is that all phenomena of language have a principled account in this sense, that language is a perfect solution to interface conditions, the conditions it must satisfy to some extent if it is to be usable at all. If that thesis were true, language would be something like a snowflake, taking the form it does by virtue of natural law, in which case UG would be very limited.

---

[20] Rizzi (2003). (Editors' note)

In addition to unbounded Merge, language requires atoms, or word-like elements, for computation. Whether these belong strictly to language or are appropriated from other cognitive systems, they pose extremely serious problems for the study of language and thought and also for the study of the evolution of human cognitive capacities. The basic problem is that even the simplest words and concepts of human language and thought lack the relation to mind-independent entities that has been reported for animal communication: representational systems based on a one–one relation between mind/brain processes and "an aspect of the environment to which these processes adapt the animal's behavior," to quote Randy Gallistel (1990b). The symbols of human language and thought are sharply different.

These matters were explored in interesting ways by seventeenth- and eighteenth-century British philosophers, developing ideas that trace back to Aristotle. Carrying their work further, we find that human language appears to have no reference relation, in the sense stipulated in the study of formal systems, and presupposed – mistakenly I think – in contemporary theories of reference for language in philosophy and psychology, which take for granted some kind of word–object relation, where the objects are extra-mental. What we understand to be a house, a river, a person, a tree, water, and so on, consistently turns out to be a creation of what seventeenth-century investigators called the "cognoscitive powers," which provide us with rich means to refer to the outside world from certain perspectives. The objects of thought they construct are individuated by mental operations that cannot be reduced to a "peculiar nature belonging" to the thing we are talking about, as David Hume summarized a century of inquiry. There need be no mind-independent entity to which these objects of thought bear some relation akin to reference, and apparently there is none in many simple cases (probably all). In this regard, internal conceptual symbols are like the phonetic units of mental representations, such as the syllable /ba/; every particular act externalizing this mental entity yields a mind-independent entity, but it is idle to seek a mind-independent construct that corresponds to the syllable. Communication is not a matter of producing some mind-external entity that the hearer picks out of the world, the way a physicist could. Rather, communication is a more-or-less affair, in which the speaker produces external events and hearers seek to match them as best they can to their own internal resources. Words and concepts appear to be similar in this regard, even the simplest of them. Communication relies on shared cognoscitive powers, and succeeds insofar as shared mental constructs, background, concerns, presuppositions, etc. allow for common perspectives to be (more or less) attained. These semantic properties of lexical items seem to be unique to human language and thought, and have to be accounted for somehow in the study of their evolution.

Returning to the computational system, as a simple matter of logic, there are two kinds of Merge, external and internal. External Merge takes two objects, say *eat* and *apples*, and forms the new object that corresponds to *eat apples*. Internal Merge – often called Move – is the same, except that one of the objects is internal to the other. So applying internal Merge to *John ate what*, we form the new object corresponding to *what John ate what*, in accord with the No-Tampering condition. As in the examples I mentioned earlier, at the semantic interface, both occurrences of *what* are interpreted: the first occurrence as an operator and the second as the variable over which it ranges, so that the expression means something like: *for which thing x, John ate the thing x*. At the sensorimotor side, only one of the two identical syntactic objects is pronounced, typically the structurally most salient occurrence. That illustrates the ubiquitous displacement property of language: items are commonly pronounced in one position but interpreted somewhere else as well. Failure to pronounce all but one occurrence follows from third-factor considerations of efficient computation, since it reduces the burden of repeated application of the rules that transform internal structures to phonetic form – a heavy burden when we consider real cases. There is more to say, but this seems the heart of the matter.

This simple example suggests that the relation of the internal language to the interfaces is asymmetrical. Optimal design yields the right properties at the semantic side, but causes processing problems at the sound side. To understand the perceived sentence

(7)   What did John eat?

it is necessary to locate and fill in the missing element, a severe burden on speech perception in more complex constructions. Here conditions of efficient computation conflict with facilitation of communication. Universally, languages prefer efficient computation. That appears to be true more generally. For example, island conditions are at least sometimes, and perhaps always, imposed by principles of efficient computation. They make certain thoughts inexpressible, except by circumlocution, thus impeding communication. The same is true of ambiguities, as in the examples I mentioned earlier. Structural ambiguities often fall out naturally from efficient computation, but evidently pose a communication burden.

Other considerations suggest the same conclusion. Mapping to the sensorimotor interface appears to be a secondary process, relating systems that are independent: the sensorimotor system, with its own properties, and the computational system that generates the semantic interface, optimally insofar as the strong minimalist thesis is accurate. That's basically what we find. Complexity, variety, effects of historical accident, and so on, are overwhelmingly restricted to morphology and phonology, the mapping to the sensorimotor interface. That's why these are virtually the only topics investigated in traditional linguistics, or that enter into language teaching. They are idiosyncracies, so are noticed, and have to be learned. If so, then it appears that language evolved, and is designed, primarily as an instrument of thought. Emergence of unbounded Merge in human evolutionary history provides what has been called a "language of thought," an internal generative system that constructs thoughts of arbitrary richness and complexity, exploiting conceptual resources that are already available or may develop with the availability of structured expressions. If the relation to the interfaces is asymmetric, as seems to be the case, then unbounded Merge provides only a language of thought, and the basis for ancillary processes of externalization.

There are other reasons to believe that something like that is true. One is that externalization appears to be independent of sensory modality, as has been learned from studies of sign language in recent years. More general considerations suggest the same conclusion. The core principle of language, unbounded Merge, must have arisen from some rewiring of the brain, presumably the effect of some small mutation. Such changes take place in an individual, not a group. The individual so endowed would have had many advantages: capacities for complex thought, planning, interpretation, and so on. The capacity would be transmitted to offspring, coming to dominate a small breeding group. At that stage, there would be an advantage to externalization, so the capacity would be linked as a secondary process to the sensorimotor system for externalization and interaction, including communication. It is not easy to imagine an account of human evolution that does not assume at least this much. And empirical evidence is needed for any additional assumption about the evolution of language.

Such evidence is not easy to find. It is generally supposed that there are precursors to language proceeding from single words, to simple sentences, then more complex ones, and finally leading to unbounded generation. But there is no empirical evidence for the postulated precursors, and no persuasive conceptual argument for them either: transition from ten-word sentences to unbounded Merge is no easier than transition from single words. A similar issue arises in language acquisition. The modern study of the topic began with the assumption that the child passes through a one- and two-word stage, telegraphic speech, and so on. Again the assumption lacks a rationale, because at some point unbounded Merge must appear. Hence the capacity must have been there all along even if it only comes to function at some later stage. There does appear to be evidence about earlier stages: namely, what children produce. But that carries little weight. Children understand far more than what they produce, and understand normal language but not their own restricted speech, as was shown long ago by Lila Gleitman and her colleagues.[21] For both evolution and development, there seems little reason to postulate precursors to unbounded Merge.

In the 1974 biolinguistics conference, evolutionary biologist Salvador Luria was the most forceful advocate of the view that communicative needs would not have provided "any great selective pressure to produce a system such as language," with its crucial relation to "development of abstract or productive thinking." His fellow Nobel laureate François Jacob added later that "the role of language as a communication system between individuals would have come about only secondarily, as many linguists believe," perhaps referring to discussions at the symposia.[22] "The quality of language that makes it unique does not seem to be so much its role in communicating directives for action" or other common features of animal communication, Jacob continues, but rather "its role in symbolizing, in evoking cognitive images," in "molding" our notion of reality and yielding our capacity for thought and planning, through its unique property of allowing "infinite combinations of symbols" and therefore "mental creation of possible worlds," ideas that trace back to the seventeenth-century cognitive revolution and have been considerably sharpened in recent years.

We can, however, go beyond speculation. Investigation of language design can yield evidence on the relation of language to the interfaces. There is, I think, mounting evidence that the relation is asymmetrical in the manner indicated. There are more radical proposals under which optimal satisfaction of semantic conditions becomes close to tautologous. That seems to me one way to understand the general drift of Jim Higginbotham's work on the syntax–semantics border for many years.[23] And from a different point of view, something similar would follow from ideas developed by Wolfram Hinzen (2006a, 2007a; Hinzen and Uriagereka 2006), in line with Juan Uriagereka's suggestion that it is "as if syntax carved the path interpretation must blindly follow" (Uriagereka 1999).

The general conclusions appear to fit reasonably well with evidence from other sources. It seems that brain size reached its current level about 100,000 years ago, which suggests to some specialists that "human language probably evolved, at least in part, as an automatic but adaptive consequence of increased absolute brain size," leading to dramatic changes of behavior (quoting George Striedter, in *Brain and Behavioral Sciences* February 2006, who adds

---

[21] See also Shatz and Gelman (1973). (Editors' note)

[22] Jacob (1977). For an insightful reconstruction of those debates see also Jenkins (2000). (Editors' note)

[23] See Chapter 10. (Editors' note)

qualifications about the structural and functional properties of primate brains). This "great leap forward," as some call it, must have taken place before about 50,000 years ago, when the trek from Africa began. Even if further inquiry extends the boundaries, it remains a small window in evolutionary time. The picture is consistent with the idea that some small rewiring of the brain gave rise to unbounded Merge, yielding a language of thought, later externalized and used in many ways. Aspects of the computational system that do not yield to principled explanation fall under UG, to be explained somehow in other terms, questions that may lie beyond the reach of contemporary inquiry, Richard Lewontin has argued.[24] Also remaining to be accounted for are the apparently human-specific atoms of computation, the minimal word-like elements of thought and language, and the array and structure of parameters, rich topics that I have barely mentioned.

At this point we have to move on to more technical discussion than is possible here, but I think it is fair to say that there has been considerable progress in moving towards principled explanation in terms of third-factor considerations. The best guess about the nature of UG only a few years ago has been substantially improved by approaching the topic "from bottom up," by asking how far we can press the strong minimalist thesis. It seems now that much of the architecture that has been postulated can be eliminated without loss, often with empirical gain. That includes the last residues of phrase structure grammar, including the notion of projection or later "labeling," the latter perhaps eliminable in terms of minimal search. Also eliminable on principled grounds are underlying and surface structure, and also logical form, in its technical sense, leaving just the interface levels (and their existence too is not graven in stone, a separate topic). The several compositional cycles that have commonly been postulated can be reduced to one, with periodic transfer of generated structures to the interface at a few designated positions ("phases"), yielding further consequences. A very elementary form of transformational grammar essentially "comes free": it would require stipulations to block it, so that there is a principled explanation, in these terms, for the curious but ubiquitous phenomenon of displacement in natural language, with interpretive options in positions that are phonetically silent. And by the same token, any other approach to the phenomenon carries an empirical burden. Some of the island conditions have principled explanations, as does the existence of categories for which there is no direct surface evidence, such as a functional category of inflection.

Without proceeding, it seems to me no longer absurd to speculate that there may be a single internal language, efficiently yielding the infinite array of

---

[24] Lewontin (1998). (Editors' note)

expressions that provide a language of thought. Variety and complexity of language would then be reduced to the lexicon, which is also the locus of parametric variation, and to the ancillary mappings involved in externalization, which might turn out to be best-possible solutions to relating organs with independent origins and properties. There are huge promissory notes left to pay, and alternatives that merit careful consideration, but plausible reduction of the previously assumed richness of UG has been substantial.

With each step towards the goals of principled explanation we gain a clearer grasp of the essential nature of language, and of what remains to be explained in other terms. It should be kept in mind, however, that any such progress still leaves unresolved problems that have been raised for hundreds of years. Among these is the question how properties "termed mental" relate to "the organical structure of the brain," in the eighteenth-century formulation. And beyond that lies the mysterious problem of the creative and coherent ordinary use of language, a central problem of Cartesian science, still scarcely even at the horizons of inquiry.

Discussion

PIATTELLI-PALMARINI: I am concerned with the parallel between the numbering system and language, and the conceptual possibility of starting with one single lexical item only and then generating the rest with something like the successor function. Peano was adamant in stressing that there can only be one empty set. This is a truth of reason, an inescapable necessary truth, that there is only one empty set. So, you form the set that contains it, and then the set that contains the previous one, and so on. The successor function and the necessary uniqueness of the empty set give you the natural numbers system. It does not seem to me to be quite straightforward to do something similar in the case of language. The necessary uniqueness of the empty set would be missing.

CHOMSKY: That's one way of doing it. If you want to generate it from set theory, that's a rich way of doing it. If you want to do it without set theory, what you have is one element, and then you have an operation that forms a successor, and it's simply repeating it. Okay, that's the numbering system. Now this system you *can* get by taking one lexical item, and one way of doing it would be with a Merge system, which does use limited trivial set theory. The one item could be, for example, the set containing 0. And then if you use internal Merge, you'll get a set which consists of 0 and the set containing 0, and you can call that 1, if you like. And you can do that again, and you get 2, and if you throw in associativity, you can get addition, and that's basically the number system. You can get addition, subtraction, and multiplication in the familiar way. So it does need just a trivial amount of set theory, just as Merge does, and in fact I don't know if you even need that; it might be possible to develop a Nelson Goodman-style nominalist alternative.[25] So that's one way of getting numbers, and there are others you can think of for just getting a numbering system by restricting language to the very narrowest sense.

HIGGINBOTHAM: Just to help clarify this. You know that in the mathematics of these things one studies semi-groups? You have groups (with a reciprocal operation) and semigroups, which are merely associative. The "free" semi-groups have certain special algebraic properties; and then, as they used to tell us at Columbia, the numbering system is just the free semigroup with one generator. That's it.

CHOMSKY: Yes, that's basically what I'm saying. That's correct, it means that the numbering system might just be a trivial case of language, which would solve Wallace's Paradox. Wallace was worried about how it could be that everybody has this number system but it's obviously never been selected; it's not very useful.

RIZZI: I have a question on the division of labor between UG and third-factor principles. In a number of cases that come to mind, it looks as if there is a highly general loose concept which applies across cognitive domains. Take locality, for instance, a concept that seems to be relevant and operative in different cognitive domains in various forms. And then if you look at language, it is very sharp, very precise. It gets implemented in an extremely sharp manner, only certain things count as interveners, only certain categories determine impenetrability, etc. So the question, related to your short comment on the fact that minimal search may be a third-factor entity, is how much of that is in UG and how much of that is derivable from external general principles.

CHOMSKY: This looks ahead to Luigi's talk in this conference,[26] so he is going to elaborate on this, but he mentions two principles that seem to be involved in these kinds of questions. One is something that comes out of sequential computation, which has strong computational reasons for it, and that could take care of some kinds of extralinguistic effects – though as an aside, I think there is good reason to suppose that computation of syntactic-semantic objects involves parallel computation as well. But there is another one, which he mentioned now and which is intervention effects, a kind which, as he points out, cross over the units of sequential computation, so they don't seem to follow directly. That is

---

[25] Goodman and Quine (1947).
[26] See Chapter 11.

more or less the story. And he raises and will suggest answers to the question of how these two things could interact. But then one may be third factor, like minimal search, and the other somehow specific to language? Now technically, if I have understood the abstract of his talk here correctly, one possible way of getting an indication (which does require work as his examples show) is that it all has to do with minimal search. Now that does require reanalysis of things like the Nominative Island Constraint and Superiority Conditions and so on, and I think there is some reason to believe that that is possible. But as you know, I am very skeptical about the Superiority Condition. I really don't think it exists; I think it's been misinterpreted, along lines I discussed a bit in my book *The Minimalist Program* (1995). There is some work on things like the Negative Island Condition which suggest that it may have an explanation in other terms, like in Danny Fox's recent papers.[27] It is possible, like some future goal, that it might all be reduced to minimal search. That is, minimal search *could* be – we have to prove this, you have got to show it – in principle it could be just a law of nature. It is just the best way of doing anything. And you would expect to find it in efficient patterns of foraging, all sorts of neural structures, and so on. If that can be worked out, then you *would* reduce it all to third-factor principles.

Of course you are exactly right. In the case of language, it is going to have very special properties, because language is apparently unique as a system of discrete infinity. So it is going to be totally different from foraging, let's say, which is a continuous system, unlike language which is a discrete system. But it would be nice to try to show that the differences that occur in the case of language, in spite of the specific things you mentioned, are just due to the fact that it is uniquely a system of discrete infinity, which is then of course going to have different effects. Probably the nearest analogue with human language in the natural world, in the non-human world, is bee communication, which is a rich communicative system. In fact many kinds of different species use different forms of it. Oddly – somebody here who knows more about this can correct me, but as far as I understand the bee literature – there are about 500 species, and some of them use the waggle dance, others use sound, and they all seem to get along about as well, from the point of view of biological success, which does raise the question of what it is all for. If you can get by without the waggle dance, then why have it? But that is a typical problem in evolutionary theory. When people produce evolutionary speculations from adaptiveness, it just doesn't mean much. If you look at the encyclopedic reviews of the evolution of communication, what you actually find is people saying how beautifully

---

[27] Fox and Hacki (2006); Fox (in press).

something works in this ecological niche. Okay, maybe it does, but that leaves open the question – it doesn't say anything about evolution.

But whatever it is, bee communication is fundamentally continuous insofar as an organism's behavior can be continuous (I mean, there are minimal perceptual effects), so they are just going to have different properties. Even with the same minimal search principle, it would show up very differently in a discrete system like language, and in a continuous system like, say, the bee dance. And maybe that's the answer. A shot in the dark, but I think it might be a direction to look.

PARTICIPANT: Could I ask you to deal a little bit with Peirce's theory of abduction, and the importance of an abductive instinct?

CHOMSKY: Peirce posed the problem of abduction in lectures which I think are from about a century ago, but as far as I know, nobody ever noticed them until about the 1960s. When I found them and wrote about them then, I couldn't find any earlier discussion of them. Those were pre-electronic days when you couldn't do a real database search, but I couldn't find any reference to Peirce's theory of abduction.[28]

Now the term abduction *is* used, Jerry Fodor has spoken about it and others, but it is a different sense;[29] it is not Peirce's sense. Peirce's sense was very straightforward and, I think, basically correct. He says you want to account for the fact that science does develop, and that people do hit upon theories which sort of seem to be true. He was also struck by the fact, and this is correct, that at a certain stage of science, a certain stage of understanding, everybody tends to come to the same theory, and if one person happens to come to it first, everybody else says "Yes, that's right." Why does that happen? You take any amount of data and innumerable theories can handle them, so how come you get this kind of convergence in a straight pattern through even what Thomas Kuhn called revolutions?[30]

Let's take, say, relativity theory, special relativity. When it came along in 1905, Einstein didn't have much empirical evidence. In fact, there was a great deal of experimentation done in the following years by all kinds of experimental scientists, who refuted it, and nobody paid any attention. They didn't pay any attention to the refutations, because it was obviously right. So even if it was refuted by a lot of experimentation, they disregarded the experiments. And that went on for many years. I remember years ago reading the Born–Einstein

---

[28] Peirce (1982).
[29] J. A. Fodor (2001).
[30] Kuhn (1962).

correspondence, and somewhere in the late 1920s (someone who knows more about this can correct me if I don't have it right, but it is something like this) a very famous American experimental physicist redid the Michelson–Morley experiment, which had provided the main evidence, and it came out the wrong way. And Born wrote to Einstein and he said "Look, do you think I'd better go over to this guy's lab and find out what mistake he made?" And Einstein said "No, it is probably not worth it. Somebody will probably figure it out sooner or later."[31] But the point is he didn't even pay any attention to the refutation of the Michelson–Morley experiment because it couldn't be right. And it couldn't be right for conceptual reasons.

That is pretty much the way science often seems to work. It is true even in our areas. You just see that some ideas simply look right, and then you sort of put aside the data that refute them and think, somebody else will take care of it. Well, Peirce was interested in that, and he asked how it happened, and I think he gave the right answer. He says we have an instinct. He says it is like a chicken pecking. We just have an instinct that says this is the way you do science. And if you look at the famous scientists reflecting, that is what they say. I remember once I was at the Institute for Advanced Studies and Dirac was giving a lecture, so I went out of curiosity. Of course I didn't know what he was talking about, but in the lecture some hotshot mathematician got up and said "You made a mathematical error in a particular point," and Dirac said "Okay, you figure out what the mistake is, I'm going on with this, because this is the way it has to be." Well, that is sort of the way things work.[32] Peirce's answer is that there is some kind of instinct, the abductive instinct, which sets limits on permissible hypotheses and says these kinds are explanatory theories, but this other kind are not, even if they work.

And that leads us onward somehow. Peirce argued that if you keep on this track indefinitely, you eventually reach truth. He thought that truth is sort of defined as the limit of scientific experimentation, and he gave a very bad evolutionary argument for this. He said that evolution has adapted us to find the right kinds of solutions to natural problems, but that cannot possibly be true. There is nothing in human evolution that led people to figure out quantum

---

[31] Einstein et al. (1971 (reprinted 2005)).

[32] Much in the same vein, Jacques Monod once said to Massimo Piattelli-Palmarini that there had been some early experiments from other laboratories apparently refuting the Monod–Jacob model of genetic regulation (Jacob and Monod 1961), a major breakthrough that won them the Nobel Prize in 1965. Monod confessed he had decided to pay no attention to them, and did not even try to replicate them, because the model was so obviously correct. He assumed, rightly as it turned out, that time would have told what was wrong with those experiments. This is especially noteworthy, because Monod professed to be a convinced Popperian falsificationist. (Editors' note)

theory, or classical mechanics, or anything, so that can't be right. That is just one of the worst kinds of pseudo-Darwinism. So maybe what it is leading us to is something totally wrong, and if somebody is looking at this, say some Martian with different cognitive structures, they could see we are just asking the wrong questions. We are not asking the right questions because they are not within our range. We can't ask those right questions; we aren't built for it. And if we can ask them, we can't answer them. So take the questions, this first-person perspective thing, which is a big issue in philosophy: what is it like to be a bat? (a famous article);[33] what is it like to be me? There are no sensible answers to those questions. I cannot tell you what it is like to be me. If something has an interrogative form and there are no sensible answers to it, it is not a real question; it just has an interrogative form. It is like "How do things happen?" You know, it sounds like a question, but there is no possible answer to it.

So I don't think these are even questions. You can give a naturalist interpretation of such matters, and maybe there is a right question and we just can't formulate it, because we're just not built that way. So if there is one, we may not find it. That is Peirce's concern. Well, to get back to your question, I can't add anything to that, and I don't think anybody has added anything to it in a hundred years. In fact, they haven't even looked at it. The term abduction has been picked up, but it is used for something else. It is used for best-theory construction or something like that, whatever that means, but that is just rephrasing the question.

It seems to me the answer has to come from some kind of study of what this organ is, this science-forming organ. Now Sue Carey, whom I mentioned, has been trying to show that it is just the natural extension of ordinary, common-sense figuring out what the world is like (Carey 1985). But that seems to me to be extremely unlikely. Of course it is interesting stuff, but it seems to me to be going in the wrong direction. Whatever this crazy thing is that scientists do, it seems to me very much disconnected from sort of finding your way in the world. I mean, people talk about it, the search for symmetry – there is a famous book about that[34] – and Galileo talked about how Nature has to be perfect and it is the task of scientists to find it. You do have these guiding intuitions and so everybody follows on, more or less, but they don't seem to have anything to do with sort of getting around in the world. So it is a serious open question, and it could be – it is an empirical question, in principle: what is the nature of Peirce's abductive instinct? Maybe somebody can tell me something. A lot of you know more about this than I do, but I don't know of any work on it, philosophical or

---

[33] Nagel, T. (1974).
[34] Weyl (1989).

empirical or anything else. It has just kind of been left to the side, and again, as far as I know, Peirce's essay wasn't even discussed for about sixty years.

DOVER: You have a long-held view that the human capacity for language is an evolved biological system and, as such, there has to be a genetic basis for it – no different in kind from any other specific feature of human biology. I don't think anyone would want to refute that, but I sense, if I understood you correctly, that you want to go beyond that.

Within the minimalist program, my understanding of which is very shaky indeed, I sense you want to bring forth something beyond the genes. That is, we have what you call principles of natural law. However, I want to point out that the whole thrust of modern-day genetics is going against such ideas of laws of form and principles of natural law, or however you want to phrase it. And indeed, in a very revealing way, Alan Turing was actually wrong with this approach. Just take this one example. He showed mathematically that if you consider a larva of an insect simply in terms of physical/chemical principles of reaction and diffusion amongst free-floating molecules, then the system falls naturally into a series of standing waves of molecular concentrations underlying the appearance of discontinuous bands of bristles along the larval axis (Turing 1952). But we now know from genetic analysis that the positioning of each band is independently determined by a band-specific handful of genes that are networking with each other in a regulatory manner, and if you mutate one or other gene you might knock out, say, bristle band 3 or band 7 and so on. However, knocking out a band does not entail a reorientation of the remaining bands according to physical principles of organization in the remaining larva as a whole – in other words, there are very local molecular interactions making each band independent of the rest, and the ensemble approach of field theory based on physical/chemical principles doesn't seem to come into it. Now we can show this over and over again for almost any aspect of phenotypic form and behavior you'd wish to consider. The evolutionarily constrained yet flexible network, seemingly unique in operation in biology, is very significant, as I shall show in my talk. Biological diversity is a consequence of local differences in the combinatorial usage of modular and versatile genes and their proteins that often stretch back to the origin of life. But nothing seems to be obeying laws of form, out of reach of the genes.

CHOMSKY: That can't be. I mean, take, say, the division of cells into spheres, not cubes. Is there a gene for that?

DOVER: Yes, of course there is. It could be your worst nightmare (!) for there are tens upon tens, if not hundreds, of genes directly responsible for very wide-ranging differences in the shapes, sizes, numbers, divisions, life spans, senescence, functions, and behavior of the several hundred types of cells in our species. Cells are not soap bubbles. There are constraints of course but these are a matter largely of history not of physics, over and above the obvious physics/chemistry of molecular contacts.

CHOMSKY: No there isn't such a gene. Cells form spheres because that is the least-energy solution. In fact, it has always been obvious that something is channeling evolution and development. It doesn't go any possible way; it goes in the ways that the laws of physics and chemistry allow. Now, Turing's particular proposal about reaction-diffusion, giving discreteness from continuity – first of all, I think it has been partly confirmed, for angelfish stripes and in other instances. But quite apart from that, whether he had exactly the right proposal back in 1952 doesn't really matter. His general formulation just has to be true. And it is presupposed by all the work you are talking about.

If particular combinations of proteins and molecules and so on do particular things, that is because of physics and chemistry. The only question is to try to discover in what ways physics and chemistry determine the particular evolution. So again, we are getting into your domain, which you obviously know more about, but take the evolution of the eye. Let's say Gehring's more or less right, okay?[35] What happens is there is a set of molecules, rhodopsin molecules, which happen to have the physical property that they turn light energy into chemical energy? One of them might randomly migrate into a cell. That, according to him, is the monophyletic origin of eyes along with a conserved master control gene, and maybe even everything phototropic.

Everything that happens after that has to do with the intercalation of genes and certain gene sequences, but that all happens in particular ways because of physical law. You cannot intercalate them in any crazy way you dream up. There are certain ways in which it can be done. And he tries to conclude from this that you get the few kinds of eyes that you get. Well, all of that is presupposing massive amounts of maybe unknown physical and chemical principles which are leading things in a certain direction, kind of like cell division into spheres. I mean, there may be a couple of genes involved, but fundamentally it is physical principles.

Now how far does that go? Well, I'm no biologist but I don't agree with your conclusion, or that that is the conclusion of modern genetics. In fact, the whole evo-devo development over the past twenty to thirty years has been moving strongly in the opposite direction, saying that it is all the same genes pretty

---

[35] Gehring (2004).

much, and that they are conserved; and you get the Hox genes going back to bacteria, and so on, but there are small shifts in the structure of regulatory circuits and the hierarchy and so on; and that through physical principles you get the observed diversity of forms. And it does give you the laws of form. I mean, it is not that the laws of form are like Newton's laws. They emerge from the principles of physics and chemistry, which say that these are the ways in which molecules can work, and not a lot of other ways.

And just conceptually, it has to be like this. I mean, there cannot be anything like selection acting blindly. It is like learning – B. F. Skinner pointed out correctly (in one of the few correct statements he made back in *Verbal Behavior*, in fact) that the logical structure of conditioning, reinforcement theory, is the same as the Darwinian theory of natural selection. He understood Darwinian theory in a very naïve way – random mutation and then natural selection with changes in any possible way; that is all there is. But it can't be true. No biologist ever believed that it was true. It is totally impossible. Something has to channel a mutation in particular ways, not other ways – according to some recent work that I mentioned, in only a few ways. And then selection is just going to have to operate in particular channels and not in others. Skinner took that to be a justification for reinforcement theory, but in fact it is a refutation of reinforcement theory. This naïve Darwinian view is all over the place in evolutionary psychology and fields that touch on the evolution of language, and so on. But it is all just nonsense, as it is often presented. There have to be presupposed physical and chemical laws, and Turing I think was right about that. Maybe reaction-diffusion doesn't explain the stripes of zebras, but the basic principle has got to be right. And it is presupposed in everything that is done. Every time you talk about molecules behaving in a certain way, or genes producing this protein and not another one, and so on, that is all because that is the way physics and chemistry works.

DOVER: Well of course. All is chemistry and physics at the level of electrons and protons, and molecular interactions in biology, always based on differences in reduction and oxidation potentials, are not exempt. We don't differ on this point. Nor do we differ on evolved diversity being constrained (life is not a free-for-all). The argument is whether constraints are a reflection of contingent history (given that our single tree-of-life just happens to occupy only a small fraction of phenotypic space), or of the workings of physics/chemistry, or of laws of form above the reach of genes. But I will examine these alternatives in my talk, as well as the other point on which we agree that there is more to the evolution of life than natural selection.

CHOMSKY: The point is that if you want to move biology from looking at things as particular cases, if you want to move it from that to a science, then you're going to ask what the guiding principles are that determine what happens – you've got to ask the Why questions: Why did it happen this way and not that way? And that is being done. That is evo-devo work, which is increasingly showing that the course of evolution to a large extent (not always) is more regulatory than structural. I mean, the structures stay and the regulatory mechanisms change, and then you get a lot of diversity. Now they don't have a lot of experimental evidence for it, but that is a leading theme of modern evolutionary developmental biology, and plenty of biologists are staking on its potentially being true, whatever the evidence is.

So I think that Turing is correct in saying that that is the way that biology ought to go as a science. True, you find all sorts of details when you look, but we know that that can't be true generally. In this case, it is very much like the case of language, I think. It looked fifty years ago, and it still sort of looks, like every language is different from every other one and that is all you can say. You study the details. But it is conceptually obvious that that cannot be true, or no-one would ever acquire a language. And it is increasingly understood that it isn't true, and that to some extent you can attribute it to natural law.

About language evolving, yes of course language evolved. We are not angels. But evolution isn't just selection. Now here is an extreme thesis: perhaps language evolved as a result of, say, the explosion of brain size, for whatever reasons that took place maybe 100,000 years ago. It could be. Striedter speculates that a consequence of that is that some neural changes took place. It is not understood well. Even the simplest computation of insects is not understood well.[36] But something is going on, and it could be that explosion of brain size led to some small rewiring which yields unbounded Merge, and everything else that it has come up with, and that yields the semantic interpretations. Then comes the problem of relating two independent systems, this one and the sensorimotor system, whatever it is, and you get complicated solutions to that problem which could be best-possible solutions – a research problem for the future. Well if that is true, then nothing in this particular domain involved selection. I don't really expect that that is going to be true. That is just an extreme speculation. But if that is true, it evolved and nothing was selected. Beyond that, there will be what residue is left in UG after you have extracted all the third-factor principles. And I think the same question arises in the development of organisms. I mean an ant may be developing and you take a look at it and it looks hopelessly complex – this gene did this, and this kind of gene did

---

[36] See Gallistel's contribution, Chapter 4.

something else, and so forth, but there has got to be some physical explanation for that. The problem is to discover it.

PARTICIPANT: I have a sort of exploratory question about the relationship of symbolic items that enter into Merge and content. One of our recent graduates wrote a dissertation on generics and he came to a conclusion where he basically just supposes a GEN operator and finds variables, and then that points him to a generalization. And while I'm sympathetic to that sort of approach, I'm not sure it is a strategy for studying mental content and its relationship to language in this way, because it sort of seems like, well, you try to work it out in a more conventional generative semantics way, but after a while you think, well, I can't really get this to work out, so let's just invent a new operator and say, hey, there's this mystery box in the brain that takes care of it. So while I think it is great to come up with answers like that, I'm just wondering about the research value of this and how to make this a little more solid.

CHOMSKY: Without going into that particular work, I think there *is* a question one has to ask about these things, and that is whether they are actually answers, or whether they are simply reformulations of questions. I mean, you have a certain phenomenon that is puzzling. You can sometimes kind of reformulate that phenomenon in technical terms, introducing certain assumptions about the nature of the mechanisms and so on. But then, the question you always have to ask yourself is whether your explanation is of the same order of complexity as the description of the phenomena. And I think it often turns out that it is. It often turns out that the explanation is approximately of the same order of complexity as saying here is what the phenomena are, in which case it is not an answer. It may be useful. Maybe it is useful to reformulate the question that way, and maybe that carries you on to some next stage, but it is a question you always have to be very aware of. Take things like work trying to explain ECP,[37] or the *that*-trace phenomena or what have you. Possibly you get things which you could call explanations, but when you look at them properly, it turns out they are not really explanations; they are reformulations because you are introducing assumptions for which you have no reasons other than the fact that they help to account for this phenomenon. And insofar as that is true, you are restating the phenomenon in an organized way. Now again, that could be a useful step, because maybe this organized way of restating it leads to

---

[37] ECP stands for Empty Category Principle, a condition designed to account for the syntactic distribution of unpronounced elements of the so-called trace variety. For a discussion of these and related topics, see infra, in Rizzi's presentation (Chapter 11). (Editors' note)

suggestions about how to get a real explanation. But my suspicion about this case is kind of like that. Like where did that operator come from? Is it anything other than just a restatement of the data that we are trying to somehow find an account of? In that case, it is not an answer, though perhaps a useful step towards one. I think it is a question that always should be asked.

CHAPTER 3

The Nature of Merge

Consequences for Language, Mind, and Biology

Cedric Boeckx

I wanted to discuss an issue that speaks to both linguists and non-linguists, and what I am going to try to do is first of all phrase a series of very general questions and then take one specific example, Merge (the most basic kind of example that I can take from the linguistic literature), in order to address particular questions of evolution with regard to that process.

To begin, let me just give you the context of my presentation. It is basically the biolinguistic perspective that Chomsky defined very well in the eighties by enumerating a series of questions that I think ought to be on everybody's agenda. The questions are as follows:

(1) What is the knowledge or faculty of language?
(2) How did this knowledge or faculty develop in the individual?
(3) How is that knowledge put to use?
(4) How is it implemented in the brain?
(5) How did that knowledge emerge in the species?

Part of what I would like to do in this paper is briefly establish a parallelism between a question that we have understood fairly well in the linguistic litera-ture, namely the developmental question (2) and its analogue or cousin in the sense of evolution.

Another thing that Chomsky did that was very useful was to trace historical antecedents for these questions and give them names. So, for example, (1) is called Humboldt's Problem, and (2) is Plato's Problem, and that is the one that we are all very familiar with. Question (3) is Descartes's Problem, in many ways still a mystery. Question (4), interestingly enough, is not easy to name. It is about the brain–mind connection, and very few people have had good intuitions as to how to go about solving that mystery. You could call it Broca's Problem or Gall's Problem, but it is very difficult to find insightful antecedents for this issue. I think there is a lesson to be learned from the fact that we cannot really name that question, despite the fact that nowadays question (4) is taken in many circles to be the one on which the future of linguistics depends. By contrast, problem (5) is very easy to name, and although no one has applied this name to my knowledge, it can easily be called Darwin's Problem. Just like Humboldt, Descartes, and to some extent Plato, Darwin was very much interested in language, and in fact if you read *The Descent of Man*, there are very interesting reflections on language. Interestingly, Darwin establishes connections between our "language instinct" (that is where the term comes from) and the abilities that for example birds display when they sing. I think if we actually read those chapters in Darwin, we would not be misled by some of the recent heat on songbirds. Darwin was ahead of his time in that context as well.

The questions that Chomsky raised defining the biolinguistic literature find very obvious correspondences with those that Tinbergen put forth in 1963 in a famous paper called "On Aims and Methods of Ethology." These are the questions:

i. What stimulates the animal to respond with the behavior it displays, and what are the response mechanisms?
ii. How does an organism develop as the individual matures?
iii. Why is the behavior necessary for the animal's success, and how does evolution act on that behavior?
iv. How has the particular behavior evolved through time?

You can see that if you decompose those questions and rephrase them, inserting language in them, you get exactly the same set of questions that Chomsky put on the agenda. When Tinbergen put forth those four questions for ethology, he was very much under the influence of Ernst Mayr, and Dobzhansky's (1973) assertion that nothing makes sense, except in the light of evolution – Darwinian evolution, that is.

In the realm of psychology or the mental properties of cognition, we are in an uncomfortable position because we have to deal with a big phenomenon called "evolutionary psychology," which sort of reduces that question of Darwinian evolution to adaptation. However, if you talk to real biologists, they know that evolution is actually much richer than just adaptation. In particular, I think that we should bear in mind three things about evolution, which are valid for everything including questions about the evolution of the language faculty. The three things are the three factors that for example Stephen Jay Gould identified in a wonderful book called *The Structure of Evolutionary Theory* (2002): first, of course, adaptation, but then there are two others that psychologists often forget, namely chance (accidents of various sorts), and then structural constraints (some of the things that fall into the laws of form, if you want: what Chomsky now calls "third-factor" effects). There is actually a good term that comes from Wallace Arthur (2004), namely "bias," in the sense of "biased embryos," meaning that embryos develop or evolve in some directions and not in others. So if you combine adaptation, bias, and chance, you get this ABC of evolutionary theory, which is worth bearing in mind, particularly in approaching questions on the evolution of language. In doing so, we should also recall some of the early results that Lenneberg put forth in his 1967 book on the biological foundations of language, where he was very much interested in questions concerning the brain–mind connection and the question of evolution.

I think we have made progress recently in linguistic theory that enables us to address those questions a little bit more precisely. In particular, it is well known to non-linguists who attend linguistics talks that the jargon is so developed that it is hard to start a conversation, let alone address questions that are of an interdisciplinary nature, much less design adequate experiments. But here I think that the minimalist program in particular has forced linguists to go more basic, that is to develop a series of questions and answers that to some extent may help us to talk to non-linguists and address those questions, in particular questions (4) and (5).

To continue with the fifth question, Darwin's Problem, I first want to note that in various ways it shares similarities to the way we approach Plato's Problem. As everyone knows, when talking about Plato's Problem, one has to mention poverty of stimulus and the fact that children face a formidable task that they have to solve within a very short window of time. The result in a very few years is uniform acquisition – very rapid, effortless, and so on and so forth. I think the only way to really answer Plato's Problem generally is to give a head start to the child and say that much of it (the ability to develop or acquire language) is actually innate and built in somehow, in the genome or elsewhere (epigenetics), but it is at least given, it does not come from the input the child receives. This way, you can make sense of the task that is being fulfilled and achieved within the very short window of time that we all encounter.

That is exactly the same problem as the issue of language evolution, because everyone who has thought about the evolution of language seems to agree that it also happened within a very short space of time. Just like in the context of Plato's Problem, it appears that human language as we know it developed very,

very rapidly; and it's uniform across the species (Homo sapiens). So the way we should try to address and solve that problem, given that short time frame, is to do exactly what we have done for Plato's Problem, namely to say that in large part you want to make the task "easy" – that is, you want to make sure that the thing that has to evolve is actually fairly simple. You also want to say that much of it is already in place when you start facing that problem. This brings us to the distinction, or the combination, of the language faculty in the broad sense (FLB) and in the narrow sense (FLN).[1] The more you put into the FLB, the easier Darwin's Problem becomes. Just as we attribute a lot to the genome for his problem, so should we try to make sure that FLB contains quite a few things already, such that the thing that has to evolve is actually plausible as an organ subject to all the pressures of evolution.

I think that the FLB/FLN distinction becomes tractable or expressible especially in the context of the minimalist program, where you can begin to try to give some content in particular to FLN. And here I am building on work that Hauser, Chomsky, and Fitch did (Hauser et al. 2002, Fitch et al. 2005) by suggesting that one of the things that seems to be part of FLN is the operation Merge, which gives you this infinite recursive procedure that seems to be central to language. But here what I would like to do is suggest a slightly different take on the issue, or rather suggest a different way of defining Merge, that I think gives a slightly different program for linguists and non-linguists when addressing Darwin's Problem. Specifically, I think that there are some advantages in trying to decompose Merge a little bit further into more basic operations, to reveal not just the very general character of the operation, but also some of the specificity that gets into Merge to give you language and not just any recursive system.[2] In particular there is one thing that is quite clear about Merge and language: once you combine two units, X and Y, the output is not some new element Z, but either X or Y. So the hierarchical structure that we get in language is a very specific sort, namely it gives rise to so-called endocentric structures. That is the role of labels in syntax. So for example, when you put a verb and a noun together, what you get (typically, say, for the sake of concreteness) is a verb, and that verb, or that unit, acts as a verb for further combination. Now this, as far as I can tell, is very, very specific to language as a kind of hierarchical structure. If you look elsewhere in other systems of cognition (music, planning, kinship relations, etc.), you find a lot of evidence for hierarchical structuring of systems, possibly recursive ones, but as far as I can tell,

---

[1] See Chapter 5 for Marc Hauser's discussion of the FLB and FLN.

[2] See pages 155–157 for Luigi Rizzi's discussion of the specificity of Merge. This relates to some of the questions that Randy Gallistel talks about in Chapter 4.

those hierarchical structures are not headed or endocentric in the same way that linguistic structures are. That, to my mind, is very specific to language, so while you find hierarchies everywhere, headed or endocentric hierarchies seem very central to language. And so of course they would be part of FLN.

As soon as you identify this as an interesting and unique property of language, the next question is how does that endocentricity come about? The brute force answer might be to say "Well, this is the way you define Merge." But I think that there is a different, more interesting way of getting endocentricity that will actually raise other questions that people like Marc Hauser can address from an experimental perspective. For example, I have suggested (Boeckx 2006) that one way of getting endocentricity is by decomposing Merge into at least two operations. The very first operation is, say, a simple grouping procedure that puts X and Y together, and that presumably is very common across cognitive modules.[3] It is not very specific to language. Putting things together is presumably so basic an operation that it is, if not everywhere, at least in many systems. The next operation is selecting one of these two members and basically using that member as the next unit for recombination. For linguists, this is actually an operation that is well known. It is typically called a copying operation, where you take X and Y and then you, for example, retake X by copying it and recombine it with something else.

Now, the combination of basic grouping on the one hand, and copying on the other, gives you endocentric structures. It gives you Merge, which is in the linguistic sense a very specific kind of hierarchical structure. Not the type of structure that you get even in phonology. If you take, say, the syllable structure in phonology, that is a type of hierarchy that is not headed in the same way that syntax is. It is not endocentric (a VP is a V, but a syllable is not a nucleus). So what we should target precisely is that process of combining those two presumably fairly basic operations or processes, namely Concatenate and Copy, and it is the result of these two operations that gives you a very specific representation of vocabulary that we call Merge. Now notice that those two operations, Basic Grouping and Copy, need not be linguistically specific. These might have been recruited from other systems that presumably exist. I haven't checked, but other systems may make use of copying operations or operations that basically combine things. But it is the combination of these two presumably general processes that gives you the specificity that linguistic structures display.

That is actually a welcome consequence of work in linguistics, trying to decompose Merge. It is an arcane question, if you want, but it should be a

---

[3] Chomsky now uses Merge to refer to this basic grouping operation (keeping the labeling algorithm separate). Merge in that sense cannot be specific to language, in my opinion.

welcome consequence for biologists because biologists have long noted that typically novel things, like novel abilities, are very rare in nature. That is, novelty as such is usually not what you find in the biological world. Typically, what you find is a recombination of old processes that are put together in new ways that give you novelty. But you do not develop novelty out of nowhere. It is typically ancient things that you recombine. Now presumably Copy and Basic Grouping are ancient processes that you find elsewhere, and it is the combination of them that could actually define a good chunk of FLN. So the specificity for language would come from the combination of old things.

Stephen Jay Gould was very fond of making a distinction between the German terms *Neubildung*, that is "new formation," which is very, very rare in the biological world, and novelty coming about by what he called *Umbildung*, "recombination," the topological variations of old things, which is very, very common. That is what I think Jacob (1977) had in mind when he was talking about tinkering. He really did not have in mind what evolutionary psychologists like to use "tinkering" for (the less than optimal connotation of the term). Instead I think that what he wanted to stress was that if you have something that emerges as a novel aspect of the world, what you should first explore is the possibility that that novelty is just the result of recombination of old parts (which is not at all incompatible with suboptimal results). I think that decomposing Merge in that sense is what linguists can contribute, by saying that there is a way of making Merge not completely novel, outlandish, and very different from everything else that we know in the cognitive world; instead we should find basic operations that, once put together, result in a unique, specific structure that can be used for language and that may be recruited for other systems.

Now admittedly, this does not give us everything that has to evolve for language to become this very special object that we have. So for example I have not mentioned anything about phonology, about parameters, or about the lexicon or things of that sort. But it seems to me that Merge is the central component that has been taken, even in the recent literature, as something that is so unique and unlike anything else, that it is hard to see how it could have evolved even in a short period. By contrast, if you decompose it into more basic components, I think you can get a better handle on that question. If you can do that, if you can reduce Darwin's Problem to more basic questions, then it seems not implausible to think that, just as we solved Plato's Problem at least conceptually (though not in detail), we may at least begin to have a better handle on Darwin's Problem. And that is the suggestion I'd like to leave on the table here.

Discussion

LAKA: I agree that headedness seems to be an outstanding formal feature of language. The point you were trying to make is that we should think of Merge as a combination of two operations, and if I understood you correctly, that these two operations are likely to be independently found in other cognitive domains; and you also said that you think headedness is a good candidate for the language faculty in the narrow sense (FLN), which I assume we agree would be that part of language where you find novelty that is specific for language. My question is, if Merge is decomposed into two different operations, you might as well say it belongs to the faculty of language broadly understood (FLB), because you could also say that all those other things we find in FLB form a constellation that is unique to human language.

BOECKX: Yes, my intention is to say that some of the very specific aspects that define language, and headedness is an obvious one, may not be the result of completely new processes as such, but of the very novel or specific combinations of things that might actually be part of FLB. So that FLN might be, say, a new representation of vocabulary that results from the combination of processes that may be part of FLB for example. So it is just a different take on the FLB/FLN distinction. I think the distinction makes an awful lot of sense, but sometimes some of the content of FLN, you don't want to make it too specific so that it becomes this weird thing that we don't know how it could have evolved. It could be that these are just a new combination of old parts basically, so they might be part of FLB, okay? But you don't want to say that FLN is an empty set. You just want to say that some of the specificity of FLN could be the result of things that are in FLB and that are recruited for FLN.

PARTICIPANT: Suppose we agree that language to some extent is conceptually innovative. It is one thing to state that, but the question is how does it do that? How would language do that? And I want to send this out as a kind of test to my fellow linguists here. What is it about current thinking about syntax that makes us expect that language could have the conceptual and semantic consequences that have been discussed here? In particular, if you have such an impoverished view of Merge, if you think that the materials that enter into structure building are so conservative and you just bundle them together in a new way, why would language lead to the new ways of seeing the world that Marc Hauser mentions, for example?[4]

---

[4] See below, Chapter 5.

BOECKX: It's not implausible to think that as soon as you have a new representation in the vocabulary – even if it builds on old processes for combining things – that once you have that, you can use it as an exaptation for other things, giving you a completely different cognitive mind. For example, the hypothesis that Liz Spelke and others have explored that once you have language as a concept booster, you could have a very different conceptual world that results from that. Namely, you would have enough with basic Merge to combine modular information that is encapsulated otherwise, yielding as a result cross-modular concepts. That's something which, for example, Paul Pietroski[5] has explored. Now, once you have that (as a result of just using those basic operations, but using those operations to cross modules that have not been crossed in other animals), you get a very different kind of mind. It is not the only possibility, but it is one possibility, I think.

URIAGEREKA: A technical question for you, Cedric. Once you have talked about concatenation and copying, an immediate question that comes to mind is that you have concatenation in Markovian systems and you have copying in loops. So I wonder if that is a possibility you have thought about, that you exapt from those?

BOECKX: A very short answer: yes, that is exactly what I had in mind when you were saying that these could be exapted from more basic systems, and once you combine them you get a much more powerful system.

PARTICIPANT: I have a question about the proposal to decompose Merge. There are a few things I didn't really understand. First of all, I'm not really clear why concatenation is somehow simpler, less mysterious than Merge. In particular I thought that, at least in the version of Merge that I'm familiar with, it's not linearly ordered for all elements. So the flow of speech, one word after another, I take this to be a feature that is due to restrictions on the phonological interface in minimalism, so you probably don't want narrow syntax to have this constraint already built in. But now concatenation, at least in my computer, is a function that is ordered. AB and BA are two different results from the same elements and the same concatenation function. It seems like you're building order into it.

BOECKX: Yes, it's unfortunately built in the notion of concatenation for some, but it's not what I intended, so if you don't like "concatenation," use "combine" or "set formation" or something else that's very simple. There is no linear order

---

[5] Pietroski (in press).

meant there. It's just putting A and B together. That I think is a very basic and general operation, but I didn't intend to put linear order into the picture.

CHOMSKY: Actually, there is a question I wanted to raise, but technically, what the last person just said was correct. "Concatenate" means order, so it is more complex than Merge. But if you take the order away from "concatenate," it just *is* Merge. Merge simply says, "Take two objects, make another object." I think you are right in saying that something ought to be decomposed, but it seems to me that there is a better way to do it. In my talk earlier,[6] I just mentioned in a phrase that you can get rid of labeling, and I didn't explain it then, but I'll try to do so now. I don't agree that headedness is a property of language. I think it is an epiphenomenon, and there is nothing simpler than Merge. You can't decompose it, and when you take order away from concatenation, well that is what you have. But the crucial thing about language is not Merge; it is unbounded Merge. So just the fact that things are hierarchic elsewhere doesn't really tell you anything. They have to be *unboundedly* hierarchic. Now there is a way to decompose it coming from a different perspective, which I think might be promising. The crucial fact about Merge – the "almost true generalization" about Merge for language is that it is a head plus an XP.[7] That is virtually everything. Now, there is a pretty good, plausible reason for that. For one thing it follows from theta-theory. It is a property of semantic roles that they are kind of localized in particular kinds of heads, so that means when you are assigning semantic roles, you are typically putting together a head and something. It is also implicit in the cartographical approach. So when you add functional structures, there is only one way to do it, and that is to take a head and something else, so almost everything is head-XP, but when you have head-XP, that kind of construction, then headedness is a triviality; it comes from minimal search. If the element that you formed, the head-XP, is going to participate in further combinatorial operations, some information about it is relevant, and the simplest way to find the information – minimal search for the information – will be to take one of the two objects. Well, one of them has no information, because you have to find *its* head, and that is too deep down, so you find the other one. So the trivial consequence of an optimization procedure (presumably nonlinguistic and not organic, or maybe the law of nature) is in H-XP, take H.

Okay, that takes care of almost everything. It takes care of selection, it takes care of probe–goal relations – virtually everything. That eliminates any need for a copying operation. I don't see any reason for a copying operation. Copying

---

[6] See page 31 above.

[7] See the comments of Jim Higginbotham below (page 143) about generalizations that are "very close to being true."

just takes two objects, one of which happens to be inside the other. That is one of the two logical possibilities. Either one is inside the other, or one is outside the other. So that is just logical. We don't need a copying operation. All that this leaves out, and it is an interesting class that it leaves out, is XP-YP structures. Well, there are two types of those. One of them is coming from Internal Merge, where you pick something from the inside and you tack it on, on the outside, but in that case again, minimal search gives you a kind of obvious algorithm for which piece of the structure is relevant to further combination – labeling. Namely, keep being conservative, i.e. pick the one that did the work. The one that did the work is the probe of what would Y be, which itself was an H-XP thing, and that, for all kinds of probe–goal reasons that we know, found the internal one. Put it on the outside; OK, just keep that as the identifying element, the label for the next thing. And here Caterina Donati's[8] discovery was important, that if the thing you are adding happens to be a head, you do get an ambiguity. You can take either the conservative one to be the head, or the new head to be the head, but that is correct, as she showed. It shows up in various ways.

Well, that leaves only one case, and it is a striking case because it is exceptional, and that is the external argument. The only other plausible case that exists (sorry, this is getting too internal to linguistics) is the external argument in the V. That is the one case that remains. We intuitively take the V, not the external argument, and you need an answer for that. But in order to answer that, we first ought to notice how exceptional this case is. For one thing, this new object that you form when you put on an external argument never behaves like a constituent, so for example it never fronts, never moves, and it cannot remain that way. Something has to pull out of it. It is an old problem, with various proposals (I don't think they are very convincing), but it doesn't act like a constituent the way everything else does. You have to take something out of it; it can't remain. Furthermore, these things have different kinds of semantic roles. Actually, there's a paper of Jim Higginbotham's,[9] about subjects and noun phrases, where Jim argues that they just don't have the same kinds of semantic roles as the subjects of verb phrases, or they may have no semantic role, but it is different than a theta-role, and that is the other case of XP-YP. It is the specifier of a noun phrase. So it is different in that respect.

Another difference – it is kind of an intuitive argument, but a powerful one – is that Ken Hale (whose intuition was better than any other human being I've ever known) thought that external arguments didn't belong inside the VP. That

---

[8] Donati (2005).
[9] Higginbotham (1983a).

doesn't sound like a very convincing argument for people who don't know Ken Hale, but he had kind of like a God-given linguistic intuition. Anyway, there is enough information around aside from that to suggest that it is something we don't understand about where external arguments fit in. And if that case is out, then every case of what we call headedness just follows from a minimal search operation, which would mean that what we have to say is, "This is correct." I agree with you about the decomposing, but we should decompose the unbounded Merge operation into the fact that essentially everything is (head, XP). That looks special to language, but then that has plausible sources, like in theta-theory and in the cartographic approach, which adds the rest of the stuff.

BOECKX: For me the Ken Hale argument is of course, given where I come from, a powerful one. So I am happy you agree with me that decomposing Merge, regardless of how we do it, is an important next step. Some of the things you said actually illustrate a few of the things that Marc Hauser and I have been running into, namely translating, for example, theta-theory, or notions like external arguments, or even head vs. XP – this is actually the hard part for the next step, i.e. testing the FLN/FLB distinction. Because how do we do, for example, theta-theory independently of the very specific linguistic structures that linguists know for sure, but people like Marc do not, or at least do not know how to test yet? That is the hard part. Similarly for notions like external arguments, or even XP – how do we go about testing that? But if you agree about the next step, about decomposing Merge (no matter how we do it), that is one point that I wanted to make.

PIATTELLI-PALMARINI: I have a question for Noam. You say the status of the head emerges somehow. So for example, if I have "red wine," how do I put together "red" and "wine"? It seems that "wine" is the head. What is the phenomenon there?

CHOMSKY: Well, first of all, it is not really true that we put together "red" and "wine." We put together an XP, which is an adjective phrase, and it could be "very red" or, you know, "formerly red," or "redder than this," or whatever. It just happens that the case that you gave is a reduced XP, but in fact it is an XP. So we are putting together the XP ("formerly red," or "redder than that") with a head, a noun, so that is a head-XP relation. And in fact just about everything you look at is a head-XP relation. We sometimes mislead ourselves, because we select as the XP something which is in fact a head, but that is just a special case. For example, that is why "many" cannot be a determiner. You can't have a determiner "many" because it could be "very many" or "more than you thought" or something like that, so it really is an XP. You look through the range of structures, and they are almost entirely head-XP. The only exceptions that I know of are internal Merge, which has reasons to be different, and then has the interesting property that Caterina Donati noticed,[10] that if it is a head, it behaves differently – the thing that is extracted, and the external argument. That is the sticking point, both for NPs and for the sorts of clauses, and in both cases it has exceptional properties, which makes one think that there is something else going on there.

PIATTELLI-PALMARINI: So what about EPP, the Extended Projection Principle?

CHOMSKY: The Extended Projection Principle remains, in my opinion, simply mysterious. Actually, since Tom Bever is not here,[11] I can maybe speak for him. He was going to give a paper with a proposal about that, and it is an interesting proposal. I don't understand exactly how to make it work, but it is a different take on the matter. The EPP is the one that says that every sentence has to have a surface subject, so for example in English you cannot just say *Is a man in the room; you have to say There is a man in the room. You have to put in a fake subject to make it look like a subject, and as a matter of fact that is a source of EPP. It is English. Now I think there is a kind of historical accident here. The first language studied in any depth was English, and English happens to be one of the very rare languages that has an overt expletive. It just is not common. Almost no language has them, and in the few languages that do appear to have them, like Icelandic, it is a demonstrative and only appears in special cases. Most of the time you don't put it in at all. And then there is an argument about whether it is really a specifier of T or whether it is somewhere in something like Luigi Rizzi's left periphery, but the point is that it is very rare. Well, when people started looking at null-subject languages, they kind of modeled it on English, and they assumed that since there is no subject (you don't hear it, if it is a null subject), there must be a null expletive because then you get EPP. But suppose there isn't a null expletive. There is really no strong evidence for it that I know of. It just satisfies EPP. So maybe EPP is just wrong, just some idiosyncrasy of English, which we could look into.

Well that suggests a different way of looking at null-subject languages, but then comes Tom Bever's proposal. I don't feel right about giving it, because I'm probably not doing it the way he would have done it, had he been present, but what he is arguing is that there are for every language what he calls

---

[10] Donati (2005).

[11] Thomas G. Bever was unable to attend the meeting, but he and Chomsky had been corresponding about these topics for a long time. Bever's updated presentation is published in this volume (Chapter 18). (Editors' note)

"canonical sentence forms," of a kind that are sort of standard, the things that you are most likely to hear, especially a child,[12] like *John saw Bill*, or something, and these canonical sentence forms are simply different for different languages. For VSO languages, they are different in that you don't hear any subjects. There may be one in Irish sometimes, but it is not the canonical sentence form. For null-subject languages the same. You don't typically hear Subject Verb Object, because they have a different canonical sentence form. Then what he argues is that there is a kind of general learning procedure of some sort that utilizes the canonical sentence form and sort of forces the other forms to look like the canonical sentence form. So in English you would stick in this pointless expletive to make it look like the canonical sentence form. When you look at the proposal in detail, it is hard to work out, because there are plenty of sentences in English…

PIATTELLI-PALMARINI: He thinks that EPP is linked to a general cognitive strategy.

CHOMSKY: It is a general cognitive strategy, coming from generalizing from canonical sentence forms. It is pretty tricky to get it to work out, because, say, English has many sentences without subjects, like every yes/no question, for example. But still, there is something there that I think is attractive.

GLEITMAN: Yes, I think it is very attractive too, but there *is* this little problem, that if you look at what an [English] input corpus looks like, it is 10 percent Subject Verb Object, but I'm only counting 10 percent of the things you would say in *sentences*. A whole lot of it is just noun phrases. So let's just take the cases that are sentences. If you look at a corpus from a mother to kids aged 0 to 3, only 10 percent of the sentences are SVO. Imperatives and questions, that's what it is. "Shut up," and "Would you shut up" – that's what most of it is.

CHOMSKY: I'll answer in the way Tom would answer, I think.[13] He has talked about it and I don't know the numbers, but I think what he would say at this point is that the child knows that some things are not declarative sentences, and they are constructing their canonical sentence form for declarative sentences. That is the attractive part of the argument; then come the nuts and bolts that make it work.

GLEITMAN: Yes, the nuts and bolts are not the reasons I study it, but I think it is a very attractive hypothesis and also I think it is probably true.

---

[12] See also Townsend and Bever (2001).
[13] Bever's contribution (see Chapter 18) was written after the San Sebastián conference, also in the light of the present exchange, of which he had read the transcript. (Editors's note)

PIATTELLI-PALMARINI: Something like that seems to come out with Broca's aphasics – some such strategy where they use a canonical order and they seem to pay attention to the canonical order. When it is inverted they are lost.

GELMAN: Yes, in languages where the subject is not first, there are people who have predicted that verbs would be preferred, and it turns out not to be the case.

CHAPTER 4

The Foundational Abstractions

C. R. Gallistel

4.1 A short history of the mind

By way of prelude, I make a rapid – and necessarily superficial – tour of familiar philosophical terrain, because the material on animal cognition that I then review has substantial bearing on long-standing philosophical issues of relevance to contemporary cognitive science.

4.1.1 *Empiricist epistemology*

In this epistemology, the newborn mind knows nothing. But it has the capacity to experience elemental sensations and to form associations between those sensations that recur together. Thus, all representation derives from experience: "There is nothing in the mind that was not first in the senses" (Locke 1690). The mind's capacity to associate sensations makes it possible for experience to mold a plastic mind to reflect the structure of the experienced world. Thus, concepts derive their form from the form of experience. The farther removed from sensory experience a concept is, the more derived it is.

In this epistemology, our concepts of space, time, and number are maximally derivative. They are so far removed from sensory experience that they do not seem to have sensory constituents at all. Nor is it clear how their highly abstract, essentially mathematical form can be derived from experience. Neither the nature of the relevant experience, nor the inductive machinery necessary to derive them from that experience are in any way apparent. And yet these abstractions seem to play a foundational role in our representation of our experience.

4.1.2 *Rationalist epistemology*

Kant famously responded to this puzzle by arguing that the empiricists were wrong in attempting to derive our concepts of space, time, and number from our experience of the world. On the contrary, Kant argued, these organizing concepts are a precondition for having any experience whatsoever. We always represent our experiences, even the most elementary, as ordered in time and localized in space. The concepts of time and space are not derivable from our experience; rather, they are the foundation of that experience.

4.1.3 *Cartesian dualism and human exceptionalism*

Descartes famously argued that the machinery of the brain explains unmindful behavior. But, he argued, some behavior – behavior informed by thought – is mindful. He further argued that the operations of thought cannot be the result of mechanical (physically realizable) processes. He was among the originators of a line of thought about mind in human and non-human animals that continues to be influential, not only in popular culture but in scholarly and scientific debate. In its strongest form, the idea is that only humans have minds. In its weaker form, it is that humans have much more mind than non-human animals. A corollary, often taken for granted, is that the farther removed from humans an animal is on the evolutionary bush, the less mind it has. The most popular form of this idea in contemporary thought is that animals, like machines, lack representational capacity. Therefore, abstractions like space, time, number, and intentionality do not inform the behavior of non-human animals.

The popularity of the view that non-human animals know nothing of time, space, number, and intentionality owes much to the lingering effects of the behaviorism that dominated scientific psychology until relatively recently, and that still dominates behavioral neuroscience, particularly those parts of it devoted to the investigation of learning and memory. The more extreme behaviorists did not think that representational capacity should be imputed even to humans. Radical behaviorism fell out of favor with the rise of cognitive psychology. The emergence of computers, and with them, the understanding of the physics and mathematics of computation and representation played an important role in the emergence of contemporary cognitive psychology. The fact that things as abstract as maps and goals could demonstrably be placed into the indubitably physical innards of a computer was a fatal blow to the once widespread belief that to embrace a representational theory of mind was to give up the hope of a material theory of mind. The realization that a representational theory of mind was fully compatible with a material theory of mind was a critical development in scientific thinking about psychology, because, by the early twentieth century, a theory of mind that made mind in principle immaterial was no longer acceptable in scientific circles.

By the early twentieth century, the progress of scientific thought made Descartes's concept of an immaterial mind that affected the course of events in a material nervous system unacceptable to the great majority of scientists committed to developing a scientific psychology. The widespread belief in a uniquely human mind did not, however, die with the belief in a materially effective immaterial mind. Rather, the belief in a uniquely human form of mental activity came to rest largely on the widely conceded fact that only humans have language. If one believes that language is *the* (or, perhaps, *a*) medium of thought, then it is reasonable to believe that language makes possible the foundational abstractions. One form of this view is that it is language itself that makes possible these abstractions. Alternatively, one may believe that whatever the unique evolutionary development is that makes language possible in humans, that same development makes it possible to organize one's experience in terms of the foundational abstractions.

4.2 The birds and the bees

The history of thought abounds in ironies. One of them is that Sir Charles Sherrington's enormously influential book *The Integrative Action of the Nervous System* (Sherrington 1906) did as much as any work to persuade many scientists that a purely material account of mental activity – an account couched in neuroanatomical and electrophysiological language – was possible. The irony is that Sherrington, who died in 1952, was himself strongly committed to a Cartesian dualism. He believed that when he severed the spinal cord he isolated the purely physical neural machinery of the lower nervous system from the influence of an immaterial soul that acted on levels of the nervous system above his cut.

Sherrington placed the concept of the synapse at the center of thinking about the neurobiological mechanisms of behavior. His student, Sir John Eccles (1903–1997), further enhanced the centrality of the synapse in neuroscientific thinking by confirming through intracellular recordings of postsynaptic electrical processes Sherrington's basic ideas about synaptic transmission and its integrative (combinatorial) role. Eccles, too, was a Cartesian dualist, even though he secured the empirical foundations on which contemporary connectionist theories of mind rest. The irony is that a major motivation for connectionism is to found our theories of mind not only on physically realizable processes but more narrowly on the understanding of neuroanatomy and neurophysiology that Sherrington and Eccles established. Indeed, the neurobiology commonly mentioned as a justification for connectionist theorizing about the mind is exactly that elaborated by Sherrington a century ago. Discoveries since then have made no contribution to the thinking of contemporary modelers.

A similar irony is that the empirical foundations for the now flourishing field of animal cognition were laid by behaviorist psychologists, who pioneered the experimental study of learning in non-human animals, and by zoologists, who pioneered the experimental study of instinctive behavior in birds and insects. Both schools were to varying degrees uncomfortable with representational theories of mind. And/or, they did not believe they were studying phenomena in which mind played any role. Nonetheless, what we have learned from the many elegant experiments in these two traditions is that the foundational abstractions of time, space, number, and intentionality inform the behavior of the birds and the bees – species that last shared an ancestor with humans several hundred million years ago, more than halfway back in the evolution of multicellular animals.

Some years ago (Gallistel 1990a), I reviewed the literature in experimental psychology and experimental zoology demonstrating that non-human animals, including birds and insects, learn the time of day (that is, the phase of a neurobiological circadian clock) at which events such as daily feedings happen, that they learn the approximate durations of events and of the intervals between events, that they assess number and rate (number divided by time), and that they make a cognitive map of their surroundings and continuously compute their current location on their map by integrating their velocity with respect to time. Here, in this paper, I give an update on some further discoveries along these lines that have been made in recent years.

4.2.1 Birds and time

The most interesting recent work on the representation of temporal intervals by birds comes from a series of brilliant experiments by Nichola Clayton, Anthony Dickinson, and their collaborators demonstrating a sophisticated episodic memory in food-caching jays (Clayton et al. 2006; Clayton et al. 2003, and citations therein; see also Raby et al. 2007). In times of plenty, many birds, particularly many species of jays, gather food and store it in more than ten thousand different caches, each cache in a different location, spread over square miles of the landscape (Vander Wall 1990). Weeks and months later, when food is scarce, they retrieve food from these caches. Clayton and Dickinson and their collaborators took this phenomenon into the laboratory and used it to show that jays remember what they hid where and how long ago and that they integrate this information with what they have learned about how long it takes various kinds of food to rot.

The experiments make ingenious use of the fact that jays are omnivores like us; they'll eat almost anything. And, like us, they have pronounced preferences. In these experiments, the jays cached meal worms, crickets, and peanuts. Other things being equal, that is the order of the preference: they like meal worms more than crickets, and crickets more than peanuts. In one experiment, hand-reared jays, with no experience of decaying food, were given repeated trials of caching and recovery. They cached two different foods in two different caching episodes before being allowed to recover their caches. In the first of each pair of caching episodes, they were allowed to cache peanuts on one side of an ice-cube tray whose depressions were filled with sand. In the second episode of each pair, they were allowed to cache either mealworms or crickets on the other side of the same tray. Thus, on some caching trials, they hid peanuts in one half of the trays and mealworms in the other, while on other trials, they hid peanuts in one half and crickets in the other.

Either 4 hours, 28 hours, or 100 hours (4 days) after each pair-of-caching episode, they were allowed to recover food from both sides of the trays. On trials with only a 4-hour delay, both the mealworms and the crickets were still fresh and tasty when retrieved. At that delay, the jays preferred to retrieve from the caches where they had hidden either mealworms or crickets (depending on whether they had cached peanuts-and-mealworms or peanuts-and-crickets). On trials where a 28-hour delay was imposed between caching and recovery, the experimenters replaced the cached mealworms with mealworms that had been artificially rotted. Thus, on the first few peanuts-and-mealworms trials with a 28-hour delay before retrieval, the jays found inedible "rotten" mealworms where they had cached tasty fresh mealworms. By contrast, on peanuts-and-crickets trials, they found crickets that were still fresh after 28 hours in their caches. On trials with a 4-day delay before recovery, both the mealworms and the crickets had rotted; the peanuts alone remained fresh.

Control birds that never encountered rotted caches preferred the caches where mealworms and crickets had been hidden no matter how long the delay between caching and recovery. The experimental birds preferred those caches when only four hours had elapsed. When twenty-eight hours had elapsed, their preference after a few trials of each type depended on whether it was mealworms or crickets that they had hidden on the "better" side of the tray. If it was mealworms, they preferred the peanut caches, but if it was crickets, they preferred the cricket caches. When four days had passed, their preference after a few trials (during which they learned about rotting) was for the peanut caches, whether it was mealworms or crickets that they had hidden on the "better" side of the tray.

In an ingenious extension of these experiments, Clayton, Yu, and Dickinson (2001) showed that the birds would adjust their retrieval preferences on the basis of information about rotting time acquired after they had made their caches. At the time the caches were made, they did not yet know exactly how long it took the meal worms to rot.

It appears from these experiments that the remembered past of the bird is temporally organized just as is our own. The birds compute elapsed intervals and compare them to other intervals in memory. They compare the time elapsed since they cached a cricket to what they have since learned about the time it takes a cricket to rot. Like us, birds reason about time.

4.2.2 Birds reason about number

There is an extensive literature showing that pigeons and rats can base behaviorally consequential decisions on estimates of the approximate number of events (Brannon and Roitman 2003; Dehaene 1997; Gallistel 1990a). In many of the experiments, the animal subjects make a decision based on whether the current number is greater or less than a target number in memory. Thus, these experiments give evidence that animal minds reason about number as well as about time. Brannon and her collaborators (Brannon et al. 2001) extended this evidence using a task that required pigeons to first subtract the current number from a target number in memory and then compare the result to another target number in memory.

In their experiment, the birds pecked first at the illuminated center key in a linear array of three keys on a wall of the test chamber. Their pecking produced intermittent flashes (blinks) of the light that illuminated the key. The ratio of the number of pecks made to the number of flashes produced varied unpredictably, for reasons to be explained shortly. After a number of flashes that itself varied unpredictably from trial to trial, the two flanking keys were illuminated, offering the bird a choice.

Pecking either of the newly illuminated side keys generated further intermittent flashes. Eventually, when the requisite number of further flashes on the side key they first chose had been produced, the bird gained brief access to a feeding hopper. For one of the side keys the requisite number was fixed. This number was one of the target numbers that the birds had to maintain in memory. For the other side key, the number of flashes to be produced was the number left after the flashes already produced on the center key were subtracted from a large initial number. This large initial number was the other number that had to be maintained in memory. The greater the number of flashes already produced on the center key, the smaller the difference remaining when it was subtracted from this large initial number; hence, the more attractive the choice of the "number-left" key relative to the "fixed-number" key. The pigeons' probability of their choosing the number-left key in preference to the fixed-number key depended strongly and appropriately on the magnitude of the number left relative to the fixed number.

The random intermittency of the flashes partially deconfounded the duration of pecking on the center key from the number of flashes produced by that pecking, allowing the authors to demonstrate that the pigeons' choices depended on number, not duration.

4.2.3 Birds and intentionality

Jays are not above stealing the caches of others (Bednekoff and Balda 1996). Experienced jays are therefore reluctant to cache when another jay is watching. They remember which caches they made while being watched and which jays were watching them (Dally et al. 2006). When no longer watched, they selectively re-cache the food that others observed them cache (Emery and Clayton 2001). "Experienced" jays are those who have themselves pilfered the caches of other jays; those innocents who have not succumbed to this temptation are not yet wary of being observed by potential thieves while caching (Emery and Clayton 2001). Thus, nonverbal animals represent the likely intentions of others and reason from their own actions to the likely future actions of others (see also Raby et al. 2007).

4.2.4 Bees represent space

The zoologist Karl von Frisch and his collaborators discovered that when a foraging bee returns to the hive from a rich food source, it does a waggle dance in the hive out of sight of the sun, which indicates to the other foragers the direction (bearing) and distance (range) of the source from the hive (von Frisch 1967). The dancer repeatedly runs a figure-8 pattern. Each time it comes to the central bar, where the two circles join, it waggles as it runs. The angle of this waggle run with respect to vertical is the solar bearing of the source, the angle that a bee must fly relative to the sun. The number of waggles in a run is a monotonic function of the range, that is, the distance to the source.

It is somewhat misleading to say that the dance communicates the solar bearing, because what it really communicates is a more abstract quantity, namely, the compass bearing of the source, its direction relative to the north-south (polar) axis of the earth's rotation. We know this because if the foragers that follow the dance and use the information thus obtained to fly to the source are not allowed to leave the nest until some hours later, when the sun has moved to a different position in the sky, they fly the correct compass bearing, not the solar bearing given by the dance. In other words, the solar bearing given by the dance is time-compensated; the users of the information correct for the change in the compass direction of the sun that has occurred between the time when they observed the dance and the time when they use the directional information they extracted from it. They are able to do this, because they have learned the solar ephemeris, the compass direction of the sun as a function of the time of day (Dyer and Dickinson 1996). Man is by no means the only animal that notes where the sun rises, where it sets, and how it moves above the horizon as the day goes on.

Knowledge of the solar ephemeris helps make dead reckoning possible. Dead reckoning is the integration of velocity with respect to time so as to obtain one's position as a function of time. Successful dead reckoning requires a directional referent that does not change as one moves about. That is, lines of sight from the observer to the directional referent must be parallel regardless of the observer's location. The farther away the point of directional reference is and the more widely perceptible from different locations on the earth, the better it serves its function. In both of these respects, the sun is ideal. It is visible from almost anywhere, and it is so far away that there is negligible change in its compass direction as the animal moves about. The problem is that its compass direction changes as the earth rotates. Learning the solar ephemeris solves that problem.

Dead reckoning makes it possible to construct a cognitive map (Gallistel 1990a: Chapter 5) and to keep track of one's position on it. Knowledge of where one is on the map makes possible the setting of a course from wherever one currently is to wherever one may suddenly wish to go. The computation involved is simple vector algebra: the vector that represents the displacement between one's current location and the goal location is the vector that represents the goal location minus the vector that represents one's current location. The range and bearing of the goal from one's current location is the polar form of that displacement vector.

There is a rich literature on navigation in foraging ants and bees, which make ideal subjects, because they are social foragers: they bring the food they find back to the communal nest, then depart again in search of more. In this literature, one finds many demonstrations of the subtlety and sophistication of the spatial reasoning that goes on in these miniature brains, which contain only on the order of 1 million neurons. For some recent examples, see Collett and

Collett (2000); Collett et al. (2002); Collett and Collett (2002); Harris et al. (2005); Narendra et al. (2007); Wehner and Srinivasan (2003); Wittlinger et al. (2007); Wohlgemuth et al. (2001). For a review of the older literature, see Gallistel (1990a: Chapters 3–6). Here, I have time to recount only two of the most important recent findings.

For many years, researchers in the insect navigation field have questioned whether ants and bees make an integrated map of their environment (e.g., Collett and Collett 2004; Dyer 1991; Wehner and Menzel 1990; but see Gould 1990). The alternative generally proposed is that they have memorized range-bearing pairs that enable them to follow by dead reckoning routes back and forth between familiar locations. They have also memorized snapshots of the landmarks surrounding those locations (Collett et al. 1998; Collett et al. 2002; Collett 1992; Collett and Baron 1994) together with the compass directions of those landmarks, and they have memorized snapshots of land-marks passed en route between these locations (Fukushi and Wehner 2004). But, it is argued, all of this information is integrated only with regard to a particular route and summoned up only when the ant or bee is pursuing that route (Collett and Collett 2004).

Part of what has motivated skepticism about whether the information from different routes is integrated into an overall map of the environment is that bees often appear to fail a key test of the integrated-map hypothesis. The question is, can a bee or ant set a course from an arbitrary (but recognizable!) location on its map to an arbitrary goal on its map? One way to pose this question experimentally is to capture foraging bees when they are leaving the hive en route to a known goal and displace them to an arbitrary point within their foraging territory. When released at this arbitrary new location, do they reset their course, or do they continue to fly the course they were on when captured? Under some conditions, they do reset their course (Gould 1986; Gould and Gould 1988; Gould 1990), but in most experiments, most of the bees continue to fly the course they were on (Dyer 1991; Wehner and Menzel 1990). This suggests that they cannot recompute the course to their old goal from their new location.

Against this conclusion, however, is the fact, often reported in footnotes if at all, that the bees who take off for the wild blue yonder on a course inappropriate to their goal (given their release location) are nonetheless soon found either at the goal they had when captured or, more often, back at the hive. They do not go missing, whereas bees released in unfamiliar territory do generally go missing, even if that territory is quite close to the hive.

The problem has been that we had no idea what happened between the time the bees disappeared from the release site flying on the wrong course to the time they reappeared, either at their intended goal or back at the hive. Menzel and his collaborators (2005) have taken advantage of the latest developments in radar technology to answer the question, what do misdirected bees do when they discover that they have not arrived at their intended goal? Radar technology has reached the point where it is possible to mount a tiny reflector on the back of a bee and track that bee at distances up to a kilometer. Thus, for the first time, Menzel and his collaborators could watch what misdirected bees did. What they did was fly the course they had been on when captured more or less to its end. This brought them to an equally arbitrary location within their foraging terrain. They then flew back and forth in a pattern that a sailor, aviator, or hiker would recognize as the sort of path you follow when you are trying to "get your bearings," that is, to recognize some landmarks that will enable you to determine where you are on your map. At some point this flying back and forth hither and yon abruptly ended, and the bee set off on a more or less straight course either for the goal they had been bound for when captured or back to the hive. In short, they can set a course from an arbitrary location (the location where they find themselves when they realize that they are not getting where they were going) to another, essentially arbitrary location (the location of the feeding table they were bound for). This result argues in favor of the integrated map hypothesis.

The final result I have time to report (Gould and Gould 1988; Tautz et al. 2004) moves the level of abstraction at which we should interpret the information communicated by the waggle dance of the returned bee forager up another level. These little-known results strongly suggest that what the dance communicates is best described as the map coordinates of the food source. Moreover, it appears that before acting on the information, potential recruits consult their map for the additional information that it contains.

In these experiments, a troop of foragers was recruited to a feeding table near the hive, which was then moved in steps of a few meters each to the edge of a pond and then put on a boat and moved out onto the pond. At each step, the table remained where it was long enough for the troop foraging on it to discover its new location and to modify appropriately the dance they did on returning to the hive. So long as the table remained on land, these dances garnered new recruits. But when the table was moved well out onto the water, the returning foragers danced as vigorously as ever, but their dances did not recruit any further foragers – until, in one experiment, the table approached a flower-rich island in the middle of the pond, in which case the new recruits came not to the boat but to the shore of the island, that is, to the nearest plausible location. In short, bees' past experience is spatially organized: like the birds, they remember where they found what, and they can integrate this spatially indexed information with the information they get from the dance of a returning forager.

4.3 Conclusions

The findings I have briefly reviewed imply that the abstractions of time, space, number, and intentionality are both primitive and foundational aspects of mentation. Birds and bees organize their remembered experience in time and space. The spatio-temporal coordinates of remembered experience are accessible to computation. The birds can compute the intervals elapsed since they made various caches at various locations at various times in the past. And they can compare those intervals to other intervals they have experienced, for example, to the time it takes a given kind of food to rot. The bees can use the dance of a returning forager to access a particular location on their cognitive map, and they can use that index location to search for records of food in nearby locations. Birds can subtract one approximate number from another approximate number and compare the result to a third approximate number. And birds making a cache take note of who is watching and modify their present and future behavior in accord with plausible inferences about the intentions of the observer.

To say that these abstractions are primitive is to say that they emerged as features of mentation early in evolutionary history. They are now found in animals that have not shared a common ancestor since soon after the Cambrian explosion, the period when most of the animal forms now seen first emerged.

To say that they are foundational is to say that they are the basis on which mentation is constructed. It is debatable whether Kant thought he was propounding a psychology, when he argued that the concepts of space and time were a precondition for experience of any kind. Whether he was or not, these findings suggest that this is a plausible psychology. In particular, these findings make it difficult to argue that these abstractions arose either from the language faculty itself or from whatever the evolutionary development was that made language possible in humans. These abstractions appear to have been central features of mentation long, long before primates, let alone anatomical modern humans, made their appearance.

Discussion

RIZZI: I was wondering how far we can go in analogy between the foraging strategy that you described and certain aspects of language. I wondered whether there is experimental evidence about strategies of rational search of this kind:

first you go to the closer spots and later to more distant spots. A particular case that would be quite interesting to draw an analogy with language would be the case of intervention, presenting intervention effects in these strategies. For instance, just imagine a strategy description of this kind, that there is a direct trajectory for a more distant cache; there is one intervening spot with a less desirable kind of food (let's say nuts rather than peanuts, or rather than worms). Would there be anything like experimental evidence that this kind of situation would slow down somehow the search for the more distant spots – or anything that would bear on the question of whether there are distance and/or intervention effects in search strategies? Because that is very typical of certain things that happen in language – in long-distance dependencies.

GALLISTEL: As regards the second part of your question, on the interfering effect of an intervening, less desirable cache, I don't know of anything that we currently have that would be relevant, although it might very well be possible to do this. The setup that Clayton and Dickinson used, as I just said, doesn't lend itself at all to that because it's not like a natural setup where this situation would arise all the time. The birds are just foraging in ice-cube trays. However, some years ago we did a traveling salesman problem with monkeys, where they very much have to take distance into account, and where they have to take into account what they are going to do three choices beyond the choice that they are currently making. That is, the monkeys had to harvest a sequence, going to a number of cache sites. This was done by first carrying a monkey around and letting it watch while we hid food, before releasing it to harvest what it had seen hidden. The question was, would it solve the traveling salesman problem by choosing the most efficient route, particularly in the interesting cases where to choose the most efficient route, the least-distance route, you would have to, in your current choice, foresee or anticipate what you were going to do in a subsequent task. And they very clearly did do that. They clearly did show that kind of behavior, so I think that's relevant.

HAUSER: One of the puzzles of some of the cases that you brought up is that lots of the intimate knowledge that the animals have been credited with seems to be very specialized for certain contexts, which is completely untrue of so much of human knowledge. So in the case of the jays, it seems to be very, very located to the context of cache recovery. Now, maybe it will eventually show itself in another domain. We're taking advantage of natural behavior so maybe it will not. But in the same way that the bees seem to be one of the only species that externalize this knowledge in the communicative signal in a richness that is totally unparalleled in any other species but humans, so you get this kind of odd thing where the bees are only really sort of talking about one specific context.

You have rich social relationships, but there is no communicative signal outwards at all. So the question is – the way I've put it in the past is – animals have this kind of laser-beam intelligence and we have this kind of floodlight, and what happens? How do you get from this very, very selective specialization to probably a promiscuous system in humans?

GALLISTEL: Well, of course the competence–performance distinction is just as important in interpreting the behavior of animals as it is in interpreting the language of humans. They have a lot of competences that they don't always choose to show us. But I agree with your basic point, and in fact it is something I have often emphasized myself. Animals show a lot of competence in a very sharply focused way. If I were to venture into perilous terrain and ask what language does for thought, one suggestion that one might offer is that, because it allows you to take these representations that arise in different contexts with, on the surface, different formal structure, and map them onto a common representational system, it may enable you to bring to bear the representational capacity of this module on a problem originally only dealt with by that module, and so this module can contribute something that the original module wouldn't have been able to do on its own. And that would be where the floodlight quality of human reasoning came in perhaps. The idea that language didn't really introduce new representational capacity, except perhaps insofar as it created a representational medium in which anything could be, to some extent at least, represented.

URIAGEREKA: At some point I would like to hear your opinion, Randy, on this *Science* report on the bees doing their dance also for the purpose of finding a new nest, so the behavior is apparently not fully encapsulated for the purposes of foraging. I had no idea that they also did that, find a viable nest with procedures akin to those involved in foraging. I don't know how plastic that is. The point I'm trying to emphasize is this: would we find more of those apparently plastic behaviors if we knew where to look? That said, in the case of plasticity that we have seen in our system, my own feeling (and this is sheer speculation) is that generalized quantification – that is, the type of quantification that involves a restriction and a scope – is certainly central to much of human expression, but may be hard to find in other species. In fact, if Elena Herburger is right in her monograph on focus, this sort of full-fledged, crucially binary quantification may even be central to human judgment, especially the way Wolfram Hinzen is pushing that idea. It may be that the type of syntax you require for that type of quantification (which is one of the best understood systems in linguistics), however it is that we evolved it, might as well liberate, if you will, a kind of richly quantificational thought that I would actually be very interested to see if animals exhibit. I mean, you know much more than I do about these things, Randy, but the experiments I have read do not get to generalized quantification. For example, in dolphin cases in the literature, it is reported that these animals get, say, *bring red ball, bring blue ball*, and so on; let's grant that much. But apparently they do not get *bring most ball* or even *bring no ball*. So maybe that would be another way to push these observations, another thing to look for, constructing experiments to test for behaviors of that truly quantificational sort.

CHOMSKY: Randy's comment sort of suggests Liz Spelke's experiment,[1] i.e. using language for intermodal transfer (visuo-spatial, for instance).

GALLISTEL: You're right, it does seem to, but in fact I'm not sympathetic to that. I don't agree with Liz on the interpretation of those experiments, but what I said does seem to point in that direction.

GELMAN: I'd like to modify what Randy said, to say that what seems to be unique to humans is a representational capacity. Language is one that can be used for a wide range of activities, but notational capacities are also representations. Drawings can be representations, plans, and so forth – there are many options. And I have yet to see data that animals can go invariably from one representational format to another.

PARTICIPANT: It's only a simple question. Do the systems of communication of bees and birds display feedback? For example, if they make a mistake and then realize that they've made a mistake, do they communicate it?

GALLISTEL: Ahhhh [scratches head; laughter]. That's tough! Sort of implying that as a result, where the bees that are following the dance consult their map, sort of implying that they conclude that the dancer didn't know what the dancer was talking about, right? [Chuckles to himself.] Because if the information conveyed by the dance is sufficiently inconsistent with the information on their map, they appear to discount the information in the dance. I'm not sure whether that isn't correcting themselves, of course. I'm not sure this is relevant, but there are recent experiments by Laurie Santos,[2] one of Marc's many good students, who has gone on to do work that Marc has also done on observing the mind sort of thing, where you have to represent whether the other animal knows what you know, in order to choose. This has been a big issue for a long, long while. But I thought her recent experiments, which I cannot reproduce (I'm sure Marc can, as they were partly or mostly undertaken with Marc)

---

[1] Lipton and Spelke (2003).
[2] Santos et al. (2002).

were very persuasive on that score. Part of Marc's genius has been to exploit naturalistic circumstances, and they exploited naturalistic circumstances in a way to make a much more compelling case that the animal knew that the other animal didn't know X.

PARTICIPANT: I was wondering if you have feedback when you have something similar to negation. It is usually claimed that negation is unique to human language...

GALLISTEL: Ohhhh, like where the catcher in a baseball game shakes off the signal? I can't quickly think of a clear example that one could regard as equivalent to negation. But negation is certainly a kissing-cousin of inversion, and animals invert all the time. I mean, they invert vectors, right? Not only do they calculate the home vector themselves when they are out there and they have found food, but when they get back, what they are dancing is not the vector they calculated coming home, but the inverse vector, the vector for going the other way. About negation, I always remember that tee-shirt that says, "What part of No don't you understand?" [Laughter]. It seems to me about as elementary as you can get.

PIATTELLI-PALMARINI: Concerning foraging, I have seen work by my colleague Anna Dornhaus, concerning some of the optimal criteria that honeybees meet in foraging,[3] which is rather astounding, because they have constructed a graph of how many bees are proactive (they go out and look for food) versus the reactive foragers that wait for the dance. So they have calculated the percentages of proactive versus reactive, and the graph you get depends on how long the food is available. And you have a triple point like in second-order phase transitions in physics and chemistry. It's extraordinary. They have a number of predictions that sound very weird, but then they observe them in nature or in the laboratory. So it seems that, when we approach foraging in a quantitative way, among other things, it is one of those fields in which the species seem to be doing the best thing that they could possibly do. Have you any comments on that, because it is a question of great current interest in linguistics. It wouldn't be the only case in which you have biological systems that are doing the best that can be done.

GALLISTEL: Yes, this question of optimality is apt to provoke very long arguments in biological circles. I can give you sort of a general view, and then my own particular view. If you look on the sensory side, you see spectacular optimality. That is, sensory transduction mechanisms are, most of them, very near the limits of what is physically possible. So the threshold for audition, for

---

[3] Dechaume-Moncharmont et al. (2005).

example, is just above the threshold set by physics – there's a slight vibration on the eardrum due to the fact that on a small surface there is stochastic variation in how many molecules of air hit that surface, and that produces a very faint vibration in the eardrum that is an ineliminable noise in the system. And the amount of additional vibration that you need from another source is just above that limit. The most essential thing is to calculate how much the eardrum is moving at that threshold. It is moving less than the diameter of an atom! So that's a lot better than you would have thought at the beginning.

Similarly with the eye. One of the proofs before it was directly demonstrated that the absorption of a single photon by a single rhodopsin molecule in a single rod generated a signal that could make its way all the way through the nervous system came from a famous experiment by Hecht, Shlaer, and Pirenne in which they showed that there was a clearly detectable effect.[4] This was subsequently studied by Horace Barlow and Barbara Sakitt,[5] and they showed that for every quantum or photon of light absorbed, there was a quite sizeable increase in the probability that a human would say that he had detected the flash. There are ten million rhodopsin molecules in the outer segment of a single rod, and there are a million rods in the retina. So it is a little bit like one of these huge soccer matches and someone burps and the referee says, "Who burped?" There are a hundred million spectators and somehow the burp is centrally detectable. That's pretty impressive.

There is wide agreement about this – the facts are extremely well established. When you come to computational considerations, that is where the arguments begin, but of course that reflects the fact that we, unlike the sensory things, don't know what's going on. Most neuroscientists think that the computations are just one spike after the next, right? But this seems to me nonsensical. Any engineer will tell you that the contradictions that follow the transduction of the signal are more important than the transduction in the first place. That is, if you've got a good signal but lousy signal processing, then you've wasted your time producing a good signal. So it seems to me that the pressure to optimize the computations is at least as great as the pressure to optimize the signal transduction, and we know that the signal transduction is very near the limits of what is physically possible. So I tend to think that the computations, or processing of the signal, are also at the limits of what is computationally possible. But since we know practically nothing about how the nervous system computes, it's hard to say.

---

[4] Hecht et al. (1942).
[5] Sakitt (1972).

CHAPTER 5

Evolingo

The Nature of the Language Faculty

Marc D. Hauser

I want to begin by saying that much of what I will discuss builds tremendously on the shoulders of giants and couldn't have been done if it hadn't been for the thinking and experimental work of people like Noam Chomsky, Randy Gallistel, and Rochel Gelman, who significantly inform what I will be telling you about. Today I want to develop an idea of a new research path into the evolution of language, which I'll call "evolingo," parasitizing the discipline known as "evo-devo," and I will tell you a little about what I think the label means. Then I want to give you a case example, some very new, largely unpublished data on quantifiers. Finally, what I will try to argue is that there is really a new way of thinking about the evolution of language that is very different from the earliest stages of working on this problem.

Definitionally, what I want to do is anchor thinking about this in terms of viewing language as *a mind-internal computational system designed for thought and often externalized in communication.* That is, language evolved for internal thought and planning and only later was co-opted for communication. This sets up a dissociation between what we do with the internal computation as opposed to what the internal computation actually evolved *for*. In a pair of papers that we published a couple of years ago (Hauser et al. 2002; Fitch et al. 2005) we defined the faculty of language in the broad sense (FLB) as including *all the mental processes that are both necessary and sufficient to support language.* The reason why we want to set up in this way is because there are numerous things internal to the mind that will be involved in language processing, but that need not be specific to language. For example, memory is involved in language processing, but it is not specific to language. So it is important to distinguish those features that are involved in the process of language computation from those that are specific to it. That is why we developed the idea of the faculty of language in the narrow sense (FLN), a faculty with two key components: (1) those mental processes that are unique to language, and (2) those that are unique to humans. Therefore, it sets out a comparative phylogenetic agenda in that we are looking both for what aspects are unique to humans, but also what aspects are unique to language as a faculty.

Evolingo, then, is a new, mostly methodological, way of thinking about the evolution of language, whose nature can be described in terms of the three core components described by Noam Chomsky in his opening remarks here and in his recent work (Chomsky 2005b) – that is, the system of computational rules, semantics or the conceptual intentional system, and the sensorimotor or phonological system, and their interfaces. What the evolingo approach then puts forward is that we are looking for the study of mind-internal linguistic computations, focusing on those capacities that are shared, meaning both in terms of homologies (traits that have evolved through direct, common descent) as well as homoplasies (traits that have evolved largely from convergence or independent evolution, but arise due to responses to common problems), looking at those aspects that are unique to humans and unique to language as a domain of knowledge.

The real change with the prior history of work on the evolution of language is that it focused almost entirely on non-communicative competencies, using methods that tap both spontaneous capacities as well as those that involve training. I want to make just one quick point here, because I think some of the work that I have done in the past has confused this. Much of the work in animal learning that has gone on in the past has involved a particular kind of training methodology that, by its design, enables exquisite control over the animal's behavior. In contrast, much of the work that we have done in the past ten or so years has departed, not intellectually, but I think methodologically, from prior approaches by looking at what animals do spontaneously, in the *absence* of training, as with an experiment that Tecumseh Fitch and I did. We did not train the animals through a process of reward or punishment to show what kinds of patterns they can extract. We merely exposed them, passively, in much the same way that studies of human infants proceed.[1] We are trying to use very comparable methods to those used with human infants so that if we find similar kinds of behaviors, we can be more confident about not only the computation, but how it was acquired and implemented. I'll pick up on these points later in the talk.

---

[1] See Lila Gleitman's description in Chapter 16.

So the two very important empirical questions that I will address in a moment are: (1) to what extent are the conceptual representations that appear to uniquely enter into linguistic computation built from nonlinguistic resources; and (2) to what extent have linguistic conceptual representations transformed in evolution and ontogeny some of our ontological commitments? The reason why I think this is important, and the reason why I think the evolingo change in approach has been important, is that almost all the work at a phylogenetic level that has addressed questions of interest to linguists about the nature of language, language structure, and computation, has looked almost exclusively at the communication of animals, either their natural communication or what we can train them to do with sign languages or symbols. What it has generally failed to do, except in the last few years, is to ask about the computational capacities that may be seen in completely different domains and never externalized. This is why, in my first paper with Noam and Tecumseh Fitch (Hauser et al. 2002), we made the analogy that some of the computations that one sees in language may well appear in something like spatial navigation – the integration of spatial information that Randy elegantly described in his talk (see Chapter 4) about the notion of landmarks and bearings. Those kinds of computations may have some similarity to the kinds of computations we see in language.

A couple of examples of how I think the structure of the questions has changed in the field, away from questions like "Can animals vocalize and refer to things in the world?" or "Do animals have any syntactic structures?" to other kinds of questions. I think in terms of conceptual evolution there are two issues, one having to do with the nature of animal concepts. And here I will just take the lead from Randy's elegant work, and argue that in general, the way that people in the field of animal cognition have thought about them is exactly the way that Randy describes,[2] namely as isomorphisms or relationships between two distinct systems of representation. Critically, and as Randy describes (I'm not going to go through this, although interestingly we picked out the same terms), they seem to be abstract, not necessarily anchored in the perceptual or sensory experiences for things like number, space, time, and mental states. Importantly, there seems to be virtually no connection in animals, perhaps with the exception of honeybees (which is why I asked that question),[3] between the sensorimotor output of signaling and the richness of the conceptual systems they have. Notice there is nothing remotely like a word in animal communication. I take it to be the case that what is debated in the field, and I think what

---

[2] See Chapter 4 above.

[3] See the discussion on pages 64–68.

should be of relevance to people working in language, are the following issues: the details of the format and content of the representations in animals; how the language faculty transforms the conceptual space; and lastly, whether there are language-specific conceptual resources. And it is really the latter question that I want to address today.

A question that will be at least somewhat debated, perhaps in the corner where Randy, Rochel, and I sit, is what the nonlinguistic quantificational systems are in animals and humans. One system that certainly is not questioned is the one that Randy and Rochel have worked on for many years, and is often called the "analog magnitude system." This is a system whose signature or definitional property is that it computes approximate number estimation with no absolute limit on number, but with discrimination limited by Weber (logarithmic) ratios. There is abundant evidence for this in the animal world, shown by studies that involve training animals, and studies that involve spontaneous methods. Such studies are complementary in the sense that they both reveal the signature of the system in animals like chimpanzees, rhesus monkeys, tamarins, lemurs, rats, pigeons, and so forth. A second system, which is perhaps more heatedly debated in terms of whether it should count as something numerical is a system that some of us have called the "parallel individuation system," or the "object file system." This system has a different kind of signature. It seems to be very precise, but it is limited in terms of the numbers that it is precise for – specifically in a range of 3 to 4. So discrimination is limited by how many individuals can be tracked at the same time in parallel. Here as well, there is evidence from some training studies and some spontaneous methods, in both human adults and infants, as well as in primates.

I want to take you now to one of my labs, the beautiful island of Cayo Santiago, off the coast of Puerto Rico, which is the sole location for 1,000 rhesus monkeys. What's beautiful about this island is that, in contrast to most studies of primates, this island has a very large number of individuals, about a thousand at a given time. They are perfectly habituated to our presence, allowing us to observe them at very close range, safely, and carry out experiments with them in a naturalistic setting. What I want to tell you about today is one kind of experiment that lends itself to asking about the capacity for numerical quantification in a functionally significant, ecologically relevant foraging task. Here is the basic nature of the design, which you will hear about over and over again in the next few pages. We find an animal who is by himself or herself; we place two boxes in front of the animal; we show them they're empty, and then we proceed to lower objects into the boxes. In most cases, what we are lowering are food objects that we know they're highly motivated to go find. In the typical experiment we are in effect asking them, "Do you prefer the box with more food or the one with less food?" Since we can assume that they are going to try to go for more food, the experiment should work.

So here is the idea for the basic experiment, counterbalancing for all sorts of necessary things. We load into the first box one apple followed by a second apple (the boxes are opaque so the monkeys can't see inside) and then we load one apple into the second box; we walk away and let the animal choose. This is one trial per animal, we don't repeat the individuals, so we are going to be comparing across conditions where every condition has 20–24 different individuals. We don't train them, we don't even cue them into what the task is until we walk away. We place the apples in the box, walk away, and let them choose a box. When we do that, here are the results we get. If we compare one piece of apple going into a box and nothing in the other, they prefer 1 vs. 0, 2 vs. 1, 3 vs. 2, and 4 vs. 3, but they fail to show a successful discrimination of 5 vs. 4, 6 vs. 4, 8 vs. 4, and 8 vs. 3. So although the ratios are favorable here relative to what they can do with 2 vs. 1, they are not using ratios to make discrimination. The discrimination is falling out precisely at 4 vs. 3. They can do no more. So under these conditions (no training, one trial per individual), this is the level of discrimination that we find, and this pattern cannot be explained by the analog magnitude system. It is, however, entirely consistent with the signature of the parallel individuation system.

Now, let us turn to a conceptual domain that might appear to be privileged for language, morpho-syntax in particular – namely the singular–plural distinction – and ask the question whether the conceptual roots upon which language was constructed over evolutionary time and in development built upon some conceptual primitives that may be seen in nonlinguistic creatures and in pre-linguistic human infants. The basic idea is that if we have one cat, or we have two, or millions of cats, we simply take the noun and add a terminal -s. The result that opens the door to the comparative angle comes from a recent study by Dave Barner, Susan Carey, and their colleagues (Barner et al. 2005). They presented infants with a version of the box-choice study I just described for rhesus monkeys. When infants in the age range of 12–20 months were tested, Barner and Colleagues found that subjects could discriminate 1 cracker from 2, as well as 3 from 2, but they failed with 4 vs. 3, 2 vs. 4, and surprisingly, even 1 vs. 4. As soon as the number of items going into one box exceeds 3, infants at this age fail the discrimination task. Of interest is that at the age of around 22 months, when infants are producing, in English, the singular–plural morphology, they now succeed on the 1 vs. 4 task. Barner and Colleagues explain these results by suggesting that the explicit formulation of the singular–plural morphology, in terms of its representational structure, enables a new form of numerical discrimination, specifically, one between singular and plural entities.

Therefore, in ontogeny we see a linguistic distinction first, and then a conceptual distinction second. Now if this interpretation is correct, and numerical discrimination of this kind depends on the singular–plural morphology, then of course animals lacking this morphology will fail on a comparable task.

To test this hypothesis, I now want to run through a series of experiments that ask the following question. If we consider the two nonlinguistic systems that I have described, the parallel individuation system, which is precise (less than 4 in rhesus monkeys), and the analog magnitude system, which is approximate but with no absolute limit, both will predict success at singular vs. plural, and for plural–plural as long as there are favorable ratios or fewer than four objects. So if both systems are operative, which we know they are, then singular–plural should work fine and so should plural–plural, as long as it has these conditions are satisfied. So we are back to the box-choice experiment, but we are going to do it in a slightly different way. Now, rather than presenting the items one by one, we present them as sets. So we show them five apples; those five apples go into the box all at once and disappear; next we show them one apple and this one apple disappears into the box; and then we allow subjects to approach and choose one box. What we do therefore is present plural sets, presented all at once as opposed to presenting individuals, and we counterbalance the order in which they go into the boxes. We test for singular–plural (1 vs. 2 and 1 vs. 5), as well as plural–plural (2 vs. 4 and 2 vs. 5). Now recall that if either the system of parallel individuation or analog magnitudes is operative, subjects will be able to discriminate values of 4 or less.

What we find in terms of the proportion of subjects picking the larger number of objects, in this case apples, is success on 1 vs. 2 and 1 vs. 5. Now this is an uninformative result, at least for analog magnitude or set-based quantification, because both could work. But here is where it gets interesting: subjects fail at 2 vs. 4, 2 vs. 3, and 2 vs. 5. These results cannot be explained on the basis of the analog magnitude system, and certainly the 2 vs. 3 and 2 vs. 4 failures cannot be explained on the basis of parallel individuation. How, then, can we explain these data? These data do not force a rejection of the systems for parallel individuation or analog magnitude. Rather, they simply indicate that under the testing conditions carried out, these mechanisms are not recruited or expressed. Why?

Let's now run the same exact experiment, but carry it out as individuals going into the box. For example, we show them five apples going into a box one at a time, followed by two apples going into another box one at a time. So now it is still 5 vs. 2, but this time presented as individuals as opposed to sets. They succeed again on 1 vs. 2, 1 vs. 5, but also on 2 vs. 3 and 2 vs. 4, while failing on 2 vs. 5. Remember that this pattern is consistent with the parallel individuation system, but inconsistent with analog magnitude. We therefore recover the pattern of results obtained in the original experiment, a pattern that is entirely consistent with the system of parallel individuation. But we can do better. We can actually turn the system on and off.

If we start out with individual apples, but we load them in as sets, what happens? Here, subjects succeed on 1 vs. 2 and 1 vs. 5, but they fail 2 vs. 3 on 2 vs. 4 and 2 vs. 5. In other words, when sets go in last, they are back to set-based quantification, even though they see them individuated. If we start out with sets, but we load them in as individuals, they succeed on 1 vs. 2, 1 vs. 5, 1 vs. 5 and 2 vs. 4, but they fail on 2 vs. 5. In other words, what is driving the system is the set-based quantificational system. If they see objects as sets as the last thing, then they use a set-based system to quantify which has more; if they see things going in as individuals, then discrimination is based on the system of parallel individuation.

What I would like to argue, therefore, is that rhesus monkeys seem to be making a conceptual distinction between singular and plural. The results I have presented today cannot be explained by the currently available mechanisms that have been discussed, either analog magnitude or parallel individuation. Again, this is not to reject those mechanisms as viable mechanisms for quantification, but they simply cannot account for the pattern of data we see today. Therefore, as a working hypothesis, what I would like to argue is that this system of set-based quantification is part of the faculty of language in the broad sense (FLB), but it is not something specific to language and is not therefore part of FLN.

Now I move to a second line of experiments that plays on the mass–count distinction, a topic of considerable interest to both semanticists and syntacticians. The question is: could this distinction, and its ontological commitments, be rooted in a nonlinguistic conceptual format, and therefore be present in other animals? We have count nouns, things that can be enumerated (cup, shovel, apple), and we have mass nouns, things that cannot be enumerated unless there is a preceding classifier or packaging term (e.g. not *waters, but cups of water, not *sands but piles of sand), so we don't say, for example, *three sands. The question is: does this kind of distinction, which appears in natural languages (not all, but many), translate into conceptual resources that are nonlinguistic, present early in evolution and ontogeny? Consider the experiments on enumeration in human infants, and specifically the classic studies by Karen Wynn (Wynn 1990, 1992) that were done initially with solid objects (e.g. Mickey Mouse dolls), using the violation-of-expectancy looking time method.[4] Wynn's results, and the many replications that followed, show that if you place one object behind a screen followed by a second one, and you pull the screen away,

---

[4] See also descriptions of similar studies by Lila Gleitman in Chapter 16.

babies will look longer at violations of those numbers. So if you place two objects behind the screen but then reveal one or three, babies look longer at these outcomes than at an outcome of two. But if you run the exact same experiment, but pour sand (one pour of sand followed by a second pour of sand) and reveal one, two, or three piles of sand, babies do not look longer at these different outcomes. This suggests that in order for enumeration to proceed, infants require individuals, discrete items that can be enumerated. There is something fundamentally different between solid objects and nonsolid masses.

To address the evolutionary or phylogenetic aspect of this problem, we (Wood et al., 2008) ran a similar experiment, using the box-choice experiment I described earlier. To motivate the animals, we used small pieces of carrot, poured out of a bucket. We filled up beakers with carrot pieces and then poured them into the opaque buckets, walked away, and gave the monkeys a choice between two buckets that had different quantities of carrot pieces. We presented 2 vs. 1, 3 vs. 2, and so forth, pouring pieces of carrot out of a beaker. The monkeys picked 2 vs. 1 beaker pours, 3 vs. 2, and 4 vs. 3, but they failed at 5 vs. 4 and 6 vs. 3. This is exactly the pattern of results I presented for objects, but now the computation is carried out over pouring of quantities or masses of carrot pieces. Now, this confounds many things including volume, so can we control for these factors and see if they are actually enumerating? To find out we poured 1 big quantity of carrot pieces vs. 2 medium ones, where volume is now equated but the actions are different. Here they picked 2 medium over 1 big, so now quantity is preferred over the number of actual pours. We showed them the identical number of actions, 1 vs. 1, but where one beaker was a full volume of carrot pieces and one a small volume, they pick the one big over small, showing they're paying attention to the volume. Regarding all the previous conditions, they could actually see the amount of carrot pieces in the beaker, because the beaker was transparent, but if we make it opaque so they actually have to attend to what is falling out of the beaker, they still picked 2 vs. 1. So they are actually tracking the amount of stuff falling out of the beaker. Together, these results suggest that rhesus monkeys are computing numerosities over solid and nonsolid entities, tapping, in these conditions into the system of parallel individuation. These patterns stand in contrast to those presented thus far for infants, where the enumerative capacities tapped for objects falls apart for masses.

Let me now end by returning to the questions I posed at the beginning. First, *to what extent are the conceptual representations that appear to uniquely enter into linguistic computation built from nonlinguistic resources?* This question is, to me, only beginning to be addressed, but the problem of quantifiers and their representational format seems ideally suited for further exploration. Can we get to the point where we can ask about whether animals have some notion of *many* vs. *all* or *some*? Are the kinds of logical quantifiers that enter into language built upon conceptual resources that have a much more ancient evolutionary trajectory? We are only beginning to ask questions such as this, and we have few answers. Secondly, *to what extent have linguistic conceptual representations transformed in evolution and ontogeny some of our ontological commitments?* The speculation I'd like to leave you with is this. If you consider the results I just presented, involving rhesus monkeys enumerating carrot pieces, and you contrast these with the baby results on pouring sand, I think there is an interesting proposal with respect to the relationship between language and ontological commitments. Specifically, although infants do not yet have, in their production or comprehension, anything like a mass–count distinction, the evolution of that distinction within language has actually transformed our ontological commitments such that infants see the world differently than do rhesus monkeys, who are happily enumerating masses in a way that at least babies seem not to. In other words, humans uniquely evolved the mass–count distinction as a parametric setting, initially set as a default, but then modifiable by the local language, leading some natural languages to make the distinction, but only optionally.

Discussion

LAKA: When you said that you think that children have a more refined singular/plural quantification system that is due to language (so the idea is that there is some conceptual part that is shared between rhesus monkeys and us humans, but there is the difference as well between babies and rhesus monkeys), your hypothesis was that this has to do with language. I realize that you are not saying that babies' knowledge of quantification is driven by language directly. My question is, do you mean to say that human babies have this capacity because they are endowed with the language faculty, or do you mean to say that they will develop this faculty as language matures?

HAUSER: I think I was referring to the former. Due to the evolution of the language faculty, babies already have ontological commitments prior to the maturation of language.

HIGGINBOTHAM: I have two remarks. One is a detailed question on children and their behavior with respect to mass/count distinctions. You know there are languages in which there is simply no plural morphology at all, e.g. Chinese, where it appears vestigially in the personal pronouns, but that's it. Moreover, the nominal (like *book*, let's say) is number neutral, so if you say *I bought book*, that could be one, two, or any number of books. So you do not get morphological marking with this thing, although, in contrast to others, I think that it is pretty clear that you have exactly the same distinction. I mean, *book* is a count noun in Chinese, and *stone* is not a count noun, but a mass noun. But that suggests, now, that the distinction is fundamentally in place, independently of any question of anybody's morphology. But then I think you are going to have to ask yourself, with respect to human beings and with respect perhaps also to the animals, what is the peculiar status of the fact that you never get numerals with mass terms. Try saying *three sands* or *three sand*, or something like that, or in Chinese *three stone* – it makes no sense. One of the interesting questions, it seems to me, is why does it make no sense? (Of course not everybody agrees to that.) A possibility which I have explored,[5] and other people are sympathetic to too, I think, is that it makes no sense because the realm of counting is simply alien to this. You do not have a domain of objects. There would be a fundamental and physical distinction there. That would be a kind of thinking that one could look for in children, I would think, and something that might provide insight into how the ontology really changes once you get language into the picture.

GELMAN: We actually have evidence to support that – Lila, myself, and two post-docs – which I will present.

URIAGEREKA: I am among the ones who are convinced that the FLB/FLN distinction is not only useful, but probably even right, but now we have another wonderful research program ahead, because as we get closer to understanding how FLN came to be, now the big question is going to be, how about FLB? In other words, thought in animals, and so on.

HAUSER: I think one of the challenges for all of us – certainly one that rings through at this Conference – is that it has been hard for us experimental biologists to do the translation from the abstractions that linguists invoke to actually flesh out the research program. I think it is going to require multiple steps. What is exciting – and a significant historical change, I hope – is that the acrimonious debates of the past between biologists and linguists are hopefully gone. But I think it is going to require more than this for the research project to be fruitful. It is going to require a way of articulating what the computational procedures are that are of relevance that enter into language (whether they are FLN or FLB doesn't matter), in such a way that there is a research program that can go forward both in ontogeny and phylogeny. That is a serious challenge. For example, I think that many of the comparative experiments conducted thus

---

[5] Higginbotham (1994).

far have focused on fairly easy problems, easy at least from an experimental perspective. Take categorical perception: this was easy to look at in animals because you could use the same materials and methods that had been used with human infants. Similarly, it was relatively easy for my lab to explore the commonalities between rhythmic processing in human infants and tamarins because we could exploit the same test materials and habituation methods. But once you move to the domains of semantics and syntax, the methods are unclear, and even with some fairly solid experimental designs, the results are not necessarily clear. In the work that I have done with Fitch, for example, in which we tested tamarins on a phrase structure grammar, we now understand that neither negative nor positive evidence is really telling with respect to the underlying computation.

Added to this is the problem of methods that tap spontaneous abilities as opposed to those that entail training. I think both methods are useful, but they tap different problems. We must be clear about this. When the work on starlings was published, claiming that unlike tamarins, these songbirds can compute the phrase structure grammar, we are left with a mess because there are too many differences between the studies. For example, though both species were tested on the same A_nB_n grammar, the tamarins were tested with a non-training habituation-discrimination method whereas the starlings were operantly trained, requiring tens of thousands of trials of training before turning to the key transfer trials. Further, the tamarins were tested on speech syllables, where the starlings were tested on starling notes. And lastly, starlings are exquisite vocal learners, whereas tamarins do not show any sign of vocal learning. The fact that starlings can learn following massive training shows something potentially very interesting about learnability, on the one hand, and the computational system on the other. I think that is extremely interesting. But it might turn out that for many of the most interesting computations observed in humans that they are available spontaneously, with no training or teaching required. Animals may require a serious tutorial. In the end, therefore, we need a comparative research program that specifies not only which kinds of computation we share with other animals, but also, how they are acquired.

CHAPTER 6

Pointers to a Biology of Language?

Gabriel Dover

It cannot be denied that the faculty of language is a part of human biological development in which the particular path taken by any one individual is influenced by a unique, interactive milieu of genetics, epigenetics, and environment. The same can be said of all other features of human biology, even though the operative poetics are not known in detail for any one process. Hence, unraveling (if that were at all possible) the route through which language gets established, whether as a problem of ontogeny or evolution, needs to take note of current advances in research into the ways of biology. No matter what the specific locus of attention might be ("broad" or "narrow" language faculty; "principles" or "parameters"; "I"- or "E"-language; "core" or "peripheral" domains; and so on), the same kinds of developmental and evolutionary factors will be concerned.

On this premise, I describe the sorts of features of evolved biological structures that dominate current research, and which can be expected to be no less involved with the biology of human language than any other known function, including consciousness and ultimately the biology of free will. But I'm getting ahead of myself.

6.1 A dog's breakfast

Although it is often said (following the lead of Theodosius Dobzhansky) that nothing makes sense in biology except in the light of evolution, the problem is that not much makes sense in evolution. Contemporary structures and processes are the result of a three and a half billion year span of time in which random and unpredictable perturbations have been the dominant contributions. Evolution is a consequence of three major recurrent operations (natural selection; genetic drift; molecular drive) each of which is essentially stochastic. Natural selection relies on the occurrence of spontaneous, undirected mutations alongside a fortuitous match (that is, a greater level of reproductive success) between such mutant phenotypes and a fluctuating environment. The process of genetic drift, whereby some mutations accumulate over others without inter- ference from natural selection, depends on the vagaries of randomly fluctuating populations, whether of haploid gametes or diploid organisms. In essence, it is due to sampling errors. The process of molecular drive, whereby some genetic elements fluctuate in number in the germ line of single individuals, and may accumulate in a sexual population with the passing of the generations, depends on a variety of mechanisms of DNA turnover (for example, transposition, gene conversion, DNA slippage, unequal crossing over, and so on).

Each process is operationally independent of the other two, although there is a complex three-way interaction between them which has led to the evolution of bizarre structures and functions, not all of whose features are optimized solu- tions to problems of adaptation, the sole prerogative of natural selection (Dover 2000). Nevertheless, such seemingly exotic features have survived and continue to survive. This is life as the cookie crumbled.

This tripartite phenomenon of evolution impinges on our discussion regard- ing the existence of "laws of form" in biology and their lower-level reliance on the laws of physics and chemistry. Such a discussion in turn impinges on the conceptualization of the faculty of language (or, at minimum, recursive syntax) as an inevitably evolved universal structure, not unlike a "law of form."

6.2 So few modules, so many permutations

There are a number of key features that have come to the fore over the last decade in the study of biology. I describe them briefly in order to indicate the general territory from which an understanding of the ontogeny and evolution of language may one day emerge.

The newer concepts are given a number of names of which modularity, redundancy, networks, turnover, and degeneracy take priority. The first, modu- larity, concerns the observation that at all levels of organization from genes through to organs, a number of basic modular units can coalesce to form a higher-level structure, and that the arrangement of such units can vary from one structure to another. In other words, with reference to genes, the structure and subsequent function of a given gene (and its encoded protein) depend on the specific combination of units that have gone into its (evolved) making. Signifi- cantly, the modular units are frequently and widely shared by other, unrelated genes and each unit may change in its number of copies from gene to gene – that is, the modular units are redundant and versatile. The combined effects of modularity and redundancy in biological structures are not unlike the game of Lego in which many elaborate structures can be constructed from a few repetitive building blocks that can combine one with another in a bewildering number of permutations. Such flexibility, stemming from pre-existing modular units, begs the question as to the meaning of "complexity" as one moves up the tree of life to "higher organisms"; and also imposes considerable caution on the notion of "laws of form" (see below).

There is no average gene or protein with regard to the types, numbers, and distributions of units that go into their making. Importantly, each module contains the sequence information that determines to what other structures it binds, whether they are sequences of DNA/RNA, stretches of protein poly-peptides, or other metabolites, and so on. Hence, multi-module proteins are capable of forming extensive networks of interaction, from those regulating the extent of gene expression in time and space, through to neuronal networks that lie at the basis of brain functions.

It is important to stress that biological interactions of whatever sort are the result of differences between the participating molecules with regard to the distribution of protons and electrons at the points of contact. In other words, the dynamics of all living processes are based on the expected laws of physics and chemistry, as is every other process in the universe (or at least in the single universe with which we are most familiar). Which particular interaction takes effect during ontogeny is a consequence of the perseverance of chemical contacts over evolutionary time. The argument that chemistry/physics provide invariant laws not "transgressable" by biology cannot lie at the level of protons and electrons – for without all the paraphernalia of fundamental physics there would be no biology. Hence, the locus of any such argument that biology reflects universal and rational laws of form, based on universal features of chemistry and physics, must need be at a "higher" level. Is there, or could there be, a higher level in biology obeying universal decrees? Or does universality stop at the level of the differences in redox at the point of contact of our fundamental modules?

6.3 What do we need genes for?

A population of biological molecules, or organisms, is unlike a population of water molecules in that there are no predictable regularities of events from which universal and timeless laws can be drawn. The liquidity of water is a property of a collection of water molecules; no single molecule is liquid. There have been attempts to explain consciousness as an emergent property of a collective of neurons on the assumption that no single neuron is conscious. Setting aside recent hints in brain research that single neurons are more consciously expressive than has been assumed, the metaphoric, or perhaps even literal, comparison with water is illegitimate. The one certain point of biological evolution is that variation is the name of the game, as a combined result of well-characterized mutagenic processes amongst the genes, the random features of sexual reproduction, and the combinatorial flexibility of interacting modules. Hence, no two neurons, from the billions on hand, are alike with regard to their inputs and outputs. Whatever the explanation of consciousness turns out to be, it will need to take on board the massive, inbuilt variation of evolved modular systems and the interactive networks to which they give rise. Consciousness, based on this heaving sea of constantly variable interactions, does not appear to be fixed according to regular, predictable, and universal laws of form.

In our current state of ignorance on the ontogeny and phylogeny of mind and all of its component parts, including the device for language, it is safer to move to simpler biological systems in our efforts to distinguish between biology based on universal principles of physics/chemistry, and biology based on local, modular, interactive promiscuity. For this I turn to the reaction-diffusion models first proposed by Alan Turing and which still form an active focus of theoretical biology. The case in hand concerns the appearance of seven stripes of activity of genes involved in segmentation of the larva of *Drosophila melanogaster* along its proximal-distal axis. Turing developed equations (taking on board differences in rates of diffusion of two interactive molecules and subject to random perturbations of Brownian motion), which showed an initial homogeneous solution settling down into a series of standing waves of concentration. The inference here being that something similar occurs during segmentation. Ingenious but wrong. In essence, as with everything else in biology, each stripe is the result of very local networks of interactions between a variety of modular units in which a particular permutation of interactants is specific for each stripe. Stripes do not arise as a consequence of gene-independent chemical and physical processes operating in a "field."

D'Arcy Thompson similarly proposed in his once influential book *On Growth and Form*[1] that the laws of growth are independent of genes in that diverse animal body plans can be circumscribed by Cartesian coordinates, with a little appropriate bending here and there.[2]

---

[1] Thompson (1917).

[2] It is perhaps in this tradition that Massimo stated in his comments on optimal foraging (see Noam Chomsky's summary, page 407): "There are some things you don't need genes for because it's the physics and chemistry of the situation that dictate the solution."

6.4 Biology: one percent physics, ninety-nine percent history

The well-known early nineteenth-century debate between Geoffroy Saint Hilaire and Cuvier has been introduced by Noam (see page 23) as another example of early antecedents in the argument for what he has called "rational morphology," a position he claims is supported by recent results derived from comparisons between species of the molecular genetics of ontogenetic processes. Geoffroy argued that there is one animal body plan embracing both vertebrates and arthropods, as any sharp morphologist could deduce by examining a lobster on its back. Over the last decade many of the networks of genes responsible for body plans have been elucidated, and many, if not all, of such genes are shared by lobsters and humans. Notwithstanding some fashionable return to Geoffroy by some biologists, does such widespread sharing support the concept of an ur-body plan? Are the tens of major body plans (phyla) in the animal kingdom, and individual biological variation in general, an illusion, as Marc Hauser has advanced? In the background of what I have introduced above the answer has to be no.

Biological variation arises from differences in combinatorial interactions between shared modular units, from genes to neurons. Such sharing does not specify a "rational morphology" of an ur-body plan, rather it indicates, as Darwin taught us 150 years ago, that life is a process of continually evolving differences and that, so far as we know, there is one tree of life on earth occupying a minuscule fraction of the totality of phenotypic space. Hence, it is not at all surprising that genetic modules are shared by all subsequent life forms once such modules were established, long ago in the ancestry of animals. As with all historical processes, subsequent steps are contingent and constrained by earlier steps. Furthermore, we are not in a position to consider the ur-modules or the ur-plan "rational" or "optimal" for we do not have an alternative tree for comparison, any more than we can say that the genetic code is "rational" or "optimal." Given what we know about the large amount of stochasticity in evolutionary processes (see section 6.1), we are on safer grounds viewing all such features, in the words of Francis Crick, as successful "frozen accidents." Noam might suggest that a biology of language as "one damn thing after another" is a "worst possible solution,"[3] but there seems no alternative in the current state of our understanding of biology in general. It is nothing but one novel permutation after another of a relatively small handful of gene/protein modules (possibly as few as 1,200) whose chemistry makes them highly susceptible to such promiscuity of interaction and co-evolution, thus leading to the generation of novel functions.

---

[3] See Chapter 2.

6.5 Is the individual an "abstraction"?

To answer this we need to explore sex – which is an odd phenomenon. From the point of view of the stresses I am making above, it is indeed odd that as a consequence of sex, all of the ontogenetic networks have to be reconstructed from scratch. Newly fertilized eggs contain randomized sets of parental genes that have never before co-existed, and that need to renegotiate, step by step, the patterns of contact required by the history of a given species. In this respect, the making of each individual is unique, in addition to the unique influences of locally expressed epigenetic and environmental factors. I have argued elsewhere that sex inevitably leads to the construction of a completely novel individual; that is to say, individual ontogeny is a highly personalized process of *total nurturing* from the moment of fertilization onwards. Importantly, it needs to be emphasized that the genes are as much part of such widespread nurturing as the more traditionally recognized environmental inputs. If, say, a given gene is participating in a network of 100 other genes, then, from the point of view of that gene, the other 100 genes are part of its nurturing environment. There is no false dichotomy between nature and nurture in this scheme of things – all is nurture in a world of modular biology; an ongoing process throughout an individual's lifetime. Furthermore, there is a sense in which the zygote (the first diploid cell) is a blank slate (give or take some epigenetic influences) in that a process of reconstruction starts at this point (Dover 2006).

It is because of sex and the constant generation of new, unique phenotypes that I emphasize the central role of individuals as units of selection or drift in evolution, and as a potential explanation for the subjectivity of consciousness and free will. Individuals produced by sex, whether uni-, bi-, or multi-cellular, are the only real units of biological operations. Their constituent genes and proteins are not: they have no functions, no meanings, in isolation. Neither have populations nor species. They are all abstractions as we willfully ignore the variation within each category.

I do not think that individuals are just my choice of "abstraction."[4] For example, there is no one "human nature" – only millions upon millions of different takes on human nature as each individual emerges, alive and kicking, from its highly personalized process of nurturing (Dover 2006). "Average" has no heuristic meaning in such a situation. Men are taller than women, on average – true – but this does not help either in the prediction of height of a given man or woman, or in the prediction of sex of a given height. Nor can we measure the height of an abstraction. We objectively measure the height of an individual at a given moment in that phenotype's real lifetime.

---

[4] As Noam suggests, see page 397 below.

Individual biological variation is not an illusion, it is at the heart of all that happens in evolution and ontogeny. And the same can be said of all sexual species – including Noam's ants[5] – for these too we can dismiss the old irrelevant nature-versus-nurture debate in terms of the individualized processes of nurturing involving all of the networking genes. There seems little need to say it, but ants too have "blank slates" at the single-cell stage of a fertilized ant egg.

6.6 "Principles" and "parameters": are there biological equivalents?

Are "principles" and "parameters" to be found in the forms and functions of networks? Networks are evolved structures and their topology (the pattern of connections between interacting units) reflects the history of successfully functioning contacts. Some network nodes are highly connected, perhaps indicative of their early origin. Other nodes form into tightly connected sub-networks which have been shown to be conserved as sub-networks across widely separated taxa. The quality of the contact between units at the nodes reflects the differences in their chemistry, as explained earlier, in addition to a large number of local influences of temperature, pH concentrations, and so on. Are topologies (or at least the widely conserved sub-networks) equivalent to "principles," and are the local influences equivalent to "parameters" of language acquisition?

In the discussion on optimization properties with reference to Massimo's and Donata's "minimax" concept, Noam suggests that "if you take a parameter, and you genetically fix the value, it becomes a principle."[6] There seems to be a clear operational distinction here, allowing us to ask the question whether network topology is the genetically fixed "core" component responsible for network functional stability, with the local parameters at the node imparting functional flexibility. Or could it be the other way round? Computer simulations, based on real networks, reveal in some cases that topology is the key to stable network function, and in other cases stability is a consequence of buffering in contact parameters. Hence, there is no clear distinction between what might be considered "core" and "peripheral" components. Both operate simultaneously during network formation and their influence on network function depends on the types and number of modular units that go into the making of each node, which are of course genetically encoded. So far, there is no obvious distinction between "principles" and "parameters" in network biology, nor with respect to "core" and "peripheral" operations.

---

[5] See page 398 below.
[6] See page 385 below.

6.7 Consciousness

My emphasis on individual personalization during ontogeny is perhaps no more relevant than in the dissection of the biological basis of consciousness, and from that the phenomenon of free will. In so far as I am less a philosopher of mind than I am a linguist (!), I have a sort of amateur freedom to join the dots where the professionals might say no lines exist. Nevertheless, I have the sense that there is general agreement that human consciousness is a first person subjective phenomenon of experiences (*qualia*) that cannot be described in their totality to another conscious mind. Whatever the correct wording might be, there is no doubt that it is a real, not illusory, biological process that can be expected to be unique and subjective in its precise operations to each individual phenotype. So, is there anything about evolved biological networks and their ontogenetic reconstruction, post-sex, which figures in the existence of consciousness?

6.8 Degeneracy

To answer this question I need to introduce one other confounding feature of biological systems, which is the phenomenon of "degeneracy." This is the capacity for different routes to be taken through a network, with each route yielding the same or similar functional outputs. Degeneracy was spotted early on in the history of molecular biology with regard to codon–anticodon patterns of recognition in which some amino acids have more than one designated codon. Degeneracy is invariably found wherever it is looked for, and one relevant new study by Ralph Greenspan (2001; and Van Swinderen and Greenspan 2005) has found degeneracy operative in a network of genes regulating neuronal behavior in *Drosophila*. He was able to show that the topology of connections in the relevant network could differ widely, depending on the mutant state of different participating units, yet with only subtle alterations of the behavioral phenotype under investigation.

Coupling widespread degeneracy with random background noise is one of the strong arguments in favor of my advocacy that development is a highly personalized set of operations from the early inception of the networks regulating gene expression through to the ever-changing neuronal connections in the brain. From beginning to end there is a subjective process of individualization that is perhaps no different in kind from that mode of first person subjectivity that is considered to be the basis of each individual's mind.

Subjectivity is the name of the game at all levels, even though we are only mindful of it in the brain.

6.9 A biological basis to free will?

Could it be then that there is some biological basis to free will residing in such personalized degeneracy? I consider free will to be the feeling that, although we make decisions based on a long series of cause-and-effect steps, there is nevertheless a gap in the chain of causality at the very last step. Acceptance of this "gap" means abandoning for a moment the basis of Western science. How can we overcome this dilemma?

According to the philosopher Ted Honderich (2002) there is a sense in which, when we look back on our lives, we have an inescapable conviction that we were always "our own man" (or woman); that "things could have been otherwise." Our subjective feeling that this is so is no illusion, any more than our subjective experiences of qualia are an illusion. The latter might be a first person phenomenon emanating from the highly personalized structures of degenerate networks, as is everything else in the totality of living processes in an individual, but this does not mean that qualia cannot be dissected, as emphasized by John Searle, using the third person, objective methods of Western science bounded by its acceptance of cause and effect. There is a real phenomenon of personalized free will that is open to scientific investigation starting with the genes, continuing with the processes of total nurturing as individualized degenerate networks are configured, and ending with the subjective reality of mind.

With all of this in mind it might not be totally off the beaten track to see free will, not as an abandonment of cause-and-effect determinism, but as a situation of rapidly and subtly changing outcomes as degenerate neuronal networks switch from one quasi-stable state of topology to others. Our sense of what is going on is that we, each and every lonely individual, feel that a freely willed, subjective decision has been made. At the level of biology (all that chemistry and physics if you will), there is an unbroken route of cause and effect passing through each and every personalized degenerate state, but at the level of our sense of what has happened, we feel that at the threshold of the final step (the gap to the one remaining degenerate state with its final functional output) is one for us alone to decide.

All is subjective, not just free will: it cannot be otherwise given the bizarre paths taken by evolved heaps of life, with their re-usable and promiscuous modular units.

Discussion

PIATTELLI-PALMARINI: It is certainly refreshing to see a geneticist saying that there is no difference between *innate* and *acquired*. In the world of language, I always receive this with grave concern. You know, some of my colleagues say the same; in linguistics a couple of people at MIT say the same, that we should abolish the *innate/acquired* distinction. I usually receive this with great concern because I can see where that's leading.

GELMAN: I can think of no worse or more unacceptable message to take back to developmental psychologists. This is that it's all right to continue thinking that the mind is a blank slate. Your reason: just because you said so. But many in my field do not understand the fundamental problem, which is that we are dealing with epigenesis and hence the interaction with mental structures and a very complicated environment that has the potential to nurture the nascent available structures. The notion of what is given has to be stated differently, in a way that does not pit innate against learned. If we buy into the standard learning account offered by various empiricists, then we are once again assuming a blank slate: that is, no innate ideas, just the capacity to form associations between sensations and do so according to the laws of association. In this case you don't need any biology. For me there is no reason to pit innate against learned. To do so is to accept the widespread idea that there is but one theory of learning. Put differently, it allows empiricists to commandeer the learning account. This is not acceptable. Our task is to delimit the theory of learning that is able to deal both with the fact that domains like language, sociality, and natural number are learned early, on the fly, and without formal tutoring and that domains like chess, computer science, art history, sushi making, etc. require lengthy efforts and organized instruction.

DOVER: I said it tongue-in-cheek, slightly, because I've been reading Pinker's book *The Blank Slate* (2003) and I don't have another term for it, basically. I would welcome one. But actually, what I'm saying is that the genes, all those individual little units – all 30,000 of them in humans – have to get their act together all over again after each moment of fertilization. And it's not just a question of epigenetic influences that are coming in from maternal cytoplasm or maternal mitochondria or parental differences in DNA methylation patterns – all that stuff. It has little to do with that, in the first instance. As I said, the genes have to start renegotiating one with another in the sequential order of interactions expected of the human genome if a human phenotype is to emerge. And there is no-one there telling them what to do. There is no-one at home saying, "Gene A, you'd better start interacting with B, and then hold hands with F, and then hold hands with X". It will naturally, inevitably unfold that way, even though you start off with the genes all blankly spread out on the slates of the two parental genomes. We mustn't misunderstand what most biologists mean by genetic regulation "programs" – programs and blueprints and recipes are metaphors that are highly misleading. *Why* there are no programs, and *why*, nevertheless, reconstruction proceeds along species-specific lines, is a matter for evolution – all those billions of steps from the origin of life onwards that led to the human genome behaving as it does during development – literally giving life from a genetic blank slate – from a completely novel, post-sex, combination of genes.

GELMAN: I totally understood what you said, I'm very sympathetic to it; it's consistent. But you asked for the return, at the beginning, to the notion of blank slate. And that's what I object to.

DOVER: Well, the genetic blank slate is this. This is the genome of a frog [holds up a piece of blank paper]. There's nothing written on it; there are no dotted lines indicating how we are going to turn that into this [holds up a paper frog]. This is a frog, a squashed frog! So how do we get from that [the blank paper] to this [the frog], when there are no instructions of any sort on this piece of paper as to how the folding should proceed? Nor are there any extraneous hands of cooks following a misconceived idea of a recipe, or anything of that sort. So that is the genetic blank slate. If we have to use a different term, that's fine by me, because it is bound to be misunderstood given the history of usage of the term. We need a term to cover the process of *total nurturing* during the highly personalized reconstruction of a phenotype and all its networks, involving novel combinations of genes, novel epigenetics, and novel environments – and all starting from the "blank slate" of a unique fertilized egg, the first diploid cell.

RIZZI: I had a comment on your puzzlement about different views of parameters. I'm not sure it is exactly the same thing, but there is a debate in linguistics between two views of parameters. This to some extent emerged in our discussions here, and probably the thing is important so I think the debate should be more lively than it actually is. There is an interesting paper by Mark Baker on that. It is between a view that considers parameters as simple gaps in universal grammar (UG), so there are certain things on which UG says nothing, and then the role of experience is to fill these gaps – this is a kind of underspecification view – and then there is an overspecification view that says that UG contains specific statements for certain choices, which must be fixed by experience, but it is an overspecified view of UG somehow.

The argument for the underspecification view, of course, is simplicity. It is a simpler concept of UG. The argument for overspecification is restrictiveness, essentially. That is to say, those who argue for the second view observe that the underspecification view is not sufficiently restrictive in that it predicts possibilities that you actually do not find. Just to take the case offered by Cedric Boeckx in this conference,[7] those who argue for a headedness parameter, something that says explicitly that the head precedes the complement or follows the complement, seek to account for what actually is found across languages. If you did not have a statement in UG about that, the effect would simply be a consequence of the fact that you have to linearize the elements, that you have to pronounce words one after the other, so you do not get what you actually find. That is to say, in one language, for instance, you could sometimes produce VO structures, and some other times OV structures, because as the only goal is linearization, there is nothing that tells you that you must always go consistently. So there are these two views, overspecification and underspecification, which somehow transpired in our discussions here. That may be a source of your puzzlement about different conceptions.

---

[7] See Chapter 3.

CHAPTER 7

Language in an Epigenetic Framework[*]

Donata Vercelli and Massimo Piattelli-Palmarini

I have to tell you a story and the story is that the reason I am here is that I can't say no to my friends. Juan Uriagereka was both very insistent and very eloquent in inviting me, so here I am, presenting something that Massimo and I have been thinking about. I have to tell you that the division of labor is such that Massimo takes all the credit and I take all the blame. So this, by way of disclaimer, that I think we acknowledge that there is a little element of absurdity in what we may be saying, but we hope that we also have something that may be relevant to you.

Today we would like you to think about a biological trait, and for reasons I hope will become clear to you, let us call it biological trait *L*. *L* has certain features. It is species-specific, and in particular is unique to humans. It has a common core that is very robust but allows for inter-individual and inter-group variation. It has both heritable and non-heritable components. It goes through critical developmental windows of opportunity: that is, its developmental patterns are time-dependent. It is very plastic, particularly in response to environmental cues. It has multiple and discrete final states, it is partially irreversible, and it is robust and stable over a lifetime.

The question we are trying to answer is, what kind of biology may underlie a trait such as *L*, or, how is a trait such as *L* implemented in our genome. Classical genetics (which I will define in a minute) can certainly account for some features of *L*: species specificity, uniqueness to humans, and a very robust common core that allows for variation. The problem is that classical genetics, we maintain, would not buy us the other features that *L* has. And this is where we think we need to go a little bit further. Let us qualify why.

---

[*] This paper was delivered at the conference by Donata Vercelli.

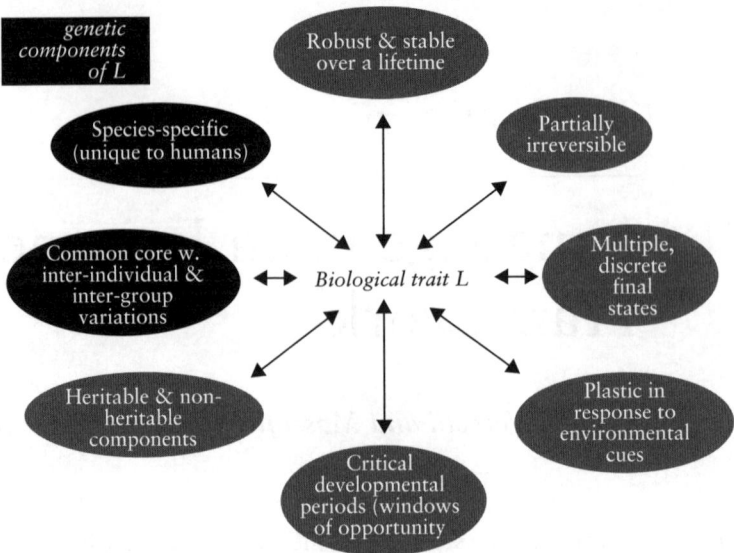

Fig. 7.1. Aspects of biological trait L

1953 is the year in which DNA, as we know it today, and classical molecular genetics were born. It is the year in which Watson and Crick published their rightly famous paper stating that the structure they proposed for DNA, the double helix, could be very effective to replicate, faithfully copy, and transmit information. The success of classical molecular genetics has been spectacular. In their labs, molecular biologists apply the paradigms of classical genetics every day. The notion that a DNA sequence is transcribed into an RNA sequence which is in turn translated into a protein is something we use, for instance, to make proteins *in vitro* starting with a sequence of DNA. This successful notion of genetics emphasizes the amount of information that is encoded and carried by the DNA sequence. What this genetics can give us is great fidelity and specificity in the transmission of information. What this genetics does *not* buy us is a fast, *plastic* response as well as environmental effects and memory of a functional state – nor does it buy us cell fate decisions. In essence, classical genetics is necessary, but not sufficient. This is where epigenetics comes in.

We are stressing the importance of plasticity, because we think plasticity is probably one of the defining features of our trait *L*. From a biological point of view, here is the puzzle. Let us consider the different stages our blood cells go through to become the mature cells circulating in our bloodstream. We have red cells and white cells, and they have quite different tasks. Red cells transport oxygen, some white cells fight infection from bacteria, some white cells fight infection from parasites. Therefore, all these cells do very different things, but they all derive from an initial common precursor cell – that is, they are genetically identical, but they are structurally and functionally heterogeneous because they have different patterns of gene expression that arise during development. Such differences are epigenetically implemented.

To talk about epigenetics, we need to introduce a difficult but fascinating concept.[1] The DNA double helix is not linear in space. It is a very long structure, if you unfold it, but it is actually very tightly packaged, to the extent that in the cell it becomes 50,000 times shorter than it is in its extended length. Packaging is a stepwise process during which the double helix initially forms nucleosomes, that is, spools in which the DNA wraps around a core of proteins (the histones). In turn, each of these beads-on-a-string is packaged in a fiber that is even more complex, and the fiber is further packaged and condensed until it becomes a chromosome. All this packaging and unpackaging, winding and unwinding, provides a way to assemble a huge amount of information within a very small space, but also makes it possible to *regulate* what happens to the information encoded in the DNA.

This is the subject of epigenetics. Epigenetics is the study of changes in gene expression and function that are heritable, but occur without altering the sequence of DNA. What changes is the functional state of the complex aggregate formed by DNA and proteins. These changes – extremely dynamic, plastic, potentially reversible – occur in response to developmental and/or environmental cues that modify either the DNA itself (by appending chemical groups to the sequence, which remains unaltered) or by changing the proteins around which the DNA is wrapped (i.e., the histones). By modifying the core proteins around which the DNA is assembled, or the chemical tags appended to the DNA, the functional state of a gene is also modified (Vercelli 2004).

Deciphering these modifications is quite complex. For DNA to become active, to release the information it carries, the molecule needs to unwind, to become accessible to the machinery that will transcribe it and turn it into a protein. This cannot happen if the DNA is very compressed and condensed, if all the nucleosomes, all the beads-on-a-string, are so close to one another that nothing can gain access to a particular region. Such a state is *silenced chromatin*, as we call it – chromatin being the complex (which is more than the sum of the parts) of DNA and proteins. When nucleosomes are very close and condensed, chromatin is silenced. That happens when methyl groups are added to the DNA or the histones bear certain chemical tags. On the other hand, when other tags are added to the histones or the DNA is no longer methylated,

---

[1] Two recent classics are: Grewal and Moazed (2003) and Jaenisch and Bird (2003). For a recent exhaustive exposition, see Allis et al. (2006). For short accessible introductions see Gibbs (2003). (Editors' Note)

the nucleosomes are remodeled and open up, the distance between them becomes greater, and the machinery in charge of transcription can get in. Now, transcription can occur. Hence, active chromatin is marked by accessibility.

That epigenetics results in real changes in how genes function is a fact. A clear example of how this happens is provided by the case of the black mice. These mice are all genetically identical, in DNA sequence, but it does not take a geneticist to see that they are quite different phenotypically, in terms of the color of their coats. What has happened is that the mothers of these mice are given diets containing different amounts of substances that provide methyl groups. As we discussed, DNA methylation is a major epigenetic regulator of gene expression. After the mothers are fed different amounts of methyl donors and the pups are born, their coat color is checked. Depending on the amount of methyl donors the mothers received, and depending on the different colors of the coats, different levels of methylation are found in the DNA locus that regulates this trait, the color of the coat, with a nice linear relationship between methylation and coat color (Morgan et al. 1999).

This may be true not only of mice; there are interesting data in humans as well, for instance the famous case of the Dutch hunger winter, the famine in the Netherlands during World War II, when mothers who were pregnant at that time had very small children. The children of those children (the grandchildren of the mothers pregnant during the famine) remained small despite receiving a perfectly normal diet.[2] It is possible that this feature, this trait, was transmitted across generations.

What we propose is that this *kind* of mechanism may account for some of the features of L at least (those in red in Fig. 7.1). Here are some cases in support of our proposal.

Plasticity is certainly a paramount feature of biological trait L. A relevant well-known case is that of the Achillea, a plant. Plants are masters at using epigenetics because they are exposed to weather and heavy environmental insults and they need to react to light and temperature. This they do epigenetically. For Achilleas, the same plant at low altitude is very tall, at medium elevation is very short, and at high elevation it becomes again very tall. Nothing changes in the genome of this plant, but the phenotype changes heavily in response to environmental cues, in this case climate and altitude.[3] This is the concept of *norm of reaction* that Richard Lewontin, in the wake of the Russian geneticist and evolutionist Ivan Ivanovich Schmalhausen (1884–1963),[4] has so

---

[2] Described in Roemer et al. (1997).
[3] Studied ever since Hiesey et al. (1942).
[4] For an analysis of the history of this notion, see Levit et al. (2006).

clearly formulated: what the genotype specifies is not a unique outcome of development, it is a *norm of reaction*. A norm of reaction is constrained by genotype, but specifies a pattern of different developmental outcomes depending on the environment.

The concept of *windows of opportunity* is quite familiar to immunologists. In the stables of a Bavarian farm, the mothers work while their children sit in a cradle. As a result of that, we now know, these children are incredibly well-protected from allergic disease, but only if they sit in the stables up to the age of one year, or even better if the mother goes and works in the stables when she's pregnant. Prenatal exposure to stables and barns has the strongest effect. If exposure occurs when the child is 5 years old, it matters much less or not at all.

For *multiple discrete final states*, we already discussed how functionally and morphologically distinct cells (in our case, red and white blood cells) can derive from a single precursor. This process stresses two points. One is about plasticity, as we said, but the other is *partial irreversibility*. Once a cell becomes highly differentiated and its epigenetic differentiation program is fully implemented, this cell cannot go back. In fact, only stem cells retain plasticity all the time. For most other cells, the features acquired through epigenetic modifications are fixed and irreversibly preserved throughout life.

Now do we need to say the *L* we have been talking about is language? We think the genetic components of *L* are species-specificity and the common core (Universal Grammar) with room for large but highly constrained parametric variation (variation is going to become important to some extent, but it requires of course a robust common core). These components may correspond to FLN (the faculty of language in the narrow sense, in the terminology of Hauser et al. 2002). All the other plastic, dynamic components of *L*, we propose, are mechanistically implemented through epigenetic mechanisms – these could be the broader language faculty (FLB). We may have to go beyond this "division of labor" for another feature – the fact that *L* is or seems to be extremely robust, resistant to degradation, and also extremely stable, at least over a lifetime. From a strictly biological point of view, this feature suggests simplicity of design, because simplicity of design gives very high effectiveness. However, a simple design is also vulnerable to stress, unless it is balanced with some redundancy. The stability of a very small system is difficult to understand without postulating that somewhere, somehow, there is some compensatory repair pathway that allows a very compact core to repair. But this is even more speculative than our previous speculations.

Our last point, and this is entirely Massimo's doing, depicts two potential (alternative) scenarios: (1) *All parameters are innately specified*. This would put a very high burden on genetic encoding, something that we immunologists are acutely aware of. And the problem of how you encode an enormous amount of diversity in a limited genome would of course come back here. This possibility would put very little or no burden on learnability. At the other end, (2) *unconstrained variability*, would however put an excessive burden on learnability. So I guess that what we are trying to say is that perhaps having principles and parameters might represent an optimal compromise.

Discussion

DOVER: Epigenetics is a very active and important research field at the moment and it is highly appropriate that you should attempt to link it to the supposed difference between FLB and FLN as I understand it. But I need to add one important caveat, which is that epigenetics is fast becoming a catch-all phenomenon covering anything that moves in the workings of biology. The turning on or off of any gene, whatever it's doing, requires the prior engagement of tens upon tens of proteins which are the products of other genes of course. Now, some of these other proteins are opening and closing the chromatin near to our gene of interest in preparation for transcription; others are involved with nearby DNA methylation; others with the initiation and termination of transcription of the gene, and so on, so you can go on forever. If that is the case, then everything is both epigenetic and genetic at one and the same time, that is, no gene exists in a vacuum, its expression is carefully regulated and depends on the state of its local chromatin, which in turn depends on the comings and goings of many other gene-encoded proteins. In such a situation we might well ask what is the real operational distinction between genetic and epigenetic? Can this really be the basis to distinguish between *core* processes, which are supposedly ancient and go way back, and the more recent *peripheral* processes?

So just to get away from language, let me say something about legs, because it is easier to make my point. We all have two legs, yet we all walk very differently. Now it has long been thought that having two legs is one of those core, basic things that universally characterizes our human species – any healthy fertilized human egg will develop into an individual with two legs. But the shape and manner of usage of legs, peculiar to each individual, is considered to be something peripheral, something that might be "epigenetically influenced" during individual development. Now the whole point of Richard Lewontin's earlier concept of "norms of reaction" (he might not have said this in precisely the same way at the time, but it is certainly the way it's being interpreted now) is that the developmental emergence of two legs, and not just the ways we use the two legs, is as much "epigenetically" modifiable, and is as much a key part of that total process of ongoing, ontogenetic nurturing that I spoke about earlier.[5] In other words, those complexes of genes that are involved in making two legs are no different in kind from the genes, or the very complex milieu of interactions of genes with genes, and genes with environment, that affect the individual shape and use of those legs. So it is very hard to distinguish between them, between "core" and "peripheral," given that this is happening from the moment a specific sperm enters a specific egg and on through each individual's highly personalized route of development.

Each individual's personal history of cell differentiation, tissue patterning, organogenesis, emergence of consciousness, language acquisition, and all the rest of it involves many complex and fluctuating networks of gene (protein) interactions, also subject to much environmental input. There is variation and constraint, simultaneously, at all times. The only thing we can be sure about is that, as a consequence of the sexual process of making sperm and eggs, we essentially get back to a genetic blank slate from which all human developmental processes, "core" and "peripheral," "genetic" and "epigenetic," "variable" and "constrained," need to re-emerge. Anything produced by evolution is bound to be a mess and even the original concepts of principles and parameters might be difficult to unravel when considering biological, ontogenetic processes and their inherently sensitive networks – but here I reach the edge of my understanding.

VERCELLI: I think we need to tread lightly because we are on tricky ground. That the development of an organism involves, as you put it, "many complex and fluctuating networks of gene (protein) interactions, also subject to much environmental input" I certainly will not deny. Nor will I argue against the continuous interplay between (and the likely co-evolution of) genetic and epigenetic mechanisms and processes, which at times may blur the distinction between them. But a distinction *does* exist and emerges when one thinks about the *kind of mechanisms* that may account for certain essential features of language as a biological trait. Some of these features (species specificity and uniqueness to humans, first and foremost) appear to be rooted so deeply and constrained so strongly that one would expect them to be inscribed in the genetic blueprint of our species – that is, to be genetically encoded. But most of the other defining features of language reveal a degree of *plasticity* in development and final states that best fits under the epigenetic paradigm. In other words, not everything in language is nurture – but not everything is nature either.

---

[5] See section 6.5 above.

PIATTELLI-PALMARINI: Let me add to this the following: take the case you present of movement and the fact that we all have two legs and yet each walk differently. There is the famous two-thirds power law;[6] all biological movement obeys this two-thirds power law. All natural movement in humans and animals obeys the law that the two-thirds power of the ratio between linear speed and radius of gyration is always constant. It is universal and we immediately perceive it. Indeed, each one of us walks in a slightly different way. You can look at someone and say "Oh that's Jim, because see the way he walks." But it's very interesting to see that there is a universal law for biological movement. So, what are we interested in? The big effort that has been going on in language – we use different words, different accents, different tones of voice – but the big effort has been to go beneath these and see at what level there may be something universal, something that is common, that is deep. And it is no mean feat. You have seen these days what is in the lexicon, what is in the syntax, what is in the morpho-lexicon, what is in semantics – very, very difficult questions, all subdivided in order to deal with them one at a time. And so the FLB/FLN distinction is complicated to make, but it is a good way of distinguishing things, seeing which components are innate and which components are not. You are a geneticist but I have been a molecular biologist and continue to follow the field, so we both know that there are certain things you can do to genes with very specific effects. Of course, the effect of a gene on a phenotype usually depends on the effect of many other genes, that is called epistasis, and sometimes subtle or not so subtle effects come from apparently unrelated genes. But there are also clear examples of the effects of only one gene. For example, there is the outstanding phenomenon of Hsp90, with its chaperone protein which, if knocked out, gives rise to all sorts of mutations, all over the body of, say, a fruitfly.[7] That is, there are very specific things you can do to specific genes with very specific effects. Moreover, the distinction between genetic core processes and peripheral (also called exploratory) processes is unquestioned these days. I find it all over the current literature, often under the label of developmental and evolutionary modularity.[8] The biochemical pathways and their enzymes, for instance, just to name one clear case, are evolutionarily strictly conserved, often all the way down to bacteria.

DOVER: I don't think I've argued against genetics, otherwise I'd be out of a job; nor have I argued against universality, in terms of human-specific features which are shared by all humans. That's not my point. The point is that the

---

[6] Viviani and Stucchi (1992).

[7] Queltsch et al. (2002).

[8] For a vast panorama, see Schlosser and Wagner (2004).

ontogeny of a given individual is a highly personalized dynamic in which many factors are involved unavoidably nurturing each other. You cannot, with regard to the ontogeny of an individual, say that the "universal genes" and all their participatory networks for two legs are more of a "core" process than the genes and all their participatory networks for the manner in which we use those two legs. The two are ontogenetically unfolding together and there are many, many diverse and interactive influences at play in each unique individual – genes, proteins, environment, culture – the whole catastrophe!

Just one final thing: about the myth of the unique relationship between a specific gene and its very specific effect. First let us set aside the confounding property of rampant pleiotropy of most genes – that is, each and every gene having widely diverse effects at one and the same time – and let's just concentrate on one gene and one of its effects. Some of the best characterized of all molecular genetic diseases are the hemoglobin thalassemias. Now if you talk to David Weatherall and all those guys who have been working several decades on these genes,[9] they tell you the following. If you take a number of individuals, each of which has the identical mutation in say the beta-globin gene, which in turn is embedded in thirty kilobases of identical surrounding DNA (presumably with identical epigenetic patterns of chromatin condensation and methylation), you can then ask the question, what is the phenotype of all these individuals sharing the identical mutation in the same sequence neighborhood? Will they all have beta-thalassemia as part of their phenotype? And the surprising answer is "No." The disease phenotype is not just a specific effect of a specific mutation in a specific gene. They all have the specific mutant beta-globin allele but their phenotypes range from no clinical manifestations through to a requirement for life-long blood transfusions. This spectrum of effects arises because the rest of each individual's genetic background – all those other interactive genes (proteins) and metabolites, whether directly involved with blood metabolism or not, plus of course the internal and external environmental milieu – is absolutely crucial for the extent to which an individual goes down with beta-thalassemia. And the same story is emerging from the etiology of the majority of human diseases, once thought to be a specific consequence of single mutant genes. I think that in biology the pursuit of genetic subdivision, hierarchy, and specificity is not necessarily the appropriate approach to the seemingly indivisible, whether of legs or language. A recipe for despair or an exhilarating challenge?

FODOR: At the end of the presentation (I think this is perhaps especially Massimo's department), you had some speculations about the biological encoding of

---

[9] Craig et al. (1996); Weatherall (1999).

parameters. I wondered if we could relate this somehow to some of the thinking we have been doing at CUNY about that huge grammar lattice of ours.[10] We worry about the biological status of this huge amount of information. I want to divide it into two aspects. One is that there is this huge amount of information, all those thousands of subsets of relationships; and then there is also the apparent specificity of the information. It codes for very particular relationships. This grammar is a subset of this one, but not this one of this other one, something like that. Now, wondering how that information got there, we should consider the possibility that it isn't really so specific at all, that in fact there are many, many other relationships equally coded but that they are invisible to us as linguists, as psychologists. We don't know about them because those languages aren't learnable, so imagine just for a moment you had two grammars in the lattice, so to speak the wrong way up, so that the superset came before the subset. Then we would never know of the existence of the subset language because nobody would ever learn it. It would be unlearnable. So you can imagine that behind the lattice that is visible to us as scientists there is a whole lot of other stuff just like it that we know nothing about because it is arranged the wrong way to be put to use by humans in learning. So: unlearnable languages. It may be that the specificity of the particular parameters that we know about is actually illusory.

PIATTELLI-PALMARINI: Well, this is really the core of the matter. I think that in the evo-devo approach to the evolution of language you have to take into account not just how we once got to the adult state; you have to take into account the whole process of getting there – how that evolved. And of course a very, very old puzzle is why we don't really have only one language. Since genetically we are predisposed to learn any language that there is, there is no specific inclination of a baby coming into this world in China to learn Chinese, nothing of the sort. So we have on the one hand the puzzle as to why we don't all literally speak the same language, and also on the other, why we don't have infinite variation beyond any limit, beyond any constraint. So the suggestion is that maybe what we have is a *minimax* solution, where you minimize the amount of genetic information and at the same time you optimize the amount of learning that there has to be in an acquisition somehow. Mark Baker (2001, 2003) has this hypothesis that the reason we don't all speak the same language is because we want to be understood by our immediate neighbors, but we don't want to be understood by people in the next tribe; which is a cute idea, but it really doesn't explain much, because you can only do that if you

---

[10] See sections 17.6–9 below.

already have an organ that is predisposed to have a large but finite set of possible languages. We could invent some codes that are different from having this parametric variation. So I think the consideration is in fact how complex the acquisition process is versus how much burden you have on the genetic or biological machinery. The guiding (and interesting) idea, in which Noam concurs, if I understand him correctly, is that you have a minimax, you have something close to the perfect compromise between loading the biology, loading the genetics, and having a reasonably complex acquisition process. You know, the things that you are doing and that Charles Yang is doing are closely related to this reflection.[11] We will have to learn from you how exactly these things developed, how much work has to be done there and then continue possibly with some data on other functions, on other species, to see if we can get a grasp on how much genetic information is needed for this or for that, and whether this hypothesis of a minimax solution can be tested.

FODOR: I guess I was trying to suggest that maybe there isn't as much biological design work to be done as we tend to think from our perspective, studying the particular cases, the particular languages that we observe, because in the case of language, if the design isn't optimal, we don't know about it, nobody is going to learn the language, nobody *has* to learn any particular language, so those languages just sort of disappear from view. So I am just wondering whether in fact there is so much specific biological design work going into what I still call universal grammar, and so the pattern of UG, as we tend to think.

VERCELLI: I can answer Janet's question only indirectly, using an intriguing analogy – that between the problem of encoding what there is in language, and the central problem my own field, immunology, faced for years. Our problem was to figure out how a large but finite genome could harbor a huge amount of information without clogging up. As you know, that problem was solved by an atomization of the encoding process, whereby the final molecular repertoire results from rearrangements of multiple, smaller units. That allows for a relatively limited core – then the information is rearranged and used, switched on and off. Systems of this level of complexity run into this kind of problem: how do you build information capacity effectively but not at the expense of everything else in a genome which is finite? The idea that you make space by erasing is a little hard for me to picture, because somehow you have to encode what you erase as well as what you don't. Thus, the encoding problem remains. I would argue a better way to solve it is, as Massimo was saying, by minimizing what you encode and then being very plastic in the way you use what you encode.

---

[11] See Yang (2002).

CHAPTER 8

Brain Wiring Optimization and Non-genomic Nativism

*Christopher Cherniak**

I will talk about combinatorial network optimization – that is, minimization of connection costs among interconnected components in a system. The picture will be that such wiring minimization can be observed at various levels of nervous systems, invertebrate and vertebrate, from placement of the entire brain in the body down to the sub-cellular level of neuron arbor geometry. In some cases, the minimization appears either perfect, or as good as can be detected with current methods – a predictive success story. In addition, these instances of optimized neuroanatomy include candidates for some of the most complex biological structures known to be derivable "for free, directly from physics" – that is, purely from simple physical energy minimization processes. Such a "physics suffices" picture for some biological self-organization directs attention to innate structure via non-genomic mechanisms, an underlying leitmotif of this Conference.

The innateness hypothesis is typically expressed in the DNA era as a thesis that some cognitive structure is encoded in the genome. In contrast, an idea of "non-genomic nativism" (Cherniak 2005) can be explored, that some biological structure is inborn, yet not genome-dependent; instead, it arises directly from simple physical processes. Not only, then, is the organism's *tabula rasa* in fact not blank, it is "pre-formatted" by the natural order: a significant proportion of structural information is pre-inscribed via physical and mathematical law.

* Acknowledgments: I am indebted to Zekeria Mokhtarzada for his collaboration on this work. NIMH Grant MH49867 supported some of the experimental research.

In his opening remarks, Noam Chomsky described a strong minimalist thesis, that "a principled account" of language is possible: "If that thesis were true, language would be something like a snowflake, taking the form it does by virtue of natural law" (Chomsky "General Introductory Remarks," this volume; see also 1965: 59). Of course, the snowflake reference calls to mind D'Arcy Wentworth Thompson's *On Growth and Form* (1917), where the paradigmatic example of mathematical form in nature was the hexagonal packing array, of which snow crystals are an instance. However, even the thousand pages of the unabridged 1917 edition of Thompson's opus contained few neural examples. Similarly, Alan Turing's study (1952) of biological morphogenesis via chemical diffusion processes opens a conversation that needs to be continued. In effect, we examine here how far this type of idea presently can be seen to extend for biological structure at the concrete hardware level of neuroanatomy. The key concept linking the physics and the anatomy is optimization of brain wiring.

Long-range connections in the brain are a critically constrained resource, hence there seems strong selective pressure to optimize finely their deployment. The "formalism of scarcity" of interconnections is network optimization theory, which characterizes efficient use of limited connection resources. The field matured in the 1970s for microcircuit design, typically to minimize the total length of wire needed to make a given set of connections among components. When this simple "save wire" idea is treated as a generative principle for nervous system organization, it turns out to have applicability: to an extent, "instant brain structure – just add wire-minimization." The main caveat is that in general network optimization problems are easy to state, but enormously computationally costly to solve exactly. The ones reviewed here are "NP-hard," each conjectured to require computation time on the order of brute-force search of all possible solutions, hence often intractable. The discussion here focuses upon the Steiner tree concept and upon component placement optimization. (For a full set of illustrations, see Cherniak and Mokhtarzada 2006.) The *locus classicus* today for neuroanatomy remains Ramón y Cajal (1909).

8.1 Neuron arbor optimization

The basic concept of an optimal tree is: given a set of loci in 3-space, find the minimum-cost tree that interconnects them, for example the set of interconnections of least total volume. If branches are permitted to join at internodal junctions (sites other than the given terminal loci, the "leaves" and "root"), the minimum tree is of the cheapest type, a Steiner tree. If synapse sites and origin of a dendrite or axon are viewed in this way, optimization of the dendrite

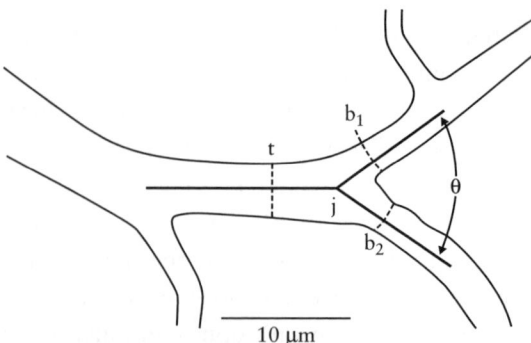

Fig. 8.1. Neuron arbor junction (cat retina ganglion cell dendrite). (a) Branch and trunk diameters conform to $t^3 = b_1^3 + b_2^3$, a fluid-dynamic model for minimum internal wall drag of pumped flow (laminar regime). (b) In turn, angle θ conforms to the "triangle of forces" law, a cosine function of the diameters: $cos\ \theta = (t^2 - b_1^2 - b_2^2)/2b_1b_2$. This yields the minimum volume for a Y-tree junction (Cherniak et al. 1999). So, "Neuron arbor junctions act like flowing water."

or axon then can be evaluated. (Such an analysis applies despite the "intrinsic-ally" driven character of typical dendrites, where leaf node loci are in fact not targets fixed in advance.) Approximately planar arbors in 2-space are easier to study. The most salient feature of naturally occurring arbors – neuronal, vas-cular, plant, water drainage networks, etc. – is that, unlike much manufactured circuitry, for each internodal junction, trunk costs (e.g., diameter) are higher than the two branch costs. The relation of branch diameters to trunk diameter fits a simple fluid-dynamical model for minimization of wall drag of internal laminar flow. Furthermore, when such micron-scale "Y-junctions" are exam-ined in isolation, positioning of the junction sites shows minimization of total volume cost to within about 5 percent of optimal, via simple vector-mechanical processes (Cherniak 1992) (see Fig. 8.1).

This Y-tree cost-minimization constitutes local optimization. Only one inter-connection pattern or topology is involved. Such small-scale optimization does not by itself entail larger-scale optimization, where local tradeoffs are often required. When more complex sub-trees of a total arbor are analyzed, the optimization problem becomes a global one, with an exponentially exploding number of alternative possible interconnection topologies. For example, a 9-terminal tree already has 135,135 alternative topologies, each of which must be generated and costed to verify the best solution. Neuron arbor samples, each with three internodal Y-junctions, minimize their volume to within around 5 percent of optimal (Cherniak et al. 1999). This optimality performance is consistent for dendrites (rabbit and cat retina cells) and also for some types of axons (mouse thalamus) (see Fig. 8.2).

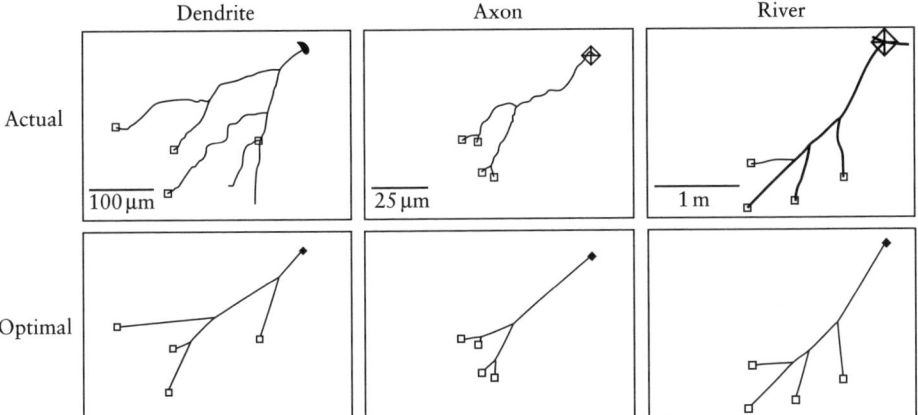

Fig. 8.2. Complex biological structure arising for free, directly from physics.–
"Instant arbors, just add water." In each case, from micron to meter scale, neural
and non-neural, living and non-living, the actual structure is within a few percent of
the minimum-volume configuration shown.

8.2 Component placement optimization

Another key problem in microcircuit design is component placement optimization (also characterized as a quadratic assignment problem): Given a system
of interconnected components, find the positioning of the components on a
two-dimensional surface that minimizes total connection cost (e.g., wirelength).
Again, this concept seems to account for aspects of neuroanatomy at multiple
hierarchical levels.

"Why the brain is in the head" is a 1-component placement problem. That is,
given the positions of receptors and muscles, positioning the brain as far
forward in the body axis as possible minimizes total nerve connection costs to
and from the brain, because more sensory and motor connections go to
the anterior than to the posterior of the body. This seems to hold for the
vertebrate series (e.g., humans), and also for invertebrates with sufficient ceph-
alization to possess a main nervous system concentration (e.g., nematodes)
(Cherniak 1994a, 1995).

Multiple-component problems again generally require exponentially exploding costs for exact solutions: for an n-component system, $n!$ (n factorial)
alternative layouts must be searched. One neural wiring optimization result is
for placement of the eleven ganglionic components of the nervous system of
the roundworm *Caenorhabditis elegans*, with about 1,000 interconnections (see
Fig. 8.3). This nervous system is the first to be completely mapped (Wood 1988),
which enables fair approximation of wirelengths of connections (see Fig. 8.4).
When all 39,916,800 alternative possible ganglion layouts are generated, the

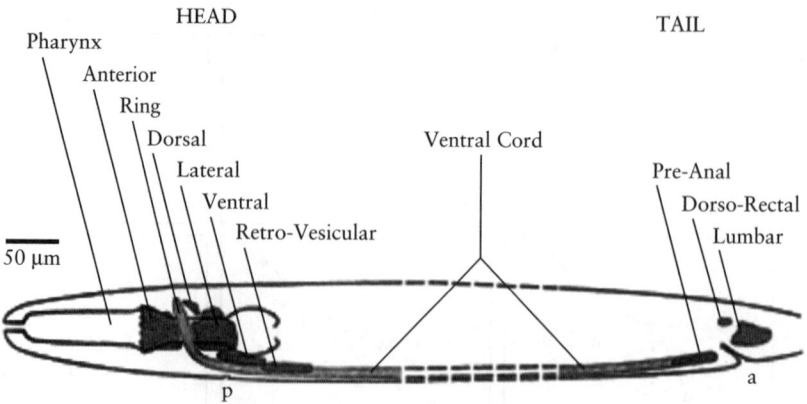

Fig. 8.3. *C. elegans* ganglion components: their body locations and schematized shapes.

actual layout turns out in fact to be the minimum wirelength one (Cherniak 1994a). Some optimization mechanisms provide convergent support for this finding: a simple genetic algorithm, with wirecost as fitness-measure, will rapidly and robustly converge upon the actual optimal layout (Cherniak et al. 2002). Also, a force-directed placement ("mesh of springs") algorithm, with each connection approximated as a microspring acting between components, attains the actual layout as a minimum-energy state, without much trapping in local minima (Cherniak et al. 2002) (see Fig. 8.5). This little nervous system can thereby weave itself into existence.

There is statistical evidence that this "brain as microchip" wire-minimization framework also applies in the worm down to the level of clustering of individual neurons into ganglionic groups, and even to cell body positioning within ganglia to reduce connection costs (Cherniak 1994a).

Finally, the wiring-minimization approach can be applied to placement of functional areas of the mammalian cerebral cortex. Since wirelengths of intrinsic cortical connections are difficult to derive, another strategy is to explore instead a simpler measure of connection cost, conformance of a layout to a wire-saving heuristic Adjacency Rule: If components a and b are connected, then a and b are adjacent. Exhaustive search of all possible layouts is still required to identify the cheapest one(s). One promising calibration of this approach is that the minimum wirecost actual layout of the nematode ganglia is among the top layouts with fewest violations of this adjacency rule. For seventeen core visual areas of macaque cortex, the actual layout of this subsystem ranks in the top 10^{-7} layouts best fitting this adjacency-costing; for fifteen visual areas of cat cortex, the actual layout ranks in the top 10^{-6} of all layouts (Cherniak et al. 2004).

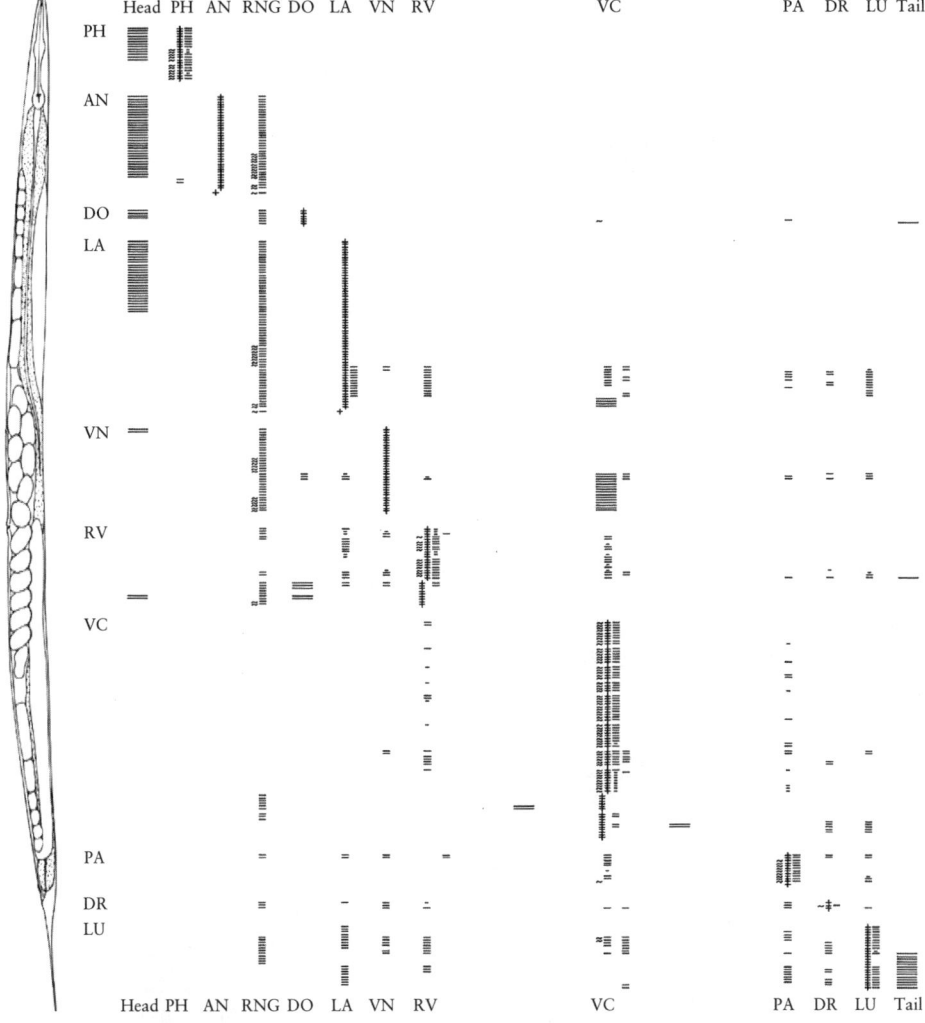

Fig. 8.4. Complete ganglion-level connectivity map for *C. elegans* nervous system (apparently, the first depiction of approximately complete connectivity of a nervous system down to synapse level). Each horizontal microline represents one of the 302 neurons. Horizontal scaling: ~ 100x. This actual ganglion layout requires the least total connection length of all ~ 40 million alternative orderings (Cherniak 1994a).

In general, a Size Law seems to apply to cases like macaque and cat (and worm) with such local–global tradeoffs: The larger the proportion of a total system the evaluated subsystem is, the better its optimization. We have observed this Size Law trend recently also for rat olfactory cortex and for rat amygdala (Rodriguez-Esteban and Cherniak 2005). For the largest systems studied (visual, auditory, plus somatosensory areas of cat cortex), there is evidence of

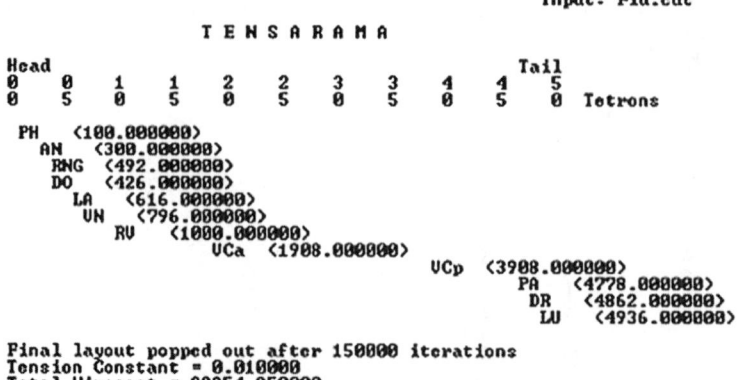

```
                                              Input: rid.cut

              TENSARAMA
  Head                                      Tail
  0     0    1    1    2    2    3    3    4    4    5
  0     5    0    5    0    5    0    5    0    5    0   Tetrons
    PH    <100.000000>
      AN    <300.000000>
        RNG   <492.000000>
         DO   <426.000000>
           LA    <616.000000>
             UN    <796.000000>
               RU    <1000.000000>
                 UCa  <1908.000000>
                             UCp  <3908.000000>
                                   PA    <4778.000000>
                                     DR    <4862.000000>
                                       LU    <4936.000000>


  Final layout popped out after 150000 iterations
  Tension Constant = 0.010000
  Total Wirecost = 88954.250000
```

Fig. 8.5. Tensarama, a force-directed placement algorithm for optimizing layout of *C. elegans* ganglia. This "mesh of springs" vector-mechanical energy-minimization simulation represents each of the worm's ∼ 1,000 connections (not visible here) acting upon the moveable ganglia PH, AN, etc. The key feature of Tensarama performance for the actual worm connectivity matrix is its low susceptibility to local minima traps (Cherniak et al. 2002) – unlike Tensarama performance for small modifications of the actual connectivity matrix (a "butterfly effect"), and unlike such force-directed placement algorithms in general for circuit design. Here Tensarama is trapped in a slightly sub-optimal layout, by a "killer" connectivity matrix that differs from the actual matrix by only one fewer connections.

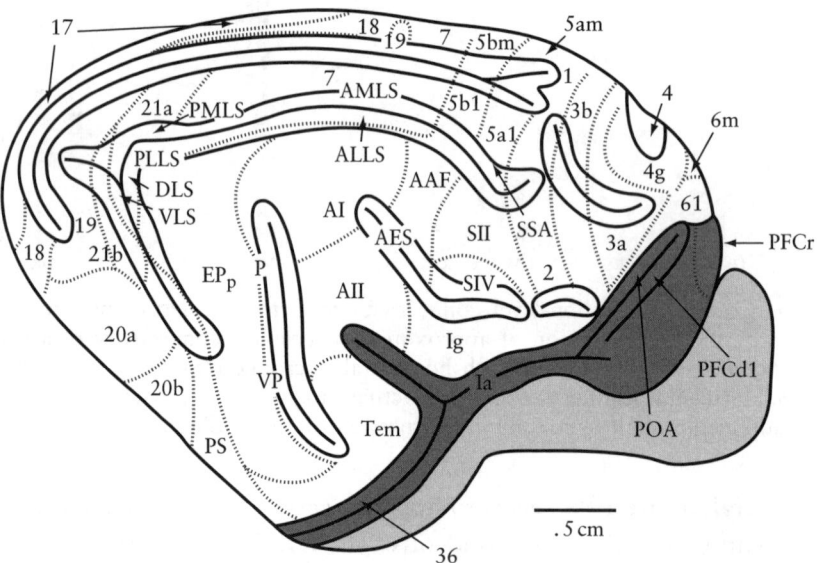

Fig. 8.6. Cerebral cortex of cat. (Lateral aspect; rostral is to right.) Placement of 39 interconnected functional areas of visual, auditory, and somatosensory systems (in white). Exhaustive search of samples of alternative layouts suggests this actual layout ranks at least in the top 100 billionth of all possible layouts with respect to adjacency-cost of its interconnections (Cherniak et al. 2004). – "Best of all possible brains"?

optimization approaching limits of current detectability by brute-force sampling techniques (see Fig. 8.6). A similar Size Law pattern also appears to hold for Steiner sub-tree optimization of neuron arbor topologies.

8.3 Optimization: mechanisms and functional roles

The neural optimization paradigm is a structuralist position, postulating innate abstract internal structure – as opposed to an empty-organism blank-slate account, without structure built into the hardware (structure is instead vacuumed up from input). The optimization account is thereby related to Continental rationalism – but for brain structure, rather than the more familiar mental structure.

The picture here is of limited connections deployed very well – a predictive success story. The significance of ultra-fine neural optimization remains an open question. That is, one issue raised by such "best of all possible brains" results is, what is the function of minimizing, rather than just reducing, neural connection costs? Wiring optimization is of course subject to many basic constraints, and so cannot be ubiquitous in the nervous system; the question is where it does in fact occur, and how good it is. Tradeoffs of local optimality for better cost minimization of a total system are one way in which global optimization can be obscured.

The high levels of connection optimization in the nervous system seem unlike levels of optimization common elsewhere in organisms. Optimization to nearly absolute physical limits also can be observed in human visual and auditory sensory amplitude sensitivities, and in silk moth olfactory sensitivity to pheromones (Cherniak et al. 2002) – that is, at the very meniscus of the neural with its environment. Why should the neural realm sometimes demand optimization, rather than the more familiar biological satisficing? (For some biological optimization phenomena elsewhere, see Weibel et al. 1998).

Mechanisms of neural optimization are best understood against the background mentioned earlier, that the key problems of network optimization theory are NP-complete, hence exact solutions in general are computationally intractable. For example, blind trial-and-error exhaustive search for the minimum-wiring layout of a 50-component system (such as all areas of a mammalian cerebral cortex), even at a physically unrealistic rate of one layout per picosecond, would still require more than the age of the Universe (Cherniak 1994b). Thus, to avoid universe-crushing costs, even evolution instead must exploit "quick and dirty" approximation or probabilistic heuristics.

One such possible strategy discernible above is optimization "for free, directly from physics." That is, as some structures develop, physical principles cause them automatically to be optimized. We reviewed above some evidence for arbor optimization via fluid dynamics, and for nematode ganglion layout optimization via "mesh of springs" force-directed placement simulation. As could be seen for each of the neural optimization examples above, some of this structure from physics depends in turn on exploiting anomalies of the computational order (Cherniak, 2008). While neuron arbors seem to optimize on an embryological timescale, component placement optimization appears to proceed much slower, on an evolutionary timescale. For component placement optimization, there is the chicken-egg question of whether components begin in particular loci and make connections, or instead start with their interconnections and then adjust their positions, or some mix of both causal directions. It is worth noting that both a force-directed placement algorithm for ganglion layout, and also genetic algorithms for layout of ganglia and of cortex areas, suggest that simple "connections → placement" optimization processes can suffice.

If the brain had unbounded connection resources, there would be no need or pressure to refine employment of wiring. So, to begin with, the very fact of neural finitude appears to drive "save wire" fine-grained minimization of connections. Another part of the functional role of such optimization may be the picture here of "physics → optimization → neural structure." Optimization may be the means to anatomy. At least our own brain is often characterized as the most complex structure known in the universe. Perhaps the harmony of neuroanatomy and physics provides an economical means of self-organizing complex structure generation, to ease brain structure transmissibility through the "genomic bottleneck" (Cherniak 1988, 1992) – the limited information carrying-capacity of the genome. This constitutes a thesis of non-genomic nativism, that some innate complex biological structure is not encoded in DNA, but instead derives from basic physical principles (Cherniak 1992, 2005).

The moral concerns not only "pre-formatting" for evolutionary theory, but also for modeling mind. Seeing neuroanatomy so intimately meshed with the computational order of the universe turns attention to constraints on the computationalist thesis of hardware-independence of mind; practical latitude for alternative realizations narrows.

Discussion

PARTICIPANT: I am a biologist and I'm interested in this concept of minimality or perfect design in terms of language. Coming from immunology, we have a mixture of very nice design and also huge waste. That is to say, every day you make a billion cells which you just throw in the bin because they make antibodies you don't need that day. And I am wondering whether in the brain there is a combination of huge waste in terms of enormous numbers of cells, and beautiful design of the cell itself and the way it copes with incoming information. Some neurons take something like 40,000 inputs, and there doesn't seem to be any great sense in having 40,000 inputs unless the cell knows how to make perfect use of them. And that seems to be something that very little is written about. The assumption is that the cell just takes inputs and adds them up and does nothing much with them. But I would suggest that there may be something much more interesting going on inside the cell, and that focusing on the perfect design of the cell might be more attractive and more productive than looking at perfect design in terms of the network as a whole, which is hugely wasteful in having far too many cells for what is needed. I wonder if you would like to comment on that.

CHERNIAK: Just to start by reviewing a couple of points my presentation garbled: anyone around biology, or methodology of biology, knows the wisdom is that evolution *satisfices* (the term "satisfice" is from Herbert Simon 1956). The design problems are so crushingly difficult that even with the Universe as Engineer, you can't optimize perfectly; rather, you just satisfice. And so, I remember literally the evening when we first pressed the button on our reasonably debugged code for brute-force search of ganglion layouts of that worm I showed you, to check on how well minimized the wiring was; I certainly asked myself what I expected. We had already done some of the work on neuron arbor optimization, and so I figured that the nematode (*C. elegans*) wiring would be doing better than a kick in the head, but that it would be like designing an automobile: you want the car to go fast, yet also to get good mileage – there are all these competing desiderata. So when our searches instead found perfect optimization, my reaction was to break out in a cold sweat. I mean, quite happily; obviously the result was interesting.

One open question, of course: it is easy to see why you would want to save wire; but why you would want to save it to the nth degree is a puzzle. One pacifier or comfort blanket I took refuge in was the work Randy Gallistel referred to on sensory optimalities (see "Foundational Abstractions," this volume). Just in the course of my own education, I knew of the beautiful Hecht, Schlaer, and Pirenne (1942) experiments showing the human retina operating at absolute quantum limits. And the similar story, that if our hearing were any more sensitive, we would just be hearing Brownian motion: you can detect a movement of your eardrum that is less than the diameter of a hydrogen atom. A third sensory case (obviously, I'm scrambling to remember these) is for olfactory sensitivity – the Bombyx silk moth, for example. Romance is a complicated project; the moths' "antennas" are actually noses that are able to detect single pheromone molecules. If you look at the titration, males are literally making Go/No-go decisions on single molecules in terms of steering when they are homing in like that. However, these are all peripheral cases of optimality, and they don't go interior; so that is one reason why I wanted to see if we could come up with *mechanisms* to achieve internal wiring minimization. Another reassurance we sought was to look at other cases of possible neural optimization. The claim cannot be that everywhere there is optimization, we cannot say that on the basis of what we are seeing. Rather, the issue is whether or not there are other reasonably clear examples of this network optimization. Now, some of the work that got lost in my talk improvisation is on cortex layout; so you are moving from the nematode's approximately one-dimensional nervous system, to the essentially two-dimensional one of the cerebral cortex (which is much more like a microchip in terms of layout). And cortex results are similar to the worm. For cortex, you need more tricks to evaluate wiring optimality. But still, when we search alternative layouts, we can argue that the actual layout of cat cortex is attaining wiring-minimization at least somewhere in the top one-billionth of all possible layouts. As an outside admirer, I find the single cell a prettier, less messy world than these multi-cellular systems. I would point out that the work I showed you on arbor optimization is at the single-cell level – actually at the sub-cellular level, in the sense that it is for the layout of single arbors. (The one caveat is that those arbors are approximately two-dimensional. The mathematics is somewhat simpler than for 3D.)

HAUSER: I may not have the story completely right, but I was reading some of the work of Adrian Bejan (Bejan and Marden 2006), an engineer at Duke, who has made somewhat similar kinds of arguments as you have about tree structure, and especially about the notion of optimal flow of energy or resources. In a section of one of his books, he makes the argument that there is a necessary binary bifurcation in many tree structures at a certain level of granularity. This is probably a leap, but in thinking about some of the arguments concerning tree structure in language, is it possible that there is more than mere metaphor here? In other words, could the fact that trees, lightning, neurons, and capillaries all show binary branching indicate that this is an optimal solution across the board, including the way in which the mind computes tree structures in language? Could this be the way language *had* to work?

CHERNIAK: Yes, that is a classic sort of inter-level connection, and I don't think it is just metaphorical. When we went into this field, all the network optimization theory, all the graph theory for arbors, had been done for what are called Steiner trees. (The usual history of mathematics story, misnamed after

Jacob Steiner of the nineteenth century; but in fact you can find work on the idea going back to the Italian Renaissance, within the research program of Euclidean geometry.) The classical models assume trunks cost the same as branches, and so we had to retrofit four centuries of graph theory to cover cases where trunks cost more than branches – as they usually do in nature. So that is the one caveat on this. But if you go back to the classic uniform wire-gauge models, then the usual theorems are in fact that optimal trees will have such bifurcating nodes; this is a completely abstract result. A caution I hasten to add is: there is another type of tree, the minimal spanning tree. With Steiner trees, you are allowed to put in internodal junctions, and you get a combinatorial explosion of alternative topologies. The largest Steiner trees that have been solved by supercomputer have perhaps around a hundred nodes. There are more towns than that in Tennessee, so the computational limits on Steiner trees are very much like the traveling salesman problem. But if you instead look at this other type of tree ("minimal spanning tree" probably approximates a standard name), in this case junctions are only permitted at nodes or terminals, which is not of course what you see for neuron arbors. However, minimal spanning trees are incredibly fast to generate, and indeed the most beautiful algorithms in the universe that I know of are for generating minimal spanning trees. You see quarter-million-node sets being solved. Anyway, if you look at the neuron cell body, you can treat that one case as a local minimal spanning tree, and the theorem there is: Not two, but six branches maximum. And indeed micrographs of retinal ganglion cells show six branches from the soma. Anyway, again, regarding your query, it's a theorem of graph theory that optimal Steiner trees have binary bifurcations. And, yes, I agree, this is germane to theorizing about tree structures in linguistics.

PART II

On Language

CHAPTER 9

Hierarchy, Merge, and Truth*

Wolfram Hinzen

9.1 The origin of truth

I'd like to speak about what I think is a rather novel problem on the scientific landscape, the origin and explanation of human semantics – the system of the kind of meanings or thoughts that we can express in language. In the last decades we have seen a very thorough description and systematization of semantics, using formal tools from logic, but moving from there to explanation requires, I believe, quite different tools and considerations. I'd like to offer some thoughts in this direction.

It is fairly clear that the realm of human meanings is highly *systemic*: you cannot know the meaning of only seventeen linguistic expressions, say, or 17,000. That's for the same reason that you can't know, say, only seventeen natural numbers, or 17,000. If you know one natural number – you really know what a particular number term means – then you know infinitely many: you master a *generative principle*. The same is true for your understanding of a single sentence: if you know one, you know infinitely many. So, this is what I call the systemic or "algebraic" aspect of number or language. The question, then, is where this system of meanings comes from, and how to explain it.

 * This paper develops what Chomsky (2006) has described as a "more radical conception of the FL–CI interface relation." This is the same position that Uriagereka (2008) identifies as "the radical option" and falls short of endorsing (so there must be something to this judgment ...). On the other hand, it is highly inspired by (my understanding of) Uriagereka (1995). I also wish to express my dear thanks to the organizers of the conference for a wonderful event where such ideas could be discussed. I specifically thank Massimo Piattelli-Palmarini, Lila Gleitman, Noam Chomsky, and Jim Higginbotham for discussion.

Actually, though, this systemic aspect of human meaning is not what is most interesting and mysterious about it. Even more mysterious is what I will call the *intentional* dimension of human semantics. You could, if you wanted to, simply use language to generate what I want to call a *complex concept*: you begin with "unicorn," say, a noun. Then you modify it by, say, "bipedal," which results in the object of thought "bipedal unicorn," and then you can modify again, resulting in "sleepless bipedal unicorn," "quick, sleepless, bipedal unicorn," "bald, quick, sleepless, bipedal unicorn," and so on, endlessly. Each of these constructions describes a discrete and novel object of thought, entirely irrespective of whether such an object ever existed or will exist: our conceptual combinatorics is unconstrained, except by the rules of grammar. It is unconstrained, in particular, by what is true, physically real, or by what exists. We can think about what does not exist, is false, and could only be true in a universe physically different from ours. We approach the intentional dimension of language or thought when we consider *applying* a concept to something ("this here *is* a bald,... bipedal unicorn"), or if we make a *judgment of truth* ("that there are no bipedal unicorns is true").

Crucially, there is an asymmetric relation between the (complex) concepts that we construct, on the one hand, and the judgments into which they enter, on the other. In order to apply a concept, we need to have formed the concept first; it is hard to see how we could refer to a person, say, without having a concept of a person. Similarly, in order to make a judgment of truth, we need to have assembled the proposition first that we make the judgment about. Progressing from the concept to the truth value also requires quite different grammatical principles, and for all of these reasons, the distinction between *conceptual* and *intentional* information seems to be quite real (see further, Hinzen 2006a).[1]

Our basic capacity of judgment, of distinguishing the true from the false, is likely a human universal, and I take it that few parents (judging from myself) find themselves in a position of actually having to explain to an infant what truth is. That understanding apparently comes quite naturally, as a part of our normal ontogenetic and cognitive maturation, and seems like a condition for learning anything. Descartes characterizes this ability in the beginning of his *Discours* (1637):

---

[1] *Here* I am rather conservative. The distinction between conceptual and intentional information is, in a rather clear sense even if in different terms, part of Government & Binding and Principles & Parameters incarnations of the generative program, by virtue of the existence of D-S and LF levels of representation. "Levels" have now been abolished, but Uriagereka (2008: Chapter 1) shows how this distinction can and should be maintained in Minimalism.

Le bon sens est la chose du monde la mieux partagée; car chacun pense en être si bien pourvu que ceux même qui sont les plus difficiles à contenter en toute autre chose n'ont point coutume d'en désirer plus qu'ils en ont. En quoi il n'est pas vraisemblable que tous se trompent: mais plutôt cela témoigne que la puissance de bien juger et distinguer le vrai d'avec le faux, qui est proprement ce qu'on nomme le bon sens ou la raison, est naturellement égale en tous les hommes.[2]

Unveiling the basis for human judgments of truth would thus seem to be of prime philosophical importance and interest. In what follows I will describe some steps which I think are needed to understand the origin of truth, and hence of human intentionality, continuing to make an assumption I have made in these past years, that the computational system of language – the generative system of rules and principles that underlies the construction of expression in any one human language – is causally responsible for how we think propositionally and why we have a concept of truth in the first place. I want to argue that if this is right, and the generative system of language underlies and is actually indistinguishable from the generative system that powers abstract thought, today's most common and popular conception of the architecture of the language faculty is actually mistaken, as is our conception of the basic structure-building operation in the language, the recursive operation Merge.

9.2 Standard minimalist architecture

Today's "standard" theory of the architecture of the human language faculty has been arrived at principally through a consideration of which features and components this faculty *has* to have if it is to be usable, in the way we use language, at all. In particular, the standard view goes, there has to be:

(i) a computational, combinatorial system that combines expressions from a lexicon, LEX (i.e., a syntax) and employs a basic structure-building operation, Merge;

(ii) a realm of "meanings" or "thoughts" that this combinatorial system has to express or "interface with";

---

[2] "Good sense is, of all things among men, the most widely distributed; for every one thinks himself so abundantly provided with it, that those even who are the most difficult to satisfy in everything else, do not usually desire a larger measure of this quality than they already possess. And in this it is not likely that all are mistaken: the conviction is rather to be held as testifying that the power of judging aright and of distinguishing truth from error, which is properly what is called good sense or reason, is by nature equal in all men (. . .)." (Translation from the online Gutenberg edition, see http://www.literature.org/authors/descartes-rene/reason-discourse/index.html.)

(iii) a realm of sound, or gesture (as in sign languages), that the system has to equally interface with, else language could not be *externalized* (or be heard/seen).

If the syntax does nothing but construct interface representations, and there are no more than two interfaces, we get the picture shown in Fig. 9.1, where PHON and SEM are the relevant representations.

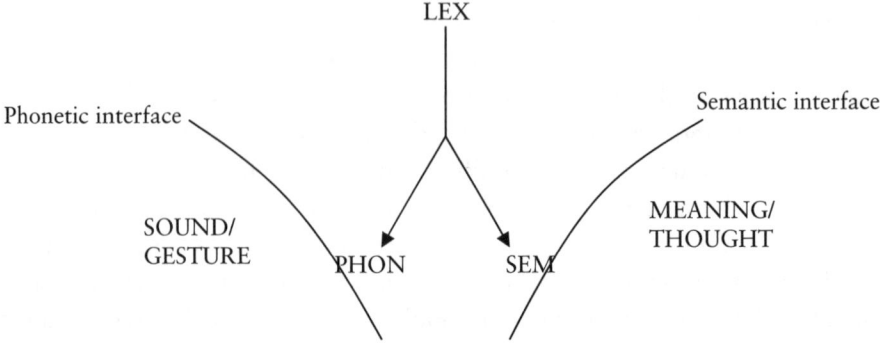

Fig. 9.1. The standard model.

From these first demarcations of structure, further consequences follow: in particular, whatever objects the computational system constructs need to satisfy conditions on "legibility" at the respective interfaces, imposed by the two relevant language-external systems (sensorimotor or "S-M"-systems, on the one side, and systems of thought, "Conceptual-Intentional" or "C-I"-systems, on the other). Ideally, indeed, whatever objects the syntax delivers at one of these interfaces should *only* contain features and structures that the relevant external system can "read" and do something useful with.

The "Strong Minimalist Thesis" (SMT) attempts to explain language from the very need for the language system to satisfy such interface conditions: language satisfies this thesis to whatever extent it is rationalizable as an *optimal solution to conditions imposed by the interfaces*. In the course of pursuing this thesis, these conditions have come to be thought to be very substantive indeed, and effectively to explain much of the diversity of structures that we find in human syntax. For example, there is said to be a semantic operation of "predicate composition" in the language-external systems of "thought" with which language interfaces, and thus (or, therefore) there is an operation in the syntax, namely "adjunction," which as it were "answers" that external condition. By virtue of that fact, it is argued, adjunction as a feature of syntax finds a "principled explanation": its answering an interface condition is what rationalizes its existence (Chomsky 2004b).[3] This example illustrates a way in which empirically certified syntactic conditions in syntax are meant to correlate one-to-one with certain conditions inherent to the "semantic component" – or the so-called "Conceptual-Intentional Systems" thought to be there irrespective of language – and how we may argue for such optimality in an effort to give substance to the SMT.

The existence of a semantic interface that plays the explanatory role just sketched is often said to be a "virtual conceptual necessity," hence to come "for free." But note that all that is really conceptually necessary here – and even that is not quite necessary, it is just a fact – is that language is used. This is a much more modest and minimal requirement than that language interfaces with "outside systems" of thought which are richly structured in themselves – as richly as language is, in fact – so as to impose conditions on which contents language has to express. Language could be usable, and be used, even if such independently constituted systems did not exist and the computational system of language would literally *construct* all the semantic objects there are. As Chomsky points out in personal conversation, at least the outside systems would have to be *rich enough to use* the information contained in the representations that the syntax constructs. Even that, I argue here, is too strong, and the more radical option is that the outside systems simply do not exist.

The new architecture I have in mind is roughly as shown in Fig. 9.2, and I will try to motivate it in the next section.

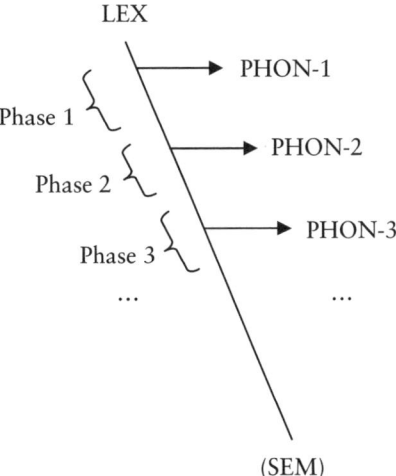

Fig. 9.2. The "radical" model.

---

[3] Chomsky offers a similar "internalist-functionalist" kind of explanation for the syntactic duality of external and internal Merge, which again is rationalized by appeal to a supposed property of language-external (independently given or structured) systems of thought, namely the "duality of semantic interpretation": argument-structure, on the one hand, discourse properties, on the other (Chomsky 2005).

The differences to the previous architecture are quite obvious: now there is no semantic component, no independent generative system of "thought," no "mapping" from the syntax to such a system, no semantic "interface." There is a computational system (syntax), which constructs derivations; periodically, after each "phase" of a computation, the generated structure is sent off to the sensorimotor systems; and there are no structured semantic representations beyond the ones that the syntax is inherently tuned to construct.

9.3 Syntax as the skeleton of thought

One way of putting this somewhat radical idea is in the form of the question: is syntax the dress or the skeleton of thought? Is syntactic complexity a contingent way of dressing up human thought, viewed as something independent from language, in a linguistic guise? Or is syntax what literally *constructs* a thought and gives it its essential shape, much as our bones give shape and structure to our body? If we stripped away syntax, would thought merely stand naked, or would it fall apart?

The former picture is far more conservative, especially in the philosophical tradition, where ever since Frege and Russell, sentence meanings are being looked at as language- and mind-independent "propositions," to which our brain, although they are external to it, somehow connects. Often they are thought to be deprived of structure altogether, sometimes they are thought to have a logical structure only; that they are not only structured, but that they can be deflated altogether into the structures that the system of human syntax provides, is, I think, a new idea.

Notice now that thought is as generative and discretely infinite as language is: there is no finite bound on the thoughts you can think, and every propositional thought (the kind of thought that can enter rational inferences) is a unique and discrete object. Such productivity is only possible if there is a generative system behind thought that powers it. Could that system really employ radically different generative principles than the ones that we now think the computational system of language (syntax) exhibits? Could it do that, after we have come to *minimalize* syntax in the course of the minimalist program, to an extent that only the barest essentials of a computational system that yields discrete infinity are left? If Merge, which is thought to be the basic computational operation of human syntax, is what is minimally needed to get a system with the basic properties of language, could it *fail* to exist in another system, the system of "thought," that exhibits these very properties as well? Having seen, moreover, that it is the generative system of language that accounts for particularly the *logical* properties of linguistic expressions (Huang 1982) – the ones that account for their behavior in rational inferences – can we really assume that the logical properties of "thought" are driven by an entirely different generative system? That there two skeletons, rather than one?

Notice also that language is *compositional*: sets of words which we informally call "sentences" contain other such sets, and the meaning of the sentences depends on the interpretation of these subsets inherently. These subsets are discrete syntactic objects in their own right, which have distinctive semantic interpretations themselves: thus, for example, a morpheme or word is interpreted differently from a sentence, a noun phrase or sentence differently from a verb phrase. Consider, to be specific, a set of words like (1):

(1) {the, man, who, left, a, fortune}

Some of its subsets, such as {the, man} or {a, fortune} or {left, {a fortune}} are discrete sub-units in the above sense. The first two have one type of semantic interpretation (they are, intuitively speaking, "object-denoting"); the third has a different type of interpretation (it is "event-denoting"). Other subsets are no such units, such as {left, a}, or {man, who}. These objects have no distinctive semantic interpretations at all – they are seriously incomplete; and they are no syntactic units either. This is an intriguing correlation that needs to be explained, along with the more general fact that "correspondences" between form and meaning are much more systematic than these sketchy remarks would let you suspect. They go far beyond 'event'-denotations for VPs and 'object'-denotations for NPs. A candidate initial list for a more detailed account of correspondences is (though I won't go into details here): Nouns correspond to kinds ('man', 'wolf,' etc.), D(eterminer)P(hrase)s to objects ('this man,' 'that wolf'), *v*Ps (verbs with full argument structure, without Tense specification) to propositions/events ('Caesar destroy Syracuse'), T(ense)P(hrase)s to tensed propositions/events, C(omplementizer)P(hrase)s to truth values, adjuncts to predicate compositions, bare Small Clauses to predications (Moro 2000), head–complement (H-XP) constructions to event-participants, possessive syntax to integral relations (Hinzen 2007a), and so on.[4]

One way of looking at lists such as this is to suppose that there exists an independently constituted semantic system or system of thought, which forces the syntax to pattern along units such as {left {a, fortune}}, but not {left, a}, say. This is a rather unattractive view, as it presupposes the semantic objects in

---

[4] Clearly, such form–meaning correspondences are highly desirable from an acquisition point of view. For syntax to help get meaning into place, it should align and condition it (see in this regard Gleitman et al. 2005, and her contributions to this volume).

question and has nothing at all to offer by way of explaining them. It is like saying that there are sentences (CPs) because there are propositions they need to express. But what are propositions? They are the meanings, specifically, of sentences. So, a more attractive and intriguing view is to say that something else, internal to the syntax, forces it to pattern around certain interpretable units. This supposition is what grounds the architecture in Fig. 9.2.

To get there, suppose, to use traditional terminology at least for a moment (like a ladder, which we will soon throw away after use), that *all linguistic representations are interface representations*, hence that *every syntactic representation and hierarchical unit in it inherently subserves (computes) a semantic task*. Different kinds of syntactic objects thus intrinsically correlate with different kinds of semantic objects, such that in the absence of the syntactic construction of the latter at the semantic interface, they would not exist. Their reality is *at* the interface and nowhere else. In that case we might as well give up speaking of an "interface" (now throw away our ladder), since on this strictly constructive view the only reality of semantic objects is due to the syntax itself. The phased dynamics of derivations is all there is. Certain semantic objects arise at phase boundaries and have an ephemeral existence at these very moments. No external demands are imposed on this dynamics. There are *executive systems* using the constructs in question, for sure, but now one wouldn't say these systems have to "match" the constructs in richness or impose conditions on them, except those imposed by executive systems that place the semantic objects in question in discourse, in line with online constraints on the construction of an ongoing discourse model.

There is thus syntax and there is discourse (and of course there is pronunciation/visualization), and that is all there is. Beyond the possible forms that the computational system of language provides, there are no thoughts that you can think. You can of course think associative, poetic, non-propositional kinds of thoughts, too. But these are not the ones we are (here) trying to naturalize (or explain). It also follows from this that to whatever extent non-human animals partake in the systematicity and propositionality of human thought, they partake in whatever fragments of the computational system are needed to think them.

9.4 Building structure: Merge

Obviously this suggestion depends on getting clearer on what kinds of structures the computational system of language actually builds, and how. It is noteworthy in this regard that recent "minimalist" theorizing in the study of language has seen a rather severe deflowering of trees. While in the early days of Government & Binding Theory they were still richly decorated, with three-layered sub-trees built by the immutable laws of X-bar theory, and in the early days of minimalism (Chomsky 1995b) at least we still had "projections" of a somewhat meagre sort, as in (2), we now are left with (3) (Collins 2002):

(2)

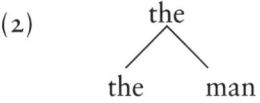

(3)

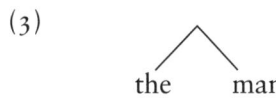

The reason for this deflowering is closely linked to the rather sad history of categorical labels (like NP, P, V', and so on), familiar from the days of Phrase Structure Grammar. First, they were demoted to the status of lexical items, and deprived of the X-bar theoretic bar-stroke that marked them as something else than that. So, for example, {the, man} would not be a D', or DP, it would just be "the": labels such as this were said to be "designated minimal elements" in a syntactic object, whose job is to carry all the information relevant for the way that object enters into further computation. But then the drive of the minimalist program in recent years has been to show that the same information follows even without designating out such elements, so that labels are eliminable after all (Chomsky 2006).

I will assume that this whole development is well-motivated within the assumptions that ground it. The deepest motivation is the elimination of a phrase-structure component in the grammar in favor of the sole operation Merge, defined as recursive set-formation. This operation I will now describe in more detail. Suppose, with Chomsky (2005a), that Merge is an operation that merely forms a set out of n elements, taken from some "lexicon." Taking $n=1$ as a special case, so that we have a one-membered lexicon, let us identify it for concreteness with the empty set. Merge then enumerates the following sequence:

(4) $\emptyset = 1$
   Merge $(1) = \{\emptyset\} = 2$
   Merge $(2) = \{\{\emptyset\}\} = 3$
   Merge $(3) = \{\{\{\emptyset\}\}\} = 4$
   Etc.

The function carrying us from any element in this series to its immediate successor is effectively the *successor function*, viewed as a generative principle that forms an immediate successor of an element simply by creating a set of which that element is the only member. We could also define this function in the way that each immediate successor of every such element is the set containing all and only its predecessors, and thus the entire history of its generation:

(5) $\emptyset = 1$

  $\text{Succ}(1) = \{\emptyset\} = \{1\} = 2$

  $\text{Succ}(2) = \{\emptyset, \{\emptyset\}\} = \{1, 2\} = 3$

  $\text{Succ}(3) = \{\emptyset, \{\emptyset\}, \{\emptyset, \{\emptyset\}\}\} = \{1, 2, 3\} = 4$

  Etc.

Clearly, both (4) and (5) give us a discretely infinite series. We could then move further from here, and define algebraic operations such as addition, by which we can combine any two such elements. The result will be a mathematical space, structured by certain relations. We could also add operations that carry us *out* of this space, such as subtraction, which opens up a new space, the space of the negatives, or division, which opens the space of the rational numbers. These spaces are not unrelated, in fact some of them come to *contain* entire other such spaces: the reals, say, entail the rationals, the rationals entail the naturals. So, it's really quite a playing-field.[5] With each operation we add, our spaces get richer, and eventually there will be a whole hierarchy of spaces ordered by a relation of containment, and depending on the space on which the objects we generate live, they behave quite differently: they are different kinds of objects, and we therefore create different kind of *ontologies*. These may relate quite regularly and systematically to one another, in the way, say, that a geometrical object such as a globe, e.g. the Earth, "contains" a surface as another, lower-dimensional kind of object, and that surface relates to the equator, a line, again a lower-dimensional kind of object (see further Uriagereka 2008: Chapter 8, for a discussion of topological notions in linguistics). The length of such a "chain" of different kinds of objects that contain one another is called the *dimension* of a space. Crucially, a space generated by the operation Merge in (4), interpreted geometrically, would be only *one-dimensional*. Geometrically, we can view it as a line.

What is the point of all this?[6] Chomsky (2005a), when discussing the above analysis of Merge, suggests that arithmetic and language are evolutionarily

---

  [5] Though, interestingly, not a limitless one: thus, in the eight-dimensional algebraic spaces inhabited by special numbers called octonions, standard algebraic operations such as associativity cease to be defined.

  [6] For a longer elaboration, see Hinzen (2007b).

linked domains of cognition in which we find the same basic operation Merge instantiated. Merge in language, on this view, is simply an instance of a more general operation that generates the natural numbers in arithmetic, too, yielding a discretely infinite space in both cases. I come to how this works for language in a moment. For now what is important is this: Chomsky's viewpoint opens up the path for looking at syntactic objects from an abstract algebraic point of view, and for asking: what kind of algebraic space do syntactic objects form or inhabit? What is its dimensionality? Obviously, a single-dimensional space will only contain one category of object. All of its objects, that is, only vary along one dimension. A multi-dimensional space, like the numbers, on the other hand, will contain multiple categories of objects, many or all of them defined in terms of operations on lower-level objects, as we saw. What we need to see here is that if we view Merge on the model of the sequence in (4), above, then it is a consequence that Merge will only ever give us one kind of object, in either arithmetic or language. Merge will never carry us outside the one-dimensional space that it constructs. Our basic computational operation, therefore, won't be, as I shall say, *ontologically productive*: it will never generate new kinds of objects, ever.

I will suggest that this is a bad result, and just as Merge is a far too poor basis to yield the rest of arithmetic (all that goes beyond the integers), a naïve adaptation of Merge or Succ in (4) and (5) to the domain of language does not give us its full richness either. In the mathematical case, other operations generating inverses, at least, will have to be added in order for mathematical knowledge to come to exist in its present form. And if arithmetic is to be an evolutionary offshoot of language, as Chomsky (2005a) plausibly suggests, basic structure-building operations in language might therefore be richer as well.

9.5 Merge in language

Let me now be more explicit about the connection between (4) and the use of the same *n*-ary operation Merge in the linguistic system. It is commonly suggested that the restriction of Merge to $n=2$ arguments follows from "interface conditions," and I shall assume so here as well, for the sake of argument. There are then two "lexical" elements to which Merge needs to apply. Say we combine the list (6) into the set (7) first:

(6)   kill, buffalos
(7)   {kill, buffalos}

Then, due to the recursiveness of Merge, this must be a Merge-partner again, which, together with, say, a new lexical item, *Hill*, yields (8), and with a further morpheme *-ed*, yields (9):

(8) {Hill, {kill, buffalos}}
(9) {-ed, {Hill, {kill, buffalos}}}

If we allow Merge to apply 'internally' (target a syntactic object inserted earlier in the syntactic object already constructed), it can target 'kill' and copy it at the root, so as to obtain (10), and it can target 'Hill' in the same way, to yield (11):

(10) {kill-ed, {Hill, {kill, buffalos}}}
(11) {Hill, {kill-ed, {Hill, {kill, buffalos}}}}

If, finally, we knock out the phonetic values of lower copies of these lexical items, we obtain the well-formed, past-Tense sentence (12), *Hill killed buffalos*:

(12) {Hill, {kill-ed, {..., {..., buffalos}}}}

As Chomsky correctly suggests, we do get hierarchy and unbounded embedding on this minimal vision of structure-building, hence discrete infinity, essentially for free. Yet, in my terms of the previous section, this hierarchy is mono-categorial. There is nothing more complex going on here than in (4) or (5). A ready defense of the minimalist conception of Merge, against the background of the standard architectural assumptions depicted in Fig. 9.1, could now be that, of course, different syntactic objects will yield categorially different semantic interpretations *at the interface* (when they are interpreted). But, in that case, there will be nothing in the syntax from which it could follow *why* this is so. All the syntax ever sees, on the standard conception, are lexical items, or else projections of lexical items, which, however, as we have seen, collapse into lexical items. If the presumed external "conceptual-intentional" or "C-I" systems make such a differentiation occur, they have to be formally *richer* than the structures we find in the human language system, as viewed on that conception. This is *highly* implausible in the light of the fact that the supposed C-I systems are thought to have whatever structure they have, independently of and prior to those we find in the language system. Looking at non-human animal accomplishments, this seems a very long shot indeed (see Penn et al. (in press) for a recent review of the comparative literature; or Terrace 2005 on iterated skepticism that propositionality is within the scope of the non-human animal mind).

    If we go the interface route, we will have merely pushed the burden of explanation. Structured thought in the putative C-I systems needs, well, structures – ones appropriate to the cognitive task. And if these structures are not formally equivalent to the ones we find in language, the danger is we won't quite know what we are talking about. Where we address the structures of thought empirically, the place where this inquiry leads us back to usually is the very structures that the computational system of language provides for our thoughts. Even if we knew how to investigate the interface in language-independent terms, and we found an entirely independent system there, the strange tightness with which specific syntactic categories get paired with specific semantic constructs will seem mysterious: if the categories are there for independent reasons, as part of the constitution of these C-I systems, why should such a syntactic specificity occur, and how could it be motivated? How could it be that we can actually study specific semantic phenomena, say predication, in syntactic terms, and that this provides advances in our understanding of the phenomena in question?

I propose, then, that we consider a radically different conclusion, that it is the *syntax* that yields a richly differentiated set of objects, as opposed to single ontology: it yields different *categories*, where each category corresponds to an ontology, and an ontology may necessarily entail or contain another: thus, a fully specified and tensed proposition ('That Caesar destroyed Syracuse') clearly entails an *event* configured in a transitive verbal phrase ('Caesar destroy Syracuse,' without Tense), which in turn entails a *state* (Syracuse's being destroyed), which in turn entails an *object* that is *in* that state, the object Syracuse itself.[7] These "vertical" hierarchies

(i) need to follow from *something*;
(ii) if interface systems are not the right place to look for them (and no empirical evidence from comparative cognition to my knowledge suggests they are), and
(iii) syntax and semantics very closely "correspond," then

---

[7] [kill Bill] will obviously be interpreted at the semantic interface as a phrase: it will surely neither be interpreted as the lexical item *kill* nor as the lexical item *Bill*. Moreover, the interpretation *will* depend on which term projects, arguing for the reality of projections. So, something different and new emerges at the phrasal level, which at least shows at the interface. Yet, on the now standard minimalist view, the syntax sees nothing of this, since it either operates with no labels, "loci" (Collins 2002), or projections (Chomsky 2006), or else only operates with labels which are lexical items. These labels *designate* complex sets (phrases), to be sure, but *what* they label has no reality in the syntax. This is precisely why "interface conditions" *need* to rise to such explanatory prominence in the minimalist reformulation (and elimination, effectively; see Chametzky 2003) of phrase structure. It is to Collins's (2002) credit that he entirely embraces this conclusion, affirming that three explanatory factors for syntax suffice:

(i) interaction of *the properties of lexical items*
(ii) economy conditions
(iii) interface ("bare output") conditions.

(iv) human syntax has to provide the vertical hierarchies in question; but,

 (v) it can do so only if it is multi-dimensional; and

(vi) it can be multi-dimensional only if it does not reduce to Merge (though it
     may *begin* there, a point to which I return shortly).[8]

In short, if we are to explain the semantic richness of language – and not merely
its systematicity – we need a multi-layered architecture, like the one we found in
the human number system (Uriagereka 1995; 2008: Chapters 7–8). The hierarchical architecture of the syntactic system will need to reflect the very architecture of *meanings* (or "thoughts"), as constructed by the computational
system of language.

9.6 Deriving the ontology of language

The specific ontology of natural language might in principle be there for purely
metaphysical reasons. A world out there might be assumed that inherently, or
by itself, and independently of human cognition or even the existence of
humans, is a very orderly place categorically: it comes structured into objects,
events, propositions, and so on, all as a matter of metaphysical fact, viewed *sub
specie aeterni*. But where does this ontology come from? And how do we
approach it? Which generative process underlies it? On standard philosophical
methodologies, they will follow from a systematization of our conceptual
intuitions. But that begs the questions. Our conceptual intuitions are what we
want to explain and to study in formal and generative terms. Will it not be
inherently *syntactic* distinctions that we have to appeal to when starting
to study these ontologies empirically, like that between a noun and a verb
phrase, or a transitive and an unaccusative verb? Would we take ourselves to
think about *propositions*, if we were not creatures implementing a computational system that, specifically, and for unknown reasons, generated *sentences*?
How would we characterize what a proposition is, *if not* by invoking syntactic
distinctions, like that between an argument and an adjunct, an event and
a proposition, a tensed proposition and one of which truth is predicated,
and so on?

I do not question here that Merge is for real, in either arithmetic or language.
The point is that it yields no ontologies, and therefore is only a subsystem of
language. I even suspect that this subsystem is quite clearly identifiable.
A linguistic subsystem that exhibits a systematic and discretely infinite semantics, but no ontology, is the adjunct system. When a syntactic object adjoins to a

---

[8] See Hinzen and Uriagereka (2006) for more on this argumentation.

syntactic object, the latter's label merely reproduces, but there is no categorial change. Moreover, an adjunct structure like (13), at least when read with a slight intonation break after each adjunct, has a flat, conjunctive kind of semantics (see Pietroski 2002; Larson 2004):

(13) (walk) quickly, alone, thoughtfully, quietly...

Walk quickly simply means, for some event, *e*, that *e* is a walking and it is quick:

(14) [walking (e) & quick (e)]

The adjunct system, therefore, contains predicates and it can conjoin them, but no matter how many predicates we add adjunctively, no new ontology emerges. This is not the kind of structure or the kind of semantics that we need in order to make a judgment of truth, or to approach what I called the intentional dimension of language. It also yields no entailments: a solitary event of walking, say, entails nothing about whether it was quick or slow. Argument structures, by contrast, lack this conjunctive semantics, and they do generate entailments: [kill Bill], say, a verb phrase, does not mean that there was an event, and it was a killing and it was Bill. As for entailments, a killing of Bill not only and necessarily entails Bill, as an event participant, it also entails, as an event, a state, like Bill's being dead.

A killing that is inherently one *of Bill* is something that adjunct syntax cannot describe. Nor could a thought structured by adjunct syntax alone ever be about any such thing. The C-I systems would thus be deprived of such thoughts or means of recognizing them, unless the computational system of language or something equivalent to it restructured them, in line with the novel architecture I proposed.

Perhaps, then, here, in the adjunctive subsystem, and *only* here, interface explanations work: for the only thing that the non-syntactic, external "semantic systems" have a chance of "motivating" or explaining is something that does not *have* much syntax. But *adjuncts* are precisely what has been argued to fall into this category (Ernst 2002). Therefore an interface explanation of the standard minimalist kind may rationalize the existence of adjuncts (or at least a sub-category of them) – and little else. In effect, adjuncts are mostly characterized *negatively*: basically, they have never really fitted into the apparatus of syntax that minimalism has tried to derive from "virtual conceptual necessities." They do not receive theta-roles, and do not take part in the agreement system; as Chomsky puts it, moreover, adjunction of α to β does not change any properties of β, which behaves "as if α is not there, apart from semantic interpretation," which makes adjunction a largely semantic phenomenon; as he further argues, the resulting structure is not the projection of any head, which makes adjunct-syntax a projection-free one; and adjunction cannot encode the argument-of relation correlated with head–complement dependencies (see Chomsky 2004b:117–118). These are properties that we may suspect a system to have that is based on unidimensional Merge. Disparities with principles of argument and A'-syntax suggest a radical dichotomy between arguments and adjuncts, however, and that their mode of attachment and connectivity with the syntactic object to which they attach is radically different.[9] This syntactic dichotomy, if I am right about strict form–meaning correspondences above, should affect the principles of semantic interpretation for adjunct structures; as we have seen, it does.

In the "extended" argument system (extended, to cover cartographic hierarchies, as in Cinque 1999), a form of hierarchy emerges that is completely different from the horizontal discrete infinity that adjuncts yield. We now see categories rigidly piling up on top of other categories, forming the quintessential V-v-T-C cycles that the sentential organization of language entails. This is not the kind of cycle that we can see in a successor-function-based system: we can cycle indefinitely in generating the natural numbers by iteratively applying the operation " + 1," with each such operation implying the completion of one cycle. In language, we are looking at a cycle that inherently constructs ultimately only one particular kind of object: a proposition, and that necessarily goes through a number of other objects along the way, such as an object, an event, a Tensed event, and so on.

Broadly speaking, what I suggest pursuing here, then, is an *internalist* direction in the explanation of semantics. Philosophy for the last one hundred years has pursued the opposite, externalist orientation: it has attempted to explain what we mean by what the world is like, or what objects it contains, and which physical relations (like causation) we stand in with respect to them.[10] Standard minimalist syntax, on the other hand, as I have pointed out, blames ontological cuts on language-external C-I systems. Neither option, I contend, seems as promising as what I have now proposed: to blame these cuts on syntax. The C-I systems are nonlinguistic ones. Ipso facto, to whatever extent the very identity of certain kinds of thoughts lies in the way they are universally structuralized in language, they wouldn't be found in the C-I systems. They would literally arise as and only as the computational system of language constructs them (i.e., endows them with the very structures

---

[9] Perhaps adjuncts *can* be structuralized as specifiers (Cinque 1999) as well, but then only after an extended argument structure system, with the relevant structural relations and a more sophisticated semantics, exists. See Hinzen (2007b) for more discussion.

[10] See Hinzen (2006b) and (2007a) on the "reference-relation," in particular its non-explanatory nature and, probably, non-existence.

and identities that define them in logical space). While the extent to which this has to happen is not total, it is not nil either. But then it will follow that for *some* of the thoughts we are thinking it will be true that we are only thinking them because the computational system of language makes them accessible to us. Fully propositional, truth-evaluated thoughts that can be placed in discourse (for example, to make a claim of truth) are a good candidate for such thoughts.

As for the externalist option above, modern physics has made virtually all of the intuitive categories that enter into our ordinary ways of understanding and talking obsolete. Early modern naturalists still found a world inconceivable where matter can act where it is not. But they didn't conclude from this that such a world could not be real, but rather that one had to give up the hope that the world will validate or find much use for human conceptual intuitions. Soon after Newton, physicists even concluded that matter was unextended, throwing overboard the one crucial "essential" feature of matter that Descartes had kept. So the intuitive ontology of language is radically different from a physical ontology, and it is not that physical ontology that will explain what we take our expressions to mean, and what categorial distinctions they entail. These could in principle also come from an entirely different module of "thought," but as I have argued, this requires, in fairness, to show that a different computational system is operative there than there is in language. If on the other hand this presumed separate module merely recapitulates syntactic distinctions under another name, it becomes explanatorily vacuous.

9.7 Conclusions

The standard formulation of the Strong Minimalist Thesis (SMT) may have misled us: in its pursuit of principled explanations of why language is the way it is, it has tended to *minimize* the contribution of the syntax to what thoughts are assumed available to the C-I systems, and thus to *deflate* syntax to an only minimally hierarchical system that is mono-categorial in the way the natural number sequence is. But this strategy is likely to succeed only if all "vertical" hierarchical cuts, whose reality is empirically manifest in language, and which intimately correlate with syntactic complexity, are, implausibly, dumped on the *non*linguistic side of the interface, in the so-called conceptual–intentional (C-I) systems. To be specific, the proposition that "C-I incorporates a dual semantics, with generalized argument structure as one component, the other being discourse-related and scopal properties" (Chomsky 2005a), hence that essentially the *entire* semantic potential of language is available *independently* of the very syntactic structures it is meant to explain or motivate, is very likely far too optimistic and unsupported by empirical evidence, as far as I can see (maybe even in principle, as there are many methodological obstacles in the empirical investigation of "thought without language").

If that optimism is unwarranted, and from one point of semantic complexity onwards I have argued it likely will be, a proper explanation for such semantic knowledge has to come from the inherent organization of syntax itself. It has to be sought in a more internalist direction. Genuine hierarchy in the system calls for dimensional shifts in the derivational dynamics, of a kind that can create necessary entailments between different kinds of objects on formal grounds. This system will generate an ontology: ontological innovativeness will lie on the *linguistic* side of the semantic interface.

Discussion

LAKA: You are arguing that there should be no intentional interface. Everything that is a little complex or relational is a part of syntax, roughly speaking. You also said that there might not be a conceptual interface either, and your examples were argument structure, discourse factors, and so forth. So my question is, what is your view of the relationship between syntax and concepts, just bare concepts. We know that animals have some sort of – I don't want to say brilliance, but something similar, maybe not the same as us, but we have evidence that there are nonverbal features that have at least something we can call concepts.

HINZEN: On the bare concepts, if we accept that word meanings are atomic, then there are atomic concepts, and if not, we will need to reduce them further. If we wish to spell out the meaning of these atomic concepts, then any appeal to a notion of reference, in particular, is I think entirely circular, so I believe we are essentially stuck with those conceptual atoms. I don't think we can reduce them further, they are primitives of reality. As for the interface with the syntax, I suppose that they are carried into the syntax as indivisible units, but I do believe in what I have elsewhere called "exploding" the lexical atom. If we explode the lexical atom, we give it structure such that specific referential properties arise. The extent to which these bare concepts are shared, and how many of them are, is, I think, a totally open question. As Chomsky emphasized earlier here (see page 27 above), the basic properties of human words seem to be so different from any other thing in existence in animal communication that I would say that at this moment, it is a totally open issue. Maybe there are a few concepts and maybe there are none. So in fact the whole enterprise of motivating language externally or semantically, by conditions imposed on it, might actually stop at concepts already, not at more complex stuff like argument structures, say. Now, as for the D-structure-like forms of complexity, in my view, if you just have adjuncts and a very simple form of combination to work with, and a very simple form of semantics correlating with that, then complexity increases very significantly as you go on to something like argument structure, because then we have at least theta-roles – and their semantics is not a conjunctive semantics any more, as with adjuncts. So, for example, if you say "John runs," this does not mean that there is a running and it is John. It's a running *of* John. There is something new there which I wouldn't know how to motivate from anything other than itself – and not from so-called interface conditions in particular. So maybe this is the place where motivations from the interface have to stop, but as I said, maybe such motivations stop earlier, at the level of word meaning already. In any case, at some specific point the external motivation does certainly stop, and my point was that wherever it does, at that point we have to start thinking more deeply about what the properties of syntax are that give us these elements, which language itself has brought into being.

PIATTELLI-PALMARINI: You presented *walks quickly* as an example, and you say something to the effect that there is no projection, or a defective one. What about adverbs, the hierarchy of different kinds of adverbs as detailed by Guglielmo Cinque in a variety of languages and dialects.[11] They each have to be inserted in a certain position in the hierarchy. *Frequently walks quickly* not *quickly walks frequently*. How do you deal with that?

HINZEN: I think that adjuncts form a class that comprises much more complex phenomena than those I evoked, and maybe adjuncts do play a crucial role in argument structure and the hierarchy of the clause. All I'm committed to is that arguments are quite radically different from adjuncts, and that within the combinatorics of language you have one very, very simple combinatorial system, which is like the one I described: it is iterative and it has an extremely simple conjunctive semantics. The adjunctal hierarchies are for real, but maybe one need not spell out or explain them in terms of phrase structure, if they are more semantic in nature. I don't think that the notion of an adjunct captures a unified phenomenon necessarily.

---

[11] Cinque (1999).

CHAPTER 10

Two Interfaces

James Higginbotham

The two interfaces that I will be talking about are (i) the interface between syntax and semantics, and (ii) the interface between what I call *linguistic semantics* (the stuff we do ordinarily, in Departments of Linguistics) and more philosophical questions about semantics – philosophical in the classical sense of raising questions about the nature of truth, and the relations of what we say to the world that we live in.

To begin with the first interface, the structure of syntax, and the relations of syntax to semantics, there has been a certain amount of literature in the last several years on the notion of compositionality. Some of this literature is highly mathematical. Some have argued that compositionality is trivial, that you can always meet that requirement; others have argued that you cannot really meet it, or you can meet it only if you include some fancy syntactic and semantic categories, and so forth. I actually think that those investigations are a little beside the empirical point of compositionality.

The basic idea of compositionality at work in current research is that semantics is locally computed, in that only a certain amount of information is used at each point. I can illustrate the thesis as follows. Consider this tree structure:

The root is the element Z, which is made up of X and Y. There are perhaps other things going on above Z, as well as things going on below both X and Y. If we are given certain information about the formal features of X and Y, and possibly also of Z, and we suppose that we have the semantics of X and Y available somehow, then the thesis is that the interpretation of Z, for any tree whatsoever in which the configuration may occur, is strictly determined by what you obtained when you got X and what you obtained when you got Y, plus those formal features. The local determination of the value of Z immediately rules out linguistic systems in which (for instance) Z refers to me if there is mention of horses four clauses down in Y, and it refers to you otherwise. That semantics is perfectly coherent, but it is not compositional in my sense. Compositionality also rules out the possibility that to get the interpretation of Z you may look ahead or "peek up" at what is higher in the tree.

Compositionality, so considered, is an empirical hypothesis, and we can test it – and in fact I think it is false. I had a long paper a while back showing that, barring special assumptions, it is even false for certain conditional sentences "B if A" (Higginbotham 2003a). The hypothesis of compositionality does however have the property of an analogous generalization that Noam mentioned to me years ago. He remarked that we all learned to say that a noun refers to a person, place, or thing. That really isn't true, Noam observed, but it is very close to being true. Similarly, compositionality should be thought of as a working hypothesis which can be assumed to be close to being true, but maybe not quite true. In terms of the present discussion, one might conjecture further that compositionality, in the sense of this very simple computation of semantics, comes in as a hypothesis that may not be peculiar to language at all – it may belong to systems of various sorts – and then the area where compositionality breaks down could be very specific to language, and in that sense special.

In one standard way of thinking about direct quotation, compositionality already breaks down. Consider (1):

(1)   Massimo said, "I'm sitting down."

We have to say that, if I speak truly in saying (1), then the words in quotation marks refer to the very words that came out of Massimo's mouth. I myself think that the same is true in indirect quotation. So for example if I say (2) (where I have put the complementizer *that* in, so the quotation must be indirect):

(2)   Massimo said that I am standing

then that first person pronoun *I* refers to me, just as if I were using it in isolation. However, I hold that the sentence *I'm standing* in (2) actually refers to itself, analogously to direct quotation, but *understood as if it were said*. That is why the word *I* continues to refer to me, just as it would if I said it in isolation.

The doctrine that indirect quotation is self-referential is sententialism (Steve Schiffer's useful term; Schiffer 2003). If the doctrine is correct, then compositionality has a certain limit, at the point at which we talk about the thoughts, wants, etc. of ourselves and other people. That doesn't mean that the semantics can't be given – on the contrary – but it can't be locally computed.

So I am interested in the compositionality question. I am also interested in linguistic parameters that might operate on the syntax–semantics side. For example, I am interested in the difference between languages like English and Chinese, on the one hand, which have resultative constructions (things like *wipe the table clean* or *come in*, etc.) and languages like Italian, Spanish, or Korean in which you don't have these constructions. Practically speaking they do not exist in those languages, and the question is: how come? Because after all, it is not as if Italians can't say *wipe the table clean*; they just can't say it that way. And I think that, if anything, the answer to this question is related to the fact that one system of languages, including the Italian and Korean, has very rich morphology, whereas English, with its cut-down morphology, can do the semantic work required for a resultative interpretation only in the syntax.

So think of it in the following way. It is an old piece of wisdom in generative grammar that in *wipe the table clean*, somehow the verb *wipe* and the adjective *clean* have to get together in some way. Let's suppose that they do that by a semantic process, which I won't describe here, which I call telic pair formation (Higginbotham 2000), and which I have elaborated partly in response to some arguments of Jerry Fodor's. The words *wipe* and *clean* get together in some way, through a semantic rule which takes an activity predicate, *wipe*, and a predicate of result, *clean*, and it puts them together to form a single unitary accomplishment predicate. In an accomplishment predicate you encode both process and end, so in *wipe clean*, you have *wipe* as the process and *clean* as the end of the activity. That is what you can do in English, and it is what you can do in Chinese, but that is what you cannot do (with some few exceptions) in Italian, Spanish, French, or Korean.

In fact, if you are a native speaker of English, you can as it were even hear the difference between the two types of languages, English and Chinese on the one hand, and Romance and Korean on the other. We have complex predicates in English in ordinary expressions such as *come in*. We also have the word *enter*, practically synonymous with *come in*, at least as far a truth conditions go. But every native speaker of the English language knows that the true English expression is *come in*, not *enter*: *enter* is a learned word (as it comes from Latin), it's more formal, and so forth. So English is a *come in* language, and Italian is an *enter* language. Similarly, English is a *give up* language, and Italian is a *resign* language.

If this is right, there is a little lesson to be learned, because there will be a difference between languages with respect to what you are allowed to do in the semantic computation. This difference will spill over into the lexicon, implying that words that may be found in one language can't exist in another. An example might be the absence of anything like the goal-driven preposition *to* in Italian, Korean, French, etc. You can't in these languages say that you walk to the store: the relevant word *to* is missing. The thought I would pursue (which agrees, I believe, with parts of what Ray Jackendoff has written, and what he has told me in personal communication) is that in *walk to the store*, it is just the word *to* that is the predicate of motion, whereas *walk* functions as a sort of adverb. It's as if one were saying: *I got to the store walkingly.* There are many similar examples. But if in Italian and similar languages that kind of semantics can't be computed, then no analogue of the English *to* can exist.

Korean speakers and linguists that I have interviewed (Professor Dong-Whee Yang and other native informants) tell me that there is exactly one verb you can say *V to the store* with, and that is the verb meaning *go*, which is presumably the empty verb. As soon as you go to a verb of motion that has some more substantial meaning to it, it is simply impossible. You can *go to the store*, but you can't *walk to the store*. So why does this happen? The explanation may be that in English you have something that is not the syntactic head, namely the preposition *to*, and you have something that is the syntactic head, namely the verb *walk*, but the semantic head, the thing that is carrying the burden of the sentence, is the preposition *to*, not the verb *walk*. And so you might suppose that English tolerates a kind of mismatch, in the sense that the syntactic head and the semantic head need not coincide, whereas in these languages they must coincide. As soon as they must coincide, we have an explanation of why you could not have in Italian or Korean preposition a with the meaning of the English preposition *to*. As soon as it was born, it would have to die, because there would have to be a certain semantic computation taking place with respect to it, and that computation couldn't happen. If that is anywhere near the right track, then it indicates a kind of limit for the view that languages really differ only lexically, because if what I have produced is a reasonable argument, it would follow that the lexical absence of *to* in Italian is principled. It is not just that it does not have it, it couldn't have it, because the principles that would be required in order to make it operate are disallowed (Higginbotham 2000).

So this is one side of a set of what I find interesting questions. How much of compositionality really belongs to general features of computation, and how much of it belongs specifically to language? In which places in human languages does compositionality break down? Also, what differences between languages should be explained in terms of parameters that act at the interface between syntax and semantics?

The second interface that I want to consider here concerns the relation between what the linguistic semantics seems to deliver, and what there is in the world. In Wolfram Hinzen's talk (see page 137 above), he gave for example the semantics of the combination *walk quickly* using the original formulation due to Donald Davidson, as *walk(e)* and *quickly(e)*, where e is a variable ranging over events (Davidson 1967). And if I understood him correctly, he was trying to have this account of modification but not eat the consequences. That is to say, he endorsed a semantics where (3) is true just in case there is an event which is a walking by John, and quick.

(3)   John walked quickly

But he didn't think there were individual events in Davidson's sense.

I think this won't do. If the interpretation of (3) is given as: *there is an event (e), it is a walking by John, and it is quick*, one cannot then turn around and say, "Oh, but I don't really believe in events." The semantic theory you are endorsing just gave you that result. It is no good saying that you are doing semantics on the one hand, but on the other hand you are really only talking.

There are many interesting problems in the relation between grammatical form classically understood, and logical form in the old sense (i.e., the structure of the proposition, or truth conditions). I have tried to deal with some of these and I will mention a couple here. Consider (4):

(4)   An occasional sailor strolled by

Suppose I am saying what happened while we were sitting at the café. An assertion of (4) could mean that Jerry Fodor came by, because he *is* an occasional sailor, but that is not what I am likely to mean in the context. What I am likely to mean is, roughly speaking, that occasionally some sailor or another strolled by. So here we have a case where the apparent adjective, *occasional*, modifying *sailor*, is actually interpreted as an adverbial over the whole sentence. The case is the same for *the average man*, as in *The average man is taller than he used to be*, and things of that kind.

Faced with such examples, there is a temptation to try to keep the syntax off which the semantic computation is run very simple, and correspondingly to complicate the semantics. I myself suspect that this move is a mistake, because complicating the semantics is bound to mean the introduction of a far more powerful logic than the language itself otherwise bears witness to. In fact, Montague's Intensional Logic, commonly deployed in semantics, is of order ω, and so allows all finite levels (Montague 1974). But it is important to stress – I'd be willing to discuss this – as there is no evidence whatsoever for such a logic outside the domain of puzzles such that I have just posed, together with the assumption (unargued for) that the linguistic level that enters semantic computation is identical to superficial syntax. There is no independent evidence in language (or in mathematics, I think, though this is a matter of serious debate) for a strong higher-order logic. Rather, language allows first-order and some weak second-order quantification, and that's it (Higginbotham 1998). Appeal to higher-order logic in linguistics constitutes the importation of machinery that is not wanted for any purpose, except to keep the syntax simple. There must be a tradeoff between components: maybe the syntax is more abstract than you think.

There is also a temptation to suppose (maybe Jackendoff is guilty of this; he thinks he is not, but certainly some people are guilty of this[1]) that once we go mentalistic about semantics, there are certain sets of problems that we don't have to worry about, like Santa Claus. So if somebody says,

(5)   It's perfectly true that Higginbotham is standing; it's also true that Santa Claus comes down the chimney on Christmas (that's what I tell my child).

you can add to the semantics at which these things come off the assembly line together, and then we can have some further note about the fact that Santa Claus doesn't really exist. But I don't think you can do semantics in this way. I mean, again, that you can't do the semantics with your left hand, and then pretend by waving your right hand that you were really only talking. Moreover, it is very important to recognize that part of knowing the interpretation, the meaning of the word *Santa Claus*, is knowing that there is no such thing. That is important, and that means that the semantics should *not* treat the two clauses in (5) in parallel, but should take account of this further dimension of meaning.

Something similar might be said about the example of generics that came up in earlier discussion here. From the point of view of early learning, these surely must be among the simplest things learned. Dogs bark, cats meow, fire burns, and so forth. From the point of view of the full understanding, as we work up our system of the world, they are in fact extremely complicated, these generic sentences. And I do agree with the critical comment, made by Nick Asher among others (Asher and Morreau 1995), that the fashionable use of a made-up "generic quantifier" for the purpose of giving them an interpretation is not an advance. Rather, what you have to do is take *dogs bark* (if x is a dog, x barks), and you have to delimit through our understanding of the world what it is that will count as a principled objection to *dogs bark*, and what it is that will count as simply an exception. All of that is part of common-sense systematic knowledge. It can't be swept under the rug just on the grounds that you're doing Linguistics.

---

[1] See Higginbotham (2003b).

So those are two kinds of things that I have been interested in, syntactic/ semantic differences amongst languages and the nature of semantic computation, and the relations of semantics to our systematic beliefs about the world. I should say that Noam and I years ago used to have discussions about whether the semantics ought to give you a real theory of real honest-to-God truth about the kind of world in which we live, which is full of independent objects that don't at all depend on my existence or that of any mind for their existence, or whether in a way it is more mentalistic than that, as he suggested. And after an hour or so of conversation, we would agree that we had reached a point where the debate was merely philosophical in the old sense. That is to say, which view we took about this probably didn't matter much for the nature of our research, whether we should be full realists or not.

David Hume once said (in the Treatise), "'Tis in vain to ask Whether there be body or not," but he added that what we can ask is what causes us to believe in the existence of bodies.[2] So similarly, we might say that it's in vain to ask whether what we systematically take there to be really exists, but we can ask what causes us to think and speak as we do. If we can do that, if we can replace one kind of question with another, then perhaps the arguments about realism and anti-realism or mentalism in semantics will go away.

What is left to the future? I think there are many interesting questions. One of them, on which I think there has been almost no progress, is the nature of combinatorial semantics. We have the notion of truth, maybe, as a nice, primitive notion, but where does the notion of predication come from? You see, if you think about it, you couldn't possibly learn a language without knowing what's the subject and what's the predicate, because these play fundamentally different semantic roles. You can't make judgments without using predicates. On the other hand, you couldn't tell a child, "Now look here, in *dogs bark*, the

---

[2] Thus the sceptic still continues to reason and believe, even though he asserts, that he cannot defend his reason by reason; and by the same rule he must assent to the principle concerning the existence of body, though he cannot pretend by any arguments of philosophy to maintain its veracity. Nature has not left this to his choice, and has doubtless, esteemed it an affair of too great importance to be trusted to our uncertain reasonings and speculations. We may well ask, What causes induce us to believe in the existence of body? *but it is in vain to ask, Whether there be body or not?* That is a point, which we must take for granted in all our reasonings.

(Part IV, Sect. II. Of Scepticism With Regard to the Senses: emphasis added)

Another relevant passage is:

Motion in one body in all past instances, that have fallen under our observation, is follow'd upon impulse by motion in another. 'Tis impossible for the mind to penetrate further. From this constant union it *forms* the idea of cause and effect, and by its influence *feels* the necessity. As there is some constancy, and the same influence in what we call moral evidence, I ask no more. What remains can only be a dispute of words. (*A Treatise of Human Nature*, 1739. [Longmans and Green reprint 1898: 187. Emphasis is Hume's.) (Editors' note)

word *bark* is the predicate and it's true or false of dogs." You couldn't do that because the child would have to already understand predication in order to understand what it was being told. Now sometimes this problem gets swept under the rug. I've had people say to me that it's simple enough, in that predicates refer to functions and names refer to their arguments. But that's not the answer to the question; that's the same question. And in fact Frege, who invented this way of talking, recognized it as the same question. What's the difference between the meaning of a functional expression and the meanings of its arguments? I guess I would like to see progress made on this kind of question, the question whether language as we have it, or perhaps must necessarily have it, must be cast in this mold, whether it must employ notions of subject, predicate, and quantification. So far we don't know any other way to do it. It would be nice to know where predication comes from and whether language makes predication possible or predication is merely an articulation of something more basic.

Those, then, are the summaries of the kinds of things that I think we might try to think about in the syntax–semantics interface, where it comes to general principles, and where it is really special to language. In the clarification of these metaphysical questions that inevitably arise about the semantics, we have a semantics of events. "But tell me more about the nature of these objects," one might say. A theory of events for semantic purposes really doesn't tell you much about their nature, it's true. And in the further articulation of the subject, which will be a really very refined discipline showing how exactly these very simple (to us) and primitive concepts get articulated, we'll see their complexity.

Let me give you another very simple example, with which I'll conclude, having to do with the English perfect (Higginbotham 2007). Every native speaker of English knows that if I have a cup of coffee and I tap it with my hand and knock it over, what I say – what I must say – is (6):

(6)   I have spilled my coffee

That is, I must use the present perfect. If somebody gives me a mop and I mop the spill up and put the mop away, I can no longer say (6). Instead, I must say (7):

(7)   I spilled my coffee

These are the sort of data that led Otto Jespersen (who regarded English as a very conservative language, relative to other Germanic languages) to say that the English perfect is not itself a past tense, but talks about "present results of past events" (Jespersen 1942). That the perfect is thus restricted, if that is true, is a rather special property of English. If you try to work out the semantics of (6) versus (7), I think you do get somewhere if you think of the perfect as a purely aspectual element, shifting the predicate from past events to present states that are the results of those events. But the investigation requires very careful probing into exactly what you are warranted in asserting and exactly when. It is not at all a trivial matter. It takes much reflection if one is, so to speak, to get inside a language and to articulate its semantics self-consciously, even if it is one's native language. As a native speaker, you get things right without knowing what it is you are getting right. Conversely, non-native speakers often have a tin ear. The English present perfect is a good example of what goes without saying in one language, but is strange in another. If you take, say, ten Romance speakers who are speaking English as a second language, eleven of them will get it wrong: they always slip in the perfect forms when they're not warranted in English.

I look, then, for considerable progress in the (as it were) backyard field of lexical semantics. I think that lexical semantics holds a great deal more promise, not only for clarifying common concepts expressed by nouns and verbs, but also clarifying notions of aspect, tense, and so forth, than it has generally been credited for. And my hope is that as that research goes on, simultaneously with combinatorial semantics, we shall succeed in reducing the burden on the combinatorics.

But there is a fond memory, and a fond quote, here. My friend Gennaro Chierchia and I once had a conversation about some of these matters, and Gennaro said, "But Jim, if you're right, then the combinatorial semantics should be trivial." And I replied, "That's right; that's the way I'd like it to be."

Goodness knows how it will turn out.

Discussion

PIATTELLI-PALMARINI: You say, and it is very interesting, that the English *to* doesn't exist in Italian, and probably the English past tense does not exist in Italian either. Now, you say that you would like such facts to be principled, not to be sort of isolated facts. Great, but my understanding of the minimalist hypothesis is that all parameters are now supposed to be morpho-lexical. Is this acceptable to you? One can stress that, even if it's lexical, the non-existence of English *to* in Italian looks like a lexical datum, and maybe also the non-existence of the English past tense in Italian may be an issue of auxiliaries. So all this can *be* principled even if it is morpho-lexical. Is it so?

HIGGINBOTHAM: Of course the absence of *to* (also *into*, *onto*, the motion sense of under (it. sotto) and so forth) has to be a matter of principle. I think the thing that was distinctive about the view that I was offering is that these words couldn't exist because a certain kind of combinatorics is not possible in Italian, specifically the combinatorics which says you take something which is not the syntactic head, and you make it the semantic head. That's something that is generally impossible, and it would be a principled absence, explained on the grounds of general language design. Conversely, to permit the semantic head to be other than the syntactic head would constitute an interface parameter that says: in this kind of language you are allowed to mesh the syntax with the semantics in such and such a way. But of course the working hypothesis in the field is that combinatorial parameters are universal. I would think that, like the compositionality hypothesis, it's probably very close to being true, but it's not entirely true, and it would be interesting to know where it breaks down. If I'm on the right track, it breaks down in this particular place.

BOECKX: I know that you have written on this extensively, but could you give me a one-line argument for thinking that the parameter that you are talking about by itself is semantic as opposed to syntactic? I guess it touches on the tradeoff between syntax and semantics and where the combinatorics, or the limitations of the combinations, come from.

HIGGINBOTHAM: Well, it's an interface phenomenon. The first part of the line of thought is the following, and is due to Jerry Fodor. Jerry pointed out that if you take a predicate and its result, and you modify the combination with an adverbial, then the position of adverbial modification becomes unique; the sentences are not ambiguous.[3] So his original argument compared *John caused Bill to die by X* (some kind of action) versus *John killed Bill by X*. In *John caused Bill to die by X* the *by*-phrase may modify *cause* or *die*. But with *kill*, you only get the modification of the whole verb. And it's the same with causative verbs, like *I sat the guests on the floor* versus *The guests sat on the floor*. Now it's also the same with *wipe the table clean*. So if to *I wipe the table clean* you add some kind of adverbial phrase, it's only the whole business – the wiping clean, not the wiping or the being clean alone – that gets modified. That's at least a consideration in favor of saying that *wipe clean* is a complex verb, just as an ordinary predicate like *cross the street*, and that the event has two parts. You don't just have an event e of crossing. There's an e1 and an e2, where in the case of *cross the street* e1 is a process, say stepping off the curb and proceeding more or less across, and e2 is the onset of being on the other side of the street, the end of the process. Similarly, in the case of *wipe clean*, you have the process signaled by *wipe* and the onset of the end, signaled by *clean*. Once you have said that, you are not just putting the verb and the adjective together, you're not just saying *I wiped the table until it became clean*, you're actually creating a

---

[3] Fodor (1970); Fodor et al. (1980); Fodor and Lepore (2005).

complex predicate, *wipe-clean* as it were. Then you would expect that, as in the case of *kill* or *cross*, you have only one position for adverbial modification, and that's in fact what you get. However, the capacity to form resultative predicates like *wipe-clean* is language-specific (common in English and Chinese, but not in Korean or Italian, for example). There is a combinatorial option, with effects on interpretation, available in some languages but not others. In that sense, the parametric difference between them is not purely syntactic, as it involves the interface between syntax and semantics.

HINZEN: I would just like to reply to some of your comments, Jim. So if we talk about *walking quickly* again, then you say that you can't talk about events or quantify over them without committing yourself to their existence. Before that, you said something related, when talking about realism and anti-realism, or mentalism/idealism as opposed to some kind of externalism. Now I have come to think that these are completely the wrong ways to frame the issue, and they are really very recent ways, which have to do with the relational conception of the mind that philosophers nowadays endorse. By and large, they think of the mind in relational, referential, and externalist terms. Realism is to see the mind's content as entirely reflecting the external world, rather than its own contents. Therefore, if you start emphasizing internal factors in the genesis of reference and truth, they think you are taking a step back from reality, as it were, and you become an anti-realist, or, even worse, a "Cartesian" philosopher. Now, early modern philosophers thought of all this in quite different terms. Realism and the objective reality of the external world was never the issue in Locke, for example, or even in Descartes, I would contend. What early modern philosophers and contemporary internalists in Noam's sense emphasize is internal structure in the mind, which underlies experience and enters into human intentional reference. But realism or denial is absolutely no issue in any of this. There is no connection between internalism in Noam's sense and an anti-realism or idealism, and that's in part because the relational conception of the mind is not endorsed in the first place. You can be a "mentalist," and believe in an objective world, realism, etc., as you please. So I don't think there is any indication in what I've said for an anti-realism or mentalism. I would really like to distinguish that.

Let's illustrate this with Davidson's event variable. I would say that as we analyze language structure, we are in this case led to introduce certain new variables, such as the E-position, a move that has interesting systematic consequences and empirical advantages. The E-position is therefore entered as an element in our linguistic representations. But it is just wrong to conclude from this that because we quantify over events, there must be events out there, as ontological entities. This move adds nothing that's explanatory to our analysis. As I understand Chomsky (though maybe I am misinterpreting him), he'd call this analysis "syntax," and so would I. The "semantic" level I would reserve for the actual relation between what's represented in the mind (like event variables) and the external physical world, which is made up of whatever it is made up of. Once we have the syntactic theory and it is explanatory, then, well, we can assume that there is something like a computation of an E-position in the mind. Again, to add to this that there are specific entities out there, events, which our event variable intrinsically picks out, doesn't explain anything. My whole point was that we should *explain* ontology, as opposed to positing it out there: *why* does our experiential reality exhibit a difference between objects, events, and propositions, say? Just to posit events out there doesn't tell me anything about why they exist (in the way we categorize the world). And I think that, probably, the answer to the question why they exist, and why we think about events *qua* events, and about the other entities I talked about, like propositions, has to be an internalist one: it is that we have a language faculty whose computational system generates particular kinds of structures. These structures we can usefully relate to the world, to be sure, but this doesn't mean we need to interpret that world ontologically as our mind's intuitive conceptions and the semantics of natural language suggest. In science, we don't, for example, and we could say there are no events and objects, because there are only quantum potentials, or waves, as I am told. So I contend there are no ontological commitments flowing from the way our mind is built, or from how we talk. I really think we should start *explaining* semantics, as opposed to doing it.

HIGGINBOTHAM: Well, let's look at two things, first of all a historical correction. The questions of realism and anti-realism can easily be traced back all through early modern philosophy. How did Kant answer Hume? Kant answered Hume on behalf of a kind of immanent realism which he called transcendental idealism, intending thereby to legitimate a version of realism about causation, the existence of bodies, and so forth. As for your second point, about events, it's not a very complicated argument. Nobody doubts that there are events. You don't doubt it, I don't doubt it, nobody here doubts it. The thing that was surprising about Davidson's work was that he located event reference in simple sentences like *John walks quickly* in order to solve the problem of modification. When Davidson's proposal first came out, people said, "My God, he proposes that there's an existential quantifier. Where in the heck did that come from?" There was of course an alternative, and sometimes it was said, "well, *quickly* is a kind of operator which takes *walk* and turns it into *walk quickly*." This was a solution within categorial grammar and higher-order logic. The solution that is proposed following Davidson is to say, "Oh no, the way we stick these guys *walk* and *quickly* together is just like *black cat*; the thing that sticks the noun and the adjective together is that the very same thing x is said to be black and a cat, and so in *walk quickly* the very same thing e is said to be a walk and to be quick." The price you pay for this solution, as Quine pointed out in an essay from many years ago,[4] is that the existence of events of walking etc. becomes part of the ontological commitment of the speakers of the language. Now, once we've taken the step Davidson suggests, for one to say, "Oh well, I'm just talking internally here" is not possible.

And the story continues. If you say that the explanation of why we derive the nominal *Rome's destruction of Carthage* from the sentence *Rome destroyed Carthage* is that *Rome's destruction of Carthage* is a definite description of an event, derived from the E-position in the word *destroy*, then you have said our predicates range over events. So in my view it's no good saying, "This is what I believe and say, but it's not for real." It's like bad faith. There used to be a movement in philosophy that Sidney Morgenbesser discussed, called methodological individualism.[5] The methodological individualist would say, "Oh there aren't really countries or peoples or anything like that. There are only individuals." This movement exemplified the same kind of bad faith. Take Hitler now. He was a dictator. Now try to explain *dictator* without bringing in objects like people or countries. If you can't, then the methodological individualism was just a pretense. Finally, if you say that this semantic theory doesn't tell me how my reference to ordinary things relates to physics, that's perfectly true and it would be interesting to find out more. But it's no good to take referential semantics on board for the purpose of linguistic explanation, and then to say, "No, well, I don't really mean it, it's all syntax." That won't go, in my opinion.

---

[4] Quine (1985).
[5] Morgenbesser (1956).

CHAPTER 11

Movement and Concepts of Locality

Luigi Rizzi

11.1 Movement as Merge

I would like to illustrate certain concepts of locality which arise in the context of the theory of movement, a very central component of natural language syntax. I will start by briefly introducing the notion of movement, on the basis of some concrete examples. When you hear a sentence like (1), starting with the wh-operator *what*, one thing that you must determine in order to understand the sentence is what verb that element is construed with, what argument structure it belongs to. And the relevant verb can come very early or be quite far away from *what*, as is the verb *buy* in our example:

(1)   What do you think...people say...John believes...we should buy ___?

In general we can say that, in natural language expressions, elements are often pronounced in positions different from the positions in which they are interpreted, or, more accurately, from the positions in which they receive certain crucial elements of their interpretation, as in the case of *what* in (1), the semantic (or thematic) role of patient of *buy*.

Research on movement has been central in the generative program over the last half-century. A significant recent development is that movement can be seen as a special case of the fundamental structure-building operation, Merge. Merge is the fundamental operation creating structure in Minimalism (Chomsky 1995); it is about the simplest recursive operation you can think of:

(2)   ...A...B...→ [A B]

or, informally, "take two elements, A and B, string them together and form a third element, the expression [A B]."

So we can put together, for example, the verb *meet* and the noun *Mary* and form the verb phrase:

(3)   [meet Mary]

Now Merge comes up in two varieties; in fact it is the same operation, but the two varieties depend on where the elements A and B are taken from. If A and B are separate objects (for instance, two items taken from the lexicon, as in (3)), the operation is called *external Merge*. The other case is *internal Merge* for cases in which you take one of the two elements from within the other: suppose that, in a structure built by previous applications of Merge, A is contained in B; then, you can take A and remerge it with B, yielding

(4)   [B...A...] → [A [B...<A>...]]

Here A occurs twice: in the remerged position and in the initial position: this is the so-called "trace" of movement, notated within angled brackets (typically not pronounced, but visible and active in the mental representation of the sentence).

Concretely, if by successive applications of external merge we have built a structure like the following:

(5)   [John bought what]

we must now take the wh-expression *what* from within the structure, and remerge (internally merge) it with the whole structure, yielding

(6)   [What [John bought <what>]]

with the lower occurrence of *what* being the trace of movement (e.g., to ultimately yield an indirect question like *I wonder what John bought* through additional applications of Merge).

The idea that movement must be somehow connected to the fundamental structure-building operation is not new, really. This is, in essence, the observation that was made by Joseph Emonds many years ago in his thesis and book under the name of "Structure Preservation Hypothesis" (Emonds 1976) – namely, the idea that movement creates configurations that can be independently generated by the structure-building component: for instance, Passive moves the object to subject position, a position independently generated by the fundamental structure-building rules. In the model in which Emonds first stated the hypothesis, movement was performed by transformations, rules clearly distinct from the phrase structure rules building the structural representations; so, the question remained why two distinct kinds of formal rules would converge in generating the same structural configurations. In the current approach, structure preservation is explained because movement *is* a particular case of the fundamental structure-building mechanism, Merge.

11.2 On delimiting chains

Movement chains are configurations that are created by movement. A′ chains are movement chains in which the moved element typically targets the left periphery, the initial part of the clause. Take familiar English constructions involving the preposing of an element to the beginning of the clause:

(7) a. Which book should I read?
     b. This book, you should really read
     c. (It is) THIS BOOK (that) you should read, not that one!

In these cases a nominal expression *which/this book* receives two kinds of interpretive properties: it is interpreted as an interrogative operator (in a), or as a Topic (in b), or as a Focus (in c), and also, in all three cases, as an argument of the verb *read*.

How are these properties expressed by the grammar? What we can say here (Chomsky 2000), is that there are two basic kinds of interpretive properties: properties of argumental semantics (typically the assignment of thematic roles to arguments); and scope-discourse properties – properties like the scope of operators, topicality, focus, and other properties that are somehow connected to the way in which information is structured and conveyed in discourse.

We can think of an A′ chain as a device to assign properties of the two kinds to an expression: in the complete representation, the expression occurs twice, in positions dedicated to the two kinds of properties:

(8) a. Which book Q should I read <which book>?
     b. This book, Top you should really read <this book>
     c. THIS BOOK Foc you should read <this book>, not that one!

The assignment of both properties is a matter of head–dependent configuration: uncontroversially, the verb assigns the thematic role "patient" to the lower occurrence of *which/this book*. More controversially, I will assume that the left periphery of the clause consists of dedicated functional heads like Q, Top, Foc (phonetically null in English, but pronounced in other languages) assigning scope-discourse properties to their immediate dependents. So, the Top head carries the instruction for the interpretive systems: "my specifier is to be interpreted as a Topic, and my complement as a Comment"; the Foc head carries the interpretive instruction "my specifier is the focus and my complement the presupposition," and so on.

This is what is sometimes called the "criterial" view on the assignment of scope-discourse properties. In some languages we observe that these criterial heads are phonetically realized. For instance, there are varieties of Dutch in which Q is pronounced and in many languages Topic and Focus heads are expressed by a particular piece of morphology, by a particular overt head. So I would like to make the rather familiar assumption that languages are uniform in this respect. All languages work essentially in the same way, all languages have criterial heads which carry explicit instructions to the interface systems; variation is very superficial in that, in some languages, these heads are pronounced and in others they are not (much as distinctions in Case morphology may superficially vary), but the syntax–interpretation interface functions in essentially the same way across languages.

The next question is to see how these structures can combine. Typically, these heads show up in a specific order, subject to some parametric variation, giving rise to complex configurations generated by recursive applications of Merge. These complex structures have attracted a lot of attention lately, giving rise to cartographic projects, attempts to draw maps as precise and detailed as possible of the syntactic complexity.[1] Once we have this view of chains, we can say that the backbone of an A-bar chain of the kind discussed so far is the following, with the two special kinds of interpretively dedicated positions:

(9) $\ldots \underline{\quad}$ X$_{\text{criterial}}$ $\cdots\cdots\cdots$ $\underline{\quad}$ X$_{\text{argumental}}$ $\cdots\cdots\cdots$

Then we may ask what general form chains can have: what other positions are allowed to occur in chains, on top of the two interpretively relevant positions? I think there is clear empirical evidence that argumental and criterial positions delimit chains – that is to say, there cannot be any position lower than the thematic position, nor higher than the criterial position, for principled reasons (Rizzi 2006a). On the other hand, much empirical evidence shows that there can be plenty of positions in between argumental and criterial positions: movement is local, each application of movement is limited to apply in a small portion of a syntactic tree by locality principles, so there is simply no way to guarantee that the argumental position and the criterial position will be sufficiently close to make sure that the distance can be covered by a single application of movement. A movement chain can indeed cover an unlimited structural space, as suggested by sentences like (1), but this is due to the fact that movement can apply in an indefinite number of successive steps, each of which

---

[1] See various essays published in Belletti (2004), Cinque (2002), Rizzi (2004).

is local. So, the apparently unbounded nature of movement chains is in fact a consequence of the fact that movement can indefinitely reapply, ultimately a consequence of the recursive nature of Merge.

11.3 Intermediate positions

The idea that movement is inherently local is not new: it was proposed many years ago by Noam Chomsky (1973) on the basis of an argument which, initially, was largely conceptual. Island constraints had been discovered in the late sixties, so it was known that some configurations were impermeable to rules, and Ross (1967/1986) had established a catalogue of such configurations. The question Chomsky asked was: why should there be such a catalogue? His approach turned the problem around. Perhaps all cases of movement are local, and the fact that in some cases we can get an unbounded dependency may be a consequence of the fact that local movement can indefinitely reapply on its own output: certain categories have "escape hatches" so that local movement can target the "escape hatch" (typically, the complementizer system in clauses), and then undergo further movement from there to the next "escape hatch"; other categories do not have escape hatches and so we get island effects, but all instances of movement are local.

At the time, the argument looked controversial. Some syntacticians thought it was too abstract and unsubstantiated. Nevertheless, empirical evidence quickly started accumulating in favor of this view. One early kind of evidence was based on French Stylistic Inversion, where the subject appears at the very end of the structure, an option triggered by the presence of an initial wh-element, as in (10). This remained possible, as Kayne and Pollock (1978) pointed out, if that wh-element is extracted from a lower clause, as in (11):

(10) Où est allé Jean?
      'Where has gone Jean?'

(11) Où crois-tu qu'est allé Jean?
      'Where do you believe that has gone Jean?'

As in general the main complementizer cannot "act at a distance" triggering inversion in the embedded clause, the most reasonable analysis, Kayne and Pollock argued, is that *où* moves stepwise, first to the embedded complementizer system and then to the main clause, and it triggers Stylistic Inversion "in passing" from the embedded complementizer system.

So, according to Kayne and Pollock we may find indirect cues of the stepwise movement by observing certain operations that are plausibly triggered by the moving element from its intermediate positions. Many other pieces of evidence of this kind have materialized since. Consider, for instance, the variety of Belfast English analyzed by Alison Henry (1995) in which sentences like the following are possible:

(12)   What did Mary claim [___ did [they steal ___]]?

with the inversion taking place also in the embedded C system. The natural analysis here is that movement is stepwise and that at each step the wh-element triggers inversion, and that can go on indefinitely. Other types of evidence, which can't be discussed for reasons of time, involve purely interpretive effects. If we want to properly analyze certain phenomena of reflexive interpretation for instance, we need certain reconstruction sites, which are in fact provided by the idea that movement takes place in successive steps, or is "successive cyclic" in traditional terminology.

So we have evidence having to do with purely syntactic phenomena, and then some evidence concerning interpretive phenomena; we also have very direct evidence having to do with morphological properties. In some cases we see a special piece of morphology that somehow signals the fact that movement has taken place in successive steps. One classical case analyzed by Richard Kayne (1989) is past participle agreement in French, where we can see the participle agreeing as a function of the fact that the object has moved. A more spectacular case is the one found in Austronesian languages like Chamorro, according to Sandra Chung's (1994) analysis: each verb in the stretch from the variable to the operator carries a special agreement, which Chung calls wh-agreement, which signals the fact that movement has taken place in successive steps, through the local complementizer system. I will come back to this phenomenon later on.

Another type of evidence for successive cyclicity is even more straightforward. In some languages or varieties the wh- trace is actually pronounced in intermediate positions (wh-copying). So there are colloquial varieties of German – not of the kind that you would find in grammar books – in which the interrogative element can be replicated and pronounced twice, so a sentence like

(13)   Who do you believe she met?

will come out as something like

(14)   Wen glaubst du [wen sie getroffen hat]?
        'Whom do you believe whom she has met?'

with the intermediate trace pronounced (Felser 2004). This phenomenon is also found in child language. If you use the skillful techniques of elicitation introduced by Crain and Thornton (1998), and you try to have children around the ages of 4 or 5 produce cases of wh-extraction from embedded clauses, then you will typically come up with structures of this sort. So if your target sentence is

(15)   What do you think is in the box?

some children will say something like the following:

(16)   What you think what is in the box?

essentially, with wh-reduplication. This phenomenon has been documented in the acquisition process of many languages, in child English, in child French, child German, child Dutch . . . and even child Basque, in work by Gutiérrez (2004):

(17)   Nor uste duzu nor bizi dela etxe horretan?
        Who think AUX who lives AUX house that-in
        'Who do you think lives in that house?'

where the wh-element *nor* gets reduplicated by the child in the embedded complementizer system.

   So there is plenty of evidence that movement actually takes place in successive steps, or is successive cyclic. We should then ask the following questions: how is stepwise movement implemented? And why does movement apply stepwise?

11.4 Implementation of stepwise movement

Let us start with the *how* question. That is, what element of the formal machinery determines the possibility of successive cyclic movements? Take a case like

(18)   I wonder [what Q [you think [___ that [I saw ___]]]]?

Here the final movement to the criterial landing site is determined by the criterial Q feature, selected by the main verb *wonder*. But what about the first step, the step from the thematic position to the Spec of the embedded complementizer *that*? At least three approaches may be considered. One is that intermediate movement is untriggered, totally free, and the only requirement on a movement chain is that the final step of movement should be to a criterial position. Another view is that movement to intermediate positions is triggered by a non-specific edge-feature, so there is something like a generalized A-bar feature that says *move this element to the edge*, and then it is only in the last step that the chain acquires its flavor as a Q chain or a Topic chain, etc. A third possibility is that intermediate movement is triggered by a specific edge-feature – that is, by the formal counterpart of a criterial feature. Thus, if the construction is a question, let's say, you have a criterial, Q feature, in the final landing site, and a formal counterpart of the Q feature in the intermediate complementizer, so that you end up with a uniform chain in that respect. The criterial and formal Q features differ only in that the criterial feature is interpretable, is visible, and triggers an explicit instruction to the interpretive systems ("my Spec is to be interpreted as an interrogative operator with scope over my complement"), whereas the formal counterpart does not carry any instruction visible to the interpretive systems, and therefore is uninterpretable.

It seems to me that some evidence in favor of this third alternative is provided by the fact that we get selective effects in the intermediate landing sites that the other approaches do not easily capture. Take for instance the inversion cases in Belfast English that we mentioned before:

(19)   What did Mary claim did they steal?

Now this inversion phenomenon in the lower complementizer is only triggered by a question, not by topicalization, etc., so that a generalized A-bar feature in the embedded C would not be sufficiently specific to account for the selectivity of the effect. And there are other pieces of evidence of the same sort supporting the view that chains are featurally uniform, and intermediate steps involve specific attracting formal features.[2]

11.5 Two concepts of locality

We now move to the question of *why* movement takes place in successive steps. The general answer is that it is so because there are locality principles preventing longer, unbounded steps in movement, so that long movement chains can only be built by successive steps each of which is local. But what kind of locality principles are operative? There are two fundamental concepts around. One is the concept of intervention, according to which a local relation cannot hold across an intervener of a certain kind, and the other is the concept of impenetrability, according to which certain configurations are impenetrable to local relations.

In essence, intervention principles amount to this: in a configuration like the following:

(20)   .... X ... Z ... Y ...

no local relation can hold between X and Y across an intervening element Z, if Z is of the same structural type, given the appropriate typology of elements and positions, as X.

---

[2] See Rizzi (2006b), and for a general discussion of the issue of intermediate movement, Boeckx (2008).

I have stated the idea, and will continue to illustrate it, basically in the format of relativized minimality, but there are many conceivable variants of these concepts, some of which (shortest move, minimal search, etc.) are explored in the literature (Rizzi 1990). Take a concrete example – the fact that certain elements are not extractable from indirect questions. So, for instance, if you start from something like

(21)   a. You think he behaved this way
       b. You wonder who behaved this way

it is possible to form a main question bearing on *this way* from (21a), but not from (21b):

(22)   a. How do you think he behaved ___?
       b. *How do you wonder who behaved ___?

How can be connected to its trace in (22a), but not in (22b). In this case, the representation is the following (where "___" represents the trace of the extracted element):

(23)   *How do you wonder [who behaved ____]?
          X   Z   Y

Here X (*how*) cannot be related to its trace Y because of the intervention of Z (*who*), which has certain qualities in common with X, namely the fact of being a wh-operator. There is a wh-element that intervenes and hence the locality relation is broken. Whereas in cases of extraction from the declarative (22a), there is no problem because *how* can reach its trace as there is no intervener of the same kind.

The second concept, impenetrability, states that certain configurations are impenetrable to rules, so that, if "HP" is such a configuration, no direct local relation can hold between X and Y across the HP boundaries:

(24)   ...X...[HP...H [...Y...]...]...

Many locality principles embody the notion of impenetrability in different forms (island constraints, subjacency, CED, etc.). The most recent version of this family of principles is Chomsky's phase impenetrability (Chomsky 2004a): if linguistic computations proceed by phases, and H is a head defining a phase, then direct movement cannot take place from Y to X in (24).

This approach correctly predicts, for instance, that extraction of *how* in (22a) necessarily proceeds in successive steps: if you try to connect *how* directly to its trace without passing through the edge of the embedded clause, you will

run into the impenetrability effect, so a stepwise derivation yielding a representation like the following is enforced:

(25)   How do you think [___ C [he behaved ___]]

In fact, there is good empirical evidence for the validity of this conclusion. For
instance, Chung (1994) observed the obligatory wh-agreement on both the main
and embedded verb in these kinds of cases in a wh-agreement language like
Chamorro, which supports the view that movement must proceed stepwise here.

11.6 A unitary approach

It is quite generally assumed that there is a certain division of labor between the
two concepts of locality. Intervention accounts for weak island effects also in
cases in which the element creating the weak island does not sit on the edge of
a plausible phase (e.g., a negation marker, a quantificational adverb, etc.), a case
that would not be covered by phase impenetrability; and, reciprocally,
phase impenetrability accounts for the obligatory stepwise movement in cases
like (25), in which intervention is apparently mute, as there is no visible
intervener.

Nevertheless, it is worthwhile to explore the possibility of a unification of the
different locality effects under a single concept. I would like to conclude by
sketching out a suggestion along these lines. Apart from conceptual considerations, I believe there is an empirical argument in favor of a unitary approach.
It is well-known that extraction across an intervener is selective, and the
same kind of selectivity is found in the possibility of directly extracting
from an embedded declarative, so it looks as if there is a generalization to be
captured here.

The selective extractability across a wh-intervener is illustrated by pairs like
the following:

(26)   a. ?Which problem do you wonder [how to solve ___]
       b. *How do you wonder [which problem to solve ___]

A wh-phrase like *which problem* is extractable from the indirect question
(marginally in English), while if we reverse the two wh-phrases and try to
extract *how* from the indirect question introduced by *which problem*, the result
is totally impossible. According to one familiar analysis, the key notion is
D(iscourse)-linking: the range of the variable bound by *which problem* is a set
assumed to be familiar from discourse (we previously talked about problems A,
B, and C, and now I want to know which one of these problems is such that . . .)

(Cinque 1990). So, cutting some corners, we could say that wh-phrases like *which problem* target positions which are featurally specified both as Q and as Topic, the latter specification expressing the familiarity of the lexical restriction; whereas wh-elements like *how* typically target positions uniquely specified as Q. So, (26a–b) have representations like the following (where "___" stands for the trace of the extracted element):

(27) a. Which problem [Q, Top] ...... how [Q] ...... ___ ...
     X   Z   Y

 b. How [Q] ...... which problem [Q, Top] ...... ___ ...
    X   Z   Y

Then I will assume a version of relativized minimality, following Michal Starke (2001) essentially, according to which an element counts as an intervener in the crucial configuration...X...Z...Y...only if the Z fully matches the feature specification of X. That is to say, if this intervener is not as richly specified in featural terms as the target, no minimality effect is determined. Then, the wh-element *which problem* is extractable in (27a) because it targets a Q Top position, so that it can jump across the less richly specified pure Q element, under Starke's interpretation of intervention. By the same logic, *how* cannot jump across another wh-element in (27b), as its target position is not more richly specified than the intervener (in fact, its specification is less rich here), so that extraction is not possible in this case.

 Now, back to the obligatoriness of stepwise movement in extraction from declaratives. What Chung has observed is that in a wh-agreement language like Chamorro, one finds the same selectivity in extraction from declaratives, as underscored by the obligatoriness or optionality of wh-agreement on the main verb:

(28) a. Lao kuantu I asagua-mu ma'a' ñao- *(ña) [___ [pära un-apasi i atumobit ___]]?
   'But how much is your husband afraid you might pay for the car?'
 b. Hafa na istoria I lalahi man- ma'a' ñao [pära uma-sangan tä'lu ___] ?
   'Which story were the men afraid to repeat?' (Chung 1998, ex.53b)

The adjunct *how much* must be extracted from the declarative through stepwise movement, as shown by the obligatoriness of wh-agreement on the main verb, while the D-linked wh-argument *which story* can also be extracted in one fell swoop, without passing from the embedded C-system, as shown by the possibility of omitting wh-agreement on the main verb in (28b), under Chung's interpretation.

In conclusion, the same kinds of elements that can be extracted from an indirect question or other weak islands in languages such as English. are also extractable in one fell swoop from an embedded declarative in Chamorro. Let me suggest a way of capturing this generalization by relying uniquely on the intervention concept. We have proposed that the left periphery of clauses consists of a sequence of dedicated heads, so we have a partial cartography of the C-system like Top, Foc, Q, etc. These elements may appear in two possible flavors: either criterial and interpretable, or their purely formal, uninterpretable counterpart. Suppose that, under general assumptions on the fundamental structural uniformity of clauses, this system is always present in the left periphery of a complete clause. This system may remain silent in a sentence in which nothing moves, but it is always activated when movement to the left periphery takes place.

Let us see how, under these assumptions, we can capture Chung's observations on Chamorro. Suppose that we are extracting a non-D-linked wh-element like *how much* in (28a). Here movement must be successive cyclic because if we try to move directly from the embedded clause to the main complementizer system, we will be skipping a Q head in the embedded clause, the Q head (uninterpretable here, as the main verb does not select an indirect question) that we now assume to be part of the left periphery of every complete clause, thus violating relativized minimality. So, we must have stepwise movement here, first to the Spec of the uninterpretable embedded Q and then to the main complementizer system, as is shown by the obligatory wh-agreement on the embedded verb in Chamorro. On the other hand, if the extractee is a D-linked, topic-like wh-phrase like *which car* in (28b), this element will be able to target a complex Q Topic position in the main clause, hence it will manage to escape the lower pure Q position in the embedded clause, under Starke's formulation of relativized minimality.[3] So, we can capture the generalization that the same elements that can be extracted from weak islands are not forced to go successive-cyclically in case of extraction from declaratives. At the same time, we capture the necessity of successive cyclicity from the sole locality concept of intervention.

In conclusion, thematic and criterial positions delimit chains: there is no position lower than the thematic position, and no position higher than the criterial position in a well-formed chain. In between thematic and criterial positions there typically are other positions, as a consequence of locality, which forces movement to proceed stepwise. It is desirable on conceptual

---

[3] We can assume that featurally complex positions like Q Top may be created by head movement, but they don't have to be, so there will always be the possibility of not creating Q Top in the embedded clause, which will permit extraction of the D-linked wh-phrase in one fell swoop, as shown by the possible lack of wh-agreement on the main verb in Chamorro.

grounds to try to unify the different notions of locality, and we have made the suggestion, based on empirical evidence, that the notion of intervention may be the relevant unifying concept.

Discussion

LAKA: My question is very small. You said something about having faulty criterial projections available for computation, even when they are not necessary for interpretation, and you said that maybe they are there in spite of this. Since often they are phonologically silent as well, could you tell us your thoughts on what kind of positions these would be?

RIZZI: Yes, in fact it is a very important question. I think the driving intuition is the idea that clauses are fundamentally uniform. This had a critical role, for instance, in the analysis of non-finite clauses: they look very different from finite clauses, in that e.g. they often lack an overt subject position, but then it turns out that if we assume that they have the same structures as finite clauses, a lot of progress is possible in understanding their formal and interpretive properties. So, uniformity is the underlying rationale for assuming scope-discourse features in the left periphery of all clauses, and then locality effects such as the obligatoriness of stepwise movement can be derived from this assumption. So the question is: what does it mean that they may remain silent in a structure in which nothing has moved? It could be that they just don't do anything, they are just there and they get activated only if you try to move something out of the structure, essentially – i.e., they give rise to minimality effects. Another possibility, at least for some of the features (maybe the answer is not the same for all of the features), is that you may have things like in-situ Focus, for instance, at least in some languages. This could be expressed by some kind of pure Agree relation without movement into the periphery, but still with some kind of relation with a left-peripheral head. I don't think this can be said for all features, because for instance the Q feature clearly would not be activated in a declarative, normally, so there would be no way of extending the analysis along these lines. So there are a number of problems, and perhaps partially different answers for different features, but I would be assuming that the features are there, expressed in the left periphery, and that their presence is somehow activated when you try to move, much in analogy with what happens in French past participle agreement, in fact. You assume the agreement feature is there, inherently, on the participial head, but it is only when you move the object that it gets morphologically activated. So that is one of the models I have in mind.

PIATTELLI-PALMARINI: I've just come from Amsterdam where I was lucky enough to sit in the morning in Mark Baker's course on Agreement, and he says that there are universals of hierarchical agreement, so you have for instance complementizers in agreement with the subject, and some in agreement with both subject and object. He also connected this rather rigid universal hierarchy with Case. How does your unification deal with the working of such parameters?

RIZZI: Basically, the system I talked about has to do with scope-discourse features, and that's a system that is relatively independent from the Case agreement system that Mark Baker refers to. Even though there are interesting interactions, for instance, again, with past-participle agreement, the case in which a property that looks like a Case agreement property shows up when you try to build a left peripheral configuration. But I would assume that in general the two systems are relatively isolated and function differently, so that whatever parameterization is to be assumed for the Case agreement system, that doesn't very directly affect the kind of system which I looked at. Of course, the scope-discourse featural system also involves parameters, which have to do with whether or not you pronounce certain left-peripheral heads, with the respective order of the heads in the left periphery (because you find some ordering differences there), and with whether or not you must, can, or can't move to the left periphery. All these parametric properties seem to be largely independent from the parameterization on the Case agreement system.

CHAPTER 12

Uninterpretable Features in Syntactic Evolution

Juan Uriagereka

As all of you know, every time I listen to a talk by Randy Gallistel, I think I have made a career mistake – I should have studied a different animal. But anyway, in the interests of interdisciplinarity, I will talk about human animals, in particular a puzzle that arises in them when considered from the minimalist viewpoint. This might offer a perspective that could be interesting for the general issues of evolution and cognition that we have been discussing.

As all of you know, in the minimalist program we seek what you may think of as *internal coherence* within the system – but *in its natural interactions* with other components of mind (its interpreting interfaces). That is, we are interested in their effective integration. The puzzle that I would like to talk about arises with a phenomenon that is actually quite central in language, namely the hierarchy of Case features – that is, the order in which values are decided within the Case system. I will give you one concrete example, but the phenomenon is general, and the reason the puzzle arises is because the hierarchy involves *uninterpretable* information, to the best of anybody's knowledge. That is, *a fortiori*, this type of information cannot be explicated in terms of interface conditions based on inter-pretability. There are very interesting stories out there for hierarchies that arise in terms of interpretable information. For instance Hale and Keyser (1993, 2002) gave us an approach to thematic hierarchy from just that point of view. But the problem I am concerned with is different. We have interesting interpretations of thematic hierarchy, but whatever featural arrangement we are going to have in terms of uninterpretable Case, such an arrangement simply cannot be the consequence of interpretive properties. So where does it come from?

I'll illustrate this through some examples in Basque, using just the abstract Basque pattern, with English words. So, in Basque, in a simple transitive structure,

(1)   [$_S$NP.subj [$_{VP}$ NP.obj   V   agrO.Trans-Aux.agrS]]
      John.subj   Mary.obj loved 'he.has.her'
      'John has loved Mary' = 'John loves Mary'

you have an NP with subject Case, an NP with object Case, and then of course
you have a verb and, importantly, an auxiliary in the transitive format, something like *V-have*, which shows agreement with subject and object. In turn,
when the expression is intransitive (in particular unaccusative),

(2)   [$_S$NP.obj [$_{VP}$ t V   agrO.Intrans-Aux]]
      John.obj   arrived 'he.is'
      'John is arrived' = 'John arrived'

then the subject, which arguably displaces from inside the verb phrase, gets
object Case, and verbal agreement is now of the intransitive sort (something like
V-be), determined by that single argument.

   Now things quickly get more complicated in an interesting way. The facts are
taken from both Laka's work on split ergativity and San Martín's thesis, adapting earlier work by Hualde and Ortiz de Urbina (2003) (for a presentation
and the exact references, see Uriagereka 2008). In essence, when you have a
transitive verb, but the object of the sentence is now *another sentence* – for
instance a subject-controlled sentence, like

(3)   [$_S$NP.obj [$_{VP}$ [S...]   V   agrO.Intrans-Aux]]
      John.obj   [to lose weight] tried   'he.is'
      'John tried to lose weight'

– all of a sudden, it is as if the object is no longer there! The object clause is
still interpreted, but it no longer behaves as a true complement, and now the
subject NP gets *object* Case, as if the structure were unaccusative, and even the
auxiliary exhibits the unaccusative pattern we saw for (2), agreeing with a
singular element. This is despite the fact that semantically you clearly have
two arguments. In effect, instead of saying 'John *has* tried to lose weight,'
you must say the equivalent of 'John *is* tried to lose weight.'

   So, in a nutshell, when the complement clause is a true subordinate clause
(you have to make sure the clause is truly subordinate, not a paratactic complement which behaves like any NP), for some reason it is pushed out of the
structural Case system and shows up without structural Case. And then the
subject, which again has a perfectly normal subject interpretation, nonetheless
receives object Case. So a way to put this is that true clauses, though they are
fine thematic arguments, just do not enter into this system of Case. It is nominal
phrases that require Case for some reason, and they do so on a first-come, first-

served basis. Simply, the first nominal (not the first interpreted argument) in a derivational cycle is the one that receives object Case, regardless actually of how "high" it is in terms of its thematic interpretation. So this Case distribution is just at right angles with semantics, in the broadest sense.

Now, an immediate question to reflect on is why it is that NPs (or more technically DPs) are subject to this structural Case system, while clauses get away without Case. This is shown by comparing (3) with a version of that same sentence having the same semantics, but where the complement clause is substituted by a pronoun:

(4) [$_S$NP.subj [$_{VP}$ that.obj V   agrO.Trans-Aux.agrS]]
     John.subj   that.obj tried 'he.has.her'
     'John tried that'

Now everything is as we would expect it: the subject gets subject Case and the object gets object Case, as is normal in a transitive construction. So what is the difference between (3) and (4), if their interpretation is not the answer? Second, how does this Case valuation mechanism enable the system to "know" that the first element in need of Case has been activated and that Case value has already been assigned, so that the next item that needs Case (which everyone agrees the grammar cannot identify interpretively, remember) can then use the next Case value?

I should say that the situation described is not at all peculiar to Basque. These hierarchies, with pretty much the same sorts of nuances, show up in virtually all other languages, if you can test relevant paradigms (Bresnan and Grimshaw 1978, Harbert 1983, Silverstein 1993; Uriagereka 2008 attempts an account of this sort of generalization). There is at least one parameter that masks things for more familiar languages (whether the first Case value assigned is inside or outside the verb phrase, basically), but if you take that into account, you find puzzles similar to the one just discussed literally all over the place. Which is why, in the end, we think of Case as an uninterpretable feature.[1] Compounding the problem as well is the notorious issue posed by dative phrases, virtually in all languages. Dative Case valuation happens to be determined, for some bizarre reason, after those two Cases I was talking about, although structurally, dative clearly appears in between them. Moreover, whereas there is only one subject and one object Case within any given derivational cycle, as just discussed, you actually can have multiple datives in between. It is almost as if you have a family

---

[1] To say that a feature is uninterpretable is to make a negative claim. A more developed theory might show us how what looks uninterpretable at this stage is in the end interpretable when seen under the appropriate light. That said, I know of no successful account of Case as interpretable that is compatible with the minimalist perspective.

affair: first the mother, last the father, and in between a bunch of children. Except this ordering is neither a result of obvious interface conditions, nor of simple derivational activation.

Anyway, this is the picture I am going to keep in mind, and in essence this strange state of affairs is what the language faculty has evolved, for some reason. For our purposes here (and I think this is probably not too far off), you must have a first or mother Case – a domain where there happens to be a parameter, as I said, depending on whether that mother Case is assigned at the edge of the VP or not. And you must have a last, or father Case, if you will – which, depending on the parameter finessing the manifestations of the mother Case, comes up at the TP or further up. And then you have what you may think of as a default Case, or, to use a third family name, the child Cases that are associated with an entirely separate system involving something like prepositions. This Case value is basically used only when the mother and the father Cases have been used, first and last, respectively. That is the hierarchy I have in mind.

These are central, although of course not logically necessary, generalizations that the derivation is clearly sensitive to. And I really mean the derivation in a serious sense, for the hierarchy is actually evaluated at each derivational cycle, meaning that every time you get, basically, a new clausal domain, you have to start all over. It is really like a family affair, relations being reset with each new generation. But it is extremely nuanced too: not simply interpretive (you must distinguish arguments depending on whether they are nominal or clausal) and not simply activated in, as it were, chronological order. True, "mother-Case" comes first, but what shows up structurally next, "child-Case," is clearly not what simply comes next in the derivation, which is "father-Case." We know that because in many instances there simply are no "child-Cases," and then it is only the father/mother-Case duality that shows up. So while this Case valuation system clearly has configurational consequences (association with the VP level or the TP level, for instance), it just cannot be seriously defined by going bottom-up in structure, the way we do, for instance, for the thematic hierarchy.

That, I should say, has an important immediate consequence, consistent with a comment in Chomsky's 2005 paper.[2] If something like this is right, then the architecture of a syntactic derivation simply cannot be of the sort that accesses interpretation fully online. The system must have enough derivational memory to keep a whole cycle in active search space, so that it knows whether, for that cycle, the mother-Case valuation has already been used, so that the father one is

---

[2] The idea "that all options are open: the edge- and Agree-features of the probe can apply in either order, or simultaneously" (Chomsky 2005a: 17).

then deployed; or when the father-Case valuation has been accessed, then you move into child Case. Without a memory buffer to reason this way, this system makes no sense. This is what Chomsky calls a "phase"-based derivation, and the present one is a pretty strong argument for it.

What role is this Case valuation playing within cycles to start with – why is it there? Here is where I am going to offer some speculations from a project that Massimo Piattelli-Palmarini and I have been working on (see Piattelli-Palmarini and Uriagereka 2004, 2005; more work is in progress). If you take all this seriously, the particular possibility I will mention has interesting consequences for the issues we have been talking about in this conference. The general question can be posed this way. If you look at the archeological record, early sapiens prior to our own species seem to have exhibited very elaborate causal behaviors, presupposing some kind of computational thought. There should be little doubt about that, especially if, following Randy Gallistel's arguments, we are willing to grant complex computational thoughts to ants or jays. But there surely is a difference between thinking and somehow sharing your thoughts, for thought, as such, can be a pretty multi-dimensional construct.

In grammatical studies alone we have shown that a simple sentence structure like the one I am using right now involves at least one "dimension" for the string of words of arbitrary length, another for labeling/bracketing going up in the phrase-marker, possibly another one for complex phrasal entanglements that we usually get through transformations and similar devices, and I would even go as far as to accept a fourth "dimension" dealing with the sorts of information-encoding that we see deployed in the very rich phenomenon of antecedence and anaphora. So these four "dimensions" at least. But as Jim Higginbotham insightfully observed in 1983, all of that has to be squeezed into the one-dimensional channel of speech.[3] Some of you might be telepathic, but I at least, and I'd say most of us have to share our thoughts in this boring way I am using, through speech, and that compression probably implies some information loss.

This actually has consequences for a very interesting study that Marc Hauser and Tecumseh Fitch did a couple of years ago with tamarins. If I understood the experiment, the tamarins failed to acquire anything that involved relevant syntactic types, and I mean by that simple context-free grammars. They only succeeded in acquiring simpler finite-state tasks, with no "type/token" distinctions. I want to put it in those terms because I want to be neutral about what it

---

[3] He observes that one "can, in point of fact, just make one sound at a time, . . . a consequence of the applications of the laws of nature to the human mouth" (Higginbotham 1983b: 151).

is that you can and cannot do as you organize your thoughts in progressively more complex computational terms.

The very simplest grammars one can think of, finite-state ones, are so rudimentary that they cannot use their own resources to code any sort of groupings, and thus have no way to express, in themselves, very elementary classifications. One could imagine other external ways to impose classifications, but the point is they would not be internal to the grammatical resources, at that level of complexity. In a grammar, it is only as you start going up in formal complexity that you can use grammatical resources – the technical term is a "stack" – to possibly group other symbols into sets of a certain type. So there is a possible issue, then: such a type/token distinction must be significant in the evolution of our line of language, and we want to figure out what sort of leap in evolution allowed us to do that, but not the tamarins. Could it have anything to do with Higginbotham's "compression" problem? In other words, could the tamarins – or other apes, or sapiens other than ourselves in evolutionary history – have been capable of real type/token distinctions in thought, but not in sharing that thought through a unidimensional channel that depends on the motor system?

I do not know, but the matter bears on what I think is a very unimaginative criticism that some researchers have recently raised against Chomsky, Hauser, and Fitch (see Jackendoff and Pinker 2005, and Fitch et al. 2005 for a response). One version of the problem goes like this. Gallistel has shown that many animals execute elaborate computational tasks, which might even reach the the context-free grammars of thought that I was alluding to a moment ago. Now simply looking at the fossil record, coupled with the detailed genetic information that we are beginning to get on them as well, tells us a similar story about pre-sapiens, or at any rate pre-sapiens-sapiens – further grist for Gallistel's mill (see Camps and Uriagereka 2006 for details and references). So here is the issue being raised: how can anyone claim that the defining characteristic of the "full" language faculty is recursion, when recursion may be a hallmark of all those computational layers of complexity that we have to grant to other thinking creatures? How can they have truly complex thoughts if they lack recursion?

I call this criticism unimaginative because I think there is a fairly simple answer to it, which starts by making a familiar, but apparently still not understood, distinction between competence and performance. Again, one thing is to have a thought, and a different one is to be able to share it. In our case, you want to ask how, in particular, a recursive thought process is also sharable. If it were not, we would find ourselves in the somewhat Kafkaesque situation of being, perhaps, truly smart – but solipsistic as well. For all we know, in large part this is what happens to other animals, and perhaps it did too in our evolutionary lineage until relatively recently. Recursive thoughts, perhaps sharing them systematically, not so obvious. Note in particular that to have a thought that is as complex as a sentence incorporating recursion, what the individual needs to know is that one X (any structure) is different from another X of the same type. That is what gives you the recursion. Observe this concretely, as in (5):

(5)   X
      / | \
    Y   ...   Z
    | / | \ |
 ... ... X ... ...

You deal with one X at the top, and another X below, inside, and then if this structure makes it as a thought, you can have recursion. But you absolutely must keep the Xs apart, and moreover somehow know that both are the same types of entity. You need two different tokens of the same syntactic type. If you could not make that distinction for some reason, say because you lacked the computational resources for it, then you would not have the recursive structure, period.

Now, one could argue that the mere generation of the various thoughts, in the thought process in time (however that is done in an actual mental computation by the animals that we are studying), actually gives you different tokenizations of X, probably in a relatively trivial sense if the generative devices are as complex as we are implying, technically a push-down automaton or PDA.[4] Plainly, if you, a PDA, are generating one X plus another X within the confines of the first, well, they must be different Xs – you are thinking them differently in the thought process. Ah, but if you want to show me your various uses of X, somehow we must share a way of determining that one X is not the same as the other X. There we may have a problem.

You may think that sheer ordering in speech, for example, does the trick, that ordering separates each token from the next – but not so fast. We have to be careful here, because of Higginbotham's "compression" problem: a unidimensional system like speech is just too simplistic to express the articulated phrasal structure that I think with, including crucially its recursive structure. To illustrate this very simply, as my speech reaches you, you may hear one X, and then

---

[4] A push-down automaton (PDA) recognizes a context-free grammar, by defining a stack within the computational memory tape, with a corresponding "stack alphabet" (e.g., non-terminals like NP or VP). This stack memory permits access only to the most recently stored symbol in making decisions about what state to go to next. See Stabler (2003).

another X – let's grant that much. But how do you know that the next X is really a part of the previous one, and not just another dangling X out there? In other words, given an object to parse like (6a) (a sequence of symbols we hear), how do we know whether to assign it the structure in (6b) or the one in (6c)?

(6) a. ...x, y, x...   b.   XP   c. XP...XP
                                   / \   / \   / \
                              ... x XP   ... x y x ...
                                   / \
                                  y x ...

In the latter instance, you would not find yourself in a truly recursive process. At best it would be an instance of a much simpler form of complexity, an *iteration*.[5] All iterations can be modeled as recursions, but you can prove that not all recursions can be modeled as iterations. Intuitively, since all you are hearing is a sequence of symbols, after they have been compressed into speech, no matter how complex a phrasal array they may have been within my own brain, you just have no way to decide whether to reconstruct the flat sequence into another, well, flat sequence (6c), or whether to somehow get ahead of the evidence and come up with a more elaborate representation that may actually correspond to what I intended (6b). Too much information is lost in the compression.

This is all to say that, if you set aside telepathy, not only do you need to ground your own Xs within a structure in relevant phrasal contexts, so that you get your own recursion off the ground; *you need to share that with me* also, if I am to reconstruct your private thought process. Without that, we won't reliably share our thoughts, we won't come up with a real lexicon of stored idiosyncrasies to tell each other things, we won't have a very rich culture, and so on and so forth. Kafka had it right, although perhaps his Gregor Samsa would have been any old roach if we grant insects the powers that Gallistel argues for!

Now, as far as I can tell, there is no way to solve Higginbotham's compression problem in full generality, particularly if the information loss is as dramatic as one literally going from many dimensions to one. That said, evolution may have found ways to cut the complexity down; perhaps not foolproof ways, but nonetheless effective enough to take us out of entire solipsism or total guesswork. A nice trick in this regard would be to come up with (sorry for the neologism) "tokenizers" of some sort, for the language system, that is. Again, a grammar can be very complex, entirely useful as a thought mechanism, yet not

---

[5] This type of operation creates arbitrarily long strings within the confines of a finite state automaton (FSA), by endlessly repeating a concrete state through a looped process. It constitutes, in effect, a form of unboundedness without internal structure.

effectively communicable if you just have this "unstructured soup" as it were, as it comes out in speech or other forms of expression that rely on motor constraints. That "unstructured soup," ordered as your thought processes, is a necessary condition for public emergence of language in some organized way, but it is simply not sufficient to succeed in sharing it. You need something else, and this is what I am calling a "tokenizer" for lack of a better term.

Whatever these gizmos turn out to be, they had better come up with a way of somehow fixing various Xs as reliable other instances of themselves, in the sense of true recursion. Moreover these devices have to anchor the structure parsed in speech as not just "another one of those," but indeed as somehow contained within. If such a nifty device can be evolved by a group of very smart creatures, then they may be on their way to reliably sharing their thoughts. From this perspective, proto-language may not have been usably recursive, no matter how recursive the thought process that sustained it was. But surely language as we understand it is not just capable of sustaining recursive thought, but also of more or less successfully *transmitting* such intricate thoughts. All right, not perfectly (effective use breaks down in garden-path situations, center-embedding, ternary branching, and I am sure much more), but enough to have managed to allow conferences like this one. And the issue is, it seems to me, what that extra step, those tokenizers, bring to the picture.

To make a very long story short (Uriagereka 2008: Chapter 8), I will simply give you an instance of what I think could have been one effective tokenizer, and this is how I come back to Case – so that you can see how a Case system would actually constitute a formal tokenizer. The story is based on what, over the years, I have called a viral theory of morphology. By that I mean, metaphorically at this point, that you introduce in a syntactic derivation an element that is actually "extraneous" to it, and crucially uninterpretable to the system. What for? Well, to eliminate it in the course of the derivation. How? That is an interesting issue. In short, linguists still do not understand this in any detail, but we have found that uninterpretable morphology, the sort Case is a prime example of, gets literally excised from the computation – not surprisingly if it has no interpretation – by way of a transformational procedure.

Actually, it is at places like this that we have convinced ourselves of Chomsky's initial insight that context-free grammars, and thus the corresponding PDA automata that execute them, are not enough to carry a syntactic computation. You also need context-sensitive dependencies, no matter how limited they turn out to be.[6] For those you plainly need a different automaton; the PDA won't do,

---

[6] In one formulation, "mild context-sensitivity," which involves polynomial parsing complexity, constant growth, and limited crossing dependencies (see Stabler 2003).

so call it a PDA +. The point is this: you observe, empirically, that the language faculty is forced into these PDA + resources precisely *when Case features are involved*. You don't just eliminate them, in other words. You go through the trouble of invoking complex agreement relations for the task, which is what forces the system into this literally higher-order PDA + computation.

In that I think the analogy with the virus is quite useful. When your organism detects one of those, you go into an internal chaos to excise it, as a result of which drastic warpings and foldings happen within your cells. In my view, this is a way to rationally account for the presence of this sort of morphology, which has very serious consequences for syntactic structuring. It is not just a little noise in the system; it is, rather, a huge issue, a virus, that the system must detect and immediately eliminate. And crucially for my purposes now, as a result of the process, new syntactic structures (literally warped phrase-structures involving new, long-distance, connections) are possible.

So anyway, as a result of immediately killing the virus, the phrase-marker is now warped in a characteristic shape that used to be called a chain, and nowadays goes by the name of a "remerged" structure, and a variety of other names to express the discontinuity of the new dependency thus formed. (It is not important what we call it though; the important issue is the discontinuous dependency.) The Case feature may be gone, thank goodness, but the aftermath is fascinating: a new phrasal dependency is now reliably created, indeed an effective way of anchoring, regardless of its meaning, a given structure X to whatever the domain was where the Case virus was excised.

Remember the mother Case, the father Case, and the child Cases? By thinking of them as viral elements that the system must eliminate immediately at given contexts, we have anchored the element X that eliminates the offending, uninterpretable, stuff *precisely to the context of the elimination*. If this is done in systematic terms within a derivation (mother Case goes first, father Case goes last, child Case is the default), then we have come up with a useful way of relating X to given phrasal contexts, and thus of tokenizing this X (say at father Case) from that X (say at mother Case), and so on.

Now, here is a crucial plus: these Case features are morphemes, not phrases. They do not need, in themselves, any fancy automata to carry their nuances – they are stupid features. Very stupid features, with absolutely no interpretation, which is what sets the entire catastrophe in motion! In other words, these things are fully parseable even at the boring level of speech, which we are granting even tamarins (at any rate, some equivalent motor control). So what did tamarins lack – or more seriously, apes or closer hominids? If we are on the right track here, probably either the resources to come up with the elimination of this Case virus, or perhaps the very virus that started it all. Be that as it may, this, I think, models a tokenizer of just the sort we were after.

I just wanted to give you a flavor of what role Case may be playing within a system where it appears to make little sense. At the level of the system itself, it is uninterpretable, but perhaps it can be rationally accounted for in some version of the story I told. Seen this way, Case – and more generally uninterpretable morphology – may have been a sort of viral element that for some reason entered a system it was not meant to be a part of. In normal circumstances, that could have been either devastating for the system – a virus of the sort our computers often get – or perhaps just a glitch that the system did not even bother to deal with. But matters seem to have been considerably more intriguing where the language faculty is concerned.

It would appear that the system deployed its full forces to eliminate the intruder, in the process emerging with new structures that, perhaps, would not have emerged otherwise. It is a fascinating possibility, it seems to me, and Massimo Piattelli-Palmarini and I have suggested that it recalls the role of transposon activity within genomes.[7] Of course, that too is a metaphor, although it emphasizes the viral connection.

It has become clear that large parts of genomes (including half of ours) have their origin in viral insertions and other "horizontal" transmissions that do not originate in the standard way we are taught in high school. Up to recently, the role of this nucleic material was thought to be irrelevant, hence terms like "junk DNA" applied to it. Well, it turns out that we have only scratched the surface, and in fact entire systems, like of all things the adaptive immune system, may have originated that way (see Agrawal et al. 1998, Hiom et al. 1998).[8] This scenario is very curious from the perspective of how the language faculty may have evolved. Viruses are species-specific, tissue-specific, and needless to say they transmit very rapidly, infecting entire populations.

The question ahead is whether the putative "viral" role of uninterpretable morphology, in more or less the sense I sketched, could be meaningfully connected to some real viral process. We shall see, but that might shed some light on such old chestnuts as why the language faculty appears to be so unique, so nuanced, and to have emerged so rapidly within entire populations, the only place where language is useful.

---

[7] Transposable elements (mobile DNA sequences inserted "horizontally" into genomes) replicate fast and efficiently, particularly when they are of viral origin.

[8] The proteins encoded by the recombination-activating RAG genes are essential in the recombination reaction that results in the assembly of antigen receptors. These proteins were once components of a transposon, the split nature of antigen receptor genes deriving from germline insertion of this element into an ancestral receptor gene.

I can't resist mentioning that the Beat generation may have had it roughly right when, in the voice of William Burroughs, it told us that "language is a virus from outer space." I don't know about the "outer space" bit, but the viral part might not be as crazy as it sounds, given the observable fact that uninterpretable morphology is simply there, and the system goes to great lengths to eliminate it.

Discussion

GALLISTEL: In computer science there is an important distinction between tail recursion and embedded recursion, because in tail recursion you don't need a stack. A stack is in effect a way of keeping track of which X is which, right? You keep track of it by where they are in the stack, and then the stack tells you where you are in your evaluation of that. And the whole point of reverse Polish in the development of the theory of computation was that it turned out you could do all of the arithmetic with this tail recursion. You could always execute your operations as they came up if you structured it the right way, and therefore you only needed a set that was three-deep, or two-deep. Does that connect with the recursion that you see as central to language?

URIAGEREKA: Well, I'm an observer here as well, but as far as I can see, the thought processes that you have shown us over the years will, I am convinced, require a lot of mind – even more mind than what you are assuming now. I mean, you could even go into quantifying, context-sensitivity, and so forth; one just has to examine each case separately. But I also think that Hauser, Chomsky, and Fitch raised a valid issue, and as you know, one of the central points in that paper was in terms of recursion.[9] But I don't think they fall into a contradiction, if we separate competence and performance. This is because in the case of the type of recursion you are talking about, not only is there recursion in the thought processes, but it is also a construct that somehow I am actually projecting outwards and that you are reconstructing as we speak. And I am projecting it into the one-dimensional speech channel, which would seem to involve a massive compression from what may well be multi-dimensional structuring to single-dimensional expression – Jim Higginbotham's point two decades ago.

If you have something like Kayne's LCA (the Linear Correspondence Axiom – Kayne 1994) you actually succeed in the task, humans do anyway, or for that matter any similar, reliable, procedure may do the trick. But I think that is what we are trying to see here. What is it that introduced that extra step, call it LCA

---

[9] Hauser et al. 2002.

or whatever turns out to be correct, that allows you to reconstruct from my speech signal all my complicated recursions? So the only point in principle that I am raising is that I disagree with Jackendoff and Pinker when they criticize the paper on the basis of something like this puzzle.

Actually, I should say they don't exactly criticize the paper on the basis of what I said – theirs would have been a better argument, actually, if they had, but I won't go into that. At any rate, I disagree with their conclusion, and think that you *can* have a recursion that is solipsistic, literally trapped inside your mind, and I would be prepared to admit that other animals have that. The issue then is how we push that thing out, making it public, and that is where I think something like this uninterpretable morphology business might have a very interesting consequence, if you have to excise it along the lines I sketched. This is why Massimo and I have often used a virus image, because a virus is an element that is crucially not part of the system, and you want to kick it out. And the way the system kicks it out (I won't go into the details, but you have to use a procedure with very convoluted consequences, much like those in adaptive immunity) is that the mechanism "forces," as a result of its workings, some kind of context-sensitive dependency. It is a bit like the RNA pseudo-knots that result from retro-viral interactions, if I understand this, which David Searls (2002) has shown have mild context-sensitive characteristics. Those presumably result from the need to eliminate the virus, or, if you wish, to modulate its activity.

The only new element in the system is on the one hand the extraneous virus, and on the other a certain topology that the system goes into in order to get rid of it – with lots of consequences. So I would argue that what Noam calls "edge features" – which at least in the early stages of minimalism he related to uninterpretable morphology – in fact are the actual push that took us to this new system, of successfully communicated recursive thought.

CHOMSKY: Well, the only comment I wanted to make is that there is a gap in the argument, which in fact is crucial, and that is that granting whatever richness you do for the kinds of things that Randy is talking about, still, to go from there to recursion requires that it be embedded in a bigger structure of the same kind and so on, indefinitely. There is no evidence for that. So however rich those thoughts or constructions may be, that's arbitrary; it doesn't carry us to recursion.

GELMAN: I actually want to repeat Randy's question in a somewhat different way. You can do the natural numbers within a recursion, in terms of competence, production, and understanding – it is always an X, not a natural number. To my knowledge, you can't do linguistics without some kind of embedded recursion. It's axiomatic.

URIAGEREKA: That's right, so if language is more than just right-branching, you have a problem in communicating those structures. So your point is completely relevant, because if you think of left-branching together with right-branching – that's actually the place where something like Kayne's LCA gets messy. Kayne's LCA for right-branching would be trivial: you just map a simple-minded c-command structure involving only right branches to precedence among the terminals, and you're done. Then there's no issue. But the minute you have left-branching as well, then you have to have an induction step in the procedure, and here different authors attempt different things. In effect, you need to treat the complex left branch with internal structure as a terminal, and linearize that as a unit including all its hanging terminals, and of course introduce some sort of asymmetry so that the mutually c-commanding branches (to the left and to the right) do not interfere with each other's linearization. That asymmetry is stipulated by everyone, and it shows you that we are dealing with a very messy procedure.

So in essence that is the question – what carried humans to that next step, which somehow introduced some, hopefully elegant, version of the procedure to linearize complex branchings? The speculation I discussed here had to do with the elimination of uninterpretable features; there might be other rationalizations, but the general point remains. Now I think Noam's point is right, you're still concerned about how you got to that larger system to start with, and I have nothing to say about that. It is a great question and I am presupposing that it may have been answered ancestrally for many other animals, not just humans.

CHOMSKY: Even with simple tail recursion, when you are producing the natural numbers, you remember the entire set that you produced. Suppose you keep adding numbers, you have to know that it is not like taking steps. When you are taking steps, one after another, the next step you take is independent of how many steps you've taken before it. However, if you really have a numbering system, by the time you get to 94, you have to know that the next one is going to be 95.

GELMAN: Right. Basically, what Noam is saying is that 94 has compressed everything up to 94, and the 1 that you now add gives you the next number, so you don't mix up the 1 you add with the first 1 that you counted.

HINZEN: I have a question about Uriagereka's conception of Case features. If you think about the number of times that you suggested what is the actual difference between talking about uninterpretable Case features and talking about morphological features that get used or signal some kind of second-order semantics, some kind of second-order computation, wouldn't it be the case that as you have this mechanics of elimination of these features, you have certain technical or semantic consequences, and it is a sequel of that? So why would we be forced to set up the morphological features as uninterpretable, as opposed to using some other kind of interpretation?

URIAGEREKA: Well, in part the question is how you manage to have access to those higher-order interpretations, to put it in your own terms. There is a stage where, in one version of the hypothesis Massimo and I are pushing, you actually do not have access to that, and there is another stage where you do – I mean in evolution. Prior to the emergence of this crazy uninterpretable morphology you arguably wouldn't have needed this very warped syntax that emerges as a result of excising the virus. You could get away with something much simpler, for better and for worse. For better in the sense that you wouldn't have all these complications we have been talking about, which serious recursion brings in (and we only scratched the surface, because the minute you introduce displacement things get even more complicated); for worse also in the sense that maybe then you wouldn't have access to these kinds of higher-order structure that your question implies, which necessitates the convoluted syntax.

But maybe when you introduce this extra element in the system, whatever you call it – a virus, edge feature, or whatever – you get this kind of elaborate syntax, but now you also gain new interpretive possibilities. I actually read Noam's recent papers in that way as well. Perhaps I'm biased by my own take, but in essence, once you get to what he calls edge features, well that plainly brings with it another bundle of things, syntactically and, consequently, in the semantics as well, criterial stuff of the sort Luigi was talking about in his talk. And again, it's a very serious separate issue whether those other things have now been literally created, or whether they were there already, latent if you wish, and somehow you now have access to them as a result of the new syntax. I personally don't have much to say about that, although I know you have a view on this. What I am saying is compatible with both takes on the matter. Simply, without a complicated syntax, you are not going to get generalized quantification, unless you code all of that, more or less arbitrarily, in a semantics that is also generative. So complicated syntax is necessary, somewhere: separately or packed into the semantics itself. The question is, how do you get that complexity? And it seems that these "viral" elements have this intriguing warping consequence, which the language faculty may have taken advantage of.

CHAPTER 13

The Brain Differentiates Hierarchical and Probabilistic Grammars

Angela D. Friederici

In a recent paper on the faculty of language, Marc Hauser, Noam Chomsky, and Tecumseh Fitch (2002) asked three critical questions stated already in the title: What is it, who has it, and how did it evolve? In their answer to the "what-is-it" question, they formulated the hypothesis that the language faculty in the narrow sense comprises the core computational mechanism of recursion. In response to the "who-has-it" question, the hypothesis was raised that only humans possess the mechanism of recursion which, interestingly, is crucial not only for language, but also, as they claim, maybe for music and mathematics – that is, three processing domains that seem to be specific to humans, at least as far as we know.

As a first attempt to provide empirical data with respect to the evolutionary part of the question, Tecumseh Fitch and Marc Hauser (2002) presented data from an experiment (see page 84 above) comparing grammar learning in cotton-top tamarin monkeys and in humans. In this study, they presented these two groups of "participants" with two types of grammars. The first was a very simple probabilistic grammar where a prediction could be made from one element to the next (AB AB), which they called a finite state grammar (FSG, Grammar I). They also tested a second, phrase structure grammar (PSG, Grammar II) whose underlying structure could be considered hierarchical. Interestingly enough, the cotton-top tamarins could learn the FSG, but not PSG, whereas humans easily learned both. So now, at least for a functional neuroanatomist, the question arises: what is the neurological underpinning for this behavioral difference? Certainly there is more to it than this one question, but today I can only deal with this one, and would be happy to discuss this with you.

In this presentation I will propose that the human capacity to process hierarchical structures may depend on a brain region which is not fully developed in monkeys but is fully developed in humans, and that this phylogenetically younger piece of cortex may be functionally relevant for the learning of PSG. I think at this point we need to take a look at the underlying brain structure of the two species. Unfortunately, however, we do not have exact data on the neural structure of the brain of the cotton-top tamarin; for the moment we only have the possibility of comparing human and macaque brains. In a seminal study Petrides and Pandya (1994) have analyzed the cytoarchitectonic structure of the frontal and prefrontal cortexes of the brain in humans and the macaque (see Fig. 13.1). Anterior to the central sulcus (CS) there is a large area which one could call, according to Korbinian Brodmann (1909), BA 6. This area is particularly large in humans and in the monkey. However, those areas that seem to be relevant for language, at least in the human brain, are pretty small in the macaque (see gray shaded areas BA44, BA45B in Fig. 13.1). According to the color coding scheme used here, the lighter the gray shading, and the more anterior in the brain, the more granular the cortex.

What does granularity mean in this context? The cortex consists of six layers. Layer IV of the cortex is characterized by the presence of particular cells. These cells are very sparse or not present in BA 6, but they become more and more numerous as one moves further anterior in the brain. The dark-colored

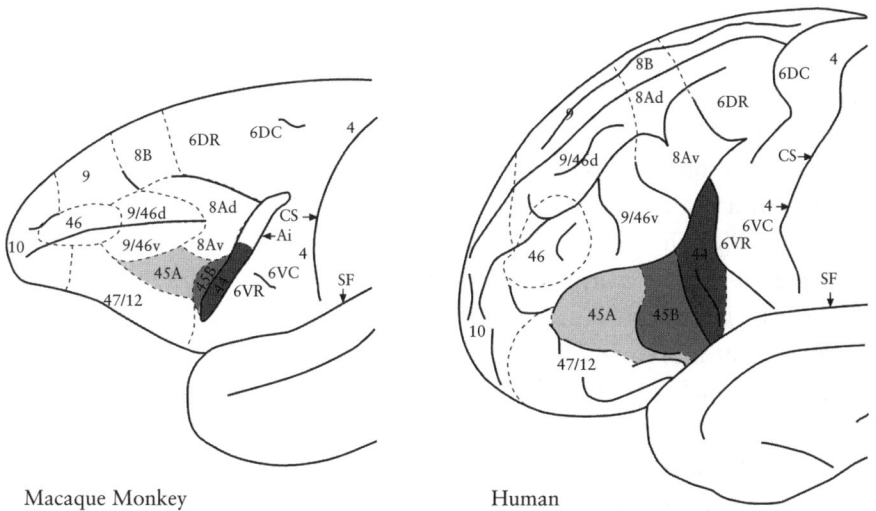

Macaque Monkey   Human

Fig. 13.1. Cytoarchitectonically segregated brain areas in the frontal cortex (indicated by numbers). Gray-shaded are those areas that make up the language-related Broca's area in the human brain and their homologue areas in the macaque brain.

Source: adapted from Petrides and Pandya 1994

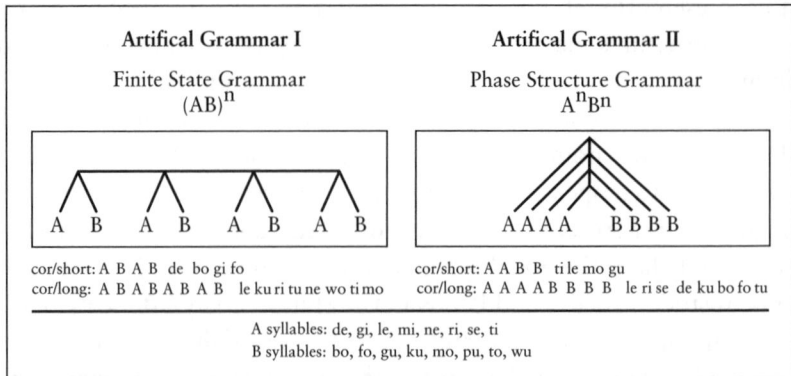

Fig. 13.2. Structure of the two grammar types. General structure and examples of stimuli in the FSG (Grammar I) and PSG (Grammar II). Members of the two categories (A and B) were coded phonologically with category "A" syllables containing the vowels "i" or "e" with category "B" syllables containing the vowels "o" or "u". The same syllables were used for both types of grammar.

Source: adapted from Friederici et al. 2006a

areas are the dysgranular part (BA 44) and the granular part (BA 45), and as you may have recognized already, this is what makes up Broca's area in humans. With respect to the evolution of these parts, the neuroanatomist Sanides (1962) has proposed a "principle of graduation," claiming that brain evolution proceeded from agranular to dysgranular and then to completely granular cortex. That is, the agranular cortex (BA 6) is not a well-developed cortex with respect to layer IV, whereas the dysgranular area (BA 44) and granular area (BA 45) are.

What could that mean with respect to the questions we are considering here? Could it be that the underlying structures of these two types of brains have something to do with the capacity to process either a simple probabilistic grammar or a hierarchical grammar? Let us assume that an FSG may be processed by a brain area that is phylogenetically older than the area necessary to process a PSG. In order to test this hypothesis, we (Friederici et al. 2006a) conducted an fMRI experiment using two types of grammars quite similar to those used by Fitch and Hauser in their experiment (see Fig. 13.2). We made the grammars a bit more complicated, but not too much. Note that we have two conditions, namely short and long sequences. This should allow us to see whether the difficulty or length of these particular sequences could be an explanation for a possible difference between the two grammar types. In our study, unlike the study with the cotton-top tamarins, we decided to use a visual presentation mode. Disregarding further details,[1] what might be of interest is that we had correct and incorrect sequences in each of the grammar types, and

---

[1] For details see Friederici et al. (2006).

we had two subject groups. One subject group learned the FSG and the other learned the PSG. The subjects learned these grammars two days before entering the scanner, where they were given correct and incorrect sequences. We then compared the brain activation of the two groups.

For the group that learned the FSG, we found activation in the frontal operculum, an area that is phylogenetically older than Broca's area, for the comparison between grammatically correct and incorrect sequences (Fig. 13.3, left). However, Broca's area is not active. Interestingly enough, difficulty cannot be an explanation here because behaviorally, no difference was found between the short sequences of the FSG and the long sequences. In the imaging data a difference was observed in the delay of the activation peak with an early peak for the short, and a later peak for the long FSG sequences. But what do we find for the PSG learning group? Here again, not surprisingly, the frontal operculum is active, but now additionally Broca's area comes into play (Fig. 13.3, right). And again, when we compare the short sequences and the long sequences, difficulty does not matter. For this first study, we concluded that the processing of FSG, or more precisely what one should call it the processing of local dependencies, only recruits the frontal operculum (a phylogenetically older

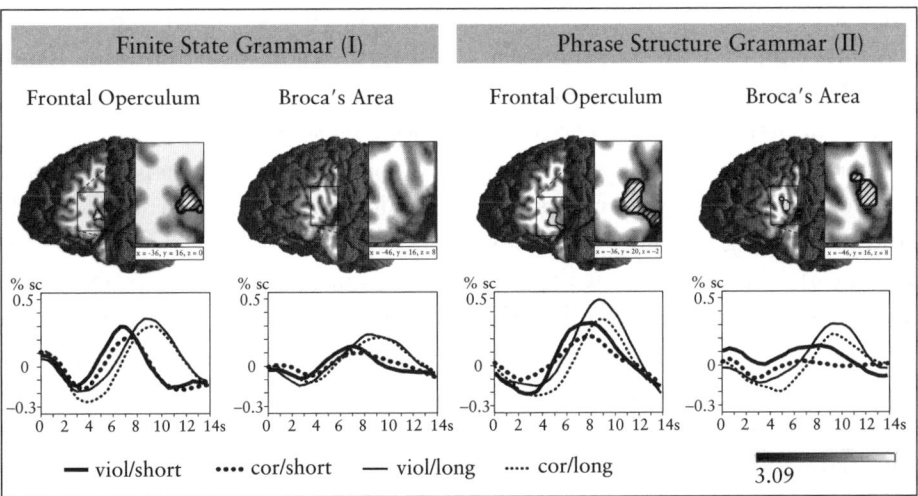

Fig. 13.3. Brain activation pattern for the two grammar types. Statistical parametric maps of the group-averaged activation during processing of violations of two different grammar types ($P<0.001$, corrected at cluster level) are displayed for the frontal operculum (FOP) and Broca's area. (*Left*) The contrast of incorrect vs. correct sequences in the FSG (Grammar I) is shown. (*Right*) The same contrast in the PSG (Grammar II) is shown. (*Bottom*) Time courses (% signal change) in corresponding voxels of maximal activation in FOP and Broca's area are displayed.

Source: adapted from Friederici et al. 2006a

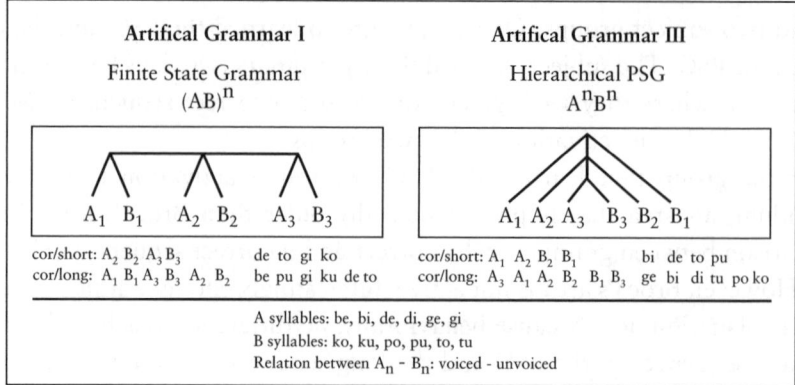

Fig. 13.4. Structure of the two grammar types. General structure and examples of stimuli of FSG (Grammar I) and hierarchical PSG (Grammar III) are displayed. Grammar III implies a rule that characterizes the dependency between related A and B elements by the phonetic feature voiced/unvoiced.

Source: adapted from Friederici et al. 2006a

cortex), whereas for the processing of minimal hierarchies as used in the present PSG, the phylogenetically younger cortex (Broca's area) comes into play.

However, there is more than one caveat to this conclusion. One argument could be the following: subjects did not really process the hierarchies, as the present PSG could be processed by a counting mechanism "plus something." I remember that Noam said this once,[2] and furthermore that this "plus something" could be memory. So, if you have a good memory, you can work with this sort of mechanism and be successful in processing such a grammar.

In order to see whether we could find a similar brain activation pattern when forcing subjects to really process the hierarchies, we conducted a second fMRI study including a more complex hierarchical grammar (Grammar III, Fig. 13.4).[3] In this study again we used two grammar types: a probabilistic and a hierarchical grammar. But the hierarchical grammar was realized such that there was a defined relation between the members of categories A and B in the sequence. In the syllables used, the consonants were either voiced or unvoiced and the fixed relation was defined over this phonological feature. This forced the subjects to establish the relation between A1 and B1, and A2 and B2. In order to learn this grammar, it took the subjects quite a bit longer (actually a couple of hours longer), but nonetheless they managed quite well after about five hours of learning. Again, learning took place two days before subjects went into the scanner, where they were given a quick refresher lesson immediately

---

[2] Discussion of a paper presented by Friederici at the Symposium "Interfaces + Recursion = Language? The view from syntax and semantics," Berlin, 2005.

[3] See Bahlmann et al. (2006) and a submitted paper.

before the scanning session. The task was once again to judge whether the sequence they were viewing was grammatical according to the rule they had learned. Moreover, and this is a second caveat you might want to raise with respect to the first experiment, we tested two different subject groups. Therefore, in the second study our subjects had to learn both grammar types in the time window of two weeks. This allowed us to do a within-subject comparison. So any difference we see now cannot be attributed to group differences. Thus, in this second fMRI study, we were able to compare directly the brain activation for the FSG and the PSG, in a within-subject design. When comparing the two grammars directly, by subtracting the activation for one grammar from the other, one should not see the frontal operculum active, because that should be active for both of the grammars. Instead, what one should see is activation in the Broca's area only.

What we found is shown in Fig. 13.5. From these functional neuroanatomical data, we concluded that two different areas (i.e., the frontal operculum and Broca's area) are supporting different aspects of sequence and grammatical processing. The frontal operculum is able to process local dependencies, whereas whenever hierarchical dependencies have to be processed, Broca's area (BA 44 and BA 45) comes into play.

However, as these two areas are located pretty close neuroanatomically in the prefrontal cortex, we thought it would be good to have additional evidence for a differentiation between these two areas in the prefrontal cortex. As one possibility, we considered structural neuroanatomy, in particular information about the structural connectivity between different brain areas. I'll explain what

Artifical Grammar III

Hierarchical PSG vs FSG
Broca's Area

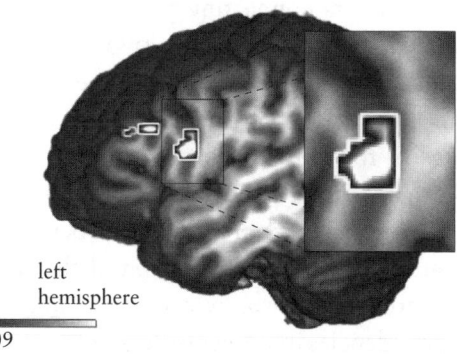

left
hemisphere

3.09

Fig. 13.5. Brain activation pattern for Hierarchical PSG (Grammar III) minus FSG (Grammar I). Statistical parametric map of group-averaged activation is shown.
Source: Bahlmann et al., in press.

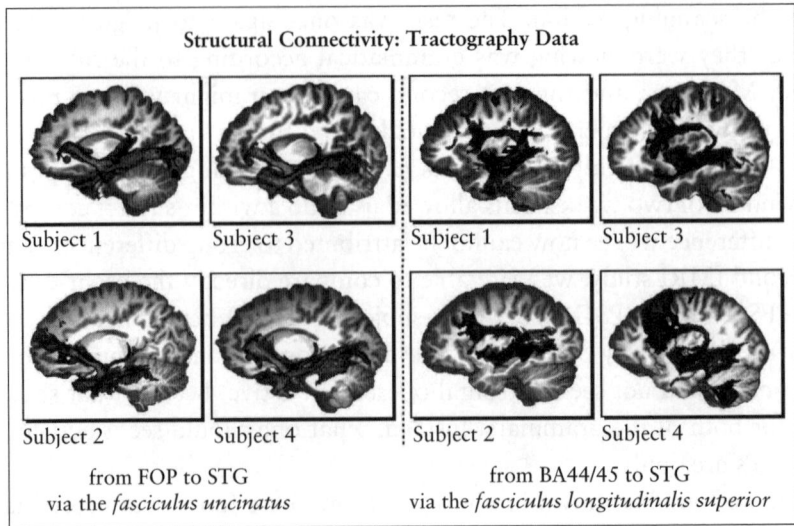

Fig. 13.6. Tractograms for two brain regions: Broca's area (BA 44/45) and the frontal operculum (FOP) for 4 different subjects are displayed. Three-dimensional rendering of the distribution of the connectivity values of two start regions with all voxels in the brain volume. (*Left*) Tractograms from FOP: the individual activation maxima in FOP as a function of the Finite State Grammar (FSG) were taken as starting points for the tractography; from the FOP connections to the superior temporal gyrus (STG) via the fasciculus uncinatus were detected. (*Right*) Tractograms from BA 44/45: individual activation maxima in Broca's area as a function of the Phrase Structure Grammar (PSG) served as starting points for the tractography: from Broca's area connections to the posterior and middle portion of the superior temporal gyrus (STG) via the fasciculus longitudinalis superior were detected.

Source: Adapted from Friederici et al. 2006a

that means. With the advent of the diffusion tensor imaging technique, we are able to image the brain fibers connecting two or more areas. Using this technique we looked at the connectivity of the two areas of interest, namely the frontal operculum and Broca's area, in order to see whether they differed with respect to their connectivity pattern (Friederici et al. 2006a). Fig. 13.6 displays the connectivity patterns for four subjects.

The left part of the figure displays the fiber tracts in four subjects, with the fiber-tractography calculation starting from the frontal operculum which connects via the fasciculus uncinatus to the anterior portion of the superior temporal gyrus (STG). Interestingly enough, we usually do see the anterior STG active in the processing of local dependencies in studies on normal language processing. On the other hand, when starting the fiber-tractography calculation in Broca's area (right part of the figure), the connecting fibers go via the fasciculus longitudinalis superior to the posterior portion of the STG, and then along the entire STG.

With these data we now have evidence for a differentiation of the two areas in the inferior frontal gyrus, not only functionally but also structurally. Basically, we can describe two separate networks, one consisting of the frontal operculum and the anterior portion of the STG, and the other including Broca's area and the posterior portion of the STG extending to the entire STG. The first network, we hypothesize, is responsible for processing local phrase structure building, while the second network may be responsible for processing hierarchical structures.

What this means with respect to the evolutionary issue is the following. The human ability to process hierarchical structures could be based on the fully developed, phylogenetically younger cortex, that is Broca's area comprising BA 44/45, whereas the older cortex, that is the frontal operculum, may be sufficient to process local dependencies.

Discussion

CHOMSKY: There were three languages. There was AB AB, $A_n B_n$, and then the third is the nested one, ABC CBA, with all the optional variations. Two questions. First, I didn't understand in the presentation whether you found a physical difference in the brain between the second type and the third type – the $A_n B_n$ and the nested one. Was there any difference between those two?

FRIEDERICI: No, for both these types of artificial languages, that is the second and the third one, we saw Broca's area activated, and I think it would be hard to make a claim of more activation in the third grammar than the second grammar on the basis of the present data because here we are looking at different subject groups. I think the conclusion from this may be that even for the processing of the second language, the $A_n B_n$, you already use Broca's area, but you certainly need it for the third grammar. So the argument that you can process the second grammar only with a simple counting mechanism perhaps cannot be ruled out, but at least for the processing of the third grammar it can.

CHOMSKY: Yes, well, there is a possible experiment here. I mean, humans do have the third type, we're sure about that. We do not know if they have the middle type. So they may only have PSG and finite state options, but not counting mechanisms. That's one possibility. So therefore, when they're doing the counting system, they may be using the richer system, which doesn't require a phrase structure grammar. The other possibility is that they also have a counting system and that it's being obscured here. But if you looked at the famous starlings, that's what you'd find, because they do not have a PSG. So is there a way to test that?

FRIEDERICI: I think the data of the third grammar may be the most conclusive of all the experiments. With respect to the second grammar I can only for the moment argue only on the basis of the similarity between the brain activation for the two grammars, that at least our subjects are not using a counting mechanism, but are going for hierarchical structure processes.

CHOMSKY: But see that's possibly in fact plausible for a subject, a human, which has the third mechanism.

FRIEDERICI: Yes, you are right, the starling data (Gentner et al. 2006) of processing the $A_n B_n$ grammar could be explained by a counting mechanism. But the prediction would be that starlings should not be able to learn the third grammar.

CHOMSKY: But you might expect that you're getting a masking effect in the humans where some might be using the counting mechanism and some might be using the richer mechanism, and get a muddled conclusion. But I'm just wondering if it's possible to tease it out? Have you done, for example, a pure counting study?

FRIEDERICI: No, we haven't done that.

CHOMSKY: That might be interesting to do, because then you could extract that out of the data for the two phrase structure types to see if they differ in that respect. The other question is just a kind of technical point. Finite state and local dependency are not the same thing. So you can have FSGs with arbitrarily long dependencies. I do not know if anybody has looked at this, but you can have a language which is $AB_n A$ and $CB_n C$, and that's an FSG but it has indefinitely long dependencies.

FRIEDERICI: Yes, but from the data we have for the moment, I think we can only draw conclusions about the local dependencies. But you are right, maybe the same sort of network also deals with the non-local probabilistic dependencies.

CHOMSKY: Just take a guess. I mean, all this confusion about finite state grammar goes back fifty years, and the things that people call FSGs are almost always ones with local dependencies. But that's just a special case. So it's possible that they're not studying FSGs at all, they're just studying kind of associationist structures, which do have local dependencies. And yes, they are a subclass of FSGs, but they're not using its capacities.

FRIEDERICI: Yes, you are exactly right, so there are at least two more experiments, if not more, that we have to do.

CHOMSKY: Notice that these are the same two mistakes. It goes way back. Technically, A_nB_n is above an FSG, so in a particular hierarchy it's a context-free grammar, but it may not be using any of the capacities of a context-free grammar. Similarly, AB AB *is* a special case of an FSG, but it doesn't tell you that when you're studying it that you're studying FSGs, in fact you're studying a special case of local FSGs, which means maybe it's just local associationist nets. I mean, that hierarchy existed for a reason, but what people have been doing for fifty years is taking sub-cases of the hierarchy and studying them and thinking they're studying the hierarchy. But they're not, because the hierarchy has different properties. So the fundamental property of context-free is your third case, nesting, and the fundamental property of finite state I do not think anybody's studied, because it does include indefinitely long dependencies. So while that hierarchy sort of made mathematical sense and so on and so forth, the psychological experiments have not been investigated. They've been investigating sub-cases of it which have different properties. And it might be worth putting all this together and studying the real properties – which you did, in fact, in the third case there.

LAKA: In the original proposal about FLN there is the suggestion that the recursion mechanism could have originated from navigation, and, as you mentioned later on, music and math perhaps use these same mechanisms. My question is whether you have run experiments or whether you are aware of studies that have looked into navigation, music, or math that might show the circuits? Secondly, do you think there might be a connection, or do you have anything to say as to electrophysiological signatures and these two circuits?

FRIEDERICI: With respect to the first question, we have done experiments on music processing, and not surprisingly, it is the Broca's area that is active. However here I must say that it is very difficult to manipulate recursion without having memory involved. So I think we have to be very careful here. There are always memory issues involved because processing stretches over a certain time. Right now we are doing mathematics and I don't have data on that, but I think it is much more easily done, because with bracketing you can easily have embeddings, and I am looking forward to those data. With respect to the electrophysiological signature, we find for the local dependencies – that is, within phrase dependencies – we do find very early negativity, which is maximal in the anterior portion of the left hemisphere. Dipole modeling of this effect using MEG shows us that we have two dipoles, one close to the frontal operculum and a second one in the anterior portion of the STG – so, exactly matching the first network I was proposing. The second network indeed involves Broca's area.[4] The involvement of the posterior portion of the STG is a bit more complicated because in the posterior STG what we usually find is activation for semantic and syntactic integration. So this may be more an integration area of semantic and syntactic information.

RIZZI: If I remember correctly, there is this literature on the activation of Broca's area in pure memory tasks, in memory tasks that are allegedly independent from language, and the question is to see if they really are. Examples would be canonical tasks, such as card identification (one, two, three, etc.). So I guess one possible interpretation of your data could be that the processing of context-free dependencies really is whatever computational capacity is in the frontal operculum plus memory. But of course there is also the opposite interpretation, which is maybe more interesting, which is that for so-called pure memory tasks, we're really using grammatical knowledge which is crucially expressed in Broca's area, so that the effect observable in card-selection type tasks is derivative, in a sense, and uses some structure that is dedicated to language but then applied in a kind of instance to other types of more abstract tasks.

FRIEDERICI: Well, happily enough, these days we can be more specific than just talking about Broca's area. I mean, there is BA 44 and BA 45. You're absolutely right, that for phonological memory issues, you get activation in Broca's area. This is the superior portion of BA 44. For our syntactic processes, we find the inferior portion of BA 44 activated, and now the question is, can you really make a secondary argument of why there should be differentiation between the inferior and the superior portions? Given that the cytoarchitectonics of this area is the same, you may not have a good argument. However, recently we have information about the receptor architechtonics of the different areas and not surprisingly to me, but surprisingly to those who look at cytoarchitec-tonics only, we find a clear separation between the inferior and the superior portions. So what we certainly need to do is an experiment within subjects where we bury phonological memory aspects and syntax.[5]

---

[4] See Chapter 22 below.

[5] Addition from June 2008. In a recent FMRI study on processing center-embedded sentences in German we varied syntactic hierarchy and memory (distance between dependent elements) as independent factors. Syntactic hierarchy was reflected in the inferior portion of BA 44 whereas working memory activated the inferior frontal sulcus. The interaction of both factors was observed in the superior portion of BA 44. The data indicate a segregation of the different computational aspects in the prefrontal cortex.

CHAPTER 14

Round Table: Language Universals: Yesterday, Today, and Tomorrow

Cedric Boeckx, Janet Dean Fodor, Lila Glertman,
Luigi Rizzi

What I will be talking about is how I think generative grammar approaches syntactic universals, and I would like to start by saying that I think the topic of linguistic or syntactic universals is actually fairly odd. A legitimate reaction upon mention of this topic could be, what else? That is, basically what we are really interested in is explanation, and not so much in statements like *there is something or other*, but rather *for all X..., such and such happens*. That is, laws, or universals.

I think that it is useful to start with an article by a psychologist in the 1930s called Kurt Lewin, who was concerned with scientific explanations in particular and tried to distinguish between two ways of going about thinking about the laws in physics, biology, and other sciences (Lewin 1935). I think that his reflections carry over to cognitive science. In particular, Lewin distinguished between Aristotelian and Galilean explanations. Aristotelian laws or explanations have the following characteristics: they are *recurrent*, that is statistically significant; they specifically (though not always) target functions, that is they have a *functionalist* flavor to them; they also *allow for exceptions*, organized exceptions or not, but at least they allow for exceptions; and finally they have to do with *observables* of various kinds. Lewin contrasts these sorts of laws or universals with what he calls Galilean laws, which are very different in all respects from Aristotelian laws. In particular, they are typically *formal* in character, and they are very abstract mathematically. They *allow for no exceptions* and they are *hidden*. That is, if you fail to find overtly the manifestation of a particular law that you happen to study, this does not mean that it is not universal. It just means that it is hidden and that we have to look at it more closely and we will eventually see that the law actually applies.

I think that the contrast between Aristotelian and Galilean laws is very relevant to the study of language because there are various ways of approaching language universals. One of the ways in which you could approach them is like what Joseph Greenberg did with his various arguments on universals. That is not the kind that I am interested in, and it is not the kind of universals that generative grammar really is interested in. The kind of typological universals that Greenberg discovered might be interesting for discovering the type of hidden universals that generative grammar is interested in, but they are not the end of the enterprise. It is worth noting that Greenberg's universals are really surfacing properties of language that typically can be explained in functionalist terms and allow for a variety of exceptions. That is, they are basically tendencies of various sorts, but that is not the kind of thing that generative grammarians have focused on in the past fifty years.

In fact generativists conceived of universals as basically properties of universal grammar (UG). This is the most general definition of universals that I could give, if you ask me what a language universal or linguistic universal (LU) is for a generative grammarian. But that definition actually depends on the specific understanding of UG, and that has been changing for the past 30–35 years. I should say though that no matter how you characterize UG, its content is defined along Galilean lines. We cannot expect universals to be necessarily found on the surface in all languages. That probably is not the case. Conversely, all languages might have a word for yes and no. (I haven't checked, but say it's true.) I don't think we would include this as part of UG, even though it is in all languages. So the understanding of universals that we have as generative grammarians is based on a theory of language that has, as I said, been changing for the past 30–35 years in many ways that do not, I think, make some people very happy as consumers because, to anticipate the conclusion that I will be reaching, the list of universals that we will reach as syntacticians or grammarians will be very refined and abstract, and not directly useful to, for example, the study of language acquisition. We should not be discouraged by that fact. This is a natural result of pursuing a naturalistic approach to language.

What I would like to stress first of all is that the study of syntactic or linguistic universals has run through various stages in generative grammar. In particular, one of the first advances that we were able to make in the understanding of linguistic universals was the distinction that Chomsky (1986b) introduced between I-language and E-language. As soon as you make that distinction, you really have the distinction between I-universals and E-universals. E-universals are the type of thing that for instance Greenberg universals could be. I-universals would be something like, for example, some deep computational principles of a very abstract sort that are only manifested in very refined and rarified phenomena. It is not something that you can observe by just walking around with a tape recorder or anything of the sort. In fact I think the study of I-universals in this sense started with "Conditions on Transformations" (Chomsky 1973), or if you want, with the discovery of the A-over-A principle – that is, an attempt to try to factor out what the abstract computational principles are, based on a fairly refined empirical view of language. It is true that "Conditions on Transformations" wouldn't have been possible before Ross's (1967) investigation of islands. It was only once you reached that very detailed empirical picture that you could try to extract from it this very abstract rule, so Galilean in nature. And so it will be, I think, with other universals.

I think that the stage of the principles and parameters (P&P) approach constitutes a serious attempt to come up with more of those universals, once you have a very good empirical map. That is, once you have attained very good descriptive adequacy, you can try to find and formulate those abstract universals. Things changed, I think, with the advance of the minimalist program, and in particular more recently with the distinction that Hauser, Chomsky, and Fitch (2002) have introduced between the narrow faculty of language (FLN) and the broad faculty of language (FLB). This further distinction basically narrows down the domain of what we take to be language, to be specifically linguistic, and that of course has a direct influence on what we take LU to be. That is, if by LU we mean specific universals for language, then we are going to be looking at a very narrow field, a very narrow set, that is FLN. And there, what we expect to find will be basically abstract general principles such as minimal search, or various refinements of relativized minimality, cyclicity, etc.

Once we reached that stage, then people began to see that perhaps those universals are not specifically linguistic, but might be generic or general principles of efficient computations belonging to third-factor properties, for example. But these would be the kind of LU that may actually be at the core of FLN. Remember that, as Chomsky has discussed recently,[1] there are basically two ways of approaching UG – from above, or from below. And these two approaches will conspire, ideally, in yielding the sources of LU, but for a while we will get a very different picture depending on which perspective we take. Notice, by the way, that if some of these LU are part of third-factor properties, then they may not be genetically encoded, for example. They may be part of general physics or chemical properties, not directly encoded in the

---

[1] Chomsky (2006).

genome. In this case, the study of LU dissociates itself from genetic nativism (the most common way of understanding the "innateness hypothesis").

The refinements that we have seen in the study of language and LU will force us to reconsider the nature of variation. In this sense, one very good and productive way of studying universals is actually studying variation.[2] Here again, recent advances in the minimalist program have been quite significant because the notion of parameter that we have currently is very different from the notion of parameter that we had, say, in the 1980s. In the 1980s we had a very rich understanding of parameters, including a fair amount of so-called macroparameters of the type that Mark Baker (2001) discussed in his *Atoms of Language*. We no longer have those macroparameters in the theory, simply because we don't have the principles on which those macroparameters were defined. However, we still have the effects of macroparameters. For example, there is something like a polysynthetic language, but I don't think we have a polysynthetic parameter, or rather I don't think we have the room for a poly-synthetic macroparameter in FLN. How to accommodate macroparametric effects in a minimalist view of grammar is a challenge for the near future. But it is a positive challenge. That is, maybe this new view of grammar is actually a good one, as I'll attempt to illustrate through just one example. Take head-edness as a parameter. We used to have a very rich structure for P&P, and one of those parameters was basically one that took care of whether complements were to the left or to the right of their heads in a given language. Now the minimalist take on UG no longer has room for such a parameter, but instead tells us that if you have a simple operation like Merge that combines alpha and beta, there are basically two ways in which you can linearize that group (either alpha comes before beta, or after). You must linearize A-B, due to the physical constraints imposed on speech, and there are two ways of doing it. Notice that there you have an effect, since you have a choice between two possibilities depending on the language, but it is no longer the case that we have to look for a parameter in the theory that encodes that. It may just be that by virtue of the physics of speech, once you combine alpha and beta, you have to linearize that set by going one way (alpha before beta) or the other way. I think that this offers new perspectives for studying parameters because LUs are different depending on your theory of language.

Now let me briefly conclude by saying that in a sense, the linguistic progress that we have seen over the past thirty years has taken us closer to a study of LU that is truly Galilean in nature. But that actually should raise a couple of flags, if language is just part of our biological world, and linguistics therefore part of

---

[2] As argued below by Luigi Rizzi (see pages 211–219 below).

biology, because biologists are typically, and by tradition, not very interested in universals in the Galilean sense; they are more interested in the Aristotelian kind of universals and tendencies. Gould, Lewontin, and others were fond of noticing two facts about biologists. First, they love details, they love diversity, the same way philologists love details. I certainly don't like diversity for its own sake. I am interested in general principles and only use the details to the extent that they can inform the study of general principles. Secondly, biologists don't usually think that there are biological laws of the kind that you find in physics, just because the world of biology is much messier than physics. But here I think linguistics has an advantage, because in a very short history (roughly fifty years) we have been able to isolate invariance amidst diversity, and this is what I was thinking of when discussing I-language vs. E-language, or FLN vs. FLB. One of the things that we have been able to do is make the study of language the study of very simple systems. By narrowing down and deepening our understanding of language we can actually exclude things that belong to details and focus on things where we can discover very deep and comprehensive principles that will be just like what you can find in Galilean laws. That is, they will be exceptionless, abstract, invariant, and hidden.

Janet Dean Fodor

For me, being asked to talk for ten minutes about universals is a bit like being asked to talk for ten minutes on the economy of northern Minnesota in 1890. That is to say, I don't know much about Minnesota and I don't know many universals either. But that's fine, because it allows me to take a very selfish perspective on the subject. I am a psycholinguist and as such it's not my job to *discover* linguistic universals, but to *consume* them.[3] I work on language acquisition, and it is very important when we are trying to understand language acquisition to assess how much children already know when they begin the task of acquiring their target language from their linguistic input. So what matters to me is not just that something is universal, but the idea that if it is universal, it can be innate. And in fact it probably is – how else did it get to be universal? So I will assume here that universals are innate, that they are there at the beginning of the acquisition process,[4] and that they can guide acquisition, increasing its accuracy and its efficiency. Language acquisition is very difficult and needs all

---

[3] I am grateful, as always, to my friend Marcel den Dikken who has exercised some quality control on my claims about syntax in this written version of my round table presentation.

[4] For evidence that some innate knowledge becomes accessible only later in child development see Wexler (1999).

the guidance UG can give it.[5] What I will do here is to highlight universals in relation to syntax acquisition. I am going to be walking into the universals store with my shopping bag, and explaining what I would like to buy for my language acquisition model, and why.

A very important point that is often overlooked is that universals (embodied in innate knowledge) play a role not only when learners are trying to find a grammar to fit the sentences they have heard, but at the very moment they perceive an input sentence and assign a mental representation to it. They have to represent it to themselves in some way or other, and it had better be the right way, because if they don't represent it correctly there is no chance that they will arrive at the correct grammar. So innate knowledge has its first impact on the acquisition process in guiding how children *perceive* the sentences in the sample of the language they are exposed to. They have to be able to recognize nouns and verbs and phrases and the heads of phrases; they have to know when a constituent has been moved; they have to be able to detect empty categories, even though empty categories (phonologically null elements) are not audible; and so forth. And that is why they need a lot of help, even before they begin constructing a grammar or setting parameters. I want to emphasize that this is so even if acquisition consists in setting parameters. In the P&P model we like to think that an input sentence (a trigger) just switches the relevant parameter to the appropriate value. But for someone who doesn't know what the linguistic composition and structure of that sentence is, it won't set any parameters, or it won't set them right. So if children get their representations right, that's a very good first step, because it will greatly limit the range of grammars that they need to contemplate as candidates for licensing the input they receive.

Learners need to know what sorts of phenomena to expect – what sorts of elements and patterns they are likely to encounter out there in this language world that is all around them. As one example, consider clitics. Children have to be alert to the possibility that they might bump into a clitic. Imagine a child who has begun to recognize that certain noises compose sentences that contain verbs and objects, and that objects consist of a noun with a possible determiner and that they normally follow (let's say) the verb, and so on. This child shouldn't be too amazed if, instead of the direct object she was expecting at the usual place in a sentence, she finds a little morpheme that seems to be attached to the beginning of the verb – in other words, a clitic. Infants need to be pre-prepared for clitics, because if they weren't it could take them a long time to catch on to what those little morphemes are and how they work. You could imagine a

---

[5] See Chapter 17 for discussion of *how* difficult it is to model what small children are doing when they are picking up the syntax of their language.

world of natural languages that didn't have any clitics, but our world of natural languages does, and infants pick them up extremely early: they are among the earliest things that they get right (Blasco Aznar 2002). So it seems that somehow they are pretuned to clitics, and to the ways in which a clitic might behave. Sometimes a clitic can co-occur with a full DP object (usually it doesn't, but it can); and there can be indirect object clitics, and locative clitics and reflexive clitics and partitive clitics; and sometimes multiple clitics have to come in a certain order before the verb, and learners should watch out for whether that order is determined by an array of properties that includes person as well as case. None of these differences from phrasal arguments seem to take children by surprise.

However, even more than being ready for what they might encounter in language, children need to have expectations about what they are *not* going to encounter. This is very important for limiting the vast number of potential hypotheses that they might otherwise entertain. Even in constrained linguistic theories which admit only a finite class of possible grammars, that still amounts to a lot of grammars for children to test against their language sample. We don't want them to waste their time on hypotheses that could not be true. Let's consider an example of movement, such as:

(1)   Which of the babies at the daycare center shall we teach ASL?

There is a missing (i.e., phonologically null) indirect object between *teach* and *ASL*, and an overt indirect object (*which of the babies at the daycare center*) at the front of the sentence, not in its canonical position. Let's suppose a learner has put two and two together and has recognized this as a case of movement: the indirect object has moved to the front of the sentence. Now why has it moved to the front? Please imagine that this is the first time that you have ever encountered a sentence with overt movement (you are a very small child), and you think perhaps the phrase was moved because it is a plural phrase, or because it is an animate phrase, or a focus phrase, or because it is a very long phrase – or, maybe, because it is a wh-phrase. Some of these are real possibilities that a learner must take seriously: in Hungarian questions, a wh-phrase is fronted because it is a focus; in Japanese a wh-phrase can be fronted by scrambling, motivated by length or by its relation to prior discourse. But other ideas about what motivated this movement are nothing but a waste of time; an infant without innate assistance from UG might hypothesize them and then would have much work to do later, to establish that they're incorrect and start hypothesizing again. So it helps a great deal to know in advance what *couldn't* be the case. To help us think this through, I'm going to make up my own universal principle: in natural language, there is no such thing as a process of fronting plural noun phrases. That is to say: a plural noun phrase may happen to be fronted, but not because it's plural; number is not a motivating factor for movement. Maybe I'm wrong, but let's pretend for the moment that this is a guaranteed universal. Then it is good for children to know it, because that makes one less hypothesis they will have to explore.

Similar points apply at all stages of learning. Imagine now a child who has correctly hypothesized that the noun phrase in our English example was fronted qua wh-phrase, not because it is plural, etc. He still needs to know how far he can generalize from this one instance, how broad he should assume this wh-fronting phenomenon to be. Do all wh-phrases front in this language? Or is it only [+ animate] wh-phrases that do, or only non-pronominal wh-phrases, or wh-phrases with oblique case, etc.? I'll assume here that part of the innate knowledge that children have is that wh-movement is sometimes sensitive to case; there are languages in which nominative but not accusative arguments can move in relative clauses.[6] But I'm supposing that wh-movement is never sensitive to number. So if a child hears a question with a singular fronted wh-phrase, he can safely assume that it is equally acceptable to have plural fronted wh-phrases, and vice versa: number is not even a conditioning factor on movement (at least, on A-bar movement). This is another fact that is very useful to know; it eliminates another hypothesis the child would otherwise have wasted time on. Note that it's a quite specific fact. There are other phenomena which are constrained by number. Obviously, anything involving number agreement is bound to be, but also some unexpected things. For example, the construction:

(2)   How tall a man is John?

has no plural counterpart. You can't say:

(3)   *How tall men are John and Bill?

That's not English. Nor is:

(4)   *How tall two men are John and Bill?

where it's clear that the movement of *how tall* isn't vacuous. So there is an odd little bit of number sensitivity here. A wh-adjunct like *how tall* can be fronted within its DP (which is then fronted in the clause), but that process *is* sensitive, it seems, to singular vs. plural. There are also phenomena that, unlike wh-movement,[7] are sensitive to whether a constituent is pronominal. In some

---

[6] This is one interpretation of the Keenan–Comrie hierarchy (Keenan and Comrie 1977).

[7] Pesetsky (1987) notes that what conditions phenomena such as superiority effects in wh-constructions is discourse-linking, not pronominality, even though the two may be related.

Scandinavian languages, for example, scrambling treats pronouns differently from non-pronominal elements. So here too, there's specific information that a learner would benefit from knowing in advance.

The general point is that if learners didn't have innate knowledge about which properties can and cannot condition wh-movement or any other linguistic phenomenon, then they would have to check out all the possibilities just in case. Many of you have probably read Steven Pinker's first book on language acquisition.[8] It is a very fat book, because what Steve was trying to do in it was to show how a child would set about checking all the possible hypotheses about which features condition a linguistic phenomenon. One of several examples he worked on was the English double NP dative construction, comparing acceptable and unacceptable instances such as:

(5) I gave Susan the book.

(6) *I donated the library a book.

The second example can only be expressed as *I donated a book to the library*, with a prepositional phrase. Which verbs permit the double NP? It takes an enormous number of pages to explain how the child would check out, one by one, all the possible features and feature combinations that might govern the extent of the double NP pattern. According to what was being proposed at that time, the key features were that the verb had to be monosyllabic (or to be of Germanic, not Romance origin; or to be prosodically one foot), and its semantics had to be such that the indirect object became the possessor of the direct object of the event described in the sentence. Pinker noted that the range of *potential* constraints on lexical alternations is large and heterogeneous, and you can imagine how far down in the child's priority list this particular combination of constraints would be. Clearly it would take a substantial amount of testing (as Pinker illustrates in detail) to discover which are the properties that matter in any particular case. Worse still: in the absence of innate guidance, a learner could imagine that there might be equally idiosyncratic phonological and semantic conditions on *any* linguistic pattern observed in the input. There would be no way to find out without trying. To be on the safe side, therefore, the child would have to go through the whole laborious procedure of checking and testing in every case – even for phenomena to which no such conditions apply at all. Surely this is not what children do. But if they don't, then it seems they must have advance knowledge of what sorts of conditions might be relevant where (e.g., no language requires the verb of a relative clause to be monosyllabic).

---

[8] Pinker (1984). For an updated approach seeking more principled and universal constraints, see Pinker (1989).

I do not know precisely how UG prepares children for acquisition challenges such as these. But that is what I am shopping for. I want to know how UG could alert children in advance to what is likely to happen in their target language, what could happen, and what definitely could not. A learner who overlooked a conditioning feature on a rule would overgeneralize the rule. And it is not just rules that are the problem; the same is true in a parameter-setting system if it offers competing generalizations over the same input examples. Overgeneralization can cause incurable errors for learners who lack systematic negative evidence. It follows that learners should never overlook a conditioning feature. But we have also concluded that they can't afford to check out every potential feature for every linguistic phenomenon they encounter. Concrete knowledge of what can and cannot happen in natural languages at this level of detail would thus be very valuable indeed for learners. Yet linguists interested in universals and innateness mostly don't map out facts at this level of detail. Why not? Perhaps just because these undramatic facts are boring compared with bigger generalizations. To be able to propose a broad structural universal is much more exciting. But another reason could be that these facts about what can be relevant where in a grammar don't seem to qualify as true universals – perhaps not even as parameterized universals unless parameters are more finely cut and numerous than is standardly assumed.[9] Therefore it appears that we may need a different concept, an additional concept, of what sorts of linguistic knowledge might be innate in children, over and above truly universal properties of languages. To the extent that there are absolute universals, that's splendid for acquisition theory; it clearly contributes to explaining how children can converge so rapidly on their target language. No learning is needed at all for fully universal facts. But it may be that there are also "soft" universals; that is, universal tendencies that tolerate exceptions though at a cost. This would be a system of markedness, which gives the child some sort of idea of what to expect in the default case but also indicates what can happen though it is a little less likely, or is a lot less likely, or is very unlikely indeed.

There certainly has been work on syntactic markedness. Noam has written about it in several of his books, including in his discussions of the P&P model,[10] but not a great deal of research on markedness has actually been done in this framework.[11] We don't have a well-worked-out system of markedness principles that are agreed on. Some linguists are leery of the whole notion. Markedness can be very slippery as a linguistic concept. What are the criteria for something being marked or unmarked? What sort of evidence for it is valid?

---

[9] See Kayne (1996).

[10] Chapter 1 of Chomsky (1981) and chapter 3 of Chomsky (1986b).

[11] For discussion of syntactic markedness within Optimality Theory see Bresnan (2000) and references there.

(Is it relevant how many languages have the unmarked form? Is the direction of language change more compelling? Or tolerance of neutralization, or ease of processing, etc.?[12]) On the other hand, if we could manage to build a marked-ness theory, it would provide just what is needed to reduce labor costs for learners. It can chart the whole terrain of possible languages, with all potential details prefigured in outline to guide learners' hypotheses. Perhaps this is extreme, but my picture is that all of the things that can happen in a natural language are mapped out innately, either as absolute principles with param-eters, or with built-in markedness scales that represent in quite fine detail the ways in which languages can differ.[13] What learners have to do is to find out how far out their target language is on each of the various markedness scales. They start at the default end, of course, and if they find that that isn't adequate for their language sample they shift outward to a more marked position that does fit the facts.[14]

To illustrate how this would work, let's consider which verbs are most likely to bridge long-distance extraction, such as wh-movement out of a subordinate clause. In some languages no verbs do: there is no long-distance extraction at all. In languages that do have long-distance extraction, the bridge verbs will certainly include verbs like *say* and *think*. English allows movement of a wh-element over the verb *say* in an example like:

(7)   Who did you say that Mary was waving to?

In some languages, such as Polish, that's about as far as it goes; there is movement across *say* but not across *consider* or *imagine*. In English the latter are acceptable bridge verbs, and perhaps also *regret*, but we draw the line at *resent* and *mumble*. It seems that there is a universal list of more-likely and less-likely bridge verbs, and different languages choose different stopping points along it – although we may hope that it is not a mere list, but reflects a coherent semantic or focus-theoretic scale of some sort.[15] If children were innately equipped with this scale, Polish learners could acquire extraction over *say* without overgeneralizing it to *imagine*, and English learners could acquire extraction over *say* and *imagine* without overgeneralizing it to *resent*. A differ-ent scale seems to control which verbs permit the passive. It's not the same set

    [12] See Chapter 1 of Klein (1993).

    [13] Chomsky (1981: 8) writes: "outside the domain of core grammar we do not expect to find chaos. Marked structures have to be learned on the basis of slender evidence too, so there should be further structure to the system outside of core grammar. We might expect that the structure of these further systems relates to the theory of core grammar by such devices as relaxing certain conditions of core grammar...".

    [14] See the "tidemark" model in Fodor (1992).

    [15] See Erteschik-Shir (1997).

in every language, but it also doesn't differ arbitrarily. In all languages the verbs most likely to passivize are action verbs like *push* or *kill*. Languages differ with respect to whether they can passivize perception verbs. We can do so in English, for example:

(8)   The boy was seen by the policeman

but many languages cannot; perception verbs are evidently further out than action verbs on the markedness scale for passive. Further out still are verbs of possession and spatial relation. Another example concerns the contexts in which binding-principle exceptions are possible, such as local binding of pronouns. This is extremely unlikely in direct object position, but less unlikely for oblique arguments of the verb; the more oblique an argument is, the less tightly the binding theory seems to hold. Thus a learner can fairly safely ignore the possibility of binding exceptions in some contexts, and yet know to keep an eye out for them in other contexts.[16]

My conclusion is that if we insist on absolute universals only, we will forgo a great deal of wisdom that all of us possess, as linguists, concerning the "personality" of natural language. We have to assume, I think, that children have that knowledge too, because otherwise they couldn't do the formidable job they do in acquiring their language. So here is my plea, my consumer's request to the "pure" (theoretical and descriptive) linguists who work on universals: Please tell us everything that is known about the sorts of patterns that recur in natural languages, even if it is unexciting, even if it is squishy rather than absolute, even if it has the "scalar" quality that I've suggested, so that we can pack it all into our learning models. They will work a whole lot better if we can do that. If we bring these facts out into the open, not just the rather small number of absolute universals, and the parameters that allow for broad strokes of cross-language variation, but all the many partial and minor trends, we will thereby strengthen the innateness hypothesis for language acquisition. I should add one comment on that last point, however. For my purposes, my selfish consumer purposes, it doesn't matter at all whether the universal trends are specific to language or whether they are general cognitive tendencies. They may be narrowly language-bound in origin, or very general psychological or biological propensities. It would be of great interest to know which is the case. Certainly we should look to see whether some of the curious trends I have cited can be derived from more general underpinnings, linguistic or otherwise. But as long as they exist, whatever their source, they will do what's needed for psycholinguistics to explain why it doesn't take a child a lifetime to learn a language.

---

[16]   See J. D. Fodor (2001).

Lila Gleitman

I would like to back up a little and point the conversation toward the case of the child learning the meaning of a word – a theme which came up in Noam Chomsky's discussion earlier in this conference, and also, in a very different way, in Wolfram Hinzen's talk about arguments and adjuncts.[17] Here's the problem. It's obvious that in deciding on the meaning of a new word, we rely at least in part on the extralinguistic situation, the context in which the word is being uttered. What's obvious, though, is only *that* this is so. What is not obvious and, rather, lies almost altogether beyond our current understanding is *how* this is so, or even how it *could be* so. The information that children – or any learners – get from the world about the meaning of a new word is often flimsy, certainly variable, and not infrequently downright misleading. This is perhaps most poignant in the case of verbs and their licensed argument structures. I got interested in this problem about thirty years ago when Barbara Landau and I studied language acquisition in a congenitally blind child (Landau and Gleitman 1985). We were very startled to discover that the first verb in this child's vocabulary, at two years old or maybe even slightly younger, was *see*, and her usage seemed much like our own from the start, referring to a perceptual accomplishment. That is, this child never seemed to have confused *look* or *see* with *touch*, even though, given her perceptual capacities, she herself necessarily touched as a condition for seeing. This case dramatizes the fact that while it is true that situational context commonly fits the intended interpretation, most of the explanatory burden for understanding learning rests on the infant's ability to represent that context "in the right way." In this instance, the contexts of the teacher/speaker (the sighted adult community) and the learner aren't even the same ones. In this brief discussion I want to illustrate the issues by showing you some findings from Peter Gordon (2003) demonstrating prelinguistic infants' remarkable capacities and inclinations in regard to the meaningful interpretation of events.

In Gordon's experiments, infants of about 10 months of age (who as yet utter no words) are shown videos depicting what to adults would be *giving* or *hugging* events. In the former case, a boy and a girl are shown approaching each other; one hands a stuffed bear to the other, and then they part. In the latter video, the two approach each other, embrace, and then part. The clever part of this manipulation is that in the *hugging* scene as well as in the *giving* scene one of the two actors is holding the stuffed bear. So crucially there are three entities involved in a motion event, in both cases. The only difference between the two events is that only in the *give* scene is this toy transferred from one participant's

---

[17] See Chapters 2 and 9 above.

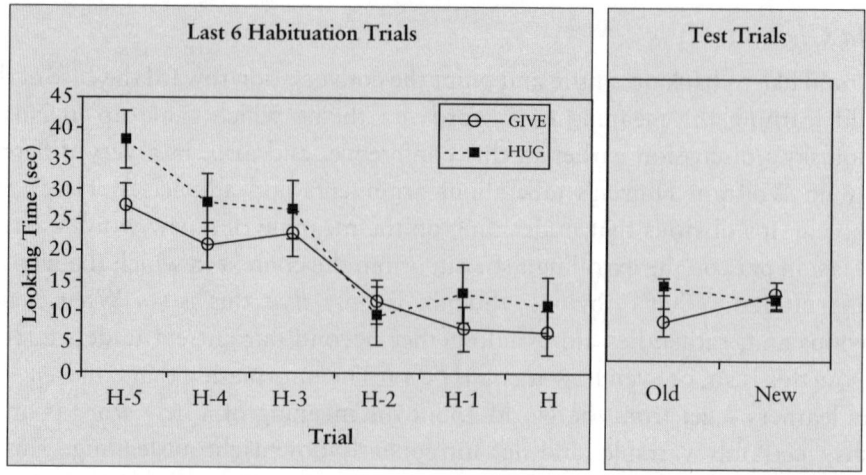

Fig. 14.1. Habituation effects for argument versus adjunct: This figure graphs habituation in infants who are watching either a scene depicting *giving* or *hugging* (panel a). When a toy animal that one character is carrying is subsequently removed from the video, dishabituation is observed for the *giving* video but not for the *hugging* video (panel b).

Source: Courtesy of P. Gordon, 2003

grasp to the other's. Gordon recycled these videos so that infants saw them again and again, leading to habituation (measured as the infant spending less and less time looking at the video at all, but rather turning away). Any individual baby in this experiment saw only the *give* scene or only the *hug* scene. Once babies were habituated, they viewed new scenes that were identical to the originals except that the toy was now absent.

As you see in Fig. 14.1, babies dishabituated (started visually attending again) in response to the new (toyless) *give* scenes but not to the new (toyless) *hug* scenes. Gordon also tracked the babies' eye movements to various scene elements during the course of the events. What is shown in the next two Figures is the proportion of time that the babies visually attended to the three entities – the boy, the girl, the toy – as the event unfolded in time, specifically, before, during, and after the two actors interacted.

For the *give* scene (Fig. 14.2) visual attention is heavily attracted to the toy as the actors encounter each other; and when the toy is removed the infants persist in looking at the actors' hands – where the toy used to be – as though searching for it. In contrast, they did not seem to notice the toy very much when it was there in the *hug* scene, as Fig. 14.3 shows.

No more did they seem to notice when it magically disappeared. That is, they hardly looked toward the hand of the hugger who previously had held it, nor provided other measurable signs that they were thinking, "Whatever happened

Eye Tracking for GIVE video

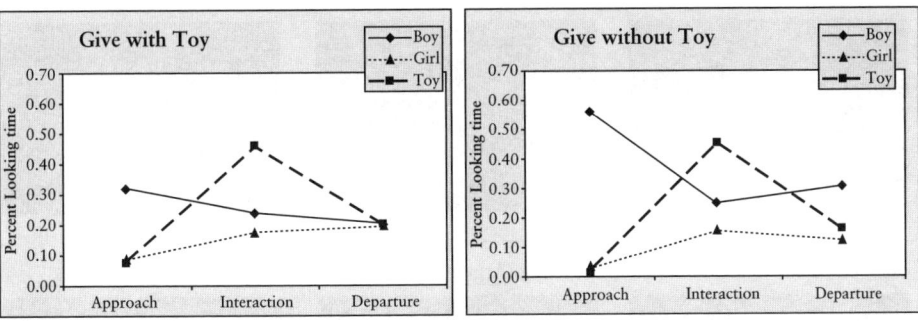

Fig. 14.2. Visual attention to argument change: This figure shows eye-tracking records for infants to the toy animal in the *give* scene as the characters approach, contact each other, and depart (panel 1) and the persistence or enhancement of visual attention when the toy (that which is given) subsequently disappears (panel 2).

Source: Courtesy of P. Gordon, 2003

Eye Tracking for HUG video

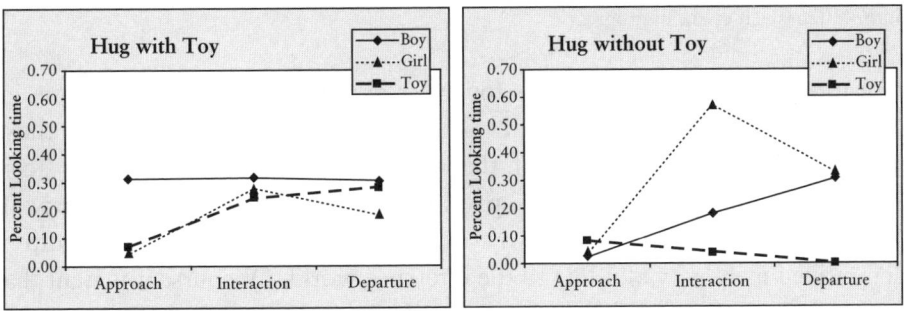

Fig. 14.3. Visual attention to adjunct change: Visual attention is diffuse across the characters in the *hug* scene (panel 1) but shifts to the hugger (the boy) and huggee (the girl) when the toy disappears. The toy itself is largely ignored (panel 2).

Source: Courtesy of P. Gordon, 2003

to that delightful stuffed animal?" Apparently, the babies' implicit supposition was that, even though stuffed bears are of great interest in everyday life, *hugging* events are not "relevantly" changed as a function of whether one of the huggers is holding one of them during the performance of this act. But an act of *giving* is demolished if the potential gift does not change hands. Bears are no more than adjuncts to *hugging* but they can be arguments of *giving*.

In one sense these charming findings are unsurprising. Of course it would have to be the case that infants could recognize these entities and represent their roles differently as a condition for acquiring *hug* and *give*. But we are very much lacking in any detailed knowledge of the conditions or procedures that underlie

Hugging (<u>Adjunct</u> Change):

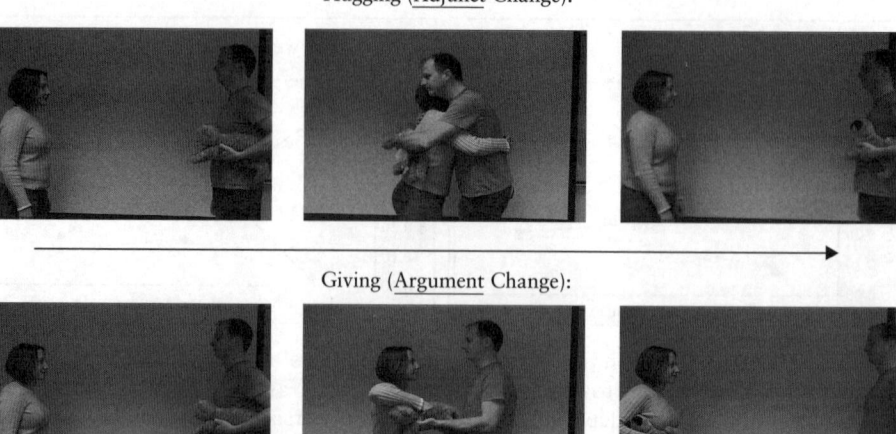

Giving (<u>Argument</u> Change):

Fig. 14.4. A change-blindness manipulation: A stuffed cat turns into a dog as it is transferred from the man to the woman.

Source: Trueswell et al., in progress

evocation of these representations for the sake of word learning. How does an infant – or for that matter an adult – select relevant representations from those made available by inspection of the world that accompanies speech acts? I believe that many developmental psychologists breezily beg or at least trivialize the questions and puzzles here by suggesting that word learning is at bottom demystified merely by alluding to the reference world. Of course it is right that in significantly many cases there is plenty of information around. The issue that Noam Chomsky has sometimes termed the "poverty of the stimulus" problem isn't always, or perhaps even usually, that there isn't any potential information. On the contrary, the problem is usually that there's enough information to drown in – sometimes I have even called this the "richness of the stimulus" problem. To understand word learning at all we have to get a lot more specific about how the relevance problem in word learning is solved with such laser-like accuracy by mere babes. To return to the present example, how does one know enough to ignore a bear held aloft while hugging?[18]

Some useful directions of research, inspired by Gordon's work, try to extend and generalize his procedures for older children and adults by using a change-blindness paradigm. Notice in Fig. 14.4, which shows three temporal points

---

[18] In Chapter 16 I discuss some first steps that I and many colleagues have tried to take in these regards.

within events, that the animal changes into another at the time of interaction. Pilot findings suggest that this change is more noticeable for *giving* than for *hugging* (Trueswell et al., in progress).

More generally, observation of the reference world, while informative for word learning, seems hardly ever to be sufficient unless the category encoded is of a basic-level object (cf. Rosch 1978). In other cases, a mosaic of conspiring cues – each of them inadequate or even obfuscating by itself – from the situation and from the surrounding speech event are exploited by learners young and old to converge almost errorlessly on the lexicon of the native tongue.

Language invariance and variation

Luigi Rizzi

In this short presentation, I would like to focus on how linguists deal with the problem of invariance and variation in natural language. If you describe and compare languages, you observe that some properties are constant and other properties vary across languages. Then the question is how we can express what is universal and what are the observed patterns of variation. The theoretical entities that are used to address this issue are the concepts of Universal Grammar and particular grammars. These concepts have undergone significant development in the last twenty-five years or so. Let us briefly go through these developments. The "traditional" approach for me, the one that I studied when I first entered the field, is the Extended Standard Theory of the early and mid-seventies. The approach is really focused on the concept of particular grammar. A particular grammar is a set of precise formal rules that are related to constructions. So the particular grammar of English, for example, is a set of rules about the form of, let's say, active sentences, passive sentences, questions, imperatives, relatives, and so on. This set of rules somehow represents, in an intrinsic manner, the knowledge of the language that the speaker has intuitively. In addition to particular grammars there is a general entity, Universal Grammar (UG), which in the framework of Extended Standard Theory would be considered a kind of grammar metatheory: if a particular grammar is a theory of a language, UG is a theory of the theory of the language. So UG specified, in this way of looking at things, the format of grammatical rules – that is, what the ingredients are that you may expect to find in the rules of specific languages. And then there were certain general conditions on rule application, like Chomsky's A-over-A Principle, principles expressing empirical generalizations like Island Constraints, and so forth.

There was a theory of language acquisition that went with this framework, more or less explicitly, according to which the language acquisition process is actually a process of rule induction. That is to say, the child, equipped with the notions of UG, has to figure out on the basis of experience what the properties are of the particular rule system pertaining to the language he is exposed to. So there is a process of rule induction, the determination of a particular rule system on the basis of experience.

There were a number of problems with this approach. One had to do with the difficulty of basing comparative syntax on this way of looking at things. What happened was that linguists would write a formal grammar concerning a particular language, and then when they started analyzing the next language, basically they had to start from scratch and write another system of rules that was in part related to the previous one, but it was truly difficult to pull out the properties that the two systems had in common. That was something that I experienced very directly because my first attempt to do syntactic research was basically to adapt to Italian what Richard Kayne had done about French. I came up with a system of formal rules for certain Italian constructions that had a sort of family resemblance to the rules that Kayne had proposed for French, but it was really hard to factor out the common properties (Kayne 1975).

Then, one major problem with this approach had to do with the acquisition model, because there weren't clear ideas on how rule induction would work.

Things changed around the late 1970s with Chomsky's lectures in Pisa (Chomsky 1981),[19] which gave rise to his 1981 book *Lectures on Government and Binding*, articulating the principles and parameters approach, based on very different ideas. The key notion really became UG, which was construed as an integral component of particular grammars: UG was conceived of as a system of principles which contain some parameters, some choice points expressing the possible cross-linguistic variation; particular grammars could be seen as UG with parameters fixed or set in particular ways. This went with a particular model of language acquisition. Acquiring a language meant essentially setting the parameters on the basis of experience. This is not a trivial task, as a number of people including Janet Fodor, for instance, have observed. In a number of cases the evidence available to a child may be ambiguous between different parametric values, there are complex interactions between parameters, etc. Still, in spite of such problems, parameter setting is a much more workable concept than the obscure notion of rule induction was. And so language acquisition studies blossomed once this model was introduced, and modern comparative syntax really started. For the first time there was a technical

---

[19] On the origins of parameter theory see also Baker (2001), and the introductory chapter of Chomsky (2003).

language that could be used to express in a concise and precise way what languages have in common and where languages differ.

Let me just mention for our non-linguist friends a couple of examples. One fundamental parameter has to do with basic word order properties. In some languages, VO languages, the verb precedes the object, as in English, for example, *love Mary*, or in French *aime Marie*. Other languages have OV, Object Verb order: Latin is one case, Japanese is another. If we are to deal with these properties we need at least a principle and a parameter. The principle is Merge, the fundamental structure-building procedure:

(1)   Merge: . . . A . . . B . . . → [A B]

It basically says "take two elements, A and B, string them together, and you will have formed a new linguistic entity, [AB] in this case." But then we need some kind of parameter to account for the difference between, let's say, English and Japanese, having to do with linear order. In some languages the head (the verb) precedes the complement, while in other languages the head follows the complement:

(2)   Head precedes/follows complement

This simple ordering parameter has pervasive consequences in languages which consistently order heads and complements one way or the other. So, two examples like the English sentence (3a) and its Japanese counterpart (3b) differ rather dramatically in order and structure, as illustrated by the two trees (4a) and (4b):

(3)   a. John has said that Mary can meet Bill
        b. John-wa [Mary-ga   Bill-ni   a- eru-   to]   itte-aru
           John-TOP [Mary-NOM Bill-DAT meet-can- that] said-has

English expressions have a fundamentally right-branching structure, Japanese expressions a fundamentally left-branching structure, not the perfect mirror image because certain ordering properties (such as the order subject–predicate) remain constant, but almost the mirror image.

We have broad parameters of this sort, having to do with the ways in which Merge works, and parameters on the other basic operations. The other fundamental operation is Move, so there are parameters on movement. Some languages have properties like Verb Second having to do with the fact that the inflected verb always occupies the second position (German, for instance, has this property), and the parameter basically amounts to the fact that there are two slots in the left periphery of these languages which must be filled by movement, one by the inflected verb and the other by any constituent. A third

(4) a.

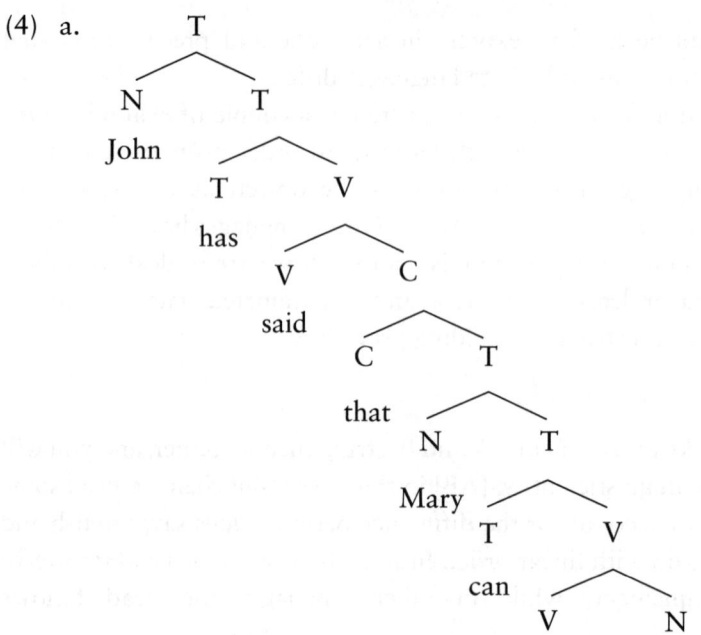

b.

kind of parameter has to do with Spell-out. There are certain elements that can or must be left unpronounced in particular configurations in some languages. One classical case is the Null Subject parameter: subject pronouns can be left unpronounced in languages like Italian, Spanish, etc. You can say things like *parlo italiano* ('*(I) speak Italian*') for instance, and this property relates in a non-trivial manner to other properties of the language (Rizzi 1982 and much subsequent work).

So the question that arose at some point, after a few years of development of these ideas, was how to express the format of these parameters. Is it the case that anything can be parameterized, or is there a specific locus for parameters? The first idea on the locus for parameters was that parameters were expressed directly in the structure of principles. This was probably suggested by the fact that the first parameter that was discussed in the late seventies had to do with a particular locality principle, Subjacency, the parameterization involving the choice of the nodes that would count as bounding nodes, or barriers for locality (the S/S′ parameter) (Rizzi 1978). On the basis of this case, it was assumed for some time that maybe parameters were generally expressed in principles, and that could be the general format. Among other things, this assumption gave a certain idea on the important question of how many parameters one should expect in UG. As the UG principles were assumed to be reduced in number, if parameters were expressed in the structure of principles one could expect an equally reduced number of parameters.

This view was abandoned fairly quickly, for a number of reasons. One reason was that some principles turned out not to be parameterized. There are certain things that don't vary at all, certain principles do not allow for any sort of variation. In no language, as far as we know, does a structure like the following

(5)   He thinks that John is crazy

allow for coreference between *He* and *John* (principle C of the Binding Theory). That seems to be a general, invariable property of referential dependencies, and many other principles seemed to work like that.

The second reason was that some macroparameters, big parameters initially assumed to characterize basic cross-linguistic differences, turned out to require reanalysis into clusters of smaller parameters. One case in point was the so-called Configurationality parameter. Some languages have a much freer word order than other languages. Originally it was thought that there was a major parameter dividing languages with free word order vs. languages without free word order, essentially. But it quickly turned out that there are different degrees of free word order: some languages are freer in the positioning of the subjects, others are freer in the reordering of the complements (scrambling), etc. You have a continuum – not in a technical sense, but in the informal sense that there are different degrees of freedom, so that the big "non-configurationality" parameters really needed to be divided into smaller parameters.

The third reason was that some parametric values turned out to be intimately related to specific lexical items. For instance, consider the Long-Distance Anaphor parameter – the fact that certain reflexives roughly corresponding to English *himself* in some languages allow for an antecedent that is not in the same local clause (in Icelandic, for example). This turned out to be the specific property of certain lexical items: if the language has such special lexical items, that is, anaphors of a certain kind, then these anaphors work long-distance. So, we are not looking at a global property of the grammatical system, but simply at the presence or absence of a certain kind of item in the lexicon. These considerations led to the general view that parameters are not specified in the structure of principles, but rather are properties specified in the lexicon of the language. In fact, assuming the fundamental distinction between the contentive lexicon (nouns, verbs, adjectives, elements endowed with descriptive content), and the functional lexicon (determiners, tense, mood, aspect specifications, auxiliaries, complementizers, etc.), parameters could be seen as specifications in the functional lexicon. So, a reasonable format for parameters would look like the following:

(6)　H has F

where H is a functional head, and F is a feature determining the possibility of one of the major operations, either Merge or Move or Spell-out, essentially. This is the general format of parameters that seems to be justified. This view implies important differences with the view expressing the parameters in the principles. For instance, the order of magnitude of parameters is now related not to the number of principles, but to the size of the functional lexicon.

If you take certain approaches, like the cartographic approach (Belletti 2004; Cinque 1999, 2002; Rizzi 2004), assuming very rich functional structures, the implication is that there can be a very rich system of parameters. Much recent work on the cartography of the left periphery of the clause has led to the identification of a rich system of functional heads corresponding to the C (complementizer) domain, a system delimited by Force and Finiteness and hosting positions for Focus, different kinds of Topics, preposed adverbials, operators for the various A′ constructions, etc. (see various papers in Belletti 2004, Rizzi 2004). And the cartography of the IP structure has uncovered a very detailed functional system for the clausal structure, with dedicated heads of Modality, Mood, Tense, Aspect, and Voice; similar conclusions hold for the structure of major phrases, DPs, etc. (Cinque 1999 and various references in Belletti 2004 and Rizzi 2004). Putting together the theory of parameters, some minimalist assumptions on linguistic computations, and cartography, we end up with something like the following typology of parameters:

(7) For H a functional head, H has F, where F is a feature determining H's properties with respect to the major computational processes of Merge, Move, and Spell-out. For instance:

Merge parameters:	– what category does H select?
	– to the left or to the right?
Move parameters:	– does H attract a lower head?
	– does H attract a lower phrase to its Spec?
Spell-out parameters:	– is H overt or null?
	– does H license a null dependent?

So we have parameters determining the capacity of a functional head to undergo merge: what categories does it select; and does it take complements to the left or to the right?[20] And perhaps even more fundamental properties, such as: does the language use that particular functional head? It may be the case that (certain) heads of the cartographic hierarchy may be "turned on" or "turned off" in particular languages.

Then we have Move parameters. Heads function as attractors: they may attract a lower head which incorporates into the attractor, or a phrase which moves to the attractor's specifier. So, does the tense marker attract the lexical verb, as it does in the Romance languages but not in English or most varieties of Continental Scandinavian? Does a head of the complementizer system attract the inflected verb, as in V-2 languages? And does the head attract some phrase to its specifier position, as the C head in V-2?

And then we have Spell-out parameters, having to do with the phonetic realization of the elements involved. Is a particular head overt or not? For instance, the topic head is realized in some languages (one particular use of Japanese *wa* seems to be analyzable along these lines), but not in others (e.g., in Romance Clitic Left Dislocation). And does a head license null dependents? For instance, does the verbal inflection license a null subject? That is one of a number of possible ways of looking at the null subject parameter in current terms.

This is the general picture that many people assume at present. Now, as there are many more parameters than we originally thought, it turns out that the different parametric choices will enter into various complex kinds of interactions,

---

[20] In the approach of Kayne (1994), the head-complement ordering property is in fact restated as a movement parameter.

generating many possible configurations of properties, so that the superficial diversity to be expected is great. Nevertheless, the deductive interactions between principles and parameters still are quite tight, so that there are many logical possibilities that are excluded even in a system which has a richer parametric specification of the kind I am describing.

I would like to conclude with a brief discussion of the reanalysis that Guglielmo Cinque (2005) proposed of one of the universals that Joseph Greenberg (1963) had identified in his very important work in the sixties. Greenberg had observed that if you look at a variety of languages, you notice that certain elements that enter into the structure of the nominal expressions can vary in order, although there are limits to order variation. If we limit our attention to cases in which the noun is either at the beginning or at the end of the string of modifiers, we basically find three types. One type is realized by English and by the Germanic languages in general, where the order is demonstrative, numeral, adjective, noun (Dem Num Adj N) giving something like:

(8)   these three nice books

One also finds quite a few other languages in which the order is the mirror image: N Adj Num Dem. Thai has that property, so a noun phrase in Thai has the order

(9)   books nice three these

– an exact mirror image to English. Then, by restricting our attention to cases in which the noun is either final or initial, a third case that is found, instantiated by the African language Kikuyu, is N Dem Num Adj, like English except for the fact that N is at the beginning of the string:

(10)   books these three nice

Apparently, we never find the fourth logical possibility given this pattern, that is to say, a language which would be like Thai, with a mirror-image order of adjective, numeral, and demonstrative, but with the noun in final position (*Adj Num Dem N):

(11)   *Nice three these books

Now Guglielmo Cinque (2005) has shown that this systematic gap can be derived from very reasonable computational principles. Just in a very simplified manner, what we can say is that we can take the Germanic order as the basic order. So (8) – demonstrative, numeral, adjective, noun – is the initial, first-merge order. Other orders can then be derived by Move, but movement is always driven by movement of the noun, so that the noun may move alone, and then you get a structure like

(10), with the same order of elements as in English except that the noun has moved stepwise to initial position. Or you have another possible instance of movement, which some linguists have called Snowballing Movement. The noun moves step-wise, but at each step it pied-pipes the whole structure it has moved to, a procedure which ends up producing the mirror-image effect. In this case, you start with something like the English order, you move the noun to the left of the adjective, and now you take the newly-created constituent, noun plus adjective, to the specifier of the numeral, and so on. If you repeat this movement a number of times, you obtain the exact mirror image of the Germanic order. But there are no other possibilities. Particularly, one cannot get the order in (11) because the noun is in final position in this case, which indicates that the noun has not moved, but noun movement is the engine of the whole process, so in the absence of noun movement the order cannot be subverted. In this case there is simply no way to get the reversal of the order with respect to the basic order. Cinque shows that the gap observed by Greenberg is not an exception, it follows from reasonable principles of linguistic computation. Following this model, it may be possible to give principled explanations to much important empirical work within the typological tradition.

In conclusion: there are more parameters than previously assumed, because parameters are properties of functional heads, and the inventory of functional heads is rich, particularly if the cartographic view is correct. Still, deductive interactions between principles and parameters are tight, and therefore the attested patterns of variation are only a fraction of the logical possibilities.

General Discussion

HIGGINBOTHAM: In relation to Luigi's point (after Cinque), you can easily derive the fact that you can say *these three nice books* but not *books nice three these* just from compositionality – you know, just from a hierarchy. It's not clear to me that we need anything else.

CHOMSKY: Part of the sequence just comes, independently of precedence and c-command, from the composition (presumably D and NP). So the D is going to remain outside anyhow, and then what is left is just the relation between *three* and *nice*. And here there seems like a fairly clear semantic property. I mean, *nice books* are a kind of books, but *three books* aren't a kind of books. There is an old paper by Tom Bever from years ago on adjectives,[21] where he tried to argue, with some plausibility, I think, that there is a kind of squishiness in adjectives and some of them are more noun-like. For instance, *red*

---

[21] Bever (1970). This is also where Bever introduced the famous garden-path sentence "The horse raced past the barn fell" that is evoked on page 287 below. (Editors' note)

can be a color, whereas *nice* can't be a something, and he argued that the more noun-like ones tend to be closer to the noun. So these kinds of considerations could be the answer to the *three nice* order, in which case you'd get the ordering.

RIZZI: Okay, so suppose you can derive the hierarchy from the needs of semantic compositionality and some related factors, as Jim and Noam suggest. This gives the Germanic order *These three nice books*. What about the other permissible orders? And the impossible one? Take the mirror image order *Books nice three these*: this could also be a direct reflection of compositionality on external merge, but here the syntactic assumptions you make become crucial. Suppose we adopt Kayne's antisymmetry, which rules out a structure like *[[[[books] nice] three] these]*: then, within Kayne's system there must be a computational procedure (snowballing movement) deriving this order from the basic order. Consider now the order *Books these three nice*: here, basically under anybody's assumptions, you need movement of N (or NP) to derive this particular order. And then you must make sure that the movement computation, which is needed anyhow, does not overgenerate, and can't give rise to the unattested order *Adj Num Dem N, a fact that Cinque plausibly tries to derive from the assumption that only N can move in this configuration (possibly pied-piping some other material), so if N doesn't move, there is no way to alter the basic order Dem Num Adj N. So, Cinque's point is that under reasonable assumptions on the fundamental hierarchy of projections in nominal expressions and on possible movement processes, one can derive the typological facts. This approach looks very plausible to me.

Then the question arises which is raised by your remarks: where does the initial hierarchy come from? Here I think it is entirely plausible that the hierarchy is grounded in semantics, that the requirements of compositional semantics impose certain orders and are inconsistent with others. The cartographic endeavor tries to determine what the functional hierarchies are for different kinds of expressions across languages, what varies and what remains constant. As far as I can tell, this is fully compatible with the attempt to trace the observed hierarchies to the interpretive considerations raised by Chomsky and Higginbotham. In fact, in my opinion, the cartographic projects and results invite such efforts to provide "further explanations" in terms of interface requirement.

PART III

On Acquisition

CHAPTER 15

Innate Learning and Beyond*

Rochel Gelman

15.1 Relevance, similarity, and attention

I usually start my presentations on this topic by asking the members of the audience to participate in an experiment. I show them slides with a pair of items and ask them to rate their similarity using a scale of 1 to 10, where 1 is, *Couldn't be less similar*, and 10 is, *Very, very similar*. Their task is simply to call out a number that reflects how similar they perceive the pair of stimuli in the slide to be. A sample stimulus pair is presented in Fig. 15.1.

As expected, they normally rate the pairs as very similar, presumably because they look very much alike on the surface. Then I inform them that the items in the slide were taken in two different places. One of the pair was taken at a zoo, and one was taken on the shelf of a store that specializes in fine ceramic copies. Now, with this as background information and a mindset that distinguishes these environments, I ask them to rate the pair of items again. This time the adult audience also does as expected: they now rate the exact same pair of stimuli as very dissimilar, switching from the top end of the similarity scale to the bottom end of it.

Let us turn now to what 3- and 4-year-olds do when they are shown the zoo and store pictures. When a child comes into the room, he finds the experimenter on her knees, surrounded by forty-two pictures, taken of twenty-one pairs of real and fabricated animals. She tells the child that she just dropped her pictures and asks if they will help to put the zoo pictures in the zoo book, and the store pictures in the store book. The child is then given the items, one at a time. Both

* Partial support for this chapter was provided by NSF ROLE Grant REC-0529579 and research funds from Rutgers University.

A   B

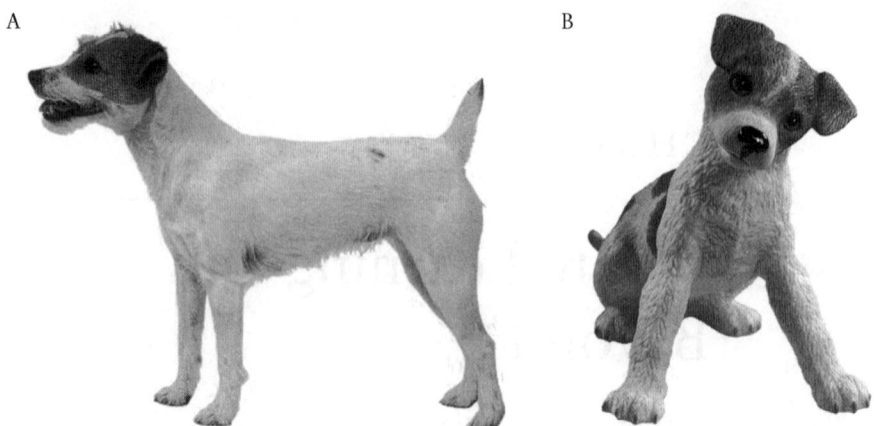

Fig. 15.1. Photographs of dogs that are similar on the surface, although one is of an animate and the other of a fabricated dog. An example of displays used in Gelman and Brenneman (2004).

age groups do this extremely well. They do not fall for the overall surface similarity as might be expected given any Piagetian, stage, or association theory about preschool competence. According to such theories, preschoolers are perception-bound. If so, our young subjects should treat pairs that are perceptually very similar on the surface as the same. Therefore their placements should be at chance. But they are not. In fact, in one such study (Gelman and Brenneman 2004), 67% and 100% of the 3- and 4-year-olds, respectively, turned in performance that met a criterion of $p < .026$. For the children to succeed on this task, they had to be able to look for details in the photographs of the live and fabricated version of the same kind that provided clues regarding their different ontological categories. But to do this, they had to have available a framework providing hints as to what constitutes relevant information for animate as opposed to inanimate objects.

Results like the above have led me to the view that there is a core domain which involves a high-level causal–conceptual distinction, one that makes principled distinctions between the nature of relevant energy sources for the movements and transformations of animate and inanimate separably moveable objects. For inanimate objects to move or be transformed, there has to be a transfer of external energy. Although animate objects obey the laws of physics, their particular motion paths and transformations are due to the generation of energy from within. I have dubbed these the Innards-Agent and External-Agent principles (Gelman et al.1995). The idea is that the children benefited from an implicit, abstract causal framework, which informs the kind of perceptual information they take to be relevant and therefore salient for descriptions of similarity and actions. Thus, the framework provides input about what kind of data are relevant to each sub-domain, in this case, cues for biological/living or inert things. The cues include ones that are relevant to the potential actions on the one hand, and potential functions, on the other hand. That is, the possible forms and details of each kind of object are part of implicit skeletal "blueprint" characterizations of the two ontological kinds.

Further evidence for this view was obtained in Massey and Gelman (1988). Children aged 3 and 4 were asked whether a series of objects could move themselves up and down a hill or whether they needed help. The objects all were novel. They included vertebrates and invertebrates, wheeled objects, statues that represented and shared parts of mythical human or animal creatures, and complex inanimate objects that resembled stick-like human figures. No graduate students could tell us what they were. Neither could the 3- and 4-year-olds, who successfully told us which objects could move by themselves both up and down a hill. What these young children said was most informative, as illustrated in the following sections from our transcripts.

> Experimenter: *Could this (a statue)* [go up the hill by itself]?
> Child: *No.*
> Experimenter: *Why not?*
> Child: *It doesn't have feet.*
> Experimenter: *But look, it does have feet!*
> Child: *Not really.*

In her own way, this child was telling us that the statue was not made up of the right kind of stuff. Another child told us that a statue was just a furniture statue, again an example from an inert category.

The results of this experiment also show that young children can use high-level, abstract causal principles, principles that outline the equivalence class of their entities, which differ for separably moveable animate and inanimate entities. Internal energy sources govern animates as well as the kinds of transformations, motions, and interactions that are permitted. External energy sources are taken as the source of the kinds of motions and transformations that inert objects exhibit. Of course animates honor the laws of physics, but they in turn have their own sources for generating goal-directed motions, responding in kind to other members of their species, and adjusting to unexpected features of the environment, such as holes, barriers, and so on (Gelman et al. 1995).

This brings me to the question of what counts as a *domain*. Randy Gallistel talked earlier about space and intentionality.[1] Simply put, a domain is a domain if

---

[1] See Chapter 4.

it has a set of coherent principles that form a structure and contains unique entities that are domain-specific. The domain of causality does not contain linguistic entities. It makes no sense to ask whether "movement" in a sentence – a linguistic variable – is due to biological energy or forces of nature. Similarly, it matters not how large an entity is when one engages counting principles (see below). When it comes to considerations of moving objects, the weight and size of an object is often paramount. To repeat: whenever we can state the principles that serve to capture the structure and the entities within it, either by themselves or ones generated according to the combination rules of the structure, it is appropriate to postulate a kind of domain-specific knowledge.

15.2 Core and non-core domains

I distinguish between *core* and *non-core domains* (Gelman and Williams 1998). The above account of a domain is neutral as to whether a given domain is innate or acquired. Like Spelke (2000), I reserve the phrase *core domain* for those that have an innate origin. I prefer to think of these as "skeletal." Of course the notion of "skeletal" is a metaphor meant to capture the idea that core domains do not start out being knowledge-rich. Nevertheless, no matter how nascent these mental structures, they are mental structures. And, like all mental structures, they direct attention and permit the uptake of relevant data in the environment. This leads me to favor structure-mapping as a fundamental learning mechanism. If we accept that young children have some core mental structures, we see that they have a leg-up when it comes to learning about the data that can put flesh on these.

Since non-core domains lack initial representational resources, it follows that learning about them will be hard. It is hard – in fact it is "hell on wheels" (HoW) – to master with understanding non-core domains. To do this, one has to both mount a structure and collect data that constitutes the knowledge in the domain. But we know that it is hard to acquire new conceptual structures. One has to work at the task for a considerable number of years and it helps to have formal tutoring. Often one's exposure to a new domain is incomprehensible. Imagine what beginning Chemistry students might think when they hear words like "bond," "attraction," and the like. They surely are not in a position to understand the technical meaning of these terms and therefore are at risk of misunderstanding them or even dropping the course. We know from research that such knowledge is the kind attributed to experts and we know that it takes a very great deal of work over many, many years to acquire expertise for any non-core domain. A characterization of non-core domains is presented below (see section 15.2.2). I now return to considerations regarding core domains from the perspective of very early learning.

Consider the domain of natural number arithmetic as an example of a core domain. Importantly, the principles of arithmetic (addition, subtraction, and ordering) and their entities (numerons and separate, orderable quantities) do not overlap with those involved in the causal principles and their link to separably moveable animate and inanimate objects. As a result examples of relevant entities and their properties are distinctly different. For no matter what the conceptual or perceptual entities are, if you think they constitute a to-be-counted collection of separate entities, you can count them. It is even permissible to decide to count the spaces between telephone poles (a favorite game of many young American children) or collect together for a given count every person, chair, and pair of eyeglasses in a room. This is because there is no principled restriction on the kinds of items counted. The only requirement is that the items be taken to be perceptually or conceptually separable.

In contrast, when it comes to thinking about causality, the nature and characteristics of the entities really do matter. One's plans about interactions with an object will be constrained by the kind of entity it is and its environments. If the entity is an animate object, I will take into account its size, whether it can bite, its posture, how fast it can move, and so on. If I want to lift two chairs, I certainly will take into account their size and likely weight. I will do the same should I be asked to also lift the two men sitting in those chairs. I know that I do not have the kind of strength it takes to transfer the relevant energy to lift and move the men in the chairs. I might be able to lift the chairs by themselves. So when it comes to considering the conditions under which objects move, their material, weight, and size do matter. This contrast accomplishes what we want – an a priori account of psychological relevance. If the learner's goal is to engage in counting, then attention has to be paid to identifying and keeping as separate the to-be-counted entities, but not the particular attributes of these, let alone their weight.

Similarly, if the learner's goal is to think about animate or inanimate objects, then attention has to be given to the information that provides clues about animacy or inanimacy: for example, whether the object communicates with and responds in kind to like objects, moves by itself, and is made up of what we consider biological material. Food surely is another core domain. We care about the color of a kind of food, even if we rarely care about the color of an artifact or countable entity. In this regard, it is noteworthy that children as young as 2 years of age also take the color of food into account (Macario 1991).

15.2.1 *What are core domains?*

(1) They are *mental structures*. However skeletal, they actively engage the environment from the start. This is a consequence of their being biological, mental organizations. As a result they function to collect domain-relevant data and hence provide the needed memory "drawer" for the build-up of knowledge that is organized in a way that is consistent with the principles of the domain.

(2) They help us solve the problem of *selective attention*. This avoids the common circular argument that selective attention is due to salience and salience directs attention. To repeat, potential relevant candidate data are those that fit the equivalence class outlined by the principles of the domain. It is the principles of the domain that offer the definition of the relevance dimensions.

(3) They are *universal*. To say that a core domain is universal is not to say that everyone will have the exact same knowledge or that learning about the domain will occur in one trial. It is well to keep in mind that linguists who assume that there are universal principles that support language acquisition do not expect children to learn their language in one trial. Further, variability across languages is taken for granted. Still, the assumption is that there are innate principles that help the child solve the learnability problem. My appeal to the universality of some small set of core domains should be thought of as being in the same vein. The principles serve to outline the equivalence classes of possible data. Since the kind of data a given culture offers young children varies as a function of geography, urbanization, etc., it follows that the range of knowledge about a domain will vary, just as do languages.

To appeal to universal innate principles is *not* to assume that learning does not take place. Instead, it forces us to ask what kind of theory of learning we need to account for early learnings and the extent to which these serve as bridges or barriers to later learnings. For a discussion of why the terms "innate" and "learned" are not opposites, given our theoretical perspective on learning, see Gelman and Williams (1998).

(4) They are akin to *labeled and structured memory drawers* into which the acceptable data "are attached." This provides an account of how it is possible to build up understanding of a coherent knowledge domain.

(5) They support *learning on the fly*. They do so because of the child's active tendencies to search for supporting environments – be these in the physical, social, or communicative worlds represented in the environment. The fact that learning occurs on the fly and is very much a function of what the child attends to is why many students of young children's early cognitive development have moved in this direction.

(6) The *principles of the structure and entities within a domain are implicit*. There is no claim that an infant or young child can state them, and I would bet that most adults cannot do so either, any more than they can state linguistic principles.

(7) Learning in these domains is *highly motivated* by the child. They ask relevant questions, including how a remote control works, why a parent says the car battery is dead, and what number comes after 100, 1000, etc. I well remember a little girl in a schoolyard telling me she was too busy to talk. She had set herself to count to "a million." I asked when she thought she would get there. Her reply was, "A very, very, very long time." She pointed out that she needed to eat, sleep, and probably would be very old.

Many young children's online inclinations to self-correct and rehearse are part of their overall tendencies to put into place the competencies that are within their purview. Examples of young children self-correcting their efforts or even rehearsing what they have just learned are ubiquitous in the developmental literature. A common report from parents has to do with their children asking "What's that?" after they have answered the question what seems like more than fifty times. Such rituals can go on for days and, then, without a clue, drop off the radar screen. In a related way, we are finding that the children in the preschools where we work are eager to have us ask more questions about unfamiliar animate and inanimate objects, no matter what the socioeconomic class represented by their families.

(8) The *number of core domains is probably relatively small*. They are only going to be as large as is necessary for us to get universal shared knowledge without formal instruction. To repeat what was presented above: just as different language communities support the acquisition of different languages, different language/cultural communities will favor differential uptake of the relevant data that they offer. Nevertheless, the underlying structure should be common – at least to start.

15.2.2 *What are non-core domains?*

(1) They are not *universal*; they have no representation of the targeted learning domain, and therefore no understanding of the data to start.

(2) They involve the *mounting of new mental structures* for understanding and require considerable effort over a very extended period of time, typically about ten years.

(3) The *number of non-core domains is not restricted*. This is related to the fact that individuals make different commitments regarding the extensive effort needed to build a coherent domain of knowledge and related skills. Success at

the chosen goal depends extensively on the individual's ability to stick with the learning problem, talents and the quality of relevant inputs, be these text materials, cultural values, and demonstrations and/or the skills of a teacher. Some examples of non-core domains include: chess, sushi-making, sailing, orchestra conductor, master chef, CEO, golf pro, car mechanic, dog show judge, discrimination learning; algebra, Newtonian physics, theory of evolution, theory of probability, composer, linguist, military general, abalone diver, and so on.

Learning about a non-core domain also benefits extensively from a teacher or master of the domain – an individual who selects and structures input and provides feedback. Still, no matter how well-prepared the teacher might be, the learner often has a major problem if she is unable to detect or pick up relationships or at least parts of relationships that eventually will relate to other relevant inputs. The task can be even more demanding if one has to acquire a new notational system, which can be hard in its own right.

Finally, early talent in non-core domains does not guarantee acquisition of expertise. It will take around ten years of dedicated work to reach the level of expert for the domain in question, be this musical composition, x-ray reading, chess, or Olympic competition, as well as a host of other areas, including academic ones. See Ericsson et al. (1993) for a review and theoretical discussion.

15.3 Early learning mechanisms

For me, the queen learning mechanism is *structure-mapping*. Given an existing structure, the human mind will run it roughshod over the environment, finding those data that are isomorphic to what it already stores in a structured way. This kind of learning of the data in a given domain need not take place in one trial. It could be that one first identifies the examples of the relevant patterned inputs and then maps to the relevant structure. Subsequently, further sections of the pattern are put in place. In any case, the details that are assimilated fit into a growing set of the class of relevant data that fill in the skeletal structure.

Importantly, input data can vary considerably on the surface, as long as they represent examples of the same principles and therefore are considered examples within the equivalence class of data that are recognizable by the principles. This carries with it the implication that the input stimuli do not have to be identical; in fact, they are most likely to be variants of the same underlying structure. Multiple examples are good for all kinds of reasons – different ways of doing the same thing, or beginning to look, compare, and contrast analogically to see if they belong together. Given an existing structure, it is possible to have online self-monitoring correction, by which I mean that the child can say "That's not right; try again." In fact, in our counting protocols, we have examples of children saying, "One, two, three, five – no, try dat again!" – for five trials, then getting it right and saying, "Whew!" Nobody told the child to do this; he or she just did it. We see a lot of this kind of spontaneous correction or rehearsal of learning that is related to the available structure.

15.4 More on core domains: the case of natural number

There is a very large literature now on whether babies or even preschoolers count or not. An ability that counts as one in the domain is arithmetic, or more precisely, natural number arithmetic on the positive integers. First of all, the meaning of a counting list does not stand alone. There is nothing about the sound "tu" that dictates that it follows the sound "won" and so on. Instead the requirements are that a list of count words follow:

(1) the *one-to-one principle*. If you are going to count, you have to have available a set of tags that can be placed one-for-one, for each of the items, without skipping, jumping, or using the same tag more than once;

(2) the *stable order principle*. Whatever the mental tags are, they have to be used in a stable order over trials. If they were not, you could not treat the last tag as

(3) the *cardinal value,* which is conserved over irrelevant changes.

The relevant arithmetic principles are ordering, add, and subtract. Counting itself is constrained by three principles. If you want to know if the last tag used in a tagging list is *understood as a cardinal number,* it is important to consider whether a child relates these to arithmetic principles; it helps also to determine how the child treats the effects of adding and subtracting.

It helps to see that count words behave differently than do adjectives, even if they are in the same position in a sentence. In Fig. 15.2, one can see that it is acceptable to say that each of the round circles is *round* or *a circle,* but one cannot say that each of the five circles is *five* or *a five circle.* The other thing we know is this: if we put several objects in front of 2-year-olds who are just beginning to speak, they are likely to label the object kind. Hence it is not clear that they are going to say "One," when there is one object. Of interest is whether it is possible to switch the child from interpreting the setting as a labeling one or one for counting. If we can switch attention, and therefore show the setting is ambiguous for the child, we might pick up some early

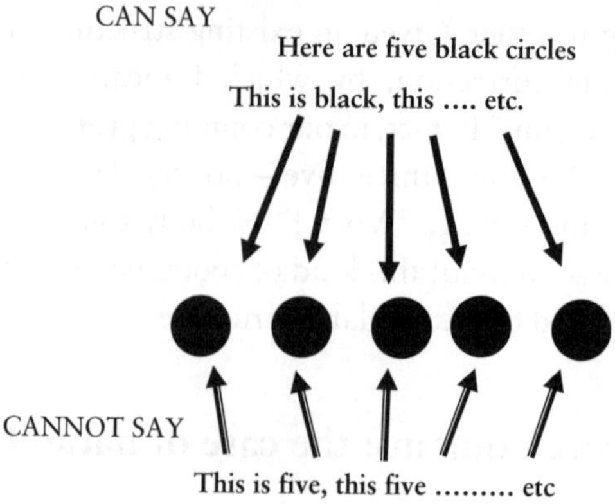

CAN SAY

Here are five black circles

This is black, this .... etc.

CANNOT SAY

This is five, this five .... etc

Fig. 15.2. A set of circles that can be labeled as five circles, black circles, or five black circles. Further, each can be called a black circle but not a five circle. This is because 'five' only refers to the set as a whole and not the individuals.

counting knowledge data. We accomplished this with a task that I call *What's on the Card?* (Gelman 1993).

We tested three age groups of children: those who ranged in age from 2 years 6 months to 2 years 11 months; 3 years 0 months to 3 years 2 months; and 3 years 3 months to 3 years 6 months. The following example of a protocol illustrates both the procedure and how our youngest children responded.

> Experimenter: *See this card? What's on this card?*
> Child: *A heart.*
> Experimenter (feedback): *That's right. There is one heart on the card.*

Next two trials first show two hearts and then three hearts in a row:

> Experimenter (with the 2-heart card): *See this card? What's on this card?*
> Child (has now shifted and taken up the instruction to shift domain mindset): *Two hearts.*
> Experimenter: *Show me.*
> Child: *One, two.*
> Experimenter: *So what's on the card?*
> Child: *Two.*

And then we get a similar pattern for three hearts. There are several points to make about the procedure. As expected, the child first answered a wh- question with a label reply. However, when offered the option to treat differently subsequent examples that showed an increasing number of the item, the child took the bait. This was so for subsequent blocks of trials with new sets of cards, each set depicting different item kinds. Indeed, the youngest age group counted and indicated the cardinal value on 91 percent of their trials.

Thus, they understood our hint that they treat the display as opportunities to apply their nascent knowledge of the counting procedure and its relation to cardinality.

What about addition and subtraction? A rather long time ago I started studying whether very young children (2 1/2 years to 5 years) keep track of the number-specific effects of addition and subtraction. In one series of experiments, I used a magic show that was modeled after discussions with people in Philadelphia who specialized in doing magic with children. The procedure is a modification of a shell game. It starts with an adult showing a child two small toys on one plate vs. three on another plate. One is randomly dubbed the winner, the other the loser. The adult does not mention number but does say several times which is the winner-plate and which is the loser. Henceforth both plates are covered with cans and the child is to guess where the winner is. They pick up a can, and if it hides the winner plate they get a prize immediately. If they do not see a winner, they are asked where it is, at which they pick up the other one and then get a prize. The use of a correction procedure is deliberate: it helps children realize that we are not doing anything unusual, at least from their point of view. This set-up continues for ten or eleven trials, at which point the children encounter a surreptitiously altered display either because items were rearranged, or changed in color, kind, or number (more or less).

The effect of adding or subtracting an object led to notable surprise reactions. Children did a variety of things; such as put their fingers in their mouth, change facial expression, start searching, and even asking for another object (e.g., "I need another mouse"). That is, they responded in a way that is consistent with the assumption that addition or subtraction is relevant, and they know how to relate them. When we do this experiment on 2-year-olds, with 1 vs. 2 and then transfer to 3 vs. 4, we get a transfer of the greater-than or less-than relationship. That is, we have behavior that fits the description of the natural number operations.

Oznat Zur developed a new procedure that involved 4- to 5-year-olds playing a game that involved putting on different hats. Each hat signaled a new game for the child and either a repeat or variation of a condition. For example, children played at being a baker by selling and buying donuts. To start, a child was given nine donuts to put up on the bakery shelf and asked how many he had. Then someone came into the store with pennies and said, "I have two pennies." The child then handed over two donuts, at which point an adult experimenter asked him to predict, without looking or counting, how many were left. After making a prediction, the child counted to check whether it was right. This sequence of embedded predictions and checks continued. The children did very well. Their answers were almost all in the correct direction. And many of their answers fell within a range of n ± 1 or 2. Further, the results were replicated in a class, the members of whom were about the same age but did not have an opportunity to play a comparable game before the experiment (Zur and Gelman 2004).

In yet another experiment, Hurewitz, Papafragou, Gleitman, and Gelman (2006) asked children ranging in age from 2 years 11 months to the late 3-year-old range to place a sticker either on a two- or four-item frame on one set of trials, or *some* vs. *many* on another set of trials. The children had an easier time with the request that used numerals as opposed to quantifiers. The word "some" gave them the most difficulties in this task, a finding that challenges the view that beginning language-learners find it harder to use numerals as compared to quantifiers.

15.5 Rational numbers are hard

I will conclude now with two contrasting numerical concepts: the successor principle and rational numbers. The successor principle captures the idea that there is always another cardinal number after the one just counted or thought about. This is because addition is closed under the natural numbers. As expected, when Hartnett and Gelman (1998) asked children ranging in age from about 6 years to 8 years of age if they could keep adding 1 to the biggest number that they could or were thinking about, a surprising number indicated that they could. Even when we suggested that a googol or some other very large cardinal number was the biggest number there could be, we were challenged by the child, who noted it was possible to add another 1 to even our number.

The successor principle is seldom taught in elementary school, whereas notions about fractions are. However, when it comes to moving on to considering rational numbers, and the idea that one integer divided by another is a rational number, we run into another example of a HoW domain. This perhaps is not surprising since there is no unique number between a pair of rational numbers. Formally, there is an infinite number of rational numbers between any two pairs of this kind of number. There is more to say about this, but I think that starts to give you the flavor that we really have moved into a different domain and that we may have a case of a conceptual change.

To end this presentation, I illustrate the kind of errorful but systematic patterns of responses we have obtained from school-aged children asked to place in order, from left to right, a series of number symbols, each one of which is on a separate card. Keep in mind that these children were given practice at placing sticks of different lengths on an ordering cloth; they were even told that it was acceptable to put sticks there of the same length but different colors and to move sticks, and then the test cards, until they were happy with their placement order. Careful inspection of the placements reveals that the children invented natural number solutions. For example, an 8-year-old started by placing each of three cards left to right as follows: 1/2, 2/2, 2 1/2, etc. The following interpretation captures these and all further placements. The child took the cards as an opportunity to apply his knowledge of natural number addition:

$$(1 + 2 = 3), (2 + 2 = 4), (2 + 1 + 2 = 5).$$

Other children invented different patterns but all invented some kind of interpretation that was based on natural numbers.

One might think that students would master the placement of fractions and rational number well before they enter college. Unfortunately, this is not the case. When Obrecht, Chapman, and Gelman (2007) asked whether undergraduates made use of the law of large numbers when asked to reason intuitively about statistics, they determined that students who could simply solve percent and decimal problems were reliably more able to do so. Those who made a lot of errors preferred to use the few examples they encountered that violated the trend achieved by a very large number of instances. This continues, unfortunately, through college. I will leave you with that. If you want to know now why your students are horrified and gasp when they are faced with a graph, it is probably because they do not understand rational numbers and measurement.

15.6 Conclusion

To conclude, humans benefit from core domains because these provide a structural leg-up on the learning problem. We already have a mental structure, albeit skeletal, to actively search the environment for relevant data – that is, data that share the structure of innate skeletal structures – and move readily onto relevant learning paths. The difficulty about non-core, HoW domains is that we have to both construct the structure and find the data. It is like having to get to the middle of a lake without a rowboat.

Discussion

HIGGINBOTHAM: There has been some interesting work in recent years by Charles Parsons on intuitions of mathematical objects – not intuitive judgment, but intuitions of the number 3.[2] What he observes is that, from some fairly simple premises, you start off making a stroke. You can envisage that it is possible that you can always add 1. If you have two sequences of strokes, then one of them is an initial segment of the other, and therefore if you took one off each one, they would be different. Now that is already all of the Peano axioms, except induction, and the question would be, when they have that, to check it by saying, "Look, here's this notation system. Can you reach any number that way?" If you can ask that question and get an answer, then you'll get the intuit, because Parsons is deliberately ambivalent or merely suggestive on this point.

GELMAN: Believe it or not, we haven't studied anything that is relevant. Before that, however, I do want to point out that I left out names of my collaborators on the study wherein young children correctly identified 2 and 4 but erred with the same arrays when their task was to identify *some* and *all*, one of whom is in the room, Lila Gleitman, and two of our post-docs at the time, Anna Papafragou and Felicia Hurewitz, who is the senior author of the paper that just came out.[3] As to your question, we ran another interview, where we said, "I am going to give you a dot-making machine that makes dots on paper and never breaks or runs out of paper. This is how many we have now. What happens if we push it (the button)? Will that be more dots on the paper?". Many children understood that the successive production of dots would never stop save for physical limits on themselves, i.e., "that that would never stop . . . [except] if you died, had to eat or go to sleep." This is an example of the nonverbal intuition about the effect of an iterative process.

HIGGINBOTHAM: Yes, to get induction, you need something more. You need the idea that for any number x, if I make enough strokes, I can get to x.

GELMAN: Yes, we didn't ask that one, but there is another one where we asked the question in the Cantorial way. That is, children who were having no trouble with our initial infinity interview were engaged in a version of Cantor's proof. We had drawings of hands in a line, each of which was holding hands with a numeral in a parallel line placed in one-to-one correspondence. We then asked whether we could keep adding hands and numerals, one at a time. This done, we went on to ask whether there were as many hands as numerals. The children agreed. In fact, they agreed at first that equivalence would hold if each person was paired with an odd number. The kids would say yes, probably because they had said yes to the first questions. "You know, they had the same answer."

---

[2] Parsons (1990).
[3] Hurewitz et al. (2006).

But then when we pointed out the contradiction, that we were skipping every even number, the reaction was, "Oh no, this is crazy, lady. Why are you wasting my time?" It probably is the case that even these children did not understand the abstract notions that follow from one-to-one correspondence. However, it is not so easy to develop a task that is free of confounding variables. The trick is to figure out exactly how to ask what you want to get at. And it isn't that easy, because you have to tell them, "I want you to tell me what the induction is," without telling them that I want you to tell me that. My bottom line? Be careful about saying that there are groups of people who cannot count with under-standing, who have only a few number words.

PIATTELLI-PALMARINI: You mentioned quantifiers versus numbers, and not surprisingly, numbers are easier than quantifiers. In fact, there is a dissertation in Maryland, by Andrea Gualmini, showing that children have a problem in understanding quantifiers until very, very late.[4] Do you have further data on the understanding of quantifiers?

GELMAN: The question of when quantifiers are understood is very much compli-cated by the task. I don't know that dissertation, but I know studies from the 1970s showing that the quantifier tasks (*all* and *some*, etc.) were not handled well until 6 years of age. We actually have been able to change the alligator task (Hurewitz et al. 2006) so that the kids do very well on *all* and *some* questions. The problem is, fundamentally, that we are talking about a set-theoretic concept. Once you make it easier, move them out of the full logic of class inclusion or one-on-one correspondence, the task does get easier, but that is in a sense the point of why I don't understand why anybody thinks the quantifiers are a primitive out of which come the count numbers. The formal rules for quantifiers, whichever formal system you go into – it is going to be different, because whatever that system is, it will have a different notation, there will be different rules about identity elements than there are in arithmetic, and the effect of adding we auto-matically know is different. I mean, if you add *some* to *some*, you get *some*. If you add 1 to 1, you don't get 1. So these are very different systems, and furthermore, the quantifiers are very context-sensitive. It depends on what numbers you are working with. So when we looked across the tasks, we could start doing task analysis, but we haven't done it completely.

URIAGEREKA: Just a brief follow-up on that. I think in principle it would be useful to bring in the notion of conservativity, which is quite non-trivial for binary quantifiers, as has been shown. So not only would you have numerals

---

[4] Gualmini (2003).

versus quantifiers, but among the quantifiers, you would have the ones where in effect you have an order restriction and a scope, versus the ones where you don't, and that probably can make a big difference too.

GELMAN: I totally agree. I should just say I have no argument with that. This is not an accidental combination of people working together. We have, now, two faculty members who specialize in quantifiers and their acquisition, and these are all issues they have written about, are going to work on, and so on. My interest was that this was a way to demonstrate experimentally what I have written about as a purely formal distinction. I had tried to show why arguments about development that involve the count words coming out of the quantifiers didn't make any sense. But that was the logical argument. It was now nice to be able to show that they do behave separately.

URIAGEREKA: This partly also relates to the claim of context sensitivity, because strictly speaking, it is when you do have to organize the part that the quantifier leaves on with regard to the scope that you need massive context sensitivity, but not the other way around.

GELMAN: Right.

CHAPTER 16

The Learned Component of Language Learning

Lila Gleitman

Isolated infants and children have the internal wherewithal to design a language if there isn't one around to be learned (e.g., Senghas and Coppola 2001). Such languages exhibit categories and structures that look suspiciously like those of existing languages. There are words like *horse* and *think*. Not only that: the mapping between predicate type and complement structure is also quite orthodox, as far as can be ascertained. For instance, even in very primitive instances of such self-made languages, *sleep* is intransitive, *kick* is transitive, and *give* is ditransitive (e.g., Feldman, Goldin-Meadow, and Gleitman 1978). This fits with recent demonstrations – one of which I mentioned during the round-table discussion (see page 207) – that even prelinguistic infants can discriminate between certain two- and three-argument events in the presence of the (same) three interacting entities (Gordon 2003). All of this considerable conceptual and interface apparatus being in place, and ("therefore") language being so easy to invent, one might wonder why it's hard to acquire an extant language if you are unlucky enough to be exposed to one. For instance, only ten or so of the required 50,000 or so vocabulary items are acquired by normally circumstanced children on any single day; three or four *years* go by before there's fluent production of modestly complex sentences in all their language-particular glory. What takes so long?

The answer generally proposed to this question begins with the problem of word learning, and is correct as far as it goes: ultimately, lexical acquisition is accomplished by identifying concepts whose exemplars recur with recurrent phonetic signals in the speech or signing of the adult community. That is, we match the sounds to the scenes so as to pair the forms with their meanings. Owing to the loose and variable relations between word use and the passing scene – the "stimulus-free property of language use," as Chomsky (1959c) famously termed this – knowledge of these form/meaning relations necessarily accrues piecemeal over time and probabilistically over repeated exposures. But in the end (or so the story goes), *horse* tends to occur in the presence of horses, and *race* in the presence of racing, and these associations eventually get stamped in. Just so. (I will return presently to mention at least a few of the questions I am begging by so saying.)

Now here is a potentially hard question. Equating for frequency of utterance in caretaker speech, and presupposing the word-to-world pairing procedure just alluded to, some words are easier to acquire than others as indexed by the fact that they show up in the earliest vocabularies of infants all over the world. One general property of these novice vocabularies illustrates this point: The first-learned 100 or so words are – animal noises and 'bye-bye's excluded – mainly terms that refer in the adult language to whole objects and object kinds, mainly at some middling or "basic" level of conceptual categorization (Caselli et al. 1995; Gentner and Boroditsky 2001; Goldin-Meadow, Seligman and Gelman 1976; Lenneberg 1967; Markman 1994; Snedeker and Li 2000). This is consistent with many demonstrations of responsiveness to objects and object types in the prelinguistic stages of infant life (Kellman and Spelke 1983; Needham and Baillargeon 2000).

In contrast, for relational terms the facts about understanding concepts do not seem to translate as straightforwardly into facts about early vocabulary. Again there are many compelling studies of prelinguistic infants' discrimination of and attention to several kinds of relations including containment versus support (Hespos and Baillargeon 2001), force and causation (Leslie and Keeble 1987), and even accidental versus intentional acts (Woodward 1998). Yet when the time comes to talk, there is a striking paucity of relational and property terms compared to their incidence in caretaker speech. Infants tend to understand and talk about objects first. Therefore, because of the universal linguistic tendency for object concepts to surface as nouns (Pinker 1984; Baker 2001), nouns heavily overpopulate the infant vocabulary as compared to verbs and adjectives, which characteristically express events, states, properties, and relations. The magnitude of this noun advantage from language to language is influenced by many factors, including ratio of noun to verb usage in the caregiver input (itself the result of the degree to which argument dropping is licensed), but even so it is evident in child speech to a greater or lesser degree in all languages that have been studied in this regard (Gentner and Boroditsky 2001). In sum, verbs as a class are "hard words" while nouns are comparatively "easy." Why is this so?

An important clue is that the facts as just presented are wildly oversimplified. Infants generally acquire the word *kiss* (the verb) before *idea* (the noun) and even before *kiss* (the noun). As for the verbs, their developmental timing of appearance is variable too, with words like *think* and *know* typically acquired later than verbs like *go* and *hit*. Something akin to "concreteness," rather than lexical class *per se*, appears to be the underlying predictor of early lexical acquisition (Gillette, Gleitman, Gleitman and Lederer. 1999). Plausibly enough, this early advantage of concrete terms over more abstract ones has usually been taken to reflect the changing character of the child's conceptual life, whether attained by maturation or learning. Smiley and Huttenlocher (1995: 20) present this view as follows:

Even a very few uses may enable the child to learn words if a particular concept is accessible. Conversely, even highly frequent and salient words may not be learned if the child is not yet capable of forming the concepts they encode . . . cases in which effects of input frequency and salience are weak suggest that conceptual development exerts strong enabling or limiting effects, respectively, on which words are acquired.

A quite different explanation for the changing character of child vocabularies, the so-called syntactic bootstrapping solution (Landau and Gleitman 1985; Gleitman 1990; Fisher 1996; Gleitman et al. 2005; Trueswell and Gleitman 2007), has to do with information change rather than conceptual change. The nature of the vocabulary at different developmental moments is taken to be the outcome of an incremental multi-cue learning procedure instead of being a reflection of changes in the mentality of the learner:

(1) Several sources of evidence contribute to solving the mapping problem for the lexicon.
(2) These sources vary in their informativeness over the lexicon as a whole.
(3) Only one such source is in place when word learning begins: namely, observation of the word's situational contingencies.
(4) Other systematic sources of evidence have to be built up by the learner through accumulating linguistic experience.
(5) As the learner advances in knowledge of the language, these multiple sources of evidence are used conjointly to converge on the meanings of new words. These procedures mitigate and sometimes reverse the distinction between "easy" and "hard" words.
(6) The outcome is a knowledge representation in which detailed syntactic and semantic information is linked at the level of the lexicon.

According to this hypothesis, then, not all words are acquired in the same way. As learning begins, the infant has the conceptual and pragmatic wherewithal to interpret the reference world that accompanies caretaker speech, including the gist of caretaker–child conversations (to some unknown degree, but see Bloom 2002 for an optimistic picture, which we accept). Words whose reference can be gleaned from extralinguistic context are "easy" in the sense we have in mind; that is the implication of point (3) above. By and large, these items constitute a stock of concrete nominals. Knowledge of such items, and the ability to represent the sequence in which they appear in speech, provides a first basis for constructing the rudiments of the language-specific clause-level syntax of the exposure language; that is, its canonical placement of nominal arguments and inflectional markings. This improved linguistic representation becomes available as an additional source of evidence for acquiring further words – those that cannot efficiently be acquired by observation operating as a stand-alone procedure. The primitive observation-only procedure that comprises the first stage of vocabulary growth is what preserves this model from the vicious circularity implied by the whimsical term "bootstrapping" (you can't pull yourself up by your bootstraps if you're standing in the boots), and is very much in the spirit of Pinker's (1984) "semantic bootstrapping" proposal, with the crucial difference that by and large the initial procedure yields almost solely concrete noun learning. Structure-aided learning ("syntactic bootstrapping"), required for efficient acquisition of the verbs and adjectives, builds upward by piggybacking on these first linguistic representations. An important implication of the general approach is that word learning is subject to the same general principles over a lifetime (for laboratory demonstrations, see Gillette, Gleitman, Gleitman and Lederer 1999; Snedeker and Gleitman 2004). For the same reasons, these principles should and apparently do apply to vocabulary acquisition in later-learned as well as first languages (Snedeker, Geren and Shafto 2007).

For the rest of this paper, I'll illustrate the explanatory power of this machinery for two kinds of case that pose principled problems for the idea that word-to-world pairing (though no doubt a necessary factor) is sufficient by itself as the information basis for vocabulary acquisition. The first case involves such perspective verb pairs as *give/get*, *chase/flee*, *buy/sell*, and the like, illustrated in Fig. 16.1. It depicts an action scene in which a dog is *chasing* a man. But literally by the same token it depicts a man who is *fleeing* (from) a dog. Suppose the adult utters a new verb – "Look! Pilking!" – in reference to such a scene. Is he or she speaking of chasing or of fleeing? Assuming that just these two interpretations come to mind, among the many that are really available and pertinent to the event, how is the listener to decide between them? At peril of belaboring the point, the next few hundreds of exposures to pursuit scenes are liable to embody the same ambiguity. Rarely do members of such pairs surface under real-world circumstances that differentiate between them. Which returns me to the problem that we are generally begging the questions at issue when we say that word-to-world pairing solves even the simplest cases of word learning –

Fig. 16.1. Dual conceptions: chasing and fleeing.

that people acquire word meanings "from" observing the world. The difficulty from the outset is that, for word learning to occur, one has to conceive of the observed world *in the right way*, under the description that fits the word that is being used. But this requirement completes the circle.

To escape from this circularity there has to be a way for the learner to focus ("zoom in" is our own favored technical term) on the right description (representation) of the scene without presupposing knowledge of the word whose acquisition is at issue. How could attention be focused on just one of these interpretations in the case of perspective verbs? For comparison, first consider another famous ambiguity, the duck-rabbit in Fig. 16.2. Perception psychologists

Fig. 16.2. Dual perceptions: duck and rabbit.

Georgiades and Harris (1997) showed that the chances of a naïve observer report-
ing seeing the duck versus the rabbit can be influenced by a subliminal visual
attention-capture cue judiciously placed on such a figure. Perhaps more surprisingly,
the same is true of chasing and fleeing depictions and other cases interpretable as
one of two paired perspective verbs, including *give* vs. *get*, *win* vs. *lose*, and *buy* vs.
sell (Gleitman, January, Nappa and Trueswell in press). Following Georgiades
and Harris, we captured our subjects' visual attention on such pictures by briefly
(60–80 msec) flashing a square on the computer screen just prior to the onset of the
picture. This square was aligned with the upcoming position of one or the other
character. Typically this caused eye movements to that character, even though the
subjects were not able to report noticing the flashed square. Fig. 16.3 exemplifies
the procedure using the intended contrast *win/lose*. This manipulation reliably
influenced the speaker's tendency in describing the scene. For the *chase/flee* case,
the tendency to describe the scene as one of chasing was enhanced when the
flash was where the dog subsequently appeared, and as one of fleeing if it was on
the man. So how the speaker "attentionally approaches" an event like this
does seem to affect its description and, consequently, verb choice.

It remains to ask how speaker choice might be related to the learning
situation for such cases. We know from the work of Dare Baldwin (1991) that
infants will attend to the direction of the speaker's gaze as a cue to the reference
of a new noun. In preliminary studies we have shown adult subjects a version of
these verbs in which a cartoon character ("John") is looking down on the scene.
"John's" eyes are directed either to the chaser or the fleer, as shown in Fig. 16.4;
and again this influences the subject's report of what she thinks John would say,
to describe the scene (Gleitman et al., in press). So here we have a hint that
social-attentive cues from the speaker might direct the listener-learner toward a

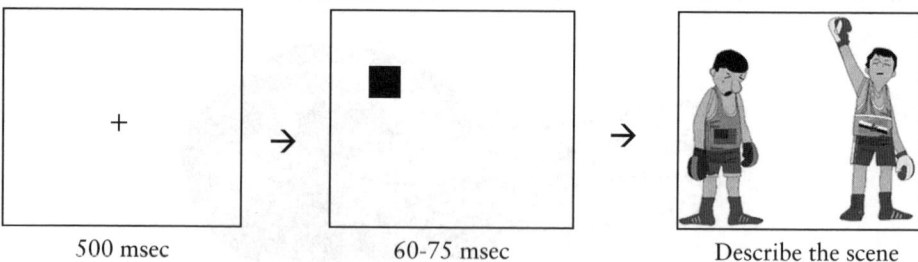

| 500 msec | 60-75 msec | Describe the scene |

Fig. 16.3. A subliminal attention manipulation: After visual fixation (panel 1), a block
is briefly flashed, situated where (on different trials) the winner, the loser, or a place in
between, will subsequently appear (panel 2). The picture then appears and the subject
describes what is seen (panel 3).

Source: Gleitman January, Nappa and Trueswell 2007

Fig. 16.4. Visual cueing of chase and flee: John's gaze direction influences subjects' utterance of chase (left image) or flee/run away (right image).

particular choice of interpretations even in these cases where on the surface the scene itself seems to provide no basis for disambiguation.

The effects of speaker-gaze direction on disambiguation of these pairs are by no means categorical even in this laboratory situation, and even with adult subjects. So I turn now to another attentional cue, evidently a more powerful one. In this experiment (Fisher, Hall, Rakowitz and Gleitman 1994) we showed 3- and 4-year-old children (and adult controls) videotaped puppet shows designed to exemplify perspective verbs, and we introduced an extra hand-held puppet, telling the children that it was a Martian puppet that talks Martian talk. We asked them if they could help us figure out what Martian words this puppet was saying. One third of the children heard the Martian (who, in company with the child subjects, was viewing the puppet show) say *Look, gorping!*; the next third of the subjects heard *Look, the skunk is gorping the rabbit!*; and the final group heard *Look, the rabbit is gorping the skunk!* The results are rendered in Fig. 16.5, collapsing across several of the scenes that the children saw and responded to. Notice first that there is a cognitive bias in all these results toward source-to-goal interpretations. This shows up strongly for both the children and adults in the no-sentence (*Look! Gorping!*) condition which does not linguistically bias the subject. For instance, *give* is heavily preferred to *get*, *chase* is preferred to *flee*, and so forth. For the subjects who heard instead *The skunk is gorping the rabbit*, this effect is enhanced – it becomes essentially categorical because the form of the sentence supports the cognitive bias. But for those subjects who heard *The rabbit is gorping the skunk*, the results reverse. The adults shift completely to the goal-to-source verb (*flee* or *run away*) dispreferred by the prior subjects. You still see the residue of the cognitive bias with the children, but the modal response has for them too now

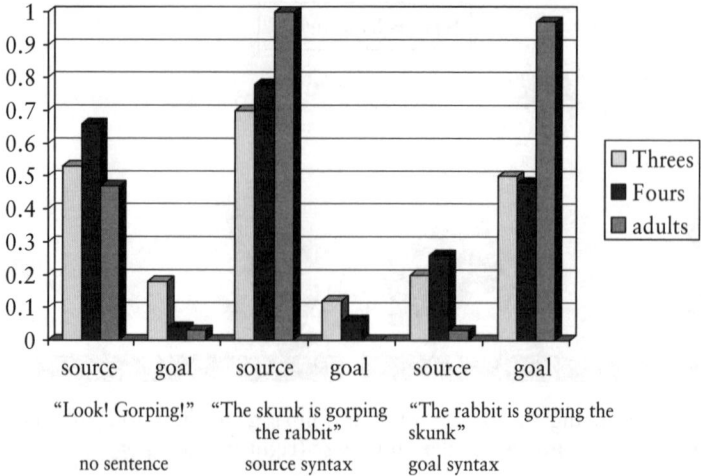

Fig. 16.5. Source versus goal by syntactic introducing context: The source is the preferred subject (e.g., the giver or chaser is preferred to the getter or evader) if the syntax is neutral. This tendency is enhanced or diminished in both adults and young children as a function of syntactic information.

Source: (Fisher, Hall, Rakowitz and Gleitman 1994)

shifted to the goal-to-source interpretations.[1] This pattern would be expected if the structural configuration chosen by a speaker is understood by the listener to reflect the speaker's attentional stance. Research on discourse coherence strongly suggests that subject position is often used to denote the current discourse center and to mark transitions from one center to another (e.g., Gordon, Grosz and Gillom 1993; Walker, Joshi and Prince 1998). This is why Fisher, Hall, Rakowitz and Gleitman (1994) described their effect as a "syntactic zoom lens" in which the structural configuration of the words in the utterance helps the child take the perspective necessary to achieve successful communication, and to infer the meaning of unknown elements in an utterance.

I want to emphasize a couple of points in wrapping up this part of the discussion. First was the idea that the word-to-world pairing procedure that is in place from earliest infancy is effective primarily for whole-object terms (Markman 1994; Gillette, Gleitman, Gleitman and Lederer 1999), accounting for the noun-dominated character of the novice vocabulary. My next ambition in this paper was to show how linguistic structure itself acts to redress these limitations once the novice (whether an infant or older language learner) has acquired its rudiments by considering the sequence of nouns against their contexts of use. To expose the problem and elements of the solution, I showed you how children and adults

---

[1] The proportions in the figure don't add up to 100% in any condition just because of the indeterminacy of what's said, given a situation. Thus children and even adults sometimes respond "They're having fun!" rather than "He's chasing him," in response to some of these scenes.

discover the interpretation of novel terms – here, the perspective verbs – whose reference is just about always ambiguous and which therefore cannot be wholly explained as observation-based learning. Because the solution to this problem must be (somehow) to draw the observer's attention toward one of the two primary interpretations, it is reassuring that attentional cues of varying kinds, including subliminal flashes but also eye-gaze direction of a cartoon figure, materially influenced these interpretations in the laboratory. Perhaps more surprising, especially in its influence on young preschoolers, is that the strongest cue of all was implicit and linguistic. They interpreted the scene in accord with the semantic information latent in the structure of the introducing sentence, specifically, according to which character captured the subject position.

It remains to say that no one of these cues (situation or syntax) can be sufficient. Obviously the subjects couldn't have learned (and therefore didn't) the meaning of "gorping" solely by hearing it used in an appropriately struc-tured sentence, any more than they could have disambiguated, say, *chase* from *flee* solely by observing the puppet shows. What does the trick for learning is the two cues working conjointly. The argument structure is revealed by the syntax, to be sure, but simultaneously the sentence is interpreted against the world to which it refers. This use of multiple cues lies at the heart of the syntactic bootstrapping procedure. With acquisition of the language-specific grammar, the learner is able to bring to bear a linguistic representation that matches in sophistication, and dovetails with, his or her natural ability to impose a predicate–argument interpretation on events. Given this narrowing of the hy-pothesis space to fit the argument-structure framework, the observed world more efficiently fills in the richer semantic content of the novel predicate.

I mentioned back at the beginning of this paper that I was going to motivate the syntactic bootstrapping approach in terms of two kinds of lexical item that pose a principled difficulty for lexical learning models that rely solely, or even very heavily, on word-to-world pairing. The first were these perspective verb pairs. Now I want to turn to the second case, which looks even harder. This is acquisition of verbs that describe unobservable acts and events, such as *think* and *believe*. Here the world is of very little value, or so it seems at first glance. You can't see thinking. And the literature tells us that these items indeed appear relatively late in the infant's verb-learning career. Even though children produce verbs describing actions or physical motion very early, often before the second birthday (Bloom et al. 1975), and appear to understand them well, they do not use mental verbs as such until about two and a half years of age (Bretherton and Beeghly 1982; Shatz, Wellman and Silber 1983) and do not fully distinguish them from one another in comprehension until around age 4. These facts are often adduced as rather straightforward indices of concept attainment (e.g., Dromi 1987;

Huttenlocher, Smiley and Charney 1983), put forward to support the view that conceptual change is what's accounting for the trajectory and contents of early vocabularies. In particular, the late learning of credal ("belief") terms is taken as evidence that the child doesn't have control of the relevant concepts, in this case the ability to entertain concepts that refer to one's own or others' mind, aka Theory of Mind. As Gopnik and Meltzoff (1997: 121) put this:

> the emergence of belief words like "know" and "think" during the fourth year of life, after "see", is well established. In this case...changes in the children's spontaneous extensions of these terms parallel changes in their predictions and explanations. The developing theory of mind is apparent both in semantic change and in conceptual change.

And in this case too I'm going to try to convince you that there is another potential explanation for why these terms are late acquired, short of saying that they are too "abstract" for young ears and minds. Specifically, I suggest that the child's problem isn't the inability to think about thinking, but only to find the evidence that the sound/word *think* is the item that expresses the concept 'think' in English: a mapping problem rather than a conceptual problem. It simply is harder to glean, by observation alone, that thinkers are thinking than that, say, jumpers are jumping. Not only is thinking invisible in the first place. Even more important, the difficulty is that it is actions that people, young and old, are inclined to think about when they interpret the world, rather than the thoughts of those performing the actions (alas, perhaps, but true nonetheless).

Now here is a parade case to introduce this topic: When one shows Rodin's famous statue, The Thinker, even to museum-knowledgeable adults and asks "What's going on here?" the respondents are disinclined to say "That's a thinker thinking." Even though, if *anything* is, this *is* a thinker thinking. They are inclined to respond instead: "He's resting his head," or "He's scratching his chin," in short to offer just about any overt act in preference to an internal one, in describing this scene – though I grant that Rodin himself was an exception to this generalization. In short this is a case of massive insalience of a concept. Nobody thinks about thinking even though it's always going on when people are around. Even here in this room, most of you are emphatically thinking, but thinking is not what you're thinking *about*. If children are to learn the word *think*, there must be circumstances in which the concept it encodes comes readily to mind.

I'll now describe just one experiment in a line we have been pursuing, focusing on this vexing class of words (Papafragou, Cassidy and Gleitman 2007; and for a theoretical review, Gleitman et al. 2005). The idea again is to assess the contribution both of syntactic cues and cues from observation. Pilot findings had provided us with the intuition that for the case of mental verbs, *it's not the truth that sets you free*. Instead, people think about thinking under

1. Lo   PILK what fimmet wifs.

2. Well, bo PILK what mippy rucky zavvy smegs
   are so far, don't bo?

3. Po PILK lo pung mo.

4. Lo PILK what lo can wif with ti?

5. Do lo PILK where the kax's lif is?

6. Do lo PILK where a fimmit is in mippy runk?

Fig. 16.6. What does PILK mean? The range of syntactic environments is revealing of the verb interpretation.
Source: Snedeker and Gleitman 2004

circumstances where someone is in a state of *false* belief. Moreover, just as was the case for the perspective verbs, there are characteristic structural environments in which such verbs leap immediately to subjects' minds. Fig. 16.6 shows an example from a study by Snedeker and Gleitman (2004). It is constructed from a random sample of mothers' natural usages of a credal verb in sentences uttered to their 18–24-month-old children, but the experimental version of these that you see here is doctored and disguised. We leave enough of the closed-class material in place so that the subject can recover the structure spontaneously, that is, without explicit instruction from us. All the other words are replaced by nonsense words. The "mystery word" (the verb) is also replaced by nonsense (in caps) and the subject's task is to recover and report its meaning, given these half-dozen *Jabberwocky*-like exemplars. People are very good at this task, evidently using the appearance of sentential complements as a giveaway clue for a credal verb interpretation.

In the Papafragou, Cassidy and Gleitman (2007) study, 4-year-old children and adults watched a series of videotaped stories with a pre-recorded narrative. At the end of each clip, one of the story characters described what happened in the scene with a sentence in which the verb was replaced by a nonsense word. The participants' task was to identify the meaning of this mystery word. The stories fully crossed type of situation (true vs. false belief) with syntactic frame (transitive frame with direct object vs. clausal that-complement) as shown in the design diagram (Fig. 16.7). For instance, in one of the false-belief stories inspired by the adventures of Little Red Riding Hood, a boy named Matt brought food to his grandmother (who in reality was a big bad cat in disguise); in the true-belief variant of the story, Matt accompanied by the big cat brought food to his real grandmother. At the end of the story, the cat offered one of these two statements:

(a) [Complement Clause condition] "Did you see that? Matt GORPS that his grandmother is under the covers!"
(b) [Transitive condition] "Did you see that? Matt GORPS a basket of food!"

	NP comp	S-comp
True belief		
False belief		

Fig. 16.7. Scene type X syntax type: This illustrates the design of an experiment in which the child hears a story in which a true or a false belief figures prominently, crossed by a verbal description in the form of a transitive construction (e.g., "The boy is eating his snack") or in a sentence-complement construction (e.g., "The boy thinks that this is his snack").

Source: Papafragou, Cassidy and Gleitman 2007

It was hypothesized that false-belief situations would increase the salience of belief states and acts and would make these more probable topics for conversation, thereby promoting mentalistic conjectures for the novel verb. It was also hypothesized that sentential complements would prompt mentalistic interpretations for the target verb. It was expected that situations where both types of cues cooperate (i.e., in the false belief scenes with a sentential complement) would be particularly supportive of mentalistic guesses. Finally, syntactic cues were expected to overwhelm observational biases when the two conflicted (e.g., in false-belief scenes with a transitive frame).

These predictions were borne out. Scene type had a major effect on the verb guesses produced by both children and adults. Specifically, false-belief scenes increased the percentage of belief verbs guessed by the experimental subjects, compared to true-belief scenes (from 7.4% to 26.5% in children's responses and from 23.5% to 46.3% in adults' responses). The effects of syntax were even more striking. Transitive frames almost never occurred with belief verbs, while complement clauses strongly prompted belief verbs (27.2% and 66.2% of all responses in children and adults, respectively). When both types of supportive cue were present (i.e., in false-belief scenes with complement clause syntax), nearly half (41.2%) of children's responses and an overwhelming majority (85.5%) of adults' responses were belief verbs.

Similar effects were obtained in a further experiment with adults, which assessed "pure" effects of syntactic environment (minus supporting content words) in the identification of mental verbs. True- and false-belief scenes were paired up with transitive or complement clause structures from which all content words had been removed and replaced with nonsense words (e.g. *He glorps the fleep* vs. *He glorps that the fleep is glexing*). Again syntax proved a more reliable cue than even the most suggestive extra-linguistic contexts. Furthermore, the combination of clausal and scene (false belief) information again resulted in an overwhelming proportion of mental-verb guesses.

Taken together, these experiments demonstrate that the syntactic type of a verb's argument (e.g., whether the object of a transitive verb is a noun phrase or a tensed sentence complement) helps word learners narrow down their hypotheses about the possible meaning of a new word. Furthermore, this type of syntactic cue interacts overadditively with cues from the extralinguistic environment (e.g., the salience of a mental state). We interpret these findings to support the presence of a learning procedure with three crucial properties: (1) it is sensitive to different types of information in hypothesizing the meaning of novel words; (2) it is especially responsive to the presence of multiple conspiring cues; (3) it especially weights the language-internal cues when faced with unreliable extralinguistic cues to the meaning of the verb.

To summarize some of the effects I've been discussing, the first general finding is that not all words are learned from the same kind of information. Certain items, including words encoding the basic-level object terms, appear early. This is one of the most robust effects in the literature of language learning, and is seen again and again cross-culturally and cross-linguistically. A popular explanation for why these items are so rapidly and uniformly learned is that they instantiate just about the only concepts that infant minds can entertain. But I have argued instead that it is these words' tractability to the first-available property of the learning procedure, word-to-world pairing, that explains why they are learned first. As support for this view, we have shown in several experiments that when adults are by experimental artifice reduced to this same information – roughly, if they are exposed to single "mystery words" in context, rather than to whole sentences in context – they too are capable of little lexical learning beyond the basic-level nominals. The information for acquiring the noun *apple* and such physical-action verbs as *jump* or *hit* resides largely in the observable world, as interpreted by both adults and very young children.

In contrast, words that describe unobservable mental states and acts are cued almost exclusively by information that resides in the semantics of syntactic structures (see Fig. 16.8, from a verb-identification task with adult subjects, which shows this effect). These adults identify action verbs largely by examining the scenes in which these are uttered, but they identify mental verbs largely from hearing nonsense-containing structures in which these occur (Snedeker and Gleitman 2004). Because children acquire the requisite (language-particular) aspects of the grammar only during the second and third years of life, they are limited until then in their word learning largely to

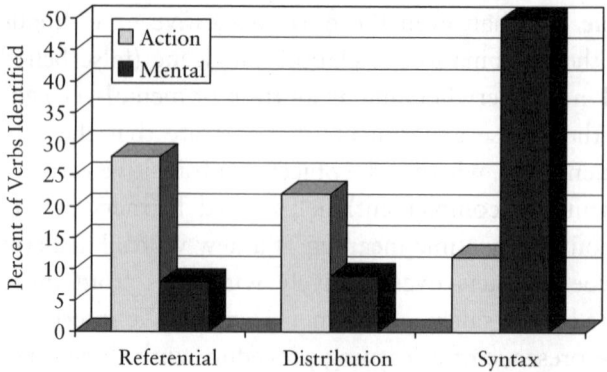

Fig. 16.8. Different verbs require different kinds of information to acquire: Referential information (the visual–situational context) provides the lion's share of information for identifying action verbs such as *jump* or *put*, but syntactic information is far more informative for mental verbs such as *think*, *see*, and *want*.

Source: Snedeker and Gleitman 2004

lexical items whose meaning can be wrested more or less directly from transactions with the referential world.

More generally, my colleagues and I have tried to explain word learning as a mapping process, one which matches sounds to their meanings. To be sure, the mapping procedure is a complex one, requiring the recruitment and integration of several kinds of linguistic and extralinguistic information. Word learners, in the special case where they are young children, may also be undergoing significant conceptual change. Even if so, these changes in mentality do not seem to be the chief limiting factors in vocabulary growth.

Discussion

PARTICIPANT: I have two questions. I think there is an important difference between saying that you need a particular structural context, a sentential complement, to solve the mapping problem for propositional attitude verbs, and saying that you need particular kinds of structural arrangements to acquire the concepts. So there are two problems: first, to solve the mapping problem for propositional attitude verbs, and for this you need a particular structural context (syntax, you said, is needed). So that is one problem. The other problem is to ask to what extent you need sentential complements – a certain structural context – to have propositional attitude concepts in the first place. To what extent is the structure actually instrumental for having the concepts in the first place? I of course would go for the latter alternative, and I was wondering about your view on that. Related to that, if you go against the conceptual change view of Gopnik (Gopnik and Meltzoff 1997) and Carey,[2] so you posit belief-type verbs in the biology (the evolution), it is obviously just pushing the problem. It's not solving any problem, I would say. So here my question is: how little Platonism do you get away with?

GLEITMAN: You are correct that there are two problems here. One has to do with where the concept *think* (or any other) comes from, how these ideas get into the mind. The second has to do with identifying the word in the exposure language that encodes each such idea; for instance, learning that *think* is pronounced /think/ in English. You, along with many others, find it congenial to suppose that hearing the sound /think/ (in some sentential context) is what – or part of what – causes the concept to grow in the mind. I myself find that position hard to understand, it seems to imbue words with some magical property. But we can't argue from what is a congenial or intuitively plausible approach on these matters, at least we won't get far that way. So, congeniality aside, what I tried to do in my talk is to show you some evidence to the effect that infant and adult word learning look very much alike. This suggests that both populations are solving the same problem, namely the mapping problem (which sound encodes the concept *think*) rather than one population solving this problem (the adults) while the other (the children) is solving two problems at once – the mapping problem and the concept acquisition problem. I tried to show you that when by experimental artifice one reduces the information that the adult has – his or her evidentiary sources for word learning – the learning trajectory and contents for child and adult look much alike. By exhibiting such laboratory effects, I invited you to consider whether information availability rather than concept availability might not hold the major key in explaining word learning.

No one doubts that there are conceptual-sophistication differences between, say, an average 3-year-old and Noam Chomsky or even the college sophomores to whom we teach *gorping* and *pilking* in the laboratory. It is the sameness in learning properties, once the task is equated for information, across these individuals and populations, that suggests that the mapping problem rather than the concept-learning problem is the chief limiting factor in word learning. But what I most wanted to show you is that observation of "the world" is insufficient as the input basis for acquiring the word /think/ – for anyone, child or adult. Even to use the situation as a constraint, one needs to narrow the search space by being told the argument-taking properties of the novel predicate. That is what the syntax does for you, and it does so for 2- and 3-year olds as well.

---

[2] Carey (1985, 2001).

PARTICIPANT: I'm not a linguist and I really want to comment on the question of language acquisition. From an interdisciplinary approach, I wanted to offer a possible alternative way of thinking about it. When for example a parent gives a child a stuffed animal, and the parent utters the sound *elephant*, the child has an experience of the joy of the moment, of possibly understanding that they are getting something and it's a toy and it's fun. Later, the parent sees an elephant on television and utters the same sound. So at this point, the child has to negotiate for a distinction. Now in another theory you look for distinctions between phenomena, but you also want to find the categories of representation. In the first case, the stuffed animal resembles an elephant – to the parent. To the child, those distinctions don't yet exist, so it could be a cat, it could be a puppy, it's a stuffed animal to the child, whatever that means to the child. The television representation actually points to an elephant in the world somewhere. So there you have this index to something in the world. Then you have a third scenario: the parent takes the child to the zoo and suddenly the child hears this same utterance while experiencing this huge object in front of him, the actual elephant in nature. It is at this point that I believe Peirce used the term *abduction*. The child is confronted with a sign, the sound *elephant*, which is used in three different contexts as a reference to an object in the world, and the child then has to negotiate the initial meaning of the sound associated with this stuffed animal, with the TV image, and now this massive object in nature. So this is where this abductive reasoning is a partial explanation of what I believe Peirce meant by abduction. This is a partial explanation of abduction where the child then has to negotiate the semantics.

GLEITMAN: Your suggested solution is a very sensible one. Your idea is to redress the insufficiencies of any one situational observation by comparing across many such observations, parsing out of scenes in which, say, /elephant/ is uttered, that which is common to all these otherwise quite variable scenarios. This cross-situational observation solution has commended itself to everyone from John Locke and David Hume to modern connectionist modelers. And as I mentioned, surely such a procedure *must* play a role, your various elephant-scenarios are probably a good sample of how this goes. Yet among the many problems of trying to do the whole job of word learning using this situation-observing procedure are the ones I concentrated on in my talk – you can't easily tell *chase* from *flee* this way because they map onto about the same scenes, and it is hard to "observe" thinking in any literal or straightforward way, no matter how many thinking scenes/utterances you are exposed to.

But there is a greater problem and that is the infeasibility of your suggested model given the rate and relative errorlessness of actual word learning. The child is learning about ten words a day. This is a very, very large number. In light of it, there doesn't seem to be enough time and varied, yet systematic, scene-observations for such a model to work, *unaided*. In fact there's considerable evidence that children are correctly inducing the meanings of words from one or a very few instances, rather than pursuing a compare/contrast procedure across many observations. And this "fast mapping" of new words goes on for a long time, probably until you're about 30–35 years of age, so you get a vocabulary of maybe 75,000 words. Though then, as we elders can tell you, it plummets [laughter]. Luckily Noam and I started with a big vocabulary [laughter].

But seriously: the speed and accuracy and persistence of word learning is something which I think influences how plausible various models should look to you. Another feature of acquisition that might influence you in this regard is the sameness of word meanings acquired by learners whose observational circumstances are wildly different, for instance, deaf, blind, and even deaf-blind persons. I and my many colleagues have offered a different solution. Though of course it involves information gleaned from word-to-world correspondences, it is not limited to this evidentiary source, at least not after the child is 18 or 24 months old and has gained some principled linguistic (as well as world) experience. What this model substitutes for sole use of a multitude of cross-cutting situational observations is a small set of exposures to a novel word, but with most such exposures *simultaneously offering evidence of different kinds*. Observations of a word's fit with the passing scene, yes, but also observations of its structural environment, its morphology, and its co-occurrence with other words (e.g., *cake* occurs more often with *bake* than with *wake*). These cues trade and conspire to overdetermine interpretation based on very small numbers of incidents during which a novel word is heard.

CHAPTER 17

Syntax Acquisition: An Evaluation Measure After All?

Janet Dean Fodor

17.1 Introduction: Evaluating grammar hypotheses

First I would like to acknowledge the contributions of my collaborators, especially my colleague William Sakas, and our graduate students. We are all part of the CUNY Computational Language Acquisition Group (CUNY-CoLAG), whose mission is the computational simulation of syntax acquisition. We have created a large domain of languages, similar to natural languages though simplified, which we use to test the accuracy and speed of different models of child language acquisition.

I will start today by taking you back to 1965, to Chapter 1 of Noam Chomsky's *Aspects of the Theory of Syntax*, which I recommend to you all. It is, I think, one of the most important fifty pages of all of the important fifty pages that Noam has written, and it is still very germane today. So that will be our beginning point, but it won't be our ending point. We are going to look at Noam's outline of a program for how to set about modeling language acquisition, and then I will tell you why we haven't actually fulfilled it. The past few decades have seen many excellent acquisition studies of real children, studies of what they know and when they know it. But our job is modeling *how* children come to know these things, and that hasn't yet progressed very far at all. I thought that this conference would be a wonderful occasion to bring a gift to Noam, so that I could say "Here, in this box wrapped up with ribbons, is the learning model that you called for in 1965." But I don't have anything to give. I'm sorry. I can offer only an apology to Noam and an excuse, which is that the problems turned out to be really difficult, much more difficult than could have been anticipated. Why that is so is what I want to explain to you today.

What Noam asked us to do back then was to consider what must be involved in any acquisition model for language. He said there must be a *representation of the input signal* (the sound waves coming to the child's ears) *in terms of linguistic derivations*. Secondly, there has to be a *specification of the class of possible grammars*, that is, all the candidate grammar hypotheses that the learner might contemplate. Third, there has to be a *method for selecting one of these grammars on the basis of the child's input*, that is, an *evaluation measure*. And that turns out to be particularly difficult. The class of possible grammars is what linguists work on, but the evaluation measure (EM) determines the sequence in which learners try out different grammar hypotheses, so it is something that psycholinguists and computational linguists should have contributed to. But we still don't have it under control. EM is important, though, as a means of explaining why all children exposed to the same language make much the same choices and arrive at much the same grammar, and why they don't get confused along the way in the vast maze of alternatives. In addition, *Aspects* Chapter 1 notes that there must be a *strategy for finding hypotheses*. Even in a tightly constrained theory, there are many, many possible grammars. (Estimating how many is easier to do in terms of parameters: if there were just thirty binary parameters, there would be more than a billion possible grammars, and that is probably an underestimate.) Because it is a huge search space, there has to be a method, as Noam observed, for finding hypotheses that fit the particular input sentences a child hears.

17.2 From rule creation to triggering

The details of the Chapter 1 blueprint for an acquisition model didn't last very long, because they were based on a notion of grammars as sets of rules and of acquisition as composing rules, and that never worked. There weren't enough constraints on the possible grammars, and there was no plausible EM for fitting grammars to the input. The next step, also from Noam (Chomsky 1981), was to shift from rule-based grammars to grammars composed of principles and parameters, which is what you have been hearing about at this conference. Languages differ in their lexicons of course, but otherwise it is claimed that they differ only in a small, finite number of parameters. (I will limit discussion to syntax here, disregarding parameters for phonology and morphology.) An example is the Null Subject parameter, which in languages like Spanish has the value [+ null subject] because Spanish permits phonologically null subjects, whereas in languages like English the setting is [− null subject] because subjects (of finite clauses) cannot be dropped. This is one binary syntactic parameter that a child must set.

The parametric model has properties that lighten the task of modeling language acquisition. Because it admits only a finite number of possible languages, the learning problem becomes formally trivial (Chomsky 1981: Chapter 1). From a psychological perspective, input sentences can be seen not as a database for hypothesis creation and testing, but as *triggers* for setting parameters in a more or less "mechanical" fashion. As Noam discussed earlier in this conference (see page 23 above), syntax acquisition then becomes simply a matter of tripping switches, a persuasive metaphor that he credits to Jim Higginbotham. A sentence comes into the child's ears; inside the child's head there is a bank of syntax switches; the sentence pushes the relevant switches over into the right *on* or *off* positions. Note that it is assumed that the triggers know which parameters to target. This will be important for the discussion that follows: the trigger sentences "tell" the learner which parameters to reset.[1] Finally, the principles and parameters model is a memoryless system, so it is economical of resources and it is plausible that a child could be capable of it. The child has to know only what the current parameter settings are, and what the current sentence is; she doesn't have to remember every sentence she's ever heard and construct a grammar that generates them all.

So the parameter model was gratefully received, a cause for celebration. But then the bad news began to come in. Robin Clark (1989) published some very important work in which he pointed out that many triggers in natural language are ambiguous between different parameter settings. One example of this is a sentence that has a non-finite complement clause with an overt subject, such as "Pat expects Sue to win." The noun phrase *Sue* has to have case, and it gets case either from the verb above it (*expect*) or the verb below it (*win*). The former is correct for English (*expect* assigns case across the subordinate clause boundary), but the latter is correct for Irish, where the infinitive verb can assign case to its subject. Thus, there is a parameter that has to be set, but this sentence won't set it. The sentence is ambiguous between the two values of the parameter. There are many other such instances of parametric ambiguity in natural language.

Parameter theory had started with the over-optimistic picture that for every parameter there would be at least one unambiguous trigger, it would be innately specified, and learners would effortlessly recognize it; when that trigger was

---

[1] Throughout this paper I will simplify discussion by assuming non-noisy input, i.e., that all input sentences are well-formed in the target language.

heard, it would set the parameter once and for all, correctly. What Clark's work made clear was that in many cases there would be no such unambiguous trigger; or if there were, a learner might not be able to recognize it because it would interact with everything else in the grammar and would be difficult to disentangle. This put paid to the notion that learners were just equipped with an innate list specifying that such-and-so sentences are triggers for setting this parameter, and thus-and-such sentences are triggers for this other parameter. Gibson and Wexler's (1994) analysis of parameter setting underscored the conclusion that triggers typically cannot be defined either universally or unambiguously.

You should bear in mind *always* that the null subject parameter is not the typical case. It is too easy. With the null subject parameter, you either hear a sentence with no subject and conclude that the setting is [+ null subject], or you never do, so you stay with the default setting [−null subject]. There are important details here that have been much studied,[2] but even so, setting this parameter is too easy because its effects are clearly visible (audible!) in surface sentences. For other parameters, such as those that determine word order, there are more opportunities for complex interactions. One parameter controls movement of a phrase to a certain position; other parameters control movement of other phrases to other positions. The child perceives the end product of derivations in which multiple movements have occurred, some counteracting the effects of others, some moving parts of phrases that were moved as a whole by others, and so on. This interaction problem exacerbates the ambiguity problem. It means that even for parameters that have unambiguous triggers, they might be unrecognizable because the relation between surface sentences and the parameter values that license them is not transparent.

To sum up: observations by Clark and others, concerning the ambiguity and surface-opacity of parametric triggers, called for a revision of the spare and elegant switch-setting metaphor. On hearing a sentence, it is often not possible, in reality, for a learner to identify a unique grammar that licenses it. At best, there is a pool of possible candidates. So either the "mechanical" switch-setting device contains overrides, such that one candidate automatically takes precedence over the others; or else the switches aren't set until after the alternatives have been compared and a choice has been made between them. In either case, this amounts to an evaluation metric within a parameter-setting model. A second important consequence is that triggering cannot be error-free. When there is ambiguity in the input, the learner cannot be expected always to guess the right answer. Thus, the original concept of triggering, though it was an

---

[2] Extensive research was initiated by Nina Hyams (1986).

extremely welcome advance in modeling grammar acquisition, proved to be too clean and neat to fit the facts of human language, and it did not free us from having to investigate how the learning mechanism evaluates competing grammar hypotheses. A problem that will loom large below is that evaluation apparently needs access to all the competitors, in order to compare them with respect to whatever the evaluative criteria are (e.g., simplicity; conservatism versus novelty; etc.), but it is unclear how a triggering process could provide the comparison class of grammars.

17.3 From triggering to decoding

All of this explains why, if you check the recent literature for models of parameter setting, you will find almost nothing that corresponds to the original Chomsky–Higginbotham conception of triggering. There are still parameters to be set in current models, but neither the mechanism nor the output of triggering has been retained. Instead of an "automatic" deterministic switching mechanism, which has never been computationally implemented, it is assumed that the learner first chooses a grammar and then tests it to see whether it can license (parse) the current input sentence; if not, the learner moves on to a different grammar. This is a very weak system, and limits the ways in which the learner can select its next grammar hypotheses. A triggering learner, when it meets a sentence not licensed by the current grammar, shifts to a grammar that is similar to the current one except that it licenses the new sentence. That seems ideal, but current models do otherwise. For Gibson and Wexler's (1994) system the principle is:

(1)　If the current grammar fails on an input sentence, try out a grammar that differs from it by any one parameter, and shift to it only if it succeeds.

For Yang's (2002) model it is:

(2)　If the current grammar fails on an input sentence, try out a grammar selected with probability based on how well each of its component parameter values has performed in the past.

Notice that in neither case does the input sentence guide the choice of the next grammar hypothesis. These are trial-and-error systems, quite unlike triggering not only in their mechanics but also with respect to the grammar hypotheses they predict the learner will consider.

By contrast, at CUNY we have tried to retain as much of the triggering concept as is possible. Although the "automatic" aspect has to be toned down, we can preserve another central aspect, which is that the input sentence should tell the learner which parameters could be reset to license it. In a sentence like *What songs can Pat sing?*, the *wh*-phrase *what songs* is at the front. How did it get there? In English, it got there by Wh-Movement, but other languages (Japanese, for example) can scramble phrases to the front, including *wh*-phrases. So as a trigger, this sentence is ambiguous between different parameter settings. Nothing can tell the learner which alternative is correct, but ideally the learner would at least know what the options are. We call this *parametric decoding*. The learning mechanism observes the input sentence and determines which combinations of parameter values *could* license it. Then it can choose from among these candidates, and not waste time and effort trying out other grammars that couldn't be right because they're incompatible with this sentence. Parametric decoding thus plays the extremely important role of guiding the learner towards profitable hypotheses. The only problem is that nobody knows how decoding can be done within the computational resources typical of an adult human, let alone a 2-year-old.

Our own learning model, called the Structural Triggers Learner, can do *partial* decoding. It uses the sentence-parsing routines for this. We suppose that a child tries to parse the sentences he hears, in order to understand them. For a sentence (a word string) that the current grammar does not license, the parsing attempt will break down at some point in the word string. At that point the parsing routines search for ways to patch up the break in the parse tree, and in doing so they can draw on any of the other parameter values which UG makes available but which weren't in the grammar that just failed. The parser/learner uses whichever one or more of these other parameter values are needed to patch the parse. It then adopts those values, so that its current grammar is now compatible with the input. For any given input sentence, this decoding process delivers *one* grammar that can license it. But it does not establish *all* the grammars that could license an ambiguous sentence, because to do so would require a full parallel parse of the sentence to find all of its possible parse trees. That is almost certainly beyond the capacities of the human parsing mechanism. The bulk of the evidence from studies of adult parsing is that the parser is capable only of *serial* processing, in which one parse tree is computed per sentence and any other analyses the sentence may have are ignored.[3]

The limitation to serial parsing entails that the learner's parametric decoding of input sentences is not exhaustive. Partial decoding is the most that a child can

---

[3] Parallel parsing is severely limited even in parsing models that permit it. See Gibson and Pearlmutter (2000); also Lewis (2000).

be expected to achieve. But partial decoding is not good enough for reliable application of EM, because among the analyses that were ignored by the parser might be the very one that the EM wants the learner to choose. In some other respects, partial decoding is clearly better than none. Our simulation experiments on the CoLAG language domain confirm that decoding learners arrive at the target grammar an order of magnitude faster than trial-and-error models. But for our present concern, which is how learners evaluate competing grammar hypotheses, partial decoding falls short. It is unclear how EM could be accurately applied by a learning device that doesn't know what the set of candidate grammars is. So in a nutshell, the verdict on parametric decoding is that only full decoding is useful to EM but only partial decoding is possible due to capacity limits on language processing. Explaining how learners evaluate grammars is thus a challenge for acquisition theory.

17.4 The Subset Principle as test case

In what follows I will use the Subset Principle (SP) as a test case for evaluation in general. SP is a well-defined and relatively uncontroversial component of the EM. It has long been a pillar of learnability theory and needs little introduction here. It is necessitated by the poverty of the stimulus – yet another major concept that Noam has given us. At CUNY we split the poverty of the stimulus (POS) into POPS and PONS (Fodor and Crowther 2002). POPS is *poverty of the positive stimulus*, meaning that learners don't receive examples of all the language phenomena they have to acquire, so they have to project many (most) sentences of the language without being exposed to them. A dramatic example is parasitic gaps, discussed by Noam in *Concepts and Consequences* (Chomsky 1982) and *Barriers* (Chomsky 1986a). More pertinent for today is the *poverty of the negative stimulus* (PONS), which is extreme. Children typically receive little information about what is not a well-formed sentence of the language, certainly not enough to rule out every incorrect hypothesis that they might be tempted by (Marcus 1993). Because of this, learning must be conservative, and SP is the guardian of conservative learning. Informally, the idea is that if a learner has to guess between a more inclusive language and a less inclusive language, she should prefer the latter, because if necessary she can be driven by further input sentences to enlarge a too-small language, but without negative evidence she could never discover that the language she has hypothesized contains too many sentences and needs to be shrunk. More precisely, SP says:

(3) When there is a choice to be made between grammars that are both (all) compatible with the available input sample, and the language licensed by one is a proper subset of the language licensed by the other, do not adopt the superset language.[4]

SP is essential for learning without negative data. Without it, incurable over-generation errors could occur. So it is evident that learners have some effective way of applying it. Our job is to find out how they do it – or even how they *might* do it, overcoming the technical snags that evaluation seems to face.

17.5 Enumeration of grammars

To get started, I must take you on another historical detour back to the 1960s. The work of Gold (1967) provides a straightforward and guaranteed solution to the problem of applying SP. Gold, a mathematical learning theorist, was not concerned with psychological reality, and you may well find his approach hopelessly clunky from a psychological point of view. Certainly it has not been taken seriously in any treatment of SP with psycholinguistic aspirations. But since it works, it is worth considering *why* it works and whether we can benefit from it. I will suggest that we can. Gold's approach needs a certain twist in order to make it psychologically plausible, but then it can solve not only the problem of how to apply SP but also another quite bizarre learnability problem that has never been noticed before: that under some very familiar assumptions, *obeying* SP can cause a learner to fail to arrive at the target grammar (Fodor and Sakas 2005).

Gold assumed an *enumeration* of all the possible grammars, in the sense of a total ordering of them, meeting the condition that a grammar that licenses a subset language is earlier in the ordering than all grammars licensing supersets of it. All the other grammars, not involved in subset-superset relations, are interspersed among these in an arbitrary but fixed sequence. (I will assume here that each grammar appears in the ordering just once.) The learner's hypotheses must respect this ordering. The learner proceeds through the list, one grammar at a time, moving on to consider a new grammar only when the preceding one has been disconfirmed by the input. The learner *thereby* obeys SP, without having to actively apply it or to know what the competing grammars for a given input sentence are. No decoding is required. The learner simply takes the next grammar in the sequence and finds out whether or not it can license

---

[4] From now on, for brevity, I will use "subset" and "superset" to mean "proper subset" and "proper superset" respectively.

(parse) the current sentence. Of course, learning in this fashion is a very slow business in a domain of a billion or more grammars, as the learner plods through them one by one. Steven Pinker wrote a very instructive paper in 1979 in which he admonished against trying to create psychology out of enumeration-based learning techniques. He wrote (p. 227): "The enumeration procedure ... exacts its price: the learner must test astronomically large numbers of grammars before he is likely to hit upon the correct one." After reviewing some possible enhancements to a Gold-style enumeration he concluded (p. 234), "In general, the problem of learning by enumeration within a reasonable time bound is likely to be intractable." From our CoLAG perspective, enumeration-based learning is an especially frustrating approach because it extracts so little goodness from the input. It has no room for parametric decoding at all. It proceeds entirely by trial and error, considering grammars in an invariant and largely arbitrary sequence that has no relation whatsoever to the sentences the learner is hearing. It is also rather mysterious where this ordering of grammars comes from. It must presumably be innate, but why or how humans came to be equipped with this innate list is unclear.

17.6 From enumeration to lattice

Despite all of these counts against it, I want to reconsider the merits of enumeration. Our CoLAG research has tried to hold onto its central advantage (fully-reliable SP application without explicit grammar comparisons) while improving its efficiency. You may find the question of its origin just as implausible for our version as for the classic enumeration, but if I can persuade you to restrain your skepticism for a little while, I will return to this point before we are through. We have taken the traditional enumeration and twisted it around into a lattice (or strictly into a *poset*, a partially ordered set) which represents the subset–superset relations among the grammars, just as Gold's enumeration did, but in a more accessible format. The lattice is huge. The 157 grammars depicted in Fig. 17.1 constitute about one-twentieth of our constructed domain of languages. The domain is defined by 13 parameters, it contains 3,072 distinct languages, and in all there are 31,504 subset–superset relations between those languages. (The real-world domain of natural languages is of course much more complex than this, which is why we have to seek an efficient mechanism to deal with it.)

This is how a learner could use the lattice. At the top of the lattice, as illustrated in Fig. 17.1, are nodes that denote the superset languages, with lines running downward connecting each one to all of its subsets, so that at the bottom there are all the languages that have no subsets. We call these

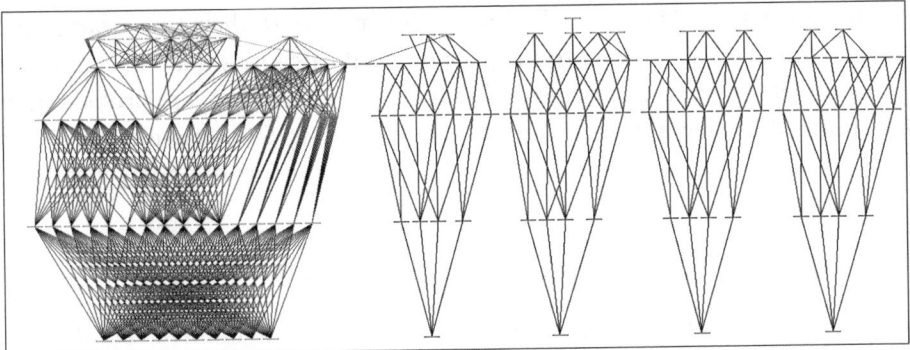

Fig. 17.1. A fragment (approximately 5%) of the subset lattice for the CoLAG language domain. Each node represents one grammar. Each grammar is identified as a vector of 13 parameter values, but the grammar labels are suppressed here because of the scale. Superset grammars are above subset grammars.

smallest languages, and by extension the grammars that generate them are *smallest grammars*. These are the only safe (SP-permitted) hypotheses at the beginning of the learning process, and the learner may at first select only from among these. Because they have no subsets, the learner thereby obeys SP. As learning proceeds, these smallest grammars are tried out on input sentences and some of them fail. When this happens, they are erased from the lattice. That is: when a grammar is disconfirmed, it disappears from the learner's mental representation of the language domain, and it will not be considered again. This means the lattice gets smaller over time. More importantly: the pool of legitimate grammars at the bottom of the lattice gradually shifts. Some of the grammars that started out higher up in the lattice because they had subsets will trickle their way down to the bottom and become accessible to the learner, as the grammars beneath them are eliminated. They qualify then as smallest languages compatible with the learner's experience, so they have become legitimate hypotheses that the learner is permitted to consider.

This lattice representation of the domain provides a built-in guarantee of SP-compliance just like a classic enumeration, but it is much more efficient than an enumeration because there is no need for the learning device to work through every language on the way between the initial state and the target language. All it has to work through are all the subsets of the target language (beneath it in the lattice), which is exactly what SP requires. Our reorganization of the domain has cleared away the intervening arbitrarily ordered grammars which merely get in the way of SP in the one-dimensional enumeration. The lattice-based approach has other good features too. The erasure of grammars incompatible with the input makes syntax learning similar to phonological learning, where it is well established that infants start by making a great many phonetic distinctions which they gradually lose with exposure to their target language, retaining only those relevant to the phonological categories that are significant in the target.[5] Also, the lattice-based model solves the other dire problem that I mentioned earlier: the fact that, although obeying SP is essential to avoid fatal overgeneration errors, it can itself lead to fatal errors of undergeneration.

17.7 Incremental learning and retrenchment

This disagreeable effect of SP stems from the assumption of *incremental learning*, that is, that the learner makes a decision about the grammar in response to each sentence it encounters. After each input sentence, an incremental learner chooses either to retain its current grammar hypothesis or to shift to a new one. It does not save up all the sentences in a long-term database, to compare and contrast, looking for general patterns. Only the current grammar (the parameter values set so far) and the current input sentence feed into its choice of the next grammar, so it can forget all about its past learning events; it does not retain either sentences previously encountered or a record of grammars previously tested. Incremental learning thus does not impose a heavy load on memory, making it plausible as a model of children. Incremental learning was clearly implied in the original parameter-setting model, and was regarded as one of its many assets. However, SP and incremental learning turn out to be very poor companions. To avoid overgeneration, SP requires the learner to postulate the smallest UG-compatible language consistent with the available data. But when the available data consists of just the current input sentence, the smallest UG-compatible language consistent with it is likely to be very small indeed, lacking all sorts of syntactic phenomena the learner had acquired from prior sentences. Anything that is not universal and is not exemplified in the *current* sentence must be excluded from the learner's new grammar hypothesis. We call this *retrenchment*. SP insists on it, because if old parameter settings weren't given up when new ones are adopted, the learner's language would just keep on growing, becoming the sum of all of its previous wrong hypotheses, with overgeneration as the inevitable result. SP thus makes an incremental learner over-conservative, favoring languages that are smaller than would be warranted by the learner's whole cumulative input sample to date. That can lead to permanent *undershoot errors* in which the learner repeatedly guesses too small a language, and never attains the full extent of the target. This doesn't happen always, but we observe undershoot failures in about 7 percent of learning trials in our language domain.

---

[5] See Werker (1989) and references there.

An example will illustrate the point. Suppose a child hears "It's bedtime." There is no topicalization in this sentence, so if the child is an incremental SP-compliant learner, there should be no topicalization in the language he hypothesizes in response to it (assuming that topicalization is something that some languages have and some do not). Similarly for extraposition, for passives, for tag questions, long-distance wh-movement, and so on. Even if the child had previously encountered a topicalized sentence and acquired topicalization from it (had set the appropriate parameter, or acquired a suitable rule in a rule-based system), that past learning is now lost. To make matters worse, this is the sort of sentence that the child is going to hear many times. So even if during the day he makes good progress in acquiring topicalization and extraposition and passives, every evening he will lose all that knowledge when he hears "It's bedtime." This is obviously a silly outcome, not what happens in real life, so we must prevent it happening in our model.

The guilty party once again is the ambiguity of (many) triggers. If the natural language domain were tidy and transparent, so that there was no ambiguity as to which language a sentence belongs to, a learner would be able to trust her past decisions about parameter settings, and hold on to them even if they aren't exemplified in her current input. Then even a strictly incremental learner could accumulate knowledge. A parameter value once set could stay set, without danger of discovering later that it was an error. But the natural language domain is *not* free of ambiguity, so a learner can't be sure that her past hypotheses weren't erroneous. Hence previously adopted parameter values cannot be maintained without current evidence for them; retrenchment is necessary. But then the puzzle is how learners avoid the undershoot errors that retrenchment can lead to.

17.8 The lattice limits retrenchment

It seems that the familiar assumption of incremental learning may be too extreme. Incrementality is prized because it does not require memory for past learning events. But even an incremental learner could profit by keeping track of grammars it has already tested and found inadequate. Then it could avoid those grammars in future, even when the evidence that disconfirmed them is no longer accessible to it. Making a mental list of disconfirmed grammars would do the job, though it would be very cumbersome. But an ideal way to achieve the same end is provided by the erasure of disconfirmed grammars from the grammar lattice, which we motivated on independent grounds earlier. Erasing grammars will block repeated retrenchment to languages that are smaller than the target. The smallest language compatible with "It's bedtime" is at first very small. But as time goes on, the smallest of the smallest languages will have been erased from the lattice, and then some larger smallest languages may be erased, and so on. As time goes by, the languages that the learner is allowed to hypothesize, the accessible ones at the bottom of the lattice, will actually include some quite rich languages. Hearing "It's bedtime" won't cause loss of topicalization and extraposition once all the grammars that don't license topicalization and extraposition have disappeared, eliminated by earlier input. Note that keeping track of disconfirmed grammars by erasing them from the innate lattice is a very economical way of providing memory to an incremental learner. The learner doesn't have to keep a mental tally of all the hundreds or thousands of languages he has falsified so far, a tally that consumes more and more memory as time goes on. Instead, memory load actually declines as learning progresses. To summarize: Like a traditional enumeration, the lattice model offers a fail-safe way to impose SP on learners' hypotheses; if combined with erasure of disconfirmed grammars it also provides a safeguard to ensure that SP doesn't get out of hand and hold the learner back too severely.

Where a lattice-based learner clearly excels over an enumeration learner is that, although it considers grammars in the right sequence to satisfy SP, it is not otherwise constrained by a rigid pre-determined ordering of all the grammars. For any input sentence, the learner must postulate a smallest language, but it has a free choice of which smallest language to postulate. Its choice could be made by trial and error, if that is all that is available. But a learner with decoding capabilities could do it much more effectively, because the input guides a decoding learner towards a viable hypothesis. And happily, for this purpose *full* decoding is not essential. Once decoding is used just to speed up learning, not for the application of the EM, partial decoding is good enough, because a lattice-based learner doesn't need knowledge of *all* the grammars that could license a sentence in order to be able to choose one that is free of subsets; instead, the lattice *offers* the learner only grammars that are free of subsets. This is the heart of the lattice solution to the problem of applying EM. The evaluation metric is inherent in the representation of the language domain, so the question of which of a collection of grammars best satisfies EM doesn't need to be resolved by means of online computations, as had originally seemed to be the case. The whole cumbersome grammar-comparison process can be dispensed with, because EM's preferred languages are now pre-identified. The Gold-type enumeration, despised though it may have been on grounds of psychological implausibility, has thus taught us a valuable lesson: that evaluation of the relative merits of competing hypotheses does not inevitably require that they be compared.

17.9 Can the lattice be projected?

We seem to be on the brink of having a learning model that is feasible in all departments: learners' hypotheses are input-guided by parametric decoding but only as much as the parsing mechanism can cope with; SP applies strictly but not over-strictly; neither online computation nor memory is overtaxed. But there are two final points that I should flag here as deserving further thought.

First, the appeal of the lattice representation in contrast to a classic enumeration is that it permits constructive grammar selection procedures, like decoding, to step in wherever rigid ordering of grammars is not enforced by EM. But I want to post a warning on this. We are in the process of running simulation tests to make sure that this ideal plan doesn't spring nasty leaks when actually put to work. The most important thing to check is that we can integrate the two parts of the idea: using the lattice to identify the smallest languages, and using partial decoding to choose among them. We think this is going to work out, but there's an empirical question mark still hovering over it at the moment.[6]

Finally, there's that nagging question of whether it is plausible to suppose that we are all born with a grammar lattice inside our heads. There's much to be said about this and about the whole issue of what could or couldn't be innate. It would be very exciting to be able to claim that the lattice is just physics and perfectly plausible as such, but I don't think we're there yet. In lieu of that, we would gladly settle for a rationalization that removes this huge unwieldy mental object from our account of the essential underpinnings of human language. If the lattice could be *projected* in a principled way, it would not have to be wired into the infant brain. It might be dispensed with entirely, if the vertical relations in the lattice could be generated as needed rather than stored. To do its job, the learning mechanism needs only (a) access to the set of smallest languages at the active edge of the lattice, and (b) some means of renewing this set when a member of it is erased and languages that were above it take its place. We are examining ways in which the lattice might be projected, holding out our greatest hopes for the system of default parameter values proposed by Manzini and Wexler (1987). But at least in our CoLAG language domain, which is artificial and limited but as much like the natural language domain as we could achieve despite necessary simplifications, we have found exceptions – thousands of exceptions – to the regular patterning of subset relations that would be predicted on the assumption that each parameter has a default value which (when other parameters are held constant) yields a subset of the language licensed by the non-default value. Many subset relations between languages

---

[6] Performance data for several variants of the lattice model are given in Fodor et al. (2007).

arise instead from unruly "conspiracies" between two or more parameters, and they can even run completely counter to the default values.[7]

If these exceptions prove to be irreducible, it will have to be concluded that as-needed projection of the lattice is not possible and that the lattice must indeed be biologically inscribed in the infant brain. We hold out hope that some refinement of the principles that define the defaults may eventually bring the exceptions under control. What encourages this prospect is the realization that the languages that linguists are aware of may be a more or less haphazard sampling from a much larger domain that is more orderly. SP concerns relations between *languages*, which do not closely map relations between grammars. So the innate *grammar* domain may be highly systematic even if the *language* domain is pitted by gaps. Gaps would arise wherever the innately given lattice contains a superset-generating grammar lower than a subset-generating grammar. The subset grammar would be UG-permitted but unlearnable because its position in the lattice happens to violate SP (or some other aspect of EM). Such grammars would be *invisible* to us as linguists, whose grasp of what is innate is shaped by observation of the languages that human communities do acquire. In that case, the priority relations among grammars in the innate domain may be much better-behaved than they seem at present, and may after all be projectable by learners on a principled basis. And there would be no need to suppose that the grammar lattice was intricately shaped by natural selection to capture just exactly the subset relations between languages.

Discussion

CHOMSKY: When the child has learned topicalization and set the topicalization parameter, why can that knowledge not be retained?

FODOR: The culprit is the ambiguity of triggers. Because the triggers are ambiguous, any parameter setting the learner adopts on the basis of them could be wrong. So the learner has to be always on the alert that sentences she projected on the basis of some past parameter setting may not in fact be in the target language. But you are right that there was a missing premise in the argument I presented. It assumed that the learner has no way to tell which triggers are ambiguous and which are not. That's important, because clearly the learner *could* hold onto her current setting for the topicalization parameter if she knew

---

[7] Chomsky (1986a: 146) observes of the approach to evaluation that relies on a default value for each parameter that "this is a necessary and sufficient condition for learning from positive evidence only, insofar as parameters are independent," but then warns that they "need not and may not be fully independent." We agree.

she had adopted it on the basis of a completely unambiguous trigger. In most current models the learner cannot know this – even if it were the case. This is because the model parses each sentence with just one new grammar (when the current grammar has failed to parse it). But parametric ambiguity can be detected only by testing more than one grammar; and *non*-ambiguity can be detected only by testing *all* possible grammars. A learner capable of full decoding would be able to recognize a sentence as parametrically unambiguous. The more psychologically plausible Structural Triggers Learners that do partial decoding can also recognize unambiguity, if they register every time they encounter a choice point in the parse. Even though the serial parser is unable to *follow up* every potential analysis of the sentence, it can tell when there are multiple possibilities. If such a learner were to set a parameter indelibly if its trigger was unambiguous, could it avoid the retrenchment problem? The data from our language domain suggest that there are so few unambiguous triggers that this would not make a big dent in the problem (e.g., 74 percent of languages have one parameter value or more which lack an unambiguous trigger). However, we are currently testing a cumulative version in which parameters that are set unambiguously can then help to disambiguate the triggers for other parameters, and this may be more successful.

PARTICIPANT: I was wondering whether any statistical measures would come in, because I think Robin Clark has suggested something of this kind in his earlier work: entropy measures, for example.[8] Also David LeBlanc at Tilburg tried to build in parameter setting in a connectionist network: there was a statistical measure before a parameter was set.

FODOR: Yes, the Structural Triggers learning model that we have developed at CUNY is actually a family of models with slight variations. The one we like best is one that has some statistics built into it.[9] What we have discovered, though, is the importance of using statistics over linguistically authentic properties. Statistical learning over raw data such as word strings without structure assigned to them has not been successful, so far anyway. Even very powerful connectionist networks haven't been proved to be capable of acquiring certain syntactic generalizations, despite early reports of success (Kam 2007). In our model – and Charles Yang's model has a similar feature – we do the statistical counting over the parameter values. A parameter value in a grammar that parses an input sentence has its activation level increased. This gives it a slight edge in the future. Each time the learner needs to postulate a new grammar, it can pick

---

[8] Clark (1992).
[9] See J. D. Fodor (1998a).

the one with the highest activation level, that is, the one that has had the most success in the past. In the lattice model we have extended this strategy by projecting the activation boost up through the lattice, so that all the supersets of a successful grammar are incremented too, which is appropriate since they can license every sentence the lower grammar can license. Then, if a grammar has been quite successful but is eventually knocked out, all of its supersets are well activated and are good candidates to try next. Preliminary results (see footnote 6 above) indicate that this does speed acquisition.

BOECKX: I am interested in knowing what the main differences are between the model that you sketched and the model that Charles Yang has been pursuing.[10] One of the things that Charles has been trying to make sense of is the ambiguity of triggers. In particular, it was obvious from the very beginning of the principles and parameters approach that if triggers were completely unambiguous, acquisition of syntax would be extremely fast. It wouldn't take three years, but three minutes, basically. That is, if all the switches are there and everything is unambiguous, it would be done almost instantaneously. We know that while it is actually fairly fast, it does take a couple of years, so one of the things that Charles has been trying to do is play on this ambiguity of triggers and the fact that there will be some sentences that will be largely irrelevant to setting the switches, so that the learner has to keep track of the complex evidence that he or she has. Therefore, the model uses the ambiguity or complexity of triggers as an advantage, to explain a basic fact, namely that it takes time to acquire syntax. Could you comment on that?

FODOR: First of all, I don't think it is true that if there were unambiguous triggers learning should be instantaneous, because there is so much else the learner has to do. At CUNY we assume that children don't learn the syntax from a sentence in which they don't know all the words; that would be too risky. So the child has to have built up some vocabulary, and as Lila Gleitman says, this can be quite slow. So that takes time, and then there is also the interaction problem – that is, the learner might not be able to recognize a trigger for one parameter until she has set some other parameter. So I doubt that parameter setting could be instantaneous anyway. However, I agree with you that it is interesting to explore the impact of the ambiguity of triggers, and this is what we have been doing for some years. My first approach to this (J. D. Fodor 1998) was to say that in order to model parameter-setting so that it really is the neat, effective, deterministic process that Noam envisaged, there *must* be unambiguous triggers; and we have got to build a model of the learner that is capable

---

[10] See J. D. Fodor (1998b).

of finding the unambiguous triggers within the input stream. As I mentioned in my paper here, a learner would have to parse all the analyses of a sentence in order to detect the ambiguities in it; but one can detect *that* it is ambiguous just by noting the presence of a choice of analysis at some point in the parse. Then the learner could say, "I see there are two potential ways of analyzing this sentence. It is ambiguous with respect to which parameter to reset, so I will throw it away. I will learn only from fully unambiguous, trustworthy triggers." We have modeled that strategy, and we have found – disappointingly – that it doesn't always work. It is very fast, as you imply, when it does work, but it often fails (Sakas and Fodor 2003). The reason is that there just isn't enough unambiguous information in the natural language domain. As far as we can tell (of course we haven't modeled the whole language world, only 3,000 or so languages), natural language sentences aren't parametrically unambiguous enough to facilitate a strategy of insisting on precise information. I think this is a puzzle. I mean, why *isn't* the natural language domain such that it provides unambiguous information for acquisition? Is there some reason why it couldn't be? Or is it just testament to the robustness of the learning mechanism that it can get by without that assistance? In any case, it suggests that Charles Yang is right to model parameter setting as a nondeterministic process, as we do too in our current models.

Now to your other point, about how our model relates to Charles's. We have worked quite closely with Charles and we do have very similar interests. However, in comparative tests on the CoLAG domain we have found that Charles's Variational Model runs about 50–100 times slower than ours. We measure learning time in terms of the number of input sentences the learner consumes before converging on the target grammar. The Variational Model is really very slow. In fact, our estimates of its efficiency are more positive than his own. In his book (Yang 2002) he says that in a simulation of the setting of ten parameters the model took 600,000 input sentences to converge. Though he doesn't describe the details of the experiment, this does seem excessive, showing signs of the exponential explosion problem that is a constant danger in parameter setting. I think the reason is that Charles was building on a seriously weak model that he inherited from the work of Gibson and Wexler (1994). The Gibson and Wexler model is a trial-and-error system. It guesses a grammar without guidance from the input as to which grammar to guess; the input serves only to provide positive feedback when a lucky guess has been made. In creating his model, Charles grafted statistical processing and the notion of grammar competition into this inherently weak model. By contrast, when we add a statistical component to our Structural Triggers models, it enhances the parametric decoding that the model engages in to identify a grammar that fits the novel input sentence. This has the property that triggering has always been thought to have, which is that the input sentence guides the learner's choice of a next grammar hypothesis. Charles has drawn interesting theoretical consequences from the statistical aspect of his model, showing how it predicts gradual learning rather than instant setting of parameters, and variable performance by children and also by adults. This is all very interesting, but we believe it deserves to be implemented in a basic learning mechanism that is closer to what Noam had in mind in proposing triggering as opposed to trial-and-error exploration through the array of all possible grammars.

RIZZI: I was wondering if it would be possible, or desirable, to incorporate into your computational model certain data from the empirical study of development which strongly suggest that it is not the case that parameters are all fixed at the same time. There is a temporal order, it seems, though we are far from having a precise temporal chart of what happens. That is a big gap in our knowledge. But at least certain things are known, particularly if one considers the critical moment when the child starts to produce syntactically relevant structures; that is to say, when he puts together at least two words so that some syntax can be observed. It is clear that some parameters have already been fixed, and others have not, at least on the basis of the productions we hear. For instance, major word-order parameters have been fixed, like Head Initial / Head Final (e.g., the verb precedes the object or follows it). That seems to have been established, because as soon as the child produces two-word sentences, if he is exposed to Japanese he'll say *Sandwich eat*, while if he's exposed to French, he'll say *Eat sandwich*. Similarly for other major word-order parameters. However for other facts it is not the case; we see a phase in production in which certain parametric properties apparently have not been determined. One relevant case that directly bears on certain things you have said is that certain types of scrambling are acquired relatively late (at least they manifest themselves relatively late). Similarly for certain kinds of grammatically determined ellipsis. There is more ellipsis (grammatically determined ellipsis, I think) in early productions, and you see a developmental effect in production. So this suggests that some parameters are fixed earlier than other parameters. And there are many stories one might propose about that. It could be that some parameters are easier; it could be that certain critical parameters come with very specific and easy triggers, as in the phonological bootstrapping hypothesis (Mazuka 1996). The infant just listens to the stress pattern and determines whether the language is head-initial or head-final. And there are other stories around. But

I wondered if you would be interested in incorporating these observations into the computational model.

FODOR: Yes, I wish we were there, but you can see we are still at a fairly primitive stage in the project of modeling real child learners. In fact I would add to the factors you mention that might determine the order of events. There is also information structure (topic, focus, etc.), which children may not be very good at; they are not very good in general at pragmatic aspects of conversation. Consider scrambling, for example. There is a study by Otsu (1994) of children's comprehension of scrambling (object before subject) in Japanese. They are very poor at it if an isolated sentence is just scrambled out of the blue. But if the scrambled sentence occurs in a conversational context where scrambling is appropriate, due to previous mention of the object, then the children perform much better. So it may be that it is not so much the syntax itself, as the work it is doing in the language. I am ashamed to admit that none of our simulation studies take meaning into account at all. We have obviously got to do so eventually, because clearly what is being learned by children is relationships between sentence forms and sentence meanings. But so far we have no interfaces in the parameter-setting models. They are treated as a pure computational system, which is interesting for us to study as psycholinguists and linguists, but in the real world the interfaces are extremely important.

I want to add one more point concerning the order in which parameters are set. There is a game that we can play with the CoLAG system, though it will be very laborious and we are just waiting until we can entice a graduate student into doing this for a dissertation. When we run our simulations, the computer keeps a record of every grammar the learning model hypothesizes along the way to final convergence on the target. Now we can do the following research project. We can order the hypothesis sequences by their length, which will tell us which sequences converged (terminated) first, and which took much longer. There is a lot of variability. So we can look to see which parameters were set first in the most efficient learning sequences, compared with which were set first in the least efficient ones. This can reveal whether (at least on purely structural grounds, not topic, focus, and so forth), there is some optimum order in which the parameters should be set. This is a huge data-crunching task, but we actually could set about doing it, and I would really like to see how it comes out.

PARTICIPANT: How do you decide, when you are going to run a simulation experiment, what a possible parameter is? I mean, doesn't it depends on your theoretical assumptions?

FODOR: Yes, you are right, the parameters are dependent on the underlying principles that you assume. There is a very interesting paper on re-parameterization of the linguistic facts, by Frank and Kapur (1996). That is, if you find that there is a learning problem somewhere, you might consider that it's because the parameterization is wrong. So you might try re-describing the facts as falling under different parameters and perhaps the learning problem disappears. For us the choice of parameters was largely a practical question. We needed to be conservative, with quite old-fashioned parameters, because we needed them to stay stable. It took three years to build the language domain, and if the syntacticians change their minds about what the parameters are tomorrow, we can't re-engineer our 3,000 languages. So we kept to very traditional sorts of parameters that any linguist would recognize (e.g., wh-movement, verb-raising, pied-piping, etc.). You are absolutely right that the results of our experiments could change if we were to shift to a different linguistic theory with different parameters. What I don't think will change are the fundamental problems that I was talking about today. I suspect those will still be with us, even when the linguistic details differ. The one thing that would make a significant difference for us is if something like the Manzini and Wexler defaults system that I mentioned for *generating* the grammar relations in the lattice could be made to square with the linguistic facts; then we could implement the Subset Principle with no lattice representation at all.

PIATTELLI-PALMARINI: The idea of subsets is one of the most interesting, I think, in the history of learning theories. It was very clear, when we had the idea of E-languages (languages as things out there), that there could be a smaller language contained in a bigger language. I am wondering what the idea of "subset" becomes in I-language.

FODOR: You have put your finger on a central problem that we face in modeling. We assume children learn *grammars* (I-languages), but the subset principle is about *languages* (E-languages). As you say, it is about one E-language being included in another one. If we had a neat translation system from grammars to languages, we could manage the SP problem a great deal better. We would love to be able to look at the grammar and say, "The language this grammar generates is going to be a subset of the language generated by this other grammar." But in fact, there doesn't appear to be a transparent correspondence between grammars and languages. Noam emphasized that a small change in a grammar can make a great change in the set of sentences generated. The Manzini and Wexler system which assumes an independently contributing default value for each parameter (which we call the 'Simple Defaults Model') does offer a transparent translation. Every subset relation between languages is due to the default value of one or more specifiable parameters in their grammars. Now that is not true of our CoLAG language domain, and so we suspect it's not true of the natural language domain at large. And we haven't yet found any alternative system for going back and forth between grammars and languages. As far we now know, the relationship between languages is not projectable from the relationship between grammars. We wish it were.

CHAPTER 18

Remarks on the Individual Basis for Linguistic Structures*

Thomas G. Bever

This paper reviews an approach to the enterprise of paring away universals of attested languages to reveal the essential universals that require their own explanation. An example, discussed at this conference, is the long-standing puzzle presented by the Extended Projection Principle (EPP, Chomsky 1981). I am suggesting an explanation for the EPP based on the learner's need for constructions to have a common superficial form, with common thematic relations, the hallmark of EPP. If one treats EPP phenomena as the result of normal processes of language acquisition, the phenomena not only receive an independently motivated explanation, they also no longer constitute a structural anomaly in syntactic theory.[1]

18.1 EPP and its implications for structural universals

EPP was initially proposed as the structural/configurational requirement that sentences must always have a subject NP, even without semantic content (cf. Chomsky 1981, Lasnik 2001, Epstein and Seely 2002, Richards 2002; see Svenonious 2002, McGinnis and Richards, in press, for general reviews). This principle was first proposed to account for subject-like phrases in sentences, so called expletives (e.g., "it"):

---

* These remarks are based on what I planned to present at this conference. What follows is influenced by extensive discussions with Noam and the editors. Of course, mistakes and infelicities are all mine.

[1] See discussion by Noam and Massimo of this, pp. 55–57.

(1)   a. "it" is raining
      b. "there" are three men in the room
      c. "it" surprised us that john left
      d. "es" geht mir gut
      e. "il" pleut

The EPP was initially proposed as a universal syntactic constraint that all languages must respect. While roughly correct for English, a number of troubling facts have emerged:

(2)   a. EPP may not be universal (e.g., Irish as analyzed by McCloskey 1996, 2001).
      b. Different languages express it differently: e.g., via focus as opposed to subject, in intonation patterns, with different and inconsistent agreement patterns.
      c. It generally corresponds to the statistically dominant form in each language.
      d. It has not found a formal derivation within current syntactic theory – it must be stipulated.

Accordingly, the EPP may be a "configurational" constraint on derivations – it requires that sentences all conform to *some* typical surface pattern. Epstein and Seeley (2002: 82) note the problem this poses for the minimalist program:

If (as many argue) EPP is in fact "configurational," then it seems to us to undermine the entire Minimalist theory of movement based on feature interpretability at the interfaces. More generally, "configurational" requirements represent a retreat to the stipulation of molecular tree properties...It amounts to the reincorporation of...principles of GB...that gave rise to the quest for Minimalist explanation...

In other words, the EPP is a structural constraint stipulated in the minimalist framework (as well as others), which violates its structural principles and simplicity. Yet EPP-like phenomena exist.

Below I outline a language acquisition model which requires that languages exhibit a canonical form, the Canonical Form Constraint (CFC) – which renders EPP phenomena in attested languages. Thus, there are two potential explanations of EPP phenomena. Either it is indeed a syntactic constraint, part of universal syntax in the narrow faculty of language; or it is a constraint on learnable languages: Sentences have to conform to the CFC – they must sound like they are sentences of the language to afford the individual child a statistical entrée into acquiring it. How can we decide between these two explanations? First, the EPP adds a stipulated constraint to grammars, undercutting their simplicity. Second, the EPP is a heterogeneous constraint, with different kinds of expressions in different languages. Third, the CFC, as we will see, is independently motivated: it explains statistical properties of language, stages of acquisition, and significant facts about adult language processing. Thus, I argue that the phenomena that motivated the EPP are actually expressions of the Canonical Form Constraint (CFC).

Syntacticians may object that this line of reasoning is circular. In many languages, the EPP constraint does not merely exert "stylistic" preferences on sentence constructions, it dictates syntactic requirements on grammatical derivations. But the issue is the source of the constraint that results in processes that conform to the EPP. On my view, the child tends to learn sentence constructions that conform to the canonical form constraint, and not other constructions. The notion of "learn" can be glossed as "discovers derivations for statistically frequent meaning/form pairs, using its available repertoire of structural devices." Thus, in individual languages the child accesses and learns specific derivational processes that conform descriptively to the EPP. But the EPP itself is merely a descriptive generalization reflecting acquisition constraints as its true cause. In the sense of Boeckx (this volume), EPP-like phenomena are among the set of E-universals (corresponding to E-language), not I-universals (corresponding to I-language). In the sense of Hauser et al. (2002), it is a property of the interface between the narrow faculty of language and the acquisition interface.

The following discussion will serve as an outline of how a simplified model of what individuals do during language acquisition, based on a general model of human learning, can explain universal properties of attested languages, such as the EPP. My argumentation strategy here is the following:

(a) a general method of paring down universals, with some non-syntactic examples
(b) a comprehension model showing how the linguistic structures are implemented in an analysis-by-synthesis comprehension model
(c) an application of the analysis-by-synthesis model as a model of acquisition
(d) implications for the Canonical Form Constraint (CFC) as a language universal
(e) implications of the CFC for a correct interpretation of EPP phenomena
(f) implications of this model in general (a potential solution to constraining the abduction of generalizations, and learning grammar as intrinsically motivated problem solving)

This line of argument follows a general research program of isolating true linguistic universals.

The concept of "language" is like those of . . . "organ", as used in biological science . . . grammatical structure "is" the language only given the child's intellectual environment . . . and the processes of physiological and cognitive development . . . Our first task in the study of a particular [linguistic] structure in adult language behavior is to ascertain its source rather than immediately assuming that it is *grammatically* relevant . . . Many an aspect of adult . . . linguistic structure is itself partially determined by the learning and behavioral processes that are involved in acquiring and implementing that structure . . . Thus, some formally possible structures will never appear in any language because no child can use [or learn] them.   (Bever 1970: 279–280)[2]

Here I focus on the dynamic role of the individual language learner in shaping properties of attested languages (aka E-languages). Certain linguistic universals that seem to be structural are in fact emergent properties of the interaction of genetic endowment, social context, and individual learning dynamics. My argument is this: Language acquisition recruits general mechanisms of growth, learning, and behavior in individual children: only those languages that comport with these mechanisms will be learned. I first review some non-syntactic universals, to outline relatively clear examples of the role of development, as background for the main focus of this paper.

18.2 Neurological foundations of language: the enduring case of cerebral asymmetries

The left hemisphere is the dominant neurological substrate for much of language – true for everyone, including the vast majority of left-handers (Khedr et al. 2002). This leads directly to *post hoc propter hoc* reasoning about the biological basis for language: the unique linguistic role of the left hemisphere reflects some unique biological property, which itself makes language possible. This argument has been further buttressed by claims that certain primates have left-hemisphere asymmetries for species specific calls (Weiss et al. 2002), claims that infants process language more actively in the left hemisphere (Mehler et al. 2000), demonstrations that artificial language learning selectively activates the left hemisphere (Musso et al. 2003; Friederici 2004, this volume). However plausible, this argument overstates the empirical case. First, we and others demonstrated that asymmetries involve differences in computational "style" ("propositional" in the left, "associative" in the right; Bever 1975, Bever and Chiarello 1974). In nonlinguistic mammals, the asymmetries may nonetheless parallel those for humans: for example, we have shown that rats learn mazes relying on serial ordering in the left hemisphere, and specific locations in the right (Lamendola and Bever 1997), a difference with the computational flavor

---

[2] See Cedric Boeckx's quote of Noam's recent reformulation of this approach, Chapter 3 above.

of the human difference. Second, the facts about asymmetries for language could follow from a simple principle: the left hemisphere is slightly more powerful computationally than the right (Bever 1980). Even the simplest sentence involves many separate computations, which during acquisition compound a small incremental computational superiority into a large categorical superiority and apparent specialization. Thus the left hemisphere's unique relation to language function accumulates from a very small quantitative difference in the individual learner.

18.3 Heritable variation in the neurological representation of language

Loss of linguistic ability results from damage to specific areas of the left neocortex. The fact that normal language depends on (rather small) specific areas suggests that it may be critically "caused" by those areas. However, certain aspects of language may have considerable latitude in their neurological representation. For example, Luria and colleagues noted that right-handed patients with left-handed relatives ("FLH+ ") recover faster from left-hemisphere aphasia, and show a higher incidence of right-hemisphere aphasia than those without familial left-handers (FLH−) (Hutton et al. 1977). They speculated that FLH + right handers have a genetic disposition towards bilateral representation for language, which often surfaces in their families as explicit left-handedness. We have found a consistent behavioral difference between the two familial groups in how language is processed, which may explain Luria's observation. Normal FLH+ people comprehend language initially via individual words, while FLH− people give greater attention to syntactic organization (a simple demonstration is that FLH+ people read sentences faster and understand them better in a visual word-by-word paradigm than a clause-by-clause paradigm; the opposite pattern occurs for FLH− people). The bilateral representation of language in FLH+ people may be specific to lexical knowledge, since acquiring that is less demanding computationally than syntactic structures, and hence more likely to find representation in the right hemisphere. On this view, FLH + people have a more widespread representation of individual lexical items, and hence can access each word more readily and distinctly from syntactic processing than FLH− people (Bever et al. 1987, 1989a; Townsend et al. 2001).

This leads to a prediction: lexical processing is more bilateral in FLH+ right-handers than FLH− right-handers, but syntactic processing is left-hemisphered for all right-handers. Recently, we tested this using fMRI brain imaging of

subjects while they are reordering word sequences according to syntactic constraints or according to lexico-semantic relations between the words. We found
that the lexical tasks activated the language areas bilaterally in FLH+ right-
handers, but activated only the left hemisphere areas in the FLH− right handers: all subjects showed strong left-hemisphere dominance in the syntactic
tasks (Chan et al. in preparation). This confirms our prediction, and supports
our explanation for Luria's original clinical observations. It also demonstrates
that there is considerable lability in the neurological representation of important aspects of language.

18.4 The critical period: differentiation and segregation of behaviors

The ostensible critical period for learning language is another lynchpin
in arguments that language writ broadly (aka E-language) is (interestingly)
innate. The stages of acquisition and importance of exposure to language at
characteristic ages is often likened to stages of learning birdsong – a paradigmatic example of an innate capacity with many surface similarities to language
(Michel and Tyler 2005). However, certain facts may indicate a somewhat less
biologically rigid explanation. First, it seems to be the case that adult mastery of
semantic structures in a second language is much less restricted than mastery
of syntax, which in turn is less restricted than mastery of phonology (Oyama
1976). This decalage invites the interpretation that the critical period is actually
a layering of different systems and corresponding learning sequences. Phonological learning involves both tuning perceptual systems and forming motor
patterns, which is ordinarily accomplished very early: linguistically unique
semantic knowledge may be acquired relatively late, draws on universals
of thought, and hence shows relatively little sensitivity to age of acquisition.

Noam suggested (in email) a non-maturational interpretation of this decalage, based on the specificity of the stimulus that the child receives, and the
corresponding amount which must be innately available, and hence not due
to different mechanisms of learning with different time courses. The semantic
world is vast: much of semantics must be universally available innately, and
hence a critical period for semantic acquisition is largely irrelevant. In contrast,
all the phonological information needed for learning it is available to the child,
and can be learned completely in early childhood.

The notorious case is syntactic knowledge of an explicit language, which is
neither determined by sensory/motor learning nor related directly to universals
of thought. I have argued that the critical period for syntax learning is a natural

result of the functional role that syntax plays in learning language – namely, it assigns consistent computational representations that solidify perceptual and productive behavioral systems, and reconciles differences in how those systems pair forms with meanings (Bever 1975, 1981). On this view, the syntactic derivational system for sentences is a bilateral filter on emerging perceptual and productive capacities: once those capacities are complete and in register with each other, further acquisition of syntax no longer has a functional role, and the syntax acquisition mechanisms decouple from disuse, not because of a biological or maturationally mechanistic change. (See Bever and Hansen 1988 for a demonstration of the hypothesis that grammars act as cognitive mediators between production and perception in adult artificial language learning).

This interpretation is consistent with our recent finding that the age of the critical period differs as a function of familial handedness: FLH+ deaf children show a younger critical age for mastery of English syntax than FLH− children (Ross and Bever 2004). This follows from the fact that FLH+ people access the lexical structure of language more readily, and access syntactic organization less readily than FLH− people: FLH+ children are acquiring their knowledge of language with greater emphasis on lexically coded structures, and hence depend more on the period during which vocabulary grows most rapidly (between 5 and 10 years: itself possibly the result of changes in social exposure, and emergence into early teenage). Consistent with my general theme, it attests to the role of general mechanisms of learning and individual neurological specialization in shaping how language is learned.

18.5 Language learning as hypothesis testing and the EPP

Of course, how language learning works computationally is the usual determinative argument that the capacity for language is innate and independent from individual mechanisms of learning or development. Typically cited problems for a general inductive experience-based empiricist learning theory are:

(3) a. The poverty of the stimulus. How do children go beyond the stimulus given?
     b. The frame problem: how do children treat different instances as similar?
     c. The motivational problem: e.g., what propels a 4-year-old to go beyond his already developed prodigious communicative competence?
     d. The universals problem: how do all languages have the same universals?

Parameter-setting theory is a powerful schematic answer to all four questions at the same time. On this theory, a taxonomy of structural choices differentiates possible languages. For example, phrases are left- or right-branching; subjects can be unexpressed or not; wh-constructions move the questioned constituent or it remains in situ. The language-learning child has innate access to these parameterized choices. Metaphorically, the child has a bank of dimensionalized "switches" and "learning" consists of recognizing the critical data setting the position of each switch: the motivation to learn is moot, since the switches are thrown automatically when the appropriate data are encountered. This is a powerful scheme which technically can aspire to be explanatory in a formal sense and has made enormous contributions in defining the minimally required data (Lightfoot 1991; Pinker 1984; J. D. Fodor 1998, 2001; Fodor and Sakas 2004; Fodor, this volume): but it is also very far removed from the motivational and daily dynamics of individual children. We are left with an abstract schema and no understanding of what the individual child might be doing, why it might be doing it, and how that activity might itself constrain possible choices of parameters, and hence, attested linguistic universals.

My hypothesis, and that of a few others who accept the idea that children in fact acquire generative grammar (e.g., Gillette et al.1999; Gleitman 1990, this volume; Papafragou et al. 2007) is that neither a parameter-setting scheme, nor inductive learning alone is adequate to the facts. On this view, acquisition involves both formation of statistical generalizations available to the child and the availability of structures to rationalize violations of those generalizations. A traditional view of this kind is "hypothesis testing," which allows for hypotheses to be inductively generated and deductively tested, and conversely.

Now to the central thesis of this discussion: there is a model of acquisition that integrates inductive and deductive processes; such a model requires the existence of canonical forms in languages; this motivates the facts underlying the Extended Projection Principle, which requires that (almost) every sentence construction maintain a basic configurational property of its language. The exposition starts with a narrowly focused discussion of how inductive and deductive processes can be combined in a model of comprehension – itself experimentally testable and tested with adults. Then I suggest that this kind of model can be generalized to a model of acquisition, with corresponding empirical predictions – at least a few of which are confirmed.

18.6 Integrating derivations into a comprehension model

The first question is, do speakers actually use a psychological representation of generative grammar – a "psychogrammar" – of the particular form claimed in derivational models, or only a simulation of it? If adult speakers do not actually use the computational structures posited in generative grammars as part of their language behavior, we do not have to worry about how children might learn it. In fact, fifty years of research and intuition have established the following facts about adult language behavior (4):

(4) a. Syntactic processes in generative models are "psychologically real": derivational representations are used in language comprehension and production (see Townsend and Bever 2001).

     b. Syntactic processes are recursive and derivational: they range over entire sentences in a "vertical" fashion (as opposed to serial) with successive reapplications of computations to their own output. These properties have been true of every architectural variant of generative grammar, from Syntactic Structures (Chomsky 1957), to the minimalist program (Chomsky 1995).

     c. Sentence behavior is instant and "horizontal" – speakers believe that they comprehend and produce meaningful sentences simultaneously with their serial input or output. Comprehension does not start only at the end of each sentence: production does not wait until a sentence is entirely formulated.

These three observations set a conundrum:

(5) a. Sentence processing involves computation of syntax with whole sentences as domain – it is *vertical*.

     b. Language behavior proceeds serially and incrementally – it is *horizontal*.

Recently, Dave Townsend and I rehabilitated the classic comprehension model of Analysis by Synthesis (AxS) that provides a solution to the conundrum (following Halle and Stevens 1962, Townsend and Bever 2001). On this view, people understand everything twice: once based on the perceptual templates; once by the assignment of syntactic derivations. In the AxS architecture the two processes are almost simultaneous. First, the perceptual templates assign likely interpretations to sentences, using a pattern completion system in which initial parts of a serial string automatically trigger a complete template. Typical templates of this kind are:

(6) a. Det . . . X → np[Det . . . N]np

     b. NP V(agreeing with NP) (optional NP) → Agent/Experiencer Predicate (object/adjunct)

Second, the initially assigned potential meaning triggers (and constrains) a syntactic derivation. The two ways of accessing meaning and structure converge, roughly at the ends of major syntactic units. That is, as we put it, *we understand everything twice*. The model has several unusual features (Townsend and Bever 2001). First, the model assigns a complete correct syntax *after* accessing an initial meaning representation. Second, that meaning is sometimes developed from an incorrect syntactic analysis. For example, syntactic passives (7a) are initially understood via the variant of the canonical sentence template in (6b) that applies correctly to lexical passives (7b); raising constructions (7c) are understood initially via the same kind of misanalysis.

(7)   a. Syntactic passive: Bill was hit
      b. Lexical passive: Bill was hurt
      c. Raising: Bill seemed happy
      d. Control: Bill became happy

The schema in (6b) initially misassigns "hit" as an adjective within a predicate phrase. That analysis is sufficient to access semantic information modeled on the interpretation template for lexical passive adjectives – a syntactic misanalysis. This analysis is then corrected by accessing the correct derivation. This sequence of operations also explains the fact that the experimental evidence for the trace appears in syntactic passives and raising constructions only after a short time has passed (Bever and McElree 1988, Bever et al. 1990, Bever and Sanz 1997). This model also explains a number of simple and well-known facts. Consider the following examples:

(8)   a. The horse raced past the barn fell
      b. More people have been to Russia than I have

Each of these cases exemplifies a different aspect of the AxS model. The first reflects the power of the canonical form strategy in English (6b), which initially treats the first six words as a separate sentence (Bever 1970). Native speakers judge this sentence as ungrammatical, often even after they see parallel sentences with transparent structure:

(9)   a. The horse ridden past the barn fell
      b. The horse that was raced past the barn fell
      c. The horse racing past the barn fell

The example is pernicious because recovering from the misanalysis is itself vexed: the correct analysis includes the garden-pathing proposition that "the horse raced" (i.e., was caused to race): thus, every time the comprehender arrives at the correct interpretation she is led back up the garden path.

   Example (8b) (due to Mario Montalbetti) is the obverse of the first example. The comprehender thinks at first that the sentence is coherent and meaningful, and then realizes that it does not have a correct syntactic analysis. The initial perceptual organization assigns it a schema based on a general comparative template of two canonical sentence forms – "more X than Y," reinforced by the apparent parallel Verb Phrase structure in X and Y (". . . have been to

Russia...I have"). On the AxS model, this superficial initial analysis triggers the derivational parse system, which ultimately fails to generate a derivation.

I do not expect to have convinced the reader of our model via such simplified examples: in our book, we organize a range of often surprising experimental and neurological facts supporting an early stage of comprehension resting on frequent statistically valid templates, followed by a structurally correct syntactic derivation (Townsend and Bever 2001, Chapters 5–8; see Friederici, this volume, for imaging data consistent with this bi-phasic model of comprehension).

This model requires languages to have certain universal features. Most important is the otherwise unmotivated fact that actual languages have a characteristic set of statistically grounded structural patterns at each level of representation (phonological, morpho-lexical, syntactic). It further requires that complex constructions be functionally homonymous with simpler constructions in ways that allow the simpler constructional analysis to convey the more complex meaning at an initial pre-derivational stage of processing. The model is inelegant in that it solves the conundrum (5) by fiat – sentence processing is both fast and complex because it is simultaneously handled by two systems, one fast and sometimes wrong, one slower but ultimately correct. This is an inelegant solution to the conundrum, but shows that humans may solve it, albeit inelegantly.

18.7 AxS in language acquisition – the Canonical Form Constraint

Two historically competing principles about the mind have alternately dominated the cognitive sciences:

(10)   a. Everything we do is based on habits.
       b. Everything (important) we do is based on creative rules.

The AxS model architecture shows how the two insights might be integrated together in adult behavior. A corresponding model holds for the acquisition of language. On that model, the child alternates (logically) between formulating statistical generalizations about the language, and assembling derivational operations that account for those generalizations. Many researchers are demonstrating that child-directed speech in fact has statistical regularities that might guide the infant and child towards language (e.g., Curtin et al. 2005, for segmentation, Golinkoff 1975; Brent 1997; Cartwright and Brent 1997; Gerken 1996; Golinkoff et al. 2005; Mintz 2002, 2003, 2006; Redington et al. 1998). At the same time, infants are quite good at detecting statistical patterns from serial strings with specific kinds of structure (Gomez and Gerken 1999;

Marcus et al. 1999; Saffran 2001, 2003; Saffran et al. 1996); older children also show statistical sensitivity in developing grammatical and lexical ability (Bates and MacWhinney 1987, Gillette et al. 1999, Moerk 2000, Naigles and Hoff-Ginsburg 1998, Yang 2006). If one component of syntax acquisition is the compilation of relevant generalizations, this model requires that the child be presented with some statistical regularities in the language he hears. This requirement explains several computationally eccentric facts about attested languages:

(11)   a. Each language has a canonical surface form: in English this is schematically as presented in the left side of the expression in (6b).
       b. Statistically, the canonical form has a dominant assignment of semantic relations: in English this is the template we found explanatory for much adult language behavior (6b).
       c. The canonical semantic interpretation is violated in a set of minority constructions: in English, this includes passives, raising, unaccusatives, middle constructions.
       d. The minority constructions that violate the form can nonetheless be approximately correctly interpreted by application of the canonical form interpretation. (This is exemplified in the initial stages of comprehending syntactic passives and raising constructions, discussed above in examples (7).)

None of these properties follows from the computational architecture of any of the last fifty years of generative grammar. Yet they are characteristic of attested languages. In English, the first property has been noted as the result of rule "conspiracies," which guarantee that sentences have the same surface form regardless of their thematic relations and derivation. The vast majority of sentences and clauses have a canonical form with a subject preceding a correspondingly inflected verb:

(12)   a. The boy hits the ball
       b. The ball was hit by the boy
       c. It is the boy who hits the ball
       d. The boy was happy
       e. The boy seems happy
       f. The boy was eager to push
       g. The boy was easy to push
       h. It was easy to push the boy
       i. The boy pushes easily
       j. Who pushed the boy?
       k. Who does the boy push?

The notion of such conspiracies is not novel, be it in syntax or phonology (cf. Ross 1972, 1973a,b). In traditional derivational terms, it reflects constraints on derivations such that they have the same general surface form regardless of differences in logical form or semantic relations. This is despite the fact that each underlying form could be reflected in a unique surface sequence or signaled by a specific marker. On our interpretation, such computationally possible languages would be allowed by generative architectures, but are not learnable: they would make it hard for the language-learning child to develop a statistically based pattern that it can internalize and use for further stages of acquisition.

The canonical form (11a) facilitates the discovery of a surface template based on statistical dominance of the pattern. The semantic schema (11b) above relates the canonical form to a standard interpretation – although a majority of individual constructions may not conform to that schema, the vast majority of actual utterances in corpora do so – another fact about languages unexplained by generative architectures. The third fact (11c) – that some cases violate the canonical semantic interpretation of the canonical form – is particularly important if the child is eventually to discover that there are actual derivations in which a given surface form expresses different patterns of thematic relations. Finally, the interpretability of the schema-violating constructions via misanalysis and homonymy with simpler constructions (11d) – contributes to the child's ability to interpret sentence types for which it does not yet have a syntactic analysis. I summarize the set of these conditions as the "Canonical Form Constraint (CFC)."

The CFC suggests a way in which the child can transcend the "poverty of the stimulus." First, the child can create and then analyze his own set of form/ meaning pairs going beyond the actual sentences he hears, based on these generalizations. Second, this solves an important problem for any learning scheme – how do children remember and understand sentences for which they do not yet have a correct syntactic analysis? (Valian 1999). It would not work for the child to maintain a list of grammatically unresolved sentences: any given list is heterogenous without prior structural ordering. The AxS model suggests that children can rely on statistical patterns and occasional false analyses to generate an internal bank of meaning/form pairs and maintain an internalized data bank to evaluate candidate derivational analyses. This reduces the need for children to access positive and negative feedback as guides to their emerging syntactic abilities. On this view, the child can attempt derivation of a construction based on a subset of sentences of a given general pattern, and then "test" the derivational structure on other sentences of a similar pattern. (For related ideas, see Chouinard and Clark 2003, Dale and Christiansen 2004,

Golinkoff et al. 2005, Lieven 1994, Moerk 2000, Morgan et al. 1995, Saxton 1997, Valian 1999). These facts and considerations offer an explanation for the CFC – peculiar in the sense that the computational architecture of syntax does not in itself require the CFC. It is reflected in attested languages because it makes them learnable, using a hypothesis formation procedure.

If this picture is correct, children should show evidence of actually learning perceptual strategies, based on statistical frequency of preponderant features of their surrounding language. We and others have found evidence supporting this (Bever 1970, Maratsos 1974, Slobin and Bever 1982). The original finding was based on having children act out simple sentences with puppets. (Typical data are summarized in Table 18.1). 2-year-old children use a simple strategy that focuses primarily on the exact sequence NounPhrase + Verb, interpreting that as Agent + Verb. Thus, at age 2, children interpret declarative and object cleft sentences, along with semantically unlikely sentences, above chance: in these constructions, the noun immediately before the verb is the agent. By age 3–4, they rely both on a more elaborated analysis of word order and semantic strategies:

(13)   a. #N . . . = Agent
        b. Animate nouns are agents, inanimate nouns are patients

(13a) represents a shift from assigning the noun immediately before the verb as agent, to assigning the first noun in the overall sequence as agent. This produces correct performance on simple declarative sentences, but a decrease in performance on sentence types in which the first noun phrase is not the agent (object clefts and passives).

The emergence of the two kinds of strategies accounts for the decrease in performance on semantically reversible sentences that violate the CFC

Table 18.1   Percentage correct interpretations of simple sentences by children[a]

	Age 2	Age 4
SEMANTICALLY REVERSIBLE		
The dog bit the giraffe –	90%	98%
It's the giraffe that the dog bit –	87%	43%
The giraffe got bit by the dog	52%	27%
SEMANTICALLY IRREVERSIBLE		
The dog ate the cookie	92%	96%
The cookie ate the dog	73%	45%
The cookie got eaten by the dog	55%	85%

[a]Children make small puppets act out short sentences. The primary measure is which noun is the agent and which the patient: chance performance is 50%.

(the giraffe was kicked by the dog). The emergence of reliance on semantic information accounts for the increase in performance on sensible sentences (the dog ate the cookie), and the decrease in performance on semantically odd sentences (the cookie ate the dog). The reliance on semantic factors at age 4 also can override the word-order strategy, leading to correct performance on irreversible passives (the cookie got eaten by the dog).

The perceptual strategies differ from language to language: we found that by age 4, children acquire processing strategies adaptive to the statistical regularities in the structure of their own language (Slobin and Bever 1982). Thus, in English what develops is sensitivity to word order, in Turkish, sensitivity to patient/object inflectional markers, in Italian and Serbo-Croatian, sensitivity to a mixture of the two kinds of linguistic signals. This reflects the fact that each language has its own CFC, which children learn.

18.8 Coda: Some broader implications of the AxS acquisition model

The following points are in large part the result of email discussions with Noam.

18.8.1 Language acquisition as enjoyable problem solving

The idea that the child acquires knowledge of syntax by way of compiling statistical generalizations and then analyzing them with its available syntactic capacities is but another instance of learning by hypothesis-testing. For example, it is technically an expansion on the TOTE model proposed by Miller et al. (1960). An initial condition (statistically grounded pattern) triggers a TEST meaning, and an OPERATION (derivation) which triggers a new TEST meaning and then EXIT. Karmilov-Smith and Inhelder (1973) advanced a different version – cognition advances in spurts, triggered by exposure to critical instances which violate an otherwise supported generalization.

The dual nature of the acquisition process is also related to classical theories of problem solving (e.g., Wertheimer 1925, 1945). On such models, the initial stage of problem organization involves noting a conceptual conflict – for example, "find a solution that includes both X and Y: if the answer is X then Y is impossible, but if Y then X is impossible": characteristically the solution involves accessing a different form of representation which expresses the relation between X and Y in more abstract terms. In language the initial conflict expresses itself as the superficial identity of all the constructions in (12) which exhibit the canonical form constraint, while assigning different semantic relations; the resolution is to find a derivational structure for the set that shows how the different surface constructions are both differentiated and related derivationally. Hence, not only is language-learning hereby interpreted in the context of a general set of learning principles, it is also interpreted as a special instance of a general problem solver. This also explains why language learning is fun, and hence intrinsically motivating: the gestalt-based model suggests that language-learning children can enjoy the "aha" insight experience, an intrinsically enjoyable sensation which may provide critical motivation to learn the derivational intricacies of language (cf. Weir's 1962 demonstration that children play with their language paradigms when they are alone).

Note that the terms "motivation" and "fun" are technical terms based in aesthetic theory, not the everyday notion of conscious desire, nor any notion of "reinforcement." Elsewhere, I have developed analyses of what makes objects and activities intrinsically enjoyable (Bever 1987). The analysis draws on the classic aesthetic definition: stimulation of a representational conflict which is then resolved by accessing a different form or level of knowledge. The formal similarity of this definition to the gestalt model of learning affords an explanation of why aesthetic objects are enjoyable: they are mini-"problems" involving conflicting representational solutions, resolved by accessing a level which creates a productive relation between those solutions, thereby eliciting a subconscious "aha." This kind of analysis is ordinarily applied to serial arts such as drama or music, in which the representational conflict and its resolution can be made explicit over time. But the analysis works for static objects, explaining the preference, for example, for the golden mean rectangle. In language, one kind of conflict is elicited by the thematic heterogeneity of superficially identical surface phrase structures: the child's resolution of that conflict requires access to an inner form of the sentences, via distinct derivational histories – a resolution which involves accessing a distinct level of representation. Thus, learning the structure of a language elicits a series of mini-ahas in the child, making it an activity which is intrinsically attractive.

The model also offers a partial answer to the frame problem (see Ford and Hayes 1993), the problem of how statistical generalizations are chosen out of the multiple possibilities afforded by any particular set of experiences. This problem was classically addressed by Peirce (1957) as the problem of abduction, who argued that there must be constraints on all kinds of hypotheses, even those ostensibly based on compilation of observations (cf. Chomsky 1959c, on the corresponding problem in S-R associative theory, and this volume). But the problem is also a moving target for the language-learning child. At any given age, the generalizations that are relevant to progress in learning are different: if the child has mastered simple declarative constructions, or some subpart of her language's inflectional system, this changes the import of further exposure to the language. Thus, we must not only address constraints on the initial state of the child (see Mehler and Bever 1968 for discussion), we must address how constraints apply to each current state of knowledge, as the child matures and acquires more structural knowledge. That is, the abductive constraints themselves have a developmental course. By what process and dynamic? Another way of putting this is, what filters (aka "frames") possible generalizations and how does the filter itself change as a function of current knowledge?

In the AxS scheme, there are two kinds of processes which filter generalizations. First is the set of salient regularities among elements that are available to the input: at a phonological level, infants have available perceptual categories that provide an initial organization of the input; this affords an innate categorization of sound sequences, available for formal derivational analysis. The other side of the filtering process is the set of computational devices available to provide a derivation. That is, those generalizations about sound sequences that endure are just those that can be explained by a set of possible computational phonological rules. Such rules must have natural domains (presumably innately determined) such as segmental features, syllabic structures, lexical templates. At the syntactic level, the corresponding problem is to isolate a natural segmentation of the potential compositional input. To put it in terms of the example we are focusing on, how does the system isolate "NP V (NP)" as a relevant kind of sequence over which to form a generalization? In the model proposed, the solution lies in the fact that the derivational component has its own natural units, namely clause-level computations. The result is that the derivational discovery component acts as a filter on the multiple possible statistical generalizations supported by any finite data set, picking out those that fit the derivational templates. Most important is that the properties of the derivational filter change as the knowledge base increases in refinement.

18.9 Finale: Biolinguistics and the individual

Recent discussions, and this conference, have clarified current linguistics as "biolinguistics," the isolation and study of genetic endowment and boundary conditions on the faculty of language. The formal approaches to isolating and explaining universals via abstracted biological constraints on what language is, or by examining the data required to set parameters in an ideal learner, clarify the relevant abstract conditions on individuals learning language. Yet it is a collection of concrete individuals that learn and use language. Thus, these boundary conditions may profit from inclusion of the motivations and actions of individual learners. I have given various kinds of examples of linguistic universals, showing how we can benefit by examining the dynamics of language learning in individuals. The extent to which individuals learn language by way of mechanisms not specific to language alone clarifies what we should take as the essential universals of language. The discussion in this paper of EPP is an example of this kind of argument.

PART IV

Open Talks on Open Inquiries

CHAPTER 19

The Illusion of Biological Variation: A Minimalist Approach to the Mind

Marc D. Hauser

19.1 The illusion of biological variation

The topic that I want to talk about today falls under the title "The illusion of biological variation." Let's consider a canonical perceptual illusion, one in which the image is completely static, with nothing moving at all, except that your visual system thinks it is. Now, no matter how many times you tell the subject that the image is static, his or her visual system won't believe it; it can't. Illusions are interesting because, no matter how aware we are of them, they simply won't go away. Similarly, and by way of analogy, I will suggest today that much of the variation that we see in the natural world is in some sense an illusion because at a different level of granularity, there are some core invariant mechanisms driving the variation.

As in any talk that attempts to go beyond one's typical intellectual limits or comfort zone, I must first make a few apologies. The first one is to Chris Cherniak and other theoretical biologists, for my gross generalizations drawn from some of the very deep facts they have uncovered about the natural world. The second one is to Noam and other linguists because I am going to generate some wild speculations about language evolution from a very fragmentary bit of evidence. The third apology is to a class of philosophers, and in particular to John Rawls, for cutting out all the subtleties of argumentation that have gone on about utilitarianism on the one hand, and deontological principles on the other, so that I can cut to the chase and tell you about how the moral faculty works. And then a final apology to John Cage and many minimalists in music and art, particularly for taking some grotesque liberties with their theories and painting a slightly different picture of what I think they really were after.

The first point to make is that when we look upon the natural world, we immediately see extraordinary variation in animal forms, what looks like limitless variation, not just in size (from extremely small animals to immensely huge animals), but in shapes, material properties, and so forth. Similarly, we see apparently limitless variation in the patterns of animal locomotion, including, most noticeably, those observed in the air, on land, and in the sea. Somebody raised a question earlier about the immune system[1] – again, a system with limitless variation in the kinds of responses that it generates to different kinds of problems in the environment. I want to call all of this observed variation, the "illusion of biological variation." It is an illusion, at least in part, because when biologists have looked deeply into the sources of variation in these different domains, as Cherniak's talk in this conference illuminated (see Chapter 8), we find something different – a common set of core mechanisms that generates the variation.

Let me put this into a historical context by quoting from two biologists who confronted the nature of biological variation. The first is Sewell Wright, who may be known to many of you. He was a distinguished evolutionary biologist who, following on from Darwin, talked about the nature of adaptation and in particular the notion of an adaptive landscape. Here is what Wright pointed out in the 1930s, which I think is very telling in terms of the story I want to paint today (Wright 1932). He says that the older writers on evolution were often staggered by the seeming necessity of accounting for the evolution of fine details. He then adds that structure is never inherited as such, but merely types of structure under particular conditions. Now, at the time Wright was discussing these matters, there were major revolutions afoot in genetics and molecular biology. If we fast-forward the story to today, here is an almost verbatim quote from Mark Kirschner, a systems biologist who makes very much the same point but takes it a little bit further and takes it in a direction that will hopefully have great appeal especially to the linguists in the audience who are interested in certain kinds of structural properties. In essence, Kirschner (Kirschner and Gerhart 2005) says that novelty in the organism's physiology, anatomy, or behavior arises mostly by the use of conserved processes in new combinations at different times, in different places and amounts, rather than by the invention of new processes. This is very much in line with some of the things that Gabby Dover says in his contribution here (see Chapter 6). Kirschner stresses that, in the 4–5 billion years of cellular life on Earth, there have been four core processes

---

[1] See page 178 above.

leading to variation: rearrangement, repetition, magnification, and division. For those of you who have been tracking what has been happening in the minimalist program, you will see a kind of family resemblance to these four core processes.

The idea that I want to push today – a project that Noam and I have been working on a bit over the last year or so, but that I will take full responsibility for in terms of errors – is to invoke three principles that extend the minimalist program in linguistics to the mind and other domains of knowledge more generally. The first is that any time we observe an open-ended, limitlessly expressive, powerful system, it will be based on a fixed set of principles or mechanisms for generating the observed variation – that is, some kind of generative, combinatorial system. Secondly, these generative mechanisms must in some sense interface with system-internal and -external processes, with nature potentially finding the optimal solution given the current conditions. This allows for lots of accidental variation that happened before, but I will talk specifically about how it allows solutions to the current conditions. And then lastly, each variant we observe will be determined by some kind of process of pruning, where the local experience tunes up the biologically given options.

That is the idea in a nutshell. Now I want to take it a little bit further. The main idea in Noam's opening remarks (Chapter 2) and alluded to in Gabby Dover's paper (Chapter 6), is that rather than having thousands and thousands of variants, we have one animal, one blueprint. I know that Gabby is somewhat opposed to this metaphor, but the idea is that we have some kind of conserved process that is generating all the variation. Of course one of the nicest stories to come out in the last twenty or so years is the account related to the Hox gene system, where we can see a direct mapping, remarkably similar from the drosophila embryo all the way up to the mouse embryo, between genes that are basically building segmentation in the body forms. Patterns of segmentation are being driven by evolutionarily ancient genetic mechanisms that have been conserved over evolutionary time. Part of the reason why this is important is because it has changed the nature of the way we think about the notion of homology. If you were simply to focus on anatomical form, and note how different things look, you would be missing the underlying genetic similarity that is extremely conserved and is homologous in that sense.

A second is a recent paper by Bejan and Marden (2006) which has received a lot of attention, especially from functional morphologists, claiming that all patterns of animal locomotion can be explained by equations relating force, energy, frequency, and mass. And just to give you one example of a beautiful fit, they consider the relationship between body mass on the X-axis and force on the Y-axis. In such a plot, it becomes evident that all the animal species that move by running (mammals, reptiles, and insects), all those that fly (birds, bats, and insects), and those that swim (fish, marine mammals, and crayfish) all align beautifully. Now much of the controversy surrounding these results is that experts in the field claim the analyses fail to account for complexities and variations observed. I am sure this is correct, but my guess is that the history of this debate will end up looking a lot like the debates in linguistics, where there are going to be some battles about the details, but what seems to be captured here are generalities.

The move that I want to make is that, given the kinds of depth of investigation that have gone on in biology over the last thirty to forty or more years, when variation has in some sense been put to the side for the purpose of looking at explanatory mechanisms, there is a common theme that seems to keep emerging. What I want to ask now is basically whether that kind of move can be adopted in thinking about the nature of the human mind. Thus, for example, it certainly appears to be the case that there is limitless cultural variation. Can we account for it by some simple, primitive mechanisms, and then use pruning as a mechanism for selecting among the possible, biologically given variants? To test this question, we need to run the universal minimalist program of research. We first look for a core set of rules or mechanisms with a generative power of expression, interfacing with specific forms of knowledge. We next explore whether these mechanisms are present in other animals and the degree to which their presence in humans is unique to a domain of knowledge or more domain-general. Then we run the comparative analysis from genes to behavior, attempting to understand what limits the phenotypic space.

This kind of approach raises a paradox to keep in mind. I don't think either Randy Gallistel or I want to be taken as saying that there is nothing unique about humans at all; only that the comparative evidence we have presented shows there are extraordinary abilities in animals and it is important to keep this in mind. Here, however, is the paradox I want to point to today. Gabby Dover mentioned the genomics of humans, and of course one of the most interesting things about the study of genomics today is the fact that if you look at the genetic relationships or similarities between chimpanzees and humans, they are far more similar to each other than are chimpanzees and humans as a cluster to gorillas. Now that is surprising again if you think about their anatomy. Chimps look much more like gorillas than they do like human beings, and yet at the level of genetic similarity chimpanzees cluster with humans and not gorillas. That said, if we leap now from the anatomical level and genetic levels to the psychological level, we are faced with a fundamental problem. If we take some of the towering intellectual achievements in our history (and even some of the less towering intellectual achievements), the gap between us and them is extraordinary; in fact I would say it is larger than the gap we see between gorillas and chimpanzees on the one side, and the humble beetle on the other. So we have to somehow come to grips with the fact that the genetic level of similarity is not accounting for the psychological variation and differences we see.

So here is the outline for what I want to say in the rest of the present paper. I want to run through three examples. I am going to first come back to language in the way that I spoke about in my previous paper here, and I will flesh out a little bit more of the argument and present some new data that bear on the conceptual richness in non-human animals. Then I will turn to some parallel arguments about the nature of the moral faculty. Then I will turn to music as another domain in which we can basically begin to ask similar kinds of questions, and finally I will end with some summary points about nature's solution to the various kinds of problems about variation and unity.

19.2 Language

So first, language. As I described earlier in this conference, I am going to think about language as *a mind-internal computational system designed for thought and often externalized in communication*, and as such, *language evolved for internal thought and planning and only later was co-opted for communication.*[2] What I want to do now is use this hypothesis as a wedge to pinpoint a disagreement in the literature which I think unfortunately misses the point. But I am going to use it as a way of showing some data that I think actually bear on the argument, capturing the difference between the way that Noam has talked (in this conference and elsewhere) about the internal computational system of language, and the way that Steven Pinker and others have talked about language as an adaptation for communication – a distinction that at some level is virtually impossible to resolve, because language is used for both functions, and the question of evolutionary origins is notoriously difficult, especially for such a complicated trait.

Let us return to the FLB–FLN distinction that I raised earlier on (see also Hauser et al. 2002) and that Cedric Boeckx picked up on in his paper here (see Chapter 3). Let us begin to think about the ways in which understanding of what goes into FLB vs. FLN can help us think about the nature of the evolutionary process vis-à-vis the internal computational system for thought and planning and its externalization in spoken language, or sign language. The hypothesis that Chomsky, Fitch, and I have been pinned with is what Pinker and Jackendoff (Pinker and Jackendoff 2005) have called "the recursion-only

---

[2] See page 74 above.

hypothesis." But that is not actually what we said (Hauser et al. 2002). What we said was that FLN – as an hypothesis – consists of the computations that enter into narrow syntax (we specifically spoke about recursion) and the interfaces to semantics and phonology. We think this is a useful way to frame the problem because it forces one to look not only at the evolution of the computational system alone, but also, how it interfaces with and is constrained by the other mind-internal systems. This move opens the door to interesting comparative issues, which I turn to next.

If we look at the songbirds, species that learn their vocalizations based on some innate structure that guides the process of acquisition with critical periods and windows of opportunity very much like language acquisition, what we see are exceptional capacities for vocal imitation. This is especially true in the open-ended song learners like starlings and lyrebirds and mockingbirds – very complex streaming together of sound patterns that looks like a rich combinatorial system; but no meaning. The variation that you see in the songbird system does not generate new meaning, it is simply "I'm-Fred-the-sparrow-from-New-York." And we're finished, that's it. Change the variation a bit and it's "I'm-Joe-from-California. But I'm still a sparrow, and the meaning or function of my song is simple: I have a territory and I am looking for a mate." *Fini*! This is equally true of humpback whale song – again, very complicated, but the variation yields no new meaning. Now, in my lab, we have recordings of a starling doing its own version of a goat and a chicken, as well as starling song material. Functionally, they use these songs in mate attraction, but they also use it as a sort of "No-vacancy" sign. They flood the habitat and say "You don't want to come here – there are goats and chickens and all sorts of other things around here. Don't bother!" Now monkeys and apes, in striking con-trast, show no evidence for vocal imitation. There is no capacity (and it has been fifty years of intensive looking by primatologists), absolutely no evidence for vocal imitation. Primates typically do not string their calls or notes together: no combinatorics evident at all, and weak meaning if at all in their vocalizations.

Thus far, most of what I have focused on concerns the sensorimotor side. Now I want to come back quickly to animal concepts. People talk about the Galilean revolution; I like "Gallistelean" for talking about concepts. I think Randy Gallistel has done a great deal to help the cause in thinking about animal concepts, especially in terms of the notion of isomorphism. For now, I want to focus on intentionality, and in particular, the puzzle concerning the richness of animal mental life and the poverty of their communicative expressions. It is what I have often described as the metamorphosis problem after Kafka's story, in which Gregor Samsa, *qua* beetle, has profound thoughts about the world, but cannot convey them.

Let's start with physiology, and mirror neurons in particular, and then build up to thought and behavior. In the mid-1990s, Giacomo Rizzolatti was recording from neurons in the pre-motor cortex of a macaque monkey when he noticed that cells firing in response to observing an experimenter grasp an object also fired when this same monkey grasped the same object, in the same way (Rizzolatti et al. 1996). Further recordings, from other cells in the premotor area, revealed a kind of gestural repertoire: cells firing when the action itself is in the repertoire of the animal, and the animal either performs the action or observes another individual performing the same action. There is a linking or coupling between perception and action. Now what I want to show you is how you can take these physiological findings and look at how they may be instantiated in real world behavior in animals trying to make decisions about goals in the world and what they pay attention to when they perceive somebody acting in certain ways.

I am going to explain a study on the island of Cayo Santiago that was carried out by one of my terrific graduate students, Justin Wood (Hauser et al. 2007; Wood et al. 2007). The star of the show, besides Justin, is the rhesus monkey again, and here is the experimental paradigm. You find an animal alone on the island. The monkeys on Cayo Santiago love coconut. Unfortunately, in over eighty years of living on this island, no single individual has ever figured out how to open one. Now this is a problem, because it is the most preferred food. If I crack open a coconut, they all come running. They call, they are very excited and so forth, but they can't work out how to open one on their own. However, they seem to understand that *we* can figure it out, so whenever we move towards some coconuts, they know that something interesting may happen, and it may be for them. This sets up a simple experiment. You show a subject two half coconuts face down. Because they are face down, but already cracked open, they can't see what is inside, but it is possible that one or both coconut halves has some flesh. For each experimental condition, the experimenter places these two half coconuts on the ground, face down, while the animal watches, and then approaches one of the coconut halves and interacts with it in some particular way before walking away. The psychologically relevant question is: does the particular form of interaction or action by the experimenter on the half coconut influence where the subject searches? The results of this study reveal the proportion of subjects selecting the coconut acted upon by the experimenter. For each condition, we use one subject per trial, but multiple animals (between twenty and twenty-four) per condition.

In the first condition, the experimenter simply grasped the top of the coconut but didn't lift it, and then walked away. Here, approximately 90 percent of the subjects approached the coconut that we grasped. Similarly, grasping the coconut with a pincer grip (i.e., index finger and thumb) also resulted in a selective approach to this coconut – approximately 85 percent of subjects. Interestingly, there are cells in the mirror neuron system that distinguish between a full hand grasp and a pincer grip; that is, cells that fire to a pincer grip do not fire to a full hand grasp, and vice versa. In a third condition, we grasped one coconut with a bare foot. Though the rhesus have never seen humans grasp in this particular way, rhesus will use their feet to pick up food, especially when they are hungry and attempt to carry as much food away as possible, using both hands, feet, and their cheek pouches. In parallel with the first two conditions, 90 percent of the subjects go to the foot-grasped coconut. In the final condition in this series, we asked whether rhesus need to see the target goal in order to infer the subject's intentions or whether they can draw this inference when the goal is occluded or out of view. Mirror neurons will fire when an agent reaches for and makes contact with a visible goal as well as when the goal is occluded. Similarly, rhesus selectively approach the occluded coconut when the experimenter reaches for it behind an occluder. Here, therefore, is a class of behaviors or actions that result in selective approaching behavior by rhesus. But there is a simple, and rather trivial explanation for all of these results, which would be that rhesus approach anything that an experimenter touches. If this is the rule they are following, then it is rather uninteresting, explained by simple associative mechanisms. If this is the proper interpretation, then any contact, intentional or not, with one coconut, should lead to selective approach. I turn next to conditions that directly explore the nature of the contact between experimenter and coconut.

In this next condition, the experimenter's hand merely flops on top of the coconut instead of grasping it. From a human perspective, it appears completely unintentional; the hand just flops on top of the coconut and then the experimenter walks away. In this condition, subjects show a 50–50 split: some go to the box associated with the flop, the others go to the non-touched box. We also failed to get selective approach when the experimenter used a pair of pliers with a pincer grip, or contacted one coconut with a pole, or a machete; rhesus never use tools, have never seen the pliers or the pole, but have seen personnel on the island occasionally cracking open coconuts with a machete. The story that we are building up to, then, is not just about contacting or attending to the object, it is about the nature of the contact, intentional or not. Next, if you use the normal grasping mode with your hand, but you touch next to, as opposed to on, the coconut, they also show no preference. Interestingly, if you kneel down and grasp a coconut to use it to stand up (so you grasp it in exactly the same way but now it is just as a way of getting up), they also show no preference.

One of the arguments that has yet to be explored in research on mirror neurons, but that we have begun to investigate, is whether rhesus understand actions that are within the repertoire, in terms of being physically possible, but irrational given environmental constraints. For example, if I have a cup in front of me, I can reach for it by stretching out my hand, or I can reach for it by passing my arm under my leg – an odd gesture. Why would I do that? If an experimenter reaches between his legs and ends up in the hand-grasp position as the terminal position, our preliminary results fail to reveal a selective approach to the target box, even though the terminal state is both intentional and has the final grasping position. We are now in the midst of running a variant of this condition, one in which an experimenter holds a brick in each hand or has both hands empty, and then bends down and contacts the coconut with his mouth. If rhesus are like human infants similarly tested, they should contact the coconut with their mouth in the hands-free condition but not in the hands-with-brick condition; that is, they should interpret the hands-free condition as "if the experimenter has his hands free, but still contacts the coconut with his mouth, then there must be something important about using the mouth in this condition." These studies, and others, suggest that there may be something like a large gestural repertoire that is being encoded for the agent's intentions, goals, and the specific details of his or her action. Cross-cutting these dimensions may also be one that maps to rational vs. irrational trajectories vis-à-vis the end-goal state.

Now before I get too carried away with my excitement over these results, I want to make the following point in order to connect up with the final part of the language section. We seem to be uncovering, in both comparative studies and studies by developmental psychologists (such as my colleagues and collaborators Liz Spelke and Susan Carey, as well as others. Barner et al. 2007), what looks like an occasional mismatch between what individuals seem to know, on some version of knowing, and how they use that knowledge to act. So far what I have shown looks like a fairly good correspondence between their knowledge or attribution of knowledge, and their action, but now what I want to show you is an interesting mismatch. Back to Cayo Santiago and the rhesus monkeys (Barner et al., 2008). An experimenter finds a lone subject and shows this individual a table, indicating by tapping that it is solid; the experimenter then places one box on top of the table and a second box below the table, and then occludes the table and boxes; the experimenter then reveals an apple, holds it above the occluder, drops it, removes the occluder, and walks away, allowing the subject to search for the apple. Where do they go? To the bottom box, almost every single time. In fact, about 15 percent of the subjects look in the bottom box and leave without ever checking the top box, as if they had decided that it must be in the bottom box, and thus, there is no point in checking the top box. Now we do the same experiment, but use the looking-time methodology that I talked about earlier. Here you remove the occluder and show that the apple is actually either in the top box or in the bottom box. Based on the search method that I just described, rhesus apparently expect to find the apple in the bottom box. Therefore, when it appears in the top box, rhesus should be surprised. From their perspective, this is a violation, so they should look longer when it appears in the top box than when it appears in the bottom box. But they don't. They look longer when the apple appears in the bottom box, which corresponds to a correct inference: that is, the apple can't appear in the bottom box as this would violate the physical principle of solidity. Thus, we see a dissociation between the knowledge that seems to be driving their looking responses as opposed to their searching behavior.

How can we tie this back into questions about the language faculty? Consider again the point I raised earlier concerning the possibility that the internal computations evolved for internal thought and then only subsequently evolved further for the purpose of externalization in communication. What seems to be critically missing in non-human primates, and therefore primate evolution, is the interface between their rich conceptual system and the sensorimotor system, but most importantly, the system of vocal imitation. Monkeys and apes do not have the capacity for vocal imitation. As a result, they could never experience a lexical explosion. There is no way to pass the information on without vocal imitation. The implication here is significant. Independently of the story that emerges for the natural vocalizations of animals, and their putatively "referential" calls – such as the vervet monkeys' predator alarm calls – none of these systems show the kind of explosion in meaningful utterances that one sees in children from a very early age. This difference could have emerged for a variety of reasons, but one in particular is that there is no vocal imitation in non-human primates. If some genius vervet monkey invented an entire vocabulary of things for the environment, there would be no way to pass it on. It would just die with that individual. I think this argues very strongly for the idea that the system of thought was evolving for a very long time without any mechanism for externalization. For externalization to emerge, one species had to evolve the capacity to both link conceptual representations to distinctive sound structures, and for these structures to be passed on to others by means of imitation. Only one species seems to have worked this one out: *Homo sapiens*.

19.3 Morality

The same sort of questions arise for morality that arise for language, and interestingly we can think about the analogy between language and morality. I am certainly not the first to have made this kind of point, and let me just give a brief historical note. Several years ago Noam was already asking why does everyone take for granted that we don't learn to grow arms but rather are designed to grow arms? Similarly he noted we should conclude that in the case of the development of moral systems, there is a biological endowment which in effect requires us to develop a system of moral judgment that has detailed applicability over an enormous range.[3] The person who really picked this up in detail was the philosopher John Rawls, who in his 1971 classic, *A Theory of Justice*, made the following point: "A useful comparison here is with the problem of describing the sense of grammaticalness.... There is no reason to assume that our sense of justice can be adequately characterized by familiar common-sense precepts..." – very much like what we have been hearing over the course of this conference about the linguistic moves and inventing of vocabulary – "...or derived from the most obvious learning principles." Again, one of the themes from today. "A correct account of moral capacities will certainly involve moral principles and theoretical constructions which go beyond the norms and standards cited in everyday life."[4]

Now this idea lay dormant for many, many years. A few philosophers, Gil Harman, Susan Dwyer, and most recently, John Mikhail, picked it up and began to argue for it more forcefully. Over the past three years, I have been exploring both the theoretical and empirical implications of the linguistic analogy with two fantastic graduate students of mine, Fiery Cushman and Liane Young;[5] I realize that I probably shouldn't wax so lyrical about my students, but, they really are as terrific as I claim! As a caveat before jumping into the empirical work, let me note that in striking contrast with the revolution in linguistics that took place fifty years ago, where there were already extremely detailed descriptions of language, there is nothing like this in the case of morality. Thus, we started our work with a significant deficit, especially with respect to achieving

---

[3] Another relevant passage is:

As in the case of language, the environment is far too impoverished and indeterminate to provide this [the moral] system to the child, in its full richness and applicability. Knowing little about the matter, we are compelled to speculate; but it certainly seems reasonable to speculate that the moral and ethical system acquired by the child owes much to some innate human faculty. The environment is relevant, as in the case of language, vision, and so on; thus we can find individual and cultural divergence. But there is surely a common basis, rooted in our nature.   (Chomsky 1988: 153)

[4] Rawls 1971: 46–47.
[5] For a detailed treatement and a complete bibliography, see Hauser (2006).

anything like descriptive adequacy. To start the ball rolling, we developed a website called the Moral Sense Test (moral.wjh.harvard.edu). It is a website that internet surfers visit on their own – if they have heard it discussed or if they google "MST" (moral sense test), they will find us. Over a period of about two years we have collected data from approximately 100,000 subjects from 120 different countries, between the ages of 13 and 70. When an individual visits the site, he or she provides some biographical information – age, education, religious background, ethnicity, nationality, and so forth – and then proceeds to read a series of moral dilemmas, followed by questions that ask about the permissibility, obligatoriness, or forbiddenness of an agent's action.

As an empirical starting point, we have made use of several artificial dilemmas created by moral philosophers to explore the nature of our intuitions concerning actions that involve some kind of harm. The use of artificial examples mirrors, in some ways, the artificial sentences created by linguists to get some purchase on the underlying principles that guide grammaticality, or in our case, ethicality judgments.

Why go the route of artificiality when there are so many rich, real-world examples in the moral domain? The first reason that I need to spell out, though probably not as necessary with this audience as with many others, is that the use of artificial stimuli is a trademark of the cognitive sciences, providing a controlled environment to zoom in on the cognitive architecture of the human mind. A second reason, and I think more important in this particular context, is that real-world moral cases like abortion, euthanasia, organ donation, etc. have been so well rehearsed that our intuitions are gone. If I ask you "Is abortion right or wrong?", you've got a view, and you've got a very principled view, in most cases. Whether I disagree with you or not is irrelevant. The main point is that you can articulate an explanation for why you think abortion is right or wrong. If you are interested in the nature of intuition, therefore, asking about real-world cases just won't do. Our moral judgments are too rehearsed. Artificial cases are unfamiliar, but if we are careful, we can manipulate them so that they capture some of the key ingredients of real-world cases. What I mean by careful is that we set up a template for one kind of moral dilemma and then clone this dilemma, systematically manipulating only a key word or phrase in order to assess whether this small change alters subjects' moral judgments. This method thus approximates a model in statistics or theoretical biology where one variable is manipulated while all others are held constant. Thus, for example, we take something like euthanasia, that relies in part on the distinction between actions and omissions, or more specifically, between killing and letting die, and then translate this into an artificial case such as the famous *trolley problems* that I will discuss in one moment. When philosophers make this move, they seem to be happy saying "Well, my intuition tells me that this is right or wrong." But for a biologically minded, empirical scientist, this claim simply raises a second question: is the philosopher's intuition shared by the "man–on–the–street" or is it a more educated decision? This is an empirical question, and one that we can answer. Let me give you a flavor of how we, and others such as Mikhail and my new colleague at Harvard, Josh Greene, have begun to fill in the empirical gaps (Hauser 2006).

Consider four classic cases of the trolley problem. Somebody logs on to our website and they get some random collection of moral dilemmas. If they are trolley problems, they always begin with something like the following: A trolley is moving down a track when the conductor notices five people ahead on the track; he slams on the brakes but they fail, and he passes out unconscious; if the trolley continues on this track it will kill the five people ahead. Here is where the dilemmas begin to change. A bystander can flip a switch killing one person on a sidetrack, but saving the five. And the question each subject will answer is, "Is it morally permissible to flip the switch?" When we ask people this question, 89 percent of our subjects say yes to this question. Okay, now here is a small change in the problem. You are standing on a bridge, and you can push this fat guy off the bridge. He's fat enough that he'll stop the trolley in its tracks, but save the five. You again ask "Is it morally permissible to push the fat guy?" Here, only 11 percent of subjects say yes. Note that the utilitarians have a real problem here, because it is one vs. five in both cases, so if you are a utilitarian, you had better start looking for alternative explanations. Similarly, those with a deontological, non-consequentialist bent, are also in trouble because adhering to the rule that killing is wrong won't work, as your actions result in the death of one in both cases.

Now the problem with these two dilemmas, looking at it scientifically, is that they have too many differences between them – there's a fat guy, there's a skinny guy, there are two tracks, there's a redirection of threat, there is direct contact with a person vs. indirect by means of a switch. What we need are cases where we reduce the variation leaving maybe only one principled distinction between the cases, enabling us to look at the nature of the judgment. So here are two cases. The fat guy's back, but now we have a loop on the track, and if you flip the switch, the train will go onto the loop, but then of course it comes back to hit the five. However, the fat guy, who's fat enough, can stop the trolley there and not kill the five. You once again ask "Is it morally permissible for the bystander to flip the switch?" The important thing to note here is that, just like the bridge case, this case can also be interpreted as using the man as an intended means for the greater good. If he's not there, just flipping the switch does you no good, because the trolley goes on, comes back, and kills the five. The fat man (or in other versions, just a man with a heavy backpack) is the intended means, and your only hope for saving the five. Here, 52 percent of the people say that flipping the switch is morally permissible. Now note, in contrast to the bridge case which only generated an 11-percent-permissibility judgment, there is a difference even though both use the intended means as a distinction. We'll come back to this difference in a minute.

Consider a very similar case: bystander, loop, man, but now the man on the looped track is irrelevant because he's too thin to stop the trolley. However, in front of this man on the loop is a weight which is heavy enough to stop the trolley. This case can be interpreted as killing as a foreseen side-effect. Aiming for the man on the looped track makes no sense as he can't stop the trolley. Aiming for the weight makes sense as it can stop the trolley. Here, 76 percent of subjects say that it is morally permissible for the bystander to flip the switch, which is significantly greater than in the previous loop case. Importantly, these two cases involve impersonal harm, the trolley is redirected, there is only one man on the looped tracks, and the greater good is five saved in both. One of the potentially significant differences is between intended vs. foreseen harmful consequence. That is, using the man as a means to save five as opposed to foreseeing the man's death to save five.

These cases are just the beginning of the story, a flavor of how we have begun to move by thinking about principles. But let me flag something crucial about the notion of a principle. My use of this term is completely different, and ultimately wrong, relative to the level of abstraction of principles that people in linguistics have moved toward. In the case of morality, this is merely a starting point. The intuition is that as we move deeper into this problem, the abstractness of the problem will surface, and the relationship between actions, intentions, and consequences will be as complex and nuanced as are the relationships between the conceptual-intentional system and the syntactic operations that provide structure and, downstream, variegated meaning. So, when I say "principle," think of it in this looser sense, at least for now.

Let me describe three principles, with the first mapping to a distinction I just called upon: the *Intention Principle*. It is basically the principle that Thomas Aquinas invoked as the "doctrine of double effect": harm intended as a means to a goal is morally worse than equivalent harm foreseen as the side effect of the goal. Second, the *Action Principle*: harm caused by action is perceived as morally worse than equivalent harm caused by omission; and lastly, the *Contact Principle*: harm caused by physical contact is morally worse than equivalent harm caused by non-contact. To explore these principles, we developed a large set of moral dilemmas (we now have some 300–400 different moral dilemmas). For each principle, we presented a set of paired dilemmas that only differed in terms of the crucial psychological dimension captured by the principle. Subjects provided judgments on a scale from 1 to 7, with 1 mapping to forbidden, 4 to permissible, and 7 to obligatory. For paired cases in which subjects noticed a difference, we both evaluated this difference statistically and also asked subjects to justify their responses.

Results showed that for both the Intention and Action principles, six out of six scenario pairings revealed support for the operative force of the principle, whereas for five out of six scenarios in the Contact principle, this was also the case. Thus, subjects judged intended harms as morally worse than foreseen harms, actions as worse than omissions, and contact harm as worse than non-contact harm. The next critical question, very much analogous to questions in linguistics, was: are these principles not only operative in that they influence people's judgments, but can they be expressed? Are they recoverable, are they used consciously in deliberations in creating these moral judgments?

For the Action principle, subjects recovered a sufficient justification 80 percent of the time, appealing to comments such as "actions are worse." For the Contact principle, subjects appealed to "contactful" harm as worse than non-contact about 50 to 60 percent of the time. Quite consistently, however, they denied the moral relevance of contact, saying such things as "Well, if you physically touch somebody and it hurts them, that is worse than if you don't touch them . . . Nah, that can't be relevant." So they rejected the principle, and often invented assumptions to explain what was driving their judgment. But perhaps most interesting of all, very few people recovered the Intention principle. People who failed would say things such as "I don't know" or our favorite, "Shit happens!" So here we have a distinction between principles that in each case are clearly operative in that they are driving the nature of the judgment, but only in some cases are they recoverable in that they seem to be expressed in people's distinctions between Case 1 and Case 2. That suggests that some principles seem to be having effects as intuitions and that maybe these intuitions are absolutely not recoverable or are inaccessible, in the same way that linguistic principles that have been discussed here in this conference are inaccessible.

One of the big questions, then, coming back to some of the themes in the conference, is the extent to which we see these kinds of principles as universally in play. To begin addressing this question, we can pinpoint different variables that have classically been invoked as causally relevant to cross-cultural variation and explore the extent to which they influence the patterns of judgment. One of our first stabs has been in terms of religious background. As a first cut, we simply contrasted all subjects indicating some kind of religious background with those marking "atheists." For this initial analysis, we didn't concern ourselves with the specific kind of religious background, but rather with its presence or absence. The clear result thus far is "no." There was not a shred of evidence that people who claim to be religious showed different patterns of moral judgment or moral justification (except that we did of course see people who were religious invoking more, "Well, God must have done something"). Furthermore, we found no differences between people who expressed different degrees of faith or religiosity: individuals who said that they were not very religious showed the same patterns of judgment as those who said that they were very religious; and within the limited sample that we collected, there were no consistent differences among the types of religions (Hauser 2006).

Let me digress for a moment to relate this finding to a recent experience I had in a class at Harvard, and in particular, during the presentation of this material. During my presentation, I could see that some students were getting extremely anxious. I therefore stopped the lecture and said, "You all seem a bit antsy. If you have concerns or questions, please pipe up and let me know." Upon finishing the last syllable of my sentence, one student exploded and said, "Look, I know where you are going with this. This is one of those biological, Darwinian explanations, but there is a clear alternative explanation: simply, God created all the universals." These are tough moments for a teacher. On the one hand, you want to respect the variety of views that people can have, and on the other hand, you want to explicate the positions, and show that issues of faith and science are entirely different ways of knowing or understanding. I responded, "We may be at an impasse here. I can either capitulate because I can't call up any evidence to show that your position is wrong, or we can take the following path together. If it is true that most, if not all religions take as inspiration some divine power, and divine power provides the intuitions that create religious doctrine, then I think you have a problem. Since religious doctrine can't explain the pattern of judgments we observe, but you want to argue that God or some divine power provides the universals, then you have to say that religion rejects divine inspiration when it comes to these moral judgments. This just strikes me as very problematic for the religious position, at least if you think that there is an empirical issue, as opposed to an issue that strictly relies on faith."

The other point I would make is that of course everyone taking the moral sense test logs on to the Internet, and thus our sample is very skewed. In fact you could say, "Even if you are not religious, you've been exposed to Christianity at some level, so of course that is why you are finding the pattern that you have." To address this problem, we have begun to present the same kinds of moral dilemmas to small-scale hunter-gatherer societies that have no explicit religious system – this doesn't mean that they lack beliefs, but rather, that their system of beliefs is not made explicit in the form of religious doctrine or accounts. And they certainly haven't been exposed to Christianity. So if we find similarities

I think it argues even more strongly for certain patterns of universality driven by some biologically set-up system. An interesting example comes from the Kuna Indians, a very small-scale hunter-gatherer/subsistence society in Panama that has had little contact with the outside world. We have given one village community various kinds of moral dilemmas, cases that in important ways mimic the trolley problems. Now here is an intriguing, albeit preliminary result. If you give them an example that is like the bystander case, a canoe going down a river which can displace crocodiles away from five onto one, most people said that it is permissible for the bystander to redirect the crocodiles. If you give them a version of the fat-man case, in which a person can push a fat man out of a tree in front of a herd of stampeding boar, saving the five, but killing the fat man, only about half say that pushing is permissible.

Now, here is the important lesson, I think. This culture, as well as others that we have been able to look at such as a Mayan community in the Chiapas area of Mexico, see the difference between intended and foreseen harms. In the case of the Kuna, however, the difference between means-based and foreseen harms seems to be less than it is in the Western and developed societies that we have tested on the internet. This is very preliminary and could be driven by all sorts of confounds, but for the moment, let us assume the pattern is real. We can explain the increased permissibility of intended harms in the Kuna by looking at their recent history of infanticide. That is, one sees almost no physical deformities in this society, primarily because those with such deformities are killed early in life. So intended killing is part of the society. What we think is happening, perhaps as a form of parametric variation, is that all societies will show the Intention principle, but each society can tune the degree of difference between means-based and foreseen harms – but not eliminate it.

I hope this provides a flavor of the argument and the work that lies ahead. I think the principles here are nowhere near where they need to be. I think in some sense we need to go back to some of the work that was started a long time ago in the philosophy of action, laying out in greater detail the nature of computation in action perception that may provide some of the primitives to our moral judgments. Even with all the empirical holes, however, I think we now have a new and important set of questions, with answers forthcoming.

19.4 Music

In this final empirical section, I will focus on music. Again, there is limitless variation in music as there appears to be for language and morality; the question is whether there are some primitives that are both driving and constraining the variation. What I don't want to spend too much time debating is a definition of music, as this could lead us down a never-ending path that would be quite fruitless. Here, however, is a quote that I like because it captures at least some of the functionality of music: "The purpose of music is to sober and quiet the mind, thus making us susceptible to divine influences." What I actually like about this quote is that it begins to capture two important aspects of music that I want to explore here, which is the interface between some kind of perceptual pattern recognition and our emotions. John Cage, of course, who really started the minimalist move in music, made exactly this kind of argument. Here is one of my favorite quotes by Cage: "I can't understand people who say I am frightened of new ideas, I am frightened of the old ones." This certainly seems to capture a flavor of the minimalist program in linguistics. There is a little piece from John Cage that relies on only three notes, over and over again, but with crucial changes in tempo and the intensity or attack. This tradition continued, for some people to their great horror, including Cage's famous "4'33"" – a piece of simple silence, lasting for four minutes and 33 seconds, precisely the length of time of typical "canned music." Taking liberties with the views espoused by the minimalist movement, I think that minimalist music focuses on breaking up the intentionality created by music, emphasizing the silences, randomness, slowness, and tempo in particular. As such, it attempts to strip music to its core, its skeletal features, and assess how such structures mediate perception. Even if this rather loose interpretation is too loose, I think it is a wonderfully ambitious and exciting project that sits at the interface of the arts and sciences.

Now here is what I want to do to show again how comparative work can bear on questions of music structure and perception. It is true that every single culture that we know about has music as part of its system, and the question is, are there invariants? Two invariants that appear to emerge, cross-culturally, are that consonant intervals are perceived as more pleasant than dissonant intervals, and that lullabies have virtually identical structures, simple, repetitive elements, slow tempos, and a restricted range of frequencies. Assuming these are invariants, part of our species' biological endowment, we can next ask: how did these perceptual–emotional biases evolve and are they uniquely human?

To address this question, we turn to studies of non-human primates. In particular, my students and I wanted to understand not only what primates perceive, but whether they spontaneously discriminate certain musical styles, and especially, like some more than others. Thus, our goal was to explore how potentially ancient perceptual mechanisms interface with the emotions to generate distinctive musical preferences.

To explore this problem, my recent graduate student Josh McDermott worked with me to design a very simple experimental approach using a V-shaped maze (McDermott and Hauser 2005). We released an animal, either a cotton-top tamarin or a common marmoset, into this maze, and while they were on one branch of the V-maze, a hidden speaker played a particular sound; as soon as they crossed over to the other branch, a different sound played. What this method provides is a kind of listening station where the animal gets to choose its musical selections, at least within the options of a session. They don't receive any physical rewards for choosing, simply the exposure to different sounds. Before we explored some of the more interesting musical contrasts, we first wanted to establish that the method would work and thus contrasted loud white noise with soft white noise. We found consistent preferences in both tamarins and marmosets: a strong preference to spend time on the soft white-noise side, as opposed to the loud. Similarly, if you present tamarins with a choice between their own, species-specific food chirps (associated with food) and their submissive screams (associated with fear), they spend more time on the chirp side than the scream side. These results reveal that the method works, providing a tool to explore spontaneous preferences for particular sounds.

Now we ask the question, if you give them dissonant intervals vs. consonant intervals, do they show a preference for consonance as would be predicted from studies of human adults and infants? Results for tamarins and marmosets failed to reveal a statistically significant preference for consonance over dissonance either at the group or individual level. This shows that neither tamarins nor marmosets show a spontaneous preference for consonance. It is unlikely that this result is due to a psychophysical constraint as several prior studies, using both behavioral and neurophysiological preparations, have revealed clear evidence of discrimination. Rather, what our studies show is that despite a physiological capacity to discriminate consonance from dissonance, this is not a meaningful distinction for these animals in that it fails to generate spontaneous preferences for one stimulus over the other.

What about lullabies? We wondered whether there would be a preference for lullabies versus something else, so we started simply, contrasting a non-vocal, flute lullaby with a non-vocal piece of German techno. The younger members of my lab were voting strongly for the techno, and I was praying secretly (though I am not religious) for the lullabies. Consistently, both species preferred the lullabies to the techno. For some, this will either represent an exceedingly trivial result or one not worth discussing because the experiment is so poorly controlled. That is, there are dozens of differences between lullabies and techno, and so the crucial question is: what acoustic properties underlie the preference for what we are describing as a lullaby? As we planned all along, the lullaby–techno contrast was simply an opening card, designed to see if we could find a systematic preference and if so, then attack the problem to determine what features are in play. I won't discuss all of the conditions, but will focus on one that is quite telling, specifically, the role of tempo. Recall that I mentioned the observation that lullabies tend to have slow tempos. As a result, perhaps the preference for lullabies merely reflects a preference for slow tempos. Thus, we presented a choice between short segments of sound played at either a fast (400 beats per minute) or slow (60 beats per minute) tempo. Consistently, subjects preferred the side playing the slow over the fast tempo. Thus, one crucial factor driving the preference for lullabies may be an evolutionarily ancient bias towards slow tempos. And one good reason for this preference is that if you look at a whole variety of species' alarm calls, they are typically associated with fast tempos. Fast tempoed sounds seem to be coupled with aversion or avoidance of what is going on in their natural vocalizations.

Following a discussion of this work, several colleagues challenged us with different versions of the following question: "Okay, your tamarins might prefer lullabies over techno, and slow over fast tempos, but do they prefer lullabies as we seem to do, and as children do, over peace and quiet?" The answer is a resounding "No!" Both species actually prefer silence to hearing a lullaby. So even though they have a preference for certain kinds of music, there seems to be a strong preference for silence over noise. Perhaps they are just ahead of their time, prescient animals who had to wait for minimalism and John Cage's "4'33"."

Coming back to some of the themes of this conference, what might be the uniquely human aspect of the music faculty is the interface between evolutionarily shared systems of tempo and frequency discrimination together with the systems that are recruited for emotional processing. That is, we share most, if not all of our capacities for frequency and tempo discrimination with other animals, and a significant proportion of our abilities for emotional processing with animals, but it is the interface between these systems that perhaps uniquely constructed our music faculty.

Two final points to wrap up. What I have tried to argue in this paper is that one way of thinking about the nature of the human mind is to take the lead from much of what is happening in biology much more generally, what has been happening in linguistics more specifically, and running with the idea of universal minimalism, the idea being to look for basic rules and computations. I think this is consistent with some of the issues that Chris Cherniak brings up in his paper (see Chapter 8). If you look at some of the core computations that have been invoked in this conference and for the minimalist program more generally – notions like Copy, Move, Merge, Hierarchical Dominance, and so forth – these are precisely the kinds of operations that are invoked by cellular and molecular biologists such as Mark Kirschner (Kirschner and Gerhart 2005). Secondly, once you invoke notions of modularity such as those that Gabby Dover brings up in his paper, you somehow need to create mechanisms that will enable interfaces between systems. The crucial question is: what is doing the translation, and how do the different representational formats "speak" to each other? In the case of language, for example, how does the representational format that codes for distinctive features in phonology interface with the representational format that codes for concepts within the system of semantics? Lastly, given the promiscuity of these systems to create the variation, ultimately what happens is that the environment is going to prune them back from the biologically given options, and this process will yield the distinctive signature observed in the local environment – thus, the move from I-language to E-language.

I hope this gives a reasonable sketch of the minimalist approach, and how it might open the door to new ways of thinking about our minds and how they evolved.

Discussion

HIGGINBOTHAM: I wanted to raise a question on intended vs. foreseen. I think it is a bit tricky to make the distinction. You may remember that Kant famously said that you intend the consequences of everything you intend. So in the sense of Kant's dictum, in using the weight to save the five people, I also know that death is a consequence and therefore I intend the death of the skinny guy. Moreover, it is a bit of a trick if you ask how these things are conceptualized. Suppose I intend to take a drink of water. So then I stand up and I walk over and I pick up the bottle. Or I flip a switch because I want to find my eyeglasses. If you ask what I intended to do, one might view the situation in the following way. I intended to move my finger like this [stretching finger out] and the rest [moving arm forward] was foreseen consequences. So I think you have to frame it in some way that is rather careful, where you speak of the intended–foreseen distinction in some way that is categorized properly for the agent, and it is not so obvious how to do this just from a description.

Also a correlative question is, I have read a number of books, all of which I think are terrible, about moral permissibility, as if this were some kind of abstract stuff that you can sort of throw out. But is it possible to change any results, or have you considered asking the question in a more first-personal way? Would *you* pull the trigger, vs. should *he* pull the trigger – the dirty-hands thing?

HAUSER: Yes, great questions, and I am sympathetic particularly to the first. I mean I think I was trying to foreshadow your question in the sense of saying that I think the notion of principles that I am picking up is really crude, and I think it is crude in precisely the way that you pointed out. For example, try pushing the analogy to language even further. Let's say that the notion of an action, a representation of an action, or what we might call an "acteme," is like a phoneme – completely meaningless in isolation, and only gaining in meaning as a function of particular sequences, underpinned by intentional states, and generating particular consequences. In this sense, bending your finger may be either meaningful or meaningless. It depends on how it is strung together with intentional states and other surrounding actemes or actions. John Mikhail, who has written a very nice thesis[6] and is really my co-collaborator in much of this, intellectually at least, has tried to make much more subtle kinds of distinctions appealing back to some of the philosophy of action, and especially Goldmanesque decision trees. I think the problem is that these trees are not at the right level of grain. And I think all the complications that have been raised in the philosophy of mind and language about the notion of intentionality are not cashed out. Frances Kamm, I think, is one of the few people actually engaged in moving these ideas forward.[7] She has created extraordinarily complex dilemmas that largely target the same scenario, the famous trolley problems. For Kamm, however, the issue is not one about empirical research or deep questions about the mind, but about probing our intuitions to decide what is prescriptively or normatively permissible. That said, I am convinced that the kind of work she has put into play will make significant contributions to the empirical studies that we are engaged with.

On the second point, we have approached this question from several other directions. Let me tell you about two of these. If everyone carries around some version of the categorical imperative, then they should answer these scenarios in the same way if they are judging (a) their own actions as the bystander, (b) a third party as the bystander, and (c) themselves or another as one of the possible victims on the track. This would be exquisite evidence of a folk theory of the categorical imperative! Now the problem is, how to dissociate what will clearly be a very strong emotional response to being on the track and saving your derrière. And this is precisely where studies of patient populations enter, and in particular, patients with damage to brain areas associated with emotional processing. This isn't going to directly answer the You/I suggestion, but let me give you a flavor of the move. Consider Antonio Damasio's classic

---

[6] Mikhail (2000).
[7] Kamm (2000).

studies of patients with damage to the ventromedial prefrontal cortex.[8] Much of the work on these patients suggests that there is a problem with the connection between the emotional areas in the amygdala and decision areas (this is crudely described) in the frontal lobes. Due to such deficits, these patients appear to have severe problems in the socioemotional domain, including moral decision making. In collaboration with Damasio and several other colleagues, including my two students Liane Young and Fiery Cushman, we have refined our understanding of this deficit by systematically exploring a broader part of the space of moral judgment.[9] Cutting a long story short, these patients seem to have a very selective deficit: they only show differences with normals on a certain class of dilemmas which are other-serving personal cases. They are true moral dilemmas in the sense that there is no adjudicating norm that clearly arbitrates between the options, and where one option is to engage an action that is aversive, but where the consequence is to maximize aggregate welfare in terms of saving more lives. Under these conditions, the frontal patients go with the utilitarian outcome, as if the aversiveness of the act was irrelevant.

HIGGINBOTHAM: You said the categorical imperative, but actually you meant the utilitarian, I think. It is the utilitarian for whom it doesn't matter who carries out the action.

HAUSER: I meant the categorical imperative in the sense of, I think this is a permissible action, I just think it is permissible in the sense of being permissible for any...

HIGGINBOTHAM: An imperative is an imperative about maxims, it is not about individual actions, it is about reasons for doing them. It is the utilitarian who has the problem here.

HAUSER: Right. More questions?

PARTICIPANT: If I didn't misunderstand you, you related the lack of lexicon in primates to an inability for vocal imitation. Is that right?

HAUSER: That is not the sole reason. What I was saying is, that no matter how rich the conceptual system, there are at least two problems, one of which is that even if they could externalize, they can't pass the information on. So there are two problems. Thinking about FLN again, there is both the problem of the mapping between sound and meaning, but there is the additional problem of being able to pass it on.

---

[8] Damasio (1994); Bechara et al. (1994).
[9] Koenigs et al. (2007).

PARTICIPANT: Yes, but then what I am questioning is your saying it just in terms of vocal imitation, because certainly they can pass on gestures, but they cannot pass on signs, or sign language.

HAUSER: Even gestural imitation is extremely impoverished in primates. "Monkey see, monkey do," just for the record, is a myth. No evidence. The best gestural imitation is weak, very very weak, relative to humans. It has taken literally thirty years to show even the most slight evidence of it. So it is absent vocally, it is weak at best visually.

CHOMSKY: On this same point, there is another form of transmission, namely by inheritance. So suppose that you get a smart ape, one that comes up with a combinatorial system. That ape has advantages. It can think, it can plan, it can interpret and so on, and its descendants will have the same advantages even without vocalization. If those advantages are sufficient, they could take over the whole breeding group. They'd all have these capacities and then vocalization could come along later because it is useful to interact. So I think there is a crucial (I'd like to expand the difference between Steve Pinker and me) – I think a possibility is that that is the way the transmission took place.

HAUSER: Yes. My quick answer to that is that that would not affect the story I told. Indeed, it would add to it, which I think is perfectly reasonable. In fact, it does enlarge the gap because it says that much of primate thought could have been really moving in quite extraordinary ways by genetic transmission, and then it may have even been a more simple trick of something about the auditory–production loop that got fused, and that could have been a trivial step.

CHOMSKY: Yes. The other question is whether you are proving something that I have always believed, namely that teenagers are a different species. [laughter]

HAUSER: Like right, man.

PIATTELLI-PALMARINI: Marc, regarding the domain of decision-making, as you know Thomas Gilovitch and Daniel Kahneman and others have shown that, in the short term at least, there is more regret for something you did than for something you didn't do, even though the consequences are exactly the same.[10] This is a traditional thing, and you seem to have it here, you know, omission vs. action. But on the other hand, Connolly and Zeelemberg[11] and others have shown that a crucial factor is whether you are somebody who is supposed to be doing something – for example a doctor is called to do something, and he either

---

[10] Gilovich and Medvec (1995).
[11] Connolly and Zeelemberg (2002).

does nothing and the patient dies, or he does something and the patient also dies. That is, the same result happens when the doctor fails to act, as when he does something but makes the wrong decision. The doctor who was called to do something and failed to act is considered worse morally. So I wonder whether you plan to extend it. It would be interesting because it has to do with counterfactuals, and it also has to do with a number of other tests that have been made, where there is something anomalous in the series of actions and you pinpoint the anomalous thing as being *the* cause of what happens.

HAUSER: Yes, we are. Take the classic case that James Rachels brought forward,[12] which some of you may well know, of the greedy uncle who wants to do away with his nephew who is first in line for the family inheritance. In Story 1, he's babysitting the nephew and he goes upstairs while the nephew is taking a bath, and he intends to kill the kid and he drowns him. So he intends to kill and he kills. In Story 2 he has the same exact intentions, he goes upstairs, the kid has flipped over in the bathtub and is drowning, and he just walks away and lets him drown. Now the first is an action, the second is an omission, but we don't want to see those cases as different, in fact we see them both as the same. So in some cases we don't see a difference between action and omission, and in some cases we do, and the question is, how much information do you attribute to the agent, that then makes you either lose it or pick it up? I think it is not clear in the philosophical literature at all. And it is also not clear to what extent we are vulnerable to the action–omission distinction. So that is what we are trying to do in two ways. One is to play around with when you get the information, whether you get the consequences first or the intentionality first, and I will come back to that in a second, and the second question is, to what extent is this distinction available early in life? We know almost nothing about action–omission in its ontogeny in young children; we know almost nothing about the means–foreseen distinction either. Oddly, even though there has been a rich literature on theory of mind, these distinctions don't enter into the discourse because they have largely been developed within moral psychology and the law. But they bear directly on the agent's mental states.

One more case. This is a nice case by a philosopher named Joshua Knobe.[13] There is a CEO of a company, and the President of the company comes to the CEO and says "Look, I've got a policy which, if implemented, will make us millions of dollars." Now there are two versions of the story. In Story 1, the President says "If we implement the policy, there is a good chance it'll

---

[12] Rachels (1975).
[13] Knobe (2005). See also Hauser (2006).

make millions of dollars, but it will probably harm the environment." In Story 2, the policy will probably help the environment. In the first case, the CEO says, "Look, I don't care about harming the environment, I just care about making money. Implement the policy." The company implements the policy, and they make millions of dollars, and it harms the environment. Now you ask people: did the CEO intend to harm the environment? Here, subjects say yes. In the help case, however, the CEO says the same thing, "I care about making money, I don't care about the environment. Implement the policy." Now you ask people: did the CEO intend to help the environment? Here, subjects say no. The idea here is that labeling an individual with some kind of moral attribute like *blame*, or *blameworthy*, actually affects the intentional attribution, at least at some level. So again, there can be all sorts of ways in which these patterns unfold, depending upon the temporal flow of them through time.

JANET DEAN FODOR: Making these moral distinctions is actually very distressing. I have to kill at least one guy if not five. And so the natural thing is to reach for a rationale, an excuse of some kind, and a very common excuse it seems to me is to blame the victim. I think we can all remember cases where we have tried to blame the victim. So this is a factor that could be introduced into the experiment so that the five guys have been told it is stupid to walk on the tracks, it is dangerous to them and everybody else; the one fat guy has been told that this is a track that is never used, it is perfectly safe to walk here, or vice-versa. Is this a universal that would make a difference to the study?

HAUSER: Yes, the problem here is that the space at some level is unconstrained in terms of the number and kind of permutations you could run. You could ask about in-group vs. out-group, you could change the numbers – there are all sorts of things you could change, and several papers have explored this part of the problem. We have taken a different route, which is to hold these personality traits constant in order to explore the causal–intentional structure of event perception in the moral domain. As soon as you put things like responsibility (like they're workmen, they should be there; or it is the conductor's job, he's got a responsibility towards the others), you are going to change lots of the dynamics. And I find these to be very difficult problems, headed more toward social psychology, and a zone that I am less familiar with. It is not that these are the wrong kinds of questions, but rather, that I have less confidence with regard to the experimental questions. I feel more comfortable with the primitives underlying causal–intentional attributions because I am quite convinced that we can explore these issues in infants, animals, patient populations, and so forth. That is, in the same way that Lila Gleitman has been exploring the foundations of giving and hugging in infants (see pages 207–211), looking at how infants dig beneath the surface dynamics, we have moved in a similar direction.

What is also of interest is how confident people can be about their judgments for one or two cases, but as they pile up, they lose this confidence, and the reason we think this is happening is because they don't really have access to the underlying principles, just the surface features of each case. Let me illustrate with my father, a very smart, rational physicist. He had asked me what I was working on, and so I decided to illustrate by giving him some moral dilemmas. I started with the bystander case and he answered, "Well of course you flip the switch." I then gave him the fat man trolley case and he said, "Well of course you push the man." This is, you will recall, a relatively rare response so I asked him why. He replied, "Well, because it is always better to save five than one." I then give him the classic organ-donor case, where there is a surgeon in the hospital and a nurse comes in and says, "We've got five people in critical care, each needs an organ, we have no time to ship out for the organs, but you know what? This guy just walked in to visit his friend. We could take his organs and save five lives. Is that okay?" My father says, "That's ridiculous, you can't just kill a healthy person off the streets!" "But wait," I say, "you just killed the fat man." He says, "Okay, you can't kill the fat man." I say, "What about the switch case where you killed the guy on the side track?" He says, "Okay, you can't do that either." So, ultimately, the whole thing unravels, because you can only locally explain one dilemma but you can't explain the cluster, because you don't have access to the underlying principles. This is the core intuition driving our work.

FODOR: I am not sure why you think the universals are likely to be about the agent and not about the patient.

HAUSER: Oh, I think the universals may come in at the patient level too. My guess is that it is a universal, and so there are studies by Lewis Petrinovich showing that if you put kinship groups as the patients, you are going to get evolutionary sociobiology to work.[14] "I will favor those who are more genetically related to me over those who are not, all else equal." You can get species effects. "I will favor human over even an endangered species like the chimpanzee." So these effects are certainly operative, and they may well be a part of what is universal, but I don't think this part is specific to morality. Ingroup–outgroup distinctions arise in all sorts of contexts, some moral and some not. More importantly, perhaps, we have tried to tackle a different set of problems by holding patient identity out of the scenario, operating under a kind

---

[14] Petrinovich (1995).

of Rawlsian veil of ignorance. By doing this, we hope to uncover the architecture of the underlying psychological cause of the agent's actual action.

PARTICIPANT: I wanted to shift to the musical section. I'd be very curious, if you could create a variable to your experiment – I would suspect that part of the preference for silence has to do with just the foreign nature of technologically produced sounds that we have *learned* to appreciate, like the flute or recorder sound in a lullaby. It may be quite offensive to the ear of some other primate. Referring back to your earlier experiments with quantification, one of the appeals of music is the structures that come with repetitious quantities – a performing musician learns to play chord progressions, for example, without physically counting them. You don't go "One, two, three, one one, two three two"; you *hear* the changes. And I wondered if there would be an appeal among primates that had a quantifying capacity, when using sounds from nature, that could be organized structurally to repetitively use sounds that they're familiar with rather than some kind of human technology that is used. Just an idea to look at whether the appeal of the recognition of repetitive quantities is a big factor in what we like about music. It's why young people like Techno.

HAUSER: In some sense I agree, but we are at such an early stage of this work that it is hard to make sense of much of it. There have been a couple of papers recently, by Smith and Lewicki, claiming that lots of the physiological firing patterns that you see to sounds have a very primitive system or structure that really taps into natural sound, and speech may simply be parasitic on this mechanism.[15] This position or perspective sets up a study that I just finished in collaboration with Athena Vouloumanos[16] – this is a slight tangent with respect to your question but it gives you an idea of what would be basic in terms of the auditory system.

There has been fifty years of research on neonates' preference for speech. The common lore is that babies are, early on, tuned to speech, preferring to listen to speech than non-speech, and showing significant abilities for speech discrimination. The problem has been that none of the studies to date have contrasted speech with other biological sounds, focusing instead on reversed speech, sine wave speech, white noise, and a variety of non-biological sounds. We therefore set out to test thirty-two neonates, less than forty-eight hours old, with a non-nutritive sucking technique where suck rate gives information about interest or attention to the material. We contrasted non-native speech with rhesus monkey vocalizations, and thus, both sets of stimuli are novel at some

---

[15] Smith and Lewicki (2006).
[16] Vouloumanos and Werker (2007); Werker and Vouloumanos (2000).

level. The result was clear as can be: no preferences at all. Neonates sucked as much for non-native speech as they did for rhesus monkey calls. By the age of 3 months, however, possibly earlier, a preference for speech is in place. These results suggest that there are general auditory biases that get tuned up quickly in development. These results also rule out all the arguments that have been put forward for *in utero* experience, because by the third trimester, the baby is certainly getting some acoustic input. But whatever that is, it is insufficient to create a preference for speech over rhesus monkey calls. So that is just a long-winded way of saying that some of the preferences in music may well derive from quite general auditory preferences. It is certainly possible that if we had played more biological sounds, perhaps structured in some musically relevant pattern, then we would have seen a different pattern of responses.

Let me add one relatively new piece of data, still preliminary in terms of our analyses. We have just completed a study in which we presented marmosets with five months of exposure, twelve hours a day, to consonant chords, and then, to samples of mozart. The idea here was to more closely approximate the kind of exposure that human infants receive during early development. When we subsequently tested our subjects for a preference for consonance over dissonance, either chords or pieces of Mozart, subjects showed no preference. Interestingly, however, infants but not adults, exposed to the same materials showed a mere exposure effect, preferring the specific sounds played over novel, but matched sounds. This provides one of the first pieces of evidence in a non-human primate for a critical period effect.

GELMAN: Just a bit on music. I expected you to be talking about something like harmonic principles, some principles of music that the mind treats as privileged. Consonance–dissonance is one of those, but if you are using chords, it matters whether you are in Western music or not. So the issue becomes what is universal across different harmonies. I believe it is the case that the octave and the fifth appear almost invariably in every harmony, where it is consonant, and that the transitions are such that they'll be very different, but you will find they are the fifth. That is not trivial because the physics is such that the first overtone is the octave, the second is the fifth, the ear is sensitive to these, etc. So this might mean that the principles are highly abstract and are harmonic principles, just as the linguistic principles that we are looking for are very highly abstract. And maybe it is not a question of whether the sounds are consonant are not, because what is consonant for us is not necessarily consonant in another culture. It is how we fill in the transitions that varies enormously.

HAUSER: Yes, it is a crude cut. And again, psychophysically there have been studies showing that animals exhibit octave discrimination and generalization.

In particular, Anthony Wright and coworkers have shown that if you train rhesus monkeys in a match-to-sample paradigm, using children's melodies, they can readily do the transpositions.[17]

GELMAN: The really interesting question is whether they will also generalize to the fifth; actually I have data I never published that show 5-year-olds will. But they're experienced.

HAUSER: Way experienced.

---

[17] Wright et al. (2000).

CHAPTER 20

What is there in Universal Grammar?

On innate and specific aspects of language*

Itziar Laka

One of the most controversial and influential aspects of Chomsky's legacy is the hypothesis that there is an innate component to language, which he named universal grammar (UG) (Chomsky 1965), in homage to the rationalist thinkers in whose footsteps he was walking. I would like to present and discuss results obtained from a variety of sources, mostly in neighboring fields within cognitive science, that bear on this central issue.

Like Janet Fodor, who mentions in her paper Chomsky's *Aspects* (1965), I also want to go back, about fifty years, and start with a piece of literature that is crucial for understanding what the research program of generative linguistics is, and also what the current research program is in the interdisciplinary study of human language. I am referring to the review that Chomsky wrote of B. F. Skinner's *Verbal Behavior* (Chomsky 1959c).

The hypothesis that there are innate organism-internal factors that constrain the languages that humans know and use sounded preposterous to most scholars in the Humanities and Social Sciences back in 1959 when Chomsky published it. The UG hypothesis, as he later named it, has since generated

* I would like to thank the organizers of this encounter for the opportunity to take part in it, and all the participants, both speakers and people in the audience, for stimulating views and discussions. Special thanks to Andreu Cabrero, Kepa Erdozia, Aritz Irurtzun, Guillermo Lorenzo, Christophe Pallier, Nuria Sebastián, and Juan Uriagereka for valuable comments and feedback. Misrepresentations and shortcomings are solely mine.

a great amount of research, discussion, and argument, a distinguished example of which is the Royaumont Debate between Piaget and Chomsky in 1975 (Piattelli-Palmarini 1980b). In other fields, however, such as biology, the claim that human languages are largely shaped by innate conditions not only did not encounter resistance, but was received with sympathy, because it naturally converged with a general view of living organisms and the importance of genetic factors in behavior (Piattelli-Palmarini 1994).[1] I think it safe to say that, fifty years later, it is widely accepted that innate mechanisms have a relevant role to play in a full understanding of the human capacity for language. Current disagreements concern the nature and specificity of those mechanisms, regarding both our species and the cognitive domain(s) where they belong.

So the question I would like to pursue is: what are the contents of UG? That is to say, what has been discovered regarding the innate component of human language since it was argued, half a century ago, to be a significant part of a human's knowledge of language? I will not engage in an exhaustive review of the variety of linguistic arguments and evidences put forward during these years to substantiate the hypothesis within linguistic theory. Rather, I will look at a variety of mechanisms that stand the sharpest tests for innateness, and discuss which ones are good candidates for UG membership and why. This will constitute the part of "what we think we know" about innateness in language, but since the organizers of this event have also urged us to think of "what we would like to know"[2] I will also briefly mention at the end an aspect of language that still appears elusive, I think, but is crucial for a thorough understanding of its whole design.

A secondary goal of this talk is to bring to the attention of linguists results and findings from neighboring fields within cognitive science that bear on the issue of innateness and specificity in language. I happen to be a theoretical linguist who has become increasingly engaged in cooperative, experimental research with cognitive psychologists. I believe the benefits of this interdisciplinary way of working largely surpass the frustrations and communication difficulties that are inevitably encountered along the way. I will discuss

---

[1] The Royaumont debate was organized by biologists, among them Piattelli-Palmarini (1994: 322) who said:

There was every reason (in our opinion) to expect that these two schools of thought should find a compromise, and that this grand unified metatheory would fit well within modern molecular biology, and the neurosciences. Both systems [Chomsky's and Piaget's] relied heavily on "deeper" structures, on universals, on precise logico-mathematical schemes, on general biological assumptions. This was music to a biologist's ears.

[2] The sentence appeared in the text sent with the invitation to this conference. (Editors' note)

discoveries related to innateness and specificity relatively well known by language researchers within cognitive psychology, but perhaps not very well
known in linguistics proper, and discuss their relevance both to the research
program that took off some fifty years ago with the birth of generative grammar,
and to our current concepts of grammar and language. I would also like to
caution against the temptation to take it for granted that any innate properties
found in language must necessarily be part of UG. As we shall see, innateness
is a necessary condition for a given mechanism to belong in UG, but not a
sufficient one: specificity is also required. UG should contain those properties of
language, if any, that cannot be fully accounted for elsewhere, for example in
the sensorimotor side of language or in the conceptual-semantic component,
both of which predate grammar. This approach, this research strategy, takes
the name of minimalism (Chomsky 1995b) and necessarily causes us to reflect
on what UG is and to try to reduce it, trim it, and pare it down to its bare
necessities.

The term universal grammar is not used in the 1959 review, but the hypothesis, though nameless, was already there, right at the start. In fact, the word
"innate" appears three times in the review, once referring to imprinting in
animals, and twice referring to human language in the context of language
acquisition. One instance is this:

As far as acquisition of language is concerned, it seems clear that reinforcement, casual
observation and inquisitiveness (coupled with a strong tendency to imitate) are important factors, as is the remarkable capacity of the child to generalize, hypothesize and
process information in a variety of very special and apparently highly complex ways
which we cannot yet describe or begin to understand, and which may be largely innate,
or may develop through some sort of learning or maturation of the nervous system.
(Chomsky 1959c: 43)

We can see that Chomsky is not saying that imitation is irrelevant for the
acquisition of language; he is simply making the point that it will not suffice
to tell the whole story. In fact imitation is a crucial, rather distinctive property of
humans, and our imitation is highly sophisticated (Meltzoff and Printz 2002).
Despite this, language acquisition researchers have found abundant evidence
that imitation alone does not account for language learning. The crucial issue in
the quote is that it appeals to (then unknown) conditions that determine the
process of language acquisition – that is, hypothetical acquisition mechanisms
which were "complex ways which we cannot yet describe or begin to understand." Today, although we still do not fully understand them, we have come a
pretty long way. Some of the "special and apparently highly complex ways" in
which infants process linguistic input have been discovered in recent years,

and have been discussed in other papers presented at this conference (see papers in Part III of this volume).

Moreover, in considering the acquisition of the lexicon, Chomsky (1959c: 42) says:

It is possible that ability to select out of the auditory input those features that are phonologically relevant may develop largely independently of reinforcement, through genetically determined maturation. To the extent that this is true, an account of the development and causation of behavior that fails to consider the structure of the organism will provide no understanding of the real processes involved.

Again, though at the time they stirred minds and thoughts, from a contemporary perspective these words do not say anything out of the ordinary; there is widespread agreement that, already at birth, infants do in fact select certain features from the auditory input. Today, few experts would disagree with the claim that it is crucial to know the structure of the human brain and its maturation in order to have a full picture of language acquisition. It is about the nature, specificity, and extent of these organism-internal conditions that the debate is taking place nowadays.

In 1959, however, none of this was so clear. In discussing Lashley's work on neurological processes, Chomsky (1959c: 55–56) proposed a research program for linguistics: "Although present-day linguistics cannot provide a precise account of these integrative processes, imposed patterns, and selective mechanisms, it can at least set itself the problem of characterizing these completely." This research program should be of relevance to the study of the brain, and vice versa: "The results of such a study [of the characterization of the mechanisms of language] might, as Lashley suggests, be of independent interest for psychology and neurology (and conversely)." These statements, which sounded extremely foreign to people in linguistics and psychology at the time, paint a landscape that has become the dwelling space of contemporary linguistics and cognitive science. This expectation of mutual importance and increasing convergence is our present: there is a vast amount of research in human language where linguists listen to what other fields can contribute about human language, and conversely. In sum, the two main conceptual seeds in the review of *Verbal Behavior* have clearly stood the test of time and bloomed. The first such seed is that there are innate aspects to our knowledge of language, and the second one is that if we want to understand them, we first need to know what language is like. Finding this out is the natural research program for linguistics.

To answer the question of what language is like, we turn now to Chomsky's 1957 work, *Syntactic Structures*. This small book, which had a hard time finding a publisher, was very successful. It proposed an approach to the study of language that set up most of the foundational issues still in the background of the discussion today, as I would like to show you. The goal of linguistics, according to *Syntactic Structures* (p. 11) is to determine

the fundamental underlying properties of successful grammars. The ultimate outcome of these investigations should be a theory of linguistic structure in which the descriptive devices utilized in particular grammars are presented and studied abstractly, with no specific reference to particular languages.

Whereas the review of *Verbal Behavior* is very much concerned with biological aspects of language, *Syntactic Structures* focuses on the formal architecture of grammar and its abstract properties, without mentioning biology or psychology. Years later, in the eighties, both sides of this research program, the biological/psychological side and the formal side, would appear hand in hand, as in this more recent quote from *Knowledge of Language* (Chomsky 1986b: 3):

The nature of this faculty is the subject matter of a general theory of linguistic structure that aims to discover the framework of principles and elements common to attainable human languages; this theory is now often called "universal grammar" (UG), adapting a traditional term to a new context of inquiry. UG may be regarded as a characterization of the genetically determined language faculty.

Universal grammar should therefore be the genetically determined part of language and would include those aspects of language that are not determined by experience. However, primitives and mechanisms involved in language that are not specific to language could (and should) be excluded from UG, because they belong to broader or related but independent cognitive domains. This naturally brings us to consider innateness and specificity in greater detail. These two properties are not synonymous, for a given trait might be innate in a species, but not specific to it, as is the case with fear of snake-like forms in mammalians. Also, there are increasingly restrictive degrees of specificity, relative to a species or relative to a cognitive domain. A given property could be human-specific, but not necessarily language-specific. This point was already discussed in the Royaumont debate in 1975, as this remark by Chomsky shows:

On this point I agree with [David] Premack. I think he is right in talking about two different problems that enter into this whole innateness controversy. The first is the question of the genetic determination of structures...the second problem concerns specificity. (Piattelli-Palmarini 1980a: 179)

There are phenomena that constitute necessary prerequisites for language, which are innate but which are clearly not specific, either to humans or to language. However, in the history of discovery, such phenomena have often

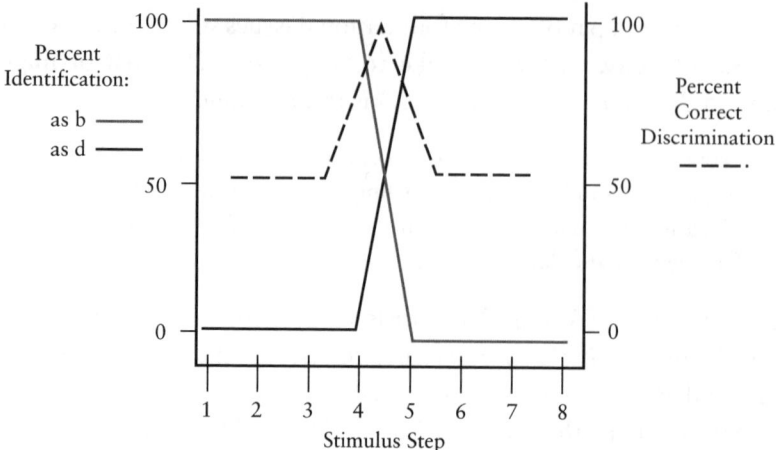

Fig. 20.1. Categorical Perceptionof /b/ and /d/ (after Liberman et al. 1957).

been thought (especially when noticed for the first time) to be specific to language. A lesson from history, therefore, is that when in our research path we find something characteristic of human language, we would be wise to check whether it is really specific to humans and specific to language. One of these, well known to psychologists but perhaps not equally well known among linguists, is categorical perception (CP).

Fig. 20.1 illustrates what CP is. This graph (made after Liberman et al. 1957), shows how native speakers of English perceive two distinct phonemes in an acoustic continuum: stimuli 1–4 are perceived as /b/, whereas stimuli 5–8 are perceived as /d/, and the perceptual change is sharp, as the different lines show. To the person's ear, the sound "changes" to another sound at one point in the acoustic continuum, so that the line goes down sharply.

Language was central in the discovery of this perceptual mechanism, which was originally explained by Liberman et al. (1957), and was taken as evidence that speech is perceived differently from other types of auditory stimuli. At that time it was thought that CP was acquired and language-specific. Later, Eimas et al. (1971) found CP in babies (1–4 months), which meant it was an innate mechanism. A few years later, Kuhl and Miller (1975) successfully trained chinchillas to perceive the voicing contrast between /da/ and /ta/ categorically. In short, CP is innate, but it is not restricted to speech or speech-like stimuli and occurs with stimuli that bear no resemblance to speech sounds (Harnad 1987). In fact, even crickets have been reported to show signs of CP (Wyttenbach et al. 1996).

So here is a perceptual mechanism that is probably essential to understanding and explaining certain architectural properties of language categories such as discreteness, a fundamental property of phonemes and words. But this perceptual mechanism is not specific to language or to our species, though it is innate and involved in language development and perception. This does not render it irrelevant or uninteresting for a language researcher, of course, but it clearly makes it a poor candidate for UG because it operates in a broader domain.

Another example of an innate mechanism that appears very significant for language is found in the study of the perceptual salience of rhythmic/prosodic properties of speech. Interestingly, the history of its discovery raises a similar point to the one in the previous example. It was originally discovered that newborns are very good at discriminating language groups based on rhythmic information: they can discriminate their mother's language-type using this information (Mehler et al. 1988, Cutler and Mehler 1993, Nazzi et al. 1998, Ramus and Mehler 1999). This capacity is already functioning at the time of birth, and it makes a good candidate for a language-specific mechanism. Recently, however, it was learned that tamarin monkeys (Ramus et al. 2000) and rats (Toro et al. 2003, Toro 2005) can detect rhythmic contrasts too, though not as well as humans. Again, here is a mechanism that appears to be a prerequisite for language, which is not specific to humans; it is a perceptual capacity that nonlinguistic beings can display.

Accordingly, when we try to determine the fundamental underlying properties of human language, we must distinguish between prerequisites that we share with other species, and those properties, if any, that are specific to language (and therefore to humans). In the words of Hauser et al. (2002: 1570), "The empirical challenge is to determine what was inherited unchanged from this common ancestor, what has been subjected to minor modifications, and what (if anything) is qualitatively new."

There are undoubtedly important discoveries to be made regarding innate, phylogenetically ancient mechanisms that our species might be using in slightly different ways, in general or in some particular domain. Usually, the debate about specificity in language is framed as a yes/no question, whereas what I would like to stress, as Marc Hauser did in his talk (see Chapter 5), is that perhaps we will increasingly find that some inherited, prelinguistic mechanisms have become specialized in humans for tasks that our biological relatives do not engage in. Both in the case of categorical perception and in the case of rhythm detection, humans appear to be particularly good at these capacities and apply them to a novel function (language) in order to select categories that are not merely perceptual, such as phonemes or words. Our task is to find out how this happens, how we push these mechanisms to take a path that other creatures do not tread – the path of language, with categories further and further removed from perception.

Let us review the acquisition of phonemes in more detail as an illustration of what I mean. What crickets and chinchillas are trained to do is acoustic discrimination, but not phoneme perception. It is relatively well known that very young toddlers are capable of fine-grained phonetic discrimination, so that a child born in a Japanese-speaking community will be able to discriminate between /r/ and /l/ even though this distinction is not phonologically relevant in Japanese, and even though the adults surrounding this baby cannot perceive the distinction. Werker and Tees (1984) showed that at about 10 months of age, children "specialize" for those contrasts that are phonologically distinctive in the language they are acquiring, and become like their parents, in that they no longer discriminate contrasts that are not phonologically relevant in their language.

From what we know, this specialization process only happens in humans. Apparently, what we humans do is build a second, higher level of representation on top of a basic, common auditory capacity.[3] This higher-order category is the phoneme, a language-specific category. We take a mechanism for auditory perceptual discrimination, perhaps refine it, and build a language category using it, in ways that are still not completely understood. In this regard, the peculiar thing about human babies is that they are able very quickly to construct something new, something different, using largely an old perceptual mechanism. If we go back to *Syntactic Structures* again, one of the central claims made there was that if you want to understand human language, the first thing you must understand is that language involves different levels of representation. Phonology and syntax, for example, have their own separate primitives and rules. This is widely agreed in linguistics today, but it was not an agreed property of language in the late fifties. In this light, what human babies do is build a repertoire for a new type of category, the phoneme, apparently using the same perceptual mechanism for acoustic perception, and presumably employing other types of cues for category membership. Accordingly, we are now talking about something that might be "qualitatively new" in human language.

To continue our search for such phenomena, let us turn from phonology to syntax, a component of language further removed from perception. Again, we start by remembering one of the main arguments in *Syntactic Structures* – namely, that phrase structure, or constituency, is an essential property of human languages that models of language must capture. The combinatorial

---

[3] The extent to which animals have phonetic discrimination capacities similar to those of humans is still unknown. I am assuming it is roughly equivalent but nothing in the argument would change if we were to find out that even auditory perception is not equivalent across chinchillas, monkeys, and humans.

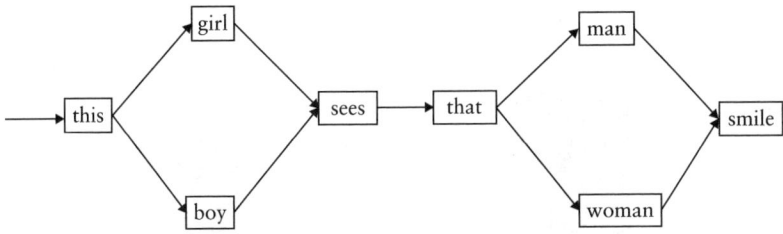

Fig. 20.2. Example of a finite state grammar.

and recursive nature of grammar that *Syntactic Structures* argued for is also common ground in linguistics today, as we can see for instance in this quote from O'Donnell et al. (2005: 285):

There are other universals, which are so basic that they are implicit in every linguistic theory and become most obvious when we compare language with other animal communication systems. These include the fact that language is built up from a set of reusable units, that these units combine hierarchically and recursively, and that there is systematic correspondence between how units combine and what the combination means.

Let us remind ourselves of the argument in *Syntactic Structures*: language cannot be captured by a model with no phrase structure. For instance, language cannot be captured by a finite state grammar (FSG). In an FSG you generate a piece of language by going from one point/state/word to the next along whichever path you choose among the ones available, until you reach the final state, at the end of the path (Fig. 20.2).

This grammar does not give you any kind of constituency, an important problem if you want to understand and explain how human language is organized. *Syntactic Structures* shows that certain aspects of English cannot be accounted for by a grammar like the one in Fig. 20.2. The reason why this is so is that the syntactic structures of human languages can resemble matryoshkas, those Russian wooden dolls you open to find smaller but identical dolls nested inside. Consider for instance the English sentence:

(1)   The girl the boy saw thinks the parrot likes cherries

Here, we find sentences nested inside sentences, and there is no grammatical limit to the number of times I can make a bigger doll, a longer sentence. Of course, this is not only a property of English, but a property of language, and the fact that all human grammars can build these matryoshka-structures tells us that this is a very essential aspect of human language. This property receives the name of recursion, and it has also been brought up in other talks and discussions

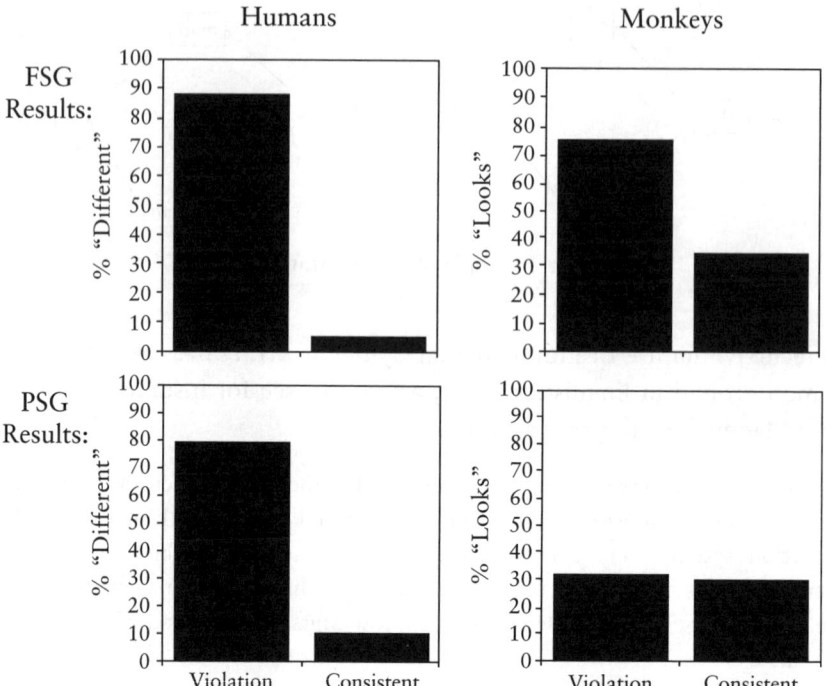

Fig. 20.3. FSG versus PSG learning results in humans and tamarin monkeys (from Fitch and Hauser 2004).

in this conference by Randy Gallistel, Rochel Gelman, and Juan Uriagereka, for instance. Here, I will focus on three recent studies that have asked whether phrase structure is qualitatively new and specific to humans and language.

For example, Fitch and Hauser (2004) have asked this very question regarding species-specificity. They taught two artificial languages to two groups of tamarin monkeys, where the difference between the two languages was precisely phrase structure. Whereas one language could be accounted for by a FSG, the other one had to be accounted for by a phrase structure grammar (PSG), so the FSG could not capture it. Fitch and Hauser found that tamarins, given time, did quite all right distinguishing grammatical versus ungrammatical sequences for the FSG, but interestingly, they could not manage to learn the PSG.

In Fig. 20.3, taken from Fitch and Hauser (2004), we can see that whereas the human group could discriminate grammatical vs. ungrammatical sequences for both grammars (results on the left), the monkeys (on the right) seemed to grasp this contrast for the FSG (top right) but not for the PSG (bottom right), where they failed to discriminate between grammatical vs. ungrammatical sequences. Does this mean that we have found a specific property of human cognition? Have we found a specific property of human language? In order to be able to answer this question, we still need to know more. For instance, we need to know whether it is only we humans who can grasp constituent structure, the unbounded combination of symbols that yields recursion in human language (Chomsky 1995b). Recently, Gentner et al. (2006) reported that starlings do in fact grasp recursion. I think the jury is still out on this claim, mainly because it is not sufficiently clear whether what the starlings do is recursion or counting, but in any event, songbirds are a good species to investigate, because their songs are long, structured, and in some species acquisition and cortical representation parallels humans in intriguing respects (Bolhuis and Gahr 2006).

Another way of determining whether phrase structure is a good candidate for UG membership is to try to determine whether our own human brain processes phrase structure in a special way. Two recent neuro-imaging studies indicate that this might be so. Musso et al. (2003) and Friederici et al. (2006a) taught human subjects human-like, and non-human-like grammars (a similar idea to the previous animal study) to see how the brain reacted to each.[4] The aim was of course to determine whether there is a property of human language that only human language has (specificity in the strongest sense). If this were the case, we could expect to find some evidence of that in the brain.

Musso and co-workers (2003) taught native German speakers three rules/constructions of true Italian and true Japanese, and three unnatural rules of a fake Italian-like language and a fake Japanese-like language. I say Italian-like and Japanese-like because the words employed in these unnatural languages were the same as in the corresponding natural language. For example, one such unnatural rule placed negation always after the third word of the sentence. The rule is trivial, but no human language does this, because a rule that counts words necessarily ignores phrase structure. The rules are easy and consistent, but they pay no attention whatsoever to phrase structure. What the authors found is that detection of violations of natural rules triggers an activation of Broca's area that is not found when subjects detect violations of unnatural rules.

Friederici and co-workers (2006a) entitle their paper "The brain differentiates human and non-human grammars," and they show that violations of FSG rules activate an area of the brain called the frontal operculum. In contrast, when subjects detect violations of the rules of a recursive grammar, this also activates Broca's area. Friederici et al. (2006a: 2460) argue that

Results indicate a functional differentiation between two cytoarchitectonically and phylogenetically different brain areas in the left frontal cortex. The evaluation of transitional dependencies in sequences generated by an FSG, a type of grammar that

---

[4] See also this volume, Chapter 13.

was shown to be learnable by non-human primates, activated a phylogenetically older cortex, the frontal operculum. In contrast, the computation of hierarchical dependencies in sequences generated according to a PSG, the type of grammar characterizing human language, additionally recruits a phylogenetically younger cortex, namely Broca's area (BA 44/45).

The area of the brain that deals with recursive grammars is phylogenetically newer than the part of the brain that deals with FSG, indicating that this might indeed be something that is qualitatively new, and specific to humans and language.

Before finishing, I would like to say something about "what we would like to know" about language. My wish list is long, but time is short, so I will choose only one wish. We have come a long way in the understanding of basic, universal aspects of language, which seemed the impossible challenge in the 1950s, when it was very much in question whether universal properties of languages even existed. However, we still need to understand much more about language variation. In his book *The Atoms of Language*, Mark Baker (2001) provides a very readable and accessible account of the principles and parameters model developed in the early eighties (Chomsky 1981).[5] This model assumes that language variation is systematic and results from the interaction of a finite number of binary parameters – aspects of grammar that must be specified according to the input. The model has been very successful in the discovery of systematic aspects of language variation, and it is largely due to this success that we can now ask certain questions about variation. I agree with the minimalist perspective that we can no longer entertain the view of a rich and highly elaborate UG, as envisaged in the principles and parameters model. Something makes language malleable, and I think we still do not understand this well enough. Progress in unraveling the mysteries of the complex phenomenon of language entails progress in unraveling the mysteries of our own nature, and I do hope that many dark mysteries of today will be shared wisdom tomorrow.

Discussion

HIGGINBOTHAM: A very brief remark about the history that you gave and the quote from O'Donnell in particular. There is nothing in that quote that couldn't have been written by William of Sherwood in the fourteenth century or the medieval magicians. There is nothing of substance in it about the reuse of familiar elements and so on that wasn't known to the Stoics. So the interesting

---

[5] For a compact synthesis, see Baker (2003).

historical question, I think, is how come that knowledge was lost in behavioral science.

LAKA: I agree with you in the sense that you could go as far back as Panini and find recursion, and there was an Icelandic monk who discovered phonemes. So if you go back, there are many people who have looked at language and have hit upon these properties.

HIGGINBOTHAM: I am sorry but I meant something stronger than that. It was actually common sense. I mean, Panini was a relatively isolated figure, but this was common sense among the relevant scholars – the medievals who were interested in language.

CHOMSKY: That's right; it was common sense up until the twentieth century. And now it is not common sense among philosophers. In fact Quine rejected it and so did the whole Quinean tradition. Behavioral science rejected it completely, and in fact if you look at what is called the advance of science, it is a little bit like learning phonology. You cut things out, but the trouble is that very often, what is cut out is the right things. I mean, if you look at the (seventeenth-century) Port Royal Grammar, it had recursion, it was explicit. It actually came from Galileo, who noticed that it had phrase structure, something like phrase structure grammar, it had something like transformational grammar, it had intension and extension almost exactly. (It was using it for explanation, it had the concept of explanation – they were trying to explain some funny descriptive fact in French which is called the rule of Vaugelas, which people spent a century on and they gave an explanation in terms of extension and intension.)[6] All of this was sort of there. Also some very important things I mentioned before and maybe I will talk about later, about meaning, which go all the way back to Aristotle and were almost totally forgotten. And it is something about the way science developed in the nineteenth and twentieth centuries that just lost lots of things. I mean, things that were pretty clear through the seventeenth and eighteenth centuries. Actually I gave an example in my talk. The observation about minds being properties of brains was standard after Newton (Locke, Hume, Priestly, Darwin). Today it is what Francis Crick called an "astonishing" hypothesis.[7] But I mean, what else could it be? It was understood right after Newton that it has got to be true. Why is it astonishing? The other quote I gave from the Churchlands – a "bold hypothesis." No, not at all. The trivialities have often been forgotten, and I think if you look at the history,

---

[6] For a historical analysis, connecting these ideas with Chomsky's work, see Miel (1969). (Editors' note)

[7] Crick and Clark (1994).

you can see why. I mean, new discoveries came along, they made it look as if what had previously been described kind of intuitively and informally was baggage and we could get rid of it. The trouble is that the baggage they were getting rid of included everything that was important.

LAKA: I certainly agree. When scholars look at language without prejudice, they hit upon these things, because they are there. If they are not objective however, they miss important insights. Bloomfield is an example you like to quote...

CHOMSKY: Yes, Bloomfield is extremely interesting, and a strikingly good example of this. He was completely schizophrenic. For those of you who don't know, he was kind of like the patron saint of modern structural linguistics in the United States and most other places. I was a student; he was God. But actually, there were two Bloomfields. There was one who was the scholar, and the guy who used common sense and thought about what language has to be. He was writing grammars in the style of Panini, like his *Menomini Morpho-phonemics*, which was economy in grammar.[8] On the other hand, there was the Bloomfield who was part of the Vienna Circle, which he mostly misunderstood, if you look closely. He was heavily involved in logical positivism. If you read his book *Language* ("the Bible"), it is logical positivism.[9] You know, anything about rule ordering is total mysticism, everything that I am doing in my other life is nonsense, etc. When we were students in the late forties, we never knew the other Bloomfield. And in fact, a little like Mark Baker's point, he published that work in Czechoslovakia, he didn't publish it in the US. I don't know what was going on in his head, but somehow this wasn't real science, because it was common sense, the whole Paninian tradition, which he knew as a good Indic scholar, and it had results. I mean, it was so extreme.

Just to give a personal example: when I was an undergraduate, I was kind of doing stuff on my own. I did it that way because what other way could you write a grammar? And not a single person on the faculty, all of whom were scholars and knew Bloomfield, not a single one told me that Bloomfield had done the same thing six years earlier. I learned about it fifteen years later when, I think, Morris Halle discovered Bloomfield's *Menomini Morphophonemics*.[10] But it was out of their range. Some of it was really remarkable, because one of them was an Indic scholar himself and knew all this stuff. But he was such a schizophrenic that he couldn't bring it together. And the same is true in philosophy and in psychology, and Jim is absolutely right, all this stuff is all

---

[8] Bloomfield (1987).
[9] Ibid (1933).
[10] Ibid (1939).

there, it somehow just got pruned away and had to get rediscovered, step by step.

URIAGEREKA: I was just going to add a footnote. In the fourteenth century, you have the exact same situation with people like Thomas of Erfurt and Radulphus Brito doing what looked like serious generative grammar, and then the philosophers going for their jugulars saying you have to study thought directly. The results of that? Well, we're still looking.

GELMAN: Just a comment. Lila, myself and Jerry Fodor ran a graduate seminar where we assigned important papers, which included Chomsky's critique of Skinner. Jerry said exactly what you just said, in a somewhat different context. He said, "Now that I've reread it, I wish Noam had pointed out that this was just a bump in history."

CHAPTER 21

Individual Differences in Foreign Sound Perception:

Perceptual or Linguistic Difficulties?

Núria Sebastián-Gallés

This talk is going to deal with variation in languages, a subject that we have heard mentioned quite often at this conference. As we know, the problem of why there are so many different languages on Earth has been solved. Genesis 11 gives us the answer with the story of the Tower of Babel – the proliferation of languages was a punishment from God. So the issue that I want to talk about here is not how all these languages came into being, but about another type of variation: why it is that when we try to learn a second language, some people are very good at it, while the rest of us are not.

Modern life seems to require that we learn different languages, but this is something new. In the old days, human beings, by definition, only needed to know one language, except for example when soldiers from different kingdoms marched off together to war, or when a wise king, such as Alfonso X, King of Spain, gathered in his court scientists and intellectuals from different cultures (Jews, Muslims, and Christians) to work together on the issues of the day. To do so, they needed to speak all in the same language, most likely Latin. Today, however, we live in situations where many, many people from different nations interact and therefore learning new languages has become imperative.

Not all of us are successful at it, however, so certain questions arise again and again when addressing the subject of second language (L2) learning. Is it more important to learn a language early or to have a lot of exposure? What is the main determinant explaining why some people are better than others at learning an L2? Is there a critical period for acquiring an L2? This latter question, which is of obvious theoretical importance, turns out to be quite controversial.

One way of describing the ability of non-native speakers is to insist on the fact that there is no evidence that anyone has ever mastered an L2 to the same degree as a native in all different domains. While this claim may be true, we can look at it from a different perspective, since the same statement seems to suggest that there may always be something that can be learned at a native level in an L2 (Birdsong 2004; Marinova-Todd 2003) – a case of the glass being either half-empty or half-full. At any rate, it is quite clear that not all aspects of second languages are equally easy to learn. Vocabulary is relatively easy, for instance, but we all know people who, despite living in a foreign country and having had years of exposure and opportunities to learn the language, still have very strong accents and a tendency to make particular mistakes. Conversely, we also know of people who move to another country and very rapidly are able to speak like natives – to the envy of most of the rest of us. The question then is, why are some people so poor at it and others so good?

One popular explanation is the importance of *age of acquisition*. Clearly, learning a language early in life increases the likelihood of doing well in that language. A second classical explanation is *amount of exposure*. Age of exposure will not ensure good learning if amount and quality of exposure are insufficient. A third explanation often given is *motivational factors*: motivated learners acquire better new skills. And then we come to the tricky question of *talent*. We know that some people have an "aptitude" for language, but what exactly is "aptitude" or "talent"?

Today, neuro-imaging techniques are beginning to provide new insights into this question, and this is what I would like to focus on for the remainder of this talk. I am going to present the results of different types of brain imaging studies that have tested L2 learners in a wide variety of situations, and explain some of the brain areas that have been found to be different between "good" learners and "poor" learners. We are going to examine two different types of evidence. The first type will present data from structural studies. In these studies differences in brain structure between different populations are analyzed. In particular, the brains of good and poor perceivers are compared using different techniques. The second type is activation or functional studies, examining which brain areas are activated while doing a particular task. All of these studies are very recent and more data is needed, but they nevertheless point in a direction that is very suggestive, albeit premature.

Mechelli and coworkers (2004) addressed the issue of whether differences in brain structure could be found as a function of age of acquisition and as a function of final attainment (proficiency). For this study, the authors chose individuals whose L1 was Italian and who learned an L2 (English) between the ages of 2 and 34 years. The way they assessed competence in the L2 was through a battery of standardized neuropsychological tests. Participants were tested in their reading, writing, speech comprehension, and production skills (the typical neuropsychological tests) and a global L2-proficiency score was computed. Using voxel-based morphometric analyses, Mechelli et al. were able to observe that the more proficient L2 learners had more grey-matter density in the left inferior parietal cortex than poor learners. It was also observed that the density of grey matter in that particular area was also a function of age of acquisition in the L2. Late learners had less grey matter density compared with early learners.

Although this study provides some clues about the relative weight of age of acquisition vs. amount of exposure, it is not possible to identify the importance of the different language subsystems in the observed results, due to the way the authors measured L2 proficiency. Indeed, as mentioned, not all aspects of a non-native language are equally easy to learn. In what particular dimensions did good and poor L2 learners differ – that is, was it a question of vocabulary, pronunciation, or syntax? What kind of linguistic (or nonlinguistic, cognitive) processes are responsible for the differences that the authors observed in grey matter in the left inferior parietal cortex? The following studies that I will discuss have focused their interest on more specific aspects of learning a new language.

Although learning new words is an ability that most human beings retain throughout life, the fact is that some people are clearly better at it than others. The next study was designed to address this particular issue. Breitenstein and colleagues (2005) showed participants in their study pictures of known objects while they heard new words being pronounced at the same time. Each picture (e.g., a book) appeared ten times with the same new word ("bini"). However, since in real life learners do not hear words in isolation every time they see a particular object, pictures also appeared, only once, with each of ten varying new words (e.g., "enas," "alep," etc). Subjects had to intuitively learn that the most frequently occurring couplings were the correct pairs.

The participants' brain activity was measured while they were learning the new words (using functional magnetic imaging). Several brain areas were differently activated in individuals who were good and poor at vocabulary learning. Three areas are of particular interest. First, good learners showed greater activation in the left inferior parietal cortex, an area very close to the one reported by Mechelli et al. (2004). In fact, Breitenstein et al. (2005) were able to observe an increase in the activation of this area as a function of learning: there was a strong correlation between the increase of correct responses during the experiment and the activation of this area. The other two areas were the left fusiform gyrus (an area previously reported to be involved in visual word recognition) and the left hippocampus (responsible mainly for short-term memory).

Short-term memory, and in particular, phonological short-term memory has often been associated with the capacity to process syntax and language comprehension in general. Chee and coworkers (2004) wanted to test the impact of differences in this particular cognitive component on the ability to learn a foreign language. In this case, Chinese–English early bilinguals were compared. The participants in this study had learned both languages before the age of 5, but they differed in their second language proficiency. They were tested in a phonological short-term working memory task. Subjects listened to French words (an unknown language for all of them) and were required to perform three different tasks. In the first task, they had to press a button every time they heard a particular word. A more difficult task required them to press a button whenever there were two successive words that were the same. Similarly, in a still harder third task, subjects were asked to compare two non-adjacent items. That is, they had to press a button whenever, in a sequence of three items, both item 1 and item 3 were the same. Behaviorally speaking, all participants performed similarly in the three tasks (no differences were observed between good and poor L2 learners). However, important differences were observed in the brain areas activated in the two groups of participants. The brain activation scans showed increased activity in the areas where the good L2 learners were better than the poor L2 learners. One of these activated areas was the left insula, a language area associated with phonological processing. However, out of the four different areas that were shown to be activated differently in the two populations, most were not typically associated with language. One area that was more activated in good than in poor L2 learners was the left cingulate. This area is known to be involved in mechanisms that control the ability to inhibit information. Therefore, the performance of individuals who managed to do the tasks better can be partly accounted for by the fact that there was enhanced processing not only in some language-related areas, but also in different areas of the brain that are responsible for attentional and inhibition processes.

The final group of studies that I want to mention is related to the ability to learn non-native contrasts. In a series of experiments conducted by Golestani and her colleagues (Golestani et al. 2002; Golestani et al. 2007), the authors tested the differences in brain structure between good and poor learners. Golestani and coworkers taught different groups of monolingual native English listeners the alveolar retroflex /da-dha/ distinction, which is very difficult for these participants to perceive. The results showed differences in white-matter volume in some parietal areas, actually very similar to the ones reported in the study of Mechelli et al. (2004). In the present study, fast learners showed greater white-matter volume than slow learners. In a subsequent study, this time with French listeners, the same findings were replicated and also, using a different analytical technique, anatomical differences between fast and slow learners were obtained in the Heschl gyrus in the left hemisphere. Approximately two-thirds of this gyrus is primary auditory cortex, which is thought to be involved in the processing of rapidly changing stimuli, and therefore supposed to be active in processing consonants, like the ones being learned in this particular experiment. But part of it is considered secondary areas, so probably related to language. It should be stressed that in this study the vast majority of the differences reported were between fast and slow learners and not between good and poor ones. That is, participants were classified according to the speed with which they reached a learning criterion. Furthermore, in these studies exposures were very short. Indeed, in one of the experiments, the training lasted 15 minutes. So, it is impossible to determine to what extent the differences reported were caused by better auditory processing, phonological processing (the ability to create new phonetic categories), or attention.

The final study that I want to present is one that we are carrying out in Barcelona. In this case, a major difference is that we did not train our participants to perceive or learn anything. We were just testing a population of individuals who had all been exposed to two languages very early in life to see whether we could find any differences in brain structure between those who managed to learn the phonology of the L2 with native proficiency and those who did not. We tested our University of Barcelona Psychology students in a variety of behavioral tasks and selected those who fell below native level in all tasks, and those who performed like natives in all tasks. To these ends, the subjects performed a categorical perception task, a gaging task, and an auditory lexical decision task, using procedures we had employed successfully in earlier experiments. The capacity of Spanish–Catalan bilinguals, who had been ex-posed only to Spanish at home, to perceive the Catalan-only /e/–/ɛ/ vowel contrast was explored. In previous studies we have shown that this is a contrast that native Spanish listeners have great difficulty in perceiving. As mentioned, we chose for the study individuals who failed at all tasks (23 percent of the population), and individuals who succeeded in all tasks (12 percent), ending with twenty participants in each group.

The scans revealed differences in brain areas not directly related to speech processing, including the fact that the right frontal operculum was much more myelinized in the poor perceivers than in the good ones. This came as a surprise, and we wondered why poor perceivers should have more myelin in this area, which is involved in an auditory attention network. Studies have shown that it is activated whenever we hear something where (a) there is a minimal difference between two different sounds, and (b) the difference is difficult, but not impossible, to perceive. That is, we have to pay attention to it, and this is what activates the area. If the difference is too small to perceive, then the area is not activated; if it is very easy to distinguish, it is not activated either. What if our poor perceivers in the L2 contrast were also poor perceivers in their L1? To test this, we measured the electrophysiological activity of our two groups of good and poor L2 perceivers. In this study participants listened repeatedly to the very same stimulus, and then from time to time one was inserted that was different, to enable us to observe electrophysiological differences in the brain when the different stimulus was heard. There is a measure known as mismatch negativity that shows how well we perceive these "odd" stimuli. Because the hypothesis was that poor L2 perceivers were going to be poor perceivers generally, we tested them with an L1 contrast: the /e/–/o/ contrast that exists in both languages. Indeed the results showed that trials with good L2 perceivers elicited a larger amplitude of mismatch negativity than trials with poor L2 perceivers, indicating that the former can perceive the difference between /e/ and /o/ more accurately. It has to be emphasized that our poor L2 perceivers exhibited a totally normal, though reduced, mismatch negativity. This suggests that the latter group probably cannot learn the L2 contrast because of a very mild deficit that is not important for the learning of the L1, but is catastrophic for learning some particular aspects of the L2.

What, then, are the reasons why some people are so poor at learning an L2? I realize that answering, even tentatively, is very premature, because there have been very few such studies, but all the data so far indicate that while there are differences in brain structure and function in the groups tested, generally speaking the differences tend not to be in language-related areas. So in most cases we find that it is not the language faculty that keeps us from learning an L2 proficiently, but our general cognitive capacities. One puzzling question for which no clue is provided by these studies is why such differences are not at all important for L1 learning. Remember, in all the Barcelona studies, the participants were University students, supposedly the percentage of the population that has proved successful, not only in passing through the educational system, but in learning language in particular. None of them reported having any difficulties in learning their L1 or difficulties in learning reading, which is also a domain where problems with the processing of speech can give rise to difficulties. Why is it, then, that the differences detected are so important to learning an L2, but not an L1? Given the way the experiments and studies reported in this talk were conducted, it is not very likely that differences in amount of exposure can play a crucial role.

In another study, we tested simultaneous bilinguals (people exposed to two languages from the very first day of their lives) (Sebastián-Gallés et al. 2005). In this case, the age of first exposure was exactly the same day. Of course there were differences in amount of exposure to the two languages, but in our experiment this was as controlled as it can be. The results demonstrated that what is heard in the first year is truly critical. Participants whose mother was a Catalan speaker performed much better than those whose mother was a Spanish speaker. Since young infants are mostly taken care of by their mothers (as opposed to their fathers), in the first months of life babies usually hear the mother predominantly, and that is when the phonemic categories are being established. The participants in our study were young men and women in their twenties, but the impact of very early L1 exposure can be traced back.

To conclude, let us return to the Tower of Babel. Genesis provides an answer to the question of the origin of language diversity, but what finally happened to the Babelians? Many of them ended up on this continent, where so many different languages are spoken. Clearly, we need to be able to talk to each other, we need to be able to build up the unity of humanity, symbolized by the Tower. Whether or not we will succeed is still an open question. Perhaps Europe will end up like the Tower in a disastrous fall. I don't know. In any case, we have no choice because we live on this particular continent, but there is some hope for us non-native speakers of English.

Discussion

PIATTELLI-PALMARINI: Several years ago Elissa Newport and Jacqueline Johnson had a very thorough study of native Korean speakers who immigrated into the US at different ages, and already it was very clear that the age at which they started acquiring the language was the only crucial factor (among e.g. motivation, intensity of exposure, etc.).[1] They also noticed that there were difficulty differences. For example, there was no big problem in learning very different word order. The really serious problem was determiners, the English definite article, which is puzzling to us who are not native speakers. So I wonder if you have data of this kind – that is, which components of language are hardest for L2 learners to acquire.

SEBASTIÁN-GALLÉS: It is not determiners, by themselves, that are difficult. The literature on second-language learning has shown that equally important are the properties of your first language. If your first language has determiners, then it is easy. [audience reaction] Okay, I didn't want to go into this, because then things

---

[1] Johnson and Newport (1989).

become extremely complex in the sense that, if something does not exist in your L1, then at the beginning it is very difficult because you need to acquire something that your language doesn't have. But later, you may benefit as you don't have interference from your first language either, because there was nothing before. In any case, this description is very general. The question is that learning determiners also means to learn many more things. I am not a linguist, but I am pretty sure you all know that learning a determiner means not only that you have to add a determiner in certain positions. It means that you have to adjust the whole system, and some adjustments are going to be easier than others. Weber-Fox and Neville (1996) have a paper showing specific aspects of the L2 that are particularly difficult for Chinese learners of English, and even the studies of Elissa Newport are interesting in this regard. I think that the first study was done with people speaking Asian languages. Jim Flege (Flege et al.1999) and others used the same materials but tested Italian and Spanish natives. Although the analyses of the results were not done in terms of what specific linguistic structures are difficult, you can deduce from the results reported in these latter studies that there were important differences between speakers of Asian languages and speakers of Romance languages, when learning some specific properties of English. The overall picture is that it is clear that the first language imposes very important constraints on the learning of the second language. So the message to take home is that you cannot make a universal foreign language textbook. You have to consider what the learner already knows.

CHAPTER 22

Language and the Brain

Angela D. Friederici

22.1 Introduction

Let me begin with a little anecdote. When I came to MIT in 1979, I was full of the energy and proud of the data derived from my Ph.D. research. Very early on, actually during my first week at MIT, I was able to take part in a workshop and there I came to sit at a table next to a person whom I didn't know, but whom I told all about my wonderful work in reading and writing, and this person said to me, "Why do you think this is interesting?" [laughter] And you guess who that person was. It was Noam Chomsky. As a result of this my entire career has focused on auditory language processing, and so in today's talk I will discuss the brain basis of auditory language comprehension.

In a lecture like this, I think we have to start from scratch, namely with Paul Broca (1865). As you all know, in 1865 he discovered a patient who was unable to produce language; he was able to produce only a single syllable, the syllable "tan." This person was well described by Broca, who later on after the patient had died was able to look at the brain, and what he found was a lesion in the inferior frontal gyrus (IFG) of the left hemisphere. This lesion was already large when looked at from the outside, but about a hundred years later the patient's brain was found on a shelf in one of the anatomy institutes in Paris, accurately labeled M. Leborgne (the name of the patient described by Paul Broca). At that time we had the first structural imaging techniques, such as computer tomography (CT), and thus Leborgne's brain was put into a CT scanner. Interestingly enough, Broca had already predicted that the lesioned area should be pretty large. He was able to do so by the following means. He had put a little metal plate on the brain and knocked on the metal plate. And from listening to how the brain tissue responded to his knocking, he concluded the brain lesion must be very deep. He described that, and the CT provided the proof (Fig. 22.1).

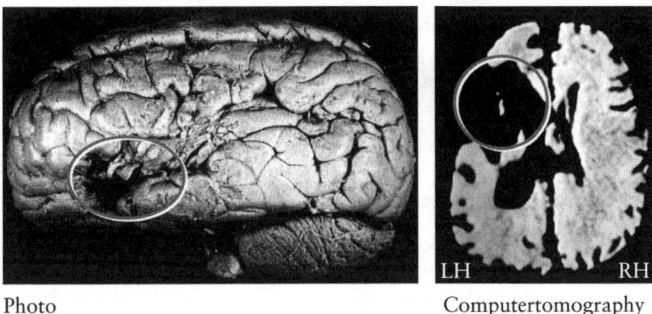

Photo   Computertomography

Fig. 22.1. Brain of the patient described by Paul Broca in 1865.

The black region on the CT scan is the lesioned area, and it was very large – much larger than what we call Broca's area today. Broca's area today is defined to include Brodmann area (BA) 44 and BA 45 (Fig. 22.2).

A couple of years later, Carl Wernicke (1874) saw and described six patients who seemed to have kind of a reverse language pattern. The deficiency of these patients was one of comprehension. They could not understand simple commands or sentences, but they had a fluent language output which, however, was without much content. In those times, such patients were often not considered as having a language problem but as having a thought problem. Wernicke described the lesions of the patients as being located in the superior temporal gyrus (STG). Later this region was called Wernicke's area (Fig. 22.2) and taken to be relevant for language comprehension. Nowadays we have to revise this

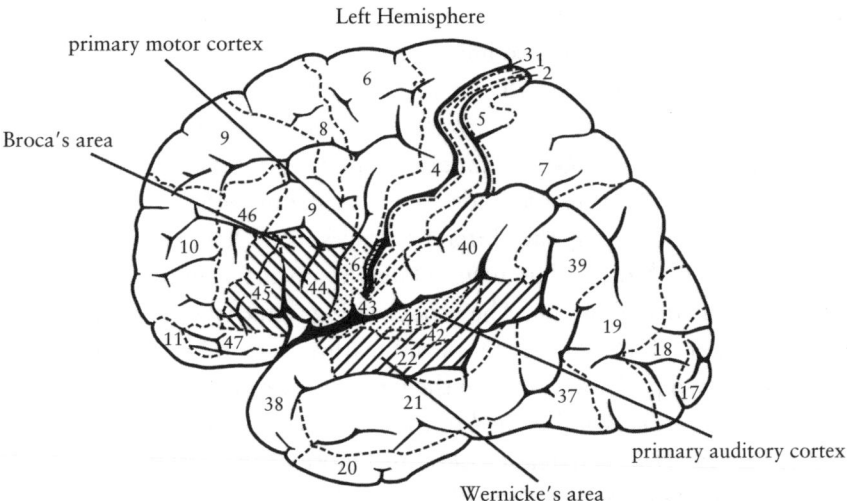

Fig. 22.2. Left hemisphere of the human brain. Numbers indicate areas which were described as cytoarchitectonically different by Korbian Brodmann in 1909.

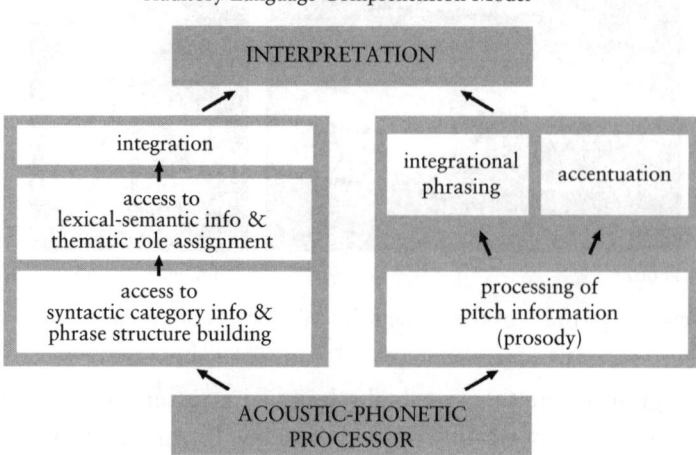

Fig. 22.3. Model of auditory language comprehension. For details see text.
Source: Friederici and Alter 2004

classical neuroanatomical model, separating comprehension and production into Wernicke's area and Broca's area respectively, because we know that Broca's area is not only involved in production, but also in language comprehension. I will specify the revised model, which is based on recent brain imaging methods, in this paper.

The research questions that we can address with the new neuroscientific imaging methods are the following. We can ask which brain areas support sentence processing, and particularly syntactic, semantic and prosodic processes. To answer these questions we use functional magnetic resonance imaging (fMRI). Moreover, we also have the possibility to look into the dynamics of brain activation, namely with methods which enable us to trace the time course of brain activation. These are electroencephalography (EEG) and magnetoencephalography (MEG). Although the spatial resolution in EEG and MEG methods is restricted, these methods can tell us something about the specific temporal relation between the different processes. What we need, however, when we want to look at language-related brain activation in a systematic manner, is a functional model. The model in Fig. 22.3 is a coarse model – no doubt about that – but it has some special features which I would like to point out. There are two pathways, one on the left side, one on the right. Later on we will see that the processes sketched in the pathway on the left side are mainly performed by the left hemisphere (LH), and those of the pathway on the right side are mainly performed by the right hemisphere (RH).[1] So what exactly are the functions of these hemispheres?

---

[1] Compare Friederici and Alter (2004).

22.2 Left-hemispheric processes

Let us first consider the left-hemispheric processes. The idea here, and it is a strong prediction in the model,[2] is that there are separate phases in processing syntactic and semantic information, and that the phases, following Lynn Frazier and Janet Fodor (1978), are sequential. In the first stage word category information is accessed and local phrase structures are built. This first processing stage is totally independent from semantic information. And then only in a second stage you access lexical-semantic information and assign thematic roles. Certainly, there are other psycholinguistic models which assume a strong interaction between these two components and at each moment in time. The model proposed here is a strong model and we can see how far we can hold up the hypothesis that the two processes are really serial. All these processes work incrementally. The system does not have to parse the entire sentence before entering the next processing stage, but can proceed in a cascade. Then at some final integration stage the system has to map the output from the two other stages to achieve comprehension.

With respect to the RH, there is the suggestion that prosodic information is processed in the RH. This holds, without any doubt, for emotional prosody, but here the focus is on linguistic prosody. Pitch information certainly provides information about intonational phrasing and also about accentuation. Today I will mainly talk about intonational phrasing and I will also discuss how intonational phrasing and syntactic phrasing go together.

Let's first concentrate on the processes assumed to be located in the LH, and see which brain areas support semantic and syntactic processes. We will do so by looking at a couple of studies using functional magnetic resonance imaging (fMRI). In our institute we usually try to scan the entire brain in order not to miss important activations in areas of the brain not predicted to respond to language. In a first experiment (Friederici et al. 2003a), we thought that one way to disentangle the semantic and syntactic information which usually comes together in a sentence would be to work with a violation paradigm. That is, we presented semantically incorrect sentences, for example sentences containing a violation of selection restrictions, such as:

(1) *Das Lineal wurde gefüttert.*
     'The ruler was fed.'

For the syntactic part, we presented syntactically incorrect sentences, for example:

---

[2] Compare Friederici (2002), and Friederici and Kotz (2003).

(2)   *Die Ente wurde im gefüttert.
      'The duck was in the fed.'

This sentence is incorrect for the following reason. In a prepositional phrase in German, the preposition *im*, which already carries a case marker (in translation: *in-the*), requires a noun or adjective + noun combination to follow. What the subjects perceive, however, is a verb; that is, we have a violation of the word category and the question is how would the brain react to this violation?

   We also included correct sentences where the prepositional phrase was fully present, e.g.:

(3)   Die Kuh wurde im Stall gefüttert.
      'The cow was in-the barn fed.'

The syntactic violation stimuli were manipulated, in order to avoid acoustic cues of "incorrectness." As speakers invariably lengthen the preposition in such incorrect sentences, providing an acoustic cue of "incorrectness" in non-spliced sentences, incorrect sentences were cross-spliced taking the preposition from a correct sentence containing a full prepositional phrase.

   When comparing the semantically incorrect to the correct condition (Fig. 22.4A) we found a significant difference in the posterior and middle portions of the superior temporal gyrus (STG), but not in its anterior portion. For the syntactic violation condition (Fig. 22.4B) we found a clear difference in the anterior portion of the STG but also in the posterior portion, and to some extent in the middle portion. Thus what really stands out for the syntactic incorrect condition is the difference of the anterior portion of the STG.

   A particular area that was predicted to also be activated when dealing with local dependencies is the frontal operculum. When considering a slice which covers the frontal operculum we found this area to be significantly more active for the syntactically incorrect condition than for the correct condition.

   From this, and a number of other studies in the literature, we can define two different networks. The first, the semantic one, which comprises the posterior and middle portions of the STG, and, under some conditions, also activation in the inferior frontal gyrus, that is BA 45 and BA 47. This latter region only comes into play when strategic semantic processes are required, that is, when asked to categorize words into particular semantic categories (Fiez et al. 1995; Thompson-Schill et al. 1997). During online sentence processing, this activation is seldom seen. For the syntactic processes, the network consists of the anterior portion of the left STG and the frontal operculum right next to, but not identical with, Broca's area in the inferior frontal gyrus (IFG). The posterior portion of

A

Semantic Processing

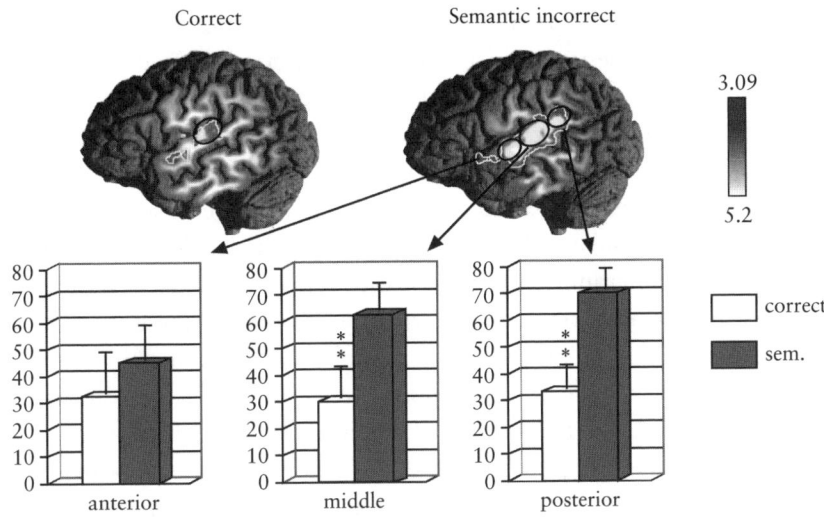

left superior temopral gyrus

B

Syntactic Processing

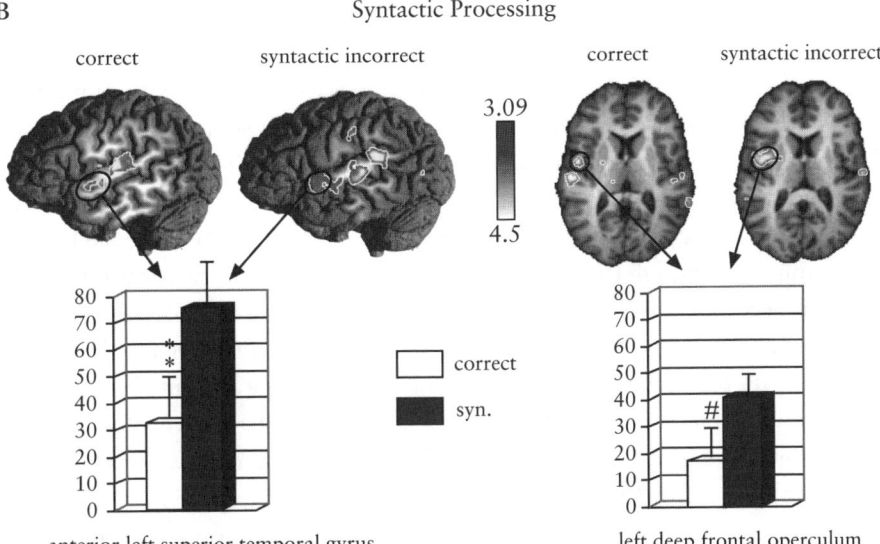

Fig. 22.4. Brain activation for different conditions versus baseline. A. Semantically incorrect condition and correct condition. B. Syntactically incorrect condition and corresponding correct condition. Bar graphs represent the activation difference between correct and incorrect conditions for relevant brain regions.

Source: Friederici et al. 2003b

the STG, which is seen to be active during semantic and syntactic processes, may be considered to be a region where these information types are integrated.

At this point the question arises: what is the function of Broca's area? At least for this type of syntactically manipulated sentence we do not see activation. From the literature we already have some suggestions as indicated by a meta-analysis of all the studies comparing different conditions of syntactic processes that were conducted over the years up to 2004 (Friederici 2004). We clustered these studies according to the particular differences they were looking at. When only comparing grammatical and ungrammatical sentences, the STG was active basically in all the studies, with frontal operculum activation in some of these. In contrast, all those studies that manipulated syntactic complexity show a massive activation in Broca's area. However, most of the studies were done in English (one in Hebrew and two in German), and for the type of sentences that were used in these English studies you could disentangle whether the activation increase was due to an increase in syntactic complexity only or to an increase in working memory. Consider an English object-first versus subject-first relative clause sentence. More memory resources are surely necessary when processing the filler–gap distance in the object-first sentences. German offers a possibility of approaching this issue in a more direct way – it is not the ideal way, but the possibility is the following.

As a scramble language German allows us to scramble different noun phrases (NPs) in the following way. In a canonical sentence, the subject (S), precedes the indirect object (IO), and the direct object (DO). By computing the operation Move or Permutation (depending on the syntactic theory you subscribe to), you can topicalize the objects. If you move the IO in front of the S, the sentence becomes more complex although the amount of working memory increase is minimal. The sentences become even complex if we move both objects in front of the subject. We conducted a visual experiment using these sentence types (Friederici et al. 2006b) in which the NPs together with the case-marked articles were presented as one chunk such that our subjects immediately knew what kind of NP they were looking at. In order to figure out how subjects would deal with these sentences, we first conducted an acceptability rating (where a score of 1 meant "good acceptability," and a score of 4 or 5 meant "not so good") and, not surprisingly, the canonical sentences were more easily accepted than the other two sentence types whose acceptability again varied as a function of the number of operations. This was a clear behavioral difference which allowed us to systematically investigate how particular brain areas would vary in their activity parametrically as a function of this gradation.

Naturally we looked at BA 44 as part of Broca's area as the crucial region of interest. Fig. 22.5 indicates that the activation is located in the inferior portion of BA 44. The timelines of the activation show that the brain response parametrically increases as a function of complexity. From this we can conclude that

Broca's Area & Syntactic Hierarchy

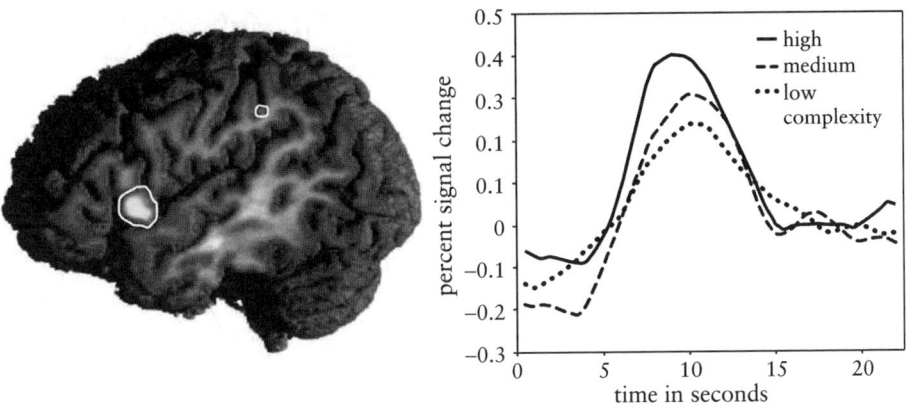

Fig. 22.5. Brain activation in Broca's area (for localization see left panel) and time lines of activation as a function of the level of syntactic hierarchy (see right panel).
Source: Friederici et al. 2006b

processing structural hierarchies activates Broca's area, and it does so parametrically as a function of the number of movements.

22.2.1 *Temporal relation between LH subprocesses*

Now let us turn to the temporal relation between the different subprocesses within the LH. Here I think we should focus on the strong claim the model makes with respect to the seriality of syntactic and semantic processes. Remember the model holds that syntactic structure-building should precede semantic processing. The temporal parameters of these processes will be investigated using electroencephalographic (EEG) recordings. Fig. 22.6 is to remind you of this method. When looking at the online EEG (top row), one cannot see very much. What one has to do is average over a couple of sentences of a similar type, and a nice event-related brain potential (ERP) wave becomes apparent (bottom). For those who are not used to looking at ERP data, be aware that negativity is plotted up.

Different language-related ERP waves have been identified over the years and they have been labeled according to their polarity (negativity/positivity), their latency (in milliseconds (ms)), and sometimes their distribution over the scalp (anterior/posterior/left/right). For example N400 is a negativity of around 400 ms.

In the critical ERP experiment we used the same sentences as for the first fMRI experiment reported (Hahne and Friederici 1999). Now the question was,

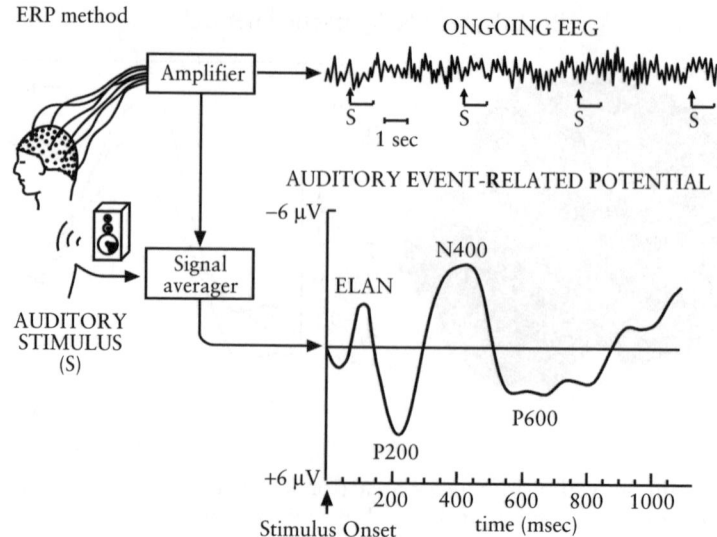

Fig. 22.6. Schematic view of ERP method. For details see text.

would we really see that the brain reacts earlier to the syntactic phrase structure (word category) violation than to the semantic violation?

For the semantic condition we see (Fig. 22.7) a more negative wave for the semantically incorrect compared to the correct condition, which peaks at around 400–500 ms. This is a well-established ERP component, the N400 known to reflect semantic processes (Kutas and Hillyard 1984).

For the syntactic violation we find a very early brain activation, namely a negativity over left anterior electrode sites around 150 ms (see Fig. 22.8). We called this component early left anterior negativity (ELAN). There is a second component, a positivity, peaking around 600–700 ms. This component, called P600, had been identified before, not only for incorrect sentences but also for garden-path sentences, whereas the early component ELAN had not been identified before.

Thus it appears that with these data (ELAN before N400 component) we have provided evidence for a seriality with respect to these first processing steps, namely syntactic structure-building and semantic processes. But then the question is what does this P600 component represent? Given that we find it for incorrect sentences, and for correct sentences when they are very difficult, and moreover for garden-path sentences, the question cannot be answered precisely based on the data in hand. For the moment I will take it to represent processes of integration. We certainly have to work on what "integration" really means under the different sentence conditions. Clearly, in this last processing phase a

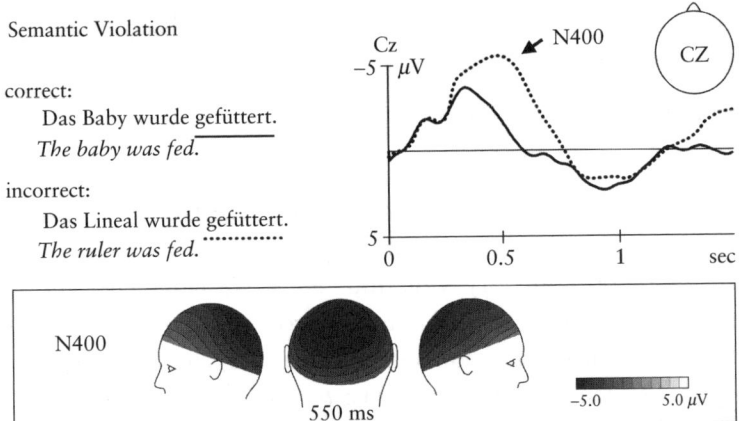

Fig. 22.7. Grand averaged ERPs for semantically incorrect (dotted line) and correct condition (solid line) plotted for the sentence-final word at electrode Cz (top right panel). Distribution of the effect displayed as the activation difference between incorrect and correct condition (bottom).

Source: Hahne and Friederici 2002

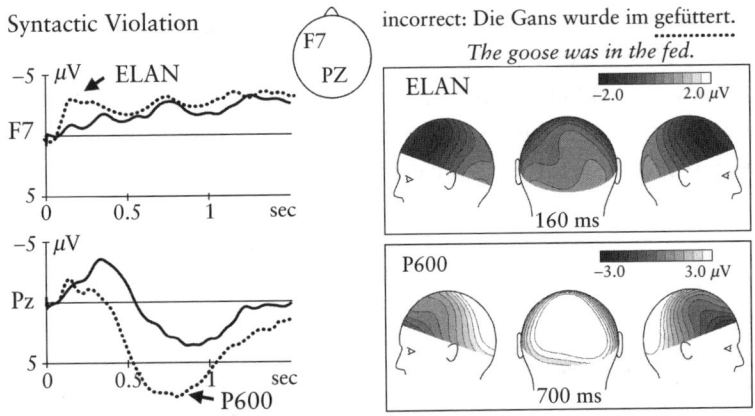

Fig. 22.8. Grand averaged ERPs for syntactically incorrect (dotted line) and correct condition (solid line) plotted for sentence-final word at electrode F7 and Pz (left panel). Distribution of the effect displayed as the activation difference between incorrect and correct condition (right panel).

Source: Hahne and Friederici 2002

lot of information types come together, and the details are not spelled out entirely yet.

But let's come back to the seriality issue concerning the first two processing phases. In order to put this hypothesis to a stronger test we conducted an additional experiment (Hahne and Friederici 2002) in which we included a condition in which the last element in a sentence is both semantically and syntactically incorrect. So for example:

(4)   *Die Burg wurde im gefüttert.*
      'The castle was in the fed.'

Here "*fed*" is the past participle translation of "*gefüttert*." The last element is clearly neither semantically nor syntactically correct – that is, there is a selection restriction and word category violation. Now we can make the following predictions. If syntactic structure building processes precede lexical-semantic processes, two detailed predictions should hold. If syntactic phrase structure building precedes semantic processes just *temporally*, because it is early, then we should probably see an ELAN, an N400, and maybe a P600, as this would simply be the sum of different effects. If however syntactic structure building precedes semantic processes *functionally*, in the sense that once the word category is realized, the system does not even make the attempt to integrate the last word semantically, then we should see an ELAN together with a P600, but no N400, because no semantic integration takes place. Thus the ERP pattern should be exactly the same as for the sentences that are incorrect only syntactically. This is exactly what we see (see Fig. 22.9).

From this we could conclude that local phrase structure-building does precede semantic processes functionally. But we thought that we should test this conclusion somewhat further, since in the sentences of the experiment just

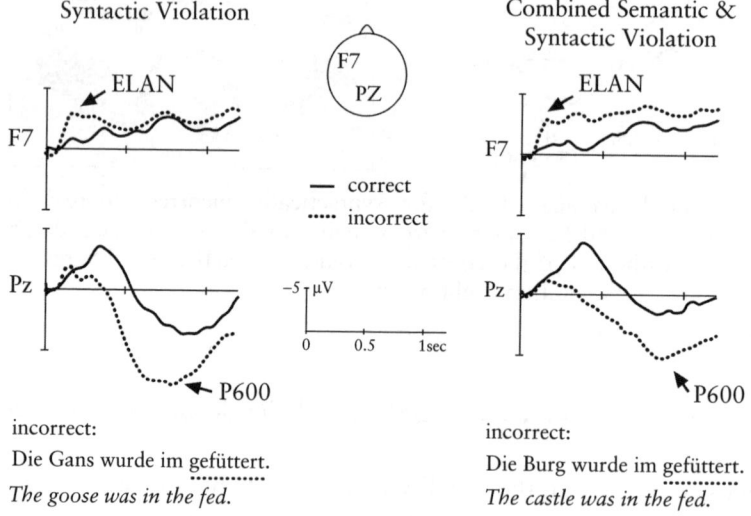

Fig. 22.9. Grand averaged ERPs for the sentence-final word in the syntactic-only violation condition (left panel) and for the double violation condition (right panel) at electrodes F7 and Pz.

Source: Hahne and Friederici 2002

reported, the critical element in the sentence is a past participle term, such as *gefüttert*. The prefix *ge-* already gives you a good indication that you are dealing with a verb and not with a noun, as the past participle forms of all nonprefixed verbs start with *ge-*, and there are very few nouns that start with the same prefix. Thus for the sentence material used, one could still argue that, given that the information is present in the prefix, the crucial syntactic process could start early and therefore it has an effect on the later semantic processes based on information available only in the word stem. Therefore, we aimed for a stronger test (Friederici et al. 2004). In German as in English, it is possible to provide word category information (noun/verb) in the suffix, so for example:

(5)   *verpflanzt* vs. *Verpflanzung*
       replant**ed** vs. "replant**ment**" (replanting)

Note that in these suffixed items, the semantic information (provided by the word stem) is available before the syntactic information (provided by the suffix). The prediction is that if syntactic structure-building precedes lexical-semantic processes functionally, even under this condition we should see only an ELAN and a P600 and no N400, and this is what we do find for the double violation condition (see Fig. 22.10). With the crucial syntactic information provided by the suffix, the early syntactic component (ELAN) is not that early when you time-lock it to the beginning of the word. But when you time-lock it to the beginning of the suffix providing the relevant word category information, it is early again. Thus we now can draw the conclusion that local structure-building processes precede lexical-semantic processes *functionally*.

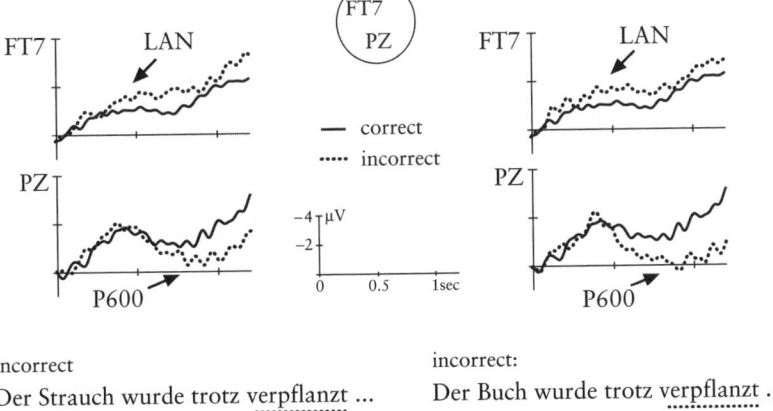

Fig. 22.10. Grand averaged ERPs for the sentence-final word in the syntactic-only violation condition (left panel) and for the double violation condition (right panel) at electrodes FT7 and Pz.

Source: Friederici et al. 2004

Localization of the ELAN Effect

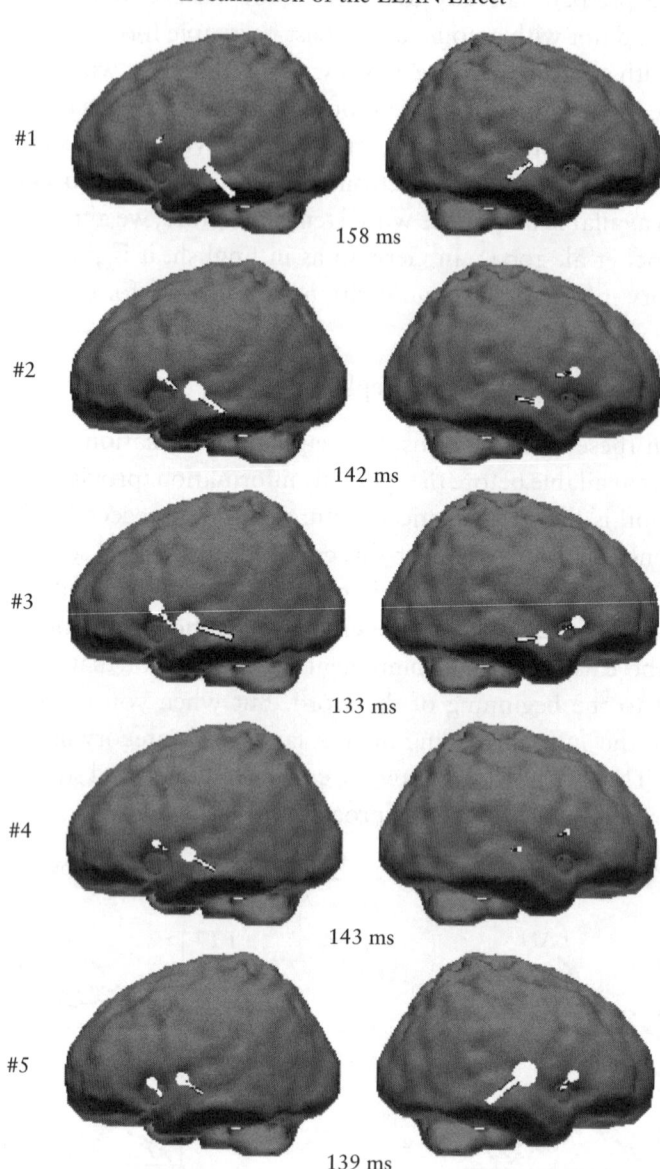

#1

158 ms

#2

142 ms

#3

133 ms

#4

143 ms

#5

139 ms

left hemisphere   right hemisphere

Fig. 22.11. MEG dipole localization results for five different subjects. Size indicates the strength of the dipole.

Source: Friederici et al. 2000

When mapping the temporal ERP data onto the spatial networks data as revealed by the fMRI, there are still open questions. In the fMRI studies we have identified at least three areas that deal with syntax, the frontal operculum, the anterior portion of the STG, and the posterior portion of the STG, independent from the hierarchical processing domain. Because the temporal resolution of the fMRI is poor, we see all three areas active, and the question remains which areas support the early syntactic processes and which areas support the late processes.

In a next step we address this issue by using MEG, because with about 150 channels, this method gives us a good opportunity to do a valid dipole localization. Using the same sentence material, we tested five subjects (Friederici et al. 2000), who had to listen to 600 of those sentences in order to get a good signature noise ratio, which allowed us to look at the single subjects data. We observed an early syntax effect and the variation between the subjects is very small. The latency range is from 133 ms to 158 ms (see Fig. 22.11). For each subject we find two dipoles in each hemisphere, one dipole in the anterior portion of the STG and one in the vicinity of the frontal operculum. These two dipoles have to work together within this early time window, but since the dipole in the former region is larger, it appears that the contribution of the anterior portion of the STG is larger than the contribution of the frontal area. Now by simple logic one can make the argument that the posterior portion of the STG is somehow involved in the late integration processes. I do not have the time to go into this issue, but because late processes are very hard to capture with MEG, the only way for us now to test this hypothesis is to test patients with lesions in the posterior portion of the STG. These patients by hypothesis should show no P600, but instead an ELAN. And one can also do the reverse test. Patients with lesions in the inferior frontal gyrus should not have an ELAN but they do have a P600. Such patient studies are always an additional critical test. We conducted those studies with patients suffering from circumscribed brain lesions, and from these studies we can say that the early process of local structure-building is supported by these two areas, the anterior portion of the STG and the inferior frontal dipole.[3] With respect to patient studies we cannot say whether the frontal operculum or BA 44 is the crucial area (as lesions are never that specific), but given all the other studies, I would dare to hypothesize that it is the frontal operculum. With the studies I presented so far we have advanced a bit further in our description of temporal and spatial representation of these processes in the brain, at least with respect to syntactic and semantic processes.

---

[3] For a review of these studies see Friederici and Kotz (2003).

22.3 Right-hemispheric processes

Now let us turn to the prosodic processes assumed to be located in the RH. When we want to look at prosody during language processing, we somehow have to manipulate the language input such that we are able to look at the different parameters of prosodic information separately. One possibility is to delete the pitch (Fo) contour, another one is to delete the segmental information so that only the Fo information remains. This is what we have done. In a first fMRI experiment (Meyer et al. 2004), as one condition, we had sentences in which all information types were present – namely semantic, syntactic, and prosodic information as in a normal sentence. For those who do not know German, the second condition probably sounds as good as the first one, but here no semantics is involved, just syntactic and prosodic information. In the third condition we have filtered out all segmental information. It sounds like some-body speaking next door. It is impossible to understand what is being said, but one can realize it is spoken language. We have called this prosodic speech, that is, we have taken out the segmental acoustic information from the signal, but a normal pitch contour is still present. What do we see when we are looking at the prosodic effect? In the fMRI data (Fig. 22.12) we see maximal activation in the RH, again in temporal structures and the frontal operculum – basically the homologue areas of what we had seen for syntactic processing, at least for local structure violations in the LH.

From these data we can at least tentatively draw some conclusions with regard to where prosodic information is processed in the RH. (Note, it is not only the RH which is active; there are also some LH structures involved, but the

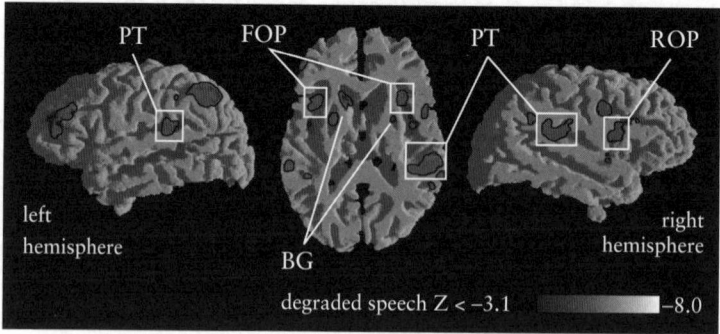

Fig. 22.12. Brain activation for prosodic effect. PT, planum temporale; FOP, frontal operculum; ROP, rolandic operculum; BG, basal ganglia.
Source: adapted from Meyer et al. 2004

maximal activation is in the RH.) Suprasegmental prosodic information elicits activation in and around the auditory cortex, that is, anterior and posterior to the auditory cortex in the STG and also the frontal operculum.

As the next issue we investigated the neural basis of the interaction between syntax and prosody. We did so by using sentence material of the following type.

(6) *Peter verspricht Anna zu arbeiten # und...*
     'Peter promises Anna to work and...'

(7) *Peter verspricht # Anna zu entlasten # und...*
     'Peter promises to support Anna and...'

Sentence (6) differs from sentence (7) only with respect to the following parameters. In a written form the two sentences are identical up to the word *Anna*, but auditorily they differ in their prosodic contour, that is with respect to their intonational phrase boundaries (#). In sentence (6), *Anna* is the object of *promise*, and in (7) *Anna* is the object of *support*. This is obvious in the English translation where the object always comes after the verb, but this is not the case in German. Interestingly, when we look at the electrophysiological response of the brain when just listening to these sentences, we find a positive wave after each of the intonational boundaries, which we called *Closure Positive Shift* (CPS) (see Fig. 22.13) (Steinhauer et al. 1999).

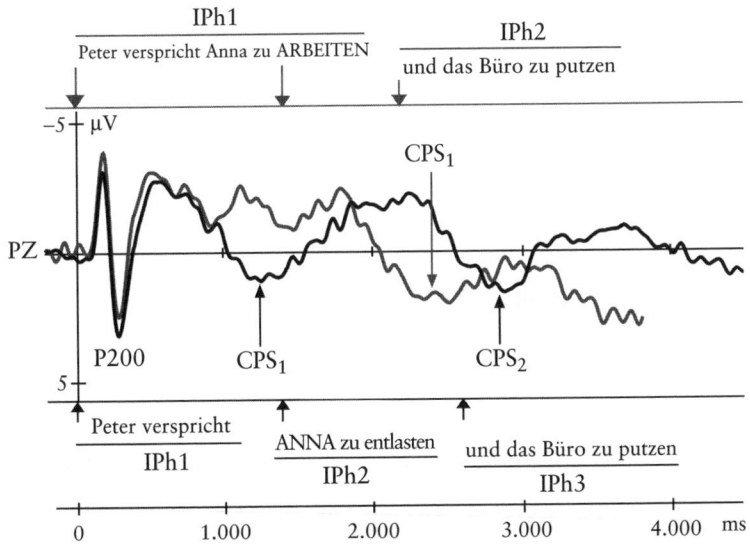

Fig. 22.13. Grand averaged ERPs for two sentence types time-locked to the sentence onset. IPh, intonational phrase boundary; CPS, Closure Positive Shift.

Source: Steinhauer et al. 1999

This is only to demonstrate that the brain takes this information about intonational phrase boundaries into consideration. Note that intonational phrase boundaries are marked by three parameters: lengthening of the syllable before the intonational phrase boundary, change in the intonational (pitch) contour, and a pause. Interestingly enough, even when taking out the pause and leaving the other two relevant parameters (pre-final lengthening and shifting the intonational contour), we find the same results. Thus the adult system does not need the pause in order to realize the intonational phrase boundary.

With this result we had an index in the ERP for the processing of prosody, in particular the processing of intonational phrase boundaries. What we tried next, in order to see if and how and when syntactic and prosodic information interact, was to cross-splice sentences (6) and (7) in order to see whether we could garden-path the listener just by the prosodic information. The crucial third sentence consisted of the first part of sentence (7) (*Peter verspricht #Anna*) and the second part of sentence (6) (*zu arbeiten...*):

(8)   *Peter verspricht # Anna zu arbeiten # und...*
      'Peter promises Anna to work and...'

This sentence now contains a verb that is not predicted, given the prosodic information of the sentence. The prediction is, if prosodic information influences syntactic processing, we expect an ERP effect on the critical verb. The parser expects a transitive verb because of the prosodic break (#) after the first verb but encounters an intransitive verb. What we find is that the brain response first shows an N400, indicating "this is a lexical element I cannot integrate,"

Prosody Mismatch Effect: Critical Verb

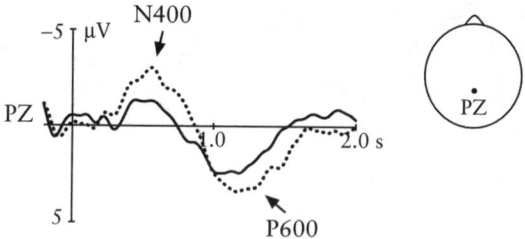

correct Prosody: [IP1 Peter verspricht] # [IP2 ANNA zu entlasten] [IP3 und ...

incorrect Prosody: *[IP1 Peter verspricht] # [IP2 ANNA zu arbeiten] [IP3 und ...

Fig. 22.14. Grand averaged ERPs for the critical verb time locked to the onset of the verb complex for prosodically correct (solid line) and prosodically incorrect (dotted line) condition. Stress is on the word ANNA in both conditions.

Source: adapted from Steinhauer et al. 1999

and secondly it shows a P600 obviously trying "to integrate the different types of information" provided by the input (see Fig. 22.14).

At this point we can formulate a tentative conclusion. We can say that auditory language comprehension is supported by separable but distinct fronto-temporal networks for semantic and for syntactic processes in the LH and for prosodic processes mainly in the RH. Syntactic structure-building precedes lexical-semantic processes and can block these. That is, when word category information is not correct, semantic integration is not licensed, and thus is not done. During normal auditory language comprehension syntactic processes interact with prosodic processes. A good prediction concerning the neural basis of this interaction might be that there must be interhemispheric communication in order to guarantee this very fast online interaction between syntactic and prosodic processes. But how can we test this?

22.4 The interaction between the LH and the RH

Ultimate evidence for interhemispheric interaction comes from patients with lesions in the corpus callosum, the neural structure connecting the two hemi-spheres (CC patients) (Friederici et al. 2007b). These are very rare patients. In our patient pool of 1,500, we found only ten subjects with those lesions, but they are interesting to study. In our subjects, the CC was not interrupted entirely but at different portions (see Fig. 22.15), and that is very interesting for the following reason. We know that the two temporal areas, namely the left and right STG, are connected by fibers crossing the CC in its posterior portion (Huang et al. 2005). The prediction here is that if the prosodic mismatch effect at the verb, which we observed in the previous experiment with normals, really is due to an interaction between the LH and RH, then such an effect should not be observable in CC patients, particularly in those with lesions in the posterior portion of the CC. We also included patients with lesions in the anterior portion of the CC. Note that those have larger lesions. Thus, if we found that those patients with lesions in the posterior portion, in contrast to those with anterior CC lesions, did not show the interaction effect, we could at least say it was not due to the size of the lesion.

Fig. 22.16 displays the results for the critical verb. For our control subjects an N400 can be observed.[4] For the anterior lesion CC patients, the N400 is

---

[4] I think we do not see a P600 here because subjects were listening passively and at the end of the sentence only had to make a prosodic judgment. Moreover, they were not answering compre-hension questions as in the previous experiment by Steinhauer et al. (1999) in which an N400 and a P600 was observed.

The Corpus Callosum and Lesion Location

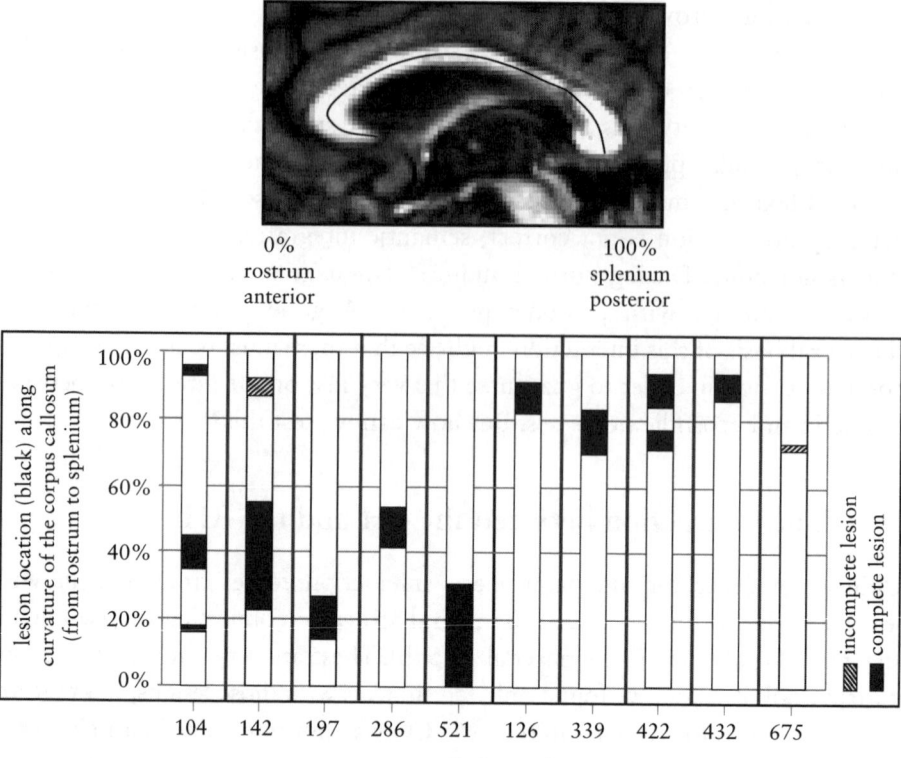

Fig. 22.15. Lesion location of the corpus callosum (CC) in the patients tested. Quantitative measures of lesions in the CC from the anterior to the posterior part are presented in the lower part of the figure.

Source: adapted from Friederici et al. 2007b

Prosody Mismatch Effect: Critical verb

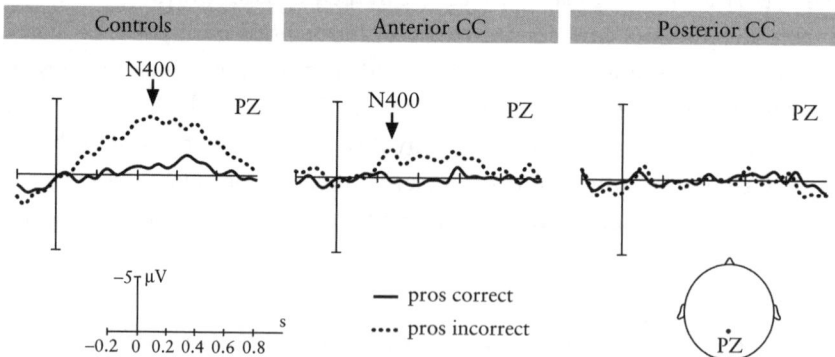

Fig. 22.16. Grand averaged ERPs for the critical verb complex in the prosodically incorrect (dotted line) and correct (solid line) condition for different groups at electrode Pz.

Source: adapted from Friederici et al. 2007b

Lexical Semantic Mismatch Effect: Critical Verb

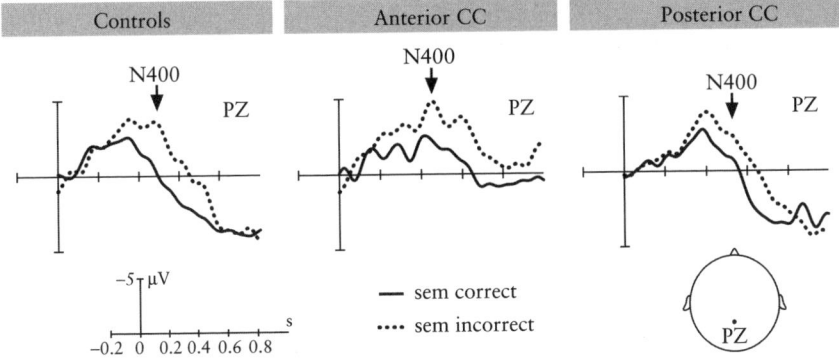

Fig. 22.17. Grand averaged ERPs for the critical verb complex in the semantically incorrect (dotted line) and correct (solid line) condition for different groups at electrode Pz.

Source: adapted from Friederici et al. 2007b

somewhat reduced but is significant. In contrast, for those with lesions in the posterior CC, there is no effect whatsoever. From this finding we may conclude that due to the lesions in the posterior portion of the CC, prosodic information (RH) cannot misguide the syntactic parser (LH). That is, patients with lesions in the posterior CC do not make a wrong prediction for a particular verb category and therefore do not show a prosody-included mismatch effect.

But before this conclusion can be drawn, it must be demonstrated that the CC patients, and in particular those with lesions in the posterior portion, do show an N400 in principle, that is, when not dependent on prosodic information. To test this we used our sentence material that in previous experiments had elicited an N400. All our patient groups, and certainly the controls, show a nice N400 (see Fig. 22.17). From this we can conclude that auditory language comprehension is supported by separable specific temporo-frontal networks for semantic and syntactic processes in the LH and for prosodic processes in the RH, and that the two hemispheres normally interact during the comprehension of spoken language. The posterior portion of the CC plays a crucial role in the interaction between syntactic and prosodic information.

22.5 Postscript: prosody and semantics

Before ending, just a little experiment to entertain you on the interaction of prosody and semantics. Going beyond language as such, we can look at emotional prosody. Earlier we showed the interaction between the LH and RH with respect to structural issues, but how about semantics? As the only semantics really encoded in prosody is emotional information, we conducted a priming study (Schirmer et al. 2008) in which our subjects were presented with sentences that had either a happy or sad intonation with quite neutral wording, for example:

(9) *Ich komme gerade vom Essen*
     'I am just coming back from lunch'

So, what would happen once we primed target words with either a happy or sad sentence prosody? The target words were either positive, like *Geschmack* (taste), or negative, like *Übelkeit* (nausea). Subjects had to listen to the sentences and then hear one of the two target words and make a lexical decision on the target words. We varied the following parameters. We had either a 200 ms lag between the sentence offset and the word onset, or a 750 ms lag. Then subjects had to do the lexical decision task. What one would expect, if the prosodic information is encoded by the semantic-conceptual system, is to see an N400. The observed results were different for men and women. Men did not show any N400 effect for the short interstimulus interval, while for the long interval they did. Women, in contrast, showed the semantic mismatch effect between the target word and the prior sentence for the short interval. From this we tentatively concluded that semantic-emotional and prosodic-emotional processes interact during language comprehension, and that women use prosodic-emotional information earlier than men. You may reach your own conclusions on that. But now the question is, is it that men cannot process prosodic information early in principle [laughter], or can they just decide whether they want to do it or not? [laughter]

   In the next experiment we used the stimulus material with the short interval between the target word and the offset of the sentence. But now in addition to the lexical decision task used in the previous experiment, all subjects also had to make an emotional judgment – that is, they had to pay attention to emotional information. Not surprisingly, now, men showed the N400 even with the short interval of 200 ms. So the conclusion is that women always process emotional prosody early [laughter], and that men only do so when required by the circumstances. I have to tell you we had a hard time trying to get that published [laughter]. We were even given the feedback that these findings and their interpretation were not politically correct. But these are the data.

   With this talk I hope to have shown you that we can look at the brain as it processes language online. In the beginning we started with a model of language processing, and in the end I think we have a good idea of how these different processes are mapped spatially and temporally within the brain.

Let me stress that all this work would not be possible without excellent colleagues and particularly without the work of a lot of excellent Ph.D. students.

Discussion

GLEITMAN: I was very puzzled, because although not brain scanned, perhaps I have been brainwashed by my very close colleagues, Trueswell and Tanenhaus, and others who I suppose are talking about rapid online interaction between syntactic and semantic processes (for instance in studies that Merrill Garrett and colleagues are carrying out at the University of Arizona). These processes are incremental and there wasn't a prior stage of simply structure-building.

FRIEDERICI: Yes, I think there are two issues here. Looking at the effects for local structure-building, they show up between 150 and 200 ms prior to semantic processes. That is one issue. The other issue concerns the material used – and I posed the question to Trueswell and Tanenhaus and everybody else working with their material.[5] I always ask them about the prosody of their material. Mostly they use auditory input, as they also apply it in studies with children, and they always tell me that prosody is "normal," and I do not know what that means. I think even with subtle prosodic cues in their material, you can influence where you do your attachment of the prepositional phrases and how you solve the ambiguity.

GLEITMAN: Well, I do not want to badger, but the first studies they did were reading studies, eye-tracking reading, so there is no question of prosody there. It is self-paced reading, so they get the same results there. Those were their first results.

FRIEDERICI: Well, I think self-paced reading is not the same thing as looking at the brain directly. During self-paced reading you have to process the information and then you have to make a reaction. I think these reading data are compatible with the third phase in our model, where we assume that all information types are interacting. And this is around 500–600 ms.

PARTICIPANT: Thanks for your talk, it has been very enlightening. Do you see a connection between your findings and work about first-language acquisition where the mother is speaking to her children and it is mainly language lessons?

FRIEDERICI: Well, I think it would be a complete lesson, to give you the relevant data on acquisition. But to answer your question briefly: yes I do, in the following sense. First of all, in the closure positive shift that we see with the

---

[5] For example "Put the frog on the towel in the box." See Trueswell and Tanenhaus (1994).

processing of the intonational phrase boundaries; we also observe this in very young infants. Secondly, we have recent data which I really think demonstrate that infants pick up the acoustic, phonological information quite early. It is in a collaborative study with Anne Christophe from Paris.[6] What we have been looking at is the age at which infants are able to detect the stress pattern of their native language. In German, as in English, two-syllable words are mostly stressed on the first syllable. But in French the stress is on the second syllable. In a mismatch negativity paradigm, where you hear for example a succession of three stimuli and then a deviant stimulus, that is stress on the first, first, first, and then on the second syllable, infants by the age of 4–5 months react to those deviant stimuli. Now here comes the interesting issue. The German infants are significantly more likely to react to the deviant with the stress on the second syllable than to the deviant with the stress on the first syllable. For the French infants by the age of 4–5 months we find the reverse pattern. So they do not react to all deviants in the experiment, but only to the deviants that are rare in their target language. So the input from the mother is really important during early acquisition.

RIZZI: A small technical question about what the P600 effect really reveals, what kind of brain computation it expresses. You made a remark in passing, if I caught it correctly, according to which in a certain task, if the task was simply passive listening, you would not see a P600 effect. Does that mean that you see a P600 only when there is some kind of metalinguistic task, or not? Because of course that would lead to other different conclusions about what the effect really indexes.

FRIEDERICI: What I can say is that the P600 is a controlled process, so for example we have done an experiment where we had just these simple syntactic violation errors, and either there were 20 percent of the sentences that were incorrect vs. 80 percent correct, or the other way around (Hahne and Friederici 1999). What subjects had to do here was they had to judge grammaticality. So maybe not surprisingly, when you have 20 percent incorrect sentences in the experimental set, you see the ELAN and a nice P600. When you reverse the proportion of correct and incorrect sentences, you see the ELAN which is not even influenced in amplitude or anything by this variation. However, when you have 80 percent incorrect sentences you don't see a P600, I think – this at least was our explanation. The system would not go into the revision process any more, even though at the end of each sentence subjects had to do a grammaticality judgment task. We also see that depending on what task we

---

[6] Friederici et al. (2007a).

use, whether we have a probe-verification task or a grammaticality judgment, the amplitude of the P600 varies as a function of that. It is larger for grammaticality judgment, as you suggested, and not so large for some other task where you do not have to process the entire syntactic structure.

FODOR: I'm interested in how much alike we all are in these respects and how much variability there is both in the location and temporal scale, because in the old days when there were only lesion studies as the data, we were taught that left-handed people had half their language in one hemisphere and half in the other, and so forth. So I'd like to know how tidy the LH–RH separation is and the time of the responses.

FRIEDERICI: I think with respect to the groups we investigated, I cannot say anything with respect to this issue as we have only looked at right-handed subjects so far. We've looked at left-handed subjects in one single fMRI experiment. In this study we also did a dichotic listening experiment on these subjects in order to figure out whether they really had the "crossed" hemisphere indication. The fMRI data revealed that only about half of the left-handers have a language dominance in the other hemisphere, that is the right hemisphere. Dominance classification based on dichotic listening worked much better than the usual handedness questionnaire (Hund-Georgiadis et al. 2002). Just looking at handedness would thus not be enough; you always have to do additional tests, and that then gives you more variables you have to consider in order to do a well-controlled experiment on language dominance. With respect to the timing of brain response, we haven't really looked at individual differences for the P600, but we did so with respect to ELAN with the MEG experiment, and I was really surprised to find that the peak of this early effect was not more than 25 ms apart between the subjects we have been looking at (Friederici et al. 2000).

FODOR: I see. So one issue is more and less advanced language skills. I mean there are scales on which you can rank people, but my real interest is actually when the syntax is over in the RH, is it crowding out the prosody? Are these trying to occupy the same space?

FRIEDERICI: As I said, we don't have data on right-dominant subjects so I cannot answer this question. But you are right in raising the issue about the RH involvement in general. In our crucial experiment concerning the prosody–syntax interaction conducted in right-handers, we were looking at the brain's reaction to an element that is not directly at the point of the critical prosodic information. You first have the intonational break and we are looking at the verb that comes two words after it.[7] So these data could mean that it needs some time for the prosodic information to influence syntactic processes. It is very difficult to find material where you can show the exact timing of the interaction of information types within these sentence structures. What we have done, therefore, is to look for material with a counterpart of the local phrase structure violation in the prosodic domain. What we have been doing is the following. In a violation sentence like the ones we were using before,[8] the prediction at the preposition, which is case-marked, could be two-fold. One is syntactic, where you predict a certain word category, but the other one would be a combination of syntactic and prosodic information. Because you know as a German speaker that the main verb should come at the end of the sentence, you predict that the next element after the preposition should not have a sentence-final prosody. In crossing these information types fully in a two-by-two design, we find that independent of the syntactic violation, the wrong prosodic intonation that an element has taken elicits an early right anterior negativity indicating RH processes. Moreover we find an interaction between prosody and syntax even for the combined violation condition (Eckstein and Friederici 2006).[9]

LAKA: I was curious about the patients that you looked at. Outside of experimental conditions, are these CC patients people who show any symptoms of lack of integration of prosody and syntax? I was trying to recall these famous patients who had the CC cut surgically and could not recall any symptoms of this sort, and I was curious as to whether the patients you looked at showed any signs of this lack of integration.

FRIEDERICI: Well, you have to test these patients very carefully. Gross testing or coarse testing would not show that, because they always are able to compensate. I didn't go into detail concerning the anterior portion of the CC, which connects the two frontal cortices. For all our syntactic and prosodic studies in normals, we have seen activation also in the frontal operculum of the two hemispheres. For the moment we do not have a really good idea of how the two anterior and the two posterior portions contribute to the observed effect of the N400 in normals. However, you may remember that the N400 was reduced in those patients who had lesions in the anterior portion of the CC, but only reduced in the second part of the N400. The first part peaked well, but then the effect flattened out. I think that also the anterior regions (these are the frontal

---

[7] For example, "Peter verspricht # Anna zu arbeiten..."
[8] For example, "The duck was in the fed."
[9] This study moreover reports an early interaction between prosody and syntax.

operculum of the RH and the LH) talk to each other but in a secondary process. I think in the N400, at least this is what you would conclude from the data here, there is an overlapping of two processes. Thus those patients with lesions in the posterior portion are perhaps able to compensate in behavioral tasks based on the anterior portion of the CC.

PARTICIPANT: Just a quick follow-up from what Janet Fodor was saying: the connection with syntax and prosody. What are your thoughts on the processing studies that have been done with sign language? One of the big issues used to be the use of the RH, but a British group seems to have managed to discard the RH effect for sign language processing. Do you have any thoughts on that?

FRIEDERICI: Well, we have thoughts and we have data. Prosodic information is very much encoded in mime and facial gestures, so if you are able to separate those out in an fMRI experiment, you should see a very similar distribution as for normal language processing. I mean, forget about the visual cortices, because the information has to go through that in the first place, but then when you only have the subjects looking exclusively at the hand movements, that is not enough, as prosody is very often signaled by eyebrows and other facial gestures. I think I know of no study that has very nicely separated those two aspects, but it is a nice idea to do that.

If there are no other questions, I would like to thank the organizers for holding this wonderful conference and for inviting me to give this talk to you. Thank you.

CHAPTER 23

Conclusion

Noam Chomsky

First of all, I'm here over my own strong objections. When I saw the program I wrote to Massimo and said that I'm not the right person to do this so somebody else ought to, and I suggested that he ought to because he's the one person who covers all of these topics and I don't. But he's very persuasive, so I fell for it, and that just made it even worse. He said I should go on as long as I liked. My children used to have a line; if they asked a question they used to say, "Please, just the five-minute lecture." So I'll just go on until you shut me up.

I've tried to think a little bit about how to organize some comments. An awful lot of fascinating material has been presented here, some of which I understood, some of which I didn't. What I'll try to do is pick out some points that come to mind, starting from the most general to the more specific, and expressing an apology in advance to everyone whose work I misrepresent. I'll try to do as little of that as possible.

The most general point was a significant one of Jim Higginbotham's presentation (see pages 142–154) which actually carries an important lesson. Namely, that if you look back in history, you find that they were often recovering ground that had been partially attained and understood. And that's true; it came up in the discussion that generative grammar goes back 2,500 years. It didn't have to be discovered in the late 1940s; it goes back to the Paninean tradition which developed for centuries.[1] And Panini himself was the result of a long, mostly unknown prehistory. And the same is true case after case; the same sort of thing happens in the sciences all the time.

So in biology, Mark Hauser gave a talk here on the illusion of variety (see Chapter 19), which was the position of Geoffroy in the famous Cuvier–Geoffroy debate.[2] Geoffroy was thought to have been demolished in the debate,

---

[1] For a historical review see Lele and Singh (1987). (Editors' note)
[2] Appel (1987). (Editors' note)

but it's coming back that he was in a deep sense right and that rational morphology, which had been derided for centuries, is somehow right.

This sort of thing continually happens, and the lesson is that science is a kind of hill-climbing. But you can get caught on the wrong hill, and you have to know that you should go down and start somewhere else and then go up; and often you find that people were higher up before you somewhere else. It's very easy to just get caught up in one's own conviction that the interesting line of work, which is raising technical problems and is fun to solve and so on, is really the answer, when it could very well be a sidetrack. We have all too many examples of that in the past – the recent past and the more remote past – and you have to constantly keep in mind the importance of knowing and remembering what happened, and keep an open mind about whether maybe those guys weren't so dumb as they looked, and that it's worth doing.

I'll just give one personal anecdote that came to mind in that discussion. Around 1960, a very famous and accomplished historian of Classical Greek Philosophy, Gregory Vlastos, came to Boston to give a talk on one of Plato's dialogues, the Meno.[3] And a couple of us from the research lab in electronics decided it would be fun to go – I can't remember exactly who, I think it was Jerry Fodor and maybe Julius Moravcsik, who was a visiting philosopher. So we went over and when Vlastos opened the talk, which was for philosophers, he was very apologetic for talking about all this stuff that we know is wrong and has been disproved. But he gave a serious talk about a serious philosopher, and after the discussion at the end we went up and talked to him, and it took him a while to figure out that we actually thought that Plato's argument was right and that it wasn't a crazy stupid thing that had been disproved. And when he finally realized, he got very excited and we went off and had lunch together and had a great discussion. He believed it, but it simply wouldn't have occurred to him that anyone in those days – in the 1950s or 60s – could possibly pay attention to this old, boring, dead stuff, which in fact turns out I think to be fundamentally right. It's come back in another form, but that can happen very often. And it's worth remembering.

The kind of work that Marc Hauser and Chris Cherniak were talking about in this conference, and the other work that's been referred to, is reconstructing and recovering consciously ideas that had been discredited. We were under the illusion that variability is limitless, the same illusion that resulted from anthropological linguistics.

I think that the broadest issues that arose in the discussion were the questions about the prerequisites for experience. So, to quote Rochel Gelman – quotes

---

[3] Vlastos (1975). (Editors' note)

here mean whatever I jotted down, probably wrongly – she made a distinction between core domains and other domains as a prerequisite for experience (see Chapter 15). The core domains involve a high-level, abstract conceptual framework, and mental structures actively engaging with the environment from the start. These core domains have several properties: they're reflexive, they're quick, they converge, they're common among people. They have many of the properties of Jerry Fodor's modules,[4] except that these are a different kind of module; these are acquisition or growth modules, not processing modules. It's not an unrelated notion but they are conceptually distinct. These are the rough properties of the core domains and they also involve from the start high-level abstract conceptual structures, not just picking out sensations and so on.

Randy Gallistel gave an amplification of this by providing a Kantian framework of foundational elements in terms of space, time, number, and so on (see Chapter 4). In ethological terms, the core domains with these foundational terms are what provided the Umwelt, the world of experience of the organism, which differs for each organism but is some kind of a complex world, and that's the kind of world that you're presented with. If we go back a century before Kant, there was rich discussion of these topics by mostly British philosophers, the neo-Platonists and the British empiricists, who talked about what they called cognoscitive powers. Somehow the organism has rich cognoscitive powers – they were only talking about humans – and these involved gestalt properties, causality, intention, and lots of others.

Thomas Hobbes argued that part of the core properties for looking at the world was characterizing things in terms of their origins, so you identified a river by its origin, or a constitution by its origin. Locke, far from being a caricature of an empiricist, assumed extremely rich cognoscitive powers. Relevant to us, his most significant contribution to this domain is, I think, his analysis of persons. Our concept of person is based critically on psychic continuity; it is continuity of the mind that individuates persons, it's not anything a physicist can find. And even what we would call science-fiction experiments – two minds in the same physical body and that sort of thing – go as far back as Locke. Some of the basic issues go back to Aristotle. He identified a house, let's say, as a combination, in his terms, of matter and form. Matter is sticks and bricks and so on, but there's also form: design, function, and standard use. It's a combination of the two. It's important to note that Aristotle was giving a metaphysical definition; he was not defining the word "house," he was defining houses. And that leads to hopeless conundrums that go right through the history of philosophy: one which came up was the ship of Theseus, a modern version of

---

[4] Fodor (1983). (Editors' note)

which is Kripke's puzzle.[5] And if you give a metaphysical interpretation to these things you run right off into impossible conundrums.

What began to happen in the seventeenth century was that these problems were restated as being essentially epistemological or cognitive rather than metaphysical, and it just turns out that our concepts don't apply in many cases. So the Ship of Theseus is simply a case where our concepts just don't give an answer.[6] And why should they? They're not supposed to answer every possible problem that comes up. The thing is still amusing to look at, but it is no longer a paradox or a conundrum. They didn't actually draw that conclusion but they should have. It ends up that the investigation of cognoscitive powers – which is quite a rich theory of meaning and still remains unexplored (and going back to Jim's lesson, it ought to be explored) – led finally to a quote of Hume's: the objects that we talk about are really objects of thought which are constructed by mental operations, and there is no peculiar physical nature belonging to them.[7] You can't identify them by some identifiable, mentally independent property. As in Locke's example, psychic continuity is not a mentally independent property. I don't know if this has been studied but we all know that infants have no problem with this. In fact, children's literature is based on these notions. In the standard fairy tale the handsome prince is turned into a frog by the wicked witch, and he is to all extents and purposes a frog until the beautiful princess kisses him and suddenly he's a prince again. The infant knows that he was the prince all along and it didn't matter if he looked like a frog. Locke's notion was much too narrow: it's not persons, it's almost anything.

My grandchildren have a favorite story about a baby donkey named Sylvester who is turned into a rock. For most of the story Sylvester the rock is trying to convince his parents that he is their baby donkey. And since children's stories always end happily – that's a law of nature – something happens at the end of the story and he turns back into the baby donkey and everybody's happy. However, the children know that the rock, which may be a rock by any physical test, is actually Sylvester because there's a psychic continuity running through it.

So Locke's distinction between person and man doesn't work; it goes to maybe anything organic, maybe beyond. But it's the typical case of some

---

[5] Kripke (1979). (Editors' note)

[6] The ship of Theseus, according to the ancient Greek legend, had to be rebuilt while continuing to sail. Otto Neurath, a prominent member and co-founder of the Vienna Circle, used it as a metaphor of science, since there too one has to proceed forward while rebuilding the theories. In fact, in the epistemological literature this is often referred to also as Neurath's Ship. For interesting discussions, see Baggaley (1999); and for Neurath's Ship, see Blais (1997) and Zemplén (2006). (Editors' note)

[7] See Chapter 10, footnote 2.

semantic or conceptual property that is impossible to identify in material terms. And Hume's conclusion is, I think, plausible. When you look at case after case you find more and more that that's exactly the way it is. And it does mean (and I'll come back to this) that there simply is no notion of reference in natural language. There is in other language-like systems, but natural language is a biological object and we can't stipulate its properties, and one of its properties seems to be that it doesn't have reference. I'll come back to that.

Alongside the core domains, to get back to Rochel Gelman, there's also what she called HoW – "hell on wheels" (see page 226). So there's another kind of domain that has none of the properties of the core domains: you have to really work on it, people's talents differentiate, it's slow, its understanding is developed over generations, it's transmitted, and so on. It's analogous in the domain of physical abilities to, say, walking versus pole-vaulting. When you go to the Olympics there's a pole-vaulting championship but there's no championship for walking across the room. And that's because everybody can do it; it may seem very easy but trying to figure out what's going on might be very hard. Or, say, reaching for something; it's extremely hard to figure out what's going on but there's no competition for it because that's a core domain. Pole-vaulting on the other hand is for freaks; very few people can do it and ability is spread all over the place, so that's why it's a game or sport. In fact, games and sports are precisely those things that people are no good at. That's one of the reasons that I've always felt that the cognitive scientists and the artificial intelligence people were barking up the wrong tree when they started to study chess, because that's something that's for freaks – like Jim Higginbotham (who notoriously is a very good chess player), but not normal people. Normal people can figure out the moves, but if you want to have championship abilities spread enormously then it's like pole-vaulting. If you want to understand an organism, you look at the core domains not the freaky things at the edges. So chess is the wrong thing to look at, just as pole-vaulting would be the wrong thing to look at if you were trying to figure out the organization of motor skills.

A first approximation to the structure of the cognitive system, and it seems to me a reasonable one, is the core domain versus "hell on wheels." We investigate these topics using capacities which allow us to carry out considered reflection on the nature of the world. It is given various names in different cultures. It's called myth, or magic, or in modern times you call it science. And they're all different but they're all sort of like that: there's some considered reflection on what's going on. It's very hard and there are all the other problems that we know about, but that's a first break.

If you look at something like Marc Hauser's father – you may remember his description of how he gave the wrong result (that is, the right result) on one of the trolley problems (see page 325) – Marc Hauser's father was, I presume, not working in the core domain where you give your intuitive reaction to what you would do. Instead, he was thinking about it and saying that in a sense here is what you *ought* to do, which is called the wrong reaction. This suggests something about that whole topic – in fact any topic like it – which is reminiscent of things like the classic case of garden path sentences (see Chapter 22). When somebody is presented with a garden path sentence, they instantly get the wrong interpretation and they may say it's not a sentence because they're doing it the wrong way. They can't tell you the processes that they're using; they are unconscious, inaccessible to consciousness (there's that same inaccessibility to consciousness). It's in a certain sense wrong, whatever that means, to get the right answer with considered reflection. If you set up a certain context and the usual things, then they'll say "Yeah, there's that other interpretation." It's a kind of performance–competence distinction, and I think all of these topics ought to be looked at that way, including the morality cases. Maybe Marc's father – for one of the cases but not the others – was in the sort of state which Jack Rawls,[8] who started this stuff off, called reflective equilibrium: not your immediate reaction but the interpretation you give when you think about it, interact with others, you figure out what your understanding and your ideas really are, and so forth. That's a distinction to keep in mind.

One of the core domains, as we get narrower, must be language. It has all the properties that Rochel Gelman talked about. To quote her again, "mental structures actively engage the world":[9] it's reflexive; it just happens without effort; it happens in exactly the same way in everyone – pathology aside; and as some evidence brought up here shows, within two days the infant has picked some of the data in the world and has decided that this is linguistic data. And as far as I know that's a pretty tricky operation. I don't know if anyone's tried a computational theory to figure out how that's done, but I suspect it wouldn't be easy to figure out how with all this mess of stuff going on in the world you decide that's linguistic data and some of it clearly isn't. But apparently this happens by two days, and even more has happened, since, as you've heard, the child is differentiating different types of linguistic data.

That's the quick development of a complex Umwelt. And one reason that no non-human animal is ever going to have anything like language is that it can't get over that first step. It's just data for your parrot or your songbird or ape or whatever. It's just not making that distinction so nothing can happen after that. What we mostly study is what happens after that – after you've taken

---

[8] Rawls (1971). (Editors' note)
[9] See section 15.2.1.

that first step, what do you do with it? And that's the rest of the core domain. The first step is tricky enough, and I think that's one reason why ape language studies are pointless from the start. There are a lot of other reasons why they're pointless, but even from the first moment they're pointless.

After that comes the growth of the system. It's called acquisition. If we go back to our discussions here, when the terrain was laid out, Lila Gleitman talked about word meaning, Janet Fodor talked about the computational system, and Núria Sebastián-Gallés talked about parameters. These are three big issues that come up in the nature of the growth of the system, which is called language acquisition.

Starting in reverse order, why parameters? The question came up again and again in our discussions here. Mark Baker, as you heard, had a proposal (see page 95). I was telling Massimo, I thought Baker was joking, frankly, when he gave that proposal, but maybe not. It's kind of amusing but it can't be right, for the reasons that Massimo said. It is true that there's evidence from cultural anthropology that groups distinguish themselves from other groups by arbitrary practices. A famous example is Jews and Muslims not eating pork. Apparently the only reason for that, that anybody can figure out, is that they do so to differentiate themselves from other people around. There are no health reasons or anything like that. And there are plenty of examples like that, so the idea that that could happen is possible, but Baker's hypothesis is logically incoherent for the reasons that Massimo mentioned – you have to have the parameters before you can use them to differentiate yourselves from others.

A second plausible proposal is one that Donata Vercelli and Massimo mentioned: there is some kind of a minimax operation going on (see page 101). This would take you back to third-factor properties – optimization properties – and the intuition is that if you take a parameter and you genetically fix the value, it becomes a principle, it moves from the domain of parameters to principles. To spell this out is not so simple, but from a certain point of view, when you add the value, you're adding genetic information. Try to work that out, it's not so trivial. There's a way of thinking about it in which it gives more information if you give the value than if you leave it open. So adding parameters is reducing genetic information from this point of view. On the other hand, it's making language acquisition harder because you have to find the value of the parameter. So you can at least imagine that there's a nice theorem out there waiting for somebody to prove which says that the choice of parameters maximized for both of these contradictory tendencies does the best possible job – it's a minimax problem. So those of you who are looking for Ph.D. dissertations or maybe Nobel prizes might try to figure that out.

There's another possibility, which I don't think should be ruled out. As far as we understand, the overwhelming weight of the parameters, almost all of them, are on the morphological/phonological side – that is, they are in the mapping from the syntax/semantics to the sensorimotor system. I mentioned before that I think there's very good evidence that this is a secondary process, and this came along later in evolution. First people sort of learned how to think, and then later when there were enough of them they somehow tried to figure out a way to externalize it. Externalization is a very non-optimal sort of process. You have two systems that have nothing to do with each other. One of the systems has evolved for basically the semantic interface (the conceptual thought system), and maybe it turned out to be almost perfect and provide a perfect matching to that system. Maybe it's even tautologous in that this system reads off it. The other system is the sensorimotor system, which has just been sitting around there for a long time. And somehow you've got to get them together and there are a lot of ways of doing this. Here's another nice theorem waiting to be proven. The ways in which this is done are optimal. That is, if you take the very messy systems of phonology and morphology, maybe they turn out to be the best possible ways of handling this very difficult problem. Conceivably, it's a long-term project.

Another possibility arises from the fact that the anthropological evidence doesn't tell us much about this group of people who underwent this amazing change. Presumably it was a small group, and small hunter-gatherer tribes tend to separate. Often pretty quickly they split up into very small groups. This means that they may not have much contact with one another – remember that it's all happening within a very small window of evolutionary time, maybe 50–100,000 years or so. There could have been enough differentiation so they started externalizing independently, and if they externalized independently they might have just solved the problem independently. And then later on they get together again and it looks as if there're a lot of languages and here are the parameters. If that's true then there wouldn't be too much rhyme or reason to the choice of parameters;[10] it would be partly historical accident – "here's the way we tried to do it and here's the way those guys tried to do it," they entangle them all and it looks like a system of parameters. And so I think there's every option open from a perfect solution to a minimax problem to a worst possible solution, which is one damn thing after another. Anywhere in there could be some kind of answer to this question. I think it's an interesting question. And then there's Janet Fodor's possibility as she explains in her paper

---

[10] Uriagereka (1998). (Editors' note)

(see Chapter 17): maybe some of them are hidden and we never see them because we just can't get to them; you just pass them by in the lattice.

The next question is the one that Janet brought up and is about the computational system. Here some clarification should be made: there's a lot of talk about recursion and it's not a mystical notion; all it means is discrete infinity. If you've got discrete infinity, you've got recursion. There are many different ways of characterizing that step, but they are all some sort of recursive operation. Recursion means a lot more than that, but that's the minimum it means. There are different kinds of recursion – partial recursive, general recursive – but we don't need to worry about them. This core notion is that if you have a discrete infinity you have to have some device to enumerate them, and in the case of language, what are the objects that you want to enumerate? Here there's confusion and it leads to trouble. From the start, say the early 1950s, all of us involved in this took for granted that the objects you want to enumerate are expressions, where expressions are structured objects. So an expression is something that has a hierarchy, has interrelations, and so on. And that's illustrated by the example that I gave earlier here to begin with. If you take the sentence:

(1) Mary saw the man leaving the store.

it's three expressions, not one expression. There are three structural interpretations that give you three semantic interpretations, and they separate when you raise the wh- word; you only get one of them. Just about every sentence is like that. There is a string formula, which is just the sequence of those words (Mary-saw-the-man-leaving-the-store), but that's a very impoverished version of the three expressions.

If we talk about generation of language, there are two kinds of generation: one is called strong generation, where you generate the expression including the objects with their structures, and that yields the meaning and gives the basis for semantic and phonetic interpretation; and there's weak generation, where you just generate the string. Weak generation has no clear meaning; strong generation has a clear meaning – it's a biological phenomenon. There is a class of structured expressions and you can figure out what they are. Weak generation is highly problematic. First of all there's no obvious interest: there's no reason why we should be interested in an impoverished version of the object that's generated. It's uninteresting as well as unclear what the class is; you can draw the boundaries anywhere you want. We talk about grammatical and ungrammatical but that's just an intuitive distinction and there's no particular reason for this; normal speech goes way beyond this. Often the right thing to say goes outside of it; there are famous cases of this, like Thorstein Veblen, a political economist who was deeply critical of the consumer culture that was developing a century ago, who once said that culture is indoctrinating people into "performing leisure."[11] We understand what that means and that's just the right way to say it but from some point of view it's ungrammatical. Rebecca West was once asked some question about possible worlds, and she said that "one of the damn thing is enough."[12] We know exactly what that means and that it's a gross violation of some grammatical rule, but there isn't any better way of saying it; that's the right way to say it.

Are such things proper strings or not proper strings? Well, it makes no difference what answer you give – they are what they are, they have the interpretation they have – it's given to you by the linguistic faculty, but they're all strongly generated. That's the only real answer.

This should be straightforward but it got to be problematic because it was intermingled with philosophical interpretations. This mostly comes from Quine, who insisted from the late 1940s that language has to be a class of well-formed formulas.[13] It's obvious that the model is formal systems, but in the case of a formal system it's unproblematic because you stipulate the well-formed formulas; you have a mode of generating the well-formed formulas and that stipulates them. And that's why Quine, for example, raised questions about the reality of phrase structure. He denied it because he said that if you have noun-verb-noun you could break it up to noun-verb versus noun or noun versus verb-noun, so it's all arbitrary and you have no evidence and so on. That's what the issue looks like if you formulate it as generating well-formed formulas or strings, but that doesn't make any sense. You're generating structures; the structure N versus VP is different from the structure NV versus object and you have empirical evidence to tell you which it is. This doesn't make it definitive, but the same is true in physics: nothing's definitive, it's just evidence.

The other problem that led to massive confusion about this, which goes on right until today (and is related to things we've talked about earlier in this

---

[11] Veblen (1899). (Editors' note)

[12] Rebecca West, the English critic, is credited with the irritated response to the "mind as a mirror of nature" that "one of the damn thing(s) is enough." The quote that "one of the damn things is enough" also appears on page 3 of Nelson Goodman's essay "Languages of Art," but as a part of the phrase: "Art is not a copy of the real world. One of the damn things is enough." Goodman says in a footnote that the phrase appears in an "essay on Virginia Woolf" but that he has "been unable to locate the source." For a discussion, see http://mindworkshop.blogspot.com/2005/11/making-it-explicit-chapter-one-part-vi.html. (Editors' note)

[13] For a first discussion of, and counters to, Quine's (and Goodman's) theories of grammar, see *Syntactic Structures* (Chomsky 1957, reprinted in 2002), then Chomsky (1968). See also Lasnik et al. (2000). A partial reconciliation with some of Chomsky's theses was made by Quine in Quine (1969). (Editors' note)

conference), is that a sort of mathematical theory came along for trying to select properties of these generative systems. That's Phrase Structure Grammar (PSG), and that theory made sense in the early 1950s. For one thing it made mathematical sense because it was an adaptation of more general ideas. At that time it had come to be understood that there were a number of ways of characterizing recursive functions (theory of algorithms): Turing machine theory, Church's lambda calculus, and others. All tried to capture the notion of mechanical procedure, and they were shown to be equivalent, so it was assumed – the assumption is called Church's thesis[14] – that there is only one such system and umpteen notations. One of the notations, by a logician named Emil Post,[15] happened to be very well adapted to looking at the specific properties of language. If you took Post's system, and you started putting some conditions on it, you got context-sensitive grammars, context-free grammars, and finite automata. Within the framework of the theory of algorithms, you did very naturally get these three levels. Why look at those three levels? It's just pure mathematics, you can get anything you want. But why look at these three levels? Because they captured some properties of language. Context-free grammars did capture the property of nested dependency (the third example that came up in the discussion of Angela Friederici's presentation – see page 191), and that's just a fact of that language. So if you look at agreement:

(2)   The men are tall.

and you put another sentence in between:

(3)   The men who John sees are tall.

you have agreement on the inner one nested within agreement on the outer one. You can't say:

(4)   *The men who John see is tall.

There's no obvious reason for that; for parsing it would be great. The first noun comes along, you take the first verb and that would work great. But it's so

---

[14] Church's Thesis (also referred to as Church–Turing's Thesis), in essence, states that a function is effectively computable (Turing-machine computable) if, and only if, it can be exhaustively and explicitly characterized. The class of these functions is identical with the class of partial recursive functions (as defined by S. C. Kleene in 1936). There is no formal proof of this thesis (that's why it is referred to as a thesis), but no counterexample has yet been found. It is now almost universally accepted by mathematicians and logicians. The classic references are: Church (1936), Turing (1936), Kleene (1936). A standard textbook is Hartley Rogers (1987). For a philosophical analysis see Mendelson (1990). (Editors' note)

[15] Post (1943). (Editors' note)

impossible it's almost impossible to say it. And all over language you find case after case of nesting: things stuck inside other things. And that property is captured by a context-free phrase structure grammar; a context-sensitive, a richer one, does it with contextual conditions. So that looked like it was capturing something about language, which is what you want from a mathematical model. A mathematical model doesn't capture the system, it just captures some properties of it.

The reason for going down to finite automata was just because they were fashionable, so fashionable in fact that they were taken to be universal. What was taken to be universal was a very particular subcase of finite automata, namely the ABAB type that Angela talked about, very local finite automata where you don't use the full capacities. The finite automata that I mentioned do allow unbounded dependencies, but nobody ever looked at them that way because the background was associationism (associating adjacent things), so nobody looked at the kind of finite automata which did yield unbounded dependencies. These narrow ones, which if you add probabilities to you get Markov sources, were taken to be universals for behavior altogether, so it was worth taking a look at those. That's the motivation for this hierarchy but no more than that, and one shouldn't be misled by it. A phrase structure grammar strongly generates a structure, such that you get the hierarchy and different levels and so on, but you can say that it weakly generates the things at the bottom, the terminal elements; it's not interesting, but you can say it. However, weak generation turns out to be mathematically feasible; strong generation is mathematically unfeasible as it's too complicated. Then comes the whole field of mathematical linguistics (Automata theory and so on), ending up being a small branch of mathematics, which completely studies weak generation; all the theorems and everything else are weak generation. I worked in it too, mainly because it was fun, but it had no linguistic significance as far as I could see.

In fact, of all the work in mathematical linguistics, I know of only one theorem that has any linguistic significance and that's about strong generation: it's a theorem that says that context-free grammars are strongly equivalent to nondeterministic push-down storage automata.[16] That's a theorem and it actually has meaning, because just about every parsing system is a push-down storage automata, and it says that there's an equivalence between these and context-free grammars. If you take a look at parsing systems they're using variants of that theorem. It is a very uninteresting mathematical theorem, so if you look at books on mathematical linguistics or computer science, they'll have

---

[16] Chomsky and Schützenberger (1963). See also Chomsky (1959a, b). (Editors' note)

a lot of stuff about context-free grammars and so on, but they'll never mention that theorem, which is the only interesting one for linguistics.[17]

All of that has again been misleading. We can get back to the starlings and you can see this. These systems (context-free grammar and finite automata) were there for a reason, but in between these, there's any number of other possible systems. One of the systems that is in between finite automata and context-free grammars is finite automata with counters. That's one of the systems that is between these two levels, but there's no point describing it. For one thing, it has no mathematical motivation and it has no empirical motivation – people don't use it, so who cares? But it's there.

When you look at the starling experiment (Gentner et al. 2006), there's every indication that this is exactly what they're using: they're just counting. What the experiment shows is that the starlings can count to three, which doesn't seem very surprising. Randy Gallistel was telling us about jays that can count to many thousands (see page 61), and if I remember correctly there was work by Ivo Kohler back around 1940, who had jays counting up to seven (if you put seven dots they'll go to the seventh cup, or something like that). And my suspicion is that if the starling people pursued their experiment a little further, they'd get up to close to seven. And there's a good reason for that: it was shown by George Miller fifty years ago in his famous paper called "The magical number seven, plus or minus two."[18] He covered a lot of literature across species, and it turns out that short term memory is right about that range. If they do this experiment they'll probably find the same thing: the starlings will get up to five, or eight, or something like that. They think it's a context-free grammar because it's above the finite automata level in that hierarchy, but that doesn't tell you anything.

It does in the third example that came up in the discussion of Angela's presentation: when you get nesting, then you're using the properties of context-free grammar. And if you experiment with human processing by reading people sentences with nestings, you can get up to about seven before the capacity breaks down. George Miller and I wrote about this in the Handbook of Mathematical Psychology in the early 1960s.[19] We didn't do the experiments, we just tried it out on ourselves: you can force yourself up to about seven and it's still intelligible, but beyond that it's just totally unintelligible. You know

---

[17] Comments about these misunderstandings and many more, instantiated in Margaret A. Boden's (2006) two-volumes history of cognitive science, are to be found in Chomsky (2007). (Editors' note)

[18] Miller (1956). (Editors' note)

[19] Miller and Chomsky (1963); also Chomsky and Miller (1953). (Editors' note)

you have the capacity because if you add time and space – like a Turing machine – then you get the right answer. For example, in your head you can multiply up to, say, 23. That doesn't mean you don't know the rules of multiplication beyond that; you just need extra time and memory. Then the same rules apply. So you know it all but you can't use it beyond that. So any simple kind of performance experiment is probably not going to distinguish humans from animals. If you can get some animal that can do nested dependencies, you're not going to be able to show the difference between them and humans by elementary performance experiments, even though the difference almost certainly is there.

This is something that has been totally missed in the connectionist literature. One of the most quoted connectionist papers is Jeffrey Elman's work on how you can get two nested dependencies.[20] This is true, you can write a program that will do that. But Elman's program totally breaks down when you get to three, and you have to rewrite the whole program. In Turing machine terms, the control unit has to be totally changed, which means you're not capturing the rules. And to make things worse, his approach also works for crossing dependencies, so in the case of the example earlier:

(4)   *The men who John see is tall.

it works just as well for those. It's not capturing the dependencies, it's just using brute force to go up to two things that you remembered. And that kind of work is never going to get anywhere. There's no point modeling performance that is bounded by time and space, just as you can't study arithmetic knowledge that way.

A last point about this: if you look at *Logical Structure of Linguistic Theory*, the 1955 manuscript of mine[21] (it was written just for friends, not for publication; you couldn't publish in this field then as it didn't exist), it was supposed to be about language and there was no mention of finite automata at all because they just don't capture enough to be worth mentioning. There is an argument against phrase structure grammar, but it's not an argument based on impossibility, like you can give for finite automata; it's an argument based on being wrong. It just gives the wrong results because it doesn't express the natural relationships or capture the principles. And that's still the main argument against it.

Over time, we've got to the point after many years where we can move to simpler systems of recursive generation of expressions, which have eliminated

---

[20] Elman (1991). (Editors' note)
[21] Chomsky (1955). Chomsky (1975). (Editors' note)

phrase structure grammar totally. The last residue are the Merge-based systems. Remember that Merge is the simplest possible mode of recursive generation; you can't get below it. Phrase structure grammar is much more complex, concatenation is more complex, and anything you can dream of is more complex. This is the absolute minimum and if you can get to that, you're finished. It looks like you can get to that. Merge automatically gives hierarchically structured expressions; you can eliminate the structure by adding an associative principle, but if you don't tamper with it, it's just a structured expression. It could be that those are the only ones they need. I can't prove it, but it could be.

Cedric Boeckx brought up an important point (see Chapter 3), namely that even if we could show that everything is just Merge-based (language is a snowflake, Merge came along, everything else is there), there's still got to be more to distinguish language from other things. He put it in terms of decomposing Merge, which I suspect is the wrong way to look at it, but you can look at it in terms of adding to Merge, which I think is the right way to look at it. There is something you add to Merge which makes it language specific and that says that reliance on Merge is (as Jim Higginbotham pointed out) "close to true" (see page 143), so close to true that you think it's really true, but there are exceptions. It's close to true that Merge is always a head and another object (a head is just a lexical item, one of the atoms, so Merge is a lexical item and some other object). To the extent that this is true – and it's overwhelmingly true – you eliminate the last residue of phrase structure grammar (projections or labels), because the head is just the thing that you find by minimal search. So a simple computational principle, minimal search (which is going to be much more general), will capture everything about headedness. And the same thing works for both its internal operations and its external relations. That also works for internal Merge, Move. The only major exception that I know is external arguments and they have all sorts of other properties and problems that I talked about. So it looks like it's close to true and probably is true.

Getting a little more explicit, Janet Fodor opened her main presentation (Chapter 17) with the sentence:

(5) Pat expects Sue to win.

This is what's called an ECM[22] structure and the interesting thing about these structures, which are pretty rare – English has them but a lot of other languages don't – is that *Sue to win* is a semantic unit, kind of like a clause. Yet *Sue* is treated as if it were in the upper sentence, as the object of *expect*, which can't be as Pat is not expecting Sue, she's expecting Sue to win. The way it functions

---

[22] Exceptional Case Marking. (Editors' note)

(quantification scope and so on) is as if *Sue* were the object of *expect*. This is a problem that goes back to the work of Paul Postal from the early 1970s.[23] There has been a lot of work on it, it's very puzzling and it doesn't make any sense. I tried for years to resist the evidence for it because it was so senseless, but by now it turns out that there's a principled argument that it has to be that way. Just from straight computational optimality measures – I can't talk about it now, but it goes into phase theory which minimizes computation and inherence of features which is required to make it work. It's a slightly involved argument but it goes back to just one principle, minimalize computation, from which it turns out that *Sue* needs to be up there. If that's the case, the child doesn't have to learn it; it's just going to follow from the laws of nature and you can knock out the problem of learning that. There *is* the parametric problem which Janet mentioned, that might be settled by earlier parameter settings, having to do with inflection and stuff like that. That's the kind of example that one should be looking for in trying to get over some of the massive difficulties of acquisition in terms of parameters.

The third of the problems that came up was Lila Gleitman's: how do you get the words? (See Chapter 16.) It doesn't really mean words, remember, it means the smallest meaning-bearing elements. In English they are word-like, but in other languages they may be stuck in the middle of long words, and so on. So how do you get the meanings of the words? One issue that comes up is whether there are parameters. Almost all the parameters that we know about are in the phonology and morphology. It's conceivable that there are none in the syntax, but are there parameters on the semantic side? There are some that Jim Higginbotham talked about, which are non-compositional, and those are very important, I think. But for the words themselves, are there parameters? The only thing I know about this has to do with what were once called semantic fields. Semantic field theory has been forgotten but it was pretty important. The last work I've seen on it was by Stephen Ullmann, who was a linguist at Leeds around forty years ago.[24] A lot of this was done by German scholars years back, and the basic idea was to try to show that there are some semantic domains which are cut up differently by different languages, but they always fill the same semantic domain. It's analogous to structural phonology: there's some domain and you pick different options. One case of it is pretty well known: colors. There is a lot of work about how colors are cut up differently in different languages and what the principles are.

---

[23] Postal (1974); see also Postal (1964), Chomsky (1995b). (Editors' note)
[24] Ullmann (1958). (Editors' note)

A more interesting case, which was studied by the German semanticists, is mental processes: words like *believe, know,* and *think.* It turns out that languages differ in how they break up the field. They seem to cover about the same domain, but in different ways. This is another one of those cases where the fact that English was studied first was very misleading as English has a very idiosyncratic way of doing this. So the English word *know,* or even *believe* is very hard to translate. *Belief* is almost impossible to translate, and *know a language* is not commonly said that way in other languages. They say you *speak a language, a language is in* you or you *have a language* whereas in English you say you *know a language.* And that has led down a huge garden path making people think that "having" a language involves propositional attitudes – you only know something if there are beliefs, which must be verified beliefs, and so forth. You know the rest of the story. But nothing like that is true of "having" language; there's no propositional attitude, there's no beliefs, there's no verification, so none of these questions arise. If only we said *I have a language* instead of *I know a language* all that probably would have been eliminated. The same is true of a word like *belief;* those who speak other languages recognize that they just don't have a word like that. But English happens to be a highly nominalizing language, so everything is nominalized and there are "beliefs."

And that can lead to the idea that there's a belief, and a belief-desire psychology, and all sorts of other things which may or may not be true but don't have the obvious linguistic anchor in other languages. The difference between *I believe that* and *I think that* . . . there are languages that have a word that really means believe. Hebrew, for example, has a word *believe* but it doesn't mean what English means by *believe* but rather something like *I have faith in it.* The word used for English *believe* is just *I think.* Lots of languages are like that. The point is that there is a semantic field there that's broken up in different ways and you can be very seriously misled if you take one of the ways of breaking it up as if it had metaphysical implications. It doesn't tell us what the world is like, it's just the way we break up the field, which goes back to Hume's point.

Lila pointed out correctly that, in the learning of words, there are questions about lexical semantics and I don't know how to answer them, but the way to look at this heuristically might be to go back to something like field theory. Lila pointed out that the learning of words is very complex, which is okay, but I think it makes more sense to say that it's not hard enough.

For example, Lila correctly remarked that there is a cue, namely the reference to the world, which gives straightforward information, like in the case of *elephant.* But in fact it doesn't, for the reasons that Locke gave. An elephant is not that thing over there, but rather it is something that has psychic continuity, like Sylvester in my grandchildren's stories. And there's nothing in the thing that tells you that. Even for a real elephant in the zoo, there's nothing that tells you it's going to be the same elephant if it turns into a rock and it ends up as in a story. That's all the things we know, basically the expansion of Locke's point, and those are things that are foundational in a cognitive sense.

So you have this huge structure of semantic space, of perceptual space, that we don't know much about and that's determining where these things are placed in it and they don't end up having any ontological character. At this point the question of Jerry Fodor's atomism came up.[25] Jerry gives a strong argument that you can't define words; you can take almost any word you like and you're not going to find a full definition of it. His conclusion is that they're atoms, but that's too strict a demand; there are positions in between there. We're familiar with them from phonology. Take, for example, my pronunciation of *ba*. There's never going to be a definition of that – it varies every time I talk, it's different if I have a cold, it's different from my brother's and so on. And nobody expects us to have a definition of it, but we don't just say it's an atom. It's different from, say, *pa*, and it's different from Arabic, which doesn't have *pa*, and you can make all kinds of observations about *ba*. This is all within the context of distinctive feature theory, which imposes a kind of grid on these systems and identifies all these relations that are real, but they don't define the act; rather they give you some kind of framework within which the act takes place.

So you neither have a definition nor an atom; you have a structure and it looks to me as if words are the same. To take Jerry's famous example, *kill* and *cause to die*.[26] He points out that they're not synonymous, but on the other hand there is something similar about them: there's a victim and he ends up dead. If we knew enough about the multi-dimensionality of this system, we'd probably say that's like a distinct feature and these things fit into a grid somehow. We don't get a full definition but we do get structure, so there is something to look at between atomism and definitions.

Let's turn to the question which came up about ontology: if I say "there is a something or other," can we introduce Quine's Principle of Ontological Commitment[27] (which Jim Higginbotham brought up – see page 154)? I think we can make some distinctions here, going back to Rochel Gelman's distinctions between core and HoW (see page 226). In the core system – the common-sense system – we'll get some answers, but we'll get different answers in the HoW systems. To take an example that's irritating me, take Madrid, where I wasted eight hours the other day, and take the sentence:

---

[25] J. A. Fodor (1998). (Editors' note)
[26] Fodor (1970). (Editors' note)
[27] Quine 1985.

(6) Madrid exists.

(Unfortunately, it does, that's why I wasted eight hours at the airport there the other day. Incidentally, for any super Basque nationalists around here, the best argument I've heard for secession of the Basque Country is that you don't have to go through the Madrid airport to get here.) Madrid certainly exists but I know that nothing exists that is simultaneously abstract and concrete. Yet Madrid is simultaneously abstract and concrete.[28] That's obvious as Madrid could burn down to the ground, so it's obviously concrete, and it could be rebuilt somewhere else out of different materials, maybe two millennia later (like Carthage could be rebuilt) and it would still be Madrid, so it's highly abstract. I know perfectly well that nothing can exist that's simultaneously abstract and concrete, so I'm in a contradiction: Madrid exists and it can't exist. That may be true at the common-sense core level – my common-sense concepts can't deal with this situation. But that's fine as there's no reason why they should. On the other hand, if I move to the HoW level, I'm not going to posit an entity, Madrid, at the same levels of abstraction from the physical world – and remember that anything you do with the HoW system is at some level of abstraction.

Gabby Dover raised the question whether there are laws of form (see Chapter 6) – you could similarly ask whether there are laws of nature. If you want to be just a string theorist or a quantum theorist, saying that there is nothing but strings or quarks, then there aren't any laws of nature of the kind usually assumed, there are just quarks moving around. Hilary Putnam once made a good comment about that: he said it's a boring law of nature that square pegs can't fit into round holes.[29] It's not a very interesting law but it's a law of nature, yet you can't state it in quantum theory, so if you're a quantum theorist, it's not a law of nature but just some freak accident. But we know that that doesn't make sense; you can't even talk unless you pick some level of abstraction. Incidentally, Gabby Dover picked a level of abstraction – individuals and phenotypes – which makes sense as you can say interesting things about them, but they are very abstract. An individual from the point of view of physics is an incredibly complex notion: particular individuals are changing every second, and so are phenotypes. Every time you take a breath, or think a thought, the phenotype is changing. However, we sensibly abstract away from all of that and we're still going to be interested in what's inside our skin. That is an individual, and we keep it that way even though it changes and so on. There's nothing

---

[28] See also Chomsky (1995b). (Editors' note)
[29] Putnam (1973). (Editors' note)

wrong with that but it is a very high level of abstraction. It makes sense because it has internal coherence, you can make comments about it and you can formulate the theory of evolution in terms of it, but the same is true of any other levels of abstraction, so why do you have to pick that one?

In terms of that level of abstraction (individuals or phenotypes), I don't think there's any problem dealing with the questions that Gabby raised; I don't see any point to the debates about nature and nurture – it seems as ridiculous as debates about chemical versus electrical. If you have some phenomenon and both electrical and chemical processes are involved in it, you don't have a war between chemical and electrical – you just try to find out what's going on. Nature and nurture have a perfectly obvious common-sense meaning, in terms of high-level abstract individuals, roughly what's in genes and what comes from the external environment – more subtle than that but that's the rough distinction. Nobody asks about a nature–nurture controversy in the case of ants; development obviously involves both. But nobody asks whether ants have a blank slate – you'd be thrown out of the department. It's just with humans where the problems arise, which is a strange form of dualism, as if somehow we have to regard humans irrationally. For any other part of the world we can be rational, but when we talk about humans, we're totally irrational. We raise questions about nature and nurture, blank slates, and so on. And I don't think that goes anywhere.

There's a difference between the cognitive quasi-ontology that comes out of our common-sense core systems, about what exists (like Madrid), and then there are other things that come out of our considered reflection (ultimately science). This doesn't have simple answers and it's going to depend on the level which we're looking at: are we looking at quarks, molecules, individuals, societies, or even square pegs in round holes? Whatever it is, we'll find things. So you just can't take sentences from ordinary language and run a Quine test on them. Take the famous pair:

(7)   a. There's a fly in the bottle.
      b. There's a flaw in the argument.

By Quine's principle, the world has flies and the world has flaws. I'm not sure that the world has flaws in common-sense understanding. You can make up some story about it, but you're going down the wrong path: it looks like it doesn't even entail that. In cases like this you can see that this doesn't even work internal to the language. You can say (8a) but not (8b):

(8)   a. There's a fly believed to be in the bottle.
      b. *There's a flaw believed to be in the argument.

Because that really requires some kind of existence. And similarly you can say (9a) but not (9b):

(9)   a. A fly is in the bottle.
       b. *A flaw is in the argument.

Because despite the sentence

(7)   b. There's a flaw in the argument.

there's no ontological commitment, even at the common-sense level. And if you look further you find more and more of this.

Furthermore, there's a lesson from Wittgenstein we should remember: language is used against a background of beliefs, and it is extremely hard to disentangle the beliefs from the meanings, maybe even impossible. His example was if you see a chair and the chair starts to talk, you don't know if it's a chair. Is it a chair that's talking, or is it a person that looks like a chair?[30] Your concepts don't give you an answer to that because all instances of language use are against a background of beliefs in which, as a special case, chairs don't talk. You have to take these things apart if you want to talk about any of this seriously. As I said, I think the traditional conundrums are resolved when you look at it this way.

I think the same kinds of consideration hold when we ask questions like those that arose about whether *Santa Claus* in our language somehow entails existence or has to be marked so as not to entail existence (see page 147). That doesn't seem to me to be the right question. As far as I can see *Santa Claus* is just any other word, like *George W. Bush*. Suppose it were proven that George W. Bush is just a creation of mirrors (which could well be since all you do is see him on television); you'd still use the word *George W. Bush* in exactly the same way. And a kid uses *Santa Claus* in exactly the same way when he thinks he's coming down the chimney and when he gets disillusioned. That's another case where your beliefs change but the language doesn't change. I still don't think those are linguistic or semantic questions: they're belief questions.

Finally, down to some really technical questions. Juan Uriagereka raised an extremely interesting question, namely, why there are uninterpretable features in language (see Chapter 12). There's a class of semantically uninterpretable features. English doesn't have it much in the externalized form, but many languages have a visibly rich case system (accusative, nominative, and so on). English probably has it too, but you just don't see it; it's visible only in the pronouns (him, us) but there's good reason to believe that it's everywhere.

---

[30] Wittgenstein (1953). (Editors' note)

And they don't have any meaning: the word *him* has the same meaning as the word *he*, but it's just in a structurally different position. And similarly for richly inflected languages where you have seven or eight cases. Another instance is agreement in verbs, so *is* and *are* have exactly the same meaning. It's just that one of these is for singulars and the other is for plurals but there's no meaning to the thing. Incidentally, even though these are the major topics that have been studied in linguistics for a couple of thousand years, this wasn't much noticed until about thirty years ago. And if you go back to the major studies – Jakobson's Kasuslehre for example,[31] a major theory of case structure in the 1930s – he tries to give a meaning to nominative and accusative, and that just can't be because it's determined by structural position. If you go back you find all sorts of long complex arguments for why singular and plural verbs have different meanings. But they don't. The basic insight came from a famous unpublished letter by the linguist Jean-Roger Vergnaud back in the 1970s.[32] (It demolished a paper that I'd just published that I was quite proud of, but he pointed this out and was kind enough not to publish it.) It led to a very rich study which a large part of modern syntax is based on.

Going back to Juan's question, why are they there? I'm not going to try to give the answer but I think there might be an answer along the following lines. The best possible answer we can get for anything is to go back to optimal computation. Can you derive it from optimal computation? What you can show is that the uninterpretable features demarcate certain units in the expression, and those happen to be the units that qualify as what are called phases, which minimize computational complexity if you do the interpretation there. So what they may be doing is picking out the smallest possible units that can minimize computational complexity. Along those lines, I think you might be able to give an argument as to why uninterpretable features ought to exist just as a pure computational mechanism to minimize computation because they pick out the elements that are the smallest ones you can use.

Luigi Rizzi rightly pointed out that there seem to be two different categories of impossible movement (see Chapter 11), what he called impenetrability and intervention. He rightly pointed out that you want to unify them somehow. We've talked about this and I think it's possible to do it in the same way in terms of minimal computation. I won't try to spell it out but I think that by going back to minimal computation you can plausibly show that these two cases ought to fall out (minimal search and so on). And you can also get the material he described about D-linking and some other topics by reasonable approaches.

---

[31] Jakobson (1936). (Editors' note)
[32] Vergnaud (1977). (Editors' note)

I'm not going to try to explain it but that's a direction to look at for dealing with the problems like this that come up – whether they be Janet Fodor's ECM cases, why there are uninterpretable features, or lots of other things – to see if you can show that the apparent anomalies and complexities of the system really do dissolve into something that will show that variability is an illusion. If you get the right level of analysis you get uniformity, simplicity, and Chris Cherniak-style principles, as well as a lot of mess, but that mess may well have to do with the later stage of the externalization of the system, meaning communication is a peripheral matter needed for language and that can be complex, but within bounds.

Discussion

HIGGINBOTHAM: It's nice to be at a meeting where there are different people representing the various disciplines interested in language. It makes me feel that maybe I belong. I remember when they opened the Whitehead Institute at MIT, which was meant to be for biologists, Luigi Rizzi and I would sometimes go there and have lunch on the grounds that we were biologists in some very abstract sense.

I wanted to remark on two things. One was about things that have remained more or less stable over the years, though a number of data have come along, and then about things that I think are changing for the better. Things that have remained stable include the sharp distinction between competence and performance. Noam disavowed the word "knowledge," but I think it's fine because what it emphasizes is that the relation of the grammatical system to what's going on is not at all to be thought of as a set of procedures; it's to be thought of as a system of principles. It's like knowing multiplication or knowing physics. A second thing that's not been touched directly was the autonomy of semantics, the fact that there is a core which is absolutely context-independent – it doesn't care about plausibility or context or how long it takes to understand it – and it is just determined by linguistic form. That's semantics, the existence proof was given a long time ago by Noam, I think, in the famous sentence:[33]

---

[33] The original sentence was "I almost had a book stolen" in Chomksy's *Aspects* (1965: 22). The sentence modified by Jim Higginbotham has, of course, the easy interpretation that it was almost the case that my wallet was stolen. The second, less easy, is that I almost commissioned someone else to steal my wallet. The third meaning, the third ambiguity, is harder to see: it can be paraphrased as I nearly managed to steal my own wallet (but something went wrong and I failed to do that). (Editors' note)

(10)   I almost had my wallet stolen

Everybody gets two ambiguities, the problem is to find the third one, and when
it's pointed out to you it immediately occurs to you. So those things have
remained stable and so I feel confident that some of the work I've done can
be continued. I do, of course, use truth-theoretic semantics. As Jerry Fodor
remarked once, there are two groups in semantics: one is the group that assumes
that the theory is a theory of reference and proof, and the problem is to find one
that works; and the other is a group of people who sit around talking about
what meaning could possibly be, but never actually do any work – "meaning as
use" and that sort of thing. I think that's still probably true, but I do think that
Rochel Gelman's talk raises some interesting questions about how to take this
kind of reference and truth. If we think of the Aristotelian tree of being as
somehow in us, then the question arises concerning notions like essence and
accident, and whether we project those from the properties of the mind, or
whether we should take a more realistic Kripkean interpretation. Maybe one
could restore a respectable notion by thinking of it in terms of something like
nominal essence in the sense of Locke; or in the sense of Hume, it's projected.

Another thing that struck me as very interesting was the relations between
number and language; I tried to raise a question about induction and so on
(see page 235). One way of thinking of it which I'd like to explore further is that
sometimes our thinking about the origin of number seems to be too closely tied
to the set-theoretic reduction. Maybe one should try to think of it in terms of
category theory. The category-theoretic foundations for mathematics are that
it's essentially algebra with bells and whistles, and sets are just another category
from that point of view. And you get number out of this algebraic property that
I mentioned, the property of being a free semi-group of a certain kind. And that
analogy between number and language is very interesting and ought to be
explored.

Finally I note how much things have changed; I really like that, and one of the
things that I think I've learned from Noam is not to dig in your heels and stay
where you are for the rest of your life, because he's managed to change his views
in very interesting ways in response to new things. I'm very glad to have heard
him do it again.

GLEITMAN: I want to address my comments to the students here, who've
listened so patiently and said so little. I wonder what they're thinking. This
has been a wonderful opportunity to see the scope and the kinds of questions
that are being asked in this field today. For me there have been a number of
revelations which have changed my own perspective in many ways, making me
see problems which I thought of as intractable. I used to think, "You can't really

look at the evolution of language. How could you even look at such a question?" I begin to see here how seriously these kinds of questions can begin to be engaged.

But back to the students; when listening to Noam just now I remembered when I first entered linguistics with the same teacher who was one of Noam's first teachers. This was Zellig Harris, a very serious person, and I'm not implying otherwise, but when I went to graduate school in linguistics, he said to me, "Okay, you'll do 'of'." But I developed a little bit of taste, and got out of the "of" business. But it shows you all how we all live on our little hills, and it's something that Noam has emphasized here – in his last talk particularly – that maybe otherwise perfectly sensible people may be sitting on a little hill and doing some funny stuff that isn't really in the end asking questions that you want in the long run to know the answers to. I also remember that not long after I got to graduate school and was trying to think about "of," I met Noam, who had graduated a couple of years later and who appeared to be much more savvy. I was doing something else, making flow charts or something, and he said to me, "Why are you doing that?" And I said, "Look at this beautiful flow chart that I'm doing. Look more closely." And he said to me, "You know, you seem to me a person who's really interested in language. So why are you doing that?" [laughter]

I hope that being here may have been useful to you as students thinking about what you want to do. The lesson is that you better be careful not to be sitting on some silly hill asking a question that nobody wants to know the answer to.

RIZZI: It has been a fantastic opportunity for us to be exposed to things that are sufficiently close to being understandable and sufficiently different to offer a slightly different perspective on the things we do. Maybe it's another case of the illusion of difference. Among the various topics that were extremely fascinating and important for the work on language that I and other people do, one thing that really caught my attention is the analogy that can be seen – at least at a certain level of abstraction – between strategies used by different species in the context of species-specific capacities, particularly optimization strategies that have relatively close analogues in language. And Gallistel's talk was illuminating for me and Mark Hauser's talk was also extremely inspiring about the possible existence of optimization strategies including something close to minimal search strategies that are found in natural languages.

The question remains whether we are still at the level of loose analogies or we are at the level of operative principles, which may have a direct causal effect on different cognitive domains, on different capacities across different species. Or maybe there is an intermediate position between the two. Years ago linguists would have said that we are definitely at the level of vague analogies; but this was partly due to an illusion generated by the technical vocabulary that we used, as well as other aspects that Noam pointed out. If you take the first version of a structured theory of universal grammar, Noam's "Conditions on trans-formations,"[34] the operative principles were called things like "Specified Subject Condition," "Tenseless Condition," and so on. They were, in a sense, locality principles. You could have said there was something similar to them in other domains and the activities of other species, but they looked so closely keyed to language that it seemed difficult to come up with some concrete operative generalization. Then things developed significantly in linguistics within the principles and parameters framework and within the minimalist program, and the units of computation are now much more abstract. This makes it much more feasible to look at other cognitive domains and pursue the question of the level of completeness of the analogy.

It seems to me that there are still a number of questions which should be asked. In linguistics we see the relevance of notions like locality and promin-ence. (Prominence being expressed in terms of notions like c-command, which may be a primitive notion or, as Noam has suggested, may be a derivative notion, but still we have a notion of prominence.) The two notions seem to interact in interesting ways. For instance, locality is computed on tree structures on which prominence is defined, hence an intervener counts only if it is in a certain hierarchical environment with respect to other things. So do we find analogues to these hierarchical properties? To put it very bluntly: given that something like minimal search can be found in other species, do we find anything like c-command in, say, foraging techniques or in the kinds of capaci-ties that have been investigated? These questions remained to be answered.

One second remark on the issue of parameters, which was raised a number of times and very interestingly so by Noam in his comments. In fact, he said something about parameters that I've never thought of before, so I guess that's one of the purposes of these meetings – to discover new things even at the very last moment. There is this basic issue of whether parameters are UG-internal or UG-external and we have heard different varieties of this story (e.g. see pages 211–219). This seems to interact with another issue, which is the locus of the parameters: where are they expressed? Is there a particular locus in our cognitive capacities where they are expressed? On the grounds of restrictive-ness, I would still strongly favor the view that parameters are in some sense UG-internal; there's some specific part of UG where parameters are expressed. The main empirical argument has to do with restrictiveness. I mentioned in previous

---

[34] Chomsky (1973). (Editors' note)

discussions that there are certain cases that indicate that there are fewer options empirically observable than the options that we could expect if parameters were conceived of as simply a lack of specifications or "holes" within UG. The head–complement parameter is one case: you would expect all sorts of solutions different from the solutions that you actually observe in languages. If UG did not contain any statement about order you would expect that language would resolve the problem of linearization in one sentence through VO order and in the next sentence through OV order, but that's not what we observe. We find fewer options. Questions of simplicity in the sense of absence of structure, and questions of restrictiveness are in tension in some interesting cases. One of our tasks is to resolve this kind of tension. From the viewpoint of these assumptions, I must say that I would be strongly in favor of the optimal scenario for the status of parameters that Noam just mentioned among the various possibilities, which would basically amount to adopting a version of Massimo and Donata's idea that parameters represent an optimal point of equilibrium concerning the amount of specification within UG (see pages 101–102) and what Noam just said about principles being parameters with a fixed value and slightly more complicated than parameters without a fixed value. This seems to be a very interesting and promising way of addressing this question.

URIAGEREKA: A couple of thoughts. For me this has been a great growing experience. I use the word "grow" and not the word "learn" because I think that there's a significant distinction that didn't get enough attention, and since Luigi just made one of the points I was going to make about parameters, I'll say little about parameters. Thinking about the two or even three types of parameters that we talked about, one possibility is that they might all be there. If this entity is complex enough, it may have enough dimensions to it that all forms of variation are there. And that might not be crazy, because languages also change. Putting aside invasions of the usual sort, which is uninteresting, they may change for interesting internal reasons of the sort David Lightfoot (1982, 1999, 2000) talked about a few years ago. So in that case there might be a possibility of drifting elements, but it's not obvious to me that you want to have the drifting part in the core part. The core part may still be really there without this drift, but you want enough messy noise to lead to internal change, though I don't know if the change would be driven by biological considerations. So the suggestion is that maybe we shouldn't eliminate one of the types of parameters in favor of another; we may need to consider all of them.

Another thought that caught my attention is Noam's case of Sylvester, the donkey turned into a rock. I also know about Sylvester because my daughters spend a lot of time talking with me about these things. I just want to mention two things here. (I tried this with them and they're aged 4 and 6-and-a-half, so they're good subjects for this kind of thing.) Sylvester can turn into a rock and back, but when you make Sylvester turn into two rocks, they get very nervous; unless, of course, you somehow have two aspects of Sylvester, like the tale of a guy who divides into two halves and each half lives an independent life and then finally at the end they get back together. So there are interesting limitations on those transformations that recall a little footnote that Noam had in *Aspects* (1965) referring back to Bertrand Russell's idea of continuity and concepts, which nowadays would be framed in terms of manifolds. There are dimensions to those meanings – of course it has nothing to do with reality but rather with internal topologies that our minds use to prevent us from going from one to two, and so on. I think similar issues also arise going between count and mass: you can get Sylvester to turn into the wind but it's more difficult to get the wind to turn into Sylvester. My only point is that there are interesting dimensions to explore for a very different internalist project, which is where the theory of reference also ought to go.

Finally, I was fascinated by Randy Gallistel's stuff and Chris Cherniak's stuff as well. My biggest challenge for the rest of my career would be to see these two notions get unified: I keep asking myself how these two notions can get together. I'm hoping that I can keep in contact with Chris and Randy to narrow down some of the big problems of unification in terms of something that Randy has said for years: the idea that memory is basically carrying information forward in time. As far as I can see, none of the models out there really help with that. That's what we need but we need to see how models would give us that notion of memory, and my only minor contribution there would be that some of the notions that Noam talked about today (going back to *The Logical Structure of Linguistic Theory* (1955/1975) and mathematical discussions), once you put away all the stuff that is of no interest, which he correctly laid out, there may be a residue for us to think about, and this actually relates to some of the issues that Luigi Rizzi was talking about. After all, when computations get interesting, when you have intervention effects, when you need to know whether there's another one of those or not, you have various notions there that speak to different kinds of memory that also seem to be hierarchical in some sense. So I think it might be time – and maybe Noam can help us with this – to rethink those hierarchies of fifty years ago in I-language terms, in the strong generative capacity terms. It's going to be a difficult task, but if that helps us understand what other memory factors are involved internal to computations, then the task of unifying what we're trying to do with the goal of what Chris Cherniak has already done with his networks might not be fifty years ahead of us but only twenty.

PIATTELLI-PALMARINI: Going back to the Royaumont meeting (Piattelli-Palmarini 1980a, 1994), there are some very interesting permanent positive trends that have developed since then. At the time, Piaget's obsession was to build up more power: more and more powerful structures. In contrast, our occupation has been to narrow down things and to constrain the search space. It goes back to the momentous Goodman's paradox: how do you constrain induction?[35] He had a pragmatic solution but the problem is very much with us still. How do you constrain down the search space? Bob Berwick, who never actually published this, made a calculation some years back. He idealized a child who hears a new type of sentence every second and has to guess a grammar with one hundred rules (in the traditional sense – she can get it basically right; or not quite right and then adjust the rule until she gets it right; or keep one rule and change another). He calculated that in order for the child to succeed she needed many thousands of years in an unconstrained search space for grammars. Maybe he got it wrong (though I doubt he did) and it's 1,500 years, or even "only" 150 years, but it's still monstrous, so something else must be happening. The principles and parameters idea really was a wonderful idea and it sounds strange to some who are outside our profession that we insist so much on them, even though we cannot say exactly that we know what all of them are. People like Janet Fodor and Charles Yang do this wonderful work of modeling parametric language acquisition without being sure yet how many there are or where they are, but there doesn't seem to be any other solution. You have to constrain the search space very powerfully. In an aside of our sessions, Noam has expressed the wish that the *minimax* hypothesis that Donata and I have suggested could actually be tested. Not an easy calculation to make, but it will be eminently interesting to try.

And it seems to be the case nowadays also in evolution. The problem is you can only select something that is selectable; you have to have stability, reproducibility, and a narrow space of possibles. What natural selection can select from must be something that can be selected, that has sufficient stability. And this is why the laws of form are coming back; we heard it from Chris Cherniak and there are other examples like optimal foraging, that I mentioned earlier (see page 88). Some species seem to be at optimal foraging and it's a very old problem: what do you need genes for? There are some things you don't need any genes for because it's the physics and chemistry of the situation that dictate the solution.

Going back again to Piaget, he postulated more and more powerful structures with all these complicated things that he invoked: thematization, reflective

---

[35] Goodman (1983).

abstraction, and so on, which a generation of psychologists have had to study. Another problem was that he was getting to abstractions, the final abstractions, but the issue is to get the initial abstractions. We know there are very basic fundamental abstractions from the very start. This is an important lesson and in linguistics we have known it for many years, and in animal behavior we heard it from Randy Gallistel: the Kantian approach. It has been beautiful to see over the years how Randy and his collaborators have had behaviorism also implode from the inside. Noam made it implode from the outside but they have seen it implode from the inside. You have to invoke very abstract structures to account for what you observe in the different species.

Giacomo Rizzolatti has discovered mirror neurons and this has been fiercely resisted over the years. Nobody could believe in mirror neurons. He couldn't get published because the model was that there were groups of neurons controlling specific muscles, and nobody could believe that one neuron is sensitive to the act of prehension, whether it's done with the right hand, the left hand, or the mouth. He has shown that that was the case, but they didn't believe it so he had to show that it wasn't just from seeing the complete action, because the mirror neuron still fires when a screen comes up and hides the completion of the action from view. But they still resisted and said it was something like grasping rather than the act of prehension. So he designed an experiment with special tweezers which only grasp if you release them (what in French restaurants they give you to eat escargots) and the neuron still fired. So, abstractions from the very, very beginning – this is a very important development and we have to continue along this line.

Finally, this is a more technical remark: E-language versus I-language. We had this discussion with Janet Fodor. Ever since Noam insisted on this distinction (it was systematized in *Knowledge of Language* (1986), but it was there all the time), it has been interesting to see how much work has been done in the context of E-language, languages that allegedly are "out there." The best example of this, which I'm not recommending, is Terrence Deacon's book (1997) on the evolution of language, in which brains are evolving and languages are also evolving and they supposedly evolve together. For Deacon languages are things out there and his idea is that our brain had been evolving with those languages out there. This is not the way to think about that; it is the computational state that we have here inside. A lot of work, notably all the learnability work – Gold's theorem and all the linguistic strings coming in, as Janet Fodor has aptly reminded us here (see Chapter 17) – has interesting aspects but the challenge is to translate those things so that they still make sense in an I-language context. Martin Nowak and other mathematicians (Nowak et al 2001a,b, 2002) have been publishing widely on the evolution of language but it's entirely on E-language evolving and some of that work may have some interest if translated into I-language. This change from E-language to I-language has been very important and, as Jerry Fodor insightfully likes to stress, we are forever bewildered by the consequences of what we know. It takes years to understand a radical change like this and all the consequences it entails, and we are looking forward to the years to come dealing with these problems.

PELLO SALABURU: I would like to take just a minute to thank all the participants here, especially Noam, because as I said the first day, it was very difficult for him to come here. So thank you, Noam, we are very, very grateful to you. I would also like to thank the other speakers and all the public who have attended the conference. I think it was a great opportunity for all of us to listen and learn. Finally, I would like to express my deep appreciation to each and every one of the participants.

Noam was telling us yesterday that it takes 25 percent longer to translate words from English into Spanish. You know that we also have a lot of redundancies in Basque too, but at this particular point, when we say "thank you very much" in Basque, we use only two words to do it: *eskerrik asko*. But unfortunately, the number of syllables is the same.

Thank you very much.

References*

Abzhanov, A., Kuo, W. P., Hartmann, C., Grant, B. R., Grant, P. R., and Tabin, C. J. (2006). The Calmodulin Pathway and Evolution of Elongated Beak Morphology in Darwin's Finches. *Nature*, 442(7102): 563–567.

Agrawal, A., Eastman, Q. M., and Schatz, D. G. (1998). Implications of Transposition Mediated by V(d)j-recombination Proteins Rag1 and Rag2 for Origins of Antigen-specific Immunity. *Nature*, 394: 744–751.

Allis, C. D., Jenuwein, T., Reinberg, D., and Caparros, M.-L. (2006). *Epigenetics*. Cold Spring Harbor Laboratory Press, Cold Spring Harbor.

Annett, M. (1998). Handedness and Cerebral Dominance: the Right Shift Theory. *Journal of Neuropsychiatry and Clinical Neurosciences*, 10(4): 459–469.

Appel, T. A. (1987). *The Cuvier–Geoffroy Debate: French Biology in the Decades Before Darwin*. Oxford University Press, USA.

Arthur, W. (2004). *Biased Embryos and Evolution*. Cambridge University Press.

Asher, N. and Morreau, M. (1995). What Some Generic Sentences Mean. In Carlson, G. N. and Pelletier, F. J., editors, *The Generic Book*. University of Chicago Press, Chicago. pp. 300–338.

Bach, E., Jelinek, E., Kratzer, A., and Partee, B. H. (1995). *Quantification in Natural Languages*. Kluwer, Dordrecht, Holland.

Baggaley, J. W. (1999). The Ship of Theseus (by John Baggaley May 10, 1999). http://www.baggaley.org/Baggaley/Essays/Entries/1999/5/10_The_Ship_of_Theseus.html

Bahlmann, J., Gunter, T. C., and Friederici, A. D. (2006). Hierarchical and Linear Sequence Processing: an Electrophysiological Exploration of Two Different Grammar Types. *Journal of Cognitive Neuroscience*, 18(11): 1829.

Bahlmann, J., Schubotz, R., and Friederici, A. D. (in press). Hierarchical Sequencing Engages Broca's Area. *NeuroImage*.

Baker, M. C. (2001). *The Atoms of Language: the Mind's Hidden Rules of Grammar*. Basic Books, New York.

—— (2003). Linguistic Differences and Language Design. *Trends in Cognitive Science*, 7(8): 349–353.

Baldwin, D. A. (1991). Infants' Contribution to the Achievement of Joint Reference. *Child Development*, 62(5): 875–890.

Barner, D. and Snedeker, J. (2005). Quantity Judgments and Individuation: Evidence That Mass Nouns Count. *Cognition*, 97: 41–66.

—— Thalwitz, D., Wood, J., and Carey, S. (2005). Overcoming the Set-size Limitation on Parallel Individuation: Plural Morphology As a Possible Source of "More Than One". Ms.

---

* Works with three or more authors are listed in date order after all other works with the same first author.

Barner, D. Thalwitz, D., Wood, J., and Carey, S. (2007). On the Relation Between the Acquisition of Singular–Plural Morpho-syntax and the Conceptual Distinction Between One and More Than One. *Developmental Science*, 10(3): 365–373.

Barner, D., Wood, J., Hauser, M., and Carey, S. (2008). Evidence for a Non-linguistic Distinction Between Singular and Plural Sets in Rhesus Monkeys. *Cognition*, 107: 603–627.

Bates, E. and MacWhinney, B. (1987). Competition, Variation, and Language Learning. In MacWhinney, B., editor, *Mechanisms of Language Acquisition*. Lawrence Erlbaum, Hillsdale, NJ. pp. 157–194.

Bechara, A., Damasio, A. R., and Damasio, H. (1994). Insensitivity to Future Consequences Following Damage to Human Prefrontal Cortex. *Cognition*, 50: 7–15.

Bednekoff, P. A. and Balda, R. (1996). Social Caching and Observational Spatial Memory in Pinyon Jays. *Behaviour*, 133: 807–826.

Bejan, A. and Marden, J. H. (2006). Unifying Constructal Theory for Scale Effects in Running, Swimming and Flying. *The Journal of Experimental Biology*, 209: 238–248.

Belletti, A., editor (2004). *Structures and Beyond. The Cartography of Syntactic Structures*. Oxford University Press, New York.

Bever, T. G. (1970). The Cognitive Basis for Linguistics Structures. In Hayes, J. R., editor, *Cognition and the Development of Language*. J. Wiley and Sons, New York. pp. 279–362.

—— (1975). Cerebral Asymmetries in Humans Are Due to the Differentiation of Two Incompatible Processes: Holistic and Analytic. *Annals of the New York Academy of Sciences*, 163: 251–262.

—— (1980). Broca and Lashley Were Right: Cerebral Dominance is an Accident of Growth. In Kaplan, D. and Chomsky, N., editors, *Biology and Language*. MIT Press, Cambridge, MA. pp. 186–230.

—— (1981). Normal Acquisition Processes Explain the Critical Period for Language Learning. Diller, K. C., editor, *Individual Differences and Universals in Language Learning Aptitude*. Newbury House Publishers, Inc., Rowley, MA. pp. 176–198.

—— (1987). The Aesthetic Basis for Cognitive Structures. In Brand, W. and Harrison, R., editors, *The Representation of Knowledge and Belief*. University of Arizona Press. pp. 314–356.

—— and Chiarello, R. J. (1974). Cerebral Dominance in Musicians and Nonmusicians. *Science*, 185(4150): 537–539.

—— and Hansen, R. E. (1988). The Induction of Mental Structures While Learning to Use Symbolic Systems. In *Proceedings of the Tenth Annual Meeting of The Cognitive Science Society*. Lawrence Erlbaum Assoc., Hillsdale, NJ. pp. 132–138.

—— and McElree, B. (1988). Empty Categories Access Their Antecedents During Comprehension. *Linguistic Inquiry*, 19(1): 35–43.

—— and Sanz, M. (1997). Empty Categories Access Their Antecedents During Comprehension: Unaccusatives in Spanish. *Linguistic Inquiry*, 28(1): 69–91.

—— Carrithers, C., and Townsend, D. J. (1987). A Tale of Two Brains; Or, the Sinistral Quasimodularity of Language. *Proceedings of the Ninth Annual Cognitive Science Society Meetings*.

—— —— Cowart, W., and Townsend, D. J. (1989a). Language Processing and Familial Handedness. In Galaburda, A., editor, *From Reading to Neurons: Issues in the Biology of Language and Cognition*. The MIT Press, Cambridge, MA. pp. 331–357.

—— Straub, K., Shenkman, K., Kim, J. J., and Carrithers, C. (1990). The Psychological Reality of NP-trace. In Carter, J., Dechaine, R.-M., Philip, B., and Sherer, T., editors, *Proceedings of NELS 20*.

Blais, A. L. (1997). *On the Plurality of Actual Worlds*. University of Massachusetts Press.

Blasco Aznar, P. L. (2002). The Truth of the I and Its Intuitive Knowledge. *Analecta Husserliana*, 76: 117–131.

Bloom, L., Lightbown, P., Hood, L., Bowerman, M., Maratsos, M., and Maratsos, M. P. (1975). Structure and Variation in Child Language. *Monographs of the Society for Research in Child Development*, 40(2): 1–97.

Bloom, P. (2002). Mindreading, Communication and the Learning of Names for Things. *Mind and Language*, 17(1 & 2): 37–54.

Bloomfield, L. (1933). *Language* (edited by Charles F. Hockett). Chicago University Press, Chicago.

—— (1939). Etudes phonologiques dédiées a la mémoire de N. S. Trubetzkoy. *Travaux du Cercle Linguistique de Prague*, 8: 105–115.

—— (1987). Menomini Morphophonemics. In Hockett, C. F., editor, *Leonard Bloomfield Anthology*. University of Chicago Press, Chicago. pp. 243–254.

Boden, M. A. (2006). *Mind As Machine: A History of Cognitive Science*. Oxford University Press, Oxford and New York.

Boeckx, C. (2006). *Linguistic Minimalism: Origins, Concepts, Methods, and Aims*. Oxford University Press, USA.

—— (2008). *Understanding Minimalist Syntax*. Blackwell, Oxford.

Bolhuis, J. and Gahr, M. (2006). Neural Mechanisms of Birdsong Memory. *Nature Reviews Neuroscience*, 7: 347–357.

Brannon, E. M. and Roitman, J. (2003). Nonverbal Representations of Time and Number in Non-human Animals and Human Infants. In Meck, W. H., editor, *Functional and Neural Mechanisms of Interval Timing*. CRC Press, Boca Raton, FL. pp. 143–182.

—— Wusthoff, C. J., Gallistel, C. R., and Gibbon, J. (2001). Numerical Subtraction in the Pigeon: Evidence for a Linear Subjective Number Scale. *Psychol Sci*, 12(3): 238–43.

Breitenstein, C., Jansen, A., Deppe, M., Foerster, A. F., Sommer, J., Wolbers, T., and Knecht, S. (2005). Hippocampus Activity Differentiates Good from Poor Learners of a Novel Lexicon. *Neuroimage*, 25(3): 958–968.

Brent, M. R. (1997). Advances in the Computational Study of Language Acquisition. Brent, M. R., editor, *Computational Approaches to Language Acquisition*. MIT Press, Cambridge, MA.

Bresnan, J. (2000) Optimality Theory. In Dekkers, J., van der Leeuw, F., and van de Weijer, J., editors, *Optimality Theory: Phonology, Syntax, and Acquisition*. Oxford University Press.

—— and Grimshaw, J. (1978). The Syntax of Free Relatives in English. *Linguistic Inquiry Amherst, Mass.*, 9(3): 331–391.

Bretherton, I. and Beeghly, M. (1982). Talking About Internal States: the Acquisition of an Explicit Theory of Mind. *Developmental Psychology*, 18(6): 906–921.

Broca, P. (1865). Sur le siège de la faculté du langage articule. *Bulletin de la Société d'anthropologie*, 6: 337–393.

Brodmann, K. (1909). *Vergleichende Lokalisationslehre Der Grosshirnrinde in Ihren Prinzipien Dargestellt Auf Grund Des Zellenbaues*. Barth, Leipzig. [English translation by Laurence Garay 1994 "Brodmann's 'Localization in the Cerebral Cortex' ", London, Smith-Gordon. Republished 2005 Springer Verlag.)

Brugos, A., Micciulla, L., and Smith, C., editors (2004). *Proceedings of the 28th Boston University Conference on Language Development*, volume 2.

Bussey, T. J., and Dickinson, A. (2003). Can Animals Recall the Past and Plan for the Future? *Nat Rev Neurosci*, 4(8): 685–691.

—— Emery, N. J., and Dickinson, A. (2006). The Prospective Cognition of Food Caching and Recovery by Western Scrub Jays (Aphelocoma Californica). *Comp Cogn Behav Rev*, 1:1–11.

Camps, M. and Uriagereka, J. (2006). The Gordian Knot of Linguistic Fossils. Ms.

Carey, S. (1985). *Conceptual Change in Childhood*. Bradford Books/MIT Press, Cambridge, MA.

—— (2001). On the Very Possibility of Discontinuities in Conceptual Development. In Dupoux, E., editor, *Language, Brain, and Cognitive Development: Essays in Honour of Jacques Mehler*. A Bradford Book/The MIT Press, Cambridge, MA. pp. 303–324.

Carroll, S. B. (2005). *Forms Most Beautiful: The New Science of Evo Devo*. Norton, New York.

Cartwright, T. A. and Brent, M. R. (1997). Syntactic Categorization in Early Language Acquisition: Formalizing the Role of Distributional Analysis. *Cognition*, 63(2): 121–170.

Caselli, M. C., Bates, E., Casadio, P., Fenson, J., Fenson, L., Sanderl, L., and Weir, J. (1995). A Cross-linguistic Study of Early Lexical Development. *Cognitive Development*, 10(2): 159–199.

Chametzky, R. A. (2003). Phrase Structure. In Hendrick, editor, *Minimalist Syntax*. Blackwell, Oxford. pp. 192–225.

Chan, S., Ryan, L., and Bever, T. G. (in preparation). Only Right Handers from Left-handed Families Have Bilateral Representation for Words, but All People Have Left Hemisphere Dominance for Syntactic Processing.

Chater, M. R. N. (1998). Connectionist and Statistical Approaches to Language Acquisition: A Distributional Perspective. *Language and Cognitive Processes*, 13(2): 129–191.

Chee, M. W. L. and Choo, W. C. (2004). Functional Imaging of Working Memory After 24 Hr of Total Sleep Deprivation. *Journal of Neuroscience*, 24(19): 4560.

—— Soon, C. S., Lee, H. W., and Pallier, C. (2004). Left Insula Activation: A Marker for Language Attainment in Bilinguals. *PNAS*, 101 (42): 15265–15270.

Cherniak, C. (1988). Undebuggability and Cognitive Science. *Communications of the ACM*, 3(4).

—— (1992). Local Optimization of Neuron Arbors. *Biological Cybernetics*, 66(6): 503–510.

—— (1994a). Component Placement Optimization in the Brain. *Journal of Neuroscience*, 14(4): 2418.

—— (1994b). Philosophy and Computational Neuroanatomy. *Philosophical Studies*, 73(2): 89–107.

—— (1995). Neural Component Placement. *Trends in Neurosciences*, 18: 522–527.

—— (2005). Innateness and Brain-wiring Optimization. In Zilhao, A., editor, *Evolution, Rationality and Cognition*. Routledge.

—— (2008). Neuroanatomy and Cosmology. In Bickle, J., editor, *Oxford Handbook of Neuroscience and Philosophy*. Oxford University Press, New York.

—— and Mokhtarzada, Z. (2006). Brain Wiring Optimization and Non-Genomic Nativism. PowerPoint slideshow. *Minds and Language* Conference, San Sebastián. Available at: www.glue.umd.edu/~cherniak/NeurOpt.ppt

—— Changizi, M., and Won Kang, D. (1999). Large-scale Optimization of Neuron Arbors. *Physical Review E*, 59(5): 6001–6009.

—— Mokhtarzada, Z., and Nodelman, U. (2002). Optimal-Wiring Models of Neuroanatomy. In Ascoli, G., editor, *Computational Neuroanatomy: Principles and Methods*. Humana, Totowa, NJ. pp. 71–82.

—— —— Rodriguez-Esteban, R., and Changizi, K. (2004). Global Optimization of Cerebral Cortex Layout. *Proceedings of the National Academy of Sciences*, 101(4): 1081–1086.

Chomsky, N. (1955). The Logical Structure of Linguistic Theory. [Partially edited 1956 version, available in microfilm and Pdf form, was published in large part in 1975, with an explanatory introduction.]

—— (1957). *Syntactic Structures*. Mouton. [Reprinted by De Gruyter, 2002.]

—— (1959a). On Certain Formal Properties of Grammars. *Information and Control*, 2: 137–167.

—— (1959b). A Note on Phrase Structure Grammars. *Information and Control*, 2: 393–395.

Chomsky, N. (1959c). Review of B. F. Skinner's *Verbal Behavior*. *Language*, 35: 26–58.

—— (1965). *Aspects of the Theory of Syntax*. MIT Press, Cambridge, MA.

—— (1968). Quine's Empirical Assumptions. *Synthese*, XIX(I (December)): 66–67.

—— (1973). Conditions on Transformations. In Anderson, S. R. and Kiparski, P., editors, *A Festschrift for Morris Halle*. Holt, Rinehart and Winston, New York. pp. 232–286.

—— (1975). *The Logical Structure of Linguistic Theory*. Plenum Press / The University of Chicago Press, Chicago.

—— (1980). *Rules and Representations*. Columbia University Press, New York.

—— (1981). *Lectures on Government and Binding*. Foris Publications, Dordrecht, Holland.

—— (1982). *Some Concepts and Consequences of the Theory of Government and Binding*. MIT Press.

—— (1986a). *Barriers*. MIT Press.

—— (1986b). *Knowledge of Language: Its Nature, Origin, and Use*. Praeger/Greenwood.

—— (1988). *Language and Problems of Knowledge: The Managua Lectures*. Bradford Books/MIT Press, Cambridge, MA.

—— (1992). *A Minimalist Program for Linguistic Theory*. MIT Working Papers in Linguistics.

—— (1993). A Minimalist Program for Linguistic Theory. In Hale, K. and Keyser, S., editors, *The View from Building 20: Essays in Linguistics in Honor of Sylvain Bromberger*, volume 20. MIT Press, Cambridge, MA. pp. 1–52.

—— (1995a). Language and Nature. *Mind*, 104(413): 1–61.

—— (1995b). *The Minimalist Program*. MIT Press.

—— (1998). Comments: Galen Strawson, Mental Reality. *Philosophy and Phenomenological Research*, 58(2): 437–441.

—— (2000). *New Horizons in the Study of Language and Mind*. Cambridge University Press.

—— (2003). *On Nature and Language*. Cambridge University Press, Cambridge.

—— (2004a). Beyond Explanatory Adequacy. In Belletti, A., editor, *Structures and Beyond: The Cartography of Syntactic Structures*, vol. 3. Oxford University Press. pp.104–131.

—— (2004b). The Biolinguistic Perspective After 50 Years. *Quaderni del Dipartimento di Linguistica, Università di Firenze (Also in Sito Web Accademia della Crusca, 2005)*, (14).

—— (2005a). On Phases. Ms.

—— (2005b). Three Factors in Language Design. *Linguistic Inquiry*, 36(1): 1–22.

—— (2006). Approaching UG from below. Ms., MIT

—— (2007). Biolinguistic Explorations: Design, Development, Evolution. *International Journal of Philosophical Studies*, 15(1): 1–21.

—— (2007). Commentary on Margaret Boden, *Mind as Machine: A History of Cognitive Science*, 2 Volumes, Oxford. 2006. *Artificial Intelligence*, 171: 1094–1103.

—— and Miller, G. (1953). Introduction to the Formal Analysis of Natural Languages. In Luce, D., Bush, R., and Galanter, E., editors, *Handbook of Mathematical Psychology*. Wiley, New York. pp. 269–321.

—— and Schützenberger, M. (1963). *The Algebraic Theory of Context-free Languages*. North-Holland, Amsterdam.

Chouinard, M. M. and Clark, E. V. (2003). Adult Reformulations of Child Errors As Negative Evidence. *Journal of Child Language*, 30(3): 637–669.

Chung, S. (1994). Wh-agreement and "referentiality" in Chamorro. *Linguistic Inquiry*, 25(1): 1–44.

—— (1998). *The Design of Agreement – Evidence from Chamorro*. Chicago University Press, Chicago.

Church, A. (1936). An Unsolvable Problem of Elementary Number Theory. *The American Journal of Mathematics*, 58: 345–363.

Cinque, G. (1990). *Types of A-dependencies*. MIT Press.

—— (1999). *Adverbs and Functional Heads: A Cross-linguistic Perspective*. Oxford University Press.

——, editor (2002). *Functional Structure in DP and IP. The Cartography of Syntactic Structures*. Oxford University Press, USA.

—— (2005). Deriving Greenberg's Universal 20 and Its Exceptions. *Linguistic Inquiry*, 36(3): 315–332.

Clark, R. (1989). On the Relationship Between the Input Data and Parameter Setting. *Proceedings of the 19th Annual Meeting of the North East Linguistic Society*, pp. 48–62.

—— (1992). The Selection of Syntactic Knowledge. *Language Acquisition*, 2(2): 83–149.

Clark, R. J. H. and Hester, R. E. (1989). *Spectroscopy of Matrix Isolated Species*. Wiley.

Clayton, N. S., Yu, K. S., and Dickinson, A. (2001). Scrub Jays (Aphelocoma Coerulescens) Form Integrated Memories of the Multiple Features of Caching Episodes. *J Exp Psychol Anim Behav Process*, 27(1): 17–29.

Clayton, P. (2006). *Mind and Emergence: From Quantum to Consciousness*. Oxford University Press.

Collett, M. and Collett, T. S. (2000). How Do Insects Use Path Integration for Their Navigation? *Biological Cybernetics*, 83(3): 245–259.

—— Collett, T. S., Bisch, S., and Wehner, R. (1998). Local and Global Vectors in Desert Ant Navigation. *Nature*, 394: 269–272.

—— Harland, D., and Collett, T. S. (2002). The Use of Landmarks and Panoramic Context in the Performance of Local Vectors by Navigating Honeybees. *Journal of Experimental Biology*, 205(6): 807–814.

Collett, T. (1992). Landmark Learning and Guidance in Insects. *Philosophical Transactions: Biological Sciences*, 337(1281): 295–303.

—— and Baron, J. (1994). Biological Compasses and the Coordinate Frame of Landmark Memories in Honeybees. *Nature*, 368(6467): 137–140.

—— and Collett, M. (2002). Memory Use in Insect Visual Navigation. *Nature Reviews Neuroscience*, 3(7): 542–552.

—— —— (2004). How Do Insects Represent Familiar Terrain? *Journal of Physiology-Paris*, 98(1–3): 259–264.

Collins, C. (2002). Eliminating Labels. In Epstein, S. and Seely, T., editors, *Derivation and Explanation in the Minimalist Program*. Blackwell Publishers. pp. 42–64.

Connolly, T. and Zeelemberg, M. (2002). Regret in Decision Making. *Current Directions in Psychological Science*, 11(6): 212–216.

Craig, J. E., Rochette, J., Fisher, C. A., Weatherall, D. J., Marc, S., Lathrop, G. M., Demenais, F., and Thein, S. L. (1996). Dissecting the Loci Controlling Fetal Haemoglobin Production on Chromosomes 11 P and 6 Q by the Regressive Approach. *Nature Genetics*, 12(1): 58–64.

Crain, S. and Thornton, R. (1998). *Investigations in Universal Grammar: A Guide to Experiments on the Acquisition of Syntax and Semantics*. MIT Press.

Crick, F. and Clark, J. (1994). The Astonishing Hypothesis. *Journal of Consciousness Studies*, 1(1): 10–16.

Curtin, S., Toben, H., Hintz, M., and Christiansen, M. H. (2005). Stress Changes the Representational Landscape: Evidence from Word Segmentation. *Cognition*, 96: 233–262.

Cutler, E. A. and Mehler, J. (1993). The Periodicity Bias. *Journal of Phonetics*, 21: 103–108.

Dale, R. and Christiansen, M. H. (2004). Active and Passive Statistical Learning: Exploring the Role of Feedback in Artificial Grammar Learning and Language. *Proceedings of the 26th Annual Conference of the Cognitive Science Society*, pp. 262–267.

Dally, J. M., Emery, N. J., and Clayton, N. S. (2006). Food-caching Western Scrub-jays Keep Track of Who Was Watching When. *Science*, 312: 1662–1665.

Damasio, A. R. (1994). *Descartes' Error*. Grossett Putnam.

Davidson, D. (1967). The Logical Form of Action Sentences. In Rescher, N. editor, *The Logic of Decision and Action*. University of Pittsburgh Press, Pittsburgh. Reprinted in Ludlow, P., editor, *Readings in the Philosophy of Language*. A Bradford Book/MIT Press, Cambridge, MA. pp. 218–232.

Deacon, T. W. (1997). *The Symbolic Species: the Co-evolution of Language and the Brain*. W.W. Norton & Company, London.

Dechaume-Moncharmont, F.-X., Dornhaus, A., Houston, A. I., McNamara, J. M., Collins, E. J., and Franks, N. R. (2005). The Hidden Cost of Information in Collective Foraging. *Proceedings of the Royal Society* (B Series), 272: 1689–1695.

Dehaene, S. (1997). *The Number Sense: How the Mind Creates Mathematics*. Penguin Putnam Inc, New York.

Descartes, R. (1637). Discourse on the Method. In *The Philosophical Writings of Descartes*, trans. J. Cottingham, R. Stoothoff, D. Murdoch, vol. 1. Cambridge University Press (1985). pp. 111–151.

Dobzhansky, T. (1973). Nothing in Biology Makes Sense Except in the Light of Evolution. *American Biology Teacher*, 35(3): 125–129.

Donati, C. (2005). *On Wh-head-movement*. The MIT Press, Cambridge, MA.

Dover, G. (2000). *Dear Mr Darwin: Letters on the Evolution of Life and Human Nature*. Weidenfeld and Nicolson, London.

—— (2006). Human Nature: One for All and All for One? In Headlam Wells, R. and McFadden, J., editors, *Human Nature: Fact and Fiction*. Continuum Press. pp. 82–99.

Dromi, E. (1987). *Early Lexical Development*. Cambridge University Press, Cambridge.

Dyer, F. C. (1991). Bees Acquire Route-based Memories but Not Cognitive Maps in a Familiar Landscape. *Anim Behav*, 41: 239–246.

—— and Dickinson, J. A. (1996). Sun-compass Learning in Insects: Representation in a Simple Mind. *Current Directions in Psychological Science*, 5(3): 67–72.

Eimas, P. D., Siqueland, E. R., Jusczyk, P., and Vigorito, J. (1971). Speech Perception in Infants. *Science*, 171: 303–306.

Einstein, A., Born, M., and Hedwig, B. (1971). *The Born-Einstein Letters 1916–1955: Friendship, Politics and Physics in Uncertain Times*. Macmillan, New York and London, reprinted 2005 edition.

Elman, J. L. (1991). Distributed Representations, Simple Recurrent Networks, and Grammatical Structure. *Machine Learning*, 7(2): 195–225.

Emery, N. J. and Clayton, N. (2001). Effects of Experience and Social Context on Prospective Caching Strategies by Scrub Jays. *Nature*, 414(6862): 443–446.

Emonds, J. (1976). *A Transformational Approach to English Syntax: Root, Structure-preserving and Local Transformations*. Academic Press, New York.

Epstein, S. D. and Seely, T. D. (2002). *Derivation and Explanation in the Minimalist Program*. Blackwell Publishers.

Ericsson, K. A., Krampe, R. T., and Tesch-Romer, C. (1993). The Role of Deliberate Practice in the Acquisition of Expert Performance. *Psychological Review*, 100 (3): 363–406.

Ernst, T. B. (2002). *The Syntax of Adjuncts*. Cambridge University Press, New York.

Erteschik-Shir, N. (1997). *The Dynamics of Focus Structure*. Cambridge University Press, Cambridge.

Fadiga, L., Fogassi, L., Gallese, V., and Rizzolatti, G. (2000). Visuomotor Neurons: Ambiguity of the Discharge or 'Motor' Perception? *International Journal of Psychophysiology*, 35: 165–177.

Feldman, H., Goldin-Meadow, S., and Gleitman, L. (1978). Beyond Herodotus: the Creation of Language by Linguistically Deprived Deaf Children. In Lock, A., editor, *Action, Symbol, and Gesture: The Emergence of Language*. Academic Press, New York. pp. 351–413.

Felser, C. (2004). Wh-copying, Phases, and Successive Cyclicity. *Lingua*, 114(5): 543–574.

Fiez, J. A., Raichle, M. E., Miezin, F. M., Petersen, S. E., Tallal, P., and Katz, W. (1995). Pet Studies of Auditory and Phonological Processing: Effects of Stimulus Characteristics and Task Demands. *Journal of Cognitive Neuroscience*, 7(3): 357–375.

Fisher, C., Hall, D. G., Rakowitz, S., and Gleitman, L. (1994). When It is Better to Receive Than to Give: Syntactic and Conceptual Constraints on Vocabulary Growth. *The Acquisition of the Lexicon*, 92: 333–375.

Fisher, C. A. (1996). Structural Limits on Verb Mapping: the Role of Abstract Structure in 2.5 Year-olds' Interpretations of Novel Verbs. *Developmental Science*, 5: 55–64.

Fitch, W. T. and Hauser, M. D. (2002). Unpacking "Honesty": Vertebrate Vocal Production and the Evolution of Acoustic Signals. In Simmons, A. M., Fay, R. R., and Popper, A. N., editors, *Acoustic Communication*. Springer Handbook Of Auditory Research 16. Springer, New York. pp. 65–137.

—— —— (2004). Computational Constraints on Syntactic Processing in a Nonhuman Primate. *Science*, 303: 377–380.

—— —— and Chomsky, N. (2005). The Evolution of the Language Faculty: Clarifications and Implications. *Cognition*, 97(2): 179–210.

Flege, J. E., Mackay, I. R. A., and Meador, D. (1999). Native Italian Speakers' Perception and Production of English Vowels. *The Journal of the Acoustical Society of America*, 106: 2973.

Fodor, J. A. (1970). Three Reasons for Not Deriving 'Kill' from 'Cause to Die'. *Linguistic Inquiry*, 1: 429–438.

—— (1983). *The Modularity of Mind: An Essay on Faculty Psychology*. Bradford Books/The MIT Press, Cambridge, MA.

—— (1998). *Concepts: Where Cognitive Science Went Wrong*. Oxford University Press, New York and Oxford.

—— (2001). *The Mind Doesn't Work That Way: The Scope and Limits of Computational Psychology*. The MIT Press, Cambridge, MA.

—— Garrett, M. F., Walker, E. C. T., and Parkes, C. H. (1980). Against Definitions. *Cognition*, 8: 263–367.

Fodor, J. A. and Lepore, E. (2005). Morphemes Matter: The Continuing Case Against Lexical Decomposition (or: Please Don't Play That Again, Sam). Ms. Rutgers University.

Fodor, J. D. and Crowther, C. (2002). Understanding Poverty of Stimulus Arguments. *The Linguistic Review*, 19: 105–145.

Fodor, J. D. (1992). Islands, Learnability and the Lexicon. In Goodluck, H. and Rochemont, M., editors, *Island Constraints: Theory, Acquisition and Processing*. Kluwer Academic Publishers, Dordrecht.

—— (1998a) Passing to Learn. *Journal of Psycholinguistic Research*, 27(3): 339–3.

—— (1998b). Unambiguous Triggers. *Linguistic Inquiry*, 29(1): 1–36.

—— (2001). Setting Syntactic Parameters. In Baltin, M. and Collins, C., editors, *The Handbook of Contemporary Syntactic Theory*. Blackwell, Oxford.pp. 730–767.

—— and Sakas, W. G. (2004). Evaluating Models of Parameter Setting. In Brugos, A., Micciulla, L., and Smith, C. E., editors, *BUCLD 28: Proceedings of the 28th Annual Boston University Conference on Language Development*. Cascadilla Press, Somerville, MA. pp. 1–27.

—— —— (2005). The Subset Principle in Syntax: Costs of Compliance. *Journal of Linguistics*, 41(03): 513–569.

—— —— and Hoskey, A. (2007). Implementing the Subset Principle in Syntax Acquisition: Lattice-based Models. In *Proceedings of the European Cognitive Science Society*, 2007.

Ford, M. and Hayes, P. J. (1993). Reasoning Agents in a Dynamic World: The Frame Problem. *International Journal of Intelligent Systems*, 8(9): 961–969.

Fox, D. (in press). Too Many Alternatives: Density, Symmetry, and Other Predicaments. *Proceedings of SALT XVII*.

—— and Hacki, M. (2006). The Universal Density of Measurement. *Linguistics and Philosophy*, 29(5): 537–586.

Frank, R. and Kapur, S. (1996). On the Use of Triggers in Parameter Setting. *Linguistic Inquiry*, 27(4): 623–660.

Frazier, L. and Fodor, J. D. (1978). Sausage Machine – New 2-Stage Parsing Model. *Cognition*, 6: 291–325.

Friederici, A. D. (2002). Towards a Neural Basis of Auditory Sentence Processing. *Trends in Cognitive Sciences*, 6: 78–84.

—— (2004). Processing Local Transitions Versus Long-distance Syntactic Hierarchies. *Trends in Cognitive Science*, 8(6): 245–247.

—— and Alter, K. (2004). Lateralization of Auditory Language Functions: A Dynamic Dual Pathway Model. *Brain and Language*, 89: 267–276.

—— and Kotz, S. A. (2003). The Brain Basis of Syntactic Processes: Functional Imaging and Lesion Studies. *NeuroImage*, 20: S8–S17.

—— Wang, Y., Herrmann, C. S., Maess, B., and Oertel, U. (2000). Localization of Early Syntactic Processes in Frontal and Temporal Cortical Areas: A Magnetoencephalographic Study. *Human Brain Mapping*, 11: 1–11.

—— Kotz, S. A., Werheid, K., Hein, G., and von Cramon, D. Y. (2003a). Syntactic Comprehension in Parkinson's Disease: Investigating Early Automatic and Late Integrational Processes Using Event-Related Brain Potentials. *Neuropsychology*, 17: 133–142.

—— Rüschemeyer, S.-A., Hahne, A., and Fiebach, C. J. (2003b). The Role of Left Inferior Frontal and Superior Temporal Cortex in Sentence Comprehension: Localizing Syntactic and Semantic Processes. *Cerebral Cortex*, 13: 170–177.

Friederici, A. D. Gunter, T. C., Hahne, A., and Mauth, K. (2004). The Relative Timing of Syntactic and Semantic Processes in Sentence Comprehension. *NeuroReport*, 15: 165–169.

—— Bahlmann, J., Heim, S., Schubotz, R. I., and Anwander, A. (2006a). The Brain Differentiates Human and Non-human Grammars: Functional Localization and Structural Connectivity. *Proceedings of the National Academy of Sciences*, 103 (February 14 no. 7): 2458–2463.

—— Fiebach, C. J., Schlesewsky, M., Bornkessel, I., and von Cramon, D. Y. (2006b). Processing Linguistic Complexity and Grammaticality in the Left Frontal Cortex. *Cerebral Cortex*, 16: 1709–1717.

—— Friedrich, M., and Christophe, A. (2007a). Brain Responses in 4-month-old Infants Are Already Language Specific. *Current Biology*, 17(14): 1208–1211.

—— von Cramon, D. Y., and Kotz, S. A. (2007b). Role of the Corpus Callosum in Speech Comprehension: Interfacing Syntax and Prosody. *Neuron*, 53: 135–145.

Fukushi, T. and Wehner, R. (2004). Navigation in Wood Ants Formica Japonica: Context Dependent Use of Landmarks. *Journal of Experimental Biology*, 207 (19): 3431–3439.

Gallese, V., Fadiga, L., Fogassi, L., and Rizzolatti, G. (1996). Action Recognition in the Premotor Cortex. *Brain*, 119: 593–609.

Gallistel, C. R. (1990a). *The Organization of Learning*. The MIT Press, Cambridge, MA.

—— (1990b). Introduction. In Gallistel, C. R., editor, *Animal Cognition*, Cognition 37.1–2, Nov.

Gates, R. R. (1916). Huxley As a Mutationist. *The American Naturalist*, 50(590): 126–128.

Gehring, W. J. (2004). Historical Perspective on the Development and Evolution of Eyes and Photoreceptors. *Int. J. Dev. Biol*, 48(8–9): 707–717.

Gelman, R. (1993). A Rational-Constructivist Account of Early Learning About Numbers and Objects. *The Psychology of Learning and Motivation*, 30: 61–96.

—— and Brenneman, K. (2004). Science Learning Pathways for Young Children. *Early Childhood Research Quarterly*, 19(1): 150–158.

—— and Williams, E. (1998). Enabling Constraints for Cognitive Development and Learning. *Cognition, Perception and Language*, 2: 575–630.

—— Durgin, F., and Kaufman, L. (1995). Distinguishing Between Animates and Inanimates: Not by Motion Alone. In Sperber, D., Premack, D., and Premack, A. J., editors, *Causal Cognition: A Multidisciplinary Debate*. Oxford University Press. pp. 150–184.

Gentner, D. and Boroditsky, L. (2001). Individuation, Relativity, and Early Word Learning. In Bowerman, M. and Levinson, S. C., editors, *Language Acquisition and Conceptual Development*. Cambridge University Press. pp. 215–256.

Gentner, T. Q., Fenn, K. M., Margoliash, D., and Nusbaum, H. C. (2006). Recursive Syntactic Pattern Learning by Songbirds. *Nature*, 440(7088): 1204–1207.

Georgiades, M. S. and Harris, J. P. (1997). Biasing Effects in Ambiguous Figures: Removal or Fixation of Critical Features Can Affect Perception. *Visual Cognition*, 4(4): 383–408.

Gerken, L. A. (1996). Phonological and Distributional Information in Syntax Acquisition. *Signal to Syntax: Bootstrapping from Speech to Grammar in Early Acquisition*.

Gibbs, W. W. (2003). The Unseen Genome: Beyond DNA. *Scientific American*, December: 107–113.

Gibson, E. and Pearlmutter, N. J. (2000). Distinguishing Serial and Parallel Parsing, *Journal of Psycholinguistic Research*, 29.2: 231–240.

Gibson, E. and Wexler, K. (1994). Triggers. *Linguistic Inquiry*, 25(3): 407–454.

Gillette, J., Gleitman, H., Gleitman, L., and Lederer, A. (1999). Human Simulations of Vocabulary Learning. *Cognition*, 73(2): 135–176.

Gilovich, T. and Medvec, V. (1995). The Experience of Regret: What, When, and Why. *Psychol Rev*, 102(2): 379–395.

Gleitman, L. (1990). The Structural Sources of Verb Meanings. *Language Acquisition*, 1(1): 3–55.

—— Cassidy, K., Nappa, R., Papafragou, A., and Trueswell, J. C. (2005). Hard Words. *Language Learning and Development*, 1(1): 23–64.

—— January, D., Nappa, R., and Trueswell, J. C. (2007). On the Give and Take Between Event Apprehension and Utterance Formulation. *Journal of Memory and Language*, 57(4): 544–569.

—— —— —— —— (in press). On the Give and Take Between Event Apprehension and Sentence Formulation. *Journal of Memory and Language* 58.

Gold, E. M. (1967). Language Identification in the Limit. *Information and Control*, 10: 447–474.

Goldin-Meadow, S., Seligman, M., and Gelman, R. (1976). Language in the Two-year-old. *Cognition*, 4(2): 189–202.

Golestani, N., Paus, T., and Zatorre, R. J. (2002). Anatomical Correlates of Learning Novel Speech Sounds. *Neuron*, 35(5): 997–1010.

—— Molko, N., Dehaene, S., LeBihan, D., and Pallier, C. (2002). Brain Structure Predicts the Learning of Foreign Speech Sounds. *Cerebral Cortex*, 17(3): 575–582.

Golinkoff, R. M. (1975). Semantic Development in Infants: The Concepts of Agent and Recipient. *Merrill-Palmer Quarterly*, 21(3): 181–194.

—— and Kerr, J. L. (1978). Infants' Perceptions of Semantically-defined Action Role Changes in Filmed Events. *Merrill-Palmer Quarterly*, 24: 53–61.

Golinkoff, R., Pence, K., Hirsh-Pasek, K., and Brand, R. (2005). When Actions Can't Speak for Themselves: Infant-directred Speech and Action May Influence Verb Learninig. In Massaro, D., Calfee, R., Sabatini, J., and Trabasso, T., editors, *From Orthography to Pedagogy: Essays in Honor of Richard L. Venezky*. Erlbaum, Mahwah, NJ. pp. 63–79.

Gomez, R. L. and Gerken, L. A. (1999). Artificial Grammar Learning by 1-year-olds Leads to Specific and Abstract Knowledge. *Cognition*, 70(2): 109–135.

Goodman, N. (1983). *Fact, Fiction and Forecast*. Harvard University Press, Cambridge, MA and London.

—— and Quine, W. V. O. (1947). Steps Towards a Constructive Nominalism. *Journal of Symbolic Logic*, 12: 105–122.

Gopnik, A. and Meltzoff, A. (1997). *Words, thoughts and theories*. MIT Press, Cambridge, MA.

Gordon, P. (2003). The Origin of Argument Structure in Infant Event Representations. In Brugos, A., Micciulla, L., and Smith, C. E., editors, *BUCLD 28: Proceedings of the 28th Annual Boston University Conference on Language Development*. Cascadilla Press, Somerville, MA. pp. 189–198.

—— Grosz, B., and Gillom, L. (1993). Pronouns, Names, and the Centering of Attention in Discourse. *Cognitive Science*, 17(3): 311–347.

Gould, J. L. (1986). The Locale Map of Honey Bees: Do Insects Have Cognitive Maps? *Science*, 232(4752): 861–863.

—— and Gould, C. G. (1988). *The Honey Bee*. Scientific American Library, New York.

Gould, S. J. (1990). *Wonderful Life: The Burgess Shale and the Nature of History*. WW Norton & Company.

—— (2002). *The Structure of Evolutionary Theory*. The Belknap Press of Harvard University Press, Cambridge, MA and London.

Greenberg, J. H. (1963). Some Universals of Grammar with Particular Reference to the Order of Meaningful Elements. *Universals of Language*, 2: 73–113.

Greenspan, R. J. (2001). The Flexible Genome. *Nat Rev Genet*, 2(5): 383–387.

Grewal, S. I. S. and Moazed, D. (2003). Heterochromatin and Epigenetic Control of Gene Expression. *Science*, 301(5634): 798–802.

Gualmini, A. (2003). The Ups and Downs of Child Language: Experimental Studies on Children's Knowledge of Entailment Relations and Polarity Phenomena. PhD Dissertation, University of Maryland, College Park, Maryland.

Gutiérrez, J. (2004). Old Issues, New Evidence: Parameter Resetting in Non-native Language Acquisition. (Presented at Eurosla 2004.)

Hahne, A. and Friederici, A. D. (1999). Electrophysiological Evidence for Two Steps in Syntactic Analysis: Early Automatic and Late Controlled Processes. *Journal of Cognitive Neuroscience*, 11: 194–205.

—— —— (2002). Differential Task Effects on Semantic and Syntactic Processes as Revealed by ERPs. *Cognitive Brain Research*, 13: 339–356.

Hale, K. and Keyser, S. J. (1993). *On Argument Structure and the Lexical Representation of Semantic Relations*. The MIT Press, Cambridge, MA.

—— —— (2002). *Prolegomenon to a Theory of Argument Structure*. The MIT Press, Cambridge, MA.

Halle, M. and Stevens, K. (1962). Speech Recognition: A Model and a Program for Research. *Information Theory, IEEE Transactions on*, 8(2): 155–159.

Harbert, W. (1983). On the Nature of the Matching Parameter. *The Linguistic Review*, 2: 237–284.

Harnad, S., editor (1987). *Categorical Perception: The Groundwork of Cognition.* Cambridge University Press, New York.

Harris, R. A., de Ibarra, N. H., Graham, P., and Collett, T. S. (2005). Ant Navigation: Priming of Visual Route Memories. *Nature*, 438(7066): 302.

Harris, Z. S. (1951). *Methods of Structural Linguistics.* University of Chicago Press, Chicago.

Hartnett, P. and Gelman, R. (1998). Early Understandings of Numbers: Paths or Barriers to the Construction of New Understandings? *Learning and Instruction*, 8(4): 341–374.

Hauser, M. D. (2006). *Moral Minds: How Nature Designed Our Universal Sense of Right and Wrong.* Ecco/Harper Collins, New York.

—— Chomsky, N., and Fitch, W. (2002). The Faculty of Language: What Is It, Who Has It, and How Did It Evolve? *Science*, 298(5598): 1569.

—— Glynn, D., and Wood, J. (2007). Rhesus Monkeys Correctly Read the Goal-relevant Gestures of a Human Agent. *Proceedings of the Royal Society B: Biological Sciences*, 274(1620): 1913–1918.

Hecht, S., Shlaer, S., and Pirenne, M. H. (1942). Energy, Quanta, and Vision. *Journal of General Physiology*, 25: 819–840.

Henry, A. (1995). *Belfast English and Standard English: Dialect Variation and Parameter Setting.* Oxford University Press, USA.

Hespos, S. J. and Baillargeon, R. (2001). Infants' Knowledge About Occlusion and Containment Events: a Surprising Discrepancy. *Psychol Sci*, 12(2): 141–147.

Hiesey, W. M., Clausen, J., and Keck, D. D. (1942). Relations Between Climate and Intraspecific Variation in Plants. *The American Naturalist*, 76(762): 5–22.

Higginbotham, J. (1983a). Logical Form, Binding and Nominals. *Linguistic Inquiry*, 14(3): 395–420.

—— (1983b). A Note on Phrase-Markers. *Revue Québecoise de Linguistique* 13 (1): 147–166.

—— (1994). Mass and Count Quantifiers. *Linguistics and Philosophy*, 17(5): 447–480.

—— (1998). On Higher Order Logic and Natural Language. In Smiley, T. J., editor, *Proceedings of the British Academy 95: Philosophical Logic.* Oxford University Press, Oxford. pp. 1–27.

—— (2000). *Accomplishments.* Nanzan University, Nagoya, Japan.

—— (2003a). Conditionals and Compositionality. In Hawthorne, J. and Zimmerman, D., editors, *Philosophical Perspectives, Language and Philosophical Linguistics*, volume 17. Blackwell, Malden, MA. pp. 181–194.

—— (2003b). Jackendoff's Conceptualism. *Behavioral and Brain Sciences*, 26 (06): 680–681.

—— (2006). Sententialism: The Thesis That Complement Clauses Refer to Themselves. In Sosa, E. and Villanueva, E., editors, *Philosophical Issues 16: Philosophy of Language.* Blackwell, Oxford. pp. 101–119.

Higginbotham, J. (2007). *The English Perfect and the Metaphysics of Events*. Springer Verlag, Berlin.

Hinzen, W. (2006a). *Mind Design and Minimal Syntax*. Oxford University Press.

—— (2006b). Spencerism and the Causal Theory of Reference. *Biology and Philosophy*, 21(1): 71–94.

—— (2007a). *An Essay on Naming and Truth*. Oxford University Press, Oxford.

—— (2007b). Succ + Lex = Human Language? In Grohmann, K., editor, *Interphases*. Oxford University Press, Oxford.

—— and Uriagereka, J. (2006). On the Metaphysics of Linguistics. *Erkenntnis*, 65 (1): 71–96.

Hiom, K., Melek, M., and Gellert, M. (1998). DNA Transposition by the Rag1 and Rag2 Proteins: A Possible Source of Oncogenic Translocations. *DNA*, 94: 463–470.

Honderich, T. (2002). *How Free Are You? The Determinism Problem*. 2nd Edition. Oxford University Press.

Hualde, J. I. and Ortiz de Urbina, J. (2003). *A Grammar of Basque*. Walter de Gruyter.

Huang, C. T. J. (1982). Logical Relations in Chinese and the Theory of Grammar. PhD thesis, MIT, Cambridge, MA.

Huang, H., Zhang, J. Y., Jiang, H. Y., Wakana, S., Poetscher, L., Miller, M. I., van Zijl, P. C. M., Hillis, A. E., Wytik, R., and Mori, S. (2005). DTI Tractography based Parcellation of White Matter: Application to the Mid-Sagittal Morphology of Corpus Callosum. *NeuroImage*, 26: 195–205.

Hume, D. (1739). *A Treatise of Human Nature Being an Attempt to Introduce the Experimental Method of Reasoning into Moral Subjects*. Longmans, Green and Co., London and New York. [Reprinted in 1978.]

Hund-Georgiadis, M., Lex, U., Friederici, A. D., and Von Cramon, Y. D. (2002). Non-invasive Regime for Language Lateralization in Right- and Left-handers by Means of Functional MRI and Dichotic Listening. *Experimental Brain Research*, 145(2): 166–176.

Hurewitz, F., Papafragou, A., Gleitman, L., and Gelman, R. (2006). Asymmetries in the Acquisition of Numbers and Quantifiers. *Language Learning and Development*, 2: 77–96.

Huttenlocher, J., Smiley, P., and Charney, R. (1983). Action Categories in the Child. *Psychological Review*, 90: 72–93.

Hutton, J. T., Arsenina, N., Kotik, B., and Luria, A. (1977). On the Problems of Speech Compensation and Fluctuating Intellectual Performance. *Cortex*, 1977: 195–207.

Huxley, T. H. (1893). *Darwiniana*. Kessinger Publishing.

Hyams, N. (1986). *Language Acquisition and the Theory of Parameters*. D. Reidel, Dordrecht.

Jackendoff, R. and Pinker, S. (2005). The Nature of the Language Faculty and Its Implications for Evolution of Language (Reply to Fitch, Hauser, and Chomsky). *Cognition*, 97(2): 211–225.

Jacob, F. (1977). Evolution and Tinkering. *Science*, 196(1): 161–171.

—— and Monod, J. (1961). Genetic Regulatory Mechanisms in the Synthesis of Proteins. *J. Mol. Biol*, 3(318): 1.

Jaenisch, R. and Bird, A. (2003). Epigenetic Regulation of Gene Expression: How the Genome Integrates Intrinsic and Environmental Signals. *Nature Genetics*, 33: Suppl; 245–254.

Jakobson, R. (1936). Beitrag Zur Allgemeinen Kasuslehre. [Translated As: General Meanings of the Russian Cases. *Russian and Slavic Grammar: Studies 1931–1981.* (1984).]

Jenkins, L. (2000). *Biolinguistics: Exploring the Biology of Language.* Cambridge University Press.

Jespersen, O. (1942). A Modern English Grammar on Historical Principles, vol. VI: *Morphology.* George Allen & Unwin Ltd, London.

Johnson, J. S. and Newport, E. L. (1989). Critical Period Effects in Second Language Learning: The Influence of Maturational State on the Acquisition of English As a Second Language. *Cognitive Psychology*, 21: 60–99.

Kam, X-N. C. (2007). Statistical Induction in the Acquisition of Auxiliary-Inversion. In *Proceedings of the 31st Boston University Conference on Language Development.* Cascadilla Press, Somerville, MA.

Kamm, F. M. (2000). The Doctrine of Triple Effect and Why a Rational Agent Need Not Intend the Means to His End, I. *Aristotelian Society Supplementary Volume*, 74(1): 21–39.

Kapur, S. and Clark, R. (in press). The Automatic Construction of a Symbolic Parser Via Statistical Techniques. *Proceedings of the Association for Computational Linguistics Workshop on Integration of Statistical and Symbolic Systems*, Las Cruces, NM.

Karmiloff-Smith, A. and Inhelder, B. (1973). If You Want to Get Ahead, Get a Theory. *Cognition*, 3: 195–212.

Kayne, R. (1989). Facets of Romance Past Participle Agreement. In P. Benincà, editor, *Dialect Variation and the Theory of Grammar.* Foris, Dordrecht. pp. 85–103.

—— and Pollock, J. Y. (1978). Stylistic Inversion, Successive Cyclicity, and Move Np in French. *Linguistic Inquiry Amherst, Mass.*, 9(4): 595–621.

Kayne, R. S. (1975). *French Syntax.* The MIT Press, Cambridge, MA.

—— (1994). *The Antisymmetry of Syntax.* The MIT Press, Cambridge, MA.

Keenan, E. L. and Comrie, B. (1977). Noun Phrase Accessibility and Universal Grammar. *Linguistic Inquiry*, 8: 63–99.

Kellman, P. J. and Spelke, E. (1983). Perception of Partly Occluded Objects in Infancy. *Cognitive Psychology (Print)*, 15(4): 483–524.

Khedr, E. M., Hamed, E., Said, A., and Basahi, J. (2002). Handedness and Language Cerebral Lateralization. *European Journal of Applied Physiology*, 87(4): 469–473.

Kirschner, M. W. and Gerhart, J. C. (2005). *The Plausibility of Life: Resolving Darwin's Dilemma*. Yale University Press, New Haven.

Kleene, S. C. (1936). General Recursive Functions of Natural Numbers. *Mathematische Annalen*, 112: 727–742.

Klein, E. C. (1993). *Toward Second Language Acquisition: A Study of Null-Prep*. Volume 17 of Studies in Theoretical Psycholinguistics. Kluwer Academic Publishers, Dordrecht.

Knobe, J. (2005). Theory of Mind and Moral Cognition: Exploring the Connections. *Trends in Cognitive Sciences*, 9: 357–359.

Koenigs, M., Young, L., Adolphs, R., Tranel, D., Cushman, F., Hauser, M., and Damasio, A. (2007). Damage to the Prefrontal Cortex Increases Utilitarian Moral Judgments. *Nature*, 446(7138): 908–911.

Kripke, S. A. (1979). A Puzzle about Belief. In Margalit, A., editor, *Meaning and Use*. D. Reidel, Dordrecht. pp. 239–283.

Kuhl, P. K. and Miller, J. D. (1975). Speech Perception by the Chinchilla: Voiced–Voiceless Distinction in Alveolar Plosive Consonants. *Science*, 190: 69–72.

Kuhn, T. S. (1962). *The Structure of Scientific Revolutions*. University of Chicago Press, Chicago.

Kutas, M. and Hillyard, S. A. (1984). Event-related Brain Potentials (ERPs) Elicited by Novel Stimuli During Sentence Processing. *Annals of the New York Academy of Sciences*, 425: 236–241.

Lamendola, N. P. and Bever, T. (1997). Peripheral and Cerebral Asymmetries in the Rat. *Science*, 278(5337): 483–486.

Landau, B. and Gleitman, L. R. (1985). *Language and Experience: Evidence from the Blind Child*. Harvard University Press, Cambridge, MA.

Lange, F. A. (1892). *History of Materialism and Criticism of Its Present Importance* (translated by Ernest Chester Thomas). Kegan Paul, Trench, Trübner and Co., London.

Larson, R. K. (2004). Sentence Final Adverbs and Scope. In Wolf, M. and Moulton, K., editors, *Proceedings of NELS*, volume 34. pp. 23–43.

Lashley, K. S. (1951). The Problem of Serial Order in Behavior. In Jeffress, L. A., editor, *Cerebral Mechanisms in Behavior*. John Wiley, New York. pp. 112–136.

Lasnik, H. (2001). A Note on the EPP. *Linguistic Inquiry*, 32(2): 356–362.

—— Depiante, M., and Stepanov, A. (2000). *Syntactic Structures Revisited*. The MIT Press, Cambridge, MA.

Leiber, J. (2001). Turing and the Fragility and Insubstantiality of Evolutionary Explanations: A Puzzle About the Unity of Alan Turing's Work with Some Larger Implications. *Philosophical Psychology*, 14(1): 83–94.

Lele, J. and Singh, R. (1987). Panini, Language Theories and the Dialectics of Grammar in Papers in the History of Linguistics. *Amsterdam Studies in the Theory and History of Linguistic Science. Studies in the History of the Language Science*, 38: 43–51.

Lenneberg, E. H. (1967). *Biological Foundations of Language*. John Wiley & Sons.

Leslie, A. M. and Keeble, S. (1987). Do Six-month-old Infants Perceive Causality. *Cognition*, 25(3): 265–288.

Levit, G. S., Hossfeld, U., and Olsson, L. (2006). From the "Modern Synthesis" to Cybernetics: Ivan Ivanovich Schmalhausen (1884–1963) and His Research Program for a Synthesis of Evolutionary and Developmental Biology. *Journal of Experimental Zoology (Mol. Dev. Evol.)*, 306B: 89–106.

Levy, J. (1980). Varieties of Human Brain Organization and the Human Social System. *Zygon. Journal of Religion and Science Chicago, Ill.*, 15(4): 351–375.

Lewin, K. (1935). *A Dynamic Theory of Personality*. McGraw-Hill, New York.

Lewis, R. L. (2000). Falsifying Serial and Parallel Parsing Models: Empirical Conundrums and an Overlooked Paradigm. *Journal of Psycholinguistic Research*, 29.2: 241–248.

Lewontin, R. C. (1998). The Evolution of Cognition: Questions We Will Never Answer. In Scarborough, D. and Sternberg, S., editors, *An Invitation to Cognitive Science: Methods, Models and Conceptual Issues*, volume 4. The MIT Press, Cambridge, MA. pp. 107–132.

Liberman, A. M., Harris, K. S., Hoffman, H. S., and Griffith, B. C. (1957). The Discrimination of Speech Sounds Within and across Phoneme Boundaries. *Journal of Experimental Psychology*, 54: 358–368.

Lieven, E. V. M. (1994). Crosslinguistic and Crosscultural Aspects of Language Addressed to Children. *Input and Interaction in Language Acquisition*.

Lightfoot, D. (1982). *The Language Lottery: Toward a Biology of Grammars*. The MIT Press.

—— (1991). *How to Set Parameters: Arguments from Language Change*. MIT Press.

—— (1999). *The Development of Language: Acquisition, Change and Evolution*. Blackwell, Oxford.

—— (2000). The Spandrels of the Linguistic Genotype. In Knight, C., Studdert-Kennedy, M., and Hurford, J. C., editors, *The Evolutionary Emergence of Language: Social Function and the Origins of Linguistic Form*. Cambridge University Press, Cambridge. pp. 231–247.

Lipton, J. S. and Spelke, E. S. (2003). Origins of Number Sense. Large-number Discrimination in Human Infants. *Psychological Science*, 14(5): 396–401.

Locke, J. (1690). *An Essay Concerning Human Understanding*. Reprinted in 1970 by Scolar Press.

Macario, J. (1991). Young Children's Use of Color in Classification: Foods and Canonically Colored Objects. *Cognitive Development*, 6(1): 17–46.

Manzini, R. and Wexler, K. (1987). Parameters, Binding Theory, and Learnability. *Linguistic Inquiry*, 18: 413–444.

Maratsos, M. P. (1974). Children Who Get Worse at Understanding the Passive: A Replication of Bever. *Journal of Psycholinguistic Research*, 3(1): 65–74.

Marcus, G. F. (1993). Negative Evidence in Language Acquisition. *Cognition*, 46 (1): 53–85.

Marcus, G. F., Vijayan, S., Bandi Rao, S., and Vishton, P. (1999). Rule Learning by Seven-month-old Infants. *Science*, 283(5398): 77.

Marinova-Todd, S. H. (2003). Know Your Grammar: What the Knowledge of Syntax and Morphology in An 12 Reveals About the Critical Period for Second/Foreign Language Acquisition. In del Pilar García Mayo, M. and García Lecumberri, M. L., editors, *Age and the Acquisition of English As a Foreign Language*. Multilingual Matters, Clevedon. pp. 59–74.

Markman, E. M. (1994). Constraints on Word Meaning in Early Language Acquisition. *The Acquisition of the Lexicon*, 92: 199–227.

Massey, C. M. and Gelman, R. (1988). Preschooler's Ability to Decide Whether a Photographed Unfamiliar Object Can Move Itself. *Developmental Psychology*, 24(3): 307–317.

Mazuka, R. (1996). Can a Grammatical Parameter Be Set Before the First Word? Prosodic Contributions to Early Setting of a Grammatical Parameter. In Morgan, J. L. and Demuth, K., editors, *Signal to Syntax: Bootstrapping from Speech to Grammar in Early Acquisition*. Lawrence Erlbaum Associates. pp. 313–330.

McCloskey, J. (1996). 8 Subjects and Subject Positions in Irish. In Borsley, R. D. and Roberts, I., editors, *The Syntax of the Celtic Languages: A Comparative Perspective*. Cambridge University Press. pp. 241–283.

—— (2001). The Distribution of Subject Properties in Irish. In Davies, W. D. and Dubinsky, S., editors, *Objects and Other Subjects: Grammatical Functions, Functional Categories and Configurationality*. Kluwer, Dordrecht. pp. 157–192.

McCulloch, W. S. (1961). What is a Number, That a Man May Know It, and a Man, That He May Know a Number. *General Semantics Bulletin*, 26(27): 7–18.

McDermott, J. and Hauser, M. (2005). The Origins of Music: Innateness, Uniqueness, and Evolution. *Music Perception*, 23(1): 29–60.

McElree, B. and Bever, T. G. (1989). The Psychological Reality of Linguistically Defined Gaps. *Journal of Psycholinguistic Research*, 18(1): 21–35.

McGinnis, M. and Richards, N., editors (in press). *Proceedings of the EPP/Phase Workshop*, Cambridge, MA. MIT Working Papers in Linguistics.

Mechelli, A., Crinion, J. T., Noppeney, U., O'Doherty, J., Ashburner, J., Frackowiak, R. S., and Others (2004). Structural Plasticity in the Bilingual Brain. *Nature*, 431(7010): 757.

Mehler, J. and Bever, T. G. (1967). Cognitive Capacity of Very Young Children. *Science*, 158: 141–142.

—— —— (1968). The Study of Competence in Cognitive Psychology. *International Journal of Psychology*, 3(4): 273–280.

—— Jusczyk, P., Lambertz, G., Halsted, N., Bertoncini, J., and Amiel-Tison, C. (1988). A Precursor of Language Acquisition in Young Infants. *Cognition*, 29:143–178.

—— Christophe, A., and Ramus, F. (2000). What We Know About the Initial State for Language.

—— —— —— (in press). What We Know About the Initial State for Language. In Marantz, A., Miyashite, Y., and O'Neil, W., editors, *Image, Language, Brain: Papers from the First Mind-Articulation Project Symposium*. MIT Press, Cambridge, MA.

Meltzoff, A. N. and Printz, W. (2002). *The Imitative Mind: Development, Evolution and Brain Bases*. Cambridge University Press.

Mendelson, E. (1990). Second Thoughts About Church's Thesis and Mathematical Proofs. *The Journal of Philosophy*, 87(5): 225–233.

Menzel, R., Greggers, U., Smith, A., Berger, S., Brandt, R., Brunke, S., et al. (2005). Honey Bees Navigate According to a Map-like Spatial Memory. *Proceedings of the National Academy of Sciences*, 102(8): 3040–3045.

Meyer, M., Steinhauer, K., Alter, K., Friederici, A. D., and von Cramon, D. Y. (2004). Brain Activity Varies with Modulation of Dynamic Pitch Variance in Sentence Melody. *Brain and Language*, 89: 277–289.

Michel, G. F. and Tyler, A. N. (2005). Critical Period: a History of the Transition from Questions of When, to What, to How. *Developmental Psychobiology*, 46 (3): 156–162.

Miel, J. (1969). Pascal, Port-Royal, and Cartesian Linguistics. *Journal of the History of Ideas*, 30(2): 261–271.

Mikhail, J. (2000). Rawls' Linguistic Analogy: A Study of the 'Generative Grammar' Model of Moral Theory Described by John Rawls in a Theory of Justice. PhD thesis, Cornell University.

Miller, G., Galanter, E., and Pribram, K. H. (1960). *Plans and the Structure of Behavior*. Holt, Rinehart and Winston Inc., New York.

Miller, G. A. (1956). The Magical Number Seven, Plus or Minus Two. *Psychological Review*, 63(2): 81–97.

—— and Chomsky, N. (1963). Finitary Models of Language Users. In Luce, R. D., Bush, R. R., and Galanter, E., editors, *Handbook of Mathematical Psychology*, volume 2. John Wiley and Sons, New York. pp. 419–491.

—— and Johnson-Laird, P. N. (1976). *Language and Perception*. Cambridge University Press.

Mintz, T. H. (2002). Category Induction from Distributional Cues in an Artificial Language. *Memory and Cognition*, 30(5): 678–686.

—— (2003). Frequent Frames as a Cue for Grammatical Categories in Child Directed Speech. *Cognition*, 90(1): 91–117.

—— (2006). Finding the Verbs: Distributional Cues to Categories Available to Young Learners. In Hirsh-Pasek, K. and Golinkoff, R. M., editors, *Action Meets Word: How Children Learn Verbs*. Oxford University Press. pp. 31–63.

Moerk, E. L. (2000). *The Guided Acquisition of First Language Skills*. Ablex/ Greenwood.

Montague, R. (1974). *Formal Philosophy* (edited by Richmond Thomason). Yale University Press, New Haven, CT.

Morgan, H. D., Sutherland, H. G. E., Martin, D. I. K., and Whitelaw, E. (1999). Epigenetic Inheritance at the Agouti Locus in the Mouse. *Nature Genetics*, 23: 314–318.

Morgan, J., and Saffron, J. (1995). Emerging Integration of Sequential and Suprasegmental Information in Preverbal Speech Segmentation. *Child Development*, 66(4): 911–936.

Morgenbesser, S. (1956). Review of "The Language of Social Research" by Paul F. Lazarsfeld. *The Journal of Philosophy*, 53(7) (March 29): 248–255.

Moro, A. (2000). *Dynamic Antisymmetry*. MIT Press.

Mountcastle, V. B. (1998). Brain Science at the Century's Ebb. *Daedalus*, 127(2).

Musso, M., Moro, A., Glauche, V., Rijntjes, M., Reichenbach, J., Buechel, C., and Weiller, C. (2003). Broca's Area and the Language Instinct. *Nature Neuroscience*, 6(7): 774–781.

Nagel, T. (1974). What is It Like to Be a Bat? *The Philosophical Review*, 83(4): 435–450.

Naigles, L. R. and Hoff-Ginsberg, E. (1998). Why Are Some Verbs Learned Before Other Verbs? Effects of Input Frequency and Structure on Children's Early Verb Use. *Journal of Child Language*, 25(01): 95–120.

Narendra, A., Cheng, K., and Wehner, R. (2007). Acquiring, Retaining and Integrating Memories of the Outbound Distance in the Australian Desert Ant Melophorus Bagoti. *Journal of Experimental Biology*, 210: 570–577.

Nazzi, T., Bertoncini, J., and Mehler, J. (1998). Language Discrimination by Newborns: Towards an Understanding of the Role of Rhythm. *Journal of Experimental Psychology: Human Perception and Performance*, 24(3): 756–766.

Needham, A. and Baillargeon, R. (2000). Infants' Use of Featural and Experiential Information in Segregating and Individuating Objects: a Reply to Xu, Carey, and Welch. *Cognition*, 74(3): 255–284.

Newport, E. L. (1990). Maturational Constraints on Language Learning. *Cognitive Science*, 14(1): 11–28.

Nowak, M. A. and Komarova, N. L. (2001). Towards an Evolutionary Theory of Language. *Trends in Cognitive Sciences*, 5(7): 288–295.

—— —— and Niyogi, P. (2001). Evolution of Universal Grammar. *Science*, 291 (5 January): 114–118.

—— —— —— (2002). Computational and Evolutionary Aspects of Language. *Nature*, 417 (6 June 2002): 611–617.

Obrecht, N. A., Chapman, G. B., and Gelman, R. (2007). Intuitive *t*-tests: Lay Use of Statistical Information. *Psychonomic Bulletin & Review*, 14: 1147–1152.

O'Donnell, T. J., Hauser, M. D., and Fitch, T. W. (2005). Using Mathematical Models of Language Experimentally. *Trends in Cognitive Sciences*, 9–6 : 284–289.

Otsu, Y. (1994). Early Acquisition of Scrambling in Japanese. In Hoekstra, T. and Schwartz, B. D., editors, *Language Acquisition Studies in Generative Grammar*. Amsterdam: John Benjamins. pp. 253–264.

Oyama, S. (1976). A Sensitive Period for the Acquisition of a Nonnative Phonological System. *Journal of Psycholinguistic Research*, 5(3): 261–283.

Papafragou, A., Cassidy, K., and Gleitman, L. (2007). When We Think About
Thinking: The Acquisition of Belief Verbs. *Cognition*, 105(1): 125–165.

Parsons, C. (1990). The Structuralist View of Mathematical Objects. *Synthese*, 84
(3): 303–346.

Peirce, C. S. (1957). The Logic of Abduction. In *Essays in the Philosophy of
Science*. Liberal Arts Press. pp. 235–255.

—— (1982). *Writings of Charles S. Peirce: A Chronological Edition* (volumes 1
and 2, edited by Max Harold Fisch). Indiana University Press, Bloomington, IN.

Pence, K., Golinkoff, R. M., Brand, R. J., and Hirsh-Pasek, K. (2005). When Actions
Can't Speak for Themselves: How Might Infant-directed Speech and Infant-
directed Action Influence Verb Learning? In Trabasso, T., Sabatini, J., Massaro,
D. W., and Calfee, R. C., editors, *From Orthography To Pedagogy: Essays In
Honor Of Richard L. Venezky*. Lawrence Erlbaum Associates. pp. 63–80.

Penn, D. C., Holyoak, K. J., and Povinelli, D. J. (in press). Darwin's Mistake:
Explaining the Discontinuity Between Human and Nonhuman Minds. *Behavioral and Brain Sciences*.

Pesetsky, D. (1987). *Wh*-in-situ: Movement and Unselective Binding. In Reuland,
E. and ter Meulen, A., editors, *The Representation of (In)definiteness*. MIT
Press, Cambridge, MA. pp. 98–129.

Petrides, M. and Pandya, D. (1994). Comparative Architectonic Analysis of
the Human and the Macaque Frontal Cortex. *Handbook of Neuropsychology*,
9: 17–58.

Petrinovich, L. (1995). *Human Evolution, Reproduction and Morality*. Plenum
Press, New York.

Piattelli-Palmarini, M. (1974). *A Debate on Bio-linguistics*. Centre Royaumont
pour Une Science de l'Homme, Endicott House, Dedham, MA.

—— (1980a). How Hard is the "Hard Core" of a Scientific Program? In Piattelli-
Palmarini, M., editor, *Language and Learning: The Debate between Jean Piaget
and Noam Chomsky*. Harvard University Press, Cambridge, MA.

—— editor, (1980b). *Language and Learning: The Debate between Jean Piaget and
Noam Chomsky*. Harvard University Press, Cambridge, MA.

—— (1994). Ever Since Language and Learning: Afterthoughts on the Piaget-
Chomsky Debate. *Cognition*, 50: 315–346.

—— and Uriagereka, J. (2004). Immune Syntax. In Jenkins, L., editor, *Universals
and Variations in Biolinguistics*. Elsevier, Amsterdam. pp. 341–377.

—— —— (2005). The Immune Syntax: the Evolution of the Language Virus.
In Jenkins, L., editor, *Variations and Universals in Biolinguistics*. Mouton
De Gruyter, Amsterdam. pp. 341–377.

Pietroski, P. (2002). Function and Concatenation. In Preyer, G. and Peters,
G., editors, *Logical Form*, volume 9. Oxford University Press. pp. 91–117.

Pietroski, P. (in press). Systematicity Via Monadicity. To appear in the *Croatian Journal of Philososphy.*

Pinker, S. (1979). Formal Models of Language Learning. *Cognition,* 7: 217–283.

—— (1984). *Language Learnability and Language Development.* Harvard University Press, Cambridge, MA.

—— (1989). *Learnability and Cognition.* The MIT Press.

—— (2003). *The Blank Slate: The Modern Denial of Human Nature.* Penguin Books, London.

—— and Jackendoff, R. (2005). The Faculty of Language: What's Special About It? *Cognition,* 95: 201–236.

Post, E. L. (1943). Formal Reductions of the General Combinatorial Decision Problem. *American Journal of Mathematics,* 65(2): 197–215.

Postal, P. M. (1964). *Limitations of Phrase Structure Grammars.* Prentice Hall, Englewod Cliffs, NJ.

—— (1974). *On Raising: One Rule of English Grammar and Its Theoretical Implications.* MIT Press.

Pray, L. A. (2004). Epigenetics: Genome, Meet Your Environment. *The Scientist,* 18 (13) (July 5): 1–10.

Putnam, H. (1973). Reductionism and the Nature of Psychology. *Cognition,* 2: 131–146.

Queltsch, C., Sangster, T. A., and Lindquist, S. (2002). Hsp90 as a Capacitor of Phenotypic Variation. *Nature,* 417(6 June): 618–624.

Quine, W. V. O. (1960). *Word and Object.* The MIT Press, Cambridge, MA.

—— (1969). Linguistics and Philosophy. In Hook, S., editor, *Language and Philosophy.* New York University Press, New York. pp. 95–98.

—— (1985). Events and Reification. In LePore, E. and McLaughlin, B., editors, *Actions and Events. Perspectives in the Philosophy of Donald Davidson.* Blackwell, Oxford. pp. 162–171.

Raby, C. R., Alexis, D. M., Dickinson, A., and Clayton, N. (2007). Planning for the Future by Western Scrub-jays. *Nature,* 445(7130): 919–921.

Rachels, J. (1975). *Moral Problems: A Collection of Philosphical Essays.* Harper & Row, New York.

Ramón y Cajal, S. (1909). *Histology of the Nervous System of Man and Vertebrates.* Translated by L. Azoulay, N. Swanson, and L. Swanson. Reprinted in 1995 by Oxford University Press, New York.

Ramus, F. and Mehler, J. (1999). Language Identification with Suprasegmental Cues: A Study Based on Speech Resynthesis. *The Journal of the Acoustical Society of America,* 105: 512.

—— Hauser, M. D., Miller, C., Morris, D., and Mehler, J. (2000). Language Discrimination by Human Newborns and by Cotton-top Tamarin Monkeys. *Science,* 288(5464): 349.

Rawls, J. (1971). *A Theory of Justice.* Oxford University Press.

Redington, M., Chater, N., and Finch, S. (1998). Distributional Information: A Powerful Cue for Acquiring Syntactic Categories. *Cognitive Science*, 22: 425–469.

Richards, N. (2002). Why There is an EPP. *Movement and Interpretation Workshop, Meikai University.*

Rizzi, L. (1978). A Restructuring Rule in Italian Syntax. In Keyser, S. J., editor, *Recent Transformational Studies in European Languages*. The MIT Press. pp. 113–158.

—— (1982). *Issues in Italian Syntax*. Foris Publications, Dordrecht.

—— (1990). *Relativized Minimality*. The MIT Press.

—— (2003). *Some Elements of the Study of Language As a Cognitive Capacity*. Routledge, London.

—— editor (2004). *The Structure of CP and IP – The Cartography of Syntactic Structures*. Oxford University Press.

—— (2006a). Selective Residual V-2 in Italian Interrogatives. *Form, Structure, and Grammar: A Festschrift Presented to Günther Grewendorf on Occasion of His 60th Birthday.*

—— (2006b). On the Form of Chains: Criterial Positions and ECP Effects, in Cheng, L. and Corver, N., editors, *On Wh Movement*. MIT Press, Cambridge, MA. 97–134.

Rizzolatti, G., Fadiga, L., Gallese, V., and Fogassi, L. (1996). Premotor Cortex and the Recognition of Motor Actions. *Cognitive Brain Research* 3(2): 131–141.

—— and Gallese, V. (1997). *From Action to Meaning: A Neurophysiological Perspective*. Paris.

Rodriguez-Esteban, R. and Cherniak, C. (2005). Global Layout Optimization of Olfactory Cortex and of Amygdala of Rat. University of Maryland Institute for Advanced Computer Studies Technical Report UMIACS-TR-2007-14.

Roemer, I., Reik, W., Dean, W., and Klose, J. (1997). Epigenetic Inheritance in the Mouse. *Current Biology*, 7(4): 277–80.

Rogers, H. (1987). *Theory of Recursive Functions and Effective Computability*. The MIT Press.

Rosch, E. (1978). Principles of Categorization. In Rosch, E. and Lloyd, B. B., editors, *Cognition and Categorization*. Lawrence Erlbaum, Hillsdale, NJ. pp. 27–48.

Ross, D. S. and Bever, T. G. (2004). The Time Course for Language Acquisition in Biologically Distinct Populations: Evidence from Deaf Individuals. *Brain and Language*, 89(1): 115–121.

Ross, J. R. (1967). Constraints on Variables in Syntax. Doctoral diss., MIT, Cambridge, MA.

—— (1972). The Category Squish. *Eighth Regional Meeting of the Chicago Linguistic Society*, 8: 316–328.

—— (1973a). Nouniness. In Fujimura, O., editor, *Three Dimensions of Linguistic Theory*. TEC Corporation, Tokyo. pp. 137–257.

—— (1973b). A Fake NP Squish. In Bailey, C. J. N. and Shuy, R. W., editors, *New Ways of Analyzing Variation in English*. Georgetown University Press. pp. 96–140.

Russell, B. (2003). *Russell on Metaphysics: Selections from the Writings of Bertrand Russell* (edited by Stephen Mumford). Routledge, Taylor and Francis, London.

Saffran, J. R. (2001). Words in a Sea of Sounds: The Output of Infant Statistical Learning. *Cognition*, 81(2): 149–169.

—— (2003). Statistical Language Learning: Mechanisms and Constraints. *Current Directions in Psychological Science*, 12(4): 110–114.

—— Aslin, R. N., and Newport, E. L. (1996). Statistical Learning by 8-month-old Infants. *Science*, 274(5294): 1926–1928.

Sakas, W. G. and Fodor, J. D. (2003). Slightly Ambiguous Triggers for Syntactic Parameter Setting. Poster presented at AMLaP-2003, Glasgow.

Sakitt, B. (1972). Counting Every Quantum. *The Journal of Physiology*, 223(1): 131–150.

Sanides, F. (1962). *Die Architektonik des menschlichen Stirnhirns: Zugleich eine Darstellung der Prinzipien seiner Gestaltung als Spiegel der stammesgeschichtlichen Differenzierung der Grosshirnrinde*. Springer.

Santos, L. R., Sulkowski, G. M., Spaepen, G. M., and Hauser, M. D. (2002). Object Individuation Using Property/Kind Information in Rhesus Macaques (Macaca Mulatta). *Cognition*, 83(3): 241–264.

Saxton, M. (1997). The Contrast Theory of Negative Input. *J. Child Lang*, 24(1): 139–61.

Schiffer, S. (2003). *The Things We Mean*. Oxford University Press, New York.

Schirmer, A., Escoffier, N., Zysset, S., Koester, D., Striano, T., von Cramon, D. Y., and Friederici, A. D. (2008). When Vocal Processing Gets Emotional. On the Role of Social Orientation in Relevance Detection by the Human Amygdala. *NeuroImage*, 40: 1402–1410.

Schlosser, G. and Wagner, G. P. (2004). *Modularity in Development and Evolution*. The University of Chicago Press, Chicago.

Searls, D. (2002). The Language of Genes. *Nature*, 420: 211–217.

Sebastián-Gallés, N., Echeverría, S., and Bosch, L. (2005). The Influence of Initial Exposure on Lexical Representation: Comparing Early and Simultaneous Bilinguals. *Journal of Memory and Language*, 52(2): 240–255.

Senghas, A. and Coppola, M. (2001). Children Creating Language: How Nicaraguan Sign Language Acquired a Spatial Grammar. *Psychological Science*, 12 (4): 323–328.

Shannon, C. E. and Weaver, W. (1949). *The Mathematical Theory of Communication*. University of Illinois Press, Urbana, IL. [Reprinted in 1998.]

Shatz, M. and Gelman, R. (1973). The Development of Communication Skills: Modifications in the Speech of Young Children As a Function of Listener. *Monographs of the Society for Research in Child Development*, 38(5): 1–38.

—— Wellman, H. M., and Silber, S. (1983). The Acquisition of Mental Verbs: A Systematic Investigation of the First Reference to Mental State. *Cognition*, 14(3): 301–321.

Sherrington, C. S. (1906). *The Integrative Action of the Nervous System*. Scribner's Sons, New York.

Silverstein, M. (1993). Metapragmatic Discourse and Metapragmatic Function. In Lucy, J. A., editor, *Reflexive Language: Reported Speech and Metapragmatics*. Cambridge University Press. pp. 33–58.

Simon, H. A. (1956). Rational Choice and the Structure of the Environment. *Psychological Review*, 63: 129–138.

Sinclair, A. (1978). *The Child's Conception of Language*, volume 2. Series in Language and Communication edition. Springer, Berlin.

Skinner, B. F. (1957). *Verbal Behavior*. Prentice-Hall, New York.

Slobin, D. I., and Bever, T. G. (1982). Children Use Canonical Sentence Schemas: A Crosslinguistic Study of Word Order and Inflections. *Cognition*, 12 : 229–265.

Smiley, P. and Huttenlocher, J. (1995). Conceptual Development and the Child's Early Words for Events, Objects, and Persons. In Tomasello, M. and Merriman, W. E., editors, *Beyond Names for Things: Young Children's Acquisition of Verbs*. Lawrence Erlbaum Associates. pp. 21–62.

Smith, E. C. and Lewicki, M. S. (2006). Efficient Auditory Coding. *Nature* 439: 978–982.

Snedeker, J. and Gleitman, L. (2004). Why It is Hard to Label Our Concepts. In Hall, D. G. and Waxman, S. R., editors, *Weaving a Lexicon*. MIT Press, Cambridge, MA. pp. 257–294.

—— and Li, P. (2000). Can the Situations in which Words Occur Account for Cross-linguistic Variation in Vocabulary Composition. In J. Tai and Y. Chang (eds.), *Proceedings of the Seventh International Symposium on Chinese Languages and Linguistics*.

—— Geren, J., and Shafto, C. L. (2007). Starting Over: International Adoption As a Natural Experiment in Language Development. *Psychological Science*, 18 (1): 79–87.

Spelke, E. (2000). Core Knowledge. *American Psychologist*, 55: 1233–1243.

Stabler, E. (2003). Notes on Computational Linguistics. UCLA Course Notes. <http://www.linguistics.ucla.edu/people/stabler/185-03.pdf>

Starke, M. (2001). Move Dissolves into Merge. PhD thesis, Doctoral dissertation, University of Geneva.

Steinhauer, K., Alter, K., and Friederici, A. D. (1999). Brain Potentials Indicate Immediate Use of Prosodic Cues in Natural Speech Processing. *Nature Neuroscience*, 2: 191–196.

Striedter, G. F. (2006). Précis of "Principles of Brain Evolution". *Behavioral and Brain Sciences*, 29: 1–36.

Svenonius, P. (2002). *Subjects, Expletives, and the EPP*. Oxford University Press.

—— (2004). On the Edge. In Adger, D., De Cat, C., and Tsoulas, G., editors, *Peripheries: Syntactic Edges and their Effects*. Springer. pp. 259–287.

Tautz, J., Shaowu, Z., Spaethe, J., Brockmann, A., Aung, S., and Srinivasan, M. (2004). Honeybee Odometry: Performance in Varying Natural Terrain. *PLoS Biology*, 2(7): e211.

Terrace, H. S. (2005). Metacognition and the Evolution of Language. In Terrace, H. and Metcalfe, T., editors, *The Missing Link in Cognition: Origins of Self-Reflective Consciousness*. Oxford University Press. pp. 84–115.

Thompson, D. W. (1917). *On Growth and Form*. Edited by J. T. Bonner. An abridged edition. Reprinted in 1992 by Cambridge University Press, Cambridge.

Thompson-Schill, S. L., D'Esposito, M., Aguirre, G. K., and Farah, M. J. (1997). Role of Left Inferior Prefrontal Cortex in Retrieval of Semantic Knowledge: A Reevaluation. *Proceedings of the National Academy of Sciences*, 94(26): 14792.

Tinbergen, N. (1963). On Aims and Methods of Ethology. *Z. Tierpsychol.*, 20(4): 1.

Toro, J. M. (2005). La extracción de regularidades rítmicas y estadísticas del habla en ratas. Universidad de Barcelona, PhD Dissertation.

Toro, J. M., Trobalon, J. B., and Sebastián-Gallés, N. (2003). The Use of Prosodic Cues in Language Discrimination Tasks by Rats. *Animal Cognition*, 6(2): 131–136.

Townsend, D. J. and Bever, T. G. (2001). *Sentence Comprehension*. MIT Press, Cambridge, MA.

—— Carrithers, C., and Bever, T. G. (2001). Familial Handedness and Access to Words, Meaning, and Syntax During Sentence Comprehension. *Brain and Language*, 78(3): 308–331.

Trubetzkoy, N. S. (1936). *Anleitung Zu Phonologische Beschreibungen*. Duke University Press, Durham, NC.

—— (2001). *Studies in General Linguistics and Language* Structure (edited by Anatoly Liberman; translated by Marvin Taylor and Anatoly Liberman). Duke University Press, Durham, NC.

Trueswell, J. C. and Gleitman, L. R. (2007). Learning to Parse and Its Implications for Language Acquisition. In Gaskell, G., editor, *Oxford Handbook of Psycholinguistics*. Oxford Univerity Press.

—— and Tanenhaus, M. K. (1994). Semantic Influences on Parsing: Use of Thematic Role Information in Syntactic Ambiguity Resolution. *Journal of Memory and Language (Print)*, 33(3): 285–318.

—— Wessel, A., McEldoon, K., and Gleitman, L. R. (in progress). The Dynamics of Event Perception and Event Participants.

Turing, A. M. (1936). On Computable Numbers: With an Application to the Entscheidungsproblem (part 2). *Proceedings of the London Mathematical Society, Series 2*, 43: 544–546.

—— (1952). The Chemical Basis of Morphogenesis. *Phil. Trans. R. Soc. Lond. B*, 237(641): 37–72.

Ullmann, S. (1958). Semantics at the Cross-roads. *Higher Education Quarterly*, 12 (3): 250–260.

Uriagereka, J. (1995). Warps: Some Thoughts on Categorization. *University of Maryland Working Papers in Linguistics*, 3: 256–308.

—— (1998). *Rhyme and Reason: An Introduction to Minimalist Syntax*. The MIT Press, Cambridge, MA.

—— (1999). Multiple Spell-out. In Epstein, S. D. and Hornstein, N., editors, *Working Minimalism*. The MIT Press, Cambridge, MA. pp. 251–282.

—— (2008). *Syntactic Anchors*. Cambridge University Press.

Valian, V. (1999). Input and Language Acquisition. In Ritchie, W. C. and Bhatia, T. K., editors, *Handbook of Child Language Acquisition*. New York: Academic Press. pp. 497–530.

Vander Wall, S. B. (1990). *Food Hoarding in Animals*. University Of Chicago Press.

Van Swinderen, B., and Greenspan, R. J. (2005). Flexibility in a Gene Network Affecting a Simple Behavior in *Drosophila melanogaster*. *Genetics*, 169: 2151–2163.

Veblen, T. B. (1899). *The Theory of the Leisure Class: An Economical Study in the Evolution of Institutions*. The Macmillan Co., New York.

Vercelli, D. (2004). Genetics, Epigenetics and the Environment: Switching, Buffering, Releasing. *Journal of Allergy and Clinical Immunology*, 113: 381–386.

Vergnaud, J.-R. (1977). Personal Letter to Howard Lasnik and Noam Chomsky. In Freidin, R. and Lasnik, H., editors, *Syntax the Essential Readings: Conditions on Derivations and Representations*, volume 5. Routledge, London. pp. 21–34.

—— (1985). Dépendance et niveaux de représentation en syntaxe. *Lingvisticae Investigationes Supplementa*, 13: 351–371.

Viviani, P. and Stucchi, N. (1992). Biological Movements Look Uniform: Evidence of Motor–Perceptual Interactions. *Journal of Experimental Psychology: Human Perception and Performance*, 18(3): 603–623.

Vlastos, G. (1975). *Plato's Universe*. University of Washington Press.

Von Frisch, K. (1967). *The Dance Language and Orientation of Bees*. Belknap Press of Harvard University Press.

Vouloumanos, A. and Werker, J. F. (2007). Listening to Language at Birth: Evidence for a Bias for Speech in Neonates. *Developmental Science*, 10(2): 159–164.

Walker, M. A., Joshi, A. K., and Prince, E. F. (1998). Centering in Naturally Occurring Discourse: An Overview. In Walker, M. A. and Joshi, A. K., editors, *Centering Theory in Discourse*. Clarendon Press, Oxford. pp. 1–30.

Weatherall, D. (1999). From Genotype to Phenotype: Genetics and Medical Practice in the New Millennium. *Philosophical Transactions: Biological Sciences*, 354(1392): 1995–2010.

Weber-Fox, C. M. and Neville, H. (1996). Maturational Constraints on Functional Specializations for Language Processing: ERP and Behavioral Evidence in Bilingual Speakers. *Journal of Cognitive Neuroscience*, 8(3): 231–256.

Wehner, R. and Menzel, R. (1990). Do Insects Have Cognitive Maps? *Annual Review of Neuroscience*, 13(1): 403–414.

—— and Srinivasan, M. (2003). Path Integration in Insects. In Jeffery, K. J., editor, *The Neurobiology of Spatial Behaviour*. Oxford University Press, Oxford. pp. 9–30.

Weibel, E., Taylor, C., and Bolis, L., editors (1998). *Principles of Animal Design*. Cambridge University Press, New York.

Weinreich, D. M., Delaney, N. F., Depristo, M. A., and Hartl, D. L. (2006). Darwinian Evolution Can Follow Only Very Few Mutational Paths to Fitter Proteins. *Science*, 312(5770): 111–114.

Weir, R. H. (1962). *Language in the Crib*. Mouton.

Weiss, D. J., Ghazanfar, A. A., Miller, C. T., and Hauser, M. D. (2002). Specialized Processing of Primate Facial and Vocal Expressions: Evidence for Cerebral Asymmetries. In Rogers, L. J. and Andrew, R. J., editors, *Comparative Vertebrate Lateralization*. Cambridge University Press. pp. 480–530.

Werker, J. F. (1989). Becoming a Native Listener. *American Scientist*, 77(1): 54–59.

—— and Tees, 1984. Cross-Language Speech Perception: Evidence for Perceptual Reorganization during the First Year of Life. *Infant Behavior and Development*, 7: 49–63.

—— and Vouloumanos, A. (2000). Who's Got Rhythm? *Science*, 288(5464): 280–281.

Wernicke, C. (1874). *Der aphasische Symptomenkomplex. Eine psychologische Studie auf anatomischer Basis*. Breslau: Max Cohn & Weigert.

Wertheimer, M. (1912). *Experimentelle Studien über das Sehen von Bewegung*. JA Barth.

—— (1925). *Drei Abhandlungen zur Gestalttheorie*. Erlangen, Enke, DE.

—— (1945). *Productive Thinking*. Harper & Brothers.

Wexler, K. and Manzini, R. (1987). Parameters and Learnability in Binding Theory. *Parameter Setting*, pages 41–76.

Weyl, H. (1989). *Symmetry*. Princeton University Press.

Wittgenstein, L. (1953). *Philosophical Investigations* (translated by E. M. Ascombe). Basil Blackwell, Oxford.

Wittlinger, M., Wehner, R., and Wolf, H. (2007). The Desert Ant Odometer: A Stride Integrator That Accounts for Stride Length and Walking Speed. *Journal of Experimental Biology*, 210(2): 198.

Wohlgemuth, S., Ronacher, B., and Wehner, R. (2001). Ant Odometry in the Third Dimension. *Nature*, 411(6839): 795–798.

Wood, J. N., Glynn, D. D., Phillips, B. C., and Hauser, M. D. (2007). The Perception of Rational, Goal-directed Action in Nonhuman Primates. *Science*, 317 (5843): 1402–1405.

—— —— Hauser, M. D., and Barner, D. (2008). Free-ranging Rhesus Monkeys Spontaneously Individuate and Enumerate Small Numbers of Non-solid Portions. *Cognition*, 106: 207–221.

Wood, W. B., editor (1988). *The Nematode Caenorhabditis Elegans*. Cold Spring Harbor Laboratory Press, Spring Harbor, NY.

Woodward, A. L. (1998). Infants Selectively Encode the Goal Object of an Actor's Reach. *Cognition*, 69(1): 1–34.

Wright, A. A., Rivera, J. J., Hulse, S. H., and Shyan, M. (2000). Music Perception and Octave Generalization in Rhesus Monkeys. *Music Perception*, 129(3): 291–307.

Wright, S. (1932). The Roles of Mutation. Inbreeding, Crossbreeding, and Selection in Evolution. In Roeper, T. and Williams, E., editors, *Proceedings of the Sixth International Congress on Genetics*, Ithaca, NY. p. 365.

Wynn, K. (1990). Children's Understanding of Counting. *Cognition*, 36(2): 155–193.

—— (1992). Addition and Subtraction by Human Infants. *Nature*, 358(6389): 749–750.

Wyttenbach, R. A., May, M. L., and Hoy, R. R. (1996). Categorical Perception of Sound Frequency by Crickets. *Science*, 273(5281): 1542.

Yang, C. D. (2002). *Knowledge and Learning in Natural Language*. Oxford University Press, New York and Oxford.

—— (2006). *The Infinite Gift: How Children Learn and Unlearn the Languages of the World*. Scribner.

Zemplén, G. (2006). The Development of the Neurath Principle: Unearthing the Romantic Link. *Studies In History and Philosophy of Science Part A*, 37(4): 585–609.

Zur, O. and Gelman, R. (2004). Young Children Can Add and Subtract by Predicting and Checking. *Early Childhood Research Quarterly*, 19(1): 121–137.

Index

Page numbers in *italics* refer to photographs or figures. '*fn*' after a page number refers to the footnote. Entries are presented in word-by-word format. For example, "semantic variables" appears before "semantics" as the first word is taken into account in the filing order.